The Indian Reorganization Act

The Indian Reorganization Act

Congresses and Bills

Edited by

Vine Deloria, Jr.

UNIVERSITY OF OKLAHOMA PRESS : NORMAN

Also by Vine Deloria, Jr.

Custer Died for Your Sins (New York, 1969; Norman, 1988)

God Is Red: A Native View of Religion (New York 1973; Golden, Colo., 1994)

Behind the Trail of Broken Treaties: An Indian Declaration of Independence (New York, 1974; Austin, 1985)

(ed.) *American Indian Policy in the Twentieth Century* (Norman, 1985)

(ed., with Raymond J. DeMallie) *Documents of American Indian Diplomacy: Treaties, Agreements, and Conventions, 1775–1979* (2 vols.) (Norman, 1999)

Library of Congress Cataloging-in-Publication Data

The Indian Reorganization Act: congresses and bills / edited by Vine Deloria, Jr.
p. cm.
Includes index.
ISBN 978-0-8061-3398-0 (Hardcover)
1. United States. Indian Reorganization Act. 2. Indians of North America—Legal status, laws, etc.—Legislative history. 3. Indians of North America—Government relations—Legislative history. 4. Tribal government—United States—Legislative history. I. Deloria, Vine.

KF8225 .I53 2002
342.73'0872—dc21

2001053466

The paper in this book meets the guidelines for permanence and durability of the Committee on Production Guidelines for Book Longevity of the Council on Library Resources, Inc.∞

CONTENTS

INTRODUCTION

Self-Government and the Indian Congresses

John Collier, after working in the field of Indian Affairs as founder and director of the American Indian Defense Association for almost a decade, was named Indian Commissioner by President Franklin Roosevelt in 1933. Inspired to assist Indians after a quasi-religious experience at Taos, Collier helped organize the Pueblos of New Mexico to oppose the Bursum Bill, which would have recognized the claims of white squatters to lands within the Pueblo land grants. Collier had proved to be a thorn in the side of Charles J. Rhoads and Joseph H. Scattergood when they administered the Bureau of Indian Affairs during the Hoover administration, and he became well acquainted with legislative procedures in the late 1920s when he devoted his time and energy to revealing the shortcomings of the Bureau of Indian Affairs in the series of hearings conducted by the Senate Indian Committee, which was surveying conditions on Indian reservations.

Indian Congresses

Collier had prepared a major reform package during his first year in office, and in January 1934 he held a conference at the Cosmos Club in Washington, D.C., inviting the various church groups and private organizations interested in reforming the Indian Service. Pretending that their recommendations were critical in formulating his Indian policy and legislative proposals, Collier had his bill introduced in February 1934 in the House of Representatives. He then announced that he would hold "congresses" in various locations in the West to consult with the tribes on his legislative proposals. Beginning in early March in Rapid City, South Dakota, with a large meeting of the Northern Plains tribes, the bureau then moved to Chemawa and then to New Mexico, Arizona, and California conducting Collier's meetings, encountering increasing Indian opposition as the consultations continued. In late March Collier held three meetings in Oklahoma, where opposition was very strong against his ideas because dissident groups of Indians had interpreted his proposals as advocating communism and segregation. The bureau completed its consultations in late April 1934 with a meeting at Hayward, Wisconsin, with the tribes of the Great Lakes. In 1935, facing discontent from the Navajos, based primarily on the crude conservation measures he had enforced on Navajo sheep grazing practices, Collier made one last effort to win Navajo endorsement for his program, which had been written into law in a vague form in June of 1934.

Contemporary scholars have not examined the Collier proposals in depth. Legal literature is generally limited to a recital of how the Indian Reorganization Act, the vastly amended bill that finally passed and was signed into law, was intended to work. Many people, unfortunately, have tended to believe that self-government began with the Collier administration and that the final form of the legislation contained basic principles of political process that enabled Indian tribes to regain powers of sovereignty that had been taken away from them earlier in the century by the United States. When the transcripts of these congresses are examined, they reveal that Collier did have certain principles in mind when he made his proposal but he had great difficulty in interpreting what he had in mind to the Indians in the various congresses. It was therefore his strong personality and refusal to surrender his dream of a revived "Red Atlantis" that made the Indian Reorganization Act work for the benefit of Indians.

The congresses reveal that most Indians had adjusted to the allotment act, and the selfishness that Senator Henry Dawes believed an essential part of civilized life had taken hold in many tribes so that they were reluctant to pool their resources and lands and try to revive the old tribal ways. Many Indian spokesmen made clear to Collier that while they wanted education for their children and better medical care, they were not prepared to welcome mixed bloods back into the tribal community in those instances in which they had sold their lands and tried to adjust to life away from the reservation.

Another prominent theme of the congresses was the insistence by many tribal groups that the United States abide by their treaties even where most of the treaty promises had been unfulfilled or even breached. Time and again Collier was confronted with the necessity of reassuring tribal leaders that he would investigate the state of their claims and other litigation pending in the federal courts and that his legislative proposals were not in conflict with treaty provisions. The Indian complaints were not as specific as the claims based on treaties that we see today. Yet it is clear that the tribes had definite rights such as hunting and fishing in mind when referring to their treaties.

Scattered through the various congresses are debates and explanations of the various credit provisions and loans that Collier saw as necessary to raise the economic level of Indians. Educational loans were understood by most of the delegates but when Collier tried to explain loans for land acquisition and economic enterprises he experienced great difficulty in getting the Indians to see how the new program would work. Collier fantasized that with tribalism as a motivating influence, Indian allottees would gladly cede their lands to the tribal government and work to restore the reservation's economic integrity, not realizing the scope of such a project or the individual attachments to the small tracts of land.

Development of Indian Self-Government

Today we mark the Indian Reorganization Act as a major event in twentieth-century Indian policy, and surely it is all of that. But organizing Indians so that the United States could deal formally with them was not a new idea. Indeed, the solution to the problem of dealing with Indians by organizing them like non-Indian governments occurred to the Pilgrims in Massachusetts who gathered their Christian Indian converts in "Praying Towns" that were initially supposed to have the same political status as townships settled by whites. When the Indians showed some degree of independence, however, "trustees" were appointed to conduct business for these towns, and the Indian lands were soon forfeited and rights extinguished, leading to some of the largest potential land claims of today.

In the 1830s the southeastern Indians were encouraged to reduce their traditional forms of government to a written constitutional format that resembled some of the colonial governments. Whereas the Indian council represented tribal members quite adequately and performed every political function except, for some tribes at least, that of declaring and conducting war, whites eager to help the southeastern Indians become "civilized" insisted that they move toward a tripartite form of government like the United States and include legislative, executive, and judicial branches of government. By the outbreak of the Civil War most of the Five Civilized Tribes had adopted written constitutions and operated within the western parameters of democratic government.

By the 1870s the Bureau of Indian Affairs was pressuring the other western tribes to adopt formal governments and was assisting in the formation of these institutions. The transition from the traditional forms of government to the new ways of governing was much slower with these Indian nations. For the most part they wanted to formalize already-existing institutions, and their primary political entity was often simply a council of traditional chiefs and headmen—the same people who would have governed had there been no effort to transform the customs of the tribes. Because the United States claimed the right of supervising the activities of Indians the standard procedure was for the council to pass laws and resolutions and forward them to the Commissioner of Indian Affairs for approval. Actually the Indians did not need the approval of the Commissioner, but when their decision affected treaty annuities or educational services, the Commissioner had to be informed so that the bureau could make changes.

During the 1880s, when the last powerful tribes had been reduced to reservation residency, and the United States began to promulgate its own rules and regulations for operating the services of the reservations, the Bureau of Indian Affairs instituted both police and judicial institutions on the reservations. The Indian police became an arm of the federal government in reality, whereas for many things the Court of Indian Affairs exercised some measure of self-government because the legal codes developed by the bureau could not cover all possible circumstances.

On some reservations the Indian agent chose the most prominent chiefs as judges for the Courts of Indian Offenses. Generally the chiefs served with distinction and fairness, but there were complaints by the chiefs that because they belonged to the tribal council or group of elders that actually governed the reservation, they felt that they could not perform judicial functions also. There was also the complaint that the tendency of the agent to interfere with their judgments made the courts less than satisfactory. Eventually most chiefs abandoned their work with the agent and turned to other matters such as claims against the government for treaty violations. Within a decade of their founding most Courts of Indian Offenses became simply tools for the agent to use arbitrarily to control the people.

Beginning in Oklahoma in the 1890s and then spreading across the country to most of the larger tribes was the movement to get admitted to a federal district court, or even better, the Court of Claims, to press suits for violation of treaties. Traditional councils and chiefs quickly understood the necessity of using the judicial system, and each Congress saw an increasing number of white lawyers lobbying to get bills passed "that would allow the tribes to sue the United States." After 1900 this movement became a deluge as lawyers saw an opportunity to garner large fees for successful prosecution of these cases. Of importance in this movement is that traditional councils that did not, as a rule, have formal constitutions and by-laws authorized the cases. We can call this period, 1890–1930, the time of the traditional governments.

People in Congress recognized the need to have formal governments on reservations so that state governments and private businesses could deal formally with Indians for services or to lease lands for mineral exploitation. Where there were weak traditional governments agents simply made the decision to lease or accept or reject services according to their own conceptions of how the reservations should be administered. The problem facing this kind of reform was where the emphasis should be lodged. Did Congress want to vest Indians with the full political powers of municipal government or arrange protective procedures to enable them to limit the powers of the agent over their lives and property? Observing that no formal political institution with rules, regulations, and administrative procedures existed on reservations, many people concluded that the Indians had no government at all. Yet during each Congress several bills were approved admitting tribes to the Court of Claims, thereby admitting that the Indians did have some form of government that was being recognized by the federal government.

Efforts at Legislative Reform of Indian Policy

In June 1912 a bill was submitted to allow Indians the right to nominate their own agents, seemingly a simple proposition that might not have needed congressional approval. A memo from the Commissioner of Indian Affairs could easily have accomplished such a reform. But the bill went far beyond a simple granting of a nominating process. Indeed, it contained the seeds of complete reform of reservation institutions, formal and informal, and foreshadowed the eventual provisions that John Collier would advocate in his proposal in 1934.

A quick analysis will demonstrate how revolutionary this bill actually was for its time. The first provision was that with a two-thirds affirmative vote the Indians of a reservation could nominate an individual to be their agent or superintendent. The Secretary of the Interior was then obligated to appoint the nominated person provided he was twenty-eight years old, was a citizen, and had been engaged in agriculture for at least five years. He must also have been a resident of the state in which the reservation was located for at least five years. It is plainly evident that the intent of the bill was to ensure that the allotment policy be strengthened by hiring a person better acquainted with local agricultural activities. The person could be removed by a majority of the tribe, so it was easier to be dismissed than to be appointed in the first place. The agent was required to file a complete report on activities on the reservation each November with the Senate and House of Representatives.

Section two basically allowed the agent to fill the various positions at the agency, with disclaimers on the employment of relatives and the prohibition of employees becoming personal servants of the agent. Indians had preference in employment in the lesser positions at the agency "if competent," which allowed the agent to exclude any Indian applicants on nebulous grounds if he wished.

Section three dealt with a cumbersome procedure for calling an election to determine the nominee. If twenty percent of the adults on a reservation petitioned for a general assembly, the agent was authorized to call a meeting of the tribe. At this meeting the people would elect a president, secretary, and treasurer to form a permanent organization, and three additional people who were designated as "electors" were approved to constitute an election board. This board would then proceed to plan and hold the election to choose an agent or superintendent. Section four forbade bureau personnel from being candidates for the office or engaging in any electioneering to obtain the position, a prohibition that would have been impossible to enforce.

The results of the election were to be certified to the Secretary of the Interior for his approval. If the individual had a notorious record the Secretary could disapprove the appointment. Successful nominees had to post bond. The Secretary would then give a sum of $300 to the agent out of funds the tribe had in the U.S. Treasury to pay for election expenses. This procedure was a somewhat backward way of handling the problem. Section seven made the election board a permanent institution, and its primary duty was to settle inheritance questions that might arise for the agent in carrying out his duties. Apparently this board was to be used to deflect the many complaints received from Indians regarding the bureau's use and administration of their lands. The incongruity here is amazing because vesting control over property interests is hardly compatible with holding an election to choose an agent.

The bill then simply departs into ad-hoc reforms of existing practices of the Interior Department. Section eight prohibited the use of tribal funds unless the business committee, formerly the election board, approved the expenditure. Section nine allowed full bloods to lease their lands with the approval of the agent and allowed mixed bloods to lease their lands with the approval of the business committee, a provision that guaranteed continuous and perhaps violent conflicts on the reservations. One-fourth Indians could lease lands at their pleasure. The racial overtones of these provisions are instantly apparent to us today but were regarded as adequate descriptions of social reality in the second decade of the twentieth century.

Section twelve exempted the Five Civilized Tribes and merged some tribes, the Kiowa and Comanche and the Osage and Kaw, into one tribe for the purposes of the act. Section fourteen extended the provisions of the act to those tribes that "have so far progressed in civilization as to be competent of organization in conformity with this act." Legislative draftsmanship was not well developed in 1912, but it boggles the mind to discover in this wording a wholly arbitrary classification that could, in the opinion of the Secretary of the Interior, have disqualified every tribe in the country. Clearly the movement for reform was a tiny seedling at this time.

We must, nevertheless, examine the proposal for the principles it attempted to articulate. Most important is the idea that Indians should have some voice in choosing the people who will assist them in making a decent life for themselves. Nearly as important is the requirement that the tribe's money cannot be spent without the permission of some formal Indian institution devised by the approval of reservation residents. The land provisions are clearly add-ons by zealous policy makers who want to require a trade of self-government for fewer protections for Indian lands. Finally, the idea of an election board transforming itself into a business committee with limited and arbitrary powers was absurd.

A number of bills were introduced during this period, most of them not as comprehensive as the 1912 bill. In May 1916 a much shorter bill was introduced seeking to confer on Indians the right to recall their agents or superintendents. According to its proposals, an agent or superintendent could be recalled, and the Secretary of the Interior was empowered to remove him, if a majority of the reservation residents voted against him. A business council was authorized of ten persons to conduct the recall election, but only adult males over twenty-one years of age could vote in the election. Here we have minimal direction from Congress regarding the creation of political institutions on the reservations, no provision for a continuing council, and the restriction of voting privileges. Presumably the power to force the removal of a federal employee was regarded as sufficient to bring about reform in the Bureau of Indian Affairs.

In the late 1920s the Klamath Indians made a bold proposal to Congress that radically changed the manner in which everyone understood the status of Indian reservations. Outraged at the continual exploitation of their timber by ineffective bureau employees, the Klamaths wanted to be organized as a federal corporation under the supervision of a federal district court judge but otherwise free of the Bureau of Indian Affairs and able to conduct their own business affairs. The timber scandals on the reservation were well known and a national disgrace, but Congress was basically shocked that a tribe with virtually no demonstrated experience in modern resource management and self-government should present such a sophisticated plan. One of the objections to the Klamath proposal was that federal judges had not been used in a supervisory capacity before. Today with judges exercising broad monitoring powers in matters such as school integration and environmental cleanup, this idea has finally taken hold.

The Klamath proposal was most traumatic for the Indian interest organizations that had made federal Indian policy for decades. John Collier, who was busy feeding the Senate Indian Committee with data on scandals in the bureau, was stunned that a tribe he and others considered rather primitive should present a well-considered proposal incorporating both self-government and economic development. The proposal was introduced in two Congresses but was never passed into law. It was regarded as too radical although it was quite similar to the arrangement of the Osage tribe in handling their oil assets. The Osage, upon being forced to surrender their self-government in 1907, had held their oil subsurface rights in common, had closed the tribal rolls, and had transformed membership into "head-rights" in the new organization.

The eventual thrust of the New Deal was to emphasize two major reforms: economic development by Indians and self-government. These two points were the essence of the Klamath proposal, and so we can see, very easily, that the Indian Reorganization Act had its roots in the Klamath corporation. Collier, at one of the Indian congresses, made mention of the Klamaths and informed the Indians that the basic transformation would be that of moving toward the status of a federal corporation. Clearly reform was in the air and the authorization of some form of self-government was inevitable. The idea only had to be floated properly in Congress.

In 1932, most probably under the influence of John Collier and others, Senator Lynn Frazier of North Dakota introduced the "Indian Tribal Councils Act." Some of the previous concepts were evident in the new proposal, and an indication that Congress had adopted the idea of self-government can be found in the greatly reduced numbers contained in the formulas for petitioning for and holding an election. Whereas two-thirds or a majority had been used in previous bills, this bill required a petition of only twenty-five percent of the adult members of an Indian tribe, the discrimination by gender having by now apparently disappeared. The bill provided for an election of a committee to draft a constitution and bylaws for the tribe instead of electing a committee to hold an election and making that committee a standing committee to handle business thereafter.

The requirements for a constitution were very specific. A council was established and its powers clearly defined, a direct election of council members every year was required, and provision for a referendum on any question of policy by fifteen percent of the members had to be included. Section two clearly stated that this council was empowered to represent the reservation before Congress, to the executive branch, and in the courts, clarifying what had been a nebulous situation on many reservations where several kinds of councils existed for specific purposes. Many of the other items clearly foreshadowed the Collier proposals for reform: land use was to be approved by the tribal council, the councils could employ their own lawyers, the Secretary of the Interior had to submit to the council estimates of expenditures from tribal funds. Tribal funds were to be under the control of the council, and all income generated within the reservation were to be deposited to the credit of the tribe in the U.S. Treasury instead of being used as "Indian moneys proceeds of labor," which was spent by the bureau as it saw fit.

The Pueblos were excluded from the application of the act, and this exclusion can be taken as evidence that Collier was involved in the drafting of the bill. Traditionally the Five Civilized Tribes, the New York Indians, and the Osage are excluded from these kinds of provisions. Collier's interest in and sympathy for the Pueblos certainly appears in this provision. Because the bill was introduced in an election year, indeed in a watershed election year, it languished and was not enacted. Its basic outline, however, would be seen two years later in the Collier proposal.

The Howard-Wheeler Bill

The original Collier proposal was the most comprehensive and far-reaching legislative vision ever offered to Congress. It covered every possible area that could have been anticipated by the government or the Indians. One can detect in its four titles an effort to respond to the findings of the *Meriam Report* of 1928, which had outlined the conditions of Indians and made recommendations for reform. It also included the best of the ideas for reform put forward in the previous decade. Its purpose, announced in the preamble, is worth repeating: "for purposes of local self-government and economic enterprise; to provide for the necessary training of Indians in administrative and economic affairs; to conserve and develop Indian lands; and to promote the more effective administration of justice to matters affecting Indian tribes and communities by establishing a federal Court of Indian Affairs."

The bill had four titles: Indian Self-Government, Special Education for Indians, Indian Lands, and the Court of Indian Affairs. Contained in these titles were radical changes in the administration of Indian affairs, and these changes reflect the perspective of the New Deal in that they provided federal funds for many activities that previously had been funded, if at all, out of tribal funds. Once organized, Indian reservations would have considerably more political and economic powers than had ever been conceded to them. But the Secretary of the Interior would also have well-defined responsibilities for monitoring Indian activities and intervening in Indian matters by exercising a trustee or supervisory function for the new governments and economic ventures.

The vision within the bill looked forward to a time when the bureau would gradually fade away as Indians developed their own institutions to perform functions that the Bureau of Indian Affairs traditionally provided. This vision, however, did not contain provisions for the withdrawal of bureau services, nor did it have any description of the criteria necessary to initiate the process of withdrawal by the government. Considering the condition of the reservations in 1934, there was no foreseeable time when Indians would be able to survive without some protection and services by the government. In this respect the bill did not move forward to articulate specific goals. If we examine the Collier bill title by title we can see the scope of Collier's vision and examine why it failed to attract support from both Indians and Congress.

Title I. Indian Self-Government

The Secretary of the Interior was authorized to issue a charter to the Indians or any reservation, or reservations, or any smaller community, upon petition by one-fourth of the adult Indians residing on the reservation. He was supposed to evaluate the condition of the Indians and design a specific charter for them, some charters being sophisticated and others being basic forms of government. Once the charter had been devised, the Secretary would call an election, and if three-fifths of the people voted to accept the charter, a charter would be issued. The charter was basically designed to be a federal municipal corporation, a new creature in federal law but probably conceived by the New Dealers as miniature versions of the Tennessee Valley Authority and other independent entities then being created by the government.

The Secretary was authorized to purchase lands for landless Indians and designate them as reservations. He could therefore issue a charter for a tract of land and, when landless Indians were willing to move to this land, set down the conditions under which Indians of one-fourth degree Indian blood could become members of the new reservation. By agreeing to move to the land, individual Indians were said to have ratified the charter. There was no provision that the Indians occupying the newly purchased reservation be of the same cultural or genetic background and heritage, so in effect new "tribes" were to be created that were "Indian" in a racial sense but shared little else in common.

Each charter was to include provisions for civil liberties guaranteeing freedom of conscience, worship, speech, press, assembly, and association to all community members. In this respect it was simply a recital of traditional liberties from the United States Constitution and, if passed into law, would have destroyed the traditional customs of the Pueblos, the very Indians after whom Collier seemed to be modeling his conception of Indians. Included within the same section was the right of expatriation by individuals and the need to pay compensation to them for their "share" of community assets. The concept strongly suggested termination and would be later adopted by the Klamaths in their termination act.

With respect to the political control of physical assets, the proposal placed control over tribal *and* individual lands in the hands of the new government, an idea that created bitter strife in Oklahoma and other places where people had come to regard their allotments as personal property. Each community receiving a charter also had to establish a court for the enforcement of ordinances passed by the new government. These ordinances were partially described in the bill and covered most of the topics that modern Indian governments handle, leading one to conclude that Collier saw the creation of powerful and efficient governments that could operate with great efficiency because these charters envisioned Indian governmental activity in areas that are divided into public and private activities in the non-Indian world.

Collier envisioned tribal governments serving as federal agencies, possessing the capabilities of condemning properties and taking them in the name of the tribe and of levying assessments and requiring the performance of labor for governmental projects. These are municipal powers not given to a single government or used by one since colonial days. The impossibility of ever enforcing these provisions seems exceedingly remote and speaks of high fantasy instead of realistic community or political planning.

Section 4(g) of this title enumerated all of the powers and liabilities of a corporation, including the adoption of a corporate seal that would have formal recognition in federal courts. It gave the right to employ counsel but it also authorized the tribes to sue and opened them to be sued for their corporate performance. One cannot, therefore, say that Collier conceived of a "government" within the historic tradition of the Indian/federal relationship, because prevailing law recognized the tribes as independent sovereigns with the protection of sovereign immunity. Seemingly Collier was willing to avoid that question altogether and make tribes vulnerable like the ordinary commercial corporations.

Section 4(i) contained curious phrasing that again confused everyone. The charter gave the power to "act in general as a Federal agency in the administration of Indian Affairs, upon the condition, however, that the United States shall not be liable for any act done, suffered to be done, or omitted to be done by a chartered Indian community." It is exceedingly difficult to conceive how this status would have worked on a practical basis. Would this provision have made Indians immune from certain kinds of interference or would it have subjected them to the same restrictions placed on all federal agencies? Would they have been required to file their ordinances in the Federal Register? The concept was positive, but no one spelled out exactly what it would mean.

Further confusing the issue was the statement that the new government, admittedly incorporated as a business venture, was to be the legal successor of the traditional councilor society that had previously represented the Indians. With respect to newly created reservations where individual Indians came to live, there would have been considerable confusion regarding whether they brought some rights and powers exercised by their former tribe that they had seemingly abandoned. Considering that the traditional tribal government retained *all* powers of self-government except those they had formally transferred to the United States via treaty (see *U.S. v. Winans*), the blithe statement that the new government was the logical if not actual successor to previous forms of government seems to defeat the purpose of organizing a government. At the least it establishes the potential for great confusion because an alert government could claim to be exercising *inherent* powers rather than *delegated* powers via its charter.

With respect to the continuing administrative powers of the Bureau of Indian Affairs, the bill provided that the Commissioner prepare budgets each year of estimated expenditures on the reservation. Tribal complaints or comments were to be forwarded to the Bureau of the Budget. Federal funds spent on Indian programs were to be gratuities and not recorded under "reimbursable debts" as appropriations before the act had been. In any year the Secretary of the Interior could delegate to the Indian community any authority it might need to perform any function of benefit to Indians, again a nebulous delegation that would have created untold confusion for everyone.

The Indian community could, by three-fourths vote, request that the Secretary of the Interior transfer a function of the Interior Department to them. They would then be granted a sum equal to the amount spent by the Bureau of Indian Affairs for that service or function so they could operate the program themselves. This provision anticipated P.L. 638, which became law in the 1970s and had the same provisions.

A more pleasing provision was that giving permission to the Secretary to transfer the title of lands previously used by the government to provide services for Indians. In fact, this provision later became an integral part of the bureau program, and many tracts of land used by the bureau for schools and other services were returned to tribal ownership and control. Nothing in the bill made Indian lands taxable; even lands that would be purchased and taken off the tax roll to create new reservations could not be taxed. But the reason they were exempt was that the tribe had now taken on a sufficient profile as to be regarded as a federal agency, not because one sovereign cannot tax another.

Title II. Special Education for Indians

A very small sum of $50,000 for scholarships for Indians in higher education and a variety of occupational programs was set aside by this title. The Commissioner was authorized to begin special training programs for Indians wishing to enter the Indian Service, but the training was generally for entry-level jobs that many Indians already had and no preference was given to Indians to enable them to move up the ladder into higher administrative jobs. The Commissioner was also authorized to begin work on curricula for government schools. Finally, school buildings could be used so that people could teach the arts and crafts of the tribe and the Commissioner could compensate the people teaching these subjects. On the whole, the Education Title did not deal with primary or secondary education or with the boarding schools or day schools on the reservations. It simply sought to open opportunities for a small number of Indians capable of entering college or attending an advanced trade school.

Title III. Indian Lands

Some of the provisions of this title were provocative and explosive in Indian country but seemed to John Collier as sophisticated ways of dealing with the declining Indian land base. The bill forbade further allotments anywhere in the United States. Actually, it did not affect that many tribes, but the idea that some Indians had received allotments whereas others would not—should the bill pass—seemed unfair to many people. The Secretary of the Interior was authorized to return lands within ceded areas that had not yet been homesteaded, and that meant a substantial amount of land that could be returned to tribal ownership.

The title also extended the trust period on allotments for an indefinite time. Previously the president had to renew the trust annually for each tribe, and there was a frantic period in late December when tribes had to make certain their lands were kept in trust for another year. Forced fee patents on allotments were also prohibited, taking pressure off Indians who feared they would have their lands sold without their permission. But section six said that allotments could only be sold to the Indian community, and that proposal proved very controversial in Oklahoma, where the tribal governments were virtually non-existent and tribal lands had already been allotted and distributed.

Sections six and seven authorized the Secretary of the Interior to designate "consolidation areas" that would form the nucleus for the development of a contiguous land base that would be economically viable for the purposes of large-scale development. A fund of $2 million was to be appropriated for the acquisition of lands to assist tribes in consolidation, although quite obviously one hundred times that amount would have been needed to do an adequate job. The land was to be taken in the name of the United States in trust for the tribe. This provision should be distinguished from taking land in the name of the tribe, the title papers to be held in trust by the United States, that applied to the Five Civilized Tribes at that time.

Any chartered Indian community or tribe could purchase lands within the reservation boundaries that meant that fee lands could be placed back in trust again. Exchanges of every kind were also authorized to make consolidation easier. Allottees exchanging with the tribe could be given life estates so that inheritance problems would not plague the next generation and interrupt consolidation. And the Secretary could promulgate new rules for inheritance if the state in which the reservation was located had laws that inhibited consolidation. Finally, heirship interests would pass to the community on the death of an allottee so that consolidation could continue.

With respect to tribes having both allotments and minerals this provision was inflammatory: even a small mineral interest was worth thousands and sometimes hundreds of thousands of dollars a year. The Secretary could issue inheritable certificates for the value of the interests, but obviously there was considerable loss involved in trading a clear interest in mineral lands for a certificate creating an obligation against the tribe.

The problem with Collier's title dealing with Indian lands is that he made it more comprehensive than he needed, thereby confusing most of the Indians attending the congresses and raising the specter of a new layer of government—the tribe—between individual lands and their use. Here more than anywhere else we can see Collier's belief that a residual cultural/religious motivation would inspire Indians to trade in their allotments and create a solid block of land for a reservation. Variations of the Collier plan were eventually devised by some of the Plains tribes to consolidate their heirship lands in the 1950s and 1960s, but it is apparent from the congresses that no one understood Collier's concept in 1934.

Title IV. Court of Indian Affairs

Here we have the best example of Collier's genius and prophetic vision for Indians. From the beginning of the Indian/federal relationship there has been no clear guide regarding litigation. For several decades Indian tribes were prohibited from suing in a federal court, and many famous cases actually arose when individuals sued or became the subject of a suit by someone else. Even today determining the proper venue for suits and ensuring that all necessary parties are involved creates much confusion. One motivation for proposing "Settlement Acts" today is to avoid long and confusing litigation over topics that might better be negotiated.

Collier proposed to establish a "Court of Indian Affairs" consisting of a chief judge and six associates. This court would accept all cases that presently go into federal district courts and handle all inheritance and competency issues. It could also order the removal of any case involving Indians in a state or tribal court, to be heard by the Court of Indian Affairs. And it would be the national appeals court for the newly authorized tribal courts. It would even handle death penalty cases and all crimes for which a term of five or more years in prison would be the penalty. State law, except where it was superseded by federal and tribal law, would prevail in civil cases.

Judges would serve for a period of ten years and would be subject to removal with the consent of the Senate for any cause. Appeals from the Court of Indian Affairs would be to circuit courts, apparently based on the residency of the parties or the geographical origin of the case. Ten special federal attorneys were to be appointed to advise and represent Indian tribes and communities. The court would also be empowered to hold hearings and conduct cases wherever the case might arise, suggesting that Collier had in mind a court that would periodically travel through Indian country and create dockets from the activities in each region. Considering the complete chaos that we presently see in the field of Indian litigation, Collier's idea sparkles with brilliance. Most essential in his idea is the degree of homogeneity this court would bring to federal Indian law. Today litigation is wholly whimsical in that the degree of representation fluctuates from bad to not-very-good, as the expertise of county, state, and even federal judges in Indian history and culture is abominable. Indian plaintiffs often do not know the background of their possible causes of action, and forum shopping by Indians and their opponents seems to be endemic. The difference in the receptions by the federal circuit courts is not predictable. The tragedy is that the self-government and land provisions of Collier's proposal created so much controversy that no one even questioned the genius of Title Four on courts.

The Collier proposal was virtually dead after the March congresses because it was difficult for Indians to conceive of, and their response was generally to oppose change, whether beneficial or not. The Indians had great faith in Collier because he had already made some important changes in the operation of the Bureau of Indian Affairs. Had he taken considerably more time and introduced the titles as separate pieces of legislation, he might have had much more success. Self-government would have been considerably easier; he would have modified his proposals on land, especially allotments; education would have sailed through Congress in a day; and while there would have been prolonged hearings on the Court of Indian Affairs, Collier might have gotten some legislation in that area that would have been worthwhile.

The two Congressional Indian Committees completely failed to deal with the issues presented in the bill and used the basic format to include all of their favorite subjects, making it one of the worst pieces of legislation ever passed by Congress. One can say at best that the committees preserved the preamble to Collier's bill and little else. Further allotment was prohibited, and the trust period on the allotments was extended indefinitely. The Secretary of the Interior was authorized to return surplus lands to the reservations, but the secretarial withdrawal of Papago [today known as Tohono O'odham] lands for mineral exploration was cancelled, opening that reservation to exploitation by the large copper interests, indicating no policy at all on the future of Indian lands. The Papagos were to be paid no more than five cents an acre for the loss of their lands, in effect reimbursing them an amount less than even grazing fees would have provided for the exploitation of their mineral lands.

The Secretary could authorize the voluntary exchange of lands within a reservation, a power that he already possessed, but a provision that echoed Collier's land proposals without enacting them. The $2 million land purchase fund survived intact except that the Navajos were excluded from using the funds to purchase lands outside their reservation, the boundaries of which were then being extended once again. Indian forests were placed on the principle of sustained yield, and soil erosion prevention measures were to be instituted for most reservations. The Secretary was authorized to purchase lands and establish new reservations for landless Indians, but the public domain allotments and homesteads were not to be touched by the Interior Department.

Section nine appropriated $250,000 for expenses in organizing the new Indian corporations. A fund of $10 million was appropriated as a revolving fund for economic development loans to Indian communities, and $250,000 annually was to be appropriated for Indian education, primarily for trade and vocational schools but with $50,000 reserved for high school and college plans. Section twelve gave preference to Indians in hiring for the Bureau of Indian Affairs. Section thirteen excluded the Oklahoma tribes completely and raised questions about Alaskan eligibility for the act. Section fourteen directed the Secretary of the Interior to continue the "Sioux benefit," which was a treaty right of enrolled Sioux Indians. (The benefit disappeared shortly thereafter.) Section fifteen disclaimed expenditures as offsets in claims.

The self-government provisions in Collier's original bill emerged in sections sixteen through nineteen, reflecting somewhat the original wording but phrased in such confused language that without the context of Collier's ideas, they would prove to be puzzles for future generations. Section sixteen provided for the organization of a government and adoption of a constitution and by-laws. Eliminating Collier's list of powers to be granted by the federal government in the charters, this section reads as follows: "In addition to all powers vested in any Indian tribe or tribal council by existing law, the constitution adopted by said tribe shall also vest in such tribe or its tribal council the following rights and powers: To employ legal counsel, . . . to prevent the sale, disposition, lease, or encumbrance of tribal lands . . . and to negotiate with the Federal, State, and local Governments."

Few people recognize how radical this phrasing was. Under Collier's original proposal the government *granted* certain powers to the newly chartered tribal governments, hence these governments would be said to have *delegated* political powers. However, the list of powers was omitted, and Congress felt it was building on already-existing powers enjoyed by Indian nations. As a result, except for the three powers listed above (which could easily have been existing powers of government as well), every power that Indian tribes had, they had possessed from the very beginning of the relationship with the federal government as a result of having been politically independent and capable of making treaties. So the tribes possessed *inherent* powers, and while Congress can limit or void delegated powers, it cannot eliminate inherent powers without the consent of the Indians.

Section seventeen provided for the election of the adult Indians living on the reservation to approve or refuse the charter of incorporation. The provisions of this section are not at all clear. Obviously this is not an election in which tribal members or people descended from tribal members can vote. It only provides that the people resident on the reservation can vote and does not even restrict eligibility to those persons having tribal relations with the tribe occupying the reservation. Theoretically a group of Indians working for the bureau all from other tribes could vote in this election. The tribal rolls necessary to create a list of eligible voters would necessarily exclude all tribal members who were recognized as members but who did not live on the reservation. In addition, it was not certain whether two tribes occupying the same reservation could organize two governments or one.

If the Indians voted down the proposed charter, according to section eighteen, the act would not apply to them—and a good many did vote against coming under the act. Section nineteen defined "Indian" in a most confusing manner. All persons of Indian descent were eligible, and all persons of one-half or more Indian blood. But how, one wonders, would individuals prove they were one-half or more Indian blood unless either the bureau or the tribe had kept accurate records? The one-half blood quantum requirement clashed directly with other laws that set the eligibility at one-quarter for education and health purposes.

Resistance to the Indian Reorganization Act

With this background of efforts to define self-government in the years prior to 1934, the reader can see that there was much confusion in Congress and the various administrations regarding the necessity of organizing modern forms of political and economic institutions on the reservations. Some scholars have suggested that the Indian Reorganization Act (IRA) governments were established to become puppets for the federal government, but considering the historical context, that accusation hardly holds water. Prior to the IRA, while tribes might have had governments, these institutions had shadowy existence and powers and most did not have any veto power over the Bureau of Indian Affairs. Most of them existed to press claims against the United States and occasionally endorse actions already done by their agents on their behalf.

The administration's thrust to avoid further allotments can be seen as a real watershed in federal Indian policy because there were provisions that allowed the Secretary of the Interior to begin to rebuild the Indian land base by returning surplus lands and purchasing new lands to consolidate tribal holdings. The price for this advance in one instance was the rape of Papago mineral lands. Nothing was said about tribal water rights, and only a token gesture was made toward modern conservation practices with forestlands.

The congresses do not reflect the sentiments of the bureau in many respects. Time and again we find Collier and his representatives puzzled by their failure to garner support from the Indians. The exchanges between Collier and individual Indians are sometimes sharp and thorough, and Collier often leads his inquisitor back to the original question and convinces him that he should support the bill. When the final tally is taken at some of these meetings, even though people have been convinced that the bill is good on every point, they nevertheless vote to reject it.

What we may have here is the failure or refusal of Indians to adopt formal institutional life. Certainly the organization of the reservations would greatly reduce the spontaneity of community life. Traditions were still very strong in 1934, and many Indians did not believe that social relationships could be or should be controlled by rules and regulations. More apparent is the idea prevalent among the delegates that they had accepted their marginal social status in white society and did not want it disturbed. The accusations of "communism" and "segregation" reflect this belief. Even higher education seemed to be a remote possibility to many of the people attending the congresses, as reflected in the expression of sentiments throughout some of the meetings that the federal schools were the best education for their children. Surely here was segregation in its highest expression being accepted as something beneficial.

Examining the names of Indians attending these congresses is enlightening in terms of understanding Indian leadership. Grandfathers and great-grandfathers, indicating prolonged involvement in tribal affairs, represent some prominent families of today. When the old chiefs speak at these congresses we find that some of them remember the days of freedom prior to the establishment of reservations, and they speak of treaties as a present reality that, for them, still endured. Above all, the transcripts of these meetings demonstrate the strong continuity of Indian life and values over many generations and continuing today.

Editorial Note

Transcriptions of the Indian congresses were mimeographed and sent out to the tribes. Editing for this volume has been kept to a minimum out of respect for their historic value.

Although the distinctive styles of the original documents have been retained, the formatting of titles, headings, and text has been standardized throughout the volume. Obvious typographical errors have been corrected, and some punctuation has been modified to reduce the likelihood of misreading. Where words or phrases are unreadable in the original, that is noted in the text.

The various pieces of legislation are preserved in their entirety in the congressional reports. Transcripts of the Indian congresses are archived at the U.S. Department of the Interior Library.

The Indian Reorganization Act

CHAPTER 1

LEGISLATIVE REFORM OF INDIAN POLICY

H.R. 25242

Right of Indians to Nominate Their Agent

June 21, 1912

Be it enacted by the Senate and House of Representatives of the United States of America in Congress assembled, That hereafter it shall be lawful for any tribe or band of Indians under the jurisdiction of any separate agency maintained for the benefit of any such tribe, tribes, band, or bands, or where several tribes or bands under the jurisdiction of any one agency may desire to act collectively, to indicate to the Secretary of the Interior by a two-thirds vote of the adult members thereof their choice and selection and nomination of their agent or superintendent, as the case may be; and it shall be the duty of the Secretary of the Interior to, in compliance therewith, appoint and designate such agent or superintendent so selected or nominated: Provided, That such selection may be made at any time after the expiration of sixty days from the passage of this act, and the person so selected, nominated, or elected by any such tribe, tribes, band or bands, shall be a citizen of the United States above the age of twenty-eight years old who shall be acquainted with agriculture and who shall have resided within the State and have been engaged in agriculture not less than five years; Provided further, That any such officer, agent, or superintendent shall not be removed from office except for good and sufficient cause and also by and with the consent of a majority of the adult voters of any such tribe or tribes, band or bands; that any such agent or superintendent so appointed shall submit to the Senate and House of Representatives on or before the first day of November of each year a report in which he shall set out in detail the increased or decreased acreage of the Indian lands under his jurisdiction and the amount of timber cut and sold therefrom, and the habits and educational progress, the number of Indian children in school, including a census of the resident Indians and non-resident Indians under his jurisdiction, giving the number of births and deaths and a general account of the progress of said Indians, including a schedule showing the names and numbers of employees, how employed, salary paid each and whether from tribal or public funds. Such agent or superintendent shall be paid the same compensation and in the same manner as now provided by law, except that no such agent or superintendent shall receive a salary in excess of one thousand eight hundred dollars per annum.

SECTION 2. That the Secretary of the Interior shall authorize the appointment or employment of such clerks, farmers, and such other employees as now authorized by law and which, in his opinion, are necessary at any such agency or superintendency, and such agent or superintendent making such appointments shall be responsible to the Department of the Interior for the efficiency and character of such employee so appointed by him: Provided, That no person so employed or appointed shall be related by blood or marriage to such agent or superintendent, and shall not act as the personal or family servant of such agent or superintendent; Provided further, That when competent to fill any position contemplated by this act persons of Indian blood shall be given the preference. Should any tribe, tribes, band, or bands nominate or elect any persons who, by reason of intemperance, immorality, or lack of qualification to fill the position of agent or superintendent as contemplated by this act is deemed unfit for such position, the Secretary of the Interior may refuse to appoint such person, and any such tribe, tribes, band or bands may immediately thereafter, or as soon as convenient to them, proceed in like manner to make another nomination or election.

SECTION 3. That prior to the first election any such tribe, tribes, band or bands shall convene in mass assembly, after due general notice for a period of not less than two weeks, such notice to be given by the agent or superintendent then in charge, upon petition being filed with him and signed by not less than twenty duly qualified Indian electors: said petition shall indicate the manner of giving such notice, and such assembly shall consist of not less than twenty per centum of all the resident electors of any such tribe, tribes, band or bands and shall select or elect a president, secretary, and treasurer from said assembly: and after so forming a permanent organization those assembled shall select three additional persons who shall be qualified electors and designated as electors, and who, in conjunction with the officers so selected, shall constitute an election board, the president of which shall give two weeks' public notice in such manner and form as to bring to general notice the time, place, and manner of holding an election for the purpose of selecting or electing such agent or superintendent; Provided, That the method or manner of election shall be free from fraud or deception and so conducted as to give each and every elector entitled to vote full and free opportunity to exercise such right.

SECTION 4. That it shall be unlawful for any person seeking the nomination or election to any such agency or superintendency to be present during the time or day of any such election or to go among the electors, after notice of such election has been given, seeking or inducing any such elector, either in person or by proxy; or if he shall give or cause to be given any article or thing of value, directly or indirectly, or by any means whatever, to secure the vote of any such Indian shall be disqualified for appointment.

SECTION 5. That the result of any such election shall be certified to the Secretary of the Interior by a certificate signed by the president and attested by the secretary of such election board, including in such certificate the number of electors, male and female, the name of the tribe, tribes, band or bands if they shall have acted either collectively or separately at such election. The confirmation or rejection of any such agent or superintendent so elected or nominated shall be made by the Secretary of the Interior within the period of twenty days of the receipt of such certificate of election or nomination; Provided, That such certificate shall be transmitted by registered mail.

SECTION 6. That the agent or superintendent, when elected or nominated and confirmed as contemplated by this act, shall give bond in manner and form as now provided by law. Immediately following the approval of the bond of any such agent or superintendent the Secretary of the Interior is directed to cause to be placed to his official credit or to be paid to him by warrant the sum of three hundred dollars out of any money in the Treasury to the credit of any such tribe, tribes, band or bands, which sum shall be used to defray the expenses of any such election when duly certified to such agent or superintendent by the secretary of such election board as herein provided. Such amount so paid by such superintendent shall be included in the annual report of the agent or superintendent.

SECTION 7. That the existence of the election board as contemplated by this act shall be continuous, and if any vacancy shall occur between elections, such vacancy shall remain until the next election, when a successor shall be voted for and such vacancy may be so filled; Provided, That should the office of treasurer, president, or secretary become vacant, such vacancy may be filled by a majority vote of the remaining members. The election board shall, when convenient, be provided with a room, a desk, a table, and eight chairs at any such agency or superintendency; and for purposes for other than election board the members shall constitute and be known and designated as a business committee. All matters of heirship affecting the rights of any member of such tribe, tribes, band or bands shall be submitted by such agent or superintendent to said board for opinion and determination, and the findings of said board shall be duly certified to the Secretary of the Interior by such agent or superintendent.

SECTION 8. That hereafter it shall be unlawful to authorize the uses of funds of any tribe, tribes, band or bands under the jurisdiction of any such elected agent or superintendent as contemplated by this act, until such proposed expenditure shall have been submitted to the business committee, who may make such report to the agent or superintendent as may be deemed by them expedient, either approving or rejecting such proposal. Such report shall be in duplicate, one copy to be forwarded to the Secretary of the Interior by such agent or superintendent, and the other copy shall be incorporated in and made a part of the annual report of such agent or superintendent.

SECTION 9. That for the protection of full-blood Indians, or others under disability, any allottee hereafter under such agent or superintendent who is a full-blood Indian, or by the agent deemed to be an incompetent Indian, may lease his allotment, subject to the approval of such agent or superintendent, for any period not exceeding five years either for cash or crop rent: in either event such crop or cash rent is to be in conformity with the prices, customs, and usages in the rental of land general in the locality.

That any allottee hereafter within the incompetent or full-blood class, or who is one-half Indian blood, may lease as now provided by law except as to crop rent, and with the modification that any such lease shall be approved by such agent or superintendent, by and with the advice and consent of the business committee. That any person who is of one-fourth Indian blood, or less, shall, at his option, have the full control and management of his allotment with respect to leasing and in all other respects than that the title to his allotment shall remain as now provided by law. That any such allottee who may exercise his right of option to control and manage his own allotment shall be paid upon application any funds to his credit now in the Treasury of the United States, and he shall hereafter in no respect be under the care, control, or jurisdiction of the Interior Department more than any other citizen of the United States.

SECTION 10. That any person who is of half Indian blood may lease his allotment for any period not exceeding one year at his own option, or if for a longer period than one year, not exceeding five years, such lease shall be approved by the agent or superintendent: Provided, That any such lease shall be free from fraud and for an equitable consideration.

The parent or next of kin having the care and custody of any minor allottee may lease his allotment, for any period not exceeding five years, or his minority, with the approval of any such agent or superintendent, and cared for as other Indian moneys are now cared for under existing law, except that such agent or superintendent may pay to such natural guardian such sums and at such times as will in his discretion best promote the interests of such minor or orphan ward.

SECTION 11. That all individual moneys now to the credit of any individual allottee under the jurisdiction of any such agent or superintendent shall be turned over to his successor or retained by him if elected, and such sums shall be cared for as now provided by law, except that such agent, by and with the approval of the business committee, shall pay to such individuals either all or in part, such sum or sums as may be due them and as it may be deemed will best subserve their interests.

SECTION 12. That this act shall not apply to the Five Civilized Tribes of Oklahoma or to the Apache band in such state, and for the purposes of this act the Kiowa and Comanche Indians shall elect an election board as herein provided, as shall also the Caddo, Wichita, and Delaware Indians within and under the jurisdiction of the Anadarko Agency, Oklahoma.

SECTION 13. That for the purposes of this act the Kaw and Osage Indians may organize as one tribe, and two members of the election board herein contemplated shall be Kaw Indians. No provision of this act shall be construed as extending any agency or superintendency, or as limiting the operation of existing law as to the rights and authority of the Secretary of the Interior to terminate any existing Indian school or superintendency within the meaning of this act.

SECTION 14. That it is further provided that any tribe or band of Indians coming within the meaning of this act shall not be entitled to its benefits unless they have so far progressed in civilization as to be competent of organization in conformity with this act and with ordinary preliminary practices in the perfection and maintenance of their organization as herein contemplated.

SECTION 15. That there be and is hereby appropriated, out of any money in the Treasury not otherwise appropriated, the sum of twenty-five thousand dollars, to be used in the discretion of the Secretary of the Interior in carrying this act into effect, and for the payment of not to exceed the sum of one thousand dollars at any one agency or superintendency in payment for counsel when requested by said business committee, to be used in the investigation by such committee of the accounts of any outgoing agent or superintendent as may be deemed expedient by said committee.

SECTION 16. That this act shall be of full force and effect from and after the date of its approval.

S. 5335

A Bill Conferring upon Tribes the Right to Recall Their Agents or Superintendents

May 2, 1916

Be it enacted by the Senate and House of Representatives in Congress assembled, That from and after the passage of this act no persons shall be retained in the capacity of agent or superintendent of any Indian agency the Indian residents of which have declared, or may declare, by majority vote of the male adults over twenty-one years of age, against the retention of any person as the agent or superintendent of such agency. And where hereunder any tribe of Indians may have declared by majority vote against the retention of an agent or superintendent, the Secretary of the Interior shall immediately remove such agent or superintendent and appoint as his successor any person whom he may select.

SECTION 2. That whenever an election is held under the provisions of this act, it shall be held as the business council or mass meeting of such tribe shall prescribe and in such manner as will show that the result of such election represents the desire of a majority of male adults of the tribe: Provided, That the word "council" as herein expressed shall mean a business council of ten members of such tribe selected biennially at a mass meeting duly advertised for a period of not less than two weeks and called for the purpose of selecting such business council at some central point in such reservation.

SECTION 3. That the Secretary of the Interior shall be notified twenty days in advance of any election, and is hereby authorized to designate a competent person to attend each polling place during the time of holding such elections, if he desires to do so.

S. 3668 [Indian Tribal Councils Act]

72nd Congress, 1st Session

(By Senator Frazier, North Dakota)

A BILL authorizing the creation of Indian tribal councils, and for other purposes.

Be it enacted by the Senate and House of Representatives of the United States of America in Congress assembled, That upon the filing with the Commissioner of Indian Affairs a written petition signed by at least 25 per centum of the adult members of any Indian tribe residing on any reservation under the jurisdiction of the United States, the Commissioner of Indian Affairs shall call a general election of the adult members of such tribe to be held within sixty days from the date of filing of such petition for the purpose of choosing a constitutional committee to draft a proposed constitution and by-laws for such tribe. Such committee shall consist of not less than nine members. Within sixty days after its election such committee shall call a general meeting of adult members of the tribe for the purpose of considering and acting upon a proposed constitution and by-laws for such tribe, and each adult member of the tribe shall be notified of the time and place of such general meeting. A copy of the proposed constitution and by-laws, together with a notice of such meeting shall be distributed to each adult member of the tribe at least two weeks prior to the time fixed for such general meeting. At such meeting the proposed constitution and by-laws may be adopted, amended, and rejected, in whole or in part, but subject to the exception contained in section 7, each such constitution shall provide for (1) the establishment of a tribal council of not less than ____ members and the powers to be conferred on such council; (2) a direct election of at least once each year of the members of the tribal council by the adult members of the tribe or of the districts to be represented by such council members, and (3) a referendum on any question of policy on the petition of at least 15 per centum of the adult members of the tribe, the action of the adult members of the tribe on such referendum to be conclusive and binding upon the tribal council. The amount of any expenses incurred by or on behalf of any tribe carrying out the provisions of this section shall be paid out of any money in the Treasury not otherwise appropriated. There is hereby authorized to be appropriated such sum as may be necessary for such purposes.

SECTION 2. Such tribal councils shall be empowered to represent their several tribes before the Congress or the executive departments of the United States or in the courts. The expenses of any such tribal council shall be paid out of any tribal funds of its tribe, or out of any other moneys over which such council may have exclusive jurisdiction under section 6 but not more than $5,000 may be expended for such purposes in any year from the funds of any tribe.

SECTION 3. All authority vested in Indian tribes or tribal councils by existing law shall be vested exclusively in the tribal councils provided for by this act. Hereafter no tribal lands, or interest in lands, belonging to any Indian tribe, shall be sold, leased, encumbered, or in any manner disposed of, nor any permit granted therefor, nor any contract made for the use thereof, by the Secretary of the Interior, except by authority of the tribal council, by authority of the general council speaking for such tribe.

SECTION 4. Said tribal councils are hereby authorized to employ legal counsel. Such employment shall not be subject to the approval or control of the Department of the Interior, but the choice of counsel and the fixing of fees paid to such counsel shall be subject to review by the Attorney General on application of any member of the tribe.

SECTION 5. The Secretary of the Interior shall submit to the tribal council for each tribe all estimates for expenditures from funds credited to the said tribe in the United States Treasury, and any recommendations made by the tribal council with respect thereto shall be transmitted to the Bureau of the Budget and to the Congress concurrently with the submission of such estimates.

SECTION 6. All funds derived from the use or sale of any tribal lands or property, including trespass fees and rights of way, shall be deposited in the Treasury of the United States to the credit of the tribe owning such property and draw interest at the rate of 4 per centum, and no such funds shall be deposited to the credit of the fund entitled "Indian moneys proceeds of labor."

SECTION 7. Funds appropriated from the Treasury of the United States for the payment of the expenses of the tribal council, or obtained through contributions by or assessments against the members of the tribe shall be under the exclusive control of the tribal councils herein authorized.

SECTION 8. The Pueblo Tribes of the States of New Mexico and Arizona may retain their traditional customs and established tribal governments in accordance with their established customs, and all provisions of this act relating to powers and functions of the tribal councils shall, so far as consistent with such governments, apply equally to such governments.

SECTION 9. The Secretary of the Interior shall dismiss any employee or officer under his jurisdiction who shall, in any manner, either directly or indirectly, interfere with any of its members in the free exercise of the powers conferred by this act.

SECTION 10. Any employee or officer of the United States who shall, in any manner, either directly or indirectly, interfere with any tribe or any of its members in the free exercise of the powers conferred by this act shall be guilty of a misdemeanor, and shall, on conviction thereof, be punished by a fine of not more than $500 or by imprisonment for not more than six months or both.

SECTION 11. All acts or parts of acts inconsistent with the provisions of this act are hereby repealed.

CHAPTER 2

DEVELOPMENT OF THE INDIAN REORGANIZATION ACT

The Original Collier Proposal

[H.R. 7902, 73rd Congress, 2nd Session]

A BILL to grant to Indians living under Federal tutelage the freedom to organize for purposes of local self-government and economic enterprise; to provide for the necessary training of Indians in administrative and economic affairs; to conserve and develop Indian lands; and to promote the more effective administration of justice to matters affecting Indian tribes and communities by establishing a federal Court of Indian Affairs.

Be it enacted by the Senate and House of Representatives of the United States of America in Congress assembled,

TITLE I—INDIAN SELF-GOVERNMENT

SECTION 1. That it is hereby declared to be the policy of Congress to grant to those Indians living under Federal tutelage and control the freedom to organize for the purposes of local self-government and economic enterprise, to the end that civil liberty, political responsibility, and economic independence shall be achieved among the Indian peoples of the United States, and to provide for cooperation between the Federal Government, the States, and organized Indian communities for Indian welfare. It is further declared to be the policy of Congress that those functions of government now exercised over Indian reservations by the Federal Government through the Department of the Interior and the Office of Indian Affairs shall be gradually relinquished and transferred to the Indians of such reservations, duly organized for municipal and other purposes, as the ability of such Indians to administer the institutions and functions of representative government shall be demonstrated, and that those powers of control over Indian funds and assets now vested in officials of the Federal Government shall be terminated or transferred to the duly constituted governments of local Indian communities as the capacity of the Indians concerned, to manage their own economic affairs prudently and effectively, shall be demonstrated. It is further declared to be the policy of Congress to assist in the development of Indian capacities for self-government and economic competence by providing for the necessary training of Indians, and by rendering financial assistance and cooperation in establishing Indian communities.

SECTION 2. In accordance with the foregoing purposes, the Secretary of the Interior is hereby authorized to issue to the Indians residing upon any Indian reservation or reservations or subdivision thereof a charter granting to the said community group any or all of such powers of government and such privileges of corporate organization and economic activity, hereinafter enumerated, as may seem fitting in light of the experience, capacities, and desires of the Indians concerned; but no such charter shall take effect until ratified by a three-fifths vote at a popular election open to all adult Indians resident within the territory covered by the charter.

Upon receipt of a petition for the issuance of a charter signed by one-fourth of the adult Indians residing on any existing reservation, it shall be the duty of the Secretary of the Interior to make the necessary investigations and issue a proper charter, subject to ratification, or shall proclaim the conditions upon which such charter will be issued; and such petition, with a record of the findings and of the action of the Secretary, shall be transmitted by the Secretary of the Interior to Congress: *Provided,* That whenever the Secretary of the Interior shall acquire land not comprised within any existing reservation for the purpose of establishing a new Indian community, pursuant to the authority granted by title III of this Act, he shall issue a charter to take effect at some future time and shall therein prescribe the conditions under which persons of at least one-fourth degree of Indian blood shall be entitled to become members of such community, and the acceptance of such membership by the qualified persons shall constitute an acceptance and ratification of such charter.

SECTION 3. Each charter issued to an Indian community shall define the territorial limits of the community and the criteria of membership within the community; shall, wherever such community is sufficiently populous and endowed with sufficient territory to make the establishment of local government possible, prescribe a form of government adopted to the needs, traditions, and experience of such community; and shall guarantee the civil liberties of minorities and individuals within the community, including the liberty of conscience, worship, speech, press, assembly, and association, and the right of any member to abandon the community and to receive some compensation for any interest in community assets thereby relinquished, the extent of which compensation and the manner of payment thereof to be fixed by chartered provision. Each charter shall further specify the powers of self-government to be exercised by the chartered community, and shall provide for the planned extension of these powers as the community offers evidence of capacity to administer them. Each charter shall likewise prescribe the powers of management or supervision to be exercised by the chartered community over presently restricted real and personal property of individual Indians or tribes, and shall provide for the bonding of any community officials or Federal employees entrusted with the custody of community funds and for such forms of publicity and accounting, and for such continuing supervision by the Office of Indian Affairs over financial transactions and economic policies as may be found by the Secretary of the Interior to be necessary to prevent dissipation of the capital resources of the community or unjust discrimination in the apportionment of income; and each charter shall further provide for the gradual elimination of administrative supervision as the Indian community shows progress in the effective utilization of its resources and the prudent disposal of its assets.

SECTION 4. The Secretary of the Interior is authorized to grant to any community which may be chartered under this Act, either by original charter or by supplement to such charter initiated or ratified by a three-fourths vote, any or all of the powers hereinafter enumerated, subject to the provisions of law fixed by section 8 of this title, or any rules or regulations promulgated pursuant thereto, respecting the terms upon which certain functions of the Federal Government shall be transferred to the chartered community, and to provide, in such original charter or supplement, for the definition, qualification, or limitation of any powers which may be granted, in any manner deemed necessary or desirable for the effectuation of the purposes and policies above set forth.

(a) To organize and act as a Federal municipal corporation, to establish a form of government, to adopt and thereafter to amend a constitution, and to promulgate and enforce ordinances and regulations for the effectuation of the functions hereafter specified, and any other functions customarily exercised by local governments.

(b) To elect or appoint officers, agents, and employees, to define the qualifications for office, to fix the salaries of officials to be paid by the community, to prescribe the qualifications of voters, to define the conditions of membership within the community, and to provide for the adoption of new members.

(c) To regulate the use and disposition of property by members of the community, to protect and conserve the property, wildlife, and natural resources of the community, to cultivate and encourage arts, crafts, and culture, to administer charity, and to protect the health, morals, and general welfare of the members of the community.

(d) To establish courts for the enforcement and administration of ordinances of the community, which courts shall have exclusive jurisdiction over all offenses of, and controversies between, members of the chartered community, under the ordinances of such community, and jurisdiction exclusive or nonexclusive over all other cases arising under the ordinances of the community, and shall have power to render and enforce judgments, criminal and civil, legal and equitable, and to punish violations of local ordinances by fine not exceeding $500, or, in the alternative, by imprisonment for a period not exceeding six months: *Provided,* That no person shall be punished for any offense for which prosecution has been begun in any other court of competent jurisdiction.

(e) To accept the surrender of the tribal, corporate, or community interests of individual members who desire to abandon the community, and to pay a fair compensation therefor, to act as guardian or to provide for the appointment of guardians for minor and other incompetent members of the community, and to administer tribal and individual funds and properties which may be transferred or entrusted to the community by the Federal Government.

(f) To operate, maintain, and equip any public improvement and, as a Federal agency, to condemn and take title to any lands or properties, in its own name, when necessary for any of the purposes authorized by charter, and to levy assessments for community purposes, or to require the performance of labor on community projects, in lieu of assessments.

(g) To acquire, manage, and dispose of property, subject to applicable laws restricting the alienation of Indian lands and the dissipation of Indian resources, to make contracts, to issue nontransferable certificates of membership, to declare and pay out dividends, to adopt and use a corporate seal which shall be judicially noticed in all Federal courts, to sue and be sued in its own name, to employ counsel and to pay counsel fees not in excess of limits to be fixed by charter provision, to have succession until its membership may become extinct, and to exercise any other privileges which may be granted to membership or business corporations.

(h) To compel the transfer from the community for inefficiency in office or other cause, of any employee of the Federal Indian Service locally assigned; to regulate trade and intercourse between members of the community and nonmembers; and to exclude from the territory of the community, with the approval of the Secretary of the Interior, nonmembers whose presence endangers the health, security, or welfare of the community: *Provided, however,* That nothing in this section or in this Act shall be construed to forbid the service in the territory of any Indian community of any civil or criminal process of any court having jurisdiction over any person found therein.

(i) To exercise any other powers now or hereafter delegated to the Office of Indian Affairs, or any officials thereof, to contract with governmental bodies of State or Nation for the reception or performance of public services, and to act in general as a Federal agency in the administration of Indian Affairs, upon the condition, however, that the United States shall not be liable for any act done, suffered to be done, or omitted to be done by a chartered Indian community.

(j) To exercise any other powers, not inconsistent with the Constitution and laws of the United States, which may be necessary or incidental to the execution of the powers above enumerated.

An Indian community chartered under this Act shall be recognized as successor to any existing political powers heretofore exercised over the members of such community by any tribal, or other native political organizations comprised within the said community, not withheld by such tribal or other native political organization, and shall, subject to the terms of said charter, further be recognized as successor to all right, interest, and title to all funds, property, choses in action, and claims against the United States heretofore held by the tribes or other native political organizations comprised within the community, or to a proportionate share thereof, except as such succession may be limited by the charter, subject to existing provisions of law with respect to the maintenance of suits against the United States, and subject further to such provision for the apportionment of such assets among nonmembers of the community having vested rights therein, as may be prescribed by the charter.

SECTION 5. When any Indian community shall have been chartered, it shall be the duty of the Commissioner of Indian Affairs to cause regular reports concerning their respective functions to be made to the constituted authorities of the community, to advise and consult with such authorities on problems of local administration and Federal policy, and to allow such authorities free access to the records and files of the local agency.

Any Indian community shall have the power to compel the transfer from the community of any persons employed in the administration of Indian affairs within the territorial limits of the community other than persons appointed by the community: *Provided, however,* That the Commissioner of Indian Affairs may prescribe such conditions for the exercise of this power as will assure to employees of the Indian Service a reasonable security of tenure, an opportunity to demonstrate their capacities over a stated period of time, and an opportunity to hear and answer complaints and charges.

SECTION 6. The Secretary shall prepare annual estimates of expenditures for the administration of Indian affairs, including expenditures for functions and services administered by an Indian community, pursuant to the authority conferred by section 8 of this title. It shall be the duty of the Secretary to transmit to the authorized representative of an Indian community any estimates and justifications thereof for expenditures to be made in whole or in part within the territorial limits of the community. Any recommendations of the authorized representatives of the community, including the approval or rejection of any item in whole or in part, or the recommendation of any other expenditure, shall be transmitted by the Secretary to the Bureau of the Budget and to the Congress concurrently with the submission of the estimates of the Secretary.

The Secretary shall also transmit to the authorized representatives of an Indian community a copy of any bill, or amendment of a bill, for the benefit of Indians, authorizing, in whole or in part, the appropriation or expenditure, within the territorial limits of such community, of any funds from the Federal Treasury for which the Secretary of the Interior has submitted no estimates, and the Secretary shall transmit their written recommendations to the Congress.

The Secretary shall also transmit to the authorized representatives of an Indian community a description of any project involving the expenditure, in whole or in part, of any funds appropriated for the general welfare within the territorial limits of the community.

No expenditure hereafter authorized or appropriated for by Congress shall be charged against any such Indian community as a reimbursable debt, unless such appropriation and expenditure have been recommended or approved by such Indian community through its duly constituted authorities; and any funds of the community deposited in the United States Treasury shall be expended only by the bonded disbursing agent of such community.

SECTION 7. The Secretary of the Interior may from time to time delegate to any Indian community, within the limits of its competence as defined by charter, the authority to perform any act, service, or function which the United States administers for the benefit of Indians within the territorial limits of the community and may enter into annual agreements with the constituted authorities of the community with respect to the terms and conditions of such delegation.

SECTION 8. The Commissioner is authorized and directed to proceed immediately after the passage of this Act, to arrange and classify the various functions and services administered for Indians by the United States into divisions and subdivisions which may be separably transferred. The Commissioner is further authorized and directed to proceed, immediately after the passage of this Act, to make a study and investigation of the conditions upon which separable functions and services may be transferred to the Indian communities and thereupon to promulgate, direct, and express rules and regulations to such given transfer.

The said rules and regulations shall set forth all conditions reasonably necessary to assure the satisfactory and continued administration of the function or service transferred. The said rules and regulations shall include standards of fitness for Indians with respect to health, age, charter, knowledge, and ability, for any position maintained, now or hereafter, before or after transfer to an Indian community, for the administration of functions or services within the territorial limits of any community, and a classification of all positions for which the requisite knowledge and training may be acquired by Indians through experience or apprenticeship in the position. The said rules and regulation shall also set forth for each separable function or services, a condition of its transfer, the positions for which Indians shall qualify and the required number of qualified Indians for each such position, provisions assuring a reasonable security of tenure, and any other conditions reasonably necessary to assure the continued and the satisfactory administration of transferred functions or services.

Any Indian community may, through procedure set up in its charter, appoint a member to any vacant position under the Indian Service maintained for the administration of functions or services for Indians within the territorial limits of the community. The appointee shall not take office until he shall have previously received the certificate of approval of his fitness for the position in question from the Commissioner. The Commissioner shall issue such certificate of approval to any member of an Indian community recommended by the duly authorized representatives of the community and who is qualified for the position under the rules and regulations prescribed pursuant to the section.

Any Indian community may, upon a three-fourths vote at a popular election open to all adult members, request the transfer of any separable function or service, and the Secretary of the Interior shall transfer such function or service and, if necessary, confer by supplement to the community charter, the legal capacity to exercise such function or service, subject only to the following terms and conditions;

(a) The community must comply with all conditions prescribed by the rules and regulations of the Secretary of the Interior pursuant to the authority of this section. The community may transmit to the Congress any objection it may have to the condition imposed, together with its budget recommendations for the next fiscal year.

(b) The Secretary of the Interior shall certify to the Secretary of the Treasury the amount of any sums or any unexpended balance of such sums theretofore or thereafter expressly appropriated, or the proportionate share of any general appropriation, for the administration of such function or service within territorial limits of the community. The Secretary of the Treasury shall place such sums to the credit of the community, to be paid out on the requisition of the bonded disbursing agent of the community. The expenditure of such funds shall be subject to all Federal laws and regulations governing the expenditures of Federal appropriations.

(c) The Commissioner shall aid and advise the community, and the local federal employees shall cooperate in any feasible manner at the request of the community, in the administration of the function or service transferred. The Commissioner shall also make available to the Indian community any facilities, including any lands, buildings, and equipment previously used but no longer needed by the United States in the administration of Indian affairs within the community.

(d) Whenever the Secretary of the Interior shall determine that the community has failed to comply with the conditions imposed for the continued administration of the function or service transferred, the Secretary or the Commissioner of Indian Affairs shall reassume the administration of such function or service and the Secretary shall report to the next regular session of the Congress with appropriate recommendations.

(e) The community, or its duly authorized representatives, shall make on or before September 1 of each year, an annual report of the fiscal year ended June 30, previously, to the Secretary, concerning the administration of the function or service transferred to the community including an account by the disbursing agent of the community of receipts and expenditures of moneys placed to the credit of the community under this section.

(f) The Secretary of the Interior shall make an annual report to Congress on the administration of the functions and services transferred to the community, and shall include in such reports the reports of the Indian communities required by paragraph (e) of this section.

SECTION 9. The Secretary and the Commissioner shall continue to exercise all existing powers of supervision and control over Indian affairs now entrusted to them or either of them which are not transferred by charter or supplement thereto or by Act of Congress to organized Indian communities and shall have power to enforce by administrative order or veto, if so provided within the charter, or, in any event, by legal process in any court of competent jurisdiction, all provisions contained in a charter for the protection of the rights of minorities within the community, all provisions that limit, qualify, or restrict the powers granted to the community.

SECTION 10. The Secretary of the Interior may, upon granting a charter to an Indian community, convey or confirm to such community, as an agency of the Federal Government, any right, interest, or title in property which may be held by the United States in trust for members of the community, and in any lands, buildings, or equipment previously used by the United States in the administration of Indian affairs within the community, and in any liens or credits of the United States held by virtue of loans to or expenditures on behalf of Indian members of the said community.

SECTION 11. Nothing in this Act shall be construed as rendering the property of any Indian community or of any member of such community subject to taxation by any State or subdivision thereof, or subject to attachment or sale under legal process, or as an expression of intent on the part of the United States to abandon the duties and responsibilities of guardianship of any Indians becoming members of chartered communities.

SECTION 12. There is hereby authorized to be appropriated, out of any funds in the Treasury not otherwise appropriated, such sums as may be necessary, not to exceed $500,000 in any one fiscal year, to be expended at the order of the Secretary of the Interior, and with the consent of the Indian communities concerned, in defraying the expenses of the organization and development of communities chartered under this Act, including the construction and furnishing of community buildings, the purchase of clerical supplies, and the improvement of community lands.

SECTION 13. The following definitions of terms used in this title shall be binding in the interpretation of this statute:

(a) The term "Commissioner" whenever used in this Act shall be taken to refer to the Commissioner of Indian Affairs, and the term "Secretary" to the Secretary of the Interior, and the terms "Commissioner" and "Secretary" whenever used in this Act in reference to the exercise of any power shall be construed as authorizing the delegation of such power to subordinate officials.

(b) The term "Indian" as used in this title to specify the persons to whom charters may be issued, shall include all persons of Indian descent who are members of any recognized Indian tribe, band, or nation, or are descendants of such members and were, on or about February 1, 1934, actually residing within the present boundaries of any Indian reservation, and shall further include all other persons of one-fourth or more Indian blood, but nothing in this definition or in the Act shall prevent the Secretary of the Interior or the constituted authorities of a chartered community from prescribing, by provision of charter or pursuant thereto, additional qualifications or conditions for membership in any chartered community, or from offering the privileges of membership therein to nonresidents of a community who are members of any tribe, wholly or partly comprised within the chartered community.

(c) The term "residing upon any Indian reservation" as used in this title to specify the persons to whom charters may be issued shall signify the maintaining of a permanent abode at the time of the issuance of a charter and for a continuous period of at least one year prior to February 1, 1934, and subsequent to September 1, 1932, but this definition may be modified by the Secretary of the Interior with respect to Indians who may reside on lands required subsequently to February 1, 1934.

(d) The term "charter" as used in this Act shall denote any grant of power by the United States, whether or not such power includes the privilege of corporate existence.

(e) The "three-fifths vote" required for ratification of a charter and the "three-fourths vote" required for proposal or ratification of any supplement thereto or transfer of any Federal function or service shall be measured with reference to the total number of votes cast; the chartered community, or, if the community has not yet been chartered, the Secretary of the Interior shall designate the time, place and manner of voting, shall declare the qualifications of voters, and shall be the final judge of the eligibility of voters and of the validity of ballots.

(f) The term "disposition of property" as used in this title shall denote any transfer of property by devise or intestate succession, as well as transfer intervivos.

(g) The term "punish" as used in this title shall not be construed to affect the amount or extent of civil judgments.

(h) The term "public" as used in this title shall include all matters affecting either the property owned or controlled by a chartered community, or the health, morals, or welfare of a considerable part of the membership of such community.

(i) The term "dividend" as used in this title shall be construed to include any distribution of funds by a chartered community out of current or accrued income and any other distribution of funds which may be approved by the Secretary of the Interior.

(j) The power "to sue and be sued" as used in this title shall not be construed to grant to the courts of any State any jurisdiction over a chartered community or the members thereof not now possessed over an Indian tribe or its members, nor to sanction execution upon the assets of the community, nor shall this power be construed to deny the right of the United States to intervene in any suit or proceeding in which it now has the right to intervene.

(k) The term "tribe" wherever used in this Act shall be construed to refer to any Indian tribe, band, nation, pueblo, or other native political group or organization.

(l) The term "reservation" wherever used in this Act shall be construed to comprise all the territory within the outer boundaries of any Indian reservation, whether or not such property is subject to restrictions on alienation and whether or not such land is under Indian ownership.

(m) The term "territory of a chartered community" wherever used in this Act shall be construed to comprise all lands, waters, highways, roads, and bridges within the boundaries of an Indian community as fixed by charter, regardless of whether the title to such property is in the United States, an Indian tribe or community, a restricted Indian or the heirs of a restricted Indian, or whether it is in a fee-patent Indian, or any other person, agency, or government.

(n) The term "transfer" as used in this title to apply to any function or service shall designate the relinquishment by the Secretary of the Interior or the Commissioner of Indian Affairs of any rights and duties incident to the performance of such function or service and the assumption of such rights and duties by the Indian community as an agency of the Federal Government.

TITLE II—SPECIAL EDUCATION FOR INDIANS

SECTION 1. The Commissioner is authorized and directed to make suitable provision for the training of Indian members of chartered communities and other Indians of at least one-fourth degree of Indian blood, in the various services now intrusted to the Office of Indian Affairs and in any additional services which may be undertaken by a chartered Indian community, including education, public-health work, and other social services, the administration of law and order, the management of forests and grazing lands, the keeping of financial accounts, statistical records, and other public reports, and the construction and maintenance of buildings, roads, and other public works. The Commissioner may use the staffs and facilities of existing Indian boarding or day schools for such special instruction, and he may provide for the training and education of Indian students in universities, colleges, schools of medicine, law, engineering, or agriculture, or other institutions of recognized standing and may subsidize such training and education under the following conditions:

(a) The Commissioner shall extend financial aid and assistance on the basis of financial need to qualified Indians for the payment of tuition and other costs of education, including necessary costs of support. One-half of the amount so expended shall be a non-interest-bearing, reimbursable loan to be repaid in installments whenever the beneficiary shall have received employment anywhere, but the obligation shall be temporarily suspended during any period of unemployment.

There is hereby authorized to be appropriated, out of any funds in the United States Treasury not otherwise appropriated, a sum not to exceed $50,000 annually to defray subsidies made under the foregoing paragraph.

(b) Notwithstanding the provisions of paragraph (a) of this section, the Commissioner may grant scholarships to any qualified Indian of special promise, no part of which shall be reimbursable.

There is hereby authorized to be appropriated, out of any funds in the United States Treasury not otherwise appropriated, a sum not to exceed $15,000 annually to defray the cost of scholarships awarded under the foregoing paragraph.

Formal contracts shall not be required for compliance with section 3744 of the Revised Statutes (U.S.C. title 41, sec. 16), with respect to the grants of subsidies or scholarships to Indian students under the foregoing provisions.

SECTION 2. It is hereby declared to be the purpose and policy of Congress to promote the study of Indian civilization and preserve and develop the special cultural contributions and achievements of such civilization, including Indian arts, crafts, skills, and traditions. The Commissioner is directed to prepare curricula for Indian schools adapted to the needs and capacities of Indian students, including courses in Indian history, Indian arts and crafts, the social and economic problems of the Indians, and the history and problems of the Indian Administration. The Commissioner is authorized to employ individuals familiar with Indian culture and with the contemporary social and economic problems of the Indians to instruct in schools maintained for Indians. The Commissioner is further directed to make available the facilities of the Indian schools to competent individuals appointed or employed by an Indian community to instruct the elementary and secondary grades in the Indian arts, crafts, skills, and traditions. The Commissioner may contribute to the compensation of such individuals in such proportion and upon such terms and conditions as he may deem advisable. For this purpose the Commissioner may use moneys appropriated for the maintenance of such schools.

TITLE III—INDIAN LANDS

SECTION 1. It is hereby declared to be the policy of Congress to undertake a constructive program of Indian land use and economic development, in order to establish a permanent basis of self-support for Indians living under Federal tutelage; to reassert the obligations of guardianship where such obligations have been improvidently relaxed; to encourage the effective utilization of Indian lands and resources by Indian tribes, cooperative associations, and chartered communities; to safeguard Indian lands against alienation from Indian ownership and against physical deterioration; and to provide land needed for landless Indians and for the consolidation of Indian landholdings in suitable economic units.

SECTION 2. Hereafter no tribal or other land of any Indian reservation or community created or set apart by treaty or agreement with the Indians, act of Congress, Executive order, purchase, or otherwise, shall be allotted in severalty to any Indian.

SECTION 3. The Secretary of the Interior is authorized to withdraw from disposal the remaining surplus lands of any Indian reservation heretofore opened or authorized to be opened, to sale, settlement, entry, or other form of disposal by Presidential proclamation, or under any of the public land laws of the United States. Any land so withdrawn shall have the status of tribal or community lands of the tribe, reservation, or community within whose territorial limits they are located: *Provided, however*, That valid rights or claims of any persons to any lands so withdrawn existing on the date of the withdrawal shall not be affected by this Act.

The Secretary of the Interior shall determine what lands, lying outside of the areas classified for consolidation under Indian ownership pursuant to section 6 of this title, are not needed by the Indians, and such lands shall be reopened to sale, settlement, entry, or other lawful form of disposal in accordance with existing law.

SECTION 4. The existing periods of trust placed upon Indian allotment and unallotted tribal lands and any restriction of alienation thereof, are hereby extended and continued until otherwise directed by Congress. The authority of the Secretary of the Interior to issue to Indians patents in fee or certificates of competency or otherwise to remove the restrictions on lands allotted to individual Indians under any law or treaty is hereby revoked.

No lands or other capital assets owned by an Indian community, or any interest therein, shall be voluntarily or involuntarily alienated: *Provided, however*, That the community may grant the use of the surface of, or any mining privileges in, any land to a nonmember, by lease or revocable permit for a period not to exceed one year, or, with the approval of the Secretary, for a longer period, and may, with the approval of the Secretary, sell or contract to sell to a nonmember any standing timber, or dispose of any capital improvements, owned by the community.

Section 5. No sale, devise, gift, or other transfer of Indian lands held under any trust patent or otherwise restricted, whether in the name of the allottee or his heirs, shall be made or approved: *Provided, however*, That such lands may, with the approval of the Secretary, be sold, devised, or otherwise transferred to the Indian tribe from whose lands the allotment was made or the chartered community within whose territorial limits they are located: *And provided further*, That the Secretary of the Interior may authorize exchanges of lands of equal value whenever such exchange is in his judgment necessary for or compatible with the proper consolidation of Indian lands classified for the purpose pursuant to the authority of section 6 of this title.

SECTION 6. The Secretary of the Interior is authorized and directed to classify areas of land allotted in whole or in part now under restricted Indian ownership which are reasonably capable of consolidation into suitable units for grazing, forest management, or other economic purposes, and to proclaim the exclusion from such areas of any lands not to be included therein. In order to bring about an orderly and sound acquisition and consolidation of lands and to promote the effective use of Indian resources and the development of Indian economic capacities, the Secretary is hereby authorized and directed to make economic and physical investigation and classification of the existing Indian lands, of Intermingled and adjacent non-Indian lands and of the other lands that may be required for landless Indian groups or individuals; to make necessary maps and surveys; to investigate Indian aptitudes and needs in the agricultural and industrial arts, in political and social affairs and in education, and to make such other investigations as may be needed to secure the most effective utilization of existing Indian resources and the most economic acquisition of additional lands. In carrying out the investigations prescribed in this section the Secretary is authorized to utilize the services of any Federal officers or employees that the President may assign to him for the purpose, and is further authorized, with the consent of the States concerned, to enter into cooperative agreements with State agencies for similar services.

SECTION 7. The Secretary of the Interior is hereby authorized, in his discretion, and under such rules and regulations as he may prescribe, to acquire, through purchase, relinquishment, gift, exchange, or assignment, lands or surface rights to lands, within or outside of existing reservations, including trust or otherwise restricted allotments, whether the allottee be living or deceased, for the purpose of providing land for Indians for whom reservation or other land is not now available and who can make beneficial use thereof, and for the purpose of blocking out and consolidating areas classified for the purpose pursuant to the authority of section 6 of this title. The Secretary is authorized, in the case of trust or other restricted lands or lands to which fee patents have hitherto been issued to Indians and which are unencumbered, to accept voluntary relinquishments of, and to cancel the patent or patents or any other instrument removing restrictions from the land.

There is hereby authorized to be appropriated, for the acquisition of such lands and for expenses incident thereto, including appraisals and the investigations provided for in section 6 of this title, a sum not to exceed $2,000,000 for any one fiscal year. The unexpected balances of appropriation made for any one year pursuant to this Act shall remain available until expended.

The Secretary of the Interior is hereby authorized to accept voluntary relinquishments from any Indian allottee or Indian homestead entryman, or from his heirs, of all rights in and to any land included in any Indian public domain allotment, homestead, or application therefor, which has heretofore or may hereafter be made, where such land lies within the exterior boundaries of any Indian reservation or area heretofore or hereafter set apart and reserved for the use and benefit of any Indian tribe or band; and the Secretary of the Interior is hereby authorized and empowered to cancel any patent which may have been issued conveying such land, or any interest therein, to any Indian allottee or Indian homestead entryman.

Title to any land acquired pursuant to the provisions of this section shall be taken in the name of the United States in trust for the Indian tribe or community for whom the land is acquired, but title may be transferred by the Secretary to such community under the conditions set forth in this Act.

SECTION 8. Any Indian tribe or chartered Indian community is authorized to purchase or otherwise acquire any interest of any member or nonmember in land within its territorial limits, and may expend any tribal or community funds, whether or not held in the Treasury of the United States, for this purpose, whenever, in the opinion of the Secretary of the Interior the acquisition is necessary for the proper consolidation of Indian lands.

The Secretary of the Interior is authorized to transfer to an Indian tribe or community, and to accept on behalf of the tribe or community, any member's interest in restricted farming, grazing, or timberlands, and shall issue a nontransferable certificate in exchange, evidencing a proportionate interest in tribal or community lands of similar quality, if in his opinion such transfer is necessary for the proper consolidation of Indian lands: *Provided, however,* That any Indian making beneficial use of such transferred lands shall be entitled to continue the occupancy and use of such lands, and to any improvements thereon, or to receive adequate compensation for such improvements, subject to the provisions of section 14 of this title. For the purpose of this section "proportionate interest" shall be construed to mean a right to use or to receive the income from an equivalent amount of tribal or community land of similar quality or to receive the money value of any lawful disposition of the interest transferred if such right of use is not exercised. A member's proportionate interest may descend to the heirs of such member but not to any nonmember, and his right of use of transferred land, if exercised, may similarly descend to the heirs of such member.

The Secretary of the Interior may sell and convey to an Indian, to an Indian tribe, or community, any restricted lands inherited by any member, whenever, in his opinion, the sale is necessary for the proper consolidation of Indian lands.

The time and mode of payment of the purchase price of any lands authorized to be sold or purchased under this section shall be governed by the agreement between parties, but insofar as practicable the purchase price shall be paid in annual installments equal to the estimated annual proceeds realizable from any lawful disposition of the land, and the vendor, if a member, may accept any right of use in tribal or community lands as satisfaction of the purchase price in whole or in part.

SECTION 9. The Secretary of the Interior shall assign the use of tribal or community lands to any member according to the right or interest of such member for a period not to exceed the life of the assignee and shall make rules and regulations governing such assignments. The Secretary of the Interior may in addition assign to any such member the right of exclusive occupancy of any community lands for farming or domestic purposes in proper economic units: *Provided*, That any Indian making beneficial use of land shall be entitled to preference in the assignment of the use of such land and to any improvements thereon or to adequate compensation for such improvements.

All rights of exclusive occupancy of, and all physical improvements lawfully created on, tribal or community lands, shall descend according to rules of descent and distribution to be prescribed by the Secretary of the Interior.

SECTION 10. Wherever the Secretary shall find that existing State laws governing the determination of heirs, so far as made applicable to any restricted Indian lands by congressional enactment, are not adapted to Indian needs and circumstances, he may promulgate independent rules governing such determination, including such rules as may be necessary to prevent any subdivision of rights to lands or improvements thereon which is likely to impair their beneficial use.

The Secretary may delegate to a chartered Indian community the authority conferred by this section.

SECTION 11. On and after the effective date of the passage of this Act, and beginning with the death of the person presently entitled, all right, interest, and title in restricted allotted lands, but not including any proportionate interest acquired pursuant to section 8 of this title or any improvements lawfully erected, shall pass to the chartered community within whose territorial limits such lands are located or, if no community has been chartered, to the tribe from whose lands the allotment was made: *Provided, however*, That individuals who would be otherwise entitled, save for the provisions of this section, shall acquire a contingent interest in such lands, and title to any such lands shall vest in such individuals when and only when the Secretary shall determine that such lands lie outside any area classified for consolidation pursuant to section 6; *And provided further*, That prior to such determination the individuals otherwise entitled shall enjoy the use and income realized from any lawful disposition of such lands.

The Secretary shall issue to the individuals otherwise entitled a nontransferable certificate evidencing a descendible interest in tribal or community lands of similar quality in the proportion which the acreage of the farming, grazing, or timber lands, whichever, passing to the tribe or community at any time bears to the total tribal or community acreage of farming, grazing, or timber lands: *Provided, however*, That such persons shall enjoy a preference in the assignment of lands passing to the tribe or community in accordance with the provisions of this action.

No will purporting to make any other disposition of such lands shall be approved.

SECTION 12. The Secretary of the Interior is authorized and directed to issue to each member of an Indian tribe or community which owns or controls lands allotted in whole or in part a nontransferable certificate evidencing the member's right to an equal interest in all tribal community assets, including the right to make beneficial use of a proportionate share thereof: *Provided, however*, That in the administration of sections 8, 9, 10, and 11 of this title, members so entitled may be given the right to actual beneficial use of more than their proportionate shares of such tribal or community lands and resources: *And provided further*, That in the administration of sections 8, 9, 10, and 11 of this title, appropriate deductions may be made from the undivided interest of any member proportionate in value to any special interest acquired or inherited by such member, in exchange for property passing, transferred, or sold, to a tribe or community, or any restricted lands retained in severalty by such member.

SECTION 13. Each certificate issued pursuant to the authority of any section of this title shall be issued in triplicate, one copy of which the Secretary of the Interior shall retain in a register to be kept for the purpose and the others of which he shall forward to the tribe or chartered Indian community. The said tribe or community shall deliver to the Indian in whose favor it is issuing one of such certificates so forwarded and shall cause the other to be copied into a register of the tribe or community to be provided for the purpose and shall file the same.

The Secretary may delegate to a chartered community the authority conferred by this section and may countersign certificates of interest issued by such community to its members.

SECTION 14. The Secretary of the Interior is authorized and directed to classify and divide the lands owned or controlled by an Indian tribe or community into economic units suitable for farming, grazing, forestry, and other purposes, and may lease or permit the use of, and may regulate the use and management of, such lands whenever in his opinion necessary to promote and preserve their economic use. The Secretary may delegate to a chartered Indian community the authority conferred by this section.

SECTION 15. The Secretary of the Interior is authorized and directed to make rules and regulations for the operation and management of Indian forestry units on the principle of sustained yield management, to restrict the number of livestock grazed on Indian range units to the estimated carrying capacity of such ranges, and to promulgate such other rules and regulations as may be necessary to protect the range from deterioration, to prevent soil erosion, and like purposes. The Secretary may delegate to a chartered Indian community the authority conferred by this section.

SECTION 16. The Secretary of the Interior is authorized to proclaim new Indian reservations on lands purchased for the purposes enumerated in this Act, or to add such lands to the jurisdiction of existing reservation. Such lands, so long as title to them is held by the United States or by an Indian tribe or community, shall not be subject to taxation, but the United States shall assume all governmental obligations of the State or county in which such lands are situated with respect to the maintenance of roads across such lands, the furnishing of educational and other public facilities to persons residing thereon, and the execution of proper measures for the control of fires, floods, and erosion, and the protection of the public health and order in such lands, and the Secretary of the Interior may enter into agreements with authorities of any State or subdivision thereof in which such lands are situated for the performance of any or all of the foregoing functions by such State or subdivision or any agencies or employees thereof authorized by the law of the State to enter into such agreements, and for the payment of the expenses of such functions where appropriations therefor shall be made by Congress.

SECTION 17. Nothing contained in this title shall be construed to relate to Indian holdings of allotments or homesteads upon the public domain outside of the geographic boundaries of any Indian reservation now existing or to be established hereafter.

SECTION 18. Whenever used in this title the phrase "a member of an Indian tribe" shall include any descendant of a member permanently residing within an existing Indian reservation.

SECTION 19. Whenever used in this title the phrase "lands owned or controlled by an Indian tribe or community" shall include all interest in land of any of its members.

SECTION 20. The provisions of this Act shall not be construed to prevent the removal of restrictions on taxable lands of members of the Five Civilized Tribes nor operate to effect any change in the present laws and procedure relating to the guardianship of minor and incompetent members of the Osage and Five Civilized Tribes, but in all other respects shall apply to such Indians.

SECTION 21. None of the provisions of this Act, except the provisions of title II, relating to Indian education, shall apply to the Indians of New York State.

TITLE IV—COURT OF INDIAN AFFAIRS

SECTION 1. There shall be a United States Court of Indian Affairs, which shall consist of a chief judge and six associate judges, each of whom shall be appointed by the President, by and with the advice and consent of the Senate, and shall receive an annual salary of $7,500 payable monthly from the Treasury.

SECTION 2. The said Court of Indian Affairs shall always be open for the transaction of business, and sessions thereof may, in the discretion of the court, be held in the several judicial circuits and at such places said court may from time to time designate. The authority of the court may be exercised either by the full court or by one or more judges duly assigned by the court to sit in a particular locality or to hold a special term for a designated class of cases.

SECTION 3. The Court of Indian Affairs shall have original jurisdiction as follows:

(1) Of all prosecutions for crimes against the United States committed within the territory of any Indian reservation or chartered Indian community, whether or not committed by an Indian;

(2) Of all cases to which any Indian tribe or chartered Indian community is a party;

(3) Of all cases at law or in equity arising out of commerce with any Indian tribe or community or members thereof, wherein a real party in interest is not a member of such tribe or community;

(4) Of all cases, civil or criminal, arising under the laws or ordinances of a chartered Indian community, wherein a real party interest is not a member of such community;

(5) Of all actions at law or suits in equity wherein the pleadings raise a substantial question concerning the validity or application of any Federal law, or any regulation or charter authorized by such law, relating to the affairs or jurisdiction of any Indian tribe or chartered community;

(6) Of all actions, suits, or proceedings involving the right of any person, in whole or in part of Indian blood or descent, to any allotment of land under any law or treaty;

(7) Of all cases involving the determination of heirs of deceased Indians and the settlement of the estates of such Indians; of all cases and proceedings involving the partition of Indian lands, or the guardianship of minor and incompetent

Indians; and of all cases and proceedings to determine the competency of individual Indians where the issuance of cancellation of a fee patent or the removal of restrictions from inherited or allotted lands, funds, or other property held by the United States in trust for such Indians may be involved: *Provided*, That the Court of Indian Affairs shall exercise no jurisdiction in cases over which exclusive jurisdiction has been granted by Congress to the Court of Claims, or to any other Federal court other than the United States district courts, or in cases over which exclusive jurisdiction may be granted by charter provision to the local courts of any Indian community.

SECTION 4. All jurisdiction heretofore exercised by the United States district courts by reason of the fact that a case involved facts constituting any of the grounds of jurisdiction enumerated in the preceding section, is hereby terminated, reserving, however, to such district courts complete jurisdiction over all pending suits and over all proceedings ancillary or supplementary thereto.

SECTION 5. The Court of Indian Affairs may order the removal of any cause falling within its jurisdiction as above set forth, from any court of any State or any Indian community in which such cause may have been instituted.

SECTION 6. The Court of Indian Affairs shall have jurisdiction to hear and determine appeals from the judgment of any court of any chartered Indian community in all cases in which said Court of Indian Affairs might have exercised original jurisdiction.

SECTION 7. The procedure of the Court of Indian Affairs shall be determined by rules of court to be promulgated by it, existing statutes regulating procedure in courts of the United States notwithstanding. Such rules shall regulate the form and manner of executing, returning, or filing writs, processes, and pleadings; the removal of causes specified in section 5; the taking of appeals specified in section 6; the joinder of parties and of causes of action, legal and equitable; the raising of questions of law before trial; the taking of testimony by examination before trial and other proceedings for discovery and inspection; the issuance of subpoenas to summon witnesses and compel the production of documents at trial; the summoning of jurors and the waiver of jury trial; the form and manner of entry of judgments; the manner of executing judgments; the conduct of supplementary proceedings; the survival of actions and the substitution of parties; the amounts and manner of payment of fees to the clerk or the marshal of the court; the practice of attorneys; and such other matters as may require regulation in order to provide a complete system of procedure for the conduct of the court. In general the rules of court shall conform as nearly as possible to the statutes regulating the procedure in the district courts of the United States, the rules of the Supreme Court governing causes in said district courts, and the practice in the courts of the State in which the controversy arises, save that the rules shall, so far as possible, be nontechnical in character and fitted to the needs of prospective litigants.

SECTION 8. The courts may provide, by rules to be promulgated by it, for appeals to the full court from judgment rendered on circuit by less than a majority of the full court.

SECTION 9. All substantial rights accorded to the accused in criminal prosecutions in the district courts of the United States shall be accorded in prosecutions in the Court of Indian Affairs. The trial of offenses punishable by death or by imprisonment for a period exceeding five years shall be had within or in the vicinity of the reservation or Indian community where the offense was committed.

SECTION 10. In both civil and criminal causes, the right to trial by jury and all other procedural rights guaranteed by the Constitution of the United States shall be recognized and observed.

SECTION 11. In criminal cases the rules of evidence shall be these prevailing in criminal cases in the United States district courts. In civil cases the commonlaw rules of evidence, including the rules governing competency of witnesses, shall prevail: *Provided, however,* That the court shall have the power to amend such rules by rule of court or judicial decision to make them conform as nearly as possible to modern changes evidenced by the statutes and decisions of the United States and the several States, and to adapt them, where necessary, to the solution of problems of proof peculiar to the cases before the court.

SECTION 12. The statutes and decisions of the several States, except where the Constitution, treaties, or statutes of the United States, or the charters or ordinances of Indian communities or orders of executive departments thereunder promulgated, otherwise require or provide, shall be regarded as rules of decision in all civil cases in the Court of Indian Affairs.

SECTION 13. The Court of Indian Affairs shall be a court of record possessed of all incidental powers, including the power to summon jurors, to administer oaths, to have and use a judicial seal, to issue writs of habeas corpus, to punish for contempt, and to hold to security of the peace and for good behavior, which may be exercised by the district courts of the

United States, and such powers shall be subject to all limitations imposed by law upon said district courts. The orders, writs, and processes of the Court of Indian Affairs may run, be served, and be returnable anywhere in the United States. The said court shall perform such administrative functions as Congress may assign to it. The said court shall have the power to render declaratory judgments, and such judgments, in cases of actual controversy, shall have the same force as final judgments in ordinary cases.

SECTION 14. The judges of the Court of Indian Affairs shall hold office for a period of ten years; they may be removed prior to the expiration of their term by the President of the United States, with the consent of the Senate for any cause.

SECTION 15. The final judgment of the Court of Indian Affairs shall be subject to review on questions of law in the circuit court of appeals of the circuit in which such judgment is rendered. The several circuit courts of appeals are authorized to adopt rules for the conduct of such appellate proceedings, and, until the adoption of such rules, the rules of such courts relating to appellate proceedings upon a writ of error, so far as applicable, shall govern. The said circuit courts of appeals shall have power to affirm, or, if the judgment of the Court of Indian Affairs is not in accordance with law, to modify or reverse the judgment of that court, with or without remanding the case for a rehearing, as justice may require; the judgment of the circuit court of appeals shall be final, except that it may be subject to review by the Supreme Court as provided in the United States Code, title 28, sections 346 and 347.

SECTION 16. The fees of jurors and witnesses shall be fixed in accordance with the provisions of law governing such fees in United States courts generally as provided in the United States Code, title 28, sections 600 to 605.

SECTION 17. The costs and fees in the Court of Indian Affairs shall be fixed and established by said court in a table of fees: *Provided*, That the costs and fees so fixed shall not exceed, with respect to any item, the costs and fees now charged in the Supreme Court.

SECTION 18. The Court of Indian Affairs shall appoint a chief clerk, a reporter, and such assistant clerk and marshals, not to exceed seven each, as may be necessary for the efficient conduct of its business. The said officials shall be under the direction of the court in the discharge of their duties; and for misconduct or incapacity they may be removed by it from office; but the court shall report such removals, with the cause thereof, to Congress, if in session, or if not, at the next session.

SECTION 19. The Attorney General shall provide the Court of Indian Affairs with suitable rooms in courthouses or other public buildings at such places as the court may select for its sessions.

Section 20. The chief clerk of the court shall, under the direction of the chief judge, employ such stenographers, messengers, or attendants and purchase such books, periodicals, and stationery as may be needful for the efficient conduct of the business of the court, and expenditures for such purposes shall be allowed and paid by the Secretary of the Treasury upon claim duly made and approved by the chief judge.

SECTION 21. The judges of the Courts of Indian Affairs and the clerks and marshals thereof shall receive necessary traveling expenses, and expenses not to exceed $5 per day for subsistence while traveling on duty and away from their designated stations.

SECTION 22. With respect to all matters relating to the receipt of fines, costs, fees, bail, and other payments to officials of the court, the custody of funds and the rendering of accounts therefor, the bonding of court officials charged with such custody, the payment of moneys for salaries, traveling expenses, clerical services, the publication of reports of opinions, and office expenses, the laws, departmental regulations, and rules of court applicable to similar matters in the Supreme Court shall apply to the Court of Indian Affairs except as otherwise provided in this chapter.

SECTION 23. The Secretary of the Interior is hereby authorized to appoint not to exceed ten special attorneys whose duty it shall be to advise and represent such Indian tribes or communities as the Secretary of the Interior may designate, and the individual members thereof. Within ten days of the institution of any proceedings on behalf of such tribes or communities or members thereof, the special attorneys provided for herein shall serve upon the appropriate United States district attorney written notice of the pendency of any such proceedings, together with a copy of all the pleadings on file in any such proceeding.

SECTION 24. As used in this title, the term "circuit court of appeals" includes the Court of Appeals of the District of Columbia.

SECTION 25. Appropriations for the Federal Court of Indian Affairs and for incidental expenses shall be made annually based upon estimates submitted by the Attorney General, and appropriations for the special attorneys shall be made annually, based upon estimates submitted by the Secretary of the Interior.

The Indian Reorganization Act

June 18, 1934

48 Stat. 984

An Act To conserve and develop Indian lands and resources; to extend to Indians the right to form business and other organizations; to establish a credit system for Indians; to grant certain rights of home rule to Indians; to provide for vocational education for Indians; and for other purposes

Be it enacted by the Senate and House of Representatives of the United States of America in Congress assembled, That hereafter no land of any Indian reservation, created or set apart by treaty or agreement with the Indians, Act of Congress, Executive order, purchase, or otherwise, shall be allotted in severalty to any Indian.[1]

SECTION 2. The existing periods of trust placed upon any Indian lands and any restriction on alienation thereof are hereby extended and continued until otherwise directed by Congress.

SECTION 3. The Secretary of the Interior, if he shall find it to be in the public interest, is hereby authorized to restore to tribal ownership the remaining surplus lands of any Indian reservation heretofore opened, or authorized to be opened, to sale, or any other form of disposal by Presidential proclamation, or by any of the public-land laws of the United States: *Provided, however*, That valid rights or claims of any persons to any lands so withdrawn existing on the date of the withdrawal shall not be affected by this Act: *Provided further*, That this section shall not apply to lands within any reclamation project heretofore authorized in any Indian reservation: *Provided further*, That the order of the Department of the Interior signed, dated, and approved by Honorable Ray Lyman Wilbur, Secretary of the Interior, on October 28, 1932, temporarily withdrawing lands of the Papago Indian Reservation in Arizona from all forms of mineral entry or claim under the public land mining laws, is hereby revoked and rescinded, and the lands of the said Papago Indian Reservation are hereby restored to exploration and location, under the existing mining entry or claim under the public land mining laws of the United States, in accordance with the express terms and provisions declared and set forth in Executive orders establishing said Papago Indian Reservation: *Provided further*, That damages shall be paid to the Papago Tribe for loss of any improvements on any land located for mining in such a sum as may be determined by the Secretary of the Interior but not to exceed the cost of said improvements: *Provided further*, That a yearly rental not to exceed five cents per acre shall be paid to the Papago Tribe for loss of the use or occupancy of any land withdrawn by the requirements of mining operations, and payments derived from damages or rentals shall be deposited in the Treasury of the United States to the credit of the Papago Tribe: *Provided further,* That in the event any person or persons, partnership, corporation, or association, desires a mineral patent, according to the mining laws of the United States, he or they shall first deposit in the Treasury of the United States to the credit of the Papago Tribe the sum of $1.00 per acre in lieu of annual rental, as hereinbefore provided, to compensate for the loss or occupancy of the lands withdrawn by the requirements of the mining operations: *Provided further*, That patentee shall also pay into the Treasury of the United States to the credit of the Papago Tribe damages for the loss of improvements not heretofore paid in such a sum as may be determined by the Secretary of the Interior, but not to exceed the cost thereof; the payment of $1.00 per acre for surface use to be refunded to patentee in the event that patent is not acquired.

Nothing herein contained shall restrict the granting or use of permits for easements or rights-of-way; or ingress or egress over the lands for all proper and lawful purposes; and nothing contained herein, except as expressly provided, shall be construed as authority for the Secretary of the Interior, or any other person, to issue or promulgate a rule or regulation in conflict with the Executive order of February 1, 1917, creating the Papago Indian Reservation in Arizona or the Act of February 21, 1931 (46 Stat. 1202).[2]

SECTION 4. Except as herein provided, no sale, devise, gift, exchange or other transfer of restricted Indian lands or of shares in the assets of any Indian tribe or corporation organized hereunder, shall be made or approved: *Provided, however*, That such lands or interests may, with the approval of the Secretary of the Interior, be sold, devised, or otherwise transferred to the Indian tribe in which the lands or shares are located or from which the shares were derived or to a successor

1. 89 Fed. (2), 312: 55 I. D. D., 16, 48, 276, 295, 984; 56 I. D. D., 3, 118, 108, 146. AS Opp. Atty Gen., 123.
2. 54 I. D. D., 559, 563; 56 I. D. D., 330.

corporation; and in all instances such lands or interests shall descend or be devised, in accordance with the then existing laws of the State, or Federal laws where applicable, in which said lands are located or in which the subject matter of the corporation is located, to any member of such tribe or of such corporation or any heirs of such member: *Provided further*, That the Secretary of the Interior may authorize voluntary exchanges of lands of equal value and the voluntary exchange of shares of equal value whenever such exchange, in his judgement, is expedient and beneficial for or compatible with the proper consolidation of Indian lands and for the benefit of cooperative organizations.[3]

SECTION 5. The Secretary of the Interior is hereby authorized, in his discretion, to acquire through purchase, relinquishment, gift, exchange, or assignment, any interest in lands, water rights or surface rights to lands, within or without existing reservations, including trust or otherwise restricted allotments whether the allottee be living or deceased, for the purpose of providing land for Indians.

For the acquisition of such lands, interests in lands, water rights, and surface rights, and for expenses incident to such acquisition, there is hereby authorized to be appropriated, out of any funds in the Treasury not otherwise appropriated, a sum not to exceed $2,000,000 in any fiscal year: *Provided*, That no part of such funds shall be used to acquire additional land outside of the exterior boundaries of the Navajo Indian Reservation for the Navajo Indians in Arizona and New Mexico, in the event that the proposed Navajo boundary extension measures now pending in Congress and embodied in the bills (S. 2531 and H.R. 8927) to define the exterior boundaries of the Navajo Indian Reservation in Arizona, and for other purposes, and the bills (S. 2531 and H.R. 8982) to define the exterior boundaries of the Navajo Indian Reservation in New Mexico and for other purposes, or similar legislation, become law.

The unexpended balances of any appropriations made pursuant to this section shall remain available until expended.

Title to any lands or rights acquired pursuant to this Act shall be taken in the name of the United States in trust for the Indian tribe or individual Indian for which the land is acquired, and such lands or rights shall be exempt from State and local taxation.[4]

SECTION 6. The Secretary of the Interior is directed to make rules and regulations for the operation and management of Indian forestry units on the principle of sustained-yield management, to restrict the number of livestock grazed on Indian range units to the estimated carrying capacity of such ranges, and to promulgate such other rules and regulations as may be necessary to protect the range from deterioration, to prevent soil erosion, to assure full utilization of the range, and like purposes.[5]

SECTION 7. The Secretary of the Interior is hereby authorized to proclaim new Indian reservations on lands acquired pursuant to any authority conferred by this Act, or to add such lands to existing reservations: Provided, That lands added to existing reservations shall be designated for the exclusive use of Indians entitled by enrollment or by tribal membership to residence at such reservations.

SECTION 8. Nothing contained in this Act shall be construed to relate to Indian holdings of allotments or homesteads upon the public domain outside of the geographic boundaries of any Indian reservation now existing or established hereafter.

SECTION 9. There is hereby authorized to be appropriated, out of any funds in the Treasury not otherwise appropriated, such sums as may be necessary, but not to exceed $250,000 in any fiscal year, to be expended at the order of the Secretary of the Interior, in defraying the expenses of organizing Indian chartered corporations or other organizations created under this Act.

SECTION 10. There is hereby authorized to be appropriated, out of any funds in the Treasury not otherwise appropriated, the sum of $10,000,000 to be established as a revolving fund from which the Secretary of the Interior, under such rules and regulations as he may prescribe, may make loans to Indian chartered corporations for the purpose of promoting the economic development of such tribes and of their members, and may defray the expenses of administering such loans. Repayment of amounts loaned under this authorization shall be credited to the revolving fund and shall be available for the purpose for which the fund is established. A report shall be made annually to Congress of transactions under this authorization.

SECTION 11. There is hereby authorized to be appropriated, out of any funds in the United States Treasury not otherwise appropriated, a sum not to exceed $250,000 annually, together with any unexpended balances of previous appropriations made pursuant to this section, for loans to Indians for the payment of tuition and other expenses in recognized vocational and

3. 54 I. D. D. 584.
4. 80 Fed. (2), 312.
5. 15 Comp. Oen. Dec., 69.

trade schools: *Provided*, That not more than $50,000 of such sum shall be available for loans to Indian students in high schools and colleges. Such loans shall be reimbursable under rules established by the Commissioner of Indian Affairs.[6]

SECTION 12. The Secretary of the Interior is directed to establish standards of health, age, character, experience, knowledge, and ability for Indians who may be appointed, without regard to civil service laws, to the various positions maintained, now or hereafter, by the Indian Office, in the administration of functions or services affecting any Indian tribe. Such qualified Indians shall hereafter have the preference to appointment to vacancies in any such positions.

SECTION 13. The provisions of this Act shall not apply to any of the Territories, colonies, or insular possessions of the United States, except that sections 9, 10, 11, 12, and 16 shall apply to the Territory of Alaska: *Provided*, That sections 2, 4, 7, 16, 17, and 18 of this Act shall not apply to the following-named Indian tribes, the members of such Indian tribes, together with members of other tribes affiliated with such named tribes located in the State of Oklahoma, as follows: Cheyenne, Arapaho, Apache, Comanche, Kiowa, Caddo, Delaware, Wichita, Osage, Kaw, Otoe, Tonkawa, Pawnee, Ponca, Shawnee, Ottawa, Quapaw, Seneca, Wyandotte, Iowa, Sac and Fox, Kickapoo, Pottawatomi, Cherokee, Chickasaw, Choctaw, Creek, and Seminole. Section 4 of this Act shall not apply to the Indians of the Klamath Reservation in Oregon.

SECTION 14. The Secretary of the Interior is hereby directed to continue the allowance of the articles enumerated in section 17 of the Act of March 2, 1889 (23 Stat. L. 894), or their commuted cash value under the Act of June 10, 1896 (29 Stat. L. 334), to all Sioux Indians who would be eligible, but for the provisions of this Act, to receive allotments of lands in severalty under section 19 of the Act of May 29, 1908 (25 (35) Stat. L. 451), or under any prior Act, and who have the prescribed status of the head of a family or single person over the age of eighteen years, and his approval shall be final and conclusive, claims therefor to be paid as formerly from the permanent appropriation made by said section 17 and carried on the books of the Treasury for this purpose. No person shall receive in his own right more than one allowance of the benefits, and application must be made and approved during the lifetime of the allottee or the right shall lapse. Such benefits shall continue to be paid upon such reservation until such time as the lands available therein for allotment at the time of the passage of this Act would have been exhausted by the award to each person receiving such benefits of an allotment of eighty acres of such land.

SECTION 15. Nothing in this Act shall be construed to impair or prejudice any claim or suit of any Indian tribe against the United States. It is hereby declared to be the intent of Congress that no expenditures for the benefit of Indians made out of appropriations authorized by the Act shall be considered as offsets in any suit brought to recover upon any claim of such Indians against the United States.

SECTION 16. Any Indian tribe, or tribes, residing on the same reservation, shall have the right to organize for its common welfare, and may adopt an appropriate constitution and bylaws, which shall become effective when ratified by a majority vote of the adult members of the tribe, or of the adult Indians residing on such reservation, as the case may be, at a special election authorized and called by the Secretary under such rules and regulations as he may prescribe. Such constitution and bylaws when ratified as aforesaid and approved by the Secretary of the Interior shall be revocable by an election open to the same voters and conducted in the same manner as hereinabove provided. Amendments to the constitution and bylaws may be ratified and approved by the Secretary in the same manner as the original constitution and bylaws.

In addition to all powers vested in any Indian tribe or tribal council by existing law, the constitution adopted by said tribe shall also vest in such tribe or its tribal council the following rights and powers: To employ legal counsel, the choice of counsel and fixing of fees to be subject to the approval of the Secretary of the Interior; to prevent the sale, disposition, lease, or encumbrance of tribal lands, interests in lands, or other tribal assets without the consent of the tribe; and to negotiate with the Federal, State, and local Governments. The Secretary of the Interior shall advise such tribe or its tribal counsel of all appropriation estimates or Federal projects for the benefit of the tribe prior to the submission of such estimates to the Bureau of the Budget and the Congress.

SECTION 17. The Secretary of the Interior may, upon petition by at least one-third of the adult Indians, issue a charter of incorporation to such tribe: *Provided*, That such charter shall not become operative until ratified at a special election by a majority vote of the adult Indians living on the reservation. Such charter may convey to the incorporated tribe the power to purchase, take by gift, or bequest, or otherwise, own, hold, manage, operate, and dispose of property of every

6. 55 I. D. D. 395, 436.

description, real and personal, including the power to purchase restricted Indian lands and to issue in exchange therefor interests in corporate property, and such further powers as may be incidental to the conduct of corporate business, not inconsistent with law, but no authority shall be granted to sell, mortgage, or lease for a period exceeding ten years any of the land included in the limits of the reservation. Any charter so issued shall not be revoked or surrendered except by Act of Congress.

SECTION 18. This Act shall not apply to any reservation wherein a majority of the adult Indians, voting at a special election duly called by the Secretary of the Interior, shall vote against its application. It shall be the duty of the Secretary of the Interior, within one year after the passage and approval of this Act, to call such an election, which election shall be held by secret ballot upon thirty days' notice.

SECTION 19. The term "Indian" as used in this Act shall include all persons of Indian descent who are members of any recognized Indian tribe now under Federal jurisdiction, and all persons who are descendants of such members who were, on June 1, 1934, residing within the present boundaries of any Indian reservation, and shall further include all other persons of one-half or more Indian blood. For the purposes of this Act, Eskimos and other aboriginal peoples of Alaska shall be considered Indians. The term "tribe" wherever used in this Act shall be construed to refer to any Indian tribe, organized band, pueblo, or the Indians residing on one reservation. The words "adult Indians" wherever used in this Act shall be construed to refer to Indians who have attained the age of twenty-one years.

Approved, June 18, 1934.

CHAPTER 3

MINUTES OF THE PLAINS CONGRESS, RAPID CITY INDIAN SCHOOL RAPID CITY, SOUTH DAKOTA, MARCH 2–5, 1934

Friday, March 2, 1934

Morning Session

Opening of meeting by James H. McGregor, Superintendent of Pine Ridge Agency, South Dakota.

Friends, we will begin this meeting and as is the usual custom of our Indian people, it will be opened by prayer. Reverend Simon J. Kirk will open the meeting with prayer. Mr. Kirk.

Invocation by Reverend Simon J. Kirk.

MR. JAMES H. MCGREGOR: Friends, if you will come to order, the greatest Council (Indian) held in recent years will be opened. Commissioner John Collier will now take charge.

MR. JOHN COLLIER: Friends, to begin with I am going to speak only of procedure. We have four days for this meeting. That will mean morning, afternoon and evening, if necessary. We have a great deal of ground to cover. I shall in a moment introduce to you others of the men from Washington who will also take part in the discussions. In fact, before I do anything else, so that you may know the other Indian Bureau staff people who have come for this meeting, I will introduce them now and I will ask them to stand up so that you will know all the Indian Bureau officials.

Mr. Walker Woehlke, Field Representative of the Commissioner of Indian Affairs.
Mr. Ward Shepard, Specialist in land policies for the Indian Office.
Mr. Siegel, Assistant Solicitor of the Interior Department.
Mr. Cohen, Assistant Solicitor of the Interior Department.
Mr. Stewart, Chief of the Land Division of the Indian Office.

A complete record will be made of everything said or done in these four days and we hope that the record of each day will be finished, and typed by the next day. In the matter of voting, or taking action on questions, the important matter is for the delegation to act; not for everybody to vote, but Congress wants to know what Rosebud wants, what Fort Peck wants, and so on. I do not say that the meeting may not vote as a whole. But very definitely, this meeting is intended to determine the options of each of the delegations, each of the tribes of the reservations. That is what Congress wants and I may add that there will probably not be any voting in the first two days. It is necessary for us to transact business with promptness because we have so much ground to cover, and inasmuch as the matter of casting votes is a matter of separate delegations voting, and a record being made of what each one thinks, it is evident that the question of Parliamentary control is not very important.

Now, I first want to ask you, and I will get this by the show of hands, whether you would like to have an Indian Chairman or have one of the Government men preside as Chairman. My own view is that it would be much better if you have an Indian Chairman, if you can choose him without taking too much time. On this we might get a show of hands. Those who favor the election of one of your own delegates, an Indian, to be chairman, hold up your hands.

Interpreted by Rosebud interpreter to Indians.

ROSEBUD INTERPRETER: Mr. Collier, if you will please, I would like to speak in Indian first and then interpret it in English myself. (*Interprets.*)

This is Mr. Collier's meeting and this is not strictly our meeting. We are here to listen, and therefore I think it is the proper thing to have a Superintendent or some Government official preside over this meeting. We are here as listeners. Each man who is here in a delegation from different reservations is here with the sole purpose of listening and we are not here to pass on questions. We are here to listen and whatever we learn we will take back with us to our own people. Therefore, I think it proper that we should have a Government official to preside over this meeting.

REPRESENTATIVE FROM FORT BERTHOLD: Mr. Collier, I wish to announce that speech to my delegation in Indian. (*Interprets.*)

MR. COLLIER: May I say that before the meeting comes to an end there will be questions put to you, to each of the delegations, because we want to know your sentiments. A delegation that does not want to answer the questions is free not to answer. A delegation that wants to answer the questions will answer them. Furthermore, it is possible that this meeting will be the beginning of meetings that will be held hereafter. This may be the first Congress to be followed by other Congresses, in a regular way. It is for these reasons that it seemed well if there was an Indian Chairman, although I do not want to insist on that. Interpret that for me, please.

Rosebud interprets the above speech to Indians.

Fort Berthold interprets Commissioner's speech to his delegation.

MR. JOHN COLLIER: Has the interpretation been understood by everybody? If not, then it should be interpreted until everybody understands.

Various O.K.'s heard throughout the hall. Shoshone? O.K. Blackfeet? O.K.

ROSEBUD INTERPRETER: Mr. Collier, please, it was my fault. I left out the most important part of that interpretation, and this is what Mr. Collier said. (*Interprets.*)

MR. COLLIER: All who desire that there be an Indian Chairman elected by you hold up your right hands. Is that understood? All who desire that there be an Indian Bureau official for Chairman hold up their right hands. There will have to be a count. It is so close. Keep your hands up, all who want an Indian Bureau Chairman. (*Count taken—101*).

Now, all who desire that there be an Indian Chairman elected by the meeting hold up their hands. (*Count taken—67.*) 101 for an Indian Bureau Chairman, 67 for an Indian Chairman. I shall ask Mr. Walter Woehlke at present to serve as Chairman of the meeting.

MR. WALTER WOEHLKE: My friends, as Mr. Collier pointed out to you, a great deal of business has to be transacted within a short time, yet that short time is twice the time that the Commissioner and his staff can give to any other of the Congresses that follow this one, but the Commissioner will have to leave here on the 5th of March because he has engagements with other Indian Congresses that can not be changed. Therefore, it is exceedingly important that this Congress transact business with as much speed as possible. I would therefore urge that the various delegations make their arrangements for interpreting the remarks and addresses here all at the same time. There are possibly seven or eight different languages represented here and if they interpret it one after the other we would be here until next fall. Therefore, it is important that each group select its official interpreter of the delegation around their interpreter so that the interpreters can go on at the same time all over the room. Will you kindly, these delegations, make that arrangement right now so that we may proceed at once? In each delegation, all those who do not speak English should get near the interpreter.

INTERPRETER FROM STANDING ROCK: Mr. Chairman.

MR. WOEHLKE: The gentlemen from Pine Ridge.

INTERPRETER: Standing Rock. The major portion of the delegates are Sioux and I believe we would save time by utilizing the services of one interpreter for the entire Sioux group.

Delegates arrange themselves near interpreters.

MR. WOEHLKE: I believe the arrangements around the interpreters have all been completed. I would now like to ask you to listen carefully and attentively to the remarks which the Commissioner is about to make. He will explain to you the purpose and the scope and the reasons for the new policy and the new legislation designed to carry out that policy. Mr. Collier will now address you.

Applause.

MR. JOHN COLLIER: It will be necessary for me and for others on the platform to do a good deal of talking, but please understand that it is just as important for you to talk as for us to talk. It is important that your views be expressed and put into the record and that any question in your mind be clearly asked and answered by us if we can answer it. The record which is being made will be immediately sent back to Washington where it will be read by the members of the House and Senate Committees on Indian Affairs by high officials of the Government. Before I begin, let me convey to you the greetings of the Secretary of the Interior, Mr. Ickes.

ROSEBUD INTERPRETER: I do not know whether I can remember all of that or not, but I will do the best I can, Mr. Collier. (*Interprets.*)

MR. JOHN COLLIER: Also the greetings of Senator Wheeler, Chairman of the Indian Committee of the Senate, and Congressman Howard, Chairman of the Indian Committee of the House. A written message to you by Congressman Howard will be received during the next day and will be read to you.

Now, my friends, I will first beg you to put out of your minds any fixed ideas that you may have brought here, based on previous reports about our policies and about the proposed legislation and that you will have open minds. A great deal is at stake for each and all Indians and there should be no hurried, careless thinking or actions. I ask you to believe that our coming to you is because we want and expect you, yourselves, to reach the final decision about these matters. That is why we come to you.

(*Sam LaPointe, Rosebud, interpreting.*) MR. LAPOINTE: I want to say to any of you English-speaking people that I am open for correction at any time.

MR. COLLIER: (*continuing*) We have not come to you because your endorsement is needed for this or that. That is not why we have come. If we were only concerned with passing a piece of legislation, we would not have to come to you. Legislation put forward by the Interior Department which is also endorsed by the President and which appeals to the common sense of Congress could be put through quickly and quietly if we wanted to do it that way. But, it is the policy and the purpose of the present Indian administration not to do things, even if they are the right things, merely because we think that they are right. We intend to act in partnership with the Indians and we are not going to act unless the Indians are willing to go with us. It also is true that within the last four or five years the members of the House Committee on Indian Affairs have taken the view that they are representatives of the Indians in Indian matters and that they want to know the views and wishes of the Indians. Hence, it is in behalf of these Committees and their Members, as well as the Administration that we have now come to meet with you.

Now, it is my belief—I may prove to be mistaken—but it is my belief that the Indians of the United States are going to be practically one hundred per cent in agreement before we are done. I am not speaking of the more than one hundred particular details of this bill when I say that you are going to be, I think, one hundred per cent in agreement. I do believe there is going to be general agreement on this bill, but when I say I believe there is going to be a complete agreement I am not necessarily referring to this bill. I am convinced that there are some things which all the Indians need and that they know those things in order to prosper, in order that their children and their grandchildren may prosper, and in order that they may be free men. Before the meeting is over, and all of the details in this bill will come up for discussion, but we would make a mistake if we began by attempting a detailed analysis of this bill, because the bill will, in any event, be amended by Congress and amended in a great many different ways.

MR. COLLIER: (*continuing; Robert High Eagle, Rosebud, interpreting.*) Therefore, with your permission, I shall not begin talking about this bill at all, but will lay it aside and forget it for the time being. And, with your permission, I shall first talk about the fundamental conditions of your life as I understand it. And what are these fundamental conditions which I shall suggest are wrong conditions and ought to be put right? What are they? They are, first, that the Indians of the United States, including your tribes, have for two lifetimes been steadily losing their property, becoming poorer and poorer on the whole. That is on the side of your property. If you take the United States as a whole, the wealth of the people has been increasing year by year steadily until the depression of three years ago. And, during those same years the wealth of the Indians, instead of increasing, has been melting away. I shall give you the exact facts after a few minutes. They are terrifying facts.

Now, the second big condition is this: That the Indians of the United States are living under a condition which puts them at the mercy of the Indian Bureau. The guardianship of the Federal Government over Indian life, which was intended to be a means of making the Indians both prosperous and free, has been having the opposite effect and has been making them poor while they were deprived of their freedom. Therefore, many people and some Indians have risen up and said that the only hope for the Indian is to put an end to the guardianship of the Government so that they may stand a chance in living. Some people have said the guardianship of the Government is injuring the Indian, is robbing the Indian, is keeping them in a condition of slavery. Therefore, the responsibility must be brought to an end. You have all heard that line of talk, and I do not hesitate to say I am speaking honestly my own feelings, that if the guardianship of the United States has to continue doing things it has been doing; if it has to go on the old way, I think it had better be stopped, thrown aside, and the Indian better do without it. But, that is not the answer. The cure for the evils done by the Government is not to abolish but to reform it and make it do good things instead of evil things, and that is true of the guardianship over Indians.

I believe that the Indians would be in agreement with us in saying that the answer to the evils of the past and the present is not to abolish the guardianship and responsibility of the Federal Government but to change it so that it will build up the property of the Indians instead of taking it away. Build up the life, the health and the liberty of the Indians instead of taking them away. The United States across centuries of time has interfered with Indian life too profoundly, has stamped its stamp on Indian life too deeply for the United States now to withdraw and disclaim its responsibility. The obligation of the United States to the Indian is not discharged. The guardianship should not come to an end. It is still possible for the United States to do the right thing, instead of the wrong thing, and I think it is fair to say, true to say, that the present Secretary of the Interior, Secretary Ickes, and the present Commissioner, myself, hold the positions that we do hold because we are expected to bring about changes and reforms in the Federal guardianship until the change becomes good instead of bad. Both—I again go back through these years gone by, almost 15 years—Secretary Ickes, Mr. Ickes as he was, and I, have stood for one thing above all which was, that it was the duty of the Indians themselves to determine what their own life shall be. It is for the Indians themselves to determine what laws Congress shall pass for them. Therefore, we are going ahead and are carrying the case to you before we attempt to procure legislation.

Applause.

I now wish to make one more general remark before going to the discussion of things in greater detail. One more general remark. There is a country north of us—Canada. There is a country south of us—Mexico, and there are Indians in Canada and there are Indians in Mexico, and Canada and Mexico both maintain Federal guardianship over their Indians. In Canada and Mexico the Indian wealth is steadily increasing in both those countries.

Interpreted to Indian delegations by Rosebud, Standing Rock, Fort Berthold and Crow Agency.

MR. COLLIER: In both those countries individual Indians are receiving every encouragement and liberty for a personal ambition and enterprise while at the same time the property of tribes and individuals is guarded against theft or foolish waste. In both of these countries the Indians and their guardian Government have a happy relationship and there are no charges of bad faith and broken contracts and treaties that are scraps of paper, and in Mexico particularly, the Indians, under the guardianship of Mexico, fill nearly all of the positions in their own Indian Service and receive such educational opportunities that they are at the top of all the professions and technical pursuits and are largely in control of the Government itself. Never in Canada, never in Mexico, do you find Indians rising up in despair to say, "Just let us alone. Quit imprisoning us. Quit driving us. Leave us to our fate." You never hear that in Canada, you never hear that in Mexico. You hear it often in the United States.

Applause.

Now it must be clear that the United States is honorable, the United States is intelligent, the United States is powerful and there is no reason why the United States, in comparison to Canada and Mexico, should go on disgracing itself in its handling of Indian matters, and it is now the intention of the President and of the Administration, and I think it is perfectly safe to say it is now the intention of Congress, that the United States shall not go on disgracing itself and wronging the Indians.

Applause.

The United States is not making a mess of its Indian guardianship because its employees are wicked or stupid. That is not the reason. They are not wicked and they are not stupid. But because the guardianship maintained by the United States is carried out under a body of laws which are wicked and stupid and which make slaves even of the Government employees hired to enforce the laws.

Applause.

There was a time when it was the policy of the United States Government to rob the Indians. There was a time when it was the policy of the United States Government to crush Indian life and even to crush the family life of Indians and during that time laws were passed and those laws are still the laws, though it is no longer the policy of the Government to rob you or to crush you, but they are the laws and by them we must work and you must live.

Rosebud interpreter asks to have last thought repeated.

MR. COLLIER: I was saying that it is not the policy of the Government to rob the Indian or to crush the Indian, but those old laws are still the laws. Therefore, the matter of deciding how to change the laws; what new laws to get, is the fundamental matter before the Indians and the country in Indian matters.

Now try to give me close attention while I talk first about your property. If we go back to the year 1887, 1887 in our thought, I will tell you about the property the Indians had then. The Indians were the owners, in that year, of 138,000,000 acres of land.

(*A gentleman speaks to the Rosebud interpreter.*) Tell them that means all the Indians, not just the Sioux. (*Interprets.*)

MR. COLLIER: I am speaking now about all the Indians. This land included the best land in the United States. It included the richest farming land, the best grazing land. It included much of the land best suited to irrigation farming and it included a great wealth of oil and lead and zinc and other minerals below the surface. In that year, 1887, Congress, over the protest of the Indians, enacted what is called the General Allotment Act. That Act is known as the backbone of the Indian law—the great basic law of Indian Affairs.

MR. COLLIER: (*continuing; Mr. LaPointe interpreting*) We come from 1887 to the present day. The amount of land now owned by the Indians is forty-seven million acres, which means that the amount of land which has been lost by the Indians since 1887 is ninety-one million acres. The best land was included in the land that was lost. If you take the forty-seven million acres that the Indians still own, twenty million acres of that land is desert or practically desert land. The facts are very much worse, as I shall now show you. The allotment law was not applied in the southwest Indian country, except in a few cases. The great Navaho tribe was spared from the allotment law. The Pueblo was spared from the allotment law both in New Mexico and Arizona. The Papago was spared and three of the four Apache tribes were spared from the allotment act. These tribes which were spared from the allotment have nearly doubled their holdings since 1887. Every one of the tribes which was spared from the allotment act has more land now than in 1887. In other words, the losses of land have fallen upon those tribes that were subjected to the allotment act, so that the allotted tribes have lost in land area more than two-thirds of their total holdings since 1887.

Mr. Red Tomahawk, Standing Rock, interpreting.

If you take the value of the land loss of the allotted tribes, it would be more than eighty per cent, or eight-tenths, or four-fifths of the total value. As you know, the allotment operation was not brought to bear everywhere at the same time. It came sooner some places and later in other places, so that the effects of the allotment system are not equal in intensity every-where. They are variable. If you take Oklahoma as an example, the amount of land owned by the Oklahoma tribes was twenty-three million acres before allotment—and all of that except three million acres has passed away. You can take individual tribes like the Oneida of Wisconsin and find that practically one hundred per cent of the land has passed from the Indians to whites and the Oneida are landless. More than one hundred thousand Indians in the allotment areas have lost all their land down to the last square foot and are entirely landless. We will later look at the allotment system in a closer way in order to understand why it has done what it has done. We will look at it closely in order to see what can be done to so change it so as to stop the loss of land. We will examine it in order to answer a very necessary question which is in your minds, so I am going to ask the question right now. The question is—how can this allotment system be changed so as, first, to stop the futile loss of land by Indians; second, increase the amount of land owned by Indians; and, third, protect the rights and equities of those Indians who have not yet lost their land?

Let me state again what we think it is necessary to do under some law to be enacted: First, that the further sale or loss of Indian lands to whites must be stopped; second, that new land—more land—must be procured in large amounts in order to supply those Indians who have lost all of their land and in order to supplement the inadequate land of those who still have some land; third, we may say what we like about the bad results of allotment, we say plenty, but allotment has created individual valid property rights in individuals. That fact is there and has to be dealt with.

Interpreter asks Mr. Collier to repeat first part of this speech.

MR. COLLIER: There must be no more land lost. There must be more land obtained. In addition, as a result of allotment, thousands of Indians live on or are the holders of parcels of land. They own that land. They were allotted it. It is their right, not only to continue to own what they own but they have the right to transmit what they own to their children, to their heirs. This right is theirs, fundamentally under the Constitution of the United States and could not be taken away from them no matter what Congress did. So that, in addition to stopping the loss of land and getting more land, any change of laws must protect these individual property rights in living allottees and their heirs.

Applause.

Right here I might as well crash into one misunderstanding that has come back to us from some Indian reservation. Deal with it at once. I went down into Oklahoma about three weeks ago, and met with a lot of Indians and among them were the Pawnee. Well, I found out that somebody had called together—I may say that among the Pawnee three out of every four have lost all of their land—somebody had called a meeting to which they had admitted only those Pawnee who had some land left. They didn't let the landless ones in. They had told those who were allowed to come in that this man Collier and Ickes, they have a scheme to take this land away from you and give it to the landless ones. So very naturally, the Pawnee came there "red hot." Of course, I was able to explain to them, as it will become clear to you. First, that anyone with a crazy plan like that could not put it into effect because the courts would not allow them to. If Congress had a crazy idea like that and passed a law like that it would be promptly thrown out by the courts. If an Indian Commissioner went to Congress with an idea like that he would just be laughed out of the building. I do not want to dwell too long on this point. Before you go away you will rightly insist on understanding clearly how the individual property rights are to be held in safety, perpetuated, protected. If there be among you Indians who are landless, it is just as important for them to be in the clear about this as for you who still have land, because if Legislation is passed which over-rides property rights, which is in violation of the Constitution, the Courts will prevent the Legislation from being put into effect. In other words, will be made null and void. In other words, what we want is Legislation so that the Courts will pass it.

Interpreters changed; Robert High Eagle from Standing Rock interprets.

MR. COLLIER: At this point may I say that the pending bill will have to pass through the Indian Committee and in addition, the Judiciary Committee of Congress and if any Indian is worried, he can rely upon those constitutional lawyers on the Judiciary Committee to see that the due process clause is not violated by any language of the Bill. I might say right here, there is nothing particularly mysterious or even experimental here. Before I referred to Canada and I referred to Mexico. They both have worked this out to the complete satisfaction of all the Indians. It can be done here. Again, let me partly turn aside now from the main argument in order to answer another misunderstanding that has come back from some reservation. We take the position that it is very necessary for Indians to be permitted to organize, to organize for many different purposes. It is necessary for Indians to be allowed to organize to do business in a modern business world in competition with the modern white world. In the world at large, the white world, the unorganized people are powerless. They are victims. Only organized groups have power in the white world.

There are many kinds of organization in the modern world. For example, there are corporations; there are cattlemen's associations and stock associations. There are co-operative societies to run, for example, creameries, to buy in quantities so as to cut out middlemen's profits; all kinds of co-operative economic organizations for mutual benefit. There are town governments which manage the local affairs of towns.

The ward Indian is shut out from all of these advantages of organization. He likewise, as you all know to your sorrow, is denied access to credit, financial credit. Now I am going to say what is almost the heart of our plan we are going to lay before you. We are proposing that Indians shall be allowed and helped to organize for mutual benefit, for local self-government and for doing business in the modern, organized way. We are proposing that there shall be set up a new financial credit system through which the Government will extend financial credit to these organized groups of Indians. We are proposing that when the Indians do organize—and they will only organize if they want to—when and if they do organize, then their organizations will be instrumentalities of the Federal Government.

Let this be very clear: When the Indians organize it will be first under Federal laws enacted by Congress to enable them to organize, under Federal laws. Second, the organized bodies of Indians will become Agencies of the Federal Government, instrumentalities, or, if you like, branches of the Federal Government. The organized Indian body then organized under Federal law, organized as an Agency of the Federal Government, would be surrounded by the protective guardianship of the Federal Government and clothed with the authority of the Federal Government.

Rosebud interpreter announces: "Mr. Clement Smith will interpret."

MR. COLLIER: I repeat, no Indian group will be required to organize, but they could organize if they wanted to. When they organized, they would be what I have told you: Agencies of the Federal Government, existing under guardianship of the Federal Government and clothed with the authority of the Federal Government.

When I say guardianship of the Federal Government and authority, what do I mean? I mean, for example, that the privilege of the Indians to be exempt from taxes will be extended to these organized groups and their operations. I mean again, that in addition to extending financial credit to these groups, the Government would subsidize them—would give them various kinds of financial assistance. This organized group, as an Agency of the Government, would, in one case, be doing one kind of thing and somewhere else would be doing another kind of thing and somewhere else would be doing another kind of thing, entirely according to the desires and needs of that Indian group.

Such a chartered Indian organization could, if it desired, take over many of the things that are now being done by the Indian Bureau and the money being spent on those things would be transferred to the organized body of Indians and they would spend the money and they would hire their own employees.

Mild Applause.

Now, we will get into the detail of this later, of course. Now I am only telling you enough that I can deal with objections that have come back from some places. For example, from one of the Pacific Northwest reservations comes in a telegram: "We don't want socialism or communism."

Applause and laughter.

From another Reservation comes in this solemn message, "We don't want anything to do with this new deal because in 1867 the Government promised rations to our people until the water ceased to flow."

Laughter.

Another phrase was brought to me by an old friend, a very good friend of mine, who I have known for 30 years. He came to me in New York to see me. He said, "Mr. Collier, I want to ask you a real question." I said, "Go to it." He said, "Are you an atheist?" because he had gotten an understanding that this plan of allowing the Indians to organize the way I have described was some scheme for doing away with Christianity; that it was some kind of thing like they do over in Russia.

It will be clear to you; if it isn't, don't go away until it becomes clear; that in the United States, if you are going to do business and make money and protect yourself, you have got to do it in an organized way. Otherwise you are just out of luck. You don't make any money, you are not protected, and the other fellow eats you alive.

Applause.

You can't govern yourselves, you can't do business, you can't protect yourself, unless you organize. That is true regarding everybody in the United States. If you look around the United States you will find some leaders of organizations who are Catholics and some who are Protestants and some who are Mormons, some who are Republicans and some who are Democrats, but every man who has got any power is organized.

MR. COLLIER: (*continuing; Rosebud interpreter*) Now, away back yonder in the old days of war when the United States was over-riding its treaties with most of you tribes—in those days the Government adopted a policy of forbidding Indians to organize at all. For Indians to organize was made seditious and an illegal act. And that tradition has come down to the present in the minds of many and the laws passed in those old days are still the laws, so that it is still illegal and it can still be considered actually seditious for Indians to organize.

In spite of that explanation from history, it does seem strange that there should be anybody in the United States who would want to forbid the Indians from organizing when everybody is organized. Many Indians have come to believe that the only way they could get power to organize, power to make contracts, power to borrow money, power to do business in the modern world, was for them to pass out of the guardianship of the Government. Indians have been taught that they had to choose between remaining like so many domestic animals being taken care of by the Indian Bureau or else thrown to the wolves. That is the choice they thought they had to make—so a misunderstanding is natural. It will pass away when everybody grasps the idea which is that the Indians who organize under this plan which we are talking about will organize under federal law, under federal guardianship. This organization will be an agency of the federal government, subsidized by the Federal Government, as well as protected by it. In other words, within the framework of guardianship, it is possible to build up for the Indians freedom as individual men, freedom as human beings, with the power that goes with organization, and there will be more Federal protection at the end than there is now.

In my remaining words I will not say any more about the details of your problem, because we will come to all that. I want rather to remind you of what is going on in the country as a whole at present under the leadership of President Roosevelt. A great body of fundamental changes are taking place swiftly at Washington and from Washington out all over the country. And, in a broad way it can be said that those changes, those reforms, are dealing with two subjects. We are dealing with what President Roosevelt in his campaign speeches called the "forgotten man." That means the rank and file of the plain people, the common people who were staggering under the burden of the rich, carrying a privileged class who ruled the country and ruled the forgotten man. But the big business which rode on the back of the forgotten man was itself blind and didn't know where it was trying to drive the common man, and, therefore, we have the great crash of 1929. And, part of the gigantic thing being done by the President is to get the blind giant off the back of the common man and to work out an economic life through which the common man is his own master and is free.

And, the other part of that thing which is going on in Washington has to do with what you may call the "forgotten land." All over the United States the great stands of timber, the forests, have been wasted by careless lumbering—cut green and burnt up—to the injury of mankind for thousands of years to come. That is being done. All over the country the soil has been neglected, over-grazed, washed away into the rivers—millions of square miles of our grazing and farming land damaged or ruined by erosion, going on every year. At this time great expenditures are being commenced, new laws are being enacted to save our forests, to restore our land, to bring the land and its productions back under the control of the people and their Government. This, what we will call a new deal for Indians, is part of all the rest. The big push that is carrying the country into a new life is the same big push that must carry the Indians into a new life.

MR. COLLIER: The time will come when the changes will be finished as far as law and Washington are concerned and the country will settle down into a new mold. Perhaps in two or three years. The chance of the Indians is now and not hereafter. It is the chance of all times for you to get whatever you are entitled to. Now and not at some future time. Now is the time of destiny for the Indians. If they will use their best brains in dead earnest on all their problems now, determine what they need, ask for it clearly, present intelligent programs, they can get the uttermost far with what they need, but that may not be true two or three years from now.

Applause.

You will understand now why we are going out to the Indians to discuss these questions of your own life.

It is time for dinner.

Interpreted by Emil Afraid of Hawk, Pine Ridge Sioux Indian.

MR. WALTER WOEHLKE, Chairman: This Congress will reconvene in this hall at 1:30. At that time photographers will be present to take pictures of this history-making group. For the purpose of that picture we would like to have the heads of the delegations and the chiefs from the various delegations seated along the center aisles and in front where the Commissioner will also be so that they can be plainly seen. We would also like to have the heads of the delegations and the chiefs to get immediately outside to have their pictures taken with the Commissioner—before dinner. The heads of the delegations are requested to obtain copies of the memorandums which explain the Bill at the boys' dormitory. They can obtain enough copies for each member of the delegation there.

The meeting is adjourned.

Afternoon Session

Afternoon session, Plains Congress, convened at 1:30 p.m., March 2, 1934. Photographs were taken of the Congress assembled.

MR. WOEHLKE, Chairman: Will the delegates arrange themselves in the same order as this morning so as to make interpreting easy. Owing to the necessity of having our picture taken we are slightly behind our schedule. I would like to announce that the Congress will convene tomorrow morning at 9:30. There will be another meeting in the afternoon at 1:30 and there will probably be an evening meeting at 7:30. We are also considering the question of holding the Sunday meeting or meetings in the auditorium of Rapid City because it affords far more space than we have here and it would allow many more of the delegates and visitors to hear and listen and talk in the proceedings. The question now is, whether the Congress would like to have a Sunday morning meeting in the Civic Auditorium of Rapid City, and I would like an expression of opinion from this Congress. Supposing that all those who are in favor of holding a Sunday morning meeting in the Civic Auditorium, raise their right hands.

INTERPRETER FROM ROSEBUD: I have interpreted what you said and I made this statement. This morning we heard that Mr. Collier had been accused of being an atheist. Now we don't want it to appear that Mr. Collier is an atheist because we are all atheists. There are many of our people that are very religious people. We belong to several different religious denominations. That is sort of a personal right. There are perhaps many of us who want to attend religious services on Sunday morning. There would be no objection to holding a meeting in the afternoon. So I make that motion against your statement.

Applause.

MR. WOEHLKE: It apparently is the sense of the meeting that we should not have a session Sunday morning in the Civic Auditorium. Is that the sense of the meeting? Let us put it this way. All those who are against holding a meeting on Sunday morning in the Civic Auditorium raise their right hand.

Quite a considerable number raise their hands.

Then we shall endeavor to arrange for a meeting Sunday afternoon in the Civic Auditorium, and as we can not get it at night, probably a Sunday evening meeting here again.

Now, with your kind indulgence, Commissioner Collier will conclude his general statement to you.

Applause.

MR. JOHN COLLIER: Friends, I do not like to do so much of the talking. When we come to discussion of details I shall yield the floor to various other people, but I suppose that it will save time if I go on myself for a little longer. I shall speak to you for a while about the most difficult part of your situation and of our problem: your property. Without repeating anything I gave you this morning about the way your land has melted away under the allotment system, not repeating that, I will go on and discuss the allotment system, a little further. As most of you know, perhaps all of you, the allotment plan was made with a view of bringing the guardianship of the Federal Government to an end.

The law clearly intended and declared that the trust period on the allotment should come to an end after a while, and the individual who owned the land should no longer be a ward of the Government, should be subject to the State laws, should pay taxes. That was the end. During the time between allotment and the end of the trust period or the declaration of competency; during that time, the Government was to act as trustee over the allotment.

It soon became apparent to the law makers that the allotment law would have to be changed, because the allottee died, the original allottee, the end of his life came and his land passed into the heirship status. After the death of the allottee the estate was probated and the heirs were determined. It then became necessary that the land either be sold and the proceeds divided among the heirs. In comparatively rare cases, the allottees were children who died and the heirs were their parents, and then there was no need of splitting up the equities, because one heir received the whole allotment.

But, as you know, the usual thing was that there would be a number of heirs; sometimes a very large number of heirs, and it frequently came about that one heir had an interest in a large number of estates. Now, if the Government did not sell these heirship lands, then the Government had to act as trustee over them; had to act as the real estate agent to sell them or lease them and handle the proceeds. An example of what happened has just been handed me by Superintendent Baker of the Sisseton Agency.

Here is one estate; that of Joseph Renville, at the Sisseton, and it is so split up that there are about sixty heirs in this case, and there are hardly two of the heirs who have an identical or equal interest.

MR. COLLIER: (*Robert High Eagle, Standing Rock, interpreting*) You can arrive at that by dividing 8,976,600 into 114,307,200. You can divide 5,200 into 114,307,200. The lowest equities are the ratio between 5,200 and 114,000,000.

Mr. Collier illustrating at blackboard.

In other words, one part in about four hundred. Now, that heir having the value of a postage stamp in one allotment may have the value of ten postage stamps in another allotment and a dollar in some other allotment. Now, understand this, every year this gets more complicated. The shares get smaller, the number of heirs becomes greater, and the number of individuals having shares in more than an allotment becomes more numerous. Now, in addition, of course, we can supply the picture that the allotments in question are scattered among a lot of white-owned land—checker-boarded with white-owned land. And that checker-boarding grows greater all the time as lands are sold. The lands themselves, because of the way they are checker-boarded, cannot be used or rented to the best advantage. There are great disadvantages in the matter of renting the land or using it.

We had hoped to have some giant maps here to show all of this. We have a number of interesting maps which we would like to have you look at before we are done. This (*indicating map*) is, as it happens, the Cheyenne River.

MR. STEWART: We have made maps of all the reservations in this part of the country and we have them here. We will pass them around sometime during the Congress to all of you. We have some picture graphs coming by airmail along this line. We want to explain them jointly with these maps. However, they have not yet arrived. The color scheme, as I mentioned before, is uniform; that is, one color—such as blue—on one map indicates the same status on all the maps. Blue represents living allotted land; that is, where the allottee is still living. On this map, this shade of green—it is green supposedly—looks like blue so don't let it mislead you. The blue is these small pieces scattered around. Green represents tribal land unallotted. Yellow represents deceased allotments where the allotment or land is still held in trust by the Government. Red represents the alienated land or white-owned land. The uncolored section here represents surplus land yet open and undisposed of. I want to qualify that remark, however. A good deal of it is undisposed of, but we have no way of putting a color here to show disposed of areas because our office does not handle that. The General Land Office handles that. This situation is true on all the reservations in this part of the country.

MR. COLLIER: While Mr. Stewart was talking I corrected my arithmetic and I find that in the case I was giving you, the heir in question has 1.1290 percent in the allotment. And, if the allotment rents for $50 a year, that heir will get a little less than two and one-half cents a year. Now let us get it clear. Under the allotment law, as it stands, the situation has to get worse every year as the original allottees die. This complicates this crazy quilt as heirship holdings increase year by year. Nothing can stop it because people insist on dying. We cannot stop them. Now, I am very anxious to get this situation, as it appears, to the people who control our annual budget and so on. It is very vital. The Indian Bureau, under the law, is compelled to be trustee and real estate agent for all of these parcels of land on behalf of all of these heirs. The number of separate equities, in bookkeeping accounts no one has ever counted, but it is probably in excess of two millions. Probably is nearly ten millions. Not merely is there the bookkeeping job, but all of the probating of heirship and then the job of renting and collecting and distributing the collected money. It does not stop the land from passing out of Indian ownership. It cannot get a good rental or a good sales price because the land is broken up by heirship. The Bureau must go on going through the motion of being the real estate agent for all these millions of acres of land. The result is, that the cost of determining these heirship lands not only exceeds the rental yields of these lands, but it often exceeds the capital value of these lands year by year. We have told Congress the truth as we know it, as all of these operations I now describe to you, which do not save the land, which do no good to the Indians, are costing us somewhere around two million dollars a year of money thrown away, wasted. This is another way of saying that it becomes a matter of administrative necessity to sell these heirship lands, no matter how much we regret it.

The person who stands pat on the allotment system has this answer. The answer is, "It was the intent of the allotment act for those lands to be sold and used. Mr. Collier can save the Government its wasted money by selling the land and then you will not have to look after the land any more." They would say, "If it is the clear intent for the allotment act for the land to be sold, why don't you go ahead and do your duty, sell the land." They further say that it is the clear intent of the allotment act to declare the Indians competent.

The allotment act has lasted 25 years. Now it is 35 years and it has been dragging on year after year so as to keep jobs in the Indian Bureau. They point out that the Secretary of Interior today has the discretion to terminate the Trust Period. They also point out what the few Indians of the allotted areas need to know, is this, that they point out that the poorest Indians are the ones living in the allotted areas. Where is the highest death rate? It is among the Indians living in the allotted areas. They point out that the Indians in the unallotted areas are costing the Government less money than the Indians living in the allotted areas. It is true, and yet they point out that the Indians in the unallotted areas are getting more services than the Indians in the allotted areas; more human services in the way of health, education and agriculture. The reason being that the Government's money in the allotted areas is so largely used up on these barren trusteeships or unallotted lands.

What I am leading up to is something that I will say to you only after a good deal of thought, whether it is wise or not, but it is the truth and therefore I am going to say it. You remember what Secretary Lane and Commissioner Cato Sells did in 1917. They used the discretion, which the Secretary of the Interior has, and they fee patented thousands of Indians in a hurry, forcibly. Those lands immediately became taxable and they were lost in a very few years to the Indians. Now the present administration, while it lasts, is not going to do anything of that kind. As you know we have even gone further and have prohibited the sale of allotted land which is temporarily a stop measure, but we must face the acknowledged fact that the Government's costs are mounting—heirship lands are increasing year by year and that an administration of the future, it would be of the near future, may submit to the pressure and simply force fee patents on all of you. They can do it and I am going to tell you they will.

This rising cost of administration for the allotted and particularly the heirship lands, which admittedly is doing no good, will stare the administration in the face and will stare the director of the budget in the face more and more every year. The Government itself, as all of you know, is getting horribly in debt as a result of the depression. Before the depression is over, the mere interest charge of the Government's bonded indebtedness probably will exceed a thousand million dollars a year.

INTERPRETER FROM ROSEBUD: How can I say a thousand million?

MR. COLLIER: A billion.

ROSEBUD INTERPRETER: You know, our arithmetic among the Sioux is very limited.

MR. COLLIER: That means that the Government is going to be compelled to economize wherever it can; at every point where money can be saved, from the regular administration costs, the Government is going to be looking for that place in saving money. That has already commenced. The Indian Bureau in the year ahead will not have as much money by $12,000,000 as it had year before last. Right now, for every dollar we get for health, for schools, etc., we have to fight like wildcats. Only last month, in order to get a little more money for our hospitals we had to go to the President himself and it took days of debate before we got an additional $75,000 for hospitals that did not have doctors and nurses. Now, I must say that you do not need to fear what Secretary Ickes is going to do; what I am going to do. We have our pledge, but we won't be there forever; not by any means. We might not be there three years from now. And now that Congress knows and now that the budget knows that this administration of these heirship lands is just throwing good money after bad; is a waste of millions of dollars a year of money needed for something else, watch out what the next Secretary of the Interior does. Watch out what the next director of the Budget does, and remember that the States and Counties may be relied on to present all of the arguments for terminating the trust period on your lands because your lands are now tax exempt.

If the trust periods were terminated your land would pay taxes. In brief, unless we can modify the land situation, then the Indians of the allotted area are in a dead end passage. There is no way through. They are clinging now to their allotments; such allotments as remain, as a last hold on a feeling of security. That hold will be taken away from them too, because as a matter of economic and administrative necessity, future administrations will carry through the thing that Franklin Lane began. If a way can be found to get out of this dead end passage in such a manner as not to disturb existing possessions, existing ownership, existing rights, in such a way as to make the trust period perpetual, and in such a way as to add land where land is needed, that clearly is the line of hope for the Indians, and that way can be found—a way which will not take away anything from any individual Indian, but which will only increase what any individual Indian has got, while giving something to the Indian who has got nothing.

Much of the time later in these sessions will, of course, be devoted to making this clear to you, but I have spoken as I have in the last half hour and told you what I have for a reason. The reason is this: That I am informed that some of your delegations consider that it may be better to do nothing at all rather than to take a risk of changing something; either that you haven't got authority to do anything or that you don't want to do anything at all to meet the situation. I am informed that some of you here, on the strength of things you heard before you came here; things that you read in the newspapers or that people have told you, have crystallized your thinking against any change, and I desire for you to realize what I know to be the truth; that beyond your power, beyond my power, beyond the power of the President himself, the forces are moving which are going to make the change in a way to destroy you unless it is made in a way to save and help you.

The allotment system is working out to its predestined conclusion; it will work on and within a comparatively few years it will force the Government into wholesale fee patenting as the only way out of a bad situation.

Now I want to say a word about another phase of the situation still connected with land. Where the land is checker-boarded in the way that you know, on most of your Sioux Reservations, checker-boarded with white holdings; where half or more of it is in the heirship status and split among an ever-increasing number of heirs; under those conditions about all that can be done is to rent the land and to rent it at a disadvantage; to rent it, that is, for rather poor returns.

The Government is not justified and cannot be expected to advance large sums of money to capitalize the Indians for the use of land when the land is in that condition. The Government program of capitalizing the Indians, extending loans to them I mean, for the effective use of their land, cannot be carried out amid such areas as, for example, the Sisseton Sioux and others that I might mention. This thing so essential for modern life, particularly modern life on the land, of credit, cannot be provided unless we find a way out of this heirship land misery.

We have amended this bill now pending before Congress with a new part, which establishes, to begin with, a five million dollar loan fund which the House Committee have stated they will raise ten million, for capitalizing the Indians in the use of their land. We can get that money. We can establish that new credit system, but it cannot be made effective until the land situation is readjusted. Once more, we propose, that the Government is, first: Buying a large amount of land for landless allotted Indians, and to add to the insufficient land of allotted Indians who haven't got enough land. That is one of the basic proposals now before Congress.

MR. COLLIER: *(continuing; Robert High Eagle, interpreting)* To begin with we are asking for two million dollars to be available each year for land purchase, that being only a beginning. In addition to that the Government is starting in to buy up millions of acres of what they call sub-marginal land, which really is grazing land, all over the country. We expect to be able to obtain large gifts of land to Indians and Indian tribes out of that sub-marginal land in order to withdraw it from farming. But here again it can be taken for granted by all of you that the Government will not buy land to get it into the condition of the allotted lands at present. It will not buy land to spend millions of dollars in this allotment business and then see it pass back to white ownership. It will not do it—only, if the Indians can get an intelligent, successful business-like land-holding system. Only then may they expect to have more land bought for them or additional lands given to them. Now we will make it clear to everyone while we are here that this improved land-holding system is necessary to get credit, necessary to acquire new land, necessary to avert fee patents. We will make it clear that this new system can be arrived at with almost no visible change from what you have, with no disturbance of any vested right of any Indian to anything.

I keep coming back to this because of things like this telegram which I hold in my hands from somebody up at Fort Peck who protests that nothing must be done to destroy the treaty rights of the Indians, so nothing must be passed on, he says. I surely do not blame any Indian or group of Indians for being like we say the man from Missouri is—he has to be shown. I don't blame you. There is not one of you tribes, I believe, that has not had the experience more than once of having high officials tell you lies. For a hundred years the usual way for the Government to dispose of a difficult situation was to tell some lie to the Indians and get them to sign up for it. Somebody here might think it bad for the Commissioner of Indian Affairs to say a thing like that. I think it is the duty of the Commissioner to tell the truth and the truth is what I said and everyone in this hall knows that it is true.

MR. LAPOINTE, Rosebud, interpreter: By the way they clap their hands, I don't think they need an interpreter.

MR. COLLIER: I, myself, have, for more than ten years before I became Commissioner struggled with repeated cases where important legislation was laid before Indian tribes all dressed up in false statements by high officials of the Government, and it was my business to strip off the untrue and help the Indians find out what was true. Therefore, I will know why no Indians anywhere will be willing to take somebody's word, Secretary Ickes' word, or anybody's word about these matters. I believe that the facts and the proposed changes are so clear and the proposals themselves are so simple, that every one of you can examine the facts, analyze the proposed relatives and reach an intelligent conclusion about them. I do think that this much is true; that in a case where there is an agreement among people who you have looked to for advice; in a case where the President, himself, joins in the assurance; in a case where the Committees of Congress give close study and are agreed on, that you can have a certain amount of confidence that you are being told the truth about them. But we have called these Indian Congresses because we want you to take our word for it only after you have made your own inquiries and arrive at your own conclusions.

Applause.

I ought to say that, which again you will all agree on, and that it is not only officials of the Federal Government in the times gone by who have misled and misinformed the Indians. Not only them. There are others who have done the same thing. There are others who have had a motive for misleading the Indians and who have misled them. Not only Government Officials. There is a group today, and speaking generally, I have no specific reference—there are today many thousands of white people living on or near the Indian owned lands who certainly will not want your lands protected.

Applause.

There are a great many lessees and cattlemen that want and intend that the Indians shall continue to be at their mercy. There are parties and groups that do not want the Indians to get their lands in shape and then have adequate talent to use their lands instead of renting them for a song. In other words I am leaving with you now that it will be your own fault really and truly that you will, and just as I do not want you to follow blindly, or neither does Secretary Ickes, still less do I want you to take your information from interested sources whose sole purpose might be the opposite of what you want. Now, before I conclude, and I have been a long time talking in general, and I am going to stop after another explanation to you, I want to refer to the element of time in the situation. To the speed in which these matters will have to happen.

The Legislation, the Bill draft, which we have put forward as our own best idea, has been before Congress since February 6th. The House Indian Committee has held four long record hearings on the bill already. The Senate hearings have begun. Our power and your power to secure legislation will be greater at the present session of Congress than we can be sure it will be at the last. We are pretty sure we can put through Congress anything reasonable that the Indians and the Administration agree on. The difficulty with Congress lies principally in getting Congress to embark upon a large program of expenditure. This five or ten million dollars as the beginning of an Indian Credit System; this two million dollars a year as a beginning for the Indian land purchasing and the five million dollars to be spent for the cost of organizing the Indian self-government, are very large amounts, but I would say that we stand a better chance of getting these large grants at this Congress than we would at the next Congress. That is because, and I have every reason to think, that the National debt will continue to roll up at an awful speed. It will increase by billions.

Again it is impossible to predict, of course, what will happen at the next Congressional election, which is not very far away as you know. Nobody knows what is going to happen next fall. I find that the need of the Indian for relief is very great. Particularly the need of those Indians whose land is gone and who really are homeless on the face of the earth. Their need is desperate and pitiful. These are all reasons in favor of moving any faster than we can move with reason and safety. Now this I should also make plain to you; that in the long run it is Congress and Congress alone which determines the passing of any Bills. First, the Indian Committee is going to take this bill and look over it very carefully and examine every line of it. The Judiciary Committee of the House and Senate will take their turn in approving the Bill and then amendment on the floor is wide open. Any amendment in either the House or Senate. So that the Bill is somewhat in the form of this paper—[*Displays paper in hands*]—as it will come out as a Bill from the House or Committee.

The way a group of Indians can meet that situation, because all of the whole Indian race cannot come to Washington and stay there, the way you can meet the situation I will now try to make clear to you, and I can best explain by an example of something like this which happened once before. Back in 1922, that is twelve years ago, there took place a great struggle dealing with the lands owned by the Pueblo Tribe of New Mexico. It was a matter that was fully as complicated as the allotment system. At least that complicated or more so. It was a condition of ancient grants from Spain and other grants that had been bought by the Indians; then of white settlers who claimed a part of the land, and any Bill in order to deal with the situation had to be a very long and complicated Bill. The Pueblo were met together and sent delegations from 17 tribes, and they stayed three or four weeks in Washington and then they came home. It was evident that the Bill would be in Congress in committee for quite a long time and they just could not stay in Washington. Then the Pueblo got together in a Congress of their own. A regular congress of delegates from every tribe, and after many days of conference, they found it possible to put in simple language in about four printed pages, they put down what they insisted on; what they would take and they would not take anything less than that. They did not try to write a great, complicated bill, with all the legal phraseology. They simply stated in one paragraph after another, and another one after another one, what they would stand for; what they demanded; their platform.

Their friends, in and out of the Government, were guided by that statement. All of the Indians themselves had copies of that statement which they themselves had drawn up and from time to time as Congress worked over the Bill and amended it, the amended drafts were sent back again and again to the tribe, and they were able to check up on the drafts to see whether it conformed to their own platform. Finally the act known as the Pueblo Lands Act was passed by Congress and signed by the President, and that act conformed to the Pueblos' Platform. It was not changed in any way but Congress worked it over into the legal language, and, as a matter of fact, all subsequent legislation; in the past ten years, every line of the subsequent legislation has conformed to the platform which the Pueblo adopted in 1924.

I believe that you will find it possible to reduce your own wishes and ideas to simple statements and then to insist that those ideas, those principles, be carried over into the legislation. I suggest also that any expression that you give here before you go away, shall be regarded as tentative, subject to change after you go back home, because what is desired; what we want and Congress wants, is the mature thought of all of the Indian people and we do not want to take your expressions of today as being binding upon you.

MR. WOEHLKE, Chairman: Before we proceed with the business of the Congress, I would like to make an announcement. There will be a meeting of all Missionary workers, Indian and white, ordained and unordained, at eight o'clock Saturday morning. They will gather in this auditorium and proceed to one of the schoolrooms. Major Case has requested the privilege of the floor to make an announcement to the Sioux delegations. Major Case.

Applause.

MAJOR CASE: Thank you, my friends. I would like to have the delegates from the eight Sioux Reservations. I will name the Reservations: Pine Ridge, Rosebud, Crow Creek, Brule, Cheyenne River, Standing Rock, Santee and the Sioux of Fort Peck of Montana, meet here in this hall at eight o'clock tonight. The Commissioner has very kindly consented to this arrangement and Mr. Staley, the head of the school, has made it possible for us to meet here. This meeting is called so that I may discuss with you the progress made in your tribal and band claims against the United States. I came here to be of service to you and to the Indian Service, and to the Commissioner of Indian Affairs, so if you have questions you want to ask me tonight, I will try to answer them.

MR. WOEHLKE: (*Mr. LaPointe, Rosebud, interpreting*) You have heard the Commissioner's general statement of the broad purposes of the new policy and of the legislation designed to make this policy effective. We now want to proceed with the discussion of the various parts of this program. There are four broad divisions. One of these divisions deals with the proposed new land policy. Another one of these divisions deals with the credit machinery that is necessary to make the land policy effective. Another division deals with the necessity and the means of providing education, and funds of this education, for Indians, to train them for the Indian Service and for leadership. And still another division deals with a matter that is and should be very close to your hearts—the right to run your own affairs. It is a most important division of this policy and I would like to have the Commissioner assign some one on his staff to give you a detailed explanation of the machinery which is set up in this legislation to make self-government possible. The Commissioner has asked Mr. Ward Shepard to present this matter to you and you will now hear from Mr. Shepard.

MR. COLLIER: (*Mr. Red Tomahawk, Standing Rock Indian, interpreting*) Before introducing Mr. Shepard to you, may I say a few words about this self-government? I want to get into your minds what your present situation is about handling your own affairs. Your present situation is that you are entirely at the mercy of the Secretary of the Interior and the Commissioner of Indian Affairs. By law, we, the officials, have final and absolute power. If you have business committees and tribal councils, they exist because we allow them to. Furthermore, what we do is in most cases final and not subject to review by the courts. That is the fact under existing law which we, ourselves, are powerless to change.

Again, if you look at the Indian Service which served you in the year 1900, that is thirty-four years ago, there were more Indians employed in the Indian Service in proportion to the total employees than there are today. After thirty-four years of education, the proportion of Indians holding positions in the Indian Service is smaller than it was in 1900. That again, in the main, is due to existing law and outside our control, due to the Civil Service, which can be changed by law—and we are proposing to change it.

I am not going on multiplying examples of how little self-move you have. We are powerless to change it in any important respect unless we get new law. In years gone by, your friends, and that included myself, have tried to get at this situation by legislation and we failed. We failed partly because the administration was against us, but that was not the only reason why we failed. We failed partly because we kept on trying to meet the situation through one blanket bill, when conditions were so varied that one blanket bill could not meet the situation.

We are now laying before Congress and before you a more carefully thought out plan—a plan according to which Indian tribes or groups may develop the kind of self-government that they want, that is fitted to them, and may take on more power or less power as they prefer. You will see that it is a plan which enables an Indian group to take over just as much of the authority of the Government, and I might add just as much of the money being spent on Indian Service, as that group after mature thought wants to take over. The machinery is such that the initiative rests with the Indians, themselves. The Secretary of the Interior is directed by Congress to present and grant the self-government as the tribes ask for it. Should the Secretary of the Interior refuse to obey the mandate of Congress, he must publicly in writing justify his position, and the tribes' appeal goes to Congress—all of this taking place within the guardianship of the Government, which is made permanent.

Now, the actual drafting of this bill, which is before you and Congress, was carried out by representatives of the Solicitors' office in consultation with members of the Indian Office, and I am going to turn over the detailed explanation to them, beginning with Mr. Ward Shepard, who is the specialist in land policy of the Indian Office, and a man who you will discover has great breadth and sympathy.

MR. WARD SHEPARD: My friends: Before we go into the details of this bill, I want first of all to get a picture of the general principles by which the self-government will be worked out.

First of all, we do not wish Indian self-government to be dependent in the future upon the whims of the Indian Bureau. We therefore have started this bill with a declaration by Congress that it is the policy of Congress to grant self-government to the Indians and that those powers of self-government will be confirmed to the Indians in charters which will be issued by the Secretary of Interior. We propose, in addition to issuing these charters of self-government and business incorporation, to provide for the gradual transfer of the functions and services of the Bureau of Indian Affairs to these organized Indian communities. We propose further, in order to permit the Indians to develop this self-government and to take over these services of the Indian Bureau progressively and gradually to set up a system of education by which Indians will be educated in all of the administrative and technical functions of their local Government. We propose further that the funds appropriated by Congress for the performance of these services which are gradually turned over to the local Indian communities; that the monies shall be turned over to be disbursed by the disbursing officer of the Indian community. We propose that the monies that belong to the Indians themselves, the monies that are in the Treasury of the United States to the credit of the Indian tribes, shall also be disbursed only through the Indian disbursing officers.

We propose further that in the future Indians themselves shall take a part in making the appropriations estimates which go to Congress for the expenditure of federal funds in their own communities, so that they themselves shall have a part in determining how this money is to be expended for their benefit. Moreover, any money expended by the Federal Government from Congressional appropriations, from gratuity appropriations, can not be made reimbursable against the Indians without the consent of the Indians. Now, let me repeat this last thing to make it perfectly clear. It means in the first place, that Indian money can no longer be spent by the Government without the consent of the Indians.

Applause.

It means further that in the future the Indians will take part in determining what appropriations that Congress will make for their benefit, and that the recommendations of the Indians will go first of all to the Bureau of the Budget and then to the Congressional Appropriations Committee and will receive the same hearing that the recommendations of the Indian Commissioner and the Secretary of the Interior receive.

Now, let us go back to the question of charters. No charters are going to be forced on any Indian community that does not want to take self-government. If any Indian community wants to go on with the present system it is up to them to determine it. If, on the other hand, an Indian community wishes to undertake self-government it has the right to petition for a charter of self-government and to help work out that charter with experts who will be furnished to help and assist them. If an Indian community petitions for charter of self-government, as the Commissioner has told you, and if the Secretary of the Interior should refuse or should lay down unreasonable conditions for the issuance of the charter, then the Secretary must report the facts to Congress and the Indians would have an appeal to Congress.

Now here is an extremely important point. This bill does not set up any one system of self-government. It does not seek to impose on the Indians a system of self-government of any kind. It sets up permission to the Indians to work out self-government which is appropriate to their traditions, to their history and to their social organization. We do not wish to force on the Indians the white man's system of Government. We want, on the other hand, to build on the old Indian traditions, on your old traditions of self-government, to make this legislation fit those old traditions and your own institutions. If, on the other hand, an Indian community wishes to adopt the white man's system of Government and to enter into the same kind of local Government you already have in your State, the Bill also permits that. This Bill permits traditions from the ancient tribal Pueblo in the Southwest to the most modernized communities.

One more final statement. This Bill guarantees what you really have under the Constitution but which we want to restate and reaffirm—namely, that all Indians shall have freedom of conscience, of worship, of speech, of press, of assembly, and of associations. Now, it is not the intention of this Bill to force upon the Indians a greater responsibility in self-government than they feel that they are able to initiate at the present time, and this Bill is not a means by which the Government, by which the Indian Bureau wishes to escape its own responsibilities. It is a means of making it possible for the Indians and the Indian Bureau to co-operate in the working out of the future of the Indians. Now this Bill gives a long list of powers which may be granted to an Indian community, and remember, please, that you are to choose in adopting this charter of self-government only those powers that I am going to enumerate which you wish to try to exercise. I will not read all of these powers but I will read the main ones slowly so that the interpreter may interpret as I read them. First:

1. Making and enforcing ordinances.
2. Electing or appointing their own officers.
3. Determining membership in the community.
4. Regulating the use and disposal of property of members of the community and of the community itself.
5. Encouraging art, culture, and education.
6. Administering charity.
7. Protecting the public health.
8. Establishing Indian Courts and enforcing your own laws.
9. Appointing guardians for minors and incompetents.
10 Constructing public works.
11 Levying assessments on members or requiring labor in place of assessments.
12. Acquiring and managing property.
13. Entering into contracts and employing attorneys.
14. To make contracts with the State or with the local Government.
15. To give to Indians, service in education, public health and such other service as states render to local communities.
16. To sue and be sued.
17. To compel the transfer from the community of unsatisfactory Federal employees.
18. To regulate trade and intercourse with non-members of the community.

Now those are the main powers which may be given under a charter to an Indian community and as I said before it is up to the Indians themselves to determine which of these they wish to take over in the beginning. Later on, you will have a chance to take over more of them as you get experience in taking care of your own affairs. This Bill proposes to appropriate five hundred thousand dollars to assist the Indian communities that wish to begin self-government, and that money would be spent to help the Indian communities to organize, to build necessary governmental buildings to carry out their functions of Government and for many other expenses necessary to inaugurate this system so that the Indians themselves would not have to pay the cost of it. Now let me repeat and emphasize that it is not compulsory on any Indian group, either to accept self-government or accept any specified system of self-government. It is up to them.

Now, I want to go on to the second important step in this bill, which is the gradual transfer of the functions of the Indian Bureau to the organized Indian Communities.

Now first of all the Commissioner is required by this law to classify all of the services and functions which may be transferred to the organized Indian community and to set up rules and regulations governing that transfer. But, I want to point out, that as a condition for the transfer of any functions to an Indian community, that community must have individual members who are capable of satisfactorily performing those functions. That does not mean that Indians who wish to go into these services which are to be turned over to the Indian communities must pass a Civil Service examination. It does mean that the Secretary and the Commissioner will define the qualifications which an Indian must meet in order to be appointed to one of those services. It means also that the Commissioner is directed to furnish financial assistance for the training of Indians so that they may become more and more qualified to take over self-government.

If the Secretary refuses to voluntarily transfer a service which the Indian community feels that it is qualified to perform, the Indians may require the Secretary to transfer that function and may appeal to Congress to require the transfer of that function. If a service is transferred to an Indian community, that does not mean that the community has to pay the cost of that service, but it means that the money appropriated by Congress for that service will be transferred with the service, itself.

The bill requires that the federal employees of the local reservation must aid and assist the Indian community in every possible way to carry out its local self-government and to administer these services that are transferred. The local Indian officials are required to make regular reports to the Indian self-government and to consult the advice of your Indian officials on all questions of administration and policy. Moreover, if there is a vacancy in the Federal Indian Service on an Indian reservation, even before the services have been transferred to your community, you have a right to appoint an Indian to that vacancy provided he has the requisite qualifications. The Indian Service will continue to administer any functions which are not transferred to the Indian community.

If an Indian community fails to administer properly a transferred service, then the Secretary or the Commissioner may reassume that service, but must report the facts to Congress. This does not mean the abolition of the Indian Bureau, or the abolition of federal guardianship and responsibility toward the Indians. It means that hereafter the Government and the Indian communities will be partners in working out all of the affairs of the Indians. And I want to say that this system will remove a great many of the causes of friction that have existed between the Indian Bureau and the Indians. The present system is equally bad for the Indians and for the employees of the Indian Bureau because it leads to constant friction and constant quarreling. This new system will give to the Indians and to the employees of the Indian Bureau a chance to work on a footing of friendly equality. It gives to the Indians a chance to become real citizens in the American community.

I think that this explains the general principles and operations of this Bill and it will be now the duty of the Chairman to announce the next proceedings.

MR. WOEHLKE: (*Mr. Red Tomahawk still interpreting*) A little while ago a lady arose in the back of the room and asked a question. Nobody understood her question. I know from just looking at you that a lot of you are just boiling over with questions. We want to answer those questions, every one of them. I, therefore, suggest that everyone who is full of questions write them out and present them at this table as soon as possible so that we all may go over them at the earliest possible moment, then proceed to answer them. And, we would like it distinctly understood that this privilege of asking questions is not confined to the official delegates—any member of the audience may ask any question and present it here at this table.

At a certain time in the future, during an early session, we shall take up those questions and answer them one by one, if they can be answered. Now, the next session of this Congress will begin tomorrow morning at 9:30. Before the session opens some motion pictures will be taken and I think it would be a good idea if you would all be here a little early.

WILLIAM BENDS (Crow Agency, Montana): I want to say a few words to the members of the council and other tribes from various States. We are now confronted with a problem affecting us which needs very careful consideration. I want to state a simple fact—that it is a known fact that once a coyote gets into a trap, very often he gets away.

MR. WOEHLKE: Before we adjourn, the Commissioner will say a few more words.

MR. COLLIER: What I wish to say will be, perhaps, a repetition of some things Mr. Shepard already has said. There are in the United States more than 200 communities or tribes of Indians. The laws concerning Indians apply to all of them. Some of these tribes are at one extreme. There are, for example, there won't be any of the grown people who talk English, and where all of the members of the tribe are pure blood. Others will be at the other extreme, where the old native language has been forgotten, everybody talks English, and where the blood is mixed, one-fourth, one-half, and one-eighth Indian blood. You would all, I think, agree that if there be an Indian tribe which wants to run its own Indian court, to select its own judges, and to control its police; if there is a tribe that wants to do that, the tribe ought to be permitted to do it.

Applause.

Maybe my tribe, your tribe, would not want to, but we would not want to forbid the other fellow from doing it if he wanted to. Again, suppose there is some tribe, maybe not here at all, whose young men believe they could qualify and hold a good many of the jobs of the Indian Service; young men who believe that they could be good foresters and good farmers and good clerks; and suppose those young men and young women are really just as well trained and just as competent as the whites that have got the jobs now. Then you surely would not want to forbid that tribe way off yonder from putting its young men and young women into the jobs.

Now, there might be here not a single tribe that wasn't completely satisfied with all of the Indian Bureau employees on the Reservation. Maybe that is the condition. But if there is a tribe in North Carolina or Oklahoma or California, that would like to take a vote on whether it wants to keep its Superintendent, you would not object to them having that privilege, would you? And just the same way, to turn the tables. If you have got any of these desires: young people that you want to put into the jobs; if you want to have a voice in choosing employees; a voice about how your money is going to be spent, you don't want some Indian in California to say you can't have it.

This arrangement that Mr. Shepard has been outlining is simply an arrangement to allow each tribe, if it wants to, to take on power—if it wants to, and to allow that tribe to take on authority without in any way risking its security as a ward of the government, and the same arrangement would enable the tribe which took over the authority also the money necessary to pay the people to do the work, and if the tribe made the experiment and then was sorry—felt that it had gone too far, the tribe would say so and turn back the authority and the jobs and the money to the Federal Government, to the Indian Bureau. Or, if the tribe made a mess of its undertaking, then Congress would have the power to take it back and put it in the hands of the Indian Bureau to straighten out, but nothing the tribe could do could bring the guardianship of the Federal Government to an end. That is made permanent by the Act.

I should mention certain safeguards. If a tribe, the majority in a tribe, became oppressive toward a minority, violated the constitutional rights of a minority, under this Bill the case would be appealed to the court of Indian Affairs. It would be the duty of the Secretary of the Interior to carry the appeal, or any Indian could carry the appeal. Minority rights are safeguarded by the Bill, especially by the creation of this Federal Court of Indian Affairs.

It is further provided that if there be an Indian who does not want to remain a part of the tribe, of his Reservation, of his community, but wants to go out into the world and break off his connection he may, if he desires, surrender his rights in exchange for compensation. He does not have to but he may. The tribe or the community would be forbidden to alienate land or to waste the capital assets, soil, forests and such. The Bill expressly prohibits the disposal of capital in a wasteful way.

Tribal funds, subject to all treaty protections, would no longer be handled by the Indian Bureau, but by the chartered community when the community got ready to handle them. You may not know this fact, but I will tell you, that even next year, beginning next July, the Indian Bureau is going to use up more than two million dollars of the Indian tribal funds for salaries and upkeep of the Indian Bureau. We are doing that in spite of our loud and continued protesting against being compelled to do it, because the Director of Budget, who controls our budget, makes it necessary that we shall go on using tribal money for Indian Bureau support. This self-government, title one, would put an end to that at once. Wherever a community accepts a charter it would be able to take over the control of the trust funds, and I do not imagine that the Indians would want those monies spent on Indian Bureau salaries.

Now, a remark about the coyote in the trap. If the Indian is a coyote he is in the trap now. It has caught his front leg. The only way he can get out is by biting off his own leg like the coyote does sometimes.

Big applause.

Biting off his own leg by declaring himself competent and starting to pay taxes.

Applause.

This whole scheme is one of opening that trap. Saving what is left of his leg. I understand the lady in the rear asked whether we wanted them to secede from our Government. That is what caused the Civil War. Do we want the Indians to secede from the Government? The answer is that same answer as about the coyote. A number of Indians have seceded in that they are worn out by the system under which they have been compelled to live. They have gone and got patents in fee and lost their land. That is the way they have seceded. Thousands of them in years gone by. The point that is being laid before you is intended to bring it about so that the Indians will not want to secede from the Government and won't need to.

WILL BENDS, Crow Agency, Montana: The Commissioner himself explained to the Council that when a Bill went to Congress and it is on the floor, it is open to amendment. In that event there is nothing to guarantee to the Indian whereby he could be sure that members of the House and Senate would not change that Bill so that when it came out, it would be the same and contain the same things as when it was sent to Congress?

MR. COLLIER: That is true. That is a very good question to bring up and it must be answered. I may say this. You have in Congress a very good House Indian Committee and Senate Committee. All Indians who have kept following the course of Legislation in the last three or four years have learned to place confidence in their Congressmen. Howard and his Committee; Senator Frazier and Wheeler and their committees. In Indian Legislation, where the Indian Committee stands solid, practically never does Congress over-ride them. It follows its committees. Particularly when the Interior Department and the Committees are in agreement, Congress would not change the Bill. He could, but it would not, and I could tell you because I did not want to seem to be persuading you too much.

MR. COLLIER: (*Robert High Eagle interpreting*) This bill, along with the memorandum accompanying it—that mimeographed memorandum, we have here—went to the President some little time ago. The President has examined the bill and favors it. That announcement was made to the House Committee on Indian Affairs by authority about five days ago. The President knows that we are taking this question back to the Indians. If the bill should become twisted into a wrong shape by Congress, if the bill should be made into something else which does not do what we are telling you but does something different, then I think you may be confident that the President will veto the bill. I have not wanted to talk about the President's part in this because that is almost overwhelming in its influence. But he is going to stand back of this thing.

CHAIRMAN: I believe we will now adjourn until 9:30 tomorrow morning.

Adjourned.

Meeting called at Alex Johnson hotel at 8:00 tonight of all superintendents and field employees.

Saturday, March 3, 1934

Morning Session

Mr. Woehlke opened the Congress at 9:50 A.M., March 3, 1934.

MR. WOEHLKE: (*Mr. LaPointe interpreting*) On account of the motion pictures we are a little behind time, so we will have to speed up to regain lost ground. I would like first to read to you a letter we have just received from the Honorable Edgar Howard, Chairman of the House Committee on Indian Affairs, with whom many of you are acquainted. Congressman Howard writes:

> Honorable John Collier,
> Commissioner of Indian Affairs,
> Rapid City, South Dakota.
>
> Great is my regret because of my inability to go with you to the Regional Conference which you have called in the several states where our Indian people largely reside. I wish I might be with you because I feel that I could help you in winning the favor of our Indian people to the new administration's Indian bill. It is a long step in advance of any legislation heretofore offered in behalf of the Indians. If I could talk with the Indians I might admit that there were some features of the bill difficult to understand. But I know I could prove to them that the bill, as a whole, will be for the welfare of the Indians in greater measure than any piece of legislation ever before presented to Congress.
>
> No doubt you will meet in the several localities many Indians who have visited me here in Washington and I will thank you to carry me in good memory to each one of them.
>
> Sincerely,
>
> Edgar Howard.

MR. WOEHLKE: I have been asked to announce that there will be a meeting of all the Cheyenne River delegates at 12:30 in Building No. 2. All delegates are requested to be present, by Luke Gilbert, Chairman of the Council.

Before we open up the preceding sections of the Bill for discussion, I am going to ask two members of the Commissioner's staff briefly to explain the two titles, two sections, two divisions of the Bill—the Court of Indian Affairs section, and the section referring to education. Both explanations will be brief and at the conclusion of these explanations we will take up the discussion of the first three titles.

ROSEBUD INTERPRETER: Mr. Chairman, I wasn't paying much attention to the first part of that. I am very sorry, but I was busy.

MR. WOEHLKE: The interpreter is fined $20.

INTERPRETER: I will have my friends raise the money. (*Asks Mr. Woehlke*:) "Law and Order section?"

MR. WOEHLKE: Court of Indian Affairs. Before I call on the next speaker I want to ask whether Mr. Joseph W. Brown is in the audience. I have a letter here for him. He may call for it.

Now, I want to ask Mr. Cohen, Assistant to the Solicitor of the Interior Department, to explain briefly the meaning of the Court of Indian Affairs section. Mr. Cohen.

Applause.

MR. COHEN: Friends, I realize that the language in the title No. 4 of the bill which you have seen is very difficult and complicated language, but I think that the processes of the Indian Court are very simple and as soon as you understand them you will feel that they are very simple. In the first place, we believe that the Indians are entitled to have a court which is convenient to them, which can settle the many disputes which arise between Indians and whites, particularly in the matters of trespass—whites trespassing on Indian lands, white bootleggers on Indian lands. At present if such a dispute arises between an Indian and a white, it is usually necessary to go to the Federal District Court which is sometimes 100 or 200 miles from the reservation. If you go to the Federal District Court you have to find a lawyer. When you come to the Federal District Court you find that the judges there are not particularly interested in the Indian. You find that the whole procedure of the Federal District Court is very complicated and difficult to understand.

What this bill would do would be to create a special court. This court would consist at first of seven judges. Each judge would have a particular region. One judge might run through two or three of the Sioux Reservations in South Dakota. Another might have two or three of the Reservations in Montana and so on. A judge would stay at one reservation for two or three weeks and all the disputes that had arisen in the last month or two would come up before that judge. The procedure before this judge might be very simple.

Furthermore this bill provides that ten special attorneys shall be assigned free to the Indian tribes and to the Indians to help the Indians before this court. This court would be of help not only to the Indian communities, which ask for a charter under this act and receive charters, but also to the tribes which do not want charters. We hope that all the Indians will be given a voice in the selection of the judges. The judges will be appointed by the President of the United States with the approval of the Senate. In these ways that I have mentioned, the Court will help all Indians, but there are some ways in which the Court will be peculiarly useful to a community that wants a charter.

Where a community receives a charter this charter is a pledge of certain rights which the community may enjoy. The Secretary of the Interior makes this pledge, but we do not think that the Secretary of the Interior should be permitted in future years to interpret this pledge. If a new Secretary of the Interior comes we do not want to be able to say that this pledge meant something very different from what the Indians understood. Therefore, we want every Indian to have the right to go into this Indian Court and insist on the rights which have been guaranteed him and his people by the Charter of the Government.

In this Charter of self-government the Secretary will give up many arbitrary rights which he now has. In this charter the Indians will be given the right to say what will happen to their tribal funds. This Charter will be a guarantee that the Secretary may not put Indian lands under State taxation as he may today by giving fee patents. These rights which are given to the Indian community in its charter must be sacred. The Indians must have the rights to go into court and sue the Secretary of the Interior if he disobeys the provisions which have been laid down in the Charter.

You know that outside of the Indian reservations, if the Secretary of the Interior or some other Government official commits an act which is unconstitutional, a private white citizen can sue that employee of the Government. A private white citizen can go into a court of the United States and sue a Federal official and say that something the Federal official has done violates his constitutional rights. There have been hundreds and thousands of cases in which the Federal Courts have held that something that an official did was wrong and that the person wronged should receive compensation for his injury.

We want to give the Indian the same right that the white man has to insist on his rights in Court. That is why we want to establish this Court of Indian Affairs. The Charter that you receive from the Secretary of the Interior is a contract. If the Secretary does not keep his promises in that contract you can sue him. So too, if the community does not keep its promise, if it injures minorities within the community; if it oppresses individuals, then the Secretary may bring a suit in this court and compel the community to live up to its contract in the Charter.

There is one more thing I must explain. That is, the relation between this Federal Court and the local Court of an Indian Community. The Indian community may be given the right to have its own local court as a community outside Indian reservations has its own local court. This court, this local court, would take the place of the present Indian judges appointed by the superintendent. This local court would be elected by the Indians of the community itself. It would administer the ordinances that the community had prepared and passed. Its punishments would be limited by the charter and, in any case, the punishment which could be inflicted, either on Indian or white, could not exceed $500 fine and six months' imprisonment. If the Indian community so desired, the limits of the punishments might be made less in the charter.

More important crimes and cases could not come before this local court but would have to come before the special federal court that has been spoken of. Also in cases before the local court, particularly if non-Indians were involved, either party could appeal from the local Indian court to the special court.

I hope I have made it clear why we need a special federal court in addition to the local Indian court. It is because there are many cases which are too important for a local court to want or to have the right to handle. It is because you want a court of the highest authority before which each community and each individual can bring any grievances that may arise in the administration of the new policies of the administration. I ask you to remember when you discuss any provisions of this bill that wherever there is a provision which seems as if it might work an injustice on an Indian, that Indian will have the right to come before this court and insist, first, on his constitutional rights as a citizen of the United States, and, second, on his special rights as are given him by the charter of his community.

MR. WOEHLKE: I want to ask you in the first place not to get scared if another bulb should fall down. We are not. I would like to illustrate the statement of Mr. Cohen by an actual example.

On the Fort Peck Reservation a few weeks ago, a young man by the name of Brown, the son-in-law of Roger Running Bear, was arrested on a charge of stealing a mare. The mare was eighteen years old and worth about $50, but the court fixed a bond of $1500. The superintendent and I looked over the evidence and we thought that it was not strong enough to convict him. The superintendent and I worked for days and days with the County Attorney, with the white man who preferred the charge and with the sheriff to get that young man out of jail. We finally had to hire an attorney for him and we got his bail reduced and got him out. Now, if there had been a court of Indian affairs, the whole thing would have been settled without any trouble, without any of this waste of time, without having the boy in jail for a month. It would have been settled in three or four days. Roger Running Bear's son-in-law would have been out again. That is what the court of Indian Affairs would have done for him.

Now I want to read you a telegram:

> Poplar, Mont.
>
> Chairman of Indian Conference:
>
> As an elected representative from the joint meeting of three districts on the Fort Peck Reservation I wish to announce that we do not agree with the new proposed Indian program which is being studied at the conference now. Reasons will be presented later in our general council.
>
> Roger Running Bear.

Now, my friends, I want to have you listen to one of the great educators of the country; to a man who is internationally known; a man of your own race. I would like to present to you Dr. Henry Roe Cloud who will speak to you on the educational features of the bill. Dr. Roe Cloud.

Applause.

DR. ROE CLOUD: The chairman has asked to speak to you on the educational features of the bill which I hold in my hand. Now, for these chartered communities that you have been hearing about, which will be located all over the Indian country, leaders for those chartered communities will be necessary. The Commissioner had anticipated—he has foreseen the need of that, and has provided for it in this bill. He is going to give leaders to every tribe. I have talked with various groups last night, and to Indians on the train, and they said, "I like this whole thing very much indeed, but there is one thing that is going to make it fall down and that is, the kind of leaders they are going to set up for this thing." One of them said last night, "We Indians are," and I agree with him, "We Indians are awfully jealous of one another and we don't follow this fellow and that fellow."

Applause.

Now, I think the reason we are jealous of one another is because in the past there have been so few leadership opportunities. Now, the way to do away with jealousy is to put so many leaders, Indian leaders, into the Indian communities themselves, that it will wear away that jealousy. Now, one reason why we have been jealous is because we don't want to follow the man who tells us what he can do, but we don't want to follow that man who has already done things. Now the Commissioner proposes to bring to us those men and women who have done things: who have accomplished certain things and who have a right to come and lead us. He proposes to give us leaders in education. Leaders in taking care of the health of our people; leaders in those things who know how to teach us to live together in groups. They call it social service in the white man's language. Leaders in law and order and not just anybody on the reservation to do this work, but those that have been taught in elementary principles of law and order. Leaders in those who know how to take care of the woods. They call it Forestry. Leaders in grazing; in cattle grazing so that the grass is not eaten off too much.

Those who sit at the desk and keep books and write on paper, they call it office work, bookkeeping, keeping of statistical records, etc. I might say that Haskell Institute has lots of those that we can give to you when you are ready. Leaders in public works, road building, and one thing and another, improvements of roads on the reservations, etc.

Now how is he going to do this? Wherever he finds one of our existing schools that will be suitable in any locality for the training of our Indian people, he will open them up and use them, and he will use also the white colleges, the law schools, medicine schools, and engineer schools, where these Indians will be sent to get the white man's technical knowledge, and he is asking Congress for fifty thousand dollars on a reimbursable plan, one half of which will bear no interest when it is paid. One half of it the student does not pay interest on and the other half is a free gift to him.

Applause.

Now in addition to this fifty thousand dollars, the Commissioner himself will have fifteen thousand which he can use to pick out other Indian youths who show special adaptation to leadership. He will select those and give them scholarships to colleges. I might say that the fifty thousand dollars will be fifty thousand a year. Now if your son got one of these monies from the Government, from the Commissioner, he can pay it back only when he is employed. When he is not employed the Government does not ask him to keep on paying. Now we spoke only of men benefiting by this arrangement. We want to emphasize that the girls will get this too. The Government does not "hog-tie" such an individual to go so far as to say in this Bill that no formal contracts will be required.

Now, there is an interesting thing in connection with this, and that is, that the Indian Tribes over all the United States have something big to give to their white brothers over all America, and the thing that he is to give is the thing that he has thought in his mind thousands of years back and passed from generation to generation, and what he has lived thousands of years back, his art, his traditions, etc., and by which the Indian himself is inspired to live. Now the Commissioner comes in this Bill and says to you, look into your minds and look into your heart. You have got great valuable things that you need to give to the world, and the world needs them. And he proposes to put teachers into the Tribes and into the schools who have sympathy with what the Indians have to give, not the white persons that come around to stamp it out and destroy, but those that are in the Indians' mind. Back of all this in his mind, is to build in us, who are Indians, the idea of our own self-respect and build up the pride of our people; that we feel that we have got a great history and great thoughts and great ideas and inspirations in our hearts, so that we can walk away with our heads up instead of looking down all the time.

Applause.

Now here is an interesting thing to think about. These leaders will bring to us the white man's way of thinking and doing things in white communities, and then the Indian race will give to the white race their own culture and that will do away to a great extent with this thing called segregation. A white man and an Indian walking down the road, nothing passing between them, the mind of the Indian is segregated. Now, just because all the Indians live in one place together, that is not necessarily segregation. Segregation is a matter of the eyes of the mind looking out all over the world, or closing them, only seeing his own people.

Now I am through. I am just going to say this and sit down. Always interesting to me is how the Navaho, although living all by himself, has made a great success of things that we who belong to other tribes have failed in. He lives all by himself but he has great thoughts and he lives by great inspiration, and I heard one of them say, when I was down there a year or so ago that he even believed that the first man that was created was Navaho.

Applause and laughter.

MR. WOEHLKE: Before proceeding I would like to read two announcements. The Rev. L. J. Sheldon, Minister of the Methodist Episcopal Church of Rapid City, extends to the people attending the Indian Conference in Rapid City an invitation to attend the Church services and worship with us Sunday. Morning worship at eleven o'clock and evening worship at seven-thirty. There will be Catholic services in the auditorium at nine o'clock a.m. tomorrow—at nine in the morning, and an invitation is extended to all Catholics in this conference to attend these services.

MR. WOEHLKE: (*Rosebud interpreter*) We have now finished with the presentation of three of the important divisions of the proposed legislation; namely, self-government, education, and the court of Indian affairs.

There is still the land division to be discussed, but before we proceed with the consideration of the land problem and the new land policy, we would like to answer the questions that have been asked regarding the three preceding titles. Commissioner Collier will take up a number of the questions that have been asked and proceed to comment on them and answer them.

MR. LAPOINTE, Chairman of the Rosebud Council: Mr. Chairman, before Mr. Collier begins his talk, may I have the privilege of reading the questions written by the Rosebud delegation? We would like to read our questions from the floor to give an opportunity to the audience to know what kind of questions we are presenting. Then we will turn them over to Mr. Collier.

MR. WOEHLKE: Do they refer to the three preceding sections or deal with the land division?

MR. LAPOINTE: They do not deal with the land. If any of them do, they can be thrown out.

MR. WOEHLKE: You may proceed, but make it brief.

MR. LAPOINTE: Question No. 1, from Rosebud delegation with respect to the ten-million-dollar credit loan—will that be a loan to the tribe or to the individuals? Will the loans be reimbursable and, if so, when and how are they to be reimbursed?

MR. WOEHLKE: I will repeat these questions so that the other delegations may have their interpreters translate them. Question No. 1, with respect to the ten-million-dollar credit loan, will that be a loan to the tribe or to the individuals—or will the loan be reimbursable and, if so, when and how is it to be repaid? The same questions arise with respect to the two-million-dollar item. Will you translate these questions?

Various interpreters translate.

MR. COLLIER: May I first ask if you all have copies of the bill now. All who have copies of the bill hold up their hands. Several copies of the bill were distributed. I will answer the first question—about the new credit system. The ten-million-dollar fund, we will call it, would be loaned to Indian communities, and through the communities to the individuals of the community. An individual might get the loan, a partnership might get it, a stock association or cattle association might get it.

The money advanced by the Government would become a revolving fund. In other words, it would never go back to the Government. But the man who borrowed from the fund would pay the money back to the fund so that it could be loaned again to another man. The loan would not bear interest. Those who borrowed would not be required to pay interest. The length of time for payment could be made as much as thirty years if the conditions justified it.

Now, what about the purposes for which loans can be made—for any purpose to build up the economic life of the individual or the community? For example, the buying of seed, the buying of implements, the buying of stock, the buying of materials to build a house. The money could be loaned to provide the capital for starting an Indian co-operative store, or an Indian co-operative creamery, an Indian sawmill, or anything like that. And, broadly, the loan could be for any business purpose that would build up the prosperity, the economic life, of the individual or the community.

I will now present a question that was asked me last night. Somebody said, what about the reimbursable loans that are now being made in the shape of seed or implements, and then the Indian pays the Government back? That system, the old reimbursable system, will not be changed, will go on. This is something else in addition. The new credit, the ten-million-dollar fund, would be supplied by preference to those Indians who organized into communities, and it would be supplied by preference to those Indians who got their lands into a condition for good business-like use. This new loan system, this ten-million-dollar fund would be provided as part of the plan for getting Indian lands into a secure condition for effective use. Unless we can get this reorganization of land system, there will be no chance of obtaining this new fund. And, when obtained, the fund will be used as a means of helping the Indians build up their life on the land.

This credit section is not found in the printed bill. It has been put in through an amendment in the House, and it will be put in the records of this meeting which will be mimeographed and sent to all of you at the earliest date. Now, the other question was about the two million dollars a year authorized by the Bill for the purchase of land. That two-million-dollar fund, we will call it two-million-dollars a year, is a gratuity and not a loan, and therefore will not have to be paid back at all. That is a thing which we are going to have to fight for in Congress, I think, to make it a gratuity and not a loan, and our justification is that the land was lost under the allotment system which the Government imposed on the Indians. In other words, the Indian lost his land under Government compulsion. The Government made him lose it. Therefore, the Government ought to buy it back.

Applause.

I may say that what I have just said appears to be agreeable to Congress as far as we have gone. There is no evidence that they will dispute this point of view.

INTERPRETER: The Rosebud delegation want to know about question No. 2, with respect to Section 13 b. What is the meaning of the word reservation? Does it include counties which were within the reservation in 1889 but which are no longer in the reservation? Why I ask that question is this, there are two words in that Bill that describe—the words Indian and reservation. Will only Indians that are within an organized county be known as Indians? We have three counties on our reservation that are organized and one unorganized. Will they be entitled to come into the community or not?

INDIAN: Mr. Chairman. We would like to make a motion at this time.

MR. CHAIRMAN: Not at this time. Let the Commissioner finish his explanation.

INDIAN: We would like to have all these questions that are submitted and let the Commissioner give an answer afterward. This will be very much appreciated.

MR. CHAIRMAN: Do I hear a second to that motion?

Motion seconded.

MR. CHAIRMAN: Any remarks to that motion? It has been moved and seconded that all questions be submitted in private to the Commissioner and be answered by him after they have been submitted in writing. Are you ready for the question? All those in favor of the motion lift their right hand.

Majority lift right hands.

MR. CHAIRMAN: All those against the motion lift their right hand.

Three or four lift right hand.

MR. CHAIRMAN: The ayes have it. The motion is carried.

GENTLEMAN FROM WINNEBAGO: I move that the last question be carried out by the Commissioner, or whoever else will explain it, and that thereafter they proceed with these questions by the various delegations. We have been killing too much time as I see it.

MR. WOEHLKE: May I explain for a moment that it is the purpose to suggest meetings with the different delegations this evening for the purpose of conferring with them; having them propound their questions right then, and have them answered on the spot. Would not that cover your idea?

GENTLEMAN FROM WINNEBAGO: That would. Yes.

MR. COLLIER: May I suggest this: Some of the questions here are in the mind of everybody. They might just as well be answered to all of you. Some of the questions are in the minds of only one particular delegation. They ought to be answered to that delegation, but some of the questions are fundamental and are of interest of all of you.

MR. WOEHLKE: I think it would be the best way, to take the written questions that are of general interest to all of you and have them answered in this general session and to take the distinctly local questions and have them answered tonight in separate delegation meetings. I believe, with this understanding, we will allow the Commissioner to proceed. I shall, however, follow the suggestion and answer this last question.

MR. COLLIER: On page 21 of the Bill the term, Reservation, is defined. The act says, "that the term 'Reservation,' wherever used in this Act, shall be construed to comprise all the territory within the outer boundaries of any Indian reservation, whether or not such property is subject to restrictions on alienation and whether or not such land is under Indian ownership." I may say that this is nothing but a repetition of the existing law as to what constitutes an Indian Reservation.

And now, the particular matter that I think is troubling the Rosebud delegation will be answered by Mr. Stewart.

INDIAN: Pine Ridge also.

MR. STEWART: The answer is, yes. For this reason. There are two classes of cessions affecting Indian lands. One class is that class where the Indians ceded their title outright. Their title was extinguished and they are paid for that land. The second class is where the Indians had their land opened to settlement under the public land laws, and the United States acts as trustee, and until the Indian lands were disposed of the Indian title remained unextinguished. We are confronted here with that second class. On page 26 of the Bill, on top, Section 3, you will find your answer. We are going to convert back into the Reservation all that surplus, undisposed of open land.

MR. DAVIDSON from Pine Pidge: Mr. Chairman.

Chairman recognizes Mr. Davidson.

MR. DAVIDSON: I am not a delegate, but I would like to have the gentleman explain the second part of that 26.

MR. WOEHLKE: Will you submit your question in writing? It has been ruled by the Congress that all questions be submitted in writing. You are out of order.

MR. DAVIDSON: All right sir, I will present my question in writing this evening.

MR. COLLIER: There is one further point about the two million dollar fund which I did not make clear. The fund for the purchase of land. That fund would be available only where the new land holding system had been put into effect.

Now, there is a question of general interest. It relates to Section 4 E of title I of the Bill. "What happens to tribal self-government if all, or a major part of the Indians, decide to withdraw at one time. How are their interests to be paid for; the interests of those who withdraw?"

The answer I will try to make simple in this way. Forget about this bill for a moment. If an Indian of any tribe is enrolled in that tribe and therefore has a share of the ownership of the tribal land and tribal funds and goes away, he continues to have his share, even though he has gone away and lives, say, in New York. Sometimes he will get a benefit from his share; that is, if there are per capita payments he will get them, even though he is living in New York. But if there is no tribal income from the property, then he loses the use of it by going to New York. There is no money being paid out on it and he is not getting the use of it.

Now, under the new plan, it would be the same, with one difference that I will state. The individual who wanted to break off his relationship with the tribe and move away permanently could bargain with the community and the community could pay him the value of his holdings and then the community would own the land or whatever there was, and he would go away with the cash. He might make a bargain in such a way that he would get cash down, or he might get installment payments to be paid over a term of years. Now, the question was, suppose there are 1,000 members of the community and 900 of them decided to go away at one time. What then? I would say that in such a case, ordinarily, there would not be enough money to buy them all out at once. They would have to wait until there was enough capital accumulated for the deal to be transacted.

It is just like with any other estate. If a family in Rapid City wants to scatter all over the country and it has got a property here it might not be possible to liquidate that property now. They may have to wait. You can't liquidate an estate the minute you want to. Some tribes have tribal funds they could use to buy out absentees. Some have no tribal funds. The only change in this point from existing law is that the individual who wants to go away is allowed to surrender his equities in exchange for compensation. The community is allowed to buy it. Neither of them is compelled. The individual may go off and keep his equities. The tribe may refuse to buy him out and then he will have to keep his equities.

We are right up against the dinner hour, and what I think I shall do now is to answer the question that is partly asked by one of the written questions. I will just answer it briefly, because it will require explanation later on, because I know it is in the minds of most of you.

Here I am going over to the land section—title 3. Is the transfer of the individual allottee's title to the community, that is, relinquishments to the community, mandatory or permissible? In other words, it is proposed simply that the allottee may relinquish his title in exchange for an equal interest or compensation?—he may do that, and he may accept it; or, is it intended that he must do it and the community must accept it? Have I asked the question in such a way that it is the question in your minds?

VARIOUS ANSWERS: Yes sir.

MR. COLLIER: Now, I will answer first just in the language of the Bill as it stands. The language now is as follows: "The Secretary of the Interior is authorized to make the transfer." That would mean, as it stands, that if a case arose where the Secretary wanted to make the transfer and the Indian did not want it, the Secretary would have the power to make it, even without the consent of the Indian. That is the effect of that language now. We have given a great deal of thought before we came here, and since we came here, to the question of where that language ought to stand or ought to be changed.

Mr. Woehlke has anticipated what I was about to say and I will just pass it on to you. Would it be interesting to have a show of hands to see whether you would like a change?

Applause.

Of course, Mr. Siegel points out that before we invite you to a show of hands we ought to make certain things clear to you. You understand that any transfer of title as planned, on this page 31, would have to be an exchange of title for compensation of a variety of kinds. In all cases adequate compensation. In other words, there should be no taking of title. There would only be a purchase of it.

SIOUX INTERPRETER: That is one of the hardest phrases to interpret that I have run across yet.

MR. COLLIER: Let us imagine the Secretary of the Interior is going to start in and transfer your title to the community. Your piece of land. If he does that he must, in the first place, give you in exchange a proportionate interest in tribal or community lands of similar quality. In other words, of equal value. In addition, you would have the right to keep the land you are living on. You would have first preference in the assignment of land; to keep the land you have got and live on it and use it. If you chose not to continue occupying that piece of land by exercising your preferential rights, and take another piece of land, then you would be entitled to be paid for the improvements on your land, as well as getting the new land.

Similarly the interests of your heirs would be protected. As a matter of fact, the protection would be so complete and the advantages would be so great that as a rule you would want to make the trade. You would want to relinquish and get in exchange the things that I have described, and because of that fact, because we were confident that the allottee himself would be the one chiefly anxious to effect the exchange, we did not worry about the result, because, as you will see, when we start discussing the land title in detail, the allottee always, would not only keep all he had but he would always get something more than what he has got. But that does not answer the question of whether the Secretary of the Interior should be given power to do this, even though the allottee is not persuaded and does not want it and it is on that point that I was going to give you my answer and then the suggestion was that we get a show of hands.

MR. WOEHLKE: Now, I would like to state the proposition that you are asked to have a show of hands on very briefly. Do you, favor giving the Secretary of the Interior the right to force a transfer? That is the question.

MR. FRANK OHLERKING of Fort Belknap: I object to your motion, Mr. Chairman, because we want to understand the conditions a little better first—the result of that transfer, or the conditions under which this transfer is to be made.

MR. COLLIER: I think that is a very wise thought. The thing ought to be viewed in the light of all the facts before you vote on it.

MR. CLEMENT SMITH of Rosebud (Yankton): Owing to the fact that we are defining the law as it is prepared and written and the discussion applies to the authority that the Secretary now has or is going to have, it is an important question to these people, and if we discuss it in that way we are just going to be taking it as a matter of course, and preparing an opinion. The definition in that bill is the question at the present time.

I make a motion to the house that we decide whether or not the Secretary shall have the power to force and coerce any allottee to transfer his property to the community or whether he shall not have that power.

Seconds are heard from various members of the audience.

MR. WOEHLKE: Now, the gentleman from Ft. Belknap has suggested that we postpone a decision on this question until a broader discussion of all the phases of this important point. I am inclined to adhere of his opinion. I believe that the entire question at this time was out of order because we had not yet reached the land subject. Therefore I rule that all motions to this effect at the present time are out of order, and that we shall give more consideration to this question at the afternoon session.

Applause.

Just prior to adjournment—and you know that dinner is waiting—I would like to ask to which delegation Ivan Griff and Mike Keith, if they are members of a delegation, belong. The Superintendent of that delegation is requested to go to the long distance telephone because they are calling from Deadwood. I do not know why.

Laughter.

I suggest also that any of the delegations or delegates who have not yet received copies of the Bill and copies of the explanation, the mimeographed explanation, come to the Chair here and receive them.

We now stand adjourned.

Afternoon Session

Congress opened at 1:45 p.m. on March 3, 1934, by the Chairman, Mr. Woehlke.

MR. WOEHLKE: I recognize the gentleman from Fort Totten, Charles White.

MR. WHITE: I make a motion to do away with all Sioux interpreters. Practically all of the Sioux speak English. Furthermore, it confuses our minds between times.

MR. WOEHLKE: Some are unable to follow the proceedings completely without the aid of an interpreter and I believe, in fairness to all the delegates, we should continue with our interpretation.

Mr. LaPointe, Rosebud interpreter, translates and requests all Indians desiring to continue with the interpreter to raise their right hands.

MR. LAPOINTE: These are the non-English-speaking Indians, so that Fort Totten can see them.

MR. WOEHLKE: There was not second to the motion. The motion was lost.

MR. WOEHLKE: (*Mr. LaPointe, Rosebud, interpreting*) I would like to explain the last ruling of the Chair because that ruling was not interpreted and a number of the delegates went out without understanding what the ruling was. At the time we closed, there was under discussion the land subject. The order of business at that time called for a concluding discussion on the three other main divisions of the bill. Therefore, the Chair ruled that the Commissioner was out of order.

However, it seems that it has been the consensus of opinion that we should get to the discussion of the land problem at the earliest possible moment. Therefore, I am now requesting the Commissioner to state the general principles, the purpose and the objectives of the proposed land policy, and I shall ask him before he does that, to answer one or two of the questions on self-government.

MR. COLLIER: (*Rosebud interpreter*) Some questions that can be answered quickly—if the Bill becomes a law what will be the voting power of the Indian who has been made a citizen? Will the Indians lose their franchise and vote? No, of course not.

A similar question. If the Bill passes can Indians run for office in a county or state when they are members of an Indian community. Yes, just as they can do now, except that they will have more training in the holding of public offices through their community organizations. Two or three delegations have said this.

Please explain the word "subsidy" as used in Title 2. Subsidy just means the same as grant—gift of money.

And then the question which is important. As to the control by Indian Tribes under this Bill over their Tribal funds? The Bill provides that when an Indian group organizes and takes a Charter, then its tribal monies cannot be spent except by the consent of the community—of the Tribe. Let me make this clear. This is not something which may be granted or withheld by the chartered members. It is fundamental and goes to all the chartered communities. Any chartered community will have the veto power over expenditures of the tribal funds belonging to that community. In addition, the community may be chartered to handle its funds completely so that it would not just have the veto power but the initiative as well. Now, I am glad this question has been brought up because I desire particularly to make it clear to these Sioux delegations.

There has been opposition against the Bill and against the vetoing idea on account of this viewpoint giving the Indians the veto over expenditure of money, and that opposition, I am advised, has come from groups who are afraid that the Tribe would not permit certain use of the money, which are good uses. As you all know, you Sioux and the Shoshone, in certain of the Mission schools—schools that are run by the churches—the tuition of the children is paid from funds which are called Treaty funds. Now this Bill would leave it for the Tribe to decide whether the Secretary of the Interior should continue to make payments of this kind. That is the case in so far as the payments are made from Tribal funds.

It is my own view, that a fundamental principle is involved in the matter of Indian tribal funds. I believe that the Tribes should be given a veto power over the expenditure of their own funds even if they might be unwise sometimes and veto something that is good. However, I point out that the contention in this matter that affected the Sioux and Shoshone grows out of a misunderstanding about its funds. The funds in question probably are not tribal funds at all. In the case of the Sioux they are called Treaty appropriations and are made annually by Congress. Actually, they are annual appropriations by Congress made gratuitously because Congress wants to make them because the Treaty in question expired many years ago.

It is therefore practically certain that these particular funds from which the tuition is paid in the Church schools are not tribal funds at all and therefore they would not come under the control of the chartered communities. But, if they are tribal trust funds and if it was so decreed ultimately by some court, then they would come under the control of the tribe and if, in fact, they are money belonging to the Sioux Tribe—if they are, which I don't think they are—then I would say the Sioux Tribe should decide how its own money is to be spent. Now, coming to the land question, in Title 3.

I shall, myself, try to outline the facts and purposes as we understand them, and then I shall ask others to take the matter up and carry on the detailed examination of Title 3. What I shall say will be a statement of what we think ought to be accomplished, and if it is not accomplished by the present draft of the Bill then the Bill ought to be changed so that it will accomplish that result and therefore, I am not going to complicate my talk by reference to section, etc. I believe that if you found yourselves in agreement with the purposes and the methods as I shall state them, then either you will find the Bill all right or you would see how to change the Bill that might make it all right.

Now, first, this loss of land by the Indians must be sharply stopped. It must be brought to an end—the loss of land. That means that the trust period on all land now held in trust must be made permanent. The power of the Secretary of the Interior to bring the trust period to an end must be taken away from him, and hereafter the trust period must be made permanent unless and until terminated by the act of Congress.

Second, in order to make the restrictions effective the exemption of Indian restricted land from taxation must be continued and made permanent until otherwise directed by Congress. You understand, of course, that the power of Congress is necessarily there always and we can not go beyond that. Now, that is No. 1, and very simple and easy to understand.

Now, No. 2. I told you yesterday that there were more than 100,000 Indians who had lost all of their land under the allotment system. Those Indians, if they desire to have land and to use land, should be supplied with the land which they need, and that land should be restricted and exempted from taxation. We do not assume that all of the landless Indians will want to have land and use it. We only say that those who do want it must be given it. There is another class of landless Indians, who have been born since allotment; all of the tribal lands have been allotted before they were born, and so they came too late.

Those Indians, also, if they want land and are prepared to use it should be supplied with land. I do not mean that these landless Indians and children born since allotment should be supplied with land by taking land that other Indians have and giving it to them. I mean that new additional land can be obtained by purchase or gift and supplied to these landless Indians.

Now, right here, before taking the next step, I am going to make two explanations. First, about this matter of exempting the new lands from taxation. How are we going to meet the objection of states and counties against taking land which is now on the tax roll and putting it over into Indian ownership where it will not bring in taxes? The answer is—by having the federal government undertake in this act to pay the cost of maintaining the public services on this newly acquired land. It will maintain the schools and the roads and so on.

The other matter is one on which I am not addressing you alone, but the general public, as we are. The question people may raise is this: Why is it the duty of the United States to supply land to these landless Indians? Why is it? The answer is—that these Indians lost their land as a result of a system of land holding forced upon them or their ancestors by the United States, a system of land holding which, admittedly, was a blunder. It is, therefore, the moral duty of the United States to retrieve the effects and repair that blunder as far as it can. And, that means to supply land and the capital or using the land. People may say why supply the capital as well as the land. The answer is—that when all of the new land is added on and given to the Indians, they will still be getting back only a very small part of what they lost under the allotment system. As for capital, we talk about a ten-million-dollar grant to the Indian communities for a revolving fund for a loan.

The United States, since the year 1900, has misappropriated more than a hundred million dollars of tribal funds, has used these funds in ways which were indefensible, which should have been illegal, and which in Canada would have been illegal and indictable. I am making only the statement that has been made on the floor of the Senate by Senators King, Frazier, and others, and reported in formal reports by its committees and is an incontestable fact. By this misappropriation I mean the diversion of Indian trust funds for the support of the Indian Bureau which ought to have been supported by the general treasury. I mean also the use of Indian trust monies without the consent of the Indians to build through highways for tourists and great irrigation systems for white farmers.

Let the Government give back to the Indians just twenty per cent of this trust money which the Government misappropriated since 1900 and it will be enough capital for the development of the Indian lands. What I am saying is not needed to convince you, but I am saying it to get it into this record so that you may use it to persuade other people—white people.

A final item, while dwelling on this point of what the Government's duty is, is that most of the Indian tribes—I believe every one of you tribes here—have valid legal claims against the Government for violated treaties. For a long lifetime the Government, by that I mean Congress and the Executive, have been using every method possible to prevent your claims from coming to judgment. The Bill we are discussing has no connection with the matter of Indian claims and I am not speaking of it for that reason. It has no connection at all, but I do say, and I want you to get this, that when a valid, legal claim could and should have been adjusted in the year 1890, and the Government by deliberate delays keeps it from being adjusted until 1950, or, let us say, 50 years too late, that is the same thing as depriving the Indians of the use of their moneys for 60 years, and the interest on a dollar in 60 years is a great deal more than the dollar.

This policy of the Government to postpone the settlement adjusting Indian claims has had the effect already of depriving the Indians of more than one hundred million dollars, of interest on trust funds which they would have gotten if the claims had been settled promptly when they should have settled. What I said is the reason why the bad practice ought to be changed, and we are going to try and change it, but it also is a reason—an additional reason—why the Government has a moral obligation to give the Indians the land they need and the capital for developing their land.

Now, I go on to the things which as we see it must be done about land. The other things. I have spoken about the policy of the government to give the Indians the new land where they need it and to give them the capital for stocking the land and developing it, but, yesterday, we saw how the existing, the present system of land holding, had cut down the

Indian land and was going to reduce them until they were all gone. And we saw, as you will see more fully, later, how the allotment arrangement has broken up the lands so that they can't be used to best advantage. We saw how it had checkerboarded the grazing land with white owned lands—

End of interpretation by Emil Afraid-of-Hawk.

MR. COLLIER: (*continues, William Fire Thunder interpreting*)—and had broken up the heirship allotments into a multitude of individual ownership almost impossible to administer.

And we saw how inevitably the thing will go on until all of the land is in the heirship status and all messed up the way the heirship lands are messed up, and that the cost to the Government for administering the system was always increasing while the land melted away. It therefore is clear, that this business of getting, or providing new land to the landless Indians and more land to the Indians that haven't got enough land; this business can not be carried out within the old land holding system. Neither can any plan of giving large grants of capital to the Indians for developing their land be carried out within this old system. It would be a waste of time to go to Congress or to the President in the matter of new land or of capital for land development if all we have got to offer is that thing on that blackboard. On the contrary, as I told you yesterday, if that is all we have got to offer—that land holding system—we may look forward to a day, 5, 7, 10, or 12 years from now when the Government will simply wash its hands of an impossible situation by fee-patenting the whole business.

Therefore, we propose a change in the land holding system as a means of saving the lands and of getting more land and capital for developing lands. Now, what is it that we have got in mind, if I can put it in language not legal at all, but just simple, plain English? We want, first, to enable the Indians holding these scattered allotments to combine their allotments if they desire, into solid blocks of land so that they can be leased or used in a profitable way. Second, we want an arrangement that will permit an heir who has a little interest in ten or twenty allotments to lump his interest into one lump so that he will have a piece of land which he can use or from which he can get a rental worth collecting that won't cost too much money to collect. Then, we want an arrangement in the matter of heirship lands that will put an end to this subdivision of the interests until it gets so small that nobody can use the subdivided parts.

Then, we want an arrangement which will allow an allotted Indian to put his title back into the tribe in exchange for a vested right to use an equivalent amount of the tribal land, or to have the rental from an equivalent amount of tribal land, as he prefers. We want him to be in possession of a guarantee, this Bill calls it a Certificate, which guarantees his property right to that amount of land, and to that particular land if he prefers to stay on it rather than to go on to another piece of land. We want him to be able to transmit this property right of his, represented by this certificate, to his heirs. We want an arrangement concerning the new land—the land newly to be acquired—the land to be bought or obtained in a new way, which will give to every member of the tribe a share of that new land. This applies not only to the landless Indian who comes in, but we conceive of every member of the tribe having a fundamental equity in the total tribal assets, but that will not be an equal share to each member of the community. It will be an unequal share, because, the Indian who transfers his allotment to the community will be entitled to the full value of that added on his equitable share in the new land.

With respect to the descent of property, heirship, making of wills. I first remind you that the Secretary of the Interior has absolute power over an Indian will at present. He can annul the will; he can compel the amendment of the will. In so far as he is guided by law, it is by the accidental laws of the state where the Reservation happens to be located. We propose to take away from the Secretary of Interior that absolute power over Indian wills, and the determination of heirs, by that proposal, is taken out of his hands and placed in the Court of Indian Affairs. We propose that if, in a given case, the State laws governing the descent of property are not satisfactory to the Indians, those laws, as applied to Indians, may be changed until they are satisfactory to the Indian.

MR. COLLIER: (*Rosebud interpreter*) I am not stopping on the details of the Bill. I am trying to give you the complete picture. We will come back to the details.

Now, I left for the last the one point in this whole program which I think will continue to be a matter of debate unless it is changed. That is the feature of the Bill which gives the Secretary of the Interior authority to transfer the individual title to the community, even without the consent of the allottee.

I am not yet going to make my own recommendation. I want to state for your consideration the reason why you might want the Secretary to have this power. If a community is proceeding by an exchange and voluntary arrangement to get its grazing lands blocked for effective use, and still more so if a community is proceeding by exchange and voluntary relinquishment to get its timber lands blocked so that they may be handled in a businesslike and conservative way, that community might find itself in a position of being held up by some one person. A man who might be willing and anxious to relinquish his land in exchange for benefits, might see a chance to demand an extortionate price. Then that community might be glad if it possessed the power, or if somebody possessed the power, to compel that individual to be reasonable and to play square.

Now, I do not present that as a reason why this compulsory feature ought to be kept in the Bill, but rather an explanation why it was put in the Bill as formally introduced. Ordinarily, in any event, the whole operation would be a voluntary one pursued by the allottees because it would be greatly to their advantage, both immediate and in the long run. Here and there, in the absence of a power of compulsion lodged in somebody, you might get a hold-up. If the Indians were tolerant and were unanimous and wanted that element of compulsion kept in the Bill, then I think it might do no harm and some good.

On the other hand, Indians might well be afraid of it because they might fear arbitrary action by the Secretary of the Interior or unwise action. All of us up here on the platform are agreed that it is a relatively unimportant point which, if we don't have it, will not seriously get in the way of the things that you all want. So, you might either vote to wipe it out of the Bill, making the whole thing voluntary, or you might vote that under certain conditions compulsion would be lodged in the Indian community with the consent of the Secretary of the Interior. You might, for example, vote that in a given tribe if four-fifths of the enrolled members wanted compulsion to be possible in that tribe, then the law will permit that tribe to use it.

Now I am going to start my presentation at this point. I am going to read you merely three questions that have been suggested to me by Mr. Woehlke. The kind of questions you might put to yourselves.

1. Do you want Legislation to stop the further loss of your land by stopping allotment and extending the trust period and tax exemptions on your land?
2. Do you want legislation and appropriations for buying land for those hundred thousand Indians who now have no land?
3. Do you want legislation that will enable you to develop your timber and grazing land, and the checkerboard system, and put your land in such condition that you can raise more stock on it or get better rent for it?
4. Do you want legislation that will end the loss of land through heirship and place deceased land back into tribal ownership with proper compensation to the heirs?
5. Do you want all of that subject to the condition that the property rights of Indians who now own land shall not be taken away or diminished, and that means that property rights shall be inheritable and descendible to your children.

Those questions merely sum up this land program. If the Indians of the country answer them with a yes, then it would be the duty of the Indian Office, of the Secretary of the Interior, of the committees of Congress to work over these principles and purposes into legislation that would accomplish these purposes and not other purposes. We would be pledged to do this as a matter of public record—to get this, or get nothing. You will note that from these questions as I have read them to you the element of compulsion has been left out. The entire matter is left as a voluntary thing with the individual Indian and the community which you are a part. (*End of Mr. Collier's speech.*)

MR. CHAIRMAN: With your permission I would like to declare a recess for ten minutes so that we can open the windows and air this place out.

Recess.

Congress convened after ten minutes recess.

MR. WOEHLKE: Chairman: I think we all enjoyed that recess. I almost feel tempted to make it permanent.

Laughter.

Now, the general session for this evening is called off. In place of the general session we will have individual sessions of the various delegations and I would suggest that all the Sioux Delegations meet here at 7:30 in order to discuss their particular problems with the Commissioner and his representatives, ask questions concerning their particular problems, and have them answered right there. For the same purpose I suggest that the Montana tribes—Blackfeet, Fort Belknap, Fort

Peck, Crow, Rocky Boy delegations—meet in the dormitory of House No. 1, at 7:30 this evening for the same purpose of close, intimate discussion of their problems and of their questions concerning this legislation with the representatives of the Commissioner, and that the other tribes, the Winnebago, and the Shoshoni and the Omaha, and all the rest of them including Turtle Mountain, meet here at 7:30 in one of the school rooms which Mr. Staley will show them and they be here promptly at 7:30 so that we may get under way, because they will have many questions to ask and it will take time. But, in that way we can speed up the proceedings and we can give various tribes information and replies concerning their particular problems; so the Sioux delegations will meet here at 7:30 in this auditorium, the Montana Tribes will meet in Dormitory of House No. 1 at 7:30 and the rest of the tribes will meet in one of the school rooms here at 7:30. The schoolroom that I mentioned is on the second floor in the northeast corner.

MR. DAVIDSON: Mr. Chairman, (*is recognized*) I am the gentleman that was out of order this morning. Mr. Chairman, I was requested this morning to put my question in writing and I have done so and it is on your table, and I desire that my question be read publicly and explained publicly before this convention concerning the second section of the land question.

MR. WOEHLKE: We have about 110 here. We have found it right here on top. Your question will be answered right away. The meeting tomorrow afternoon will take place in the Civic Auditorium in Rapid City, beginning at 2 o'clock. We expect a very large attendance there and we feel that we should have at least one meeting when this auditorium is available where we can accommodate all those who want to come in and listen or speak and at this meeting tomorrow afternoon we want to do the listening and we want you to do the talking, so I hope you will all be there.

Now, continuing with the discussion of land questions, the Commissioner wishes to conclude his remarks and to read Mr. Davidson's question and give him his reply.

MR. COLLIER: I will first read Mr. Davidson's question: "Turn to page 26 of the Bill, title 3, beginning of Section 3. Section 3, as you will note, authorizes the Secretary of the Interior to withdraw any surplus or ceded land and bring them back into tribal ownership." The fourth line of the paragraph in question reads, "Such lands shall be reopened to sale, settlement, and entry." That means these surplus or ceded lands, if it is found that they are not needed, shall be sold under existing law and the proceeds deposited to the credit of the tribe. In order to clear up any possible misunderstanding of the paragraph, these words ought to be inserted on line 11, to read: "The Secretary of the Interior shall determine what lands, referred to in the above paragraph, lying outside. . . ."

In other words, any surplus or any of this land that is already let open for entry, that is brought back and then found that the Indians have no need for it, shall be sold under existing law and the money given to the Indians.

Now, my staff points out that I have neglected to make one thing clear. Mineral land and oil lands are not dealt with in this Bill. The allottee who owns an oil well would hold his oil well in severalty, though it could be arranged that, if he wanted to part with it to the tribe, the tribe could buy it.

Then, in my statement concerning the new lands bought for the landless Indians, I stated that, in such a way that apparently, I gave a misunderstanding to some of you when I said that all members of the community would have an equity in all the land, including the new lands. That statement, of course, is corrected. But, obviously, it is the landless Indians who have the preferential right to use the new land. I suppose that will be clear.

Then, to state again the matter of descent of heirship as proposed in this new Bill. Upon the death of an allottee, his heirs would inherit first the right to use or receive the rental value of an equal amount of land. In the second place, the heirs, by a will, could be given the exclusive occupancy of the identical piece of land in question, the title going to the tribe. This will be more fully clear as the details are explained, but I simply wanted to avoid giving any misunderstanding on my own part.

MR. DAVIDSON: I never referred to any ceded land. I referred to the reservation land which we are now occupying and my question has not been read and I believe I am still in order.

MR. COLLIER: Mr. Davidson's question is as follows: "Concerning the second section of Section 3, of title 3, Page 26." That is the second paragraph which I read a while ago. Then he proceeds to quote that paragraph which I read.

I explained that that paragraph related to the ceded lands, did not relate to reservation lands, could not relate to reservation lands, because it says about these lands, "Such lands shall be reopened to sale, settlement, entry, or other lawful form of disposal in accordance with existing law."

I am explaining that Mr. Davidson's construction of this paragraph is an incorrect construction, but I added that, in order to make the undesirable construction impossible, there ought to be added the words referred to in the paragraph above. In other words the surplus and ceded lands. The paragraph as printed is nothing in clearness. Mr. Davidson's point is well taken, although there could be no doubt as to how the courts could construe the language. To make sure, we are suggesting that those words be added.

MR. CHAIRMAN: I would like to ask Mr. Davidson whether the explanation of the Commissioner is satisfactory now?

MR. DAVIDSON: Mr. Chairman, I was asked to put my question in writing to be presented before this meeting, and I have done it and it has not been read yet.

Applause.

MR. COLLIER: We will proceed with the minutes of the meeting. Mr. Davidson yesterday quoted the paragraph which we now read twice then he asks a question which I have answered twice, and I will read the asking of it again—"does this paragraph, which he states off-sets Section 3, construe to mean that the Secretary of the Interior will be empowered to re-open all lands lying outside the boundaries of communities to be determined by the Secretary of the Interior, as provided in the Senate Bill 255 and does the Bill further construe that the Indians will not need such surplus lands outside such community areas should Bill S-2775 become a law?"

Now as I have explained, the language in question does not affect any Tribe in or out of a community or any allotted land in or out of a community. It deals, as it is clear, only with these surplus or ceded lands now in the hands of the land office for disposal. It directs the Secretary of the Interior to take those lands away from the land office and restore to the Tribes such portion of these surplus or ceded lands as the Indians need, and then with respect to those surplus or ceded lands, which they don't need, to re-open them under existing laws, and I said that in order to avoid any misunderstanding, we added new words explaining that the language refers to these surplus or ceded lands and not to any other lands.

MR. CHAIRMAN: I believe it is very clear now and I would like to call on Mr. Marshall, Chief of the Forestry Division, to speak to you about the consolidation of grazing lands and timber lands, what they mean, why, and how these consolidations are to be accomplished. Mr. Marshall.

MR. MARSHALL: I think that I have about the easiest job on the program today, because I have got to say principally what is wrong, and particularly I have to say what is wrong with the way lands are blocked out in individual ownership. I am going to tell you a little bit about why the Indians lose money when their timber lands are all broken up into small hunks of land but I am going to tell you mostly why the Indians lose money when their grazing lands are all broken up into individual allotments.

I believe that there are very few of the tribes here who have got allotted timber lands, but so you will understand everything that is in the Bill. I will try to make this clear, even though it does not apply to your particular Reservation.

There are many Reservations in the country where the allottees have lands right in among the timber. On one of the Washington Reservations, the allottees sold about $2,000 worth of timber, and because this timber was sold and the unit was partly cut over, the lumber company which had formerly offered $20,000 worth had been cut out and they could get a better proposition where no cutting had been done. Now this case is just an example, and perhaps an extreme example.

SOME INTERPRETER: Mr. Marshall, I think they would prefer it on the Plains. This timber proposition does not concern us.

SIOUX INTERPRETER: Yes, but it concerns us, I want to interpret that.

MR. MARSHALL: So now, I will leave the timber and woods and go out on the plains.

Laughter.

I can think of at least six different disadvantages—six different ways in which the Indians of the country lose money where their grazing lands are all broken up into small units. The first and most obvious way is the amount it costs to administer the land. Now, I have just talked to a couple of the Superintendents on the platform, here, and one of them estimates that it takes about 10 per cent of his time just in connection with grazing leases and permits, and the other estimates it takes about 50 per cent of his time. Now, all of that costs money because there is a lot more money besides that involved.

I will give you an example and it isn't an extreme example at all. There are, in the Indian Reservations, allotments of 160 acres with as many as 100 different heirs.

INTERPRETER: We would like to get that example.

MR. MARSHALL: This is the example, about that allotment with so many heirs. It has cost, on the average, as much as 50 cents, figuring all the costs of stockmen and others in and out of the Office, to get the signature of an heir, and those connected with the land. Or, in other words, the administration of the leasing of this one allotment has, in cases, cost as much as $50. Now, the receipts have been perhaps about 10 cents per acre, which would be about 16, so, when the land is broken up that way by heirship and allotment, it sometimes costs as much as $50 to administrate for a return of $16.

Now, I admit that is an unusual case today, but it does happen that way today sometimes, and twenty years from now and thirty years from now, if the present system continues, we will have cases a whole lot worse than that one.

We have grazing allotments today from which each heir receives less than one cent. Thirty years from now, if the present system continues, each heir will get enough money to buy himself about one toothpick.

Laughter.

Now, a second evil of the present system, I have tried to show on this blackboard here. It is a fact that unless you have close administration, and on many Reservations unless you have a permit system, the stockmen will not lease all the land. Until a few years ago, this situation was true on practically every Reservation. Today it is still true on a good many Reservations. In the future, if the present system continues, it will be true on a lot more Reservations where we can not possibly have enough men to take care of and check up on all the leased lands.

Now, this is the situation. A stockman comes in and first of all makes a lease on where the water hole is. Then, he finds that there are some Indians on this unit, a 60 acre tract here, and there. Perhaps 640 acres where the water hole is. Then, he finds that there are some Indians on this unit of grazing land he wants to use who know very well how to handle their own business affairs. He knows he can't get away with trespassing on their lands, so he comes out and pays them lease money, and those lands I have shown by these lots scattered throughout here without the yellow dots. But, all in between these lands he finds Indians who might not know enough about the white man's way of doing business to protect themselves from being cheated. They may be old people who can't get out to the land, or children who can't take care of themselves, and the stockman will go ahead and trespass his sheep or cattle on those lands and take a chance on getting away with it. If he is caught he may pay a fine of $1 a head. But, as I have heard from a good many of you here, in many cases when he trespasses he is not caught.

Applause.

So, what actually happens is that unless permits are granted, the stockman gets away with using the range and only paying for perhaps one-half or three-fourths of it, and the people who suffer this way are the old people and the children and the ones who are not used to the white man's way of doing business and who cannot protect themselves.

MR. MANDAN: Who is responsible for that?

MR. MARSHALL: The superintendent is responsible for that. The question which Mr. Mandan raised is the one which is the worst trouble with this whole administration of grazing allotments. Mr. Mandan said it was the superintendent's business to see that allotments are not trespassed upon. I am thinking of one Reservation in this region, the Crow Reservation, which has 3,668 different allotments. Now, I think Mr. Mandan can imagine how many men it would take as line riders to be hired by the superintendent to check up on trespass on 3668 different allotments.

It is very easy and very cheap to prevent trespass when you have one unit all under one control, but when you have it all broken up, like this picture on the blackboard, with the stockmen permitted to go into the squares which are marked, but not permitted to go into the area in the center, it would take hundreds of dollars just to administer the trespass on one unit. And, on all the Reservations in the country it would take thousands of dollars and probably even tens or hundreds of thousands of dollars to take care of this trespassing, and that money would come from the Indians whether it was taken directly from tribal funds or from gratuity appropriations. Because the Government only has a certain amount of money it can spend, if it is spent on useless things it will mean there is that much less money to spend on things the Indians really want.

Another thing that we find happening on many of the Reservations is if that one Indian who has an allotment on which there is water refuses to lease or grant a permit or put his allotment into a permit unless he is given an exorbitant price. Now, as all of you know, you can't run either sheep or cattle without water. So, on this particular diagram I have shown here, if the two Indians with the water holes I have depicted here, refuse to lease those water holes or throw them into the permit for the whole unit, then all the rest of the Indians on this unit, who may own a thousand times as much land as these two men put together, will be held up from leasing or granting permits on their land. This is not a case that I am imagining. It is something that really happens time and again.

Then there is still another point. It is much easier to run anything in a businesslike way if you run it altogether and at once. You can imagine what would happen in an automobile factory, for instance, if each workman in the factory did just exactly what he wanted to do without any reference to the other workmen. If the factory, instead of being run as one unit, was run with each workman going about putting on a wheel or tightening a screw without anybody directing the whole business, I don't think the factory would make very much money and I don't think many people would want to ride in the car even though they were able to buy it.

MR. MARSHALL: (*William Fire Thunder interpreting*) Well, it is exactly the same way with running the business of a grazing unit. If each part of the unit is run by a different person just the way he wants it, it will make so much confusion that a cattle man or a sheep man, who wants to lease it will not pay as much money as they will when it all comes in as one unit. Now that is a point which we can also prove with figures. Now, perhaps the most important reason, in my mind, anyway, why it is good, why the present system of different allotments scattered over the Indian country is good, is the matter of Indians themselves going into the stock business.

As Mr. Collier mentioned, it is the desire to encourage all the Indians to make use of their own range. I think it can be said that the tribes having ranges have the most satisfactory life and the most money for themselves, and the ones who are actually using it. The Navaho out on a desert such as most of you would consider absolutely impossible land to use, have actually made a better living than most of you have, and the reason they have made that better living is that they have not only gotten the lease from their land but they have also gotten the money from their livestock which brings more money than just range, and they have also raised food for their own use. Now the reason that the Navaho got to this is because they have had their range in solid lands. If each Indian who wanted to run stock had to come to separate terms with allottees, the way they expect the white stockmen to do on these Reservations, it would make the situation so complicated that very few would go into the stock business at all.

We have a case—we have at least two cases in this Northwest country where Indian allottees have refused to lease their lands to Indian stockmen, preferring to lease to white stockman. Yet I think it is everybody's desire here that the Indians should be given preference in the use of the range. The only way that I can see that this can be done without interfering with individual rights of allottees is to block the land up into units that can be put up for one bid instead of depending on the good will of the allottees, some of which may have a grudge against the particular allottee and not be willing to lease their land to him, so for all these reasons I think that the present system has been a failure and that a new system, which will block up the land for the Indian, which will make them more usable, which will give them more money, more returns, and more satisfaction to the Indian.

Applause.

MR. FRANK OHLERKING (Fort Belknap Indian): Now we have heard quite a little talk about range, and I would like to have Mr. Marshall explain what would happen where there is about one-third of the range within a unit which is needed by the Indians for their cattle and the remaining two-thirds of the range subject to lease to sheep. I do not care where they are from, but you cannot tell me that sheep and cattle can range on the same range, so if an Indian couldn't afford a fence, what protection would the Indians' cattle have on this unit?

MR. MARSHALL: The answer is, that the only adequate way to keep sheep and cattle separate is by putting up a fence and all the money spent for the useless administration of these broken up range units could then be spent to build that fence for the Indians.

MR. CHAIRMAN: Now, my friends, I do not think that the seating capacity of this hall is very small, but very hard, but I would like to have Mr. Stewart, Chief of the Land Division, talk to you now for not longer than four minutes and thirty-two seconds.

MR. STEWART: I am to address you about the land matter. Before doing so I would like to tell you of a little experience I had in the Southwest with a large group of Indians. I was to address this large group of Indians. There was a total in the neighborhood of 600. The meeting was held in the open air and this particular day it was raining very hard. There were four Superintendents and several more field men there. After they had gotten through addressing the Indians I found there was nothing left for me to say. I was in, or on, what is commonly known as a tough spot. Somewhat along the lines that I am now in. However, more from nervousness than from desperation I was fumbling with my watch chain and happened to pull my watch out and see the time. Thereupon I got up and made the shortest and most pleasing speech to Indians I think ever was made in that part of the country. I merely got up and said two words, and I say them to you now. Let's Eat.

Applause and laughter.

MR. WOEHLKE: It is not that easy. You have got to listen to me first. I would like to ask the Sioux delegations tonight to postpone their meeting from 7:30 to 8:00 because there will be a small meeting in advance of the main meeting here, and then I want to warn you. If you read the papers, don't believe them.

Laughter.

The afternoon paper says that tomorrow's meeting will be held here and invites all the white people to come and meet with us. We will meet at the Civic Auditorium in Rapid City at two o'clock and I wish you would tell all your friends that the information in the papers is wrong, and that we will meet in the Civic Auditorium, and now I echo the sentiment of Mr. Stewart, and say, "Let's Eat."

Adjourned.

Night Session

Special evening meeting of all Sioux Tribe delegates, convened at 8:00 p.m. March 3, 1934, called to order by Supt. James H. McGregor of the Pine Ridge Agency. Mrs. Dumarce, delegate from Sisseton, the only woman delegate at the Congress, makes the following address to the special meeting.

MRS. DUMARCE: My friends, I am unprepared I must say, but I want to tell you that it is an honor and I want to thank Mr. LaPointe for saying, as he did.

We are here, my friends, on a question, and nothing like this has ever been brought to us people before. Now, let us think. This trap as Mr. Collier said, above our ankles; is it going to hit higher or are we going to step out of it completely? Let us think and think some more.

MR. MCGREGOR: Now, some of you men have been asking for an opportunity to talk. The Commissioner says now is your time. Get up right now and ask the Commissioner some things, anything, or the thing that you are most worried about this question.

GEORGE WHITE BULL from Standing Rock: Mr. Chairman. We have such a good interpreter that I am going to say a few words. I wish to extend my appreciation to the Officials for all the good things that they have done for us. But, in the middle there, there are some things that are detrimental to us and we fear them. Under the allotment system they have been after us for quite a number of years, using every means, employing fraud and deceit and eventually made us accept and go into allotment system, under which we are now being governed. We believed in the allotment system as presented and we are now kind of getting accustomed to that way of being governed. All the officials are interested in the passage of the now proposed Bill or the new Bill, which contains some very good provisions in that Bill.

Now, if, as a precaution and safeguard, if they will make a law guarding that Bill with a penalty of so many years' imprisonment and a fine of so many dollars attached to anyone who violates or breaks up this Bill, annuls or voids this Bill, I believe that nobody shall attempt to break up this Bill. What I have reference to is the regulations governing the allotment system of which are now past. I believe that something is not very clear in our minds and that is this, that the passage of the new bill would in turn jeopardize our interests in some of the allotment and treaties that are known by the year '68, '78, and '89. Treaties that are known by those years would be jeopardized and that part of those will be relinquished if we accept the new proposed Bill.

I also believe that immediate action concerning this Bill is unnecessary as I just mentioned that some of the contents of the Bill are not clearly understood by all of us and there are a large number waiting at home and I feel that the delegations should take the matter home on their respective jurisdictions and there acquaint themselves, study the Bill, analyze it to the fullest extent. It may seem simple to you English speaking people, in whose language the Bill is constructed, but on the other hand the Indians that are involved, by the gift of God, they have an entirely different dialect, or language, of their own and some of them do not speak the English language so I think that the matter should be referred back to the people at home and there digested fully and then acted upon according to the wishes of the entire people after they have thoroughly acquainted themselves with the provisions.

One more thing I wish to say. Something that is to be readily observed by the delegates present here is that among the delegates are some who are landless that are very anxious for the passage and the acceptance of the Bill, and the reason for this anxiety, I believe, is that in the provisions of the Bill a credit system or the loan of money was mentioned. As I said awhile ago, we are getting, some of us are getting accustomed to the allotment system; that is, live on our allotments, utilize that land for their livelihood, utilize the water, the wood, timber and grass and maybe a garden spot and, more, a majority of these people that are utilizing their allotments are full bloods and can not speak English and they are reluctant about hasty acceptance of the Bill, fearing that some authority would come and take away what they now hold and claim as their own. That is all I wish to say.

I have some claims and suits against the U.S. Government. We are looking forward to the day when a judgment shall be reached in connection with our claims that we may realize some compensation on behalf of the claims. How does it happen there are no monies to settle our claims and reach judgment on our claims or pay the amount of those claims, but when a time comes for the transfer of our allotments into another system then we are told that a large amount of money—millions—would be appropriated for this purpose? I believe that it would be an easy matter for us to reach an early decision in this matter had the Government been anxious to settle our claims and pay up our claims in full than if a new proposition were presented. I believe we would have been just as anxious to answer just as readily and go into it whole-heartedly. Also, because by the settlement of our just claims we know our rights and we would have no fear towards any other matter that they may present. I believe that if they go into an immediate decision on this matter and take final action on it here it would be just the same as taking bread and butter out of the mouths of the younger generation and taking it from the old and indigent Indians.

MR. COLLIER: My friend says that he, and other full bloods especially, are getting used to their lands, that is, planting it and all that. They want to keep what they have and they want to stay where they are. We agree with them. This Bill would permit that and would help them to do it. Our friend says that maybe some abuse would be committed under the new plan. We must be careful that there will be no abuse and there would not be under the present plan. Does our friend remember that tomorrow if he wanted to, the Secretary of Interior could issue him a fee patent to declare him competent and then issue him a patent? He knows that the Secretary of Interior is not going to do that because he trusts the Secretary of Interior not to do a bad thing of that kind. But the Secretary of Interior could do it if he wanted to do it and he could have no escape nor redress.

Under this new plan the Secretary could not do that any more even if he wanted to. Now I am more anxious that we be clear about this matter of treaty and suits in the Court of Claims. Your lawyer is here tonight as well as I am here and I wish that he would correct me if he thinks that I am in error in anything I am going to say. This Bill that was before you now has no effect upon your suit in the Court of Claims. This Bill does not take away any right that you are seeking in your suit. This is something else; not a bill dealing with a Court of Claims question. Your suit is before the court and is being presented by your attorney, in my judgment, with energy and loyalty. This Bill will neither hinder nor help in the matter of that suit. Any right which you possess under treaty remains unaltered on the terms of this Bill. Now I do want to say a word about the matter of claims against the Government.

William Fire Thunder, Pine Ridge, interpreting.

This Bill that is before you is very important, but does not do everything that needs to be done. Speaking for myself, for more than ten years I have been denouncing the Government's policy about Indian claims and trying to get it changed. In order to change it, we must get legislation and probably more than one piece of legislation. You understand of course that the Sioux Tribe is not the only tribe with claims against the Government. More than half of all the tribes are either prosecuting suits or asking authority to prosecute claims against the Government, and the Government is handling the matter in such a way that more than one hundred years will go by in the future before most of these claims are tried in court, and each year that goes by while the Government delays, means that your efforts are decreased and your judgment is cut down. This is one of the worst things about the Government Indian policy.

You Indians of the Sioux Tribe are not suffering at all as much as many other Indians are suffering. You have obtained your jurisdictional half. You have been able to get competent lawyers to represent you and they are working for you. Your case is moving toward judgment with good prospects of a very good substantial victory for you. Most of the tribes have not even got their jurisdiction act yet, as our Assiniboine friends across the aisle here last year got a judgment in court and came out one million dollars in debt to the Government and nothing for themselves.

Now, some of you, I believe, have read the hearings of the Senate Indian Committee. Some of you no doubt have those writings. If you possess them you will find one volume devoted to Indian claims against the Government. In that volume you will find that a draft of a proposed bill was prepared by Mr. Nathan Margold. Mr. Margold was the man who I wanted to have been made Commissioner of Indian Affairs this year. Instead of that he was made solicitor of the Department of the Interior. He now is the chief law official of the Interior Department and of the Indian Bureau. That Bill draft or something like it, will shortly be introduced as a departmental bill and pushed with all their energy in Congress, and it will enable all Indian tribes to get their day in court without delay, and will enable them to plead, not only breach of treaties of the Government, but violations of equity rights and moral rights by the Government, and it will limit the authority of the Government to plead what you call the off-sets. Incidentally, that same measure, if it is passed, will put your own case in a very much better position than it can be put by the jurisdictional act. We do not expect to be able to pass that Bill at this session of Congress.

That Bill will be resisted by a great many interests. It will cost the Government, before it is finished, I wouldn't like to say how much because the newspaper men are here, what it would cost the Government. It will cost the Government so much that Mr. Douglas, Director of the Budget, would faint. We are going to stand for it because the Indians are entitled to have their cases tried and settled. If the Government is subject to judgment, then the Government has no right to hide out and to keep the court from filing judgment. We have been asked in the House Indian Committee why we do not put these two things together, why we didn't take this plan of Government, land credit, and self-government, and put them in one bill with this other thing that would bring all these claims to judgment, and our answer is very simple.

This Bill we have got before you is a big mouthful, and if we threw it into the Omnibus court of claims bill, then it will choke us to death. There must be relief for the Indians in the matter of their lands. We must get credit for the Indians and we do not want to tie that down to the general claims bill. I anticipate that if we succeed in getting relief in the matter of their land and credit and so on that year then the battle-ground in Government will be this claim matter. But to take them both on at the same time and as a part of one bill would be too heroic, it is too much, we couldn't get away with it.

Now, what I earnestly hope is that you will not take the position that because we can't right every wrong in one bill, therefore we ought not to right any wrong but ought to leave them all as they are. Don't mix up the two things which are settled and thereby confuse both of them.

There is one very real connection between this proposed Bill that we are discussing and your claim. One real connection, and it has to do with what will happen to your judgment after it is paid to you. Maybe you think, "We Sioux are going to get $100,000,000 net," and that is a lot of money. But, I have told you today how the Government, without the consent of the Indian, has misappropriated more than that much Indian trust money since 1900. If you just take one tribe of Indians alone: the Osage Tribe in Oklahoma. Since 1915, $245,000,000 has been paid into the Tribal fund of the Osage Tribe: $240,000,000. And do you know how much of that is gone already, thrown away, eaten up, wasted? 220,000,000 of that is gone. If you want to find out how it went, get the issue of *Collier's Weekly* that is on the stands right now and you will read all about how the Osage tribal fund has been misappropriated, or ask Mr. Henry Roe Cloud; he will tell you about it.

Now, if this Bill becomes law, this Bill we are discussing at this Congress, and then if you Sioux Indians go ahead under the Bill and take your charters and then, if you get your judgment from the Court of Claims, then not a dollar of that money can be spent by the Government except with your consent. You can protect your fund from misappropriation. Under existing law you would be powerless to protect your tribal fund from misappropriation. That is the only connection that this Bill would have with your claim.

Change of interpreters.

I may say, that all of the Indians, in the matter of their tribal funds, are at present defenseless under existing law. There is one exception which we obtained last May. There is one group of tribes who are protected in their tribal funds. Last May the Pueblo Tribes of New Mexico were able to get a law through Congress which requires the consent of those tribes before any of their tribal money can be used. No other tribe has that protection. This Bill, which we deal with, extends that protection to all of the tribes. Now, I am very anxious for us to understand one another about the relation of this Bill to you Sioux and to Indian treaty rights and to Indian claims generally. It is very important that we understand each other. If my understanding is incorrect, if I have not stated the matter correctly or if there is disagreement, I am very anxious to have it brought out now, so that I would like to yield the floor either to any of you or to your Attorney who is here tonight.

A GENTLEMAN rises: Mr. Chairman. There is one thing I want to ask you.

INTERPRETER: There is a question as to who had the floor first.

MR. MCGREGOR: I will recognize Mr. Oliver Prue from Rosebud.

MR. OLIVER PRUE: There is a thing that I want to question in regard to this petition, but before I make any statement I want to make a general statement on it. From times gone by, the Secretary of the Interior has been empowered with authority to act and to do as he pleases in all matters relating to Indians. We are selected as delegates to come to this Congress and listen on both sides of the question and thresh out the matters and try to understand it thoroughly and then without taking any action on our part, to take the case home, back to the people whom we represent. Therefore, it is believed, those being the conditions under which we came. If it is just a little matter of local concern right at this meeting that the whole Congress is requested to act on, our delegation is not at liberty to take part even in that case.

Last night, our Attorney, Major Case, gave us a nice talk and he complimented Mr. Collier, the Commissioner, on the character of the man and his sincerity in everything and his earnest desire to do something worthwhile for our people, and we also, our Rosebud Delegation, believe with Mr. Case. From past experience in years gone by, we have come to learn to distrust all Government officials that come out here to negotiate with our people and we really have been fooled so many times, time and again, that we just simply distrust every Government official that came out here, however true they may be.

Applause.

We have listened to Mr. Collier for two days now and he has presented some very good material for us to listen to, but we have had so much experience in the past and even right now, maybe one matter brought up sounds good, looks good, and pleasant to hear about, etc., and yet we hear another thing again and then another thing. The matter has been passed along like a basketball. Thrown from one player to another until we don't know what it is.

On page 31, line 6, there is a matter that he wants to ask a question about. He says that it is a mouthful and we cannot swallow it. That is, from the fact that our property will be exempt from taxes—we ought to be able to swallow it. For this very reason it is harder for us to swallow it and we would like to have Mr. Collier explain that if he can. And we would like to have Mr. Collier explain said section of this Bill and we would also appreciate it if Major Case would give his legal opinion on this question.

MR. COLLIER: It is going to take us the rest of the evening, I am afraid.

SAM LAPOINTE, Rosebud: Mr. Commissioner, I was just going to take up this subject myself. I think it is a very good point. We had the understanding from the Chairman when he announced tonight that we were going to meet here tonight and the Sioux were going to be given a chance to talk and most of them are gone and I think this is the desire and opinion of the majority here tonight. We came here with the hope that you would read those questions that came from the Sioux delegates and you would answer them tonight.

CHARLEY RAMSEY, Standing Rock: We are all delegates to this Congress and I am one of the delegates from Fort Yates. We have taken particular care in choosing the tribal councilman and I am the chairman of that council, and if I see things running in this manner in any of my meetings I am going to talk. One thing I want to know is whether the people on the outside of the delegation assembled here have any voice in this meeting. I want an answer to my question right away so I can go home and go to bed.

MR. COLLIER: Yes, they can ask questions and make remarks, although the meeting is primarily, of course, for your business council. If there were going to be any voting each delegation would do his own voting or not vote, as it preferred to do. Do you want your questions read and then answered?

MR. MCGREGOR: The question is—do you want your questions answered right now, or do you want to talk?

FRANCIS RED TOMAHAWK, Standing Rock Delegate: I noticed during the proceedings of this meeting the method used in running this council—personally, to me, I do not like it. For this reason—I realize the chairman is trying to hold us down to the subject in order to prevent backwardness from the subject—that I realize. And yet the explanation of the Bill in question—various titles which were discussed at this stage, the majority of the delegates are not fully acquainted with and hence do not want to commit themselves in any form, no matter how mild it is.

I noticed during the conference that questions submitted were laid on the table and we do not know what was put on the table. If we are going to act intelligently for our constituents at home we want to be fully informed of everything that is on that table. It is for that very reason our delegations had a number of questions all prepared before we came down here and we have, since coming here, picked up some more which would be supplementary to the original questions prepared for explanation. We are not prejudiced against the plan of changing from the old system to a new system. We came here with an open mind; we want to listen to everything—we have no bias whatsoever and upon the explanation given and upon the attitude taken by the majority of the delegates attending this council we want to base our best judgment on that before we act. Now I ask that we be permitted to read these questions into the record and become a part of the record.

MR. COLLIER: Do you refer to the questions I have here, or the questions you have with you.

MR. RED TOMAHAWK: All the questions we have at this time. It is requested that the Commissioner answer these questions at this time.

MR. FOSTER THUNDER: This is not the original council that is supposed to meet so I object to the questions asked which are upon the table for the reason that the council is not fully represented, that is why I object.

MR. COLLIER: Many of the questions will be answered as we go along. We have not got an unlimited amount of time and sometimes one question overlaps another and in that way we will do nothing else until adjournment. I also point out that we have been answering these questions right along. Here we have for example, the Pine Ridge list of questions. "We want your frank statement of the Bill in its relation to our tribal claims." That is the answer as fully as I can answer it, and as we go along we find that many of them have been answered.

Now, at the moment I can't find those questions concerning Tomahawk. They have not been answered. Now we should know whether you want us to go ahead answering questions, or what you do want for the meeting this evening.

MR. JOE IRVING of Fort Thompson, South Dakota: It has been announced by the chairman, he said we were going to have a meeting in the City Auditorium, and I understood him to say that we were going to do all the talking and that you fellows were going to do the listening. If that is the case I will save my speech until tomorrow. I want to make a motion that the written questions on the table be read and answered.

MR. MCGREGOR: It has been moved by Joe Irving of Fort Thompson, S. Dak., that the questions on the table be read and answered tonight. Is there a second to that motion?

Motion seconded by Mr. Frank Wilson of Pine Ridge, S. Dak.

MR. MCGREGOR: You have heard the question; all in favor of the question hold up your right hand.

Majority hold up right hands.

Contrary—a few. Motion is carried.

MR. MCGREGOR: Let me just say this, let us get down to the meat of this meeting and not stray away from the questions. The Commissioner is our Commissioner tonight.

First Question, ROSEBUD: Commissioner Collier said that the Government should give back to the Indian 20 per cent of the hundred million dollars admittedly misappropriated since 1900, meaning tribal funds. Why not give back the full 100 per cent?

ANSWER: Yes.

ROSEBUD QUESTION: Suppose the Bill passes and title 3, the land title, becomes law, so that the land becomes tribal, then suppose that some Secretary of the Interior refuses to grant any charters, would not then the control of the use of the land be completely in the Government?

ANSWER: In such an event, the control over the use of all Indian lands would be completely in the Government in exactly the way that the control of tribal land is now in the Government. However, such action by the Secretary of the Interior, who we will say, refuses to grant any charters, would be a violation of the act itself. The Act expressly declares what the policy of Congress is. Do not stop to read the first three pages but you will find it all there. The Act expressly sets up the procedure for issuing charters. The initiative is put in the Indians themselves. If in the event the Secretary refuses to issue a charter after the tribe has asked for it, he must issue a written explanation why he refuses and transmit that to Congress. I also point out that the first lines of this question presume something which may not be the case.

ROSEBUD QUESTION: Suppose the Bill passes, title 3 becomes law, so that all the land becomes tribal?

ANSWER: On a basis of transfer and relinquishments being voluntary the land would not become tribal until the Indians made it so. They would organize their chartered communities before they transferred title, and then the chartered community would have the power and not the Secretary.

ROSEBUD QUESTION: How much Indian land remains unsold of whites? This refers to ceded and surplus lands.

ANSWER: We do not know. These ceded lands are under the jurisdiction of the general land office. That office has not yet compiled statistics so we can't give them to you. This Bill would direct that all of this information be compiled by the Secretary and they would have to provide the money to do it.

COMMISSIONER COLLIER: Rosebud again. "Who determines what is the fair value of land which is in a community; that is, a consolidated area, and which is to be exchanged for non-communal, that is, for individual land. Suppose the Indian thinks the value placed on the land is not a fair value, what then?" Then he does not make the exchange until he has satisfied himself that it is a fair value. The matter could be referred to an arbitration board; between an arbitration board to settle the thing between the community and the Indian. If compulsory transfer were kept in the law and then the Indian felt that he was not getting fair value, the courts would arbitrate: the Court of Indian Affairs.

I am getting away from Rosebud now for a minute. There is a lot more Rosebud yet, but I will jump around. Here is one I don't know where it is from, but not Rosebud. "Should the Indians be disfranchised if they are to adopt the self-government principle?" I do not see why that follows at all. The Indians are citizens of the United States and as such they are entitled to vote and the fact that they take over partial or complete self-government in their own business is no reason why they should not vote in the elections. That same question goes on, "Isn't it a fact that our troubles on the Indian Reservation begin when politics enters?" I do not know, but down in Washington we hear that there is lots of politics in there already.

Laughter.

Now we have come to Sisseton. This is a very practical question: "An Indian who has made his home on a trust allotment; has made much improvement on his allotment, wants to continue to live as he has. He does not want to go into the community area and he wants his children to enjoy the ownership of his land with all of the improvements after his death. Will the Secretary of the Interior ignore this man's good intentions by virtue of the Wheeler Bill and compel him to submission?"

That is a question that might be raised from any Reservation where there are allotted Indians. Now, without stopping now to again analyze Title three, I will just answer the question. This Indian described in this question, under the new plan, would continue to occupy his land if he wanted to, and his heirs would occupy that land if they wanted to. He would own his improvements and his heirs would inherit his improvements. That would be true even with the compulsory transfer feature kept in the law. If the compulsory feature be taken out of the Bill, then he would do whatever he wants to. Mr. Stewart reminds me that I want to explain here again that suppose the heirs do not want the improvements and do not want to live on that land, then they will be entitled to the value of the improvements. They can sell it, and they are entitled to the rental value or the use of either this land or any equivalent amount of land anywhere else, if they prefer.

A VOICE FROM THE AUDIENCE: Mr. Collier, supposing the community did not want those improvements?

MR. COLLIER: Well, if a fellow has got something he wants to sell and nobody will buy it, he is out of luck.

Now, we jump to Pine Ridge. There is a whole series of questions here of which I have already read No. 1, about the claims Bill, and whether this Bill affects it. The second one relates peculiarly to your Sioux situation. The English of this is not clear, so I will just read you the sense. The question is, "What is going to happen to the matter of Sioux Benefits if this Bill passes?"

The Sioux Benefit, as I understand the law, is a payment made under treaty. It is a curious thing because it has been so worked out that the benefit, which is a payment in money, goes to the allotted Sioux Indian when and if that Indian reaches a certain age. I believe it is 18 years, isn't it?

ANSWER: Yes.

MR. COLLIER: Now the question is this. It is a very practical one. Your allotted young person who has got an allotment, if that young person should relinquish his or her allotment, does that destroy his or her claim to the Benefit? I am subject here to correction by the lawyers. I believe that it is necessary in order to protect these Sioux Benefits to adopt legislation expressly protecting them. I think it is a matter on which we ought to have the opinion of your lawyers. This is the question, as to whether the pending Sioux Benefit would be endangered in the event that allotments became relinquished to the community and if so, whether we do not need to amend the Bill or pass supplemental legislation.

MR. CASE: Sioux Benefits, my friends, are payable under section 17 of the Act of March 2, 1889, only to those people who were living on the date when the President authorized allotments to be made on each Reservation. Now, those children that were born after the President ordered the allotments to be made were not even entitled to allotment under the act of '89. Now, all of your Reservations had a good deal of land, well, say in 1900 up to 1906. And all of the poor people came to the Congress and asked the Congress to open up, make allotments to the new-born children, and by the act of May 29, 1908, it was provided that the land remaining on the Reservations should be allotted as long as the land lasted, and the allotments went right on from that time and the Government seemed to think that the new-born children, when they got an allotment, that they were entitled to Sioux Benefits.

It took until 1925 until the Comptroller General stopped it, to find out that the Government was wrong in paying you Sioux Benefits, and then your attorneys went to the Congress and asked them to pass an act that would authorize the payment of Sioux Benefits to these new-born children, and that became the act of May 21, 1928. Now, you see, there are two kinds of Sioux Benefits. The old timer—1889 allottees are one kind, and 1928 is another kind. Now, the 1889 Sioux Benefits are part of the contract made by the United States and Sioux Tribes for the cession of the land between the Cheyenne River and the White River, known as the Crook's Treaty, and that belongs to you and some of you old timers and some of the old men haven't got it yet, but we have got part of them since we started this fight. Young Eagle, stand up; how many did you get on Standing Rock?

ANSWER: Something over 134.

MAJOR CASE: All right. 134. We got 134 on Standing Rock. We haven't got through yet, so I tell you, there is nothing in this Bill as far as I can see it that changes it except this. There will be no more allotments and that only affects Cheyenne River.

MR. CASE: Now I could talk to you all night about Sioux Benefits, I could talk to you all night on that one subject—and I have been laying to catch the Commissioner of Indian Affairs so I could tell him what I wanted to say about the Sioux Benefits, but I will wait until I get him in Washington. I do not want to take up the time to talk to you about it and to talk to him about it here; now.

FIRE THUNDER, Pine Ridge: The question he wants to submit to you is the payment of the Sioux Benefits under the 1928 act, whether or not the funds used will not be taken out of the claims.

MR. CASE: No. Not unless they have a better man on the other side, on this lawsuit.

FIRE THUNDER, Pine Ridge: The reason I asked the question is because some information has been received whereby the Government paid the Sioux Benefits as a loan to the tribe to be deducted from funds that may have accrued from judgment of our claims.

MR. CASE: No, that is not so. The act of May 21, 1928, simply says—the Secretary of the Interior is hereby authorized to continue making payments of Sioux Benefits to children allotted under section 19, under the Act of May 29, 1908. It simply says he can go ahead and do it.

MR. FIRE THUNDER, Pine Ridge: Is this money appropriated, or is it taken from the United States Treasury?

MR. CASE: From the United States Treasury.

MR. COLLIER: I am going to read the question which seems to be the most important. Will all monies appropriated for counting off division of this Bill be chargeable to the Indians, to be reimbursed from tribal funds?

No. All of the appropriations are gratuitous, except that where money is provided for scholarship for young Indians—One half of that money is a loan—as a gift. It is loaned to the individual Indian.

How much land would be purchased for landless Indians under the proposed amount of two million? If each family of four were to receive eighty acres of this agricultural land then there would be two thousand families put on the land each year.

MR. COLLIER: (*continues*) Could each be provided with 80 acres of agricultural land? Here are two questions almost identical, one from Pine Ridge and one from Rosebud. I will read the Rosebud question. With respect to section 13-b, title one; what is the meaning of the word Reservation?

ANSWER: I find that Mr. Stewart makes a note that this was answered this morning.

PINE RIDGE QUESTION: Clarify the intended boundary lines for a Reservation in an Indian community, in the case where a county has been thrown open for settlement and homestead purposes and the county has been organized, and where there are vested rights therein, fee patented land, or white owned land subject to taxation?

ANSWER: I think I will ask Mr. Stewart to answer that question.

MR. STEWART: In a situation of that kind, it will be our plan under the consolidation and acquisition program outlined in the Bill to acquire or reacquire some of that alienated land, fee patented land, if it is feasible to block it out for Indian purposes, and also if it is desirable to block it out. If on the other hand it is not needed or desired for Indian purposes, we will of course not attempt to obtain it. Therefore, the county jurisdiction over the land will remain undisturbed. If, however, we do acquire it, county jurisdiction would cease.

MR. RALPH H. CASE: May I have the floor a minute to explain what is in the minds of these delegates? Everybody knows that the Act of March 2, 1889, laid down the boundary lines of the several Sioux Reservations in court. Since that time, quite a number of counties have been opened up and sold out and the jurisdiction and the law over those counties has been turned over to the State. Not everybody moved out of that county. Hence Bennett County with a number of Indians living in there, and the same is true of Gregory County, Tripp County, Corson County, Mellette and Ziebach counties.

Now, what is the status of those living in those open counties where the jurisdiction has been ceded by the county over to the state? Residence is an essential factor in that matter. In the Act of 1913 all of the surplus land on Standing Rock was opened up for sale and settlement. Is Standing Rock a Reservation now? A little simple amendment that would lay down the boundaries of the Reservations as fixed by the Act of March 2, 1889 as Reservations within the minimum of this Bill would correct this situation. I am answering my own question. (*Speech interpreted by Robert High Eagle.*)

MR. STEWART: I would like to further go into that matter as to whether that open land is Reservation or is it not. This morning you recall that the undisposed of open land in Indian Territory remains undisturbed. That was a ruling by the Supreme Court of the United States laid down in a Crow case of a similar nature in connection with the Ash Sheep Company case.

Therefore, there is a dual jurisdiction of control over those lands, in this respect: The Federal Government has control over the undisposed of surplus land. The state laws prevail as to the disposed of land. Now then, as to a white man living within one of these areas that we may consolidate who refuses to remove or sell to the Indians, we would have no control and there is nothing I know of that could be done to force him out. Does that cover the general situation?

INTERPRETER: Mr. Chairman: If you please, it is now quarter of eleven and no matter how strong the Camel's back is, if you put one more straw on that Camel's back, it will break that Camel's back. Mr. Collier may be able to stand it because he is a strong man, but we are not.

MR. MCGREGOR: It is proposed that we adjourn.

MR. FRANK WILSON, Pine Ridge Agency: I would like to have that question answered. If you do not answer my question—that question is my question before the house—I will not be able to sleep tonight. There have been a lot of important things put through here and that is a very important question and we want it answered. It involves lots of Indians. It will exclude about 1500 Indians because we are not inside of the Reservation jurisdiction according to your program.

MR. COLLIER: Let me answer that question, and see if I can answer it. The way it is now on the Reservation all over the Indian country there are areas of land that once were solid Indian areas and now there are white people here and there among them. Now what is the jurisdiction of the Federal Government now? First, it has the exclusive jurisdiction over that land where the title is in the Government laws as to relations with Indians, how is this Government to regulate relations with Indians? What a white man does on his own land, that is not under the Government. What he does now within the Reservation, he is under the State Courts, but if he does something on his own land that affects an Indian, it may come under the Federal courts and if he sells liquor to an Indian, he can be prosecuted under the Federal laws for selling liquor to an Indian.

Now, under this Bill it would be actually the same as it is now. A great deal of Reservation land would never be organized under an Indian community. The Indians might not want to organize as a chartered community, and again if their land is scattered out too far from one another, they can't organize as a chartered community. If they do organize as a chartered community, then they exercise the powers of self-government, laid down in the Bill. Its powers cannot be greater than the powers that the Federal Government exercises, and those powers of the Federal Government are exercised in all Indian country regardless of whether Indian communities exist or not, but it is not the power of the Federal Government to extend its control over the fee patented land owned by white men in or out of an Indian community. And, therefore, it is the white people of Dakota need not fear that the Indians are going to eat them alive.

I do not know whether I have yet answered it. All that is Reservation land remains Reservation land. Any new land to which the Government secures title becomes Reservation land under the Federal Government. That Reservation land is just as much Reservation if it is not under an Indian community as if it is under an Indian community, and in addition, the Government's power reaches to the Indian himself in so far as he is injured by things done on white owned land, and can protect him. No bill can go beyond constitutional limits. The Federal Government can not assert a power that it does not possess, and it does not have power over land that it does not own or control, where white people are living, and we can't give that power to the Government and the Government can not give it to an Indian community.

ANTOINE DEROCKBRAINE from Standing Rock: Mr. Chairman, I would like to ask one question while we are on this subject in regard to this land. Now, under the Act of 1908, all land was thrown open for settlement and on the land that is still remaining not taken by homestead within that area of land or territory, there is section 16 and 36 out of each township sold to the State of South Dakota for $2.50 an acre by the Government. What would we do to get that land in case of a community organization within that area of unsettled portion?

MR. COLLIER: You would have to buy it. It could not be taken back. You would have to buy it back.

MR. MCGREGOR: Meeting adjourned.

Sunday, March 4, 1934

Afternoon Session

The session was opened at 2:15 P.M., by Mr. Woehlke, at the Civic Auditorium at Rapid City, South Dakota.

MR. WOEHLKE: Friends, we would like to open this session of the Congress with an invocation by the Reverend Doctor Henry Roe Cloud.

Invocation by Dr. Roe Cloud.

MR. WOEHLKE: As I stated yesterday, at this session of the Congress we have come here to listen, to hear from you. Time, unfortunately, is very short because today this auditorium will be in use again at 6:00 p.m., and we have to wind up by that time.

I shall call on the various delegations from the different Reservations to have one member of that delegation express unofficially and wholly informally what he and his fellow members of the delegation think of either the various phases of the proposed program or of the program as a whole. As there are eighteen delegations it is absolutely necessary to limit the time given to each delegation so that we may give all of them a chance to express their opinions. Now, a simple problem in arithmetic will show you what has been done. Eighteen delegations, with ten minutes for each one, means a hundred eighty minutes or three hours. We have about three and a half hours at our disposal. Therefore, the Chair must insist that the remarks of the spokesman for each delegation be limited to ten minutes, including the interpretations, though by agreement between two or three delegations they may nominate one spokesman who would have the combined time of the two or three.

Before we begin this presentation of the views, I would like to call on Commissioner Collier for a brief restatement of the general objectives and purposes of the new program, but I must limit him to not more than twenty minutes. I, therefore, call on the Commissioner who will speak and take no more than twenty minutes, but before he begins I would like to ask whether you have made arrangements for interpreters.

MR. COLLIER: Where is the Sioux interpreter? Will you be ready to interpret?

Sioux interpreter, William Fire Thunder.

I am not going to repeat things that we have been saying for the last two days. I would like to add to what the Chairman has said, this statement. We shall be in session tomorrow morning, afternoon, and if necessary, at night. There will be time for all necessary discussions tomorrow about any question. Therefore, those who may arise today in order to speak should not feel that they are being called on for any final expression or any verdict that they can't change tomorrow.

To the white friends who are here and not at the other meetings, I will merely explain that the Indians at this Congress are studying a proposal by the Administration in connection with their land and their self-government. This proposal is embodied in a Bill that has been introduced into Congress. The Bill is still being improved and when it is finally enacted, it will embody the wishes of the Indians themselves. The general purposes being sought I will state in a few words. We want to stop the continued loss of the land by Indians. We want to make it provide new land for Indians who have lost their land and who desire to farm or grow stock on lands of their own. We want to make it possible for the Indians to get their land into condition for the best use. We want to supply the necessary capital so that the Indians can restock their land and buy the necessary implements and build homes and generally can put their life on a model basis. We expect that this result can be obtained while giving complete protection to each Indian who has got property.

In addition, we want laws which will permit the Indians to organize for self-help and mutual aid, and to take part in the management of the Indian Bureau, itself. Now, in the discussions of the last two days, it has been made clear that everybody is agreed that the present situation is bad. The difficult part has been to build up a clear picture of the new plan and how it will work. In order that we can make that picture a little more clear than it is now, I shall ask the permission of the Chair to allow me to give the balance of my time to one of the Indians from the Fort Belknap Reservation in order that he may tell about the Stock Association that is now being carried on up there. That will convey a picture of what sort of thing we are aiming at in general.

MR. WOEHLKE: Will the delegate from Fort Belknap come here and take the balance of the Commissioner's time, 7 minutes? He may also take his own delegation's time in addition if he so desires.

Applause.

MR. KING of Fort Belknap, Montana: Mr. Chairman, ladies and gentlemen. Our Commissioner of Indian Affairs, Mr. Collier, has requested me to devote the rest of his time, which was allowed him, to tell about the stock organization which is organized on our Reservation of Fort Belknap, Montana. We have approximately 500,000 acres of grazing land on the Fort Belknap Reservation and we have a little less than 1,200 individual allotments, and we have eighteen grazing range units in that area. Out of these 18 units, two are leased by the Stock Association of the members of the Fort Belknap Reservation.

These lands are all allotted and some of the members of the stock association happen not to have their particular allotment in this range unit but have their allotments in some other unit. In order to work this out, a member of the stock association has so many head of cattle running inside this range unit. Maybe his land would be in another range unit somewhere.

It requires record keeping as to how many acres this man has in another range unit, and we collect the rentals from that unit and apply it to the range unit where he keeps his cattle. This requires a lot of clerical work because it requires the land description of the individual's land and if it is subdivided, it requires more land descriptions to describe the exact acreage, and the money collected is applied to the land where the cattle are grazed.

After this is all done, then the man that has land in this Indian range unit but does not have any cattle in it would be able to get his rentals. This stock association was organized something like two years ago and the members had so many cattle in there. In order to comply with the regulations of the Government, it was necessary to comply with the carrying capacity of the range—so many acres per head—so as to protect the grazing range and not overstock it. The first year we had to take in some other cattle that did not belong—we took them from off the Reservation—and filled in the carrying capacity in full so as to pay for the lands there. Last year we introduced approximately over 300 head of cattle from the outside so as to fill in the requirements of this unit.

This year there were some applications that came in from the outside from some cattlemen who wanted to bring their cattle in and have them run on the association range but we told them we could not bring them in as we wanted to use the whole range ourselves this year. We have this range unit fenced up and the way we take care of the expense is by assessing each man so much per head, so as to defray the expenses of the fence.

We assess enough so as to take care of the man who is the fence rider and the man who rides through the range and sees that the cattle are all right and sees that the range is taken care of. Next year we will have to take additional land as it will require quite a bit of land to run the increase for next year. Mr. Chairman—I asked the Chairman if it would be all right to go ahead and tell the way our delegation from Fort Belknap feel about this land policy and he asked me to go right ahead and tell about that too. Well, I have only five minutes left so I will make it short, as short as I can. Mr. Collier and his staff have been trying to tell us how this new policy will work and we have been listening very carefully and closely and in viewing it from the standpoint of our situation on that Reservation we discussed the matter among the Council and we believe it is a good thing for our Reservation to adopt this land policy.

Applause.

Our Reservation is all under trust yet up to this time and there are four patent in fee lands on our Reservation. The mortgage has been foreclosed on two of them and the Indians got their money all spent and they have no land. And we feel that from other Reservations, this also has been going on since the allotment system has been carried on; most of the Reservations in other states, even in our state, we hear that their lands have all been gone through which is like this patent in fee land that I spoke of on our Reservation. We could see that this new policy will not hurt us at all, and hereafter instead of hurting us it will add to what we got and it will protect what we got, so we are glad to hear that we have a Commissioner now that is willing to come out and protect our lands and our delegation from Fort Belknap, Montana, is willing to accept the land policy.

MR. WOEHLKE: The Fort Belknap delegation has now used up its time. I shall now begin to call on the other delegates in alphabetical order and the first I shall call upon is the Blackfeet Delegation.

MR. BROWN, Chairman, Blackfeet Delegation: The part that the Blackfeet delegation has taken in this meeting; and the part that a portion of the Blackfeet delegation took in some more of this same kind of meetings in Washington; our part in this, has been that of a good listener, trying to learn what we can and trying to figure out whether this is a good thing for our people or not. In the most part of this Bill we are in favor of it, and I believe that if we can get together with some of the Bureau officials to work over the objectionable features that we have we are not so far apart.

Our Reservation is getting so now that it is so checker-boarded with white settlers that it looks like a man with the smallpox. I want to take this opportunity to express publicly our sincere and heartfelt sympathy for the way our new Commissioner and those of his staff have treated this delegation while in Washington. Notwithstanding rumors that naturally go about the country the Blackfeet have every faith and confidence in our new Commissioner, and it is just too bad that our law permits a Commissioner to be appointed according to political affiliations—

Applause.

—because, since we have one in there now that we have faith in, it is just too bad that we can't keep him there so that with his new program he can see it through and follow it up. I thank you for your attention.

Applause.

MR. WOEHLKE: I am learning that a great many things can be said in less than ten minutes. The next delegation to speak will be the Cheyenne River delegation.

VOICE FROM AUDIENCE: Mr. Chairman, just a minute. I would like to ask you, your honor, if this meeting is confined to delegations or for open public discussion. I object, before this is open for public discussion I object to any acceptance of this Bill of any delegation confined to this meeting.

MR. WOEHLKE: *(repeatedly)* You are out of order. You shall have an opportunity for public discussion later in the meeting.

GENTLEMAN: *(ignoring the chair)* This is the first time my voice has been heard in this hall. This thing is being carried out in too much autocratic manner and I am not going to stand for it. I am not going to be the victim of this Bill and I am entitled to a voice as a citizen of the United States and I am going to have it. I object. I solemnly object to any acceptance of this Bill that is being requested by Wheeler of Montana, and I am an Indian and I am not going to put up with any confinement of speech. I realize that I am out of order but I reserve right of voice.

Applause.

MR. WOEHLKE: I want to insist that this is an expression of opinion on the part of various individuals and delegations which is not binding on them or anyone else. It is an unofficial expression of opinion.

MR. LUKE GILBERT, Chairman of Cheyenne River Reservation Delegation: Mr. Chairman, Mr. Commissioner, Official Staff, ladies and gentlemen: I represent the Cheyenne River Sioux Indians as their Chairman and I am also a member of the delegation who are there.

Voice from audience asks for speaker's name—Mr. Woehlke gives name.

We have been here now for two days listening and trying to get the true meaning and understanding of the Bill in question. The Cheyenne River Sioux Indians believe that this Bill has greatly affected them in this way. We have and still retain a vast area of tribal lands, somewhere in the neighborhood of 250,000 acres which is subject to allotment as well as the individual land holdings of the allottees.

We think we know our problems and the conditions under which we live on the Cheyenne River Reservation. We do not want an improved administration that covers health and educational facilities and other things that go with it.

We feel as though this Bill, while it may be of benefit to some Reservations, will not be of much benefit to the Cheyenne River Reservation as far as land holdings are concerned. As I said before, we think we know our problems; we know what to ask for, we know what we want. After getting the understanding of this Bill, the Cheyenne River delegation will take these views back to their people and leave it to their people to decide.

MR. WOEHLKE: My friends: Perhaps there is an apprehension and mistaken impression in the minds of some of you, especially of the gentleman who arose and spoke out of turn a little while ago. We are not asking for a vote of any delegation for or against the Bill now. We are merely asking the spokesmen of the various delegations to tell us what they think about the Bill and what is right or wrong with it.

I would now like to have the spokesman for the Crow delegation step forward. Following the Crow delegation, the Crow Creek delegation will speak.

MR. HARRY WHITE MAN, Crow Reservation: Mr. Chairman, Honorable Commissioner of Indian Affairs and Members of the Commissioner's Staff, fellow members of the Indian Race: Once an Assistant Commissioner of Indian Affairs called me the most ungrateful Indian in the United States. He said that because I was trying to voice the sentiment of my people before the Senate Committee of Indian Affairs.

MR. CHAIRMAN: Mr. White Man, please step forward so the crowd can hear you.

MR. WHITE MAN: We admire and we respect the present Commissioner of Indian Affairs for his endeavors to try to place the Indians upon a stable basis. In spite of our respect for him I want to say that when I was recently at Washington I was told that the Commissioner's heart was in this Bill, but I want to tell you that I also have a heart and that heart is the welfare of my people. I believe that we have come to the road where it forks off. Today we are confronted with the fact that among the wise men that tried to shape the destiny of the Indians and one of the most brilliant Senators the policy of the Indian Office toward Indians was adopted and pursued for the last 47 years. Those people who launched this policy said that the Reservation system was a vicious system.

Our present Commissioner of Indian Affairs says that the allotment system is a vicious system. President Roosevelt said that he was going to give us a new deal, and the Commissioner of Indian Affairs, I believe, is an advocate of the new deal. I do not want to go home and keep mum about the sentiment of my people regarding this legislative program that is brought before us. If the President and the Commissioner are sincere in giving us a new deal all that I ask in behalf of my people is to give us something to say about the shaping of this Bill and not try to cram down our throat something that we do not like.

The Commissioner of Indian Affairs told us that there were a bunch of wicked and vicious laws affecting the Indians and I want to say that we did not have a chance to say anything about the making of those laws. If you people who are drafting this Bill will give every Tribe of the United States a chance to voice their opinion and desires in the shaping of these Bills and a three-fourths vote is taken by every tribe of the United States when this legislation is made, then we will certainly be for it, otherwise we will not.

Mr. Chairman, if I have any more time left, let Max Big Man take that time.

MR. MAX BIG MAN: Mr. Chairman, the Northern Cheyenne Indians, which is a neighboring friend of ours, has elected Mr. White Man as our spokesman for this time.

MR. WHITE MAN: I want to thank my neighboring Cheyenne friend for giving me this time. I realize the fact that my neighboring tribe, the Cheyenne, who are adjacent to our Reservation, has had a great difficulty in getting their allotments made. After the allotments were made, then comes the new program. A new program as I see it takes away from us initiative and private ownership that we all desire so much to possess. It takes away from us the spirit of independence so essential and so badly needed by the members of the Indian race. Unless this Bill is made voluntary I believe the Crow Indians and Cheyenne will fight this Bill to the last measure, and, if necessary, call on our constitutional rights which says that no person shall be deprived of their rights and due process of law for Government. I believe the adopting of this Bill should be voluntary on the part of the Indians and if an Indian wants it, let him have it, and if he does not want, he does not have to have it.

Now, Mr. Chairman, if I have any time left I would like to have Mr. Big Man take the balance of my time.

MR. SHEPARD: You have five minutes left. I will give the balance of the time to Mr. Big Man.

MR. MAX BIG MAN from Crow Agency: Mr. Chairman, Commissioner and Staff and my American friends. I am very happy to be here in your presence. I want to tell our Great White Father that if my spokesman step on their toes a little bit they will have to excuse us because he is a Democrat.

Applause.

I want to tell my people that I have recently visited Washington, D.C., the home of our Great Father, and he is a real white man.

Applause.

His heart is good, and he gives an opportunity to his children, among some refuse to take it whether it is good or not.

Applause.

It may be so whether the plan is working now, but we want him to excuse us when we refuse. If it is for the wrong and if any of the Tribes refuse it I think it will make a man of them. It takes competition and big knocks to make a man. So, it is rather hard as a step that I made to learn to eat the white man's food. Now, you take me, I dress in my Indian clothes, but the progress that I make is on account of my parents. I now have push my children ahead and I can not live in a community and live altogether away from my white friends.

Now, only a little bit more and as I learn the white man's way I have learned to talk a lot, and which I want to say again, as a lot of people in their speeches when they repeat the speech they always take it wrong, but among our people we always repeat in our speech, and I want to ask the Commissioner and his staff if they step on their toes a little bit to excuse us just because he is a big Democrat and he knows more in his speeches in the thoughts of the white man.

I thank you for your kind attention and, my friends, I am very thankful for the privilege of sounding my words to you in this great hall here. I am directly talking to the Rapid City people. Of course, you have seen me before for I have done work for you Rapid City people in the days of the past. I thank you for your kindness.

MR. COLLIER: Mr. Chairman: I think at this point a reply from me would be expected. Mr. White Man will not be called an ungrateful Indian. We want plain speech. We don't care if it is very emphatic. But Mr. White Man will not object if I correct one of his own statements. The proposed new policy of legislation will not be rammed down the throats of the Indians.

What is the meaning of this Congress and of the other Congresses that are to be held all over the Indian country? What is the meaning of our statement to you that we are not even interested in your endorsing the Bill? We are meeting with you in order that you and we may think out this question and improve the Bill in any way that it can be improved, or change it in any way it ought to be changed. Now, I want to go further in my reply to my friend, Mr. White Man.

Several times during yesterday's meeting, I brought up the subject of compulsory transfer by the Secretary of the Interior, leading up to the question of whether there ought to be any compulsion. That precise question is one on which we shall seek a referendum of the Indians. But I clearly explained to you yesterday my own views which were that this feature of the compulsory transfer of the allotment to the community is not necessary to the Bill, although I pointed out that there might arise conditions where a tribe might wish there were some compulsion.

Now I will speak both to Mr. White Man and to our friend who was out of order. If and when this compulsory feature is stricken from the Bill and transfer is made wholly voluntary so that an allottee may stay in or stay out, entirely as he prefers, then the decision as to whether or not this Bill goes into effect rests with the individual allottee whose property is in question—not even with the tribe but the ultimate individual can veto it.

Coming around to tribal action, I remind all of you that there are Indians in many states who are profoundly concerned with this Bill—in Oklahoma, California, Arizona, North Carolina, in the country all over as well as in the Northwest. If at the end there should be tribes who do not want this Bill that is their own affair. Such tribes would not have the right and I am sure they would not have the desire to forbid other tribes from having the Bill if other tribes wanted it. Let me be explicit. It would be the easiest thing in the world to simply put an amendment at the end of this whole Bill and say that, just as the New York State Indians are not included, so the Crow Indians are not included in it.

And, I assure the Crow Delegation and any other delegation that when they go back to their people and take a referendum and if the majority of their people want to be shut out of this Bill, we will do all in our power to get them shut out.

Applause.

Of course, they will have to know, that, as we say, "You can't be both in and out at the same time" and the tribe which finally chooses, after this Bill is perfected, not to take advantage of it and not to have anything to do with it, would be making a serious choice—wise or unwise—and important. I would make the suggestion that before any tribe decides whether to stay in or get out of this Bill, the thing to do is to work over the Bill and try to get it the kind of Bill the tribe wants.

Applause.

I believe you will all agree that this is the first time in the history of the Indians that an administration which also controls both houses of Congress came to the Indians on an important legislative matter, requesting them to assist in drafting the Bill; submitted the Bill to them for a referendum, and told them that it was just up to them. The power was in them. It never happened before.

Applause.

Now, we don't want any praise or gratitude on account of this. We are only doing our duty.

Applause.

What we do want is that the Indians and their councils and their leaders shall do the thing we are asking: study the Bill, help us make it right if it is not right; help us change it so that it is right and will meet conditions, and we desire that they shall do that and not simply close their minds and say, "We are not going to do anything." And, this Congress is working just the way that I want you to work. I am not suggesting that you are not working. You are working on the Bill. And I want to wind up by saying again, when a large crowd of people gather about an important thing; when the ideas begin to bank up in their heads and their feelings become intense, they are not always polite. There is no reason why they should be. Let us just be ourselves and kick each other around as much as we want to. That is all good.

Applause.

MR. SHEPARD: I now call on the Chairman of the Crow Creek Delegation.

CROW CREEK CHAIRMAN: Mr. Chairman, I will have to ask you to excuse me. I will have one of my delegates speak for me. Mr. Joe Irving.

MR. SHEPARD: That is quite all right. Mr. Joe Irving will you come forward please?

MR. IRVING: Mr. Chairman. I often thought of what Mr. Collier's politics was. Some told me he was a Democrat and others told me he was a Republican. I always thought he was a Socialist, because the whole idea as to self-government, according to what it says in the Bill, is Socialism. Now, as my time is very limited I am going to come right to the point. The main objectionable point in this Bill. I have had a taste of community life. When I was a little boy my tribe used to live in a community, and I am pretty sure I would not like to go back to it. Now, it is a rather long discussion about the part of the Bill, but time is getting short and I am not going to say any more, and in the other section of the Bill, the second section, ahead of section three, is all hinged on the third section.

If that part of the Bill was cut off I do think that more would be willing to adopt this new policy. I do not believe that in a highly civilized country they would stand to give one man too much power over a downtrodden people. In this Bill it gives the Commissioner of Indian Affairs power to take away from one Indian and give to another Indian, if he so desires. Now everybody knows that is not right. That is the United States, and according to this Bill if it were passed we could not exercise our own rights and we might just as well live in Russia. Well, I have not got much time for further discussion. If I had to discuss this matter in detail it would take me until tomorrow. It is that point that Fort Thompson and Crow Agency is now objecting to. If that point from the Bill is removed, I do not think that we would object to the Commissioner's policy. That is all. I thank you.

MR. CHAIRMAN: If the chair may have the liberty of speaking half a minute, I want to say, with full respect to Mr. Irving's right to say anything he wishes to, the one thing the Bill does not do is to take land away from somebody and give it to somebody else. Now, I want to call on the Chairman of the Flandreau delegation. Who is speaking for Flandreau?

MR. JESSE WHITE MAN, Flandreau, S. Dak.: Mr. Chairman, Commissioner, Staff and Delegates, ladies and gentleman: I am a representative for the delegation of the Flandreau Indians. Flandreau is a very small place, just like myself. I will leave the land question to the other delegates. It seems to me that the next in importance or even greater importance to all Indians is the matter of their future education. The education today needs quite a bit of repairing. We have already found out from our present system of education that the Indian as a student going into the colleges—the result is so many of our Indian boys and girls are failures in college. It would be wrong to blame the student. Something must be done, as something is wrong in regard to the previous training. So therefore it is just as important for all parents to look into it and they should have a voice in regard to their education. We should have a better system, better preparation for the student to enter college, or university.

Some years ago, I do not remember how long—three or four years ago—Congress ordered that all academic or vocational and non-reservation schools should have teachers with degrees and did we get them? I will say no. I want to mention just one school and that is where I came from. We have some instructors that are not even high school graduates. From some particular departments when the students go into colleges they are failures because of their improper instruction.

At this point I wish to say that I am very much in favor of the new program that is being put out. The program indicates that Indians will have a voice in their property or anything else that concerns them. Therefore, I believe I am very much in favor of the new system, especially of education. That is the only way we will have a voice in our education. In the present system, those people who are in the Civil Service will have jobs to go on unless their status is changed.

One more thing and I will be through. I want to say that if I am not mistaken, according to the new program the Indians of the United States, as a whole, will have an increase of land in the amount of something like forty thousand acres each year, instead of a decrease.

I said enough now because I belong to a small country and I am a small man myself. I thank you for your kind attention.

MR. SHEPARD: I will now call on the Chairman of the Fort Berthold delegation.

FROM AUDIENCE: Mr. Beauchamp is our spokesman.

Mr. Beauchamp chooses interpreter.

MR. BEAUCHAMP, Fort Berthold: Friends: The Fort Berthold delegation is not prepared to make any expression one way or another at this time. We are enjoying, however, the talks and the discussions that we have had in this convention. The more we learn from you and the more instructions we get from our Government officials, the more we believe we are getting the very best information we can secure so that we will be able to go back to our homes and take up these things seriously with every individual of our Reservation. Now the rest of our time allotted to this delegation we will donate to the tribe.

MR. SHEPARD: That is the shortest speech of the afternoon but as we are a little behind time we will go right ahead and call on the next delegation, from Fort Peck.

MR. WETSIT, Fort Peck: Mr. Chairman and Honorable Commissioner of Indian Affairs and his staff and my fellow Tribesmen: I am very grateful to present here at this great gathering today. There are 2,550 Indians of the Fort Peck Reservation of which I am a representative here today. But, I want you to understand that I am speaking as an individual and not to make any final decision or to make any endorsement of any program at this time.

Well, on the Fort Peck Reservation we own at this time 1,250,000 acres of land today, in the last 20 years up to today, there are 111 landless Indians living on the Fort Peck Reservation, and I just stated a while ago we own one and a quarter million acres—that is the last property we have got today. Therefore, we feel that something must be done to safeguard further loss of our property. We feel that if we can live all these years—eighty some odd years since the Government has been keeping us in the corrals, and living up to this time, why we feel we can take another chance.

Applause.

We feel a drastic change is necessary and if we can live on that old policy we can take our chance on another policy. I want to remind you of our great grandfathers in the history. Take in the year 1851, there was eight or nine tribes here gathered at Fort Laramie, just similar to this gathering here today, and I am thankful that we are fortunate enough, after eighty some odd years, that we are called here and recognized as human beings, to consider our business for the future. You all know, recently the white people were hollering about "New Deal" and now I think it is about time that we are entitled to a new deal for our Indian people. Now, what I want to state to you at this time is, we came here for business and for the last two days Mr. Collier, our Commissioner, has made it very clear to us. He told us that he framed a Bill which would make life a little bit easier than what it has been in the past, and now, I think we should all get down and put on our thinking caps and see if we could frame up something.

This is the past, and now, I think we should all get down and put on our thinking caps and see if we could frame up something.

This is the first time in the history of our Indian people that they are recognized. They come to us and say "What is it you want now?" Now, Mr. Collier has said we can throw the Bill to one side. What do we offer in its place that is better? Now it is on behalf of the Fort Peck delegation that I want to state that we haven't got together. There is different objectionable features in the Bill that we are not quite clear on and therefore we have not decided to take any final action at this time, but in any action we are going to take, it would be subject to the approval of our people at home, after we make them understand what is made to us understood here at this convention. I thank you.

MR. SHEPARD: Now, the next speaker is the representative of the Fort Totten delegation. 10 minutes. Come right up.

MR. CHARLIE BLACKBIRD, Fort Totten: Mr. Chairman, Honorable Commissioner and official executives. For the past two days we have been taking up the work of having the Howard-Wheeler Bill interpreted to the delegates from the different tribes of different Reservations, and I am sure that each and every member of the delegations from the different Reservations have at least understood parts of the Bill as it is presented and as near as I can understand the interpretation of the Bill there are parts in the Bill I suppose that each member of the delegations have a little difficulty in understanding, simply for the reason that parts of the Bill, what effect will it have on the different Reservations.

I do not commit myself to say that I am opposed to the new land policy program of the Commissioner of Indian Affairs, and neither does the other members of my delegation who represent the Indians of the Devils Lake Indian Reservation have any objections to the Bill. Before we were delegated to come to the regional tribes conference, members of our local Indian Reservation stated that before we were sent here be sure and listen to it. "The effects of the Bill, if it has anything to do with our Reservation we would like to hear something about it when you get back."

I noticed that before we were sent here there were many of the people from my Tribe who stated that if the Bill had no tendency to deprive the Indians of the holdings, that he has on certain Reservations, well, it would be agreeable. We have at one time previously taken up the work under the Circular letter of January 20, 1934 and the problems that were brought up before the General Council on Devils Lake Indian Reservation had also to deal with Indians' interest on other Indian Reservations, and under that question we merely took up the work of answering the Circular of January 20, 1934. This work was done before we had any knowledge of what Howard and Wheeler was giving to us.

So I, myself, have wondered as to just what effect this Bill will have on the interests of Indians on other Reservations. We have still tomorrow to discuss the balance of the work that is still left in the Bill, and from the work of tomorrow, explaining or interpreting the balance of what is left in the Bill, I suppose we can all learn something more so that when we leave here we will be able to go back to our Indian Reservation and say that the work being done here was in accordance with the work that we had taken up previously. At the conclusion of the Plains Indians' Congress I hope that there will be attached in the meetings of the Congress that the Government can guarantee us in some way that it will live up to its obligations and everything that was taken up in regard to their new land policy.

DR. ROE CLOUD: Now, while we are getting ready for the next speaker, who will be from the jurisdiction of the Pine Ridge Agency, South Dakota, if the employee who has charge of the lights is here, I wish he would turn on the lights. Let's have more light on the subject.

MR. JACOB WHITE COW KILLER, Pine Ridge: If the chairman does not object, I would like to talk in the Indian language. (*William Fire Thunder interprets the English.*) When the Pine Ridge council selected me as a delegate to come to attend this Congress, it was with the idea of coming here and listening so that I could take back to them what the policies were. I was not sent here to pass on any questions that were discussed. I wish to tell here just how I see the picture according to the presentation made by Mr. Collier.

The question that confronts us and all the Congress is that Mr. Collier draws us a picture of the Bill and presents the acceptable features, or good features, to us all the way through. Now, if that Bill becomes a law and is accepted by the people what will happen then? The question I see is that what has been presented by Mr. Collier as the good features of the Bill will never get through Congress as a whole. There will be some features added and some stricken off it before it reaches its final end. Will the Commissioner go behind this Bill supporting it as it is all the way through?

I also observe another thing and that is this: After I take back the provisions of the Bill to my people and present the good points to them and we accept it whole-heartedly and the Bill becomes a law in an entirely different form. I see that Mr. Collier will be criticized. I also observe another probable thing and that is this: That what the Republican Party has been doing in the past has been all torn to pieces by the Democratic Party, and naturally there will be a large opposition to what Mr. Collier is trying to do.

What is in the minds of the delegation that has been sent here from Pine Ridge is this: That when this Congress comes to an end, we will go back to our people and present to them all the different discussions that have taken place here. Then we will take final action as to whether we shall accept or reject the program.

I also feel that this Bill may be constructed for the best interests of the Indians and yet within four years from now there will be the biggest battle that has ever taken place in the administration of our affairs, and Mr. Collier's program will be fought by the Republican Party to a bitter end. I also know another thing to be a fact and that is this: That if we go back to our people and present to them the discussions here—discuss them among ourselves, analyze them, and digest them—then when the Bill comes out in a law in entirely different form, I know that my people will call me a big liar.

I do not want to take up any more of my allotted time because the Pine Ridge delegation has submitted some questions to be answered. When those questions are to be answered I will use the reminder of my time then.

DR. ROE CLOUD: The Chair acknowledges its mistake in omitting one of the delegations. The promise was that they should come in alphabetical order. The delegation omitted was Lower Brule and, if they are here, we shall hear from them now, apologizing for our mistake.

MR. GEORGE YELLOW, Lower Brule: I have nothing to say to the audience on this side, but I have to these people up here on the platform and I am going to face them and I want the interpreter to face them too. The first thing I want to say is this: I want to thank these officials for bringing to us a gigantic measure which, to me, is very important. In my heart I believe that it is the right thing for an Indian and a white man to stand together. What I have reference to is that in the past we have never had a friend. I believe that we have a friend that we can stand together with now. It is unbelievable that he can call such a Congress here of the Plains tribes to discuss this important matter and I do not believe there is any fraud or wrong concerning it.

I also observe with reference to the allotment system that ever since we have been governed by the white people, the white man has been reaching into my pockets and robbing me of everything except the soles of my shoes. I want to talk right straight to the Commissioner and tell him that the people I am representing are living in conditions that are very deplorable. According to the allotment system, trust patents were issued and some fee patents have been issued, but I have found that the land for which a trust patent was issued does not actually belong to me. What I fear is this: That within three or four years from now I will lose all of my holdings and my interests and my property.

I wish to thank my people for sending me here to listen and observe what has taken place here so that I can take it back to them for action.

SUPT. TIDWELL: The question arises with me that the Winnebago Tribe, having four delegations here, might be entitled to four representative speakers.

DR. ROE CLOUD: I am instructed as Chairman to say that we will hear from the Winnebago jurisdiction as one.

SUPT. TIDWELL: That was not true of the Crow Creek and Lower Brule Reservations. That is one jurisdiction.

DR. ROE CLOUD: The Chair rules that we will hear from Winnebago as one this time because we have only seventy minutes left and there are a certain number to be heard from.

SUPT. TIDWELL: We will abide by your ruling.

DR. ROE CLOUD: The next delegation to be heard is Rocky Boy.

MR. MALCOM MITCHELL from Rocky Boy: I can't say very much because our land is different from those of other tribes. Our land is not allotted. It is tribal land, and what this new plan, what we hear, it is nothing that is going to hurt our Reservation, so we are just going to put our foot in it. That is all I have to say.

Applause.

The Chairman, DR. ROE CLOUD: The next delegate to be heard from is Rosebud Indian Agency under Supt. Roberts, and unless we have time enough to hear from both this representative will speak for Yankton.

MR. SAM LAPOINTE of Rosebud: Mr. Chairman, may I have the privilege of interpreting for myself.

DR. ROE CLOUD: Granted.

MR. LAPOINTE: I haven't very much to tell you because we don't know yet what we are going to do. We are in the deep sea and for the last two days, this is the third day, we have been hearing, listening to the discussions and propounding of Mr. Collier. I don't know but what we should give an Indian name to Mr. Collier. I think we had better call him the Iron Man because I know he has worn out every interpreter we have got. The Rosebud delegation is not at liberty to make any decision one way or another here, and whatever individual opinions we may have, I don't think we dare express that.

The instructions we have from home are that we are to listen, thresh out the whole thing and bring the meat home and leave the bones up here and so that is what we are going to do, and I am very sorry, Mr. Collier, that we can not say, one way or the other at this time. Now, we have heard quite a bit about this new program of the Commissioner's. He was at Rosebud in the last six weeks. I tell you Rosebud put one over you fellows because we had the Commissioner the first part of December at our Agency. We put one over on you fellows. Pine Ridge got a taste of that too, so we know something about the program since the first of December, and individually and collectively different times we have tried to study and study and study and the more we study the less we know.

That is the situation we have, but now I think, since I have been here for the past two days and this is the third day, and personally, I am not talking for the tribe, I am talking not for the delegation, but personally, this is my decision. So far in the last three days, I have been convinced that there are two sections that could be worked on our Reservation to good advantage. One is the education system. We need it, oh! The worst way. We know it and nobody knows that as well as ourselves. Then the land tenure, with a few modifications. That could be worked on our Reservation too. Now, then the other two, I hate even to look at them. I don't know whether we can look at it at all or not: self-government at this time because we are very lacking in material—good material—men as leaders.

We have now on our Reservation a population of 6200 Indians. I do not think we can find any man that would take hold of or that will make a success of it at this time. Now, I tell you, in every critical crisis point in history there has always been the rise of the man of the hour and now for the last three or four months we have tried to find some man that will rise up to be the man of the hour and we cannot find him. This is very sad. I am sure that there are some phases that could be worked, so the only thing I got to tell you now is that we cannot come to any decision soon.

Personally, I want to tell you this makes me feel pretty bad; back two or three days, Friday I guess it was, this program according to what Mr. Collier was repeating at that time, he said that he heard that some of our Missionaries had felt that this program was going to put our Indians back, way back 50 years into Heathenism and savagery. Well, I just laughed to myself. Imagine Henry Roe Cloud going back 50 years. I would just like to see him. I remember the first time I saw Henry was when he was a little boy and I was a young man and we were going to Santee. I guess he did not change much but I would like to see how we would look to go back 50 years, back to Heathenism. That is clear out of the question, for our Indian people of today. I am going to tell you something. If you white people were in our position 50 years ago you could not make as much advancement as we have made in the last 50 years. It took you people 2,000 years to be where you are now and you know we are almost up to you now. Here is the sad feature of the whole thing. Mr. McGregor is a good friend of mine, Mr. Roberts is a good friend, Mr. Baker is a good friend, I think a lot of them. I do not want to say anything to hurt their feelings. The Indian used to be at one time a self-supporting citizen, had his own government, had his own system of living. Under their own system they were intelligent people. They lived independently, depending on nobody. Initiative was something natural with them, but here today look at our Indian race. No initiative whatever there, and when I look at my people I almost cry to think that we had no man to take hold and go on. We have not degenerated below that, but that has been taught us through our people by the systems, bureaucracy, absolutism, holding the Indians down. You know I worked for the Government 26 years and served in the war and look at my condition now, but I am no longer working for the Government, thanks to Mr. C. J. Rhoads. After 26 years in the Service, because you have no college degree, therefore you are dismissed from the Service.

MR. CHAIRMAN: You have about one minute to go.

MR. LAPOINTE: I have ten minutes because I have been interpreting for myself.

MR. CHAIRMAN: Your using the interpreter's time is like using the tribal funds for administration purposes.

MR. CHAIRMAN: Next jurisdiction to be heard from is the Shoshone, Mr. Haas, Superintendent, and the representative will come forward and speak for the Shoshone delegation.

CHARLES A. DRISCO: Mr. Chairman, Members of the Washington Staff, ladies and gentlemen: At this time we are noncommittal but we are going to do our utmost to convey the interpretations of this Bill to our folks back home.

MR. CHAIRMAN: We thank the Shoshone delegate for giving us that time. Now we will hear from the Sisseton people.

MR. AMOS ONE ROAD, Sisseton, S. Dak.: Mr. Chairman, fellow members of the Aborigines. I am happy to be here, and I want to say that I am not an Atheist. The Arians and the Anglo Saxon are here. Plato made this remark one thousand years B.C.: "The acquisition of knowledge is a good thing. The cultivation of Science and Philosophy is a good thing, but there is something infinitely more important than all these, it is the rectification through that mysterious operation we call sympathy, emotion." That is why you are here. My delegates, the Sisseton and Wahpeton people are here, and I wish to say that my mind goes back into the history of the past.

I am like Will Rogers, all that I know is what I read in the papers, and I want to say that this problem, this Indian solution, is and was begun when those Puritans landed at Plymouth Rock and fell upon their knees and then upon the Aborigines and said—"We thank thee God that we can whirl these Savages to Eternity."

I want to say that the Sioux Indians have been in contact for many years, ever since the early French explorers, and I want to make it short. I could talk here all afternoon, but that is not the question. There was a settlement known as the Hazelwood Republic from 1851 to 1862 at Granite Falls. That was wiped out by the outbreak of 1862, and thereby all our treaties, the ten mile strip, was confiscated by the Federal Government. But this Robert E. Lee, the Revolutionary general, was in the same category. His land was stripped off and yet the heirs received that land back again. Why could we not then? I am going right down to this place. In March 3, 1872, Congress ceased to recognize the American Indian as a separate nation. It ceased to recognize their treaties.

What I am getting at is this; we have our Commissioner of Indian Affairs here and the Secretary of the Interior is not here, but way back in 1871, the Secretary of the Interior, Delano, and Commissioner of Indian Affairs, Smith, came to Sisseton and consulted with those people and promised to make a codified set of laws governing those Indian people in Dakota Territory, doing away with Indian chiefs and substituting a form of government towards American civilization. In 1876 the Sissetons went to Washington. Gabriel Renville was elected head chief. After his speech around; and only yesterday it was the great figure of allotment in which the heirs were so numerous; he arose and made his resignation as head chief of those bands. Those people elected their magistrates, their officers, constables, their farmers and other ones.

They had ox teams, hitched them to their plows, and their women went out with little babies on their backs and went forth with joy. With their ox teams and with the brush of a certain tree they harrowed the land. What I am getting at is this. In the 1867 treaty there is a clause which says that the man who fences and plows two or three acres will receive an allotment, and it was. That allotment is different from the Dawes act, and what I am getting at is this; that under the allotment system this land will be handed down to the descendants of the owner and will never be sold. When the blood expires, it will return to the United States for a consideration. That was good, but we ought to substitute that treaty of 1867 with that allotment, in order to live. The officials tell me, "Hold on to your land," and I am going to do it. Now, am I going to throw my land into that jackpot? I am a citizen I think, and so are my people and yours. I stood here on the mountain top, looking at the profile of Washington, who said years ago, "They, the poor wretches have no press through which their grievances may be related," and when one side of the question is related, it becomes obviously unbalanced and I want to say this. That if the Bill becomes true this is the last and greatest treaty that will be made and it will terminate all previous treaties and it will be defunct and the mighty dinosaur, which has been defunct for ten thousand.

Applause.

MR. CLEMENT SMITH: Friends, I have been listening to Mr. Collier's description of this Bill for several days.

FRANCIS RED TOMAHAWK from Standing Rock: Mr. Chairman, Standing Rock Delegation protests their position. They are next in alphabetical order.

MR. SMITH: I withdraw because you precede me.

MR. TOMAHAWK: Mr. Chairman, ladies and gentlemen of the audience. Before starting, we had a list of questions which we wanted to read into the record but our time is so limited at this time and the meeting is limited also, and we are therefore handing these questions in to be incorporated into the records, and as I want to speak on something else in connection with these, outside of these questions, I will not read them. Now then. We are here, a great many people from different Reservations all together here to consider a piece of legislation which the Commissioner himself, upon being questioned last night, could not give an explanation clear enough to clear the issue. How can people who have no legal training understand a piece of complicated legislation intended for them and for them to discuss in a short, very brief period, and understand the whole situation clearly, I can not understand.

We, the Standing Rock Delegation present here, considered the plans as outlined to us in a circular under date of January 20, this year. Up to that time we had not received a copy of that Bill. We did not know what the contents of that Bill were. How were we to know what the provisions were? But, in spite of that handicap we desired a change from the old policy. We wanted something new, something constructive, something that would elevate the status of the Indian of the United States to become a part of the economic life of the nation, and not dead weight upon that economic factor. Now, before the allotments on our Reservation the whole Reservation belonged to all of us. We each and every one had an equal share in that Reservation. Whatever we derived from that particular land out of leases, etc., right of ways, etc., was equally distributed and it worked to our advantage.

About 1904 after the Milwaukee [Railroad] had penetrated into our Reservation and cut it in two, the United States officials came out there and began to preach allotment to us. They, you might say, coerced our people into the allotment system which was their downfall at this time. At that time we had about three million acres or more. Today we have not got half of that. That is the evil of the allotment system. Now, the question uppermost in the minds of the Standing Rock people, which is worrying them, is this. The United States, through the provisions in various treaties entered into with the Sioux nations, provides that they would give us a certain amount of land, that they would hold that land under restriction for a stated period of time. Upon the expiration of that trust period they would give a patent in fee free of all charge and encumbrance. That time arrived, and the officials saw that the people were not in a condition to take a patent in fee and assume the burdens of responsibility of the citizens of the state, and therefore, under Presidential proclamation by President Hoover, the trust period was extended to cover a number of states for a period of ten years.

Now then, how long have we got before that trust patent is to end. Not very far. About eight years or a little more, and at the end of that time our people will not have become very much more educated than they are now, and it will necessitate another extension of the trust period as I see it. Now then. The Standing Rock face a change from the old system to a new system, but the provisions contained in the first title of this proposed legislation are too drastic a change. It is too abrupt a change from the present order of things, and it will do a certain amount of harm I believe which, while not being permanent, will do quite a little bit of injustice. I think that the order that we ought to adopt would be to salvage the very best parts of the old, cut out the undesirable parts, and what our people want is this. They are not adapted to the white man's culture. They live under a different culture of their own and within a short space of time in which they are trying to adapt themselves to the white man's culture they can not compete with the white people, and therefore a certain amount of protection must be given our people, and therefore what we want is this. A permanent trust placed upon all lands owned by the Indians. Somewhat on the order that the preceding speaker stated just a little while ago.

And, the educational features of that provision of the proposed law. We have no objection to that at all, because we need something like that, and I think it is just the thing we need. Now then, the other provision, the fourth provision. I do not know. That has to do with law, and as I said a bit ago, we haven't got legal training and how far we can carry that to a success is doubtful. Now, Mr. Chairman, I ask for an extension of time to explain what I have just said.

CHAIRMAN: There are only fourteen minutes left to hear two more delegations so we can not allow you any more time.

DR. ROE CLOUD: A while ago I was empowered to say from high authority that if any tribe wants to accept any part of this Bill and initiate that portion on their Reservation, the problem of lack of leadership which Sam LaPointe spoke of need not interfere. Adoption of some parts may be deferred until you have leaders and introduced them.

The next jurisdiction is Turtle Mountain.

FRANK WILSON, Pine Ridge: We don't want an interpreter in Indian. That is a waste of time.

MR. LAPOINTE: I will interpret for the speaker.

DR. ROE CLOUD: The time is very short. Please speak very fast.

JOHN AZURE, Turtle Mountain: Friends: At the present time our Reservation is twelve miles long and six miles wide and in that Reservation there are more than three thousand people. The better half of this Reservation is now owned by the white people. So we are having a hard time. Something must be done so that we can get along better than this.

We have been here for three days now trying to understand the explanation of Commissioner Collier. But we did not learn so very much because we do not have the education. When I was first elected to our council I could hardly spell my own name, but still I am trying to do the best I can for my people.

Now the way we understand Mr. Collier's explanation, it sounds rather good to us delegates, but we are not going to say that we are in favor of the new policy or against it. We would like to take the news back to our Indian people and explain everything we have learned to them. After that, if the majority wants to take up this new policy it is up to them.

The only thing now we wish from the Government is to give us help or relief to get a start. The first thing of all we need is education. We have no education on our Reservation. If the Government can work out a plan that helps us out, some way to get us on our feet—that is what we want. I thank you.

DR. ROE CLOUD: The next speaker is from Winnebago.

MR. FELIX WHITE, Winnebago: Mr. Chairman: I want to say that there are four different tribes under this jurisdiction, so that if each of their representatives may say something at this time I won't say very much. They each have different problems. I will just take a half-minute.

DR. ROE CLOUD: The speaker is going to divide his ten minutes among the other speakers from this Reservation.

MR. FELIX WHITE: We were sent up here to be open-minded and we have tried our best to be, although some things are not clear. I am praying that tomorrow I will have a clear vision of all things.

I want to express appreciation that the Commissioner brought this ball of light out here. We are probably the last on the list—last but not least. I believe Adam and Eve were Winnebagos. We are thankful that we came up here. We have learned a lot and will learn some more.

MR. ELWOOD HARLAN, Winnebago: Mr. Chairman: I might say here that our jurisdiction did not get a square deal. I want to state that in 1874 we had a land proposition similar to the one that is now under consideration by all of you. At that time we were given a certificate of occupancy title which would allow you to live on your land, die and allow your future generations to occupy it, but could not sell it. But what happened? The treaty that we had negotiated with the Government gave Congress the power—the Treaty of 1865. Politicians changed the good law we had into an allotment law in 1882. We had 300,000 acres of the most valuable agricultural land in the State of Nebraska. Today we have 25,000 acres.

I want to say for my people that I am not going to make any decision. I am going to go home with the good news of what I have learned here, that we are not going to be losing anything to try this new deal.

MR. WILLIAM WHIPPLE, Santee: For the reason that we Santee did not have any tribal council about this Bill at all as the rest of the Reservations did. More than half our tribe is scattered among other tribes. We feel that we ought to get the opinion of all the others before we give a decision.

DR ROE CLOUD: The next speaker will be from Yankton.

MR CLEMENT SMITH, Yankton.

Mr. Wilson objected to Mr. Smith, saying that Yankton was represented by Rosebud.

MR SMITH: Is there another Indian who wants to take my place or is my time up?

DR. ROE CLOUD: Go ahead.

MR. SMITH: Mr. Chairman: I don't like to say very much but I have been listening to Mr. Collier the last few days, and, to be brief, he has been telling us that the Bill which has been under discussion has as its purpose to make it as hard as possible to do wrong and as easy as possible to do right. We have also been talking about the allotment system. He tells us about the allotment system and says that the purpose of the allotment system and the laws that govern the allotment system were made as easy as possible to do wrong and as hard as possible to do right. That is my understanding of what he has conveyed to this council.

Of course, I realize that the things that are contained in that Bill would baffle the brains of a Huxley or a Darwin, and I contend that it must be revised. But, if Mr. Collier will listen to us Indians and let us revise it, I think we will strike pay dirt.

DR. ROE CLOUD: I want to thank you Indians for listening and I think there are controversial matters in this program. I am glad you are going home to submit the whole thing to the councils. I pronounce this meeting adjourned.

Adjourned.

Questions from Crow Creek Delegation.

QUESTION: This Bill abrogates the treaty laws agreements, and laws of Congress, especially the allotment system, but the Indian became a citizen under the Act of June 2, 1924 (Public Law No. 175, 68th Congress). Thereby he has the full privilege of any other citizen of the United States, and is bound by the United States Constitution, and is protected by the constitution, amendment Article 5, which among other things said, "Nor be deprived of life, liberty or property without due process of law nor shall private property be taken for public use without just compensation." How will this Bill affect individual property and land?

ANSWER—MR. COLLIER: The constitution guarantees that just compensation must be given for any private property taken for public use. The new Bill and any act under the new Bill must conform with the constitution. If this act did not conform with the constitution the Courts would hold that it was void. I have already explained that the provision for transferring Indian lands to the community in Section 8 of title 3 will be amended so as to make such transfers voluntary. In any case the Courts would protect the right of any person to fair compensation for any lands transferred to the community.

QUESTION: Government will buy land for the landless Indians. From what funds will these additional lands be bought?

ANSWER—MR. COLLIER: The Bill provides that a fund of $2,000,000 may be appropriated each year to buy lands for landless Indians and Indians with insufficient lands. This money will be paid out of the United States Treasury.

QUESTION: Will the Government give the money on gratuity or a reimbursable basis?

ANSWER—MR. COLLIER: The Bill provides that the money will be appropriated on a gratuity basis. That is with respect to money for the purchase of land. The Bill also provides for a $10,000,000 fund which will be loaned to Indians for the purchase of cattle, the improvement of land and other purposes. This money will be handled through chartered communities and loaned without interest for periods not more than thirty years.

QUESTION: If this Bill passes would it stop our suit now pending before the Court of Claims and would it be a deadline of claiming any damages for property and land?

ANSWER—MR. COLLIER: This Bill would not interfere in any way with any claims or suits against the Government.

QUESTION: What advice would you give if any money is recovered—what will you do with the money?

ANSWER—MR. COLLIER: I assume that you are referring to the General Sioux claims. Any recovery would probably be apportioned among the different Reservations. If any of the Indians entitled to any of this money are in a chartered community, they will be given the right to veto any expenditure of this money, and the money may be turned over to the community to be distributed or spent as the community charter may provide. Claims collected by tribes to which no charters have been granted may be spent by the United States Government for administrative expenses and other purposes, as has been the case in the past.

QUESTION: Will the Administration try to push this Bill through regardless as to the wants of this Congress, or is it optional and awaiting results?

ANSWER—MR. COLLIER: The Bill itself is optional in nearly all its provisions and Indians who do not wish to take advantage of these provisions are not under any compulsion to do so. However, if a majority of the members of your Reservation after thoroughly discussing and understanding this Bill want to submit an amendment that this Bill shall not apply to that Reservation, I will recommend to Congress that such an amendment be accepted. It should be understood however that none of the benefits of the Bill will be available to an Indian Reservation that is excluded by such an amendment. Of course if any Indian Reservation thinks that it can get a special law applicable to itself, instead of this Bill, it can try to do so, but the experience that several tribes have had in trying to get such special legislation shows that Congress is too busy to pass a special law for each tribe that wants a special treatment.

Monday, March 5, 1934

Morning Session

Morning Session opened by Mr. Woehlke, Chairman, at 9:45 a.m.

MR. WOEHLKE: The session of the Congress is now open. Are the interpreters ready; have they their throats oiled?

Answers: "Yes."

Now, my friends, the Government is considering this Congress of such importance that the wheels of the Government in Washington have almost stopped. Everybody is here. The last arrival from Washington came this morning and I now have the pleasure to introduce to you the Assistant Commissioner of Indian Affairs, the Honorable William Zimmerman.

Before we proceed to the business of the day, I would like to tell you very briefly what the Northern Cheyenne said to me last night and what I said to them. They said, "We are allotted only two years, and our Reservation is now in the condition into which you would like to put a lot of other Reservations which already have lost their land. We were allotted only two years ago and we have lost only four allotments through fee-patents." The Superintendent rises to correct me and says only two.—None, still better.

But, he says, "Already we have a large number of dead allotments and these dead allotments mostly cover good land, farming land in the creek bottoms." "Now," he says, "If the land section of that Bill will keep our lands for us and save the dead allotments for us, we are for it, and if the credit is to build new houses with, then we are for it." "But," they said, "We are afraid of that self-government section. We are afraid of those chartered communities and we are afraid of them because we have no young men yet who can do all that work that we have to do under this self-government section, and we are afraid of that."

So I said to them, "Under this Bill your land in that Reservation, that is all yours now. Your tribal land and your allotted land will be protected." As I said, if this Bill is adopted the credit section was made for people like you who are in a position to and willing to help themselves. I said to them, "You don't have to be afraid of self-government. All of that self-government comes into force only as you want it. This Bill, if it were passed just as it is, merely sets the self-government table. It puts out a table and puts all kinds of self-government dishes on from pie and roast beef down to a plate of soup. The Government says to you, 'Here it is, all the dishes. Step up to the table and eat if you want to.' And the Government says to you, 'Be careful. You have not had a dish of self-government for a hundred years; so don't eat too much at the start. It might make you sick. You don't have to eat anything on that self-government table unless you want to, and if you want to you can start with a plate of soup and gradually work your way up to the roast beef as you are able to digest it.'" So that is what the Northern Cheyenne said to me and what I said to them and that is all. But it took us four and a half hours to say it.

Now, I have heard that a great many of the old warriors feel that because this is an Indian Congress and not a white man's congress, we should have some talks in the Indian languages and I think that is a good request. So beginning at ten o'clock we will hear from the old men in their own language for brief periods each. We are now asking the various delegations to unite and select the older man who is to speak between eleven and twelve.

FRANK WILSON, Pine Ridge: Mr. Chairman: We put questions here on this table in the last gathering and we want to continue on that.

MR. WOEHLKE: We will.

MR. RED TOMAHAWK, Standing Rock: Mr. Chairman: During yesterday's council I asked the Commissioner that we be allowed to put into the record a report of the tribal business council and he said we could.

MR. WOEHLKE: That will be done.

MR. RED TOMAHAWK: I have the minutes here and will turn them in.

MR. WOEHLKE: Yesterday afternoon I was sorry I had to be a little harsh with a gentleman who spoke out of turn and I believe that this gentleman who was out of turn yesterday should be given an opportunity to speak his mind. Therefore, if that gentleman, who was out of order yesterday afternoon, is in the house, I would be glad to have him come to the platform here and, with your consent, speak five minutes. Is he here? Is Mr. Davidson here?

MR. FIRE THUNDER, Pine Ridge: I think he went home.

MR. WOEHLKE: I am sorry.

Now, a large number of questions that were submitted in writing have so far remained unanswered. We said that we would answer them and we do not want to speak with two tongues. Therefore, I am asking the Commissioner to show us that he is like an iron man and answer some more questions now.

MR. COLLIER: A question from many of the Sioux delegates, about the meaning of section 11, in paragraph E, page 18, of the Senate Bill. This question says: what Indians shall be eligible for membership in a chartered community? What they are troubled about are those Sioux Indians who have allotments and who are living in areas that are now surplus and ceded lands. In order to make the meaning clear we are changing the language. I will read it in the changed form and I think it will be clear to you. "The term Indian as used in this title, specifying the persons to whom charters may be issued, will include all persons of Indian descent: 1st—who are members of any recognized Indian Tribe, band, or nation. 2nd—

who are descendants of any such members of any recognized Tribe, band or Nation, actually residing within the present boundaries of any Indian Reservation." We add this language: "including surplus areas opened to settlement and homestead entry." That is the new language which I think will meet the questions in the minds of the Sioux.

Now in addition to all of those classes, any Indian with one-fourth or more Indian blood may be put into a chartered community if he wants to and in addition still, members may be brought into the community by adoption, by admission if the community wants them. This all has to do with title one, about being a member of a chartered community, and has nothing to do with land holdings. An Indian need not be a member of a chartered community at all and many will never be. Their lands are not disturbed. This only has to do with the self-government feature.

NEXT QUESTION—Lower Brule: Will the Bill affect the rights of Indians in any given Reservation or community to minerals, or anything in the land, oil, gas, etc?

ANSWER: No, but I told one of the delegations last night, I think it was the Blackfeet, that in order to make it clear we had better put in language saying so. If an Indian made relinquishment of his allotment to the community and took title in the community land, he could simply reserve any mineral rights so that they would not go into the community. The title to the minerals would remain with him individually.

STANDING ROCK QUESTION: In the matter of forming a chartered community, the question is what would be considered a reasonable number of adults to justify forming a community?

ANSWER: There is no fixed number. Anything from ten to ten thousand. That is entirely a matter of the local people and the desire of the Indians in the matter of organization.

MR. COLLIER: It is suggested that regarding this amendment about membership in the chartered community that I ask Major Case whether he thinks that meets the situation of the Sioux.

MAJOR CASE: I have gone over the language now proposed as an amendment by the Commissioner of Indian Affairs and I will tell you what I think about it.

This language will protect the people, allottees, in all country or areas opened up out of the 1889 Reservation. It is very clear that the people who live in Bennett, Tripp, Gregory or Mellette counties or the Northern counties opened up out of Cheyenne River or Standing Rock are protected. Now, while I am on my feet I would like to tell the Winnebago delegates that I would like to see them just after we have our mid-day meal, right here.

MR. COLLIER: Now, continuing my answer about the size of the chartered community. It might be some tiny group of Indians who have a body of land. There are tribes with fewer than 100 members in the United States. Again, a whole large jurisdiction might decide to take out a charter as a self-government jurisdiction or a large jurisdiction might decide to break itself down into two, three or four town governments, or again a group of Indians might decide to get a charter for some special purpose, such as forming a stock running association, and the size of the group would be determined accordingly by the Indians.

Another STANDING ROCK QUESTION: This relates to Section 3 of the Bill, Land Title. "Can the community lawfully take jurisdiction over severally owned land and personal property within its confines?" This question has to do with allotments that are kept separate but are continued within the boundaries of an organized community.

The answer is, "Yes," by which I mean this, that the community is an instrumentality of the Federal Government and by agreement between the Community and the Secretary of the Interior the Secretary could delegate to the community his own regulative powers over allotments in severalty. Remember always that the communities are things which the Indians can have or not have and they can take a power of this kind or they can not take it. It is entirely optional. Of course, with respect to the land which the community owns, obviously the community can manage that land, and in this connection Mr. Cohen says it may be well to remind you that an Indian having an allotment which has been fee patented and is therefore unrestricted, could if he desired, exchange that for an allotment of land restricted and under trust and therefore tax exempt.

Under Section 4, a question. "How can judgments against the Indian community be enforced since the property is all in trust or a restricted status?" This means that if an Indian community is sued and judgment obtained against it, how could it be collected, since the lands are not subject to judgment? The answer is, that the judgments could not be enforced if their enforcement meant taking land or capital from the tribe. However, if a tribe wanted to enter into a contract, thereby to take on obligations, and wanted to pledge some income against that contract, and to stipulate that, then with the consent of the Secretary of the Interior, that future income might be made subject to judgment.

Again, under Title 4. The question is difficult to state and may be difficult to answer. It is really under title one because it relates to membership in the community—rights in the community. "Where there is a husband and wife and one of them abandons the community, then what is the status of the children?" The answer is that the children remain members of the community unless the children individually, themselves, abandon it. Any Indian may abandon the community and so may the children, but they are members unless they abandon it.

Then a question concerning the participation of members of the Indian communities in funds derived from suits in the Court of Claims. The answer there is that, as you know, judgments obtained in the Court of Claims are paid into tribal funds. Every member of the tribe—every enrolled member—has his equal equity in those funds. That holds good regardless of whether an Indian is in a community or not in a community, so that the rights of the Indian, in and out of the community, in the matter of these funds would be equal. There would, however, be one important advantage in this matter to those who are in communities, as I explained to the Sioux the other night, in the matter of their Black Hills judgment, if and when they get it. The shares of the tribal fund belonging to the members of the committee would no longer be subject to appropriation by Congress for any and every purpose, but could be sent only with the consent of the community.

Under Section 8 of title one; about chartering of communities, and the question relates to this situation that might arise under the Bill, which provides that when a charter is issued to a tribe, the Secretary of the Interior can not revoke the charter. Only the tribe can revoke its own charter, or Congress can revoke it. The Secretary of the Interior can report a recommendation to Congress recommending that the Charter be revoked.

Now, suppose Congress does not agree with the Secretary and rejects his recommendations and refuses to revoke the charter. The answer is that the charter stands. The Indians can always revoke it. In general throughout this self-government clause, the effort is to put the Secretary of the Interior in a position where, if he wants to change what the Indians are doing under the charter, he has either to convince the Indians or convince Congress. He can not be arbitrary about it.

Another question which is again asked is, "Will Indian restricted land be subjected to attachment?" And the answer has already been given, "No, it will not."

A question is handed in by Foster Thunder Hawk, Rosebud, addressed to Mr. Stewart.

MR. COLLIER: (*reads question*) "Mr. Stewart: I wish you would explain in regard to the exchange of restricted land for a deeded land and where the Indian clog the title and where the state jumps in and says the Indians must pay tax."

MR. FOSTER THUNDER HAWK: The State might say it has to be taxed.

MR. STEWART: Does that involve deed land—alienated land, or land held under restrictions?

MR. THUNDER HAWK: Land held under restrictions to be exchanged for deeded land.

MR. STEWART: The note says, in regard to the exchange of a restricted piece of land for deeded land or a fee patented land—Now, as I asked before, does that involve any alienated land—by alienated I mean taxable land?—and it further goes on and says, where the State jumps in and says the Indians must pay taxes, what will be the outcome?

Now, if I understand the question correctly—

MR. THUNDER HAWK: I think you misunderstood it.

MR. STEWART: I think I have too.

MR. THUNDER HAWK: Restricted land is exchanged for restricted land, but if Mr. McGregor puts the deeded land back into a trust, the Supreme Court says this deeded land could not be put back in trust and there is a tax against it. Would that be involved in this community organization?

MR. RED TOMAHAWK, interpreter, Standing Rock: What he is trying to drive at is this: In exchanges of land between an Indian and a white man, trust land and deeded land, he says that the Supreme Court has held that the State had a right to tax the land and that they could not remove or attach to the deed a clause restricting the alienation of that land once it had been deeded. He says, "Would that matter be involved in any transactions of that kind in the future?"

MR. STEWART: Under the terms of this Bill, I am subject to correction by the lawyers here, provision is made for an Indian on restricted land outside a community or an Indian area we propose to consolidate, to exchange that restricted land with any white owner of land within the area. Now, if you have some restricted land outside and you want to exchange it for land inside that is taxable owned by a white man, you would take over his land unrestricted but he would have to continue to pay taxes on the land that you turned over to him outside the area.

MR. LAPOINTE: That answers the question.

MR. SIEGEL: I would like to add a few words to what Mr. Stewart has already said. The Supreme Court has held that where fee patented land, once subject to taxation, has been purchased for an Indian with restricted funds, the land continues to remain subject to taxation. The Supreme Court did not say that Congress could not exempt that land from taxation. The Supreme Court ruled that whether or not the land should be subjected to tax exemption was a question for Congress to determine. The Supreme Court held that it was not the intention of Congress, after construing the various acts of Congress, to exempt such land from taxation.

Some one asked that this be repeated.

Mr. LaPointe asks to interpret this.

The Supreme Court in this case referred to held that it was not Congress' intention to exempt from taxation land which was once subject to taxation but purchased for an Indian out of funds which were restricted. But the Court made it plain that if Congress intended to exempt the land from taxation it could do so.

Under this act, restricted land is exchanged for fee patented land, the Indian will receive in exchange the right to use the same amount of land or the rental from that land and that land will be free from taxation, or the restricted exchange for a similar piece, land of equivalent value, and it should be made plain in the Act, if it is not plain now, that that land should be free from taxation. I think the gentlemen's question brings up a good point. As the Act reads now, only lands which are acquired for the community or tribe are specifically exempted from taxation. In order to make our intention perfectly plain I think the Act ought to be amended so that restricted land exchanged for fee patented land and not transferred to the community should also continue to remain free from taxation just as the restricted land before.

Applause.

MR. COLLIER: Now we are nearing eleven o'clock and there will be a new order of business. We have only about four minutes more. We are done with answering questions, but I wanted to give one answer which covers a great many questions that have come in. They relate in one way or another to this proviso in land title 3, Section 8, page 31. The matter we have discussed repeatedly. The Bill as drawn gives to the Secretary of the Interior authority to transfer the title of an individual allotment, to transfer that to the community, and compensation without the consent of the allottee.

I have been telling you that we are leading up to a vote on that question as to where you wanted the power to be, whether you want the Secretary to have power to do that, or whether you wanted the Indian to have authority to do it if he wanted to. I am not meaning to say that you will vote on particular proposals in the Bill now, therefore, I am going to pass that over and make an announcement instead. Of course, if you want to vote on this or anything, that is up to the meeting. I am speaking now for the Indian Office. We are going to recommend to the Committees of Congress that this transfer of title by the allottee to the community, this transfer shall be exclusively voluntary and that the compulsion feature shall be stricken out.

Great applause.

I tell you this as a means of not having to answer a large number of separate questions on that point.

DR. ROE CLOUD: We come now to that part of the program where we are to hear from the older Indians in their own language, and it has been suggested that because the Sioux delegation is very large, that we hear from two representatives of the Sioux people. I hope you have talked this over among yourselves and have selected your speaker. Each speaker will be allowed five minutes and we understand that it will be put into the English language for the benefit of the people here.

SAM LAPOINTE: I want to mention that the Rosebud Sioux have selected the son of the oldest Chief on our Reservation, Mr. Edgar Quick Bear.

DR. ROE CLOUD: Interpreter please tell him that when he hears one tap he has only one more minute. When he hears two taps that means it is the end of his speech.

EDGAR QUICK BEAR: (*interpreter, Sam LaPointe*) Mr. Chairman, Honorable Commissioner, my friends on the platform and my people—delegates from all over the country. I see a good many good men here. I am glad to see you. My friends, we of the Indian race are yet very far behind in matters of education, and when it comes down to thinking faculty, you know that we can not compete with the white man. We are not up to the top notch of educational ability.

Applause—mild.

As far back as the Indian race may recall history, and all the dealings with the Government of the United States; in all the treaties and agreements there has always been inserted one insertion that has been a detriment to the Indians all the way through, and that is the insertion of "at the discretion of the Secretary of the Interior." One of the faults arising from the misunderstandings, etc., of the old treaties and agreements, has been this. We have not had the efficient interpretation of all these treaties in the past.

Now, the interpreters will tell us one thing and the real wording of the law when it becomes a law is different from the interpretation, and therefore our people are caused to misunderstand and suffer for it later on. Now, at this meeting, if we are going take action, transact any business, or come to any agreements, let us have a full understanding. The powers and the authority that the Indian may have and that can be exercised; let us have a full understanding of the relationship that we may have with those powers and the authorities he may gain.

There is one thing that I feel thankful for. In the last few minutes of the speaking of Mr. Collier, the proposition is brought up that they will eliminate this giving unlimited power to the Secretary of the Interior as far as Indian matters are concerned. If they would eliminate that, how thankful I would be. Our fathers have instructed us, our fathers have told us, that we must watch our step, every step; there are hundreds and thousands of unscrupulous white men, deceitful. They will deceive us.

Applause.

INTERPRETER speaks: Now, I want to tell my own people. He said this. "Watch your step—because it has come to light that if we had gone on ahead under the same system that we had been coming under, there was an end to that trail not very far ahead, and wisely, somebody has thought out a new way for us. Now, if we are going to accept this new way be careful, think slow, because your action will not only affect us but for generations to come. I thank you."

MR. LUKE GILBERT from Cheyenne River rises: Mr. Chairman, I would like to introduce Joseph Long from Cheyenne River Reservation.

Chairman, DR. ROE CLOUD: I believe it would be well to take this up in the order they are listed on this sheet of paper. Someone asks that they be taken up in alphabetical order.

Slight confusion while several ask for the floor at the same time.

DR. ROE CLOUD continues: We will take them up in the order I have them listed here regardless of alphabetical order.

GENTLEMAN from Standing Rock: Mr. Chairman, Rosebud and Pine Ridge are neighboring Reservations. In fact they are the same locality and conditions that prevail there are about the same. They are so close together that we would like to get a representative opinion from the different localities. I would suggest that we hear from Mr. Daniel Grass Rope of Lower Brule. We have a delegation from Standing Rock but we don't want to hog the whole thing.

Several objections are heard to Mr. Daniel Grass Rope being permitted to speak, but objections are not recognized.

MR. DANIEL GRASS ROPE, Lower Brule: First I want to say, that I see some fine men on the platform and I want to thank them for all that they have done. I do not think I ever saw an assembly, white or otherwise, as big as this, and I am glad to meet you all. I see this great gathering here and I am asked to speak and remember that, and I will remember it, and I remember at the time that I was asked to speak here some time ago that I said this: "Now, my friends, I see many faces and I see that they are all Indians. They may not be Sioux but just the same they are all Indians."

At that time I said there were two or three things for which I came and in that little short talk I gave the other day I said, "My friends, whatever you do, think of the rising generation because it is coming to the time when we have no place for our rising generation." I was afraid, my friends, that we would grasp this thing in a hurry, take hurried action, and suffer from the results later on. That is why I cautioned my people to go slow.

Now I have been hearing the Bill explained and all the good talk and I hear them all through my ears, and I think understand fairly well what it means. For the last few days you have been discussing and listening to this great proposition before us. When I was selected to come here, before started from home there were a number of people, men and women, who came to me and said this to me, "You go there. You represent a lot of people. Be careful what you do. Use your best judgment, and see that you decide for the best interests of the people at home."

Now, my friends, on the platform, I want to address you. All the words that I have heard, my thoughts have been going back to my people at home. In generations back, I know, we know, that there was wild game on which we could live and we could always depend upon that. So, in those days I grew up as a buffalo eater and deer meat was common, but I can see now and look around and there is none of that left. When thinking about these things, I come back to this new deal, your program, and then my thoughts change from what they used to be, and if this talk, all they told us, and if this is good, I hope my friends, the other Indians, will all throw in with me and help me now.

I have just told you a little while ago, that misunderstandings, the inability to grasp these ideas, was among so many of us who did not know where we were. Now, your plan seems to be to enlarge the areas in which we live and in that area our younger generation will have room to roam and do what they please and this is what I want to say to you. Now, I have advised my people to go slow, and think right, and do what is right. I want to say also to those who are in authority that they advised us to join these communities, and our boys will work in these communities. Our boys are unprepared. There is nothing to work with, and I want you to remember that. Thank you.

Applause.

Chairman, DR. ROE CLOUD: Now we come to the next group of speakers, the Blackfeet. We are through with the Sioux Indians. If this man (*meaning Mr. Grass Rope*) is through, they have lost their chance for further speaking.

GENTLEMEN from Blackfeet: We take pleasure in introducing Rides At The Door, representing the Blackfeet.

VOICE FROM AUDIENCE: Mr. Chairman. We have a spokesman from Sisseton and would like to have the chance to get up and talk. He will speak for Sisseton and Devils Lake, practically the same tribe.

Chairman, DR. ROE CLOUD: We can not allow him to speak at this time, but if we have time later, we will give him a chance to speak.

RIDES AT THE DOOr, Blackfeet:

Applause.

Natural Americans and my brothers, who are assembled in this great Congress, and to the gentlemen representing the Interior Department. I hope this great assembly will sympathize with me for this reason. That I am handicapped. I do not understand your English language and I do not know how to write.

We are here because we have gone over the past. When we reach this crisis of our lives we want to be careful always and want to listen very closely. We always want to use our best judgment to forge ahead, and to use it in that way.

The Blackfeet Nation, whom I represent, have cautioned me thus, to listen to everything that is said here and any move that is made in this place, to do it very wisely. I have been here and I have listened very carefully to the things that have been said here, and now I know what to do for myself and my people.

We have been advised by the representative of the Interior Department that community policy which means a new history and a new event in our lives now forthcoming. If we stand by the policy as it is advocated to the Indians of the Northwest—if what is said here is true, it is a word of salvation in our future lives and for our children. If the things that have been said to us here in this assembly, as I have stated before, if they are purely the truth, if the ideas of the program are true in every way, shape or form, it is the best thing that we could abide ourselves by. I have no other way if it is true. I have no other system, no other road by which I could go around it, but I must go into it.

One of the most important things that brought me here is what I am going to say to you today. My people now own a large area of oil land and we have now on our Reservation three producing wells and that is the reason I came here, and I want some law or protection whereby I can always hold that property intact so that no white man can take it away from me.

Applause.

There is one thing that we have here, an opportunity which many of us do not have, and that is the opportunity of being here with these gentlemen from the Interior Department. You know we can not always go to Washington, but today we are all in Washington with these gentlemen. I would like to say to these gentlemen who are here today, that I am holding my property in my hand just like that, and with their protection and support, their guidance, we are not going to let any white man do like that to us.

Now, my friends, my brothers, Americans of this country. When we return to our people on various and different Reservations, when we get back there, let us call a big medicine and let us call on the Great Spirit to support our wishes and those of the Interior Department.

GUS HEADRICK: Do I understand the Chair that each delegation of the various tribes are allowed to select two speakers from each delegation to speak.

DR. ROE CLOUD: One speaker is to be selected from each delegation except in the case of the Sioux. They will select two speakers on account of there being eight divisions represented from the Sioux country.

GUS HEADRICK: Our delegation are all English speaking and therefore will not need interpreters and we can turn our rights over to some of the other delegations.

DR. ROE CLOUD: The Crow delegation is next on the roster.

SAM LAPOINTE: Mr. Chairman, I happen to know both of those people and the speaker can talk better English than Jasper Long, the interpreter. I would suggest that he do his own talking.

JASPER LONG: I have been asked by this man to interpret his speech.

DR. ROE CLOUD: If any of the speakers can speak English and does not need an interpreter I suggest that they do so as it will save time.

JASPER LONG: There are in our delegation old people that cannot understand English. He requested that I interpret for him.

ARNOLD COSTA, Speaker for the Crow delegation: Mr. Chairman and members of the Interior Department and fellow American Indians. I am glad to be here and express my sentiments. In years past we did not meet in a Congress of this kind, and our wishes today have come true. In all these years we have come under the administration of the Indian Bureau where regulations have been prescribed and we have not been given any voice in the matter and at this time we are given this opportunity to voice our sentiments in the regulations to be put into the Bill.

I do not want to take up too much time at this Congress as there are delegations from other Reservations that wish the opportunity of saying a few words and I am very thankful to the Commissioner of Indian Affairs in giving me an opportunity to say that we should be excluded from the Bill. We have a number of buffalo eaters on our Reservation, since the younger generation has been up at this age of time; it was for that reason that I am speaking.

It is at this time that we understood that this tribe should be excluded from this proposed Bill. I do mean to say that any action should not be taken upon as our final decision at this present Council, because when I was selected as a delegate I was not given the authority to make any final decision in respect to the proposed Bill but we are going to take it home to our people and let our people decide and give their decision on this question. On behalf of my delegation I wish to express my thanks to the Indian Commissioner and his staff and also to the Indian people in this assembly. That is all.

DR. ROE CLOUD: The next speaker is from Fort Berthold.

ARTHUR MANDAN: There are two Gros Ventre Tribes, one is up in Montana and the other tribe is from the Fort Berthold Reservation, although they are different tribes. We have selected Chief Drags Wolf to speak for the Fort Berthold delegation. I will attempt to interpret for him.

CHIEF DRAGS WOLF, Fort Berthold: I have had the pleasure of being called on to say a few words by the Commissioner of Indian Affairs to this great assembly of the Plains people. We have heard the deliberations on this Bill for a few days now. The past administrations did not fulfill their promises. The Indians did not have a voice in the proposed legislation. Even if they were never carried out. It was always subject to Congress.

I want to say this much. On all the Reservation there has been about 360 allotments that have been sold right back to the Indians. On these allotments we have put on a program where we have established our homes, our barns, and improvements that are necessary.

There is one objectionable point that I want to bring up in this new proposed measure and that is inheritance. Today, the Commissioner of Indian Affairs and all his staff here are sitting on the platform. I want to say that we do not know whether or not we own the improvements on our own land. They may bury us six feet under the ground and we are not sure that that land can be inherited for future generations so that we can lie in peace under this six feet of soil.

There is another thing I would like to be informed about. There are over 360 allotments which have been sold directly to the Indians and that applies mostly to our children. They have paid for those lands in cash value. When this new government system comes we would like to find out whether these children are going to be reimbursed for whatever they have paid for these lands.

This branch of the Government, the Indian Bureau, is our protector and guardian. Eighty-three years ago we made peace with the United States Government and we have abided by the treaty but the Government has not. When we have brought suit against the Government there was nothing in that treaty to provide for giving this money back to the Indians. They (the Government) went to work and every cent that was spent, the Government took it back. Since then the Government and the Indian Bureau are trying to rectify all the evils of the past and we would like these to be rectified.

There are only a few complaints that I had brought here about these treaty rights and this proposed measure. We are considering this proposed measure from day to day and we would like to take home what has been said in the minutes of the meeting and what has been explained here in the last few days and tell it to our people at home and let them decide on this proposed measure. We will abide by the wishes of the majority of the people and not the minority.

MR. COLLIER: I just want to reassure the Chief there is nothing in our minds and there is nothing in the Bill to keep the children from inheriting the house and barn and stock, the improvements, the property. What the Chief wants is the thing he will get.

I don't want to take any more time from the old men.

DR. ROE CLOUD: The white man in the years gone by and even today is rushing everything. That is why he has tried to rush the American Indian into civilization long before he was prepared. Fort Belknap.

THE BOY, Fort Belknap: My friends, white men and Indians here in this assembly: I greet you.

Away back in 1855 my forefathers made a treaty with the United States Government and one of the objects of that treaty was to make peace with the white man, so that there would be peace from then on. The treaty made in 1885 was an extending of the right hand of friendship by the white man and the Indians accepted it.

They have been living under those conditions ever since although they were very trying. Many of the promises made to them in that treaty have been broken. After that treaty was made and signed and executed this souvenir was made (indicating what he holds in his hand) with a picture of two hands shaking together and two peace pipes. That represented the things that we had to do, that we were to be friends all the time. The descendants of those forefathers down to me always tried to live that way.

We are assembled here today something on that same order to keep on being peaceful and try and think up something that will do us good in the future.

According to that treaty of 1855, the white man put on a piece of paper certain things that he was to do along with what the Indian had to do. It wasn't long before the white man came down and ignored and tramped on his side of that agreement. And since that day he has laid down a lot of one-sided rules and regulations and laws that he compels the Indians to live under because they are hopelessly in the minority. When they make an attempt to have these one-sided laws corrected, the white man grabs him by the face and turns him right about face.

I have served my people a good many years now and this is one of the things I have tried to do—to change those one-sided laws. But I have failed because I have met with the same opposition. I have looked around and planned and laid awake nights hoping for some friend who would help us. Today in this assembly I think I am facing face to face with people who are our friends. I have always heard that there was one particular white man who has fought in behalf of the Indians for a long time and today I think I see him in the midst of these white men seated on the platform. And that particular white man has a program that this assembly is considering and getting an explanation of and this program is what has come from this white man's experience over a long period of time.

This white man has a program which he is presenting to us which is very good as a whole, to try to remedy these sad conditions under which we are living today.

As a representative of the Fort Belknap Indians I was told to listen closely to everything that took place in this Congress. I am going to take the news back to my people, everything that I heard. But, I say that personally I think it is a very good program as a whole.

Asks the chair for permission to say something else in one breath to the Indians.

My friends: I want to tell you something. This something is one of the downfalls of the Indian. When they get assembled in council or some meeting they always disagree. There is always a friction and there is no co-operation and there is no united action and there is no serious thought given to the question that caused that particular meeting. From now on, let us try and co-operate. Let us try to work as a whole, lay our individual desires aside and work for something that concerns everybody. In this assembly there is a wire in the middle that is not the dividing line. We are all one because we are Indians. There is another group of Indians who use their privileges as full-fledged citizens of the United States and have squandered their homes and are now penniless. Don't exclude that class of Indians.

DR. ROE CLOUD: Rocky Boy next.

MAN FROM AUDIENCE: I am a delegate from the Shoshone delegation. We have seemed to overlook that we have a tribe of Indians from Wyoming who have not been given a chance to express their views. We would like to give them a chance—the Arapahoe from Wyoming.

DR. ROE CLOUD: Just as soon as we get through they can speak. We will give the speaker five minutes.

SAMATT, Rocky Boy: I have been here four days to listen to this Congress. They say they have set the table and that everything is on it. When you eat too much you got to get medicine to cure you. He is going to doctor us. That is the first thing I am setting on the table. Every year we want the chance to take the cake and pies. We got to have a man to help us do that. We got to have a man who has the education to help me from behind. I have been trying quite a few times. I am tied up just like I was staked at the rope. I hope you have good luck on your trip.

DR. ROE CLOUD: Now the Arapahoe chief, Chief Groesbeck.

CHIEF GROESBECK: My friends: Representing this Reservation and the different tribes, I am merely wanting to ask a few questions in regard to my Reservation that I do not understand.

Back in 1904 the Government sent a representative from Washington to buy, or have the Tribe of Shoshone and Arapahoe cede, a large portion of what is known as Big Wind River, located in Shoshone Reservation in Wyoming. There were agreements made between the Government and tribes located there and only two of those agreements have been fulfilled. Now I am asking the Honorable Commissioner Collier to see about the other agreements that have not been fulfilled. Look to that.

I, as one of the representatives at that time, signed and consented to cede that portion. In one of the agreements there was to be a certain portion of monies received from this portion toward the educational use of the Indians of those particular tribes. In one of the agreements there was to be a certain portion of the money set aside toward building an irrigation canal from streams flowing or originating on these Reservations, but it was stipulated in the agreement that the Indian was to have a free use of the water. Up to this time, we understand that the water is a lien on the land. That is the question I wish to ask the Commissioner to explain. At the present time the ceded portion, not being occupied, not being taken up, and I wish to ask the Department of the Interior Secretary to withdraw all the portions not being occupied at the present time back to the Indian Status.

DR. ROE CLOUD: It is almost dinner time and these questions that have been raised by the Chief will be answered after dinner. Now I call for the last speaker—from the Winnebago jurisdiction that has several Sioux areas in it. Is the speaker here?

MAN FROM AUDIENCE: Mr. Chairman, have you omitted the Turtle Mountain Chippewa?

DR. ROE CLOUD: We omitted them because of lack of time. Please remain seated. This is the last speaker. We will be through in a few minutes.

MR. KENICK, Turtle Mountain Reservation: I am glad to meet the Commissioner of Indian Affairs. My greatest desire was to see him. I am a poor man. I am just as glad to see the Commissioner, as I would be to see him in Washington. The reason why I am so glad to meet him is because of what I have heard which is all for the benefit of the people. Of course, when I get up they all look at me as a poor man.

Upon my return the people will be looking to me to find out what I have learned from this meeting. I will tell my people what this great man had told me.

By the way I understand these Bills, the Commissioner of Indian Affairs wants to help me. The reason I am glad to meet him is that I have seen the Bill which he has presented to me. I am going to report it to the people that have sent me and I am pretty sure they will be pleased with it.

Concerning this self-government I am not quite ready to accept it yet because my people are just starting. I desire to say I will recommend to extend it a few years. That is my desire. Thank you.

DR. ROE CLOUD: The meeting will resume here at this hotel at 1:45 p.m. for the afternoon session. If business is not completed there will be an evening session. We stand adjourned for the dinner hour.

Afternoon Session

The afternoon session of the Plains Congress brought to order by Chairman Woehlke at 1:45 p.m.

Mr. Brown of Blackfeet requests five minutes to make an announcement from the platform. Granted. Members of the Blackfeet tribe come on the stage and announce that they are going to adopt Commissioner Collier into their tribe. One of the tribesmen speaks:

My friends, my fellow Americans. There are several different tribes assembled in this auditorium. You people are a little too slow; we are going to adopt the Commissioner into the Blackfeet Indians.

Applause.

And we are going to have him a leader in this community plan. Now, our Honorable Commissioner, when we adopt him in this tribe, we expect him to do more for us.

Applause.

The name which we are going to give our leader here, and you may call him by his Indian name when you meet him, is Spotted Eagle. That name, Spotted Eagle, represents the Indian Reservations, the way they are checkerboarded. We hope that those spots will be rubbed off so that every Indian Reservation will be all in one spot. The Commissioner is going to be our Chairman. We further invite the Commissioner to come out in our Reservation, which is bordering on the Glacier National Park. When he comes out there he can have a snowball in one hand and a bunch of flowers on the other hand.

Here they sing a native song, closing the ceremony, after presenting Commissioner Collier with a native headdress.

CHAIRMAN WOEHLKE: I believe we are all greatly appreciative of the honor the Commissioner has been shown by the Blackfeet tribe. I just want to suggest that if there is another tribe that wants to honor the Assistant Commissioner they might name him the man who is silent in all languages. Now, I believe that the Commissioner wishes to continue where the session was left off at 12:00 o'clock this morning.

MR. LAPOINTE, Rosebud: Mr. Chairman: Just two minutes please. There is something that we would like to insert into the record at this time. It won't take but just two minutes. Every Sioux Reservation, so far; I do not know of one Reservation among the Sioux that has actually accepted the program, but this is the position that we are in so far as the Sioux are concerned: we want to go on record that we have all been instructed to take the matter back to our people for their final decision; that our delegates are not taking any action in this matter here. Thank you.

MR. WOEHLKE: That will go into the record.

MR. COLLIER: There is only one thing on which we are going to invite a show of hands at this meeting. It hasn't got anything to do with this Bill. We are going to ask you whether you would be interested in having this Plains Indian Congress become a regular annual gathering. I can't promise that it would be, because we have to get the funds for paying the expenses, but if the plains tribes desire it, we will try and get the funds so that the Congress may become an annual event hereafter.

Interpreted by Mr. LaPointe.

MR. WOEHLKE: Now, I would like to ask those who are in favor of having this Plains Congress made an annual affair to stand up.

Great number stand.

Opposed are requested to stand. One stands.

Carried, that one delegate had the courage of his convictions.

CHAIRMAN of Blackfeet Council: He can't help himself, his name is Standing Bear.

MR. COLLIER: We will now take up the question asked just before lunch and then I am going to pass on to a matter of great final importance. He asked two or three questions and I will try to answer them. One question was about the ceded lands which were signed away by treaty to be disposed to whites, but they were not disposed of and now they are lying idle. Under existing laws there is nothing we can do about that. Under the new Bill if it becomes law, then undisposed, ceded and surplus lands will be restored to the Tribe.

Another question was connected with the use that had been made of tribal funds derived from the Cession of this land or from some land cession. Where the treaty promised that they would be used for education but they were not used, but they were used for something else. Answer: I do not know about the particular facts, but it sounds like what we have been doing all over. I assume the money was diverted to administrative costs, just as another hundred million dollars of tribal funds had been diverted in the last 34 years. This Bill would not correct a thing that took place in the past. It would only prevent that kind of thing from happening in the future. For the past happenings the tribe would have to seek redress in the Court of Claims.

Then the other question was about a water system where the Government had promised free water but a charge has been piled upon the Indians for that water. Answer: under the act passed two years ago, the Leavitt Act, we have power to cancel the reimbursable debts which have been placed on Indian tribal and allotted lands. These reimbursable debts have totaled several million dollars against the various Indian lands. To date about four million dollars of reimbursable charges have already been written off under the Leavitt Act. We shall proceed and write off more of them. The new Bill would prohibit the Government from making reimbursable charges against Indian lands except with the consent of the Indian community.

Now I am going to turn aside from the answering of written questions for a few minutes in order to answer what may be called an unasked question that is in the minds of many people, and I am now going to address myself not only and primarily to you here but rather to the Indians all over the country and to their white friends. First I want you to let me tell you about the Indians in another part of the country for a reason that you will soon understand. I refer to the Indians of the State of Oklahoma. The Oklahoma Indians possessed twenty-three million acres of land before allotment. All of their land except about three million acres is now lost, and nearly half of that three million acres have been brought under taxation by a special act of Congress. There are 100,000 members of the Five Civilized Tribes of Oklahoma and they all got land. Our latest information is that 72,000 of them have now lost all their land. Many thousands of the Oklahoma Indians now live in desperate poverty, and in addition to losing their land and their money they have been victimized in all kinds of cruel ways in Oklahoma. Probably the Indians in Eastern Oklahoma are worse off than the rest of the Indians in the whole country. This Bill we are discussing extends protection to the Oklahoma Indians and there is a companion Bill, the Howard Bill, which extends other protection to them.

Now I said yesterday in the meeting in the Civic Hall, in the Auditorium, that we all wanted the greatest freedom of expression and opinion about all these Indian matters. We do want all views to have the fullest expressions whether we agree with them or not and in the same way, we who are speaking for the Administration feel free to state our views and state the facts as we understand them. There is discussion of this Indian Bill going on all over the United States among the whites as well as the Indians, and in a sense we are compelled to discuss the Bill before the American public. I now want to read to you a dispatch that went out to the newspapers all over the country, an Associated Press Dispatch. It bears the date of February 24, and it went out from the headquarters of the Five Civilized Tribes in Oklahoma, Muskogee. From that area where the Indians are in the condition I have described to you. I ask your very close attention to what I have read, this Associated Press Dispatch.

> "Dr. Lindquist Denounces Collier's Indian Policy" Dr. E.E. Lindquist of Lawrence, Kans., a former advisor to Indian Department Officials, said here today that Commissioner John Collier's new Indian Bill is "socialism and communism in the rankest sense."

Interpreter SAM LAPOINTE: Please explain communism.

MR. COLLIER: I will continue to read.

> "It is a total reversal of the former policy of the Indian department in tending to bring Indians into the general body of citizenship" said Dr. Lindquist, who is in the Five-Civilized Tribes territory for a week's visit. "It would put them back on reservations and in blankets."
>
> He said Oklahoma has solved the Indian problem Better than any other state and is most threatened by Collier's new bill which, Dr. Lindquist contended, proposes to give the Indian commissioner authority to set up communistic settlements, not subject to State courts or laws, but answerable only to a new federal Indian court of seven judges.

I have read this to you because it represents what has been expressed by other people besides my good friend Dr. Lindquist, who is here today, who is with us now, and who gives expression to a view that is not confined to himself. And that is the only reason why I read this to you and why I shall refer to it.

The American people have never adopted a communistic or socialistic philosophy or policy, and if this Indian policy is described as being communistic or socialistic, then the American people will be against it. Several years ago the Indian Bureau of that day was promoting legislation to take away the land titles belonging to some of our Southwestern tribes, the Pueblo Tribes. The plan was to take their titles and give them to the whites. These tribes organized for self-defense. They carried their case and their battle to Congress and into the courts. In the middle of this battle the Indian Bureau gave out a statement that these tribes were being financed by Soviet Moscow. They were guilty of communism and socialism in trying to hold on to their lands. Down the years every so often this thing flames up again that the effort of the Indians to hold on to their lands is communism or socialism, and now we find that this Administration, because it is determined to help Indians hold on to their lands, is guilty of rank communism and socialism.

Now, we will just make a series of straight propositions and I will stand on them. This United States government has an obligation to its Indians. It is the guardian and they are its wards. To assert that obligation and fulfill it is plain honest Americanism and not communism. It is not communistic to extend the trust period on our Indian lands and keep you free from taxes. It is not communistic to extend to you the constitutional rights possessed by the other citizens of the United

States. It is not communistic to extend to you the right to organize for mutual aid. It is not communistic to allow you to have the same instruments of power which are possessed by all of the other people, but not you.

Local self-government was not instituted by the Communists, but is the oldest institution in the United States, founded in the New England towns of long ago. White people all over the United States own land in partnerships and companies and corporations. It is not communism to allow Indians to do the same if they want to. The jurisdiction over the Indians by the United States Government was declared by Congress and by the Supreme Court of the United States more than one hundred years ago. When we propose that that jurisdiction shall be continued and that the Indians shall not be turned over to the State of Oklahoma or any state, and to the tax collectors of Oklahoma, and the other States, we are not proposing something that we learned from Russia or any other communist place, but are following the counsel of John Marshall, the greatest of the Supreme Court Judges and the policy of the United States for the last hundred years. If it were true that civil constitutional rights are communism, and that old-fashioned American home rule was communism, and that all of the other rights and advantages which Indians are entitled to; if they are all communism, then there would be nothing for the Indians to do but become communists. It is not true and these rights and privileges have nothing to do with communism and therefore the Indians do not need to become communists. Those who tell the Indians that for them to assert their rights is to be communists are inciting the Indians to become communists.

Applause.

And, as for holding up the Oklahoma Indian record as the model of what we want for the rest of the Indians, that is condemning the Indians of the United States to ruin and humiliation and extinction. I have spoken, as I said, not primarily to you here, but in order that my words may be carried on the wires to the Indians over the whole country. But also I am speaking to you, that there will be increasing efforts to frighten you Indians and to stampede you. Throughout the local communities around the Indian Reservations there are interests that do not want the Indian property protected and you all know that.

Applause.

Your interests are, of necessity, in opposition to many local interests around you. You want to keep your lands, and of course there are other people who want to get your lands. That is inevitable. You want your lands to be exempt from taxation, and of course there are people who want to put taxes on them. You want to have the capital to put stock on your own lands and yourself enjoy the profits of the cattle business, and of course there are white cattlemen and lessors and banks that don't want you to do it.

I think we have made clear that we do not want you to follow us blindly or believe anything we tell you without investigating it. And, when you go back to your local communities, remember that you ought not to follow anybody else blindly or believe what he tells you without your own investigation.

Applause.

MR. LAPOINTE: Mr. Chairman, will you give Francis Red Tomahawk of Standing Rock the floor for several minutes. He has a resolution which he would like to read to the convention.

Granted.

> RESOLUTION
>
> Whereas it is the sense of the entire group of delegates assembled here in Rapid City from the various Reservations represented in the "Great Plains Congress" held at the Indian school at the above named city, that we owe our obligations to the Honorable Commissioner of Indian Affairs and his staff and to Superintendent Staley of the Rapid City Indian School and his efficient corps of employees, together with the Boy Scouts, and last but not the least the girls of the institution who gave of their time unselfishly to make our stay here one long to be remembered, and,
>
> Whereas, in recognition of each and every service and courtesy extended in our behalf we hereby unanimously thank each and every person for their untiring efforts to make our stay as near home-like, as possible, that we could not receive anywhere, service superior to that which has been accorded us while we were here, now there be it

Resolved. That we again heartily thank you all, that words fail to fully convey to you all our deep and heartfelt thanks and appreciation and may the "Great Spirit" who rules the Universe keep and guide you safely through all your lives, is the wish of your friends, the Delegates to the "Great Plains Congress," held at the Indian School in Rapid City, South Dakota, this 5th day of March, 1934.

HENRY STANDING
Chairman, Pine Ridge Delegation
C. T. ROWLAND, Chairman
Tongue River Council
MALCOM MITCHELL, Chairman
Rocky Boy Council
ALBERT HEMINGER, Chairman
Sisseton Council
ARTHUR MANDAN, Chairman
Fort Berthold Council
CHARLES RAMSEY, Chairman
Standing Rock Council
GEORGE EASTMAN, Chairman
Flandreau Council
RUSSELL HARRISON, Chairman
Crow Creek Council
JOSEPH W. BROWN, Chairman
Blackfeet Council
GUS M. HEADRICK, Chairman
Fort Peck Council
ELWOOD HARLAN, Chairman
Omaha Council
ED. W. PENISKA, Chairman
Ponca Council

BEAR JOHN BUCKMAN
Chairman, Fort Belknap Council
CHARLES M. DUSKELL
Chairman, Shoshone Tribal Council
JOHN B. AZURE No. 1
Chairman, Turtle Mountain Council
LOUIS MYRICK, Chairman
Fort Totten Council
GEORGE YELLOW, Chairman
Lower Brule Council
WILLIAM WHIPPLE, Chairman
Santee Council
LUKE GILBERT, Chairman
Cheyenne River Council
SAM LaPOINTE, Chairman
Rosebud Council
MAX BIG MAN, Chairman
Crow Tribal Council
FRANK BEAVER, Chairman
Winnebago Council
Delegates, "Great Plains Congress."

MR. WOEHLKE: I am not a member of this Congress, I am only the Chairman, but I would suggest, if you will accept it, an amendment to this resolution to include in your gratitude with special force, the two young women and the young man who, for four days now, have been embalming our words; who have been working harder than anybody else in this congress and who, within ten minutes after you have said your words, had them down on paper. Will you include this in your resolution?

Mr. Red Tomahawk agrees to have the amendment included.

Gentleman asks to delay the procedure a moment to interpret to the Blackfeet. Granted by the Chair.

MR. WOEHLKE: All those in favor of Mr. Red Tomahawk's resolution will answer by saying "aye." Those opposed; the "ayes" have it.

MR. RED TOMAHAWK still having the floor continues: Mr. Chairman, I have a letter here for the consideration of the delegates of this Congress also.

Rapid City, S. Dak.
March 5, 1934

Hon. John Collier
Commissioner of Indian Affairs
Rapid City, South Dakota

Dear Mr. Commissioner: We the combined delegates from the various reservations, assembled here attending the "Great Plains Congress" do hereby take this opportunity to extend to you our appreciation and gratitude for your effort to make it possible for us to gather here with you to discuss the important legislative matters proposed for our future welfare, for your every manifestation of your great interest in our affairs. For your sincerity in all your efforts toward making us better citizens and the preservation of all that is good within us; for the freedom you had accorded in exercising our native customs, and particularly for the great opportunity by your proposed legislation to better our conditions in every respect.

May the same "Great Spirit" who has taken care of his Red Children, bless you in your efforts to enable us to get on our feet in acquiring civilized lives, education and Christianity is the wish of

Your friends.

JOSEPH W. BROWN
ARTHUR MANDAN
MAX BIG MAN
CHARLES RAMSEY
GEORGE EASTMAN
RUSSELL HARRISON
GUS M. HEADRICK
GEORGE YELLOW
FRANK BEAVER
ELWOOD HARLAN
JOHN B. AZURE, No. 1
MALCOM MITCHELL
ED. W. PENISKA
LUKE GILBERT
SAM LAPOINTE
WILLIAM WHIPPLE

MR. MANDAN: I was to ask that we give the Sioux interpreters as well as some interpreters over here who have been interpreting on these last few days a vote of thanks.

MR. WOEHLKE: You have heard the remarks. Do you want to extend a vote of thanks to the indefatigable interpreters who have been serving you so beautifully without cost to you for the last few days? All those who want to include the gratitude of the Congress in a resolution of thanks, please say "aye."

Appeared to be unanimous.

MR. WOEHLKE: It is done.

MR. LAPOINTE: We want to include Mr. Case, our attorney, who has come out here. We want to thank him.

MR. WOEHLKE: You have heard the letter which Mr. Red Tomahawk has just read to you. What is the pleasure of the Congress? Do you want to authorize the chairmen of the various delegations to sign that letter? I suggest that it might perhaps be the best way to have every delegation which agrees with the spirit of this letter to authorize its Chairman to sign that letter. Mr. Red Tomahawk informs me that the letter will be in the school room in the North wing and that all those Chairmen of the various delegations who are authorized by their members to sign that letter are requested to step in to that room before they go and put their signatures down on the paper. Now what is the pleasure of the Congress? Would you like to have the Commissioner and his staff answer more of the questions which have been handed to us, or would you prefer to have your various delegations speak further and state their opinions concerning this Bill to the rest of the delegates and to the Commissioner? What would you prefer to have us do?

MR. STANDING BEAR: Mr. Chairman. I would suggest the Chairman to continue these questions that have been filed. There have been a number of questions prepared by the various delegations. A number of them have not been answered.

FRANK WILSON: To eliminate a great deal of time that would be consumed here on these questions, I wish to have the last part of this Bill turned over to the attorneys, Mr. Ralph Case, Mr. Hastings Robinson, and Mr. A. G. Granger. It will eliminate a great deal of discussion if these attorneys can take up this matter.

MR. WOEHLKE: If Mr. Case and the other attorneys will come to the office of the Indian Bureau in Washington, our attorneys will be glad to talk with them.

MR. ELWOOD HARLAN: I think we have submitted questions to Mr. Shepard the other night which I believe very different from any of these Sioux matters here. We have been here three days and we would like to hear something about our Nebraska problems.

MR. WOEHLKE: We have those Winnebago questions right here and if it is the pleasure of this Congress, we will proceed to answer them now.

MR. WILSON: I want that committee to take action this evening because they are all here, not at Washington, but here.

MR. WOEHLKE: Some of our attorneys have left, but it will be done tonight.

We will now discuss some of the questions submitted by the Winnebago delegation. I would like to point out to the members of this Congress that a great many questions have been answered two or three times and that we have more questions on the same points before us. All these answers will appear in the record which is to be printed by Dr. Roe Cloud's Haskell Institute and which will reach you in a short time. You will also have available a transcript of the hearings before the House Committee on Indian Affairs in a short time. In this Hearing a great many of the same questions, which you have been asking, have been asked by the Members of Congress and have been answered in far greater detail than we could answer them. So, from the record here and the record of the House Hearings and the record of future Congresses, you will be able to find an answer to every possible conceivable question that you could ask. I just wanted to bring that to your attention.

Now, I think we will proceed to the Winnebago questions.

MR. COLLIER: Several of your delegates have told me that there is a general wish among the delegations to hold a general meeting tonight just for the Indians in order to talk everything over. If that is your desire, I think that is the thing to do. I think, however, it should be determined so as to enable us to decide what else is to be done.

MR. LAPOINTE: I think that is a misunderstanding. The party who came to me at noon to make the request had in mind pleasure. A dance is what they want. They want to wind up with a big dance but we did not know what your plans are. If you have planned for a night session we will have that, but if not they want to use the gymnasium for a dance.

MR. COLLIER: That is for you to decide. We will be here, but maybe everybody is tired out.

DR. ROE CLOUD: Now, does the Chair understand that the Congress wants the answering of questions continued by the Commissioner? If so, now he will proceed.

MR. COLLIER: The Winnebago delegation had submitted thirteen questions. They are different from most of the other questions in that they call for an expression of opinion rather than a statement of fact. I shall try to answer them just as briefly as it is possible.

The first question is this: What does the experience of the best educated Indians prove? Did they receive more help on segregated Reservations or away from them? Did they get more help from the Reservation or off the Reservation?

ANSWER: I do not know what it proves. In the past the Indians have gotten their education mostly from non-Reservation boarding schools. Some of them have gone off to college. Some of the best brains are found among the Indians and among the people who have lived all their lives on the Reservation, so I do not know how to answer that by yes or no. I would like to state what it seems to me ought to be looked forward to. We ought to try to have real good schools near the homes of the Indians first, and then when the Indian young man or woman wants to go ahead with education, we ought to enable them to go on in places like Haskell where Dr. Roe Cloud is in charge, or into the agricultural colleges and universities, medical school, and nursing schools, but I believe that the home, the family and the home are the beginning of life and that they are important to every child. Now the next question is similar. Do we need any legislation for the old people, or rather should we look forward and do what is best for future generations? I answer this, that it is quite clear that we need new legislation for old people and the young people. Third question, Shall we again build on worn out traditions and superstitions, or on an enlightened civilization? Answer: I will have to preach you a sermon if I go ahead on this.

FRANK WILSON of Pine Ridge, S. Dak.: We object to those questions because they are taking up our time and deal with things that do not pertain to our discussions.

ELWOOD HARLAN: I believe those questions were asked by the Winnebago Indians. I think Dr. Roe Cloud knows about them. They took them when we had our meeting the other night at the dining hall.

DR. ROE CLOUD: He is referring to the very same paper that was taken from me the other night. Most of them are expressions of opinion and have very little to do with this.

MR. COLLIER: *(continuing to read questions)* Question No. 12. Who will support the old people after their lands have been sold to the community and no more rental received?

MR. HARLAN: Mr. Collier, I handed the Omaha questions to Mr. Shepard and they were in pencil. I was the Chairman of the group meeting that night in that hall. We are different from these people in allotment laws. We offer them because they are different land titles. On the Winnebago and Omaha Reservation under the Brown Bill of 1916 the trust lands are taxable.

DR. ROE CLOUD: On the Winnebago and the Omaha Reservation under the Brown Bill of 1916 the lands are taxable. The question that was expressed the other night was this—Since the Omaha Tribe was not allotted under the law of 1887 like other tribes, but allotted under a different act of Congress, does this new Bill cover the Winnebago and Omaha Indians?

MR. COLLIER: It makes no difference. This Bill would cover them all.

MR. HARLAN: Will it take a special act to repeal the tax law of December 30, 1916?

MR. STEWART: Yesterday afternoon at the Auditorium one of your delegates came to me with some penciled questions. I would like to have that man stand up.

Frank Beaver, Winnebago Indian, stands up. MR. STEWART continues: I am now working on this and drafting a new Bill to fit the Omaha and Winnebago land alone.

MR. HARLAN: When I get home that is one question the Indians will want to know, whether this new Bill would repeal that Bill?

MR. STEWART: Another question raised was concerning title to some accretion land.

MR. HARLAN: I asked another question. This is the special act of Congress of May 11, 1912 and that land to be sold and proceeds divided equally to the children living on the date of the passage of the act. This act was amended in 1925. Would we have to get special legislation to repeal that act?

MR. STEWART: Special legislation is not necessary in this case.

RALPH H. CASE: Mr. Chairman, I am the attorney for the Winnebago as well as the Sioux. We are studying legislation now to repeal the Brown Act which affects the Winnebago and Omaha lands regardless of the fact that this new Bill is being proposed. Mr. Stewart – will you in your repeal legislation put in there a provision for the repayment to the Winnebago and Omaha people for the taxes that have been collected from them illegally?

MR. STEWART: I suggest that Major Case and I get together in Washington on that point and work out something together.

DR. ROE CLOUD: The Chair wants to say that your remarks are very much in point and also that of Mr. Case and I hope that repayment provisions will be made in this new Bill.

MR. WOEHLKE: I would like to interpose at this time.

As you have also seen in the educational section of this Bill, provision is made for the encouragement of native Indian artists when you people have a great many talented young artists who need encouragement; for instance, there is among the Northern Cheyenne a young man, D. C. Wheeler, who has painted a portrait of the Northern Cheyenne Chief, Victor Little Chief, and he has asked that this portrait be presented to the Commissioner in appreciation from the Northern Cheyenne.

MR. COLLIER: I want to most heartily thank Mr. Wheeler for his gift and through him to thank the Northern Cheyenne. The picture will be sent to Washington and will there be looked at by a great many people, and in acknowledging this picture I would like to remind you all of a fact which is that a number of the most famous and greatest painters living in the United States today are Indians. What I mean is, that the people who know the art of Europe and the art of China and Japan consider that some of your Indian artists are great artists and compare favorably with a great number in China and Japan.

I want to remind you also that in some parts of the country a very large income is received by the Indians from their works of art. In ordinary years, the Navaho Indians receive an income of more than a million dollars every year from their blankets and their turquoise jewelry. There are many hundreds and perhaps thousands of your young men and women who with the proper chance for training in the arts can go out into the world, and establish themselves in the matter of income and with the respect of the whole country. It is one of the purposes of this Bill and of the present administration both to extend this educational market for your arts and craft products so that you can be seen advantageously all over the world.

I know that you are all feeling fatigued and you are certainly tired of hearing from me. I am perfectly willing to remain here and answer questions without end. It might be better if they are answered to the delegations that are asking them rather than in the whole audience, and I want to say that we hope you will not consider that you are bound by courtesy to come here again tonight and listen to us. The work connected with this new legislation must go on through weeks and months ahead, back in every one of your own tribes. You will have, and you will read over all of these proceedings here. Already the hearings, the printed hearings of the House Committee on Indian Affairs, have been sent to your different Reservations. You will find them there when you get home, and there is no possibility of exhausting this subject even though we stay here till midnight and even though we remain here the rest of this week, and I think that probably you would rather adjourn at an early hour. I do not know. We are at your service. I want to try, finally, to make clear to you some things about the Bill and how we are proposing to proceed with the legislation.

In the first place, as to the matter of how fast things are likely to move. The hearings have been adjourned in both the House and Senate Indian Committees. We asked that they be adjourned until Congress could know more about the desires of the Indians themselves. We have ahead of us either eight or nine Congresses in different parts of the Indian country before we go back to Washington, so that the hearings of the committees in Congress cannot be resumed until at least the end of the present month, and those hearings, when they are resumed, will go forward probably for several weeks. In other words, there will be abundant time for you and all of the other Indians to go over the whole thing back home—send in any ideas and Congress will not move ahead of you. Therefore it is important for you to keep right on studying the Bill and discussing it but do not feel that you are being hurried too much.

And second. As I stated yesterday, this legislation as a whole is not going to be forced on a tribe which does not want it. The tribe whose members desire to be excluded from the operations of the Bill has only got to let us and to let Congress know that they desire to be excluded. I would hope that no tribe would reach such a decision in a hurry, because I believe that all tribes, or at least most of them, will want the Bill and want it with all their hearts when they understand it thoroughly. I believe you will find that it takes nothing from you or from any individual among you; but that it adds a great deal that you want and have long wanted.

There are some of you in greater need than others. I merely now desire to emphasize that the tribe which, after mature thought, decides that it wants to be excluded, will be excluded, insofar as we have power in Congress. I think you will find a great many points at which you will be able to suggest improvements in the Bill. I expect that after all of the improvements are put in, if the Bill is passed, still there will be other improvements put in by amendment the next year, but I think that as you study the Bill and trace out exactly the way it will work in your case, you will find that we have already taken out of the Bill the one thing which you might object to. Namely, this feature of compulsion, so that the Bill in its essence is wholly an optional matter. Not only optional with the community and the tribe but with the individual. That is not wholly true because the Bill would forbid an Indian from getting a fee patent and disposing of his land. It would forbid that.

Now, one thing more before I stop. The men from the Indian Office who are with you here at this meeting are in most cases men who have been brought in by the present administration, except Mr. Stewart, who was placed at the head of the Land Division by the Administration. We are not in any way concerned with defending any element of the past record of the Indian Bureau. In fact we hold office precisely because the president knew and the Secretary of the Interior knew, that we were not going to protect the old record, but were going to try to make a new one. Otherwise we would not hold office at all. Now, I do not know that we are particularly wise. I do not suggest that at all, but I do know that we all value one thing more than any other thing. We want the Indians to continue to believe that we have been truthful and faithful. Should we, at some future date, appear to have misinformed you, to have told you things that were not true, as we understood the truth, then we should consider that we had failed and lost the most precious thing that we possess, which is your confidence. To me it would be the failure of my life and the ruin of my ambitions and hopes if I lost the confidence of the Indians. I am merely trying to convey to you that we have a stake of our own, just as much as you have, in making good, in playing fair, and in telling truth.

Now, if we haven't by this time put all our cards on the table and told you everything that we really think, it is just because we haven't had time enough or haven't known how to get it in words, and you may be sure that before these Congresses with the Indians get finished, everything we know will have been put into the record, if it hasn't already, because, just as you men here have gone right on probing down, down to the heart of this thing, and demanded straight answers from us, you have done that—so will other Indian Congresses do.

More important than this Bill, more important than any particular proposal is one other thing, and it is that the Indians shall realize that we are placing their case in their own hands, that we are doing that in dead earnest; that not merely are we willing, we are determined that the Indians shall do their own thinking and reach their own conclusions about these important matters, and that purpose, though it might result in our not getting results that we want, is still more important than getting those results. I can only here convey a feeling to you rather than state it in any words; that you are now your own judge and your own jury in these legislative and all other important matters, and from the point of view of the future of Indian life, there is something even more important than this land legislation. It is that the Indians shall take the responsibility, here and now, of thinking out their own problems and arriving at their own conclusions and determining their own future, and we are determined to be nothing but your agents in carrying out your own natural conclusions. That is all I shall say now.

Applause.

Chairman, DR. ROE CLOUD: Now, there is one thing that the Chairman would like to settle before we go any further, and that is the question of whether tonight there should be sectional meetings to discuss the technical affairs on each special group, as we had other nights, or whether we should have some entertainment. Now, the technical affairs of one group, however interesting they be to that group, are of no importance to another. Therefore it is a question if whether there should be tonight, these divisional meetings or whether there should be some entertainment.

MR. LABAN WHITE, Rosebud: Mr. Chairman,

He is granted the floor.

We, the delegates from the various Reservations, would like to say that we want to continue Mr. Collier's answering questions for the reason that we were sent here to study this matter out, and if we had something else the rumor would go out back home that we went up as delegates and instead of continuing in the examination of this Bill, why, we got into some pastime and that would be a reflection on us as delegates back home.

THE CHAIRMAN: I have just been informed that due to the fact that the Commissioner's voice is very nearly played out, he can not answer any more questions. It is a physical impossibility. So it is a question of whether we have divisional group meetings or entertainment. Those in favor of divisional meetings raise their right hands.

Considerable number do.

Opposed the same sign.

About the same number vote.

The Chair will decide. It is just about even, so the Chairman will decide on recreation tonight with the provision that those that want to meet in divisional meetings can do so.

Applause.

DR. ROE CLOUD: The Chair has something to say to you. Mr. Lindquist has asked for the privilege of the floor and I know of no man who likes to give everyone a chance to present his views more than the commissioner himself, even though those views may be averse to his. We asked Mr. Lindquist to stick to the actual provisions of the Bill in their relation to the life of the Indians, the States, and the United States.

I would also ask him to make his talk as brief as possible because there are more things coming on.

MR. LINDQUIST: Mr. Chairman, ladies and gentlemen. Just a very brief statement, my friends, and in order not to be misquoted or the statement misrepresented, I have put it in writing in a single paragraph. This is the statement.

The Muskogee, Oklahoma, paper, according to the report of February 24, made an editorial addition to my remarks, saying that Commissioner Collier's plan is socialistic or communistic. I did not say that. While I do not agree with many of the provisions of the Howard-Wheeler Bill, I consider it neither communistic nor socialistic, nor both in one. As to Oklahoma, this was my statement. From Venita, in the north, to Durant in the south, omitting those who failed to make adjustment and drifted back to the hills, you have one of the best examples of racial assimilation anywhere. I am thinking of those who made this adjustment; the Commissioner, of those who did not. Both groups are facts. Thank you.

DR. ROE CLOUD: I want to call on Mr. Stewart to make an important announcement at this time.

MR. STEWART: Many of you probably have some of your allotted land subject to sale on deferred payment plan. I know that many Indians of other Reservations than are here represented do. Under existing law, a sale made under that plan requires the white purchaser to pay 25 per cent of the sale price down at the time and the balance in installments. Under the regulations and law, if he pays his first payment and he pays his second payment or his third payment, and then does not want to continue paying out, he can ask for a refund for all but the first 25 per cent payment and get it.

A short time before I left for this trip a Bill came down to the Office for report. Major Case, the attorney here, largely aided in its introduction. Mr. Collier favorably passed that Bill to the Committee.

Now, the terms of that Bill were to this effect: That in future cases where a white purchaser of your allotment who wants to stop payment after he has made the first 25 per cent will not get any refund. You allottees involved will keep all the money. The progress that that Bill is now making in Congress is reflected in this telegram which I will now read to you. This telegram is dated March 5 and is addressed to the Honorable George J. Crilly, Rapid City, South Dakota.

> "HR 5075 introduced by me was unanimously passed by the House this afternoon. STOP. This law will give the Indian greater protection in land sales made on deferred payments in that all sums paid before default will be forfeited. STOP. Advise Case who is thoroughly familiar with the provisions of my bill and also Indians gathered there.
>
> Theodore B. Werner

Before handing this to the interpreter to read to you, I am going to invite Major Case to follow the interpreter with a few remarks. This telegram is signed by the Honorable Theodore B. Werner.

DR. ROE CLOUD: The Chair will now recognize Ralph H. Case, attorney for the Sioux and Winnebago, for a brief remark. Ralph H. Case.

MR. RALPH H. CASE: My Friends, there is nothing I like better than to bring you good news. While we have talked for four days about this Commissioner's Bill, remember we have been talking about things that are going to happen in the future, they are not here yet and the old laws still press us down; the old law is still a burden to us. There is one particular matter and that in section one of the Act of June 25, 1910, was very, very oppressive. If a man bought heirship land and paid more than one-fourth of the purchase price he could get his money back from the heir if he could not pay any more, but if he bought land from a white man or from the Government and he paid 90 per cent, if he made three out of four payments, and didn't pay any more, then he forfeited everything he had paid.

Pointing to men in the audience.

Some of the people that are sitting right here came to Washington and said why should they treat us different than they treat the man that buys land from the Government or buys land from the white man. I said, there is no reason why they should not be treated the same, so you got to change the law and the only way you can change the law is first to get a Congressman that will try to get it through for you, and at the same time you have got to have a Commissioner of Indian Affairs that will say what he honestly thinks about the proposed change. Now this just shows you that is possible that you have got some friends in Washington. I went into this gentleman's office, of the Commissioner of Indian Affairs, and sat down with him and told him just what ought to be done.

Applause.

Now do not think that this Bill affects only the Sioux and Winnebago Tribes; it affects every tribe in the United States of America who has any inherited tribal land. I went to the Congressman from this district because I know him better than any other man in the House and I said "Werner, will you put this bill in?" and he said, "Yes, I will." Now here is a good one. That bill passed the House of Representatives. That means it is half way through. Now I have just a final word that is good news. That bill is half way through. I am not asking you gentlemen what you want to do, but before I leave here I want to tell all you friends that you ought to give Mr. Collier a rising vote and thank him for all he has done as he certainly has earned the name of Iron Man.

Applause.

DR. ROE CLOUD: Now the Commissioner wants a brief word again, but before he speaks I want to say that the Chairman of each delegation is appointed by the Chair to provide the entertainment for tonight. You are to meet here right after the meeting is over with.

MR. COLLIER: I only want to say that I gladly accept Dr. Lindquist's correction of the Associated Press Report which I read to you. The fact that a detailed elaborate misquotation went over the wires all over the United States merely serves to indicate what you have to contend with, and I know that the Oklahoma Indians will be glad to learn that he will be in the foreground with fighting to correct those unjust laws for Oklahoma.

DR. ROE CLOUD: Now I have one or two things that I want to announce. Here is a notice left with me; "Left in the Alex Johnson Hotel, 317, a brief case, if found send to Porcupine, collect, to F. S. Fielder." Now a while ago Francis Red Tomahawk introduced a resolution and also a letter of thanks and warm commendations of what the Commissioner has done for us and requested that the Chairmen of the delegations sign those resolutions and I have them in my hand and will hand them to the Commissioner. I want to make this announcement, which is very gratifying to me, and that is that the Santee Mission School, of which I am a graduate, has offered to translate the Howard-Wheeler Bill into the Indian language so that you will have this Bill in the Indian language before very long.

I have a notice here of particular interest: "Honorable Commissioner of Indian Affairs, Mr. Collier—Not one Indian woman had a voice in this Indian council and may I submit in writing—this new plan is our only salvation. Let's all join in and accept the new Bill and make the best of our advantages." She said more in that one line than all the speeches put together. This is a member of the Pine Ridge Sioux delegation. She does not give her name.

Now before I go on to the next thing, I want to say just a word myself. I am in favor of this Bill, although it will be of no benefit to me whatsoever, either way it goes. The Commissioner announced a while back that now is the time to get active and do something because the thing is in a fluid condition and has not been made solid yet, has not been set. If we are to get anything done for the American Indians, now is the time to do it.

Friends, there is only one John Collier in the United States. I do not believe he is a twin. He has the brain, the personality, the friendship, the sympathy and possesses the technique to put all this into proper form for the benefit of the Indians. We will never have another John Collier as Commissioner of Indian Affairs. I have always felt sorry for the Commissioners of Indian Affairs in years gone by. They have always seemed to me men who were bound by ropes round and round their bodies, wishing to do something in their heart but unable to do anything. Here for the first time a Commissioner of Indian Affairs has broken that rope from his body and finding abundant freedom early in his career to work out good things for the Indian race. Now I have many other things I would like to say but Mr. Woehlke wants to take the stand on behalf of the Commissioner of Indian Affairs and I will call on him now. Mr. Woehlke.

INDIAN from Fort Berthold: I would like to call on Mr. A. F. Johnson to explain to us how they are going to handle the translation of the Bill into the Dakota language and how it is to be distributed.

DR. ROE CLOUD: Mr. Johnson, you may tell us.

MR. JOHNSON: The Bill is going to be put into the Dakota language and this gentleman wants to know after it is translated how it is to be distributed after it has been put into the Indian language. We are going to send copies to all Indians, missionaries, etc.

MR. WOEHLKE: Just a few words. I am taking the place of the Commissioner's throat. Now we will all get together again a year from now when the next Plains Indian Congress will be held, but before that Congress convenes next year, in all probability this new legislation will have passed, and if it passes that is when the real work begins. The Commissioner wants me to tell you that if this legislation passes, he, himself, and his representatives will come out to visit and consult with each tribe that is here represented. So that he and his representatives will discuss with your business committees and with your general councils of each tribe just what you want to do and just how much you want to do in your specific Reservation to take advantage of this new legislation.

He and his representatives want to listen to what you have to say concerning the reorganization of your Reservation or of your tribe under this new legislation, as to how much of it you want – if you want anything at all, and how to go about getting what you want on each specific Reservation. As was said this morning, the table will be set for you and he wants to find out then from each tribe, from each Reservation whether you want to eat, and what kind of fork you want to use, and I can tell you on behalf of the Commissioner's staff that we all hope to be able to get together with your various tribes and your general councils before the snow begins to fly next year.

Loud applause.

DR. ROE CLOUD: In the absence of any further announcements and seeing the audience is getting very restless, the chair is ready to dismiss if someone will put it into a motion.

REV. DAVID CLARK: Words of appreciation have come to me to be presented to Mr. Collier and to Mr. Staley from the delegates. I would like on behalf of many people who are here, both whites and Indians, Missionaries and others, to express our appreciation of his courtesy in allowing us to sit in and listen to these discussions. We appreciate it very much and are glad that we have been here and we have enjoyed it all and would like to carry back home our appreciation of the courtesy of the Iron Man. We appreciate Mr. Collier, the intentions of your interest and effort in behalf of all the Indian people. I believe I speak the voice of all these people.

DR. ROE CLOUD: The Chair will order those remarks into the records.

MR. LAPOINTE: Have Mr. Clark speak in Indian so that the Indians will understand.

Mr. Clark speaks in Indian.

DR. ROE CLOUD: On behalf of the Commissioner and all his staff we wish to thank you for your patience and cooperation in making this great Congress a great success.

MR. SAM LAPOINTE: Mr. Chairman, I move we adjourn.

DR. ROE CLOUD: Is there a second to that motion?

Motion seconded unanimously.

All in favor rise. (*All rise.*)
Congress is adjourned.

Exhibits

Letter of Tribal Business Council of Standing Rock Sioux Reservation, handed to Chairman by Francis Red Tomahawk of Standing Rock.

Fort Yates, North Dakota
February 8, 1934

Mr. John Collier
Commissioner of Indian Affairs
Washington, D.C.

Sir: We the Tribal Business Council of the Standing Rock Sioux Reservation of North and South Dakota, have the honor to submit the report of the action taken in connection with Circular dated January 20, 1934, Re "Indian Self-government" addressed to Superintendents, Tribal Councils and Individual Indians.

For the purpose of promoting the success of the proposed new policy outlined in the circular and to further the efforts of the administration to secure beneficial legislation which will enable it to realize its objective, the complete reconstructing of the whole Indian problem, we hereby endorse the plans contained in the above mentioned circular with certain reservations, which will be shown under the heading "Land Problems."

1. Evils of the Allotment System: After a thorough and comprehensive survey of the evils of the allotment system as we have experienced them on the Standing Rock Sioux Reservation we have listed the various sources of evils by which we have sustained losses in land sales and other benefits as will be seen in attached report dated February 7, 1934.

Land Problems

Under this heading we favor legislation positively prohibiting Indian land sales to outside parties, that no more patents be granted, that complicated heirship land and other heirship of like character be sold and purchased for the use of the tribe, that deeded lands located in areas predominated by Indian allotments be purchased for the use of the tribe, that timber lands lost to the tribe through land sales and opening of the Reservation be restored to tribal status which shall include mineral land also, that lands sold for taxes be restored to original allottees wherever justifiable. The legislation to conform to the white man's land sale law be enacted and the present Indian land sale law be discarded for good.

We reserve all rights as to trust land owned by the original allottees and all heirship lands not complicated so long as they retain the status of "complicated heirship lands."

We believe that the plan to acquire land for the use of our tribe, landless and future generations, is one worthy of consideration by every Indian; the health improvement plan; the establishment of self-government and the stabilization of community life; the development and preservation of Indian land in Indian ownership; and the provision of opportunity for economic livelihood for Indian community life.

The action of the Tribal Business Council of the Standing Rock Sioux Reservation of the states of North and South Dakota is for all of the foregoing and for the express purpose of supporting the present administration in securing enabling legislation to better the status of the Indian, that in the end he may take his place in the economic life of the nation and not be a dead-weight economically.

As to the "program of Administration" and "Suggested Problems and Possible Solutions" we endorse the verdict of our sub-committee unanimously.

Respectfully submitted,

(Signed) CHARLES RAMSEY
Chairman, Tribal Business Council
(Signed) FRANCIS RED TOMAHAWK
Secretary, Tribal Business Council
Fort Yates, North Dakota
February 7, 1934

Business session of the Sub-Committee of the Tribal Business council.

The above named sub-committee met at the Agency Hall and decided to organize by electing Edward Young Eagle as Chairman, and Francis Red Tomahawk Secretary.

The first matter taken up in connection with the Indian Office Circular in regard to "Indian Self-Government, dated January 20, 1934," was the "Evils of the Allotment System," which committee after careful survey of the land losses find as follows:

1. Opening of Reservation by Congress.
2. Allotment of Reservation.
3. Voluntary Land Sales.
4. Forced patents without knowledge of allottees.
5. Sale of heirship allotments.
6. Loss of large tracts of valuable grazing land through sales and plowing for agricultural purposes.
7. Loss of timber allotments through land sales and opening of Reservation.
8. Loss of mineral lands through opening of Reservation and land sales.
9. Loss of land by granting school land to the States of North and South Dakota for school purposes.
10. Loss of land through tax sales.
11. Loss of land through mortgage foreclosures.
12. Loss of land through right of ways for railroad and Federal and State and County Highways.
13. Loss of land sale proceeds through present land sale law which calls for refund of all payments except the original 25 per cent and interest.
14. Loss of land by establishment of Government reserves.
15. Loss of land through grants to Missions and other Religious organizations.

Land Problems

We favor in the fullest degree the purchase of complicated heirship lands and other lands which will become complicated and deeded lands located in areas predominated by Indian allotments for the use of the tribe.

We favor the abolishment of the land division as operated on the Reservation as soon as suitable municipal or tribal means can be worked out to satisfactorily handle its work.

Program of Administration

We favor the program of the Administration as outlined in Indian Office Circular "Indian Self-Government, dated January 29, 1934" appearing on pages 3, 4, and 5, by unanimous vote.

Suggested Problems and Possible Solutions

In connection with this portion of the Commissioner's circular we agree and hereby vote unanimously in favor of the proposed plans as outlined in this section of the communication.

Respectfully submitted:
Sub-committee

EDWARD YOUNG EAGLE
LOUIS H. THIEF
WILLIAM CLAYMORE
JOHN IRONBOULDER

FRANCIS RED TOMAHAWK
JOSEPH HUFF
EUGENE YOUNGHAWK

Approved February 8, 1934 by the Tribal Business council, Standing Rock Reservation, Fort Yates, North Dakota.

CHARLES RAMSEY
Vice-Chairman
F. R. TOMAHAWK
Secretary

LOUIS H. THIEF
JOSEPH HUFF
VITAL BEARFACE
LUKE EAGLEMAN

RALPH WHITE
JOSEPH WHITE TEMPLE
PIUS BIGSHIELD
GEORGE GABE
FRED WHITE COAT.

CHAPTER 4

PROCEEDINGS OF THE CONFERENCE AT CHEMAWA, OREGON MARCH 8 AND 9 TO DISCUSS WITH THE INDIANS THE HOWARD-WHEELER BILL

MINUTES OF THE NORTHWEST INDIAN CONGRESS

March 8, 1934

Thursday, A.M.

MR. MARSHALL: I guess everybody is in the hall. We wil now start our first session of Congress at Chemawa. We are here to discuss the bill introduced by Senator Wheeler and Representative Howard. Now in saying that we want to discuss that bill and criticize that bill I mean exactly that. The Indian Bureau doesn't feel that this bill is the final word. It is being introduced to get criticisms and comments on this bill from all of you so if this bill is passed it will be an improvement over any former bill that has been passed in Congresses. But before we discuss this bill there are a few announcements to be made. First I had better introduce myself. My name is Bob Marshall. I am just starting with this meeting until some of the other men from Washington arrive by train later on this morning.

In the beginning I have to offer sincere apologies from Commissioner Collier who had intended to come out here but had to go to another place. In his place will be Mr. Zimmerman, who will be here at 10:30 and who will take charge of the proceedings, and Mr. Woehlke who is Mr. Collier's field representative. Mr. Siegel, who just slipped out of the room a few minutes ago, was one of the lawyers who helped write the bill; he will be here and will help explain what it is all about. But again before beginning the discussion of the bill we have a few announcements to make. I hope that you are all seated in such a way that those who don't understand English will have someone near to you to interpret it. From now on I will stop for the interpreter to interpret. Maybe I had better stop right now so that those of you who don't understand will have what has just been said explained to you by those who are sitting near you.

SPOKANE DELEGATE: Mr. Chairman, may I suggest that as a delegate of the Nez Perce Tribe, and since the Nez Perce Indians have had visitations of missionaries for a number of years, we have an invocation of prayer from Mr. Parson?

MR. MARSHALL: I think that would be a very good suggestion. Will Mr. Parson please come up?

DELEGATE: Is Mr. Parsons here? I suggest that Mr. Wheeler go forward.

MR. MARSHALL: Will Mr. Wheeler come up?

DELEGATE: Wheeler?

MR. MARSHALL: Yes.

Wheeler of the Nez Perce tribe gives prayer in Indian.

MR. MARSHALL: Before proceeding with the meeting there is one announcement I would like to make. That is, that Dr. Earl Prichard would like to meet all Superintendents who have I.E.C.W. work on their reservations at one o'clock at the Practice House for a few minutes' conference.

Now I think I had better tell you about the program. We want to start this morning to give you a brief outline of the bill and then briefly explain why this legislation is necessary. And then take the bill and try to see the terms or more closely understand what the bill is; then in the afternoon we are going to thrust the matter off to questions and criticisms and I am sure we are going to try to find out if the bill meets those criticisms. We had better have a little interpretation.

I had better ask how many of you would like to go ahead in English and how many of you would like to wait after every few sentences to explain what has been said. I will ask for a show of hands. How many of you would like for the meeting to go straight ahead? Can you raise your hands? How many of you want to wait for the interpreters to interpret? That's fine. We'll wait. Each group that doesn't understand English can get close to an interpreter. We won't have an interpreter come up in front to give his interpretation as there are about 20 languages spoken here at the meeting and it would take up a great deal of our time. The Warm Springs interpreter, for instance, will talk to those around him whenever you need to interpret and in that way we won't have to break up the meeting.

SPOKANE DELEGATE: Mr. Chairman: I just want to say that within this room with all these different tongues talking at the same time, it will sound like a Babels house; so many different tongues, will be almost impossible.

MR. MARSHALL: At Rapid City, where there were 16 tongues which all live within 150 miles it was done that way and there wasn't much confusion. We will see how it works.

SPOKANE DELEGATE: Mr. Chairman: Since I have been here—I have been appointed to interpret—I feel unable to interpret as fast as you talk, and the interpreters themselves can't interpret as fast as you speak.

MR. MARSHALL: Thank you very much.

COLVILLE DELEGATE: I suggest as being one of the delegates that you have many words that even an interpreter needs an interpreter for; the average Indian understands English to some extent. If you will use more simple English I am positive that the average Indian in this group will understand.

MR. MARSHALL: What is your name please?

COLVILLE DELEGATE: I am Christine Galler from the Omak Colville District Association.

MR. MARSHALL: We will try both of those suggestions and use simple language and talk slower. It was announced earlier in the meeting that we would like any of you who have questions to offer or criticisms to please write them out and send them up to the desk.

KLAMATH DELEGATE: At this time *(and he was interrupted)*—

MR. MARSHALL: This afternoon we will start to accept the questions. We are not going to read the bill. Anybody here can read the bill. We are going to make an explanation of what the bill means to us.

VOICE FROM THE AUDIENCE: Is it compulsory to write the questions on a piece of paper?

MR. MARSHALL: It is not compulsory. It is just a suggestion which will make it clear to us.

VOICE FROM THE AUDIENCE: Don't you think we could criticize part of them?

MR. MARSHALL: Well, we are going to criticize them, but we are to start out by getting a more orderly beginning, then we are going to explain separately all the different parts. But, we are going to have an oral discussion in large group tomorrow with every tribe. When anyone gets up to speak hereafter, please give your name so that the reporter will get it down so we will have a full record. What was the name?

DELEGATE: N. Minthorn from Umatilla.

MR. MARSHALL: There is one more announcement that was just handed in here. All Carlisle ex-students will meet at noon with Mr. and Mrs. Wade Crawford at the Delegates' headquarters.

Now I think it is time to begin to explain to you why we thought it was necessary and desirable to introduce this bill into Congress. At the start I want to say that Congress could have passed this bill without having us come out here to explain it at all. Bills that affect the Indians have been passed in other years without even consulting with the Indians. The present Congress, including both the Senate and the House of Representatives, recognize the need for some legislation; the President of the U.S. has indicated that he believes in the plans in the bill, and the Secretary of the Interior is very much for the bill, and so is the Secretary of Agriculture. However, Mr. Collier has always believed and has for years fought for the plan that any bill in any action affecting the Indians should receive the consideration and approval of the Indians. Your criticisms and your suggestions are to be listened to and accepted and the bill is to be changed where necessary in order to make it what the Indians want. This bill is just for one purpose, to help the Indians and give them a better sort of legislation.

YAKIMA DELEGATE: It is almost impossible for the interpreter to interpret as fast as you are speaking. Make the sentences a little shorter, and give a little more time to interpret.

MR. MARSHALL: Yes sir. So what we want at this meeting today and tomorrow is for all of you to ask us regarding anything which you don't fully understand. We want you to tell us anything in this bill with which you do not agree and which should be changed. We want to change it for you, to help make this bill the sort of bill you really do want.

MR. THOMAS: I understand that you start in to have your men up to explain the bill. That is what I would like to know. We do not wish to be put on the defensive.

MR. MARSHALL: That is all going to take place. I am first going to tell why the bill was made, and then, Mr. Siegel will explain just what the bill says. Now Mr. Collier himself, as I said before, wanted to be out here to hear all these things which you will say but it was circumstances which were beyond his control which kept him from getting here, but nevertheless everything that is being said here today is being taken down in the minutes and he will read it all. He will also hear what we tell him about the meeting and so you can feel assured that everything that happens here will come to his attention.

Now I know that some of you here have come with opposition to this bill and that is fine, we don't mind that a bit. At the meeting held last week in Rapid City, among the Plains Indians, almost all of those who attended the conference when they came were against the bill. However very few of them really understood the bill at the time, and there had been those among them who had been going around saying things which it really didn't say, so they were against it at first. But before they had all left, we took a vote, a standing vote, on the bill on the attitude of the delegations and some 13 delegations were for the bill if a few minor changes were made and some four delegations were against it.

Now we know that all of you have come here with open minds and have not made up your mind definitely one way or the other, and that you will listen carefully to the explanations we give and judge the bill on what it really says. Now there are several reasons we felt why new laws were needed for the Indians. In the first place, we felt all over the country that the Indian lands had become so broken up by the allotment system that the cost of administering it was so high that most of the money that the Indians made from their lands went into paying for the necessary expense of taking care of it.

Now when the allotment law was originally passed back in 1887 there were several reasons behind it. Some of the reasons were very good reasons, very high reasons, very noble reasons, and some of them were very bad and low reasons. The good reasons were that if the Indians, if each Indian owned his own piece of land he would be getting better protection from the white man who might want to steal it from him, than if it were in tribal ownership. That was the reason given, but, let us see how it has really worked. When the allotment law was passed, the Indians had 138,000,000 acres of land. Of this 138,000,000 acres in the 47 years since the allotment law was passed, the Indians have lost 91,000,000 acres of that land. So all they have left today of what they possessed when the allotment system went into effect is 47,000,000 acres of land. The result of the allotment system which was supposed to save land for the Indians has been to make them lose almost two acres out of every three they had. This process of land loss is still continuing, and at as rapid a rate as ever. It was therefore felt that in order to keep land at all for the Indians it was necessary to do something to stop this loss of land. At the Rapid City meeting last week for the Indians of the Plains one of the Indians from the Lower Brule reservation, George Yellow Robe, made the following remark: "I have observed that ever since the allotment system went in, the white man has been reaching in and robbing me of everything but the soles of my shoes." Now that has been the pretty general experience all over the country—that the allotment system has robbed the Indians of their lands. So that is one thing this bill just introduced is trying to prevent.

Now in the administration of allotments we have some reservations in the country where there are over 4,000 different allotments. If they are going to be leased to white men it takes a tremendous amount of time and office work and money to get them leased because they have to make a separate deal for each piece of land. It is enough to take care of it when the original allottees are still living, but when they die and their heirs inherit the land, then there are still more people who are coming in, and the land is broken up into still smaller pieces.

Some pieces of land which only amounted to about 160 acres in the first place have got over 200 heirs to them at present. We have the actual record of one allotment of 160 acres which was leased to stockmen for 10¢ an acre.

VOICE FROM THE AUDIENCE: Where was that?

MR. MARSHALL: That was out on the Crow Reservation. That gave a return of $16.00 for the allotment.

VOICE FROM THE AUDIENCE: Did they get it?

MR. MARSHALL: Yes, they got it, but there were a hundred different heirs who were concerned with this allotment. So each one got 164. But that isn't the whole story by a long shot. Before this lease could be made each heir had to sign his name. Now then, getting all of these signatures, going out into the field, and the office work connected with it cost about 50¢ for each signature. So it cost about $50.00 to take care of the lease which brought the Indians $16.00. Now perhaps you will say that this cost was paid by the Government so it really didn't do them harm. But really, it wasn't paid by the

Government at all but by the Indians. And I will tell you why. If the Government hadn't spent all that money on this useless work that the Indians didn't want, which didn't do them any good, and would have done just as well if all the land were in one piece, they would have spent the money on something the Indians really did want. So actually the Indians paid for this as much really as if the money had been deducted from their own funds. The same sort of thing comes up all the time.

When the Indians sell their timber lands they get less for them than they would if they were in one solid block and then the lumbermen would not have to bother with each contract with one hundred different allottees. The same is true of Indian farming lands, which are so often broken up by inheritance, divisions made necessary by inheritance, that the Indians can't use their farms at all, but have to lease them or sell them. Wherever the Indians have gone in and actually used their own lands for themselves, either logging them or grazing their stock on them, or farming them, they have been held in large enough blocks that they could be used. On the Menominee Reservation where the Indians have for years logged their timber and made money on it, they made $1,600,000 on it in the past 25 years. The land is all tribal. On the grazing reservation where the Indian Stock Association, where the Indians have almost all been using the land, some system as proposed here has almost been found necessary. And when the Indians have been operating their own farms, it has always been in places where the farms have been big enough to live on. Where they have been broken up into tiny parcels to be used, they have either been sold or else have been leased to white men. All this bill tries to do is to put the land in such shape, that the Indians can use it themselves but if they don't use it they can lease it or rent it or give permits on it so that they can make the most possible money from it. Now that brings up another point which this bill is aiming at—to permit the Indians to use their property themselves instead of always leasing it or selling to the white men. If the Indians sell their timber, their stumpage to some lumbermen, they will give just as little money as they can get away paying for it.

I was speaking with Mr. Markishtum, a delegate from Neah Bay, this morning and we were talking about the lumber company that had bought their timber and were only paying $1.00 a thousand stumpage for it. That was all. That seems like a very small amount of money for their tribe to get as the sole return of their most valuable resources. If this bill were passed it would be possible for such tribes as wanted to do so to operate and develop their own timber. In this way they would not only get the little $1.00 or $2.00 or $3.00 a thousand for their lumber which the lumbermen will consent to give them but they will also get all the wages which come out of the operation of this timber and they will also get whatever percentage now goes to the lumber companies for its development. This bill makes that possible by providing loans to Indians, to Indian tribes and industrial developments which will add to the well being and the moeny they can make in their lives.

GEORGE ADAMS, Taholah Delegate from Hoods Canal: Have you any idea how much money it will require to progress and start up a logging operation to a point where it would successfully operate?

MR. MARSHALL: It would vary on different reservations. It would range from $300,000 to $500,000.

MR. ADAMS: I just wanted to satisfy myself if you were really acquainted with the amount of money. I am from Puget Sound and I was raised in the lumbering communities and I feel that you can go ahead and continue successfully your speech on logging operations.

VOICE FROM THE AUDIENCE: Would this mean that if this lumber is given the Indian, I want to know who is going to protect their right.

MR. MARSHALL: That will be explained later. The same will go to the Indians developing their resources and will also go for their range lands. The Indians, if they want to be given encouragement to get their own stock instead of leasing or giving their land to someone else and letting someone else make all the profit, will be able to get loans so that they will be able to build fences, wells, homes, and barns instead of now leasing to the white men and getting the lease rentals and nothing else. That will all happen if the bill is passed. Now the lady from the front row, from the Colville reservation.

COLVILLE DELEGATE: I ask the question whether the Indian funds are to be spent with their consent. Or at least that is what I understood. So I am trying to say is this, when the Indians are given the right to develop their timber, or is he just given control.

MR. MARSHALL: At first he is still protected and later on he is given full control. But anyway one of the things that concerns us under this bill is the fact that the Indians could have their money spent for them without their consent. One thing which we don't like about the present laws was the fact the Government could spend the Indian's money without asking for the Indian's consent. This law will make the abominable situation impossible anymore. The Government cannot anymore invest the tribal money in things that the Indians do not want or care for. Under this bill every expenditure of Indian money, money belonging to Indians, has to get the approval of the Indians. The final big point in the present set-up which seemed bad to us and which we wanted to have changed was the fact that the Indian has almost no voice in his affairs. Practically everything of importance which happens to him is decided by some white person who has been appointed to his reservation. He has practically no more voice to decide the thing which concerns him than he had back in 1887. He is still treated as if he were a little child with a parent who had to tell him everything that he should do. Now this bill proposes that gradually all the things connected with the Indians will have to be handled by the Indians themselves, if they want to handle them.

It won't happen all at once of course; it will take place as this bill shows, gradually and step by step but it *will happen*. So those are the major things we have been trying to change by this legislation which you are going to criticize and ask questions and discuss with us today and tomorrow. We want to put the Indians' land in solid enough blocks that the Indians can use it themselves or if they lease it can get a decent amount of money for it. We want to stop the sale of Indian lands to white people by homesteading and to buy up for these tribes who haven't enough land, more land. We want as much as we can to make it possible for the Indians to use their land themselves instead of just leasing it to some white men. We want to stop the use of Indian funds without the consent of the Indians, and we want as rapidly as possible to give the Indians the government of their own affairs,

During the course of this long talk I have just given, the Assistant Commissioner of Indian Affairs has come into the hall and I will introduce you to Mr. Zimmerman, who will have something to say to you.

MR. ZIMMERMAN: I am sorry that I am here in place of John Collier but there is only one John Collier and he cannot be in two places at any one time, but his spirit goes with us. He has prepared for you a message. I won't attempt to make a speech, I will read you the words that he wanted me to say.

VOICE FROM THE AUDIENCE: Will you speak louder Mr. Commissioner?

MR. ZIMMERMAN: All right, I'll try. I want also to bring you friendly greetings from Secretary of the Interior Ickes, and from Senator Wheeler of Montana, Chairman of the Senate Committee on Indian Affairs. I don't know whether or not Mr. Marshall emphasized the importance of this meeting but it seems to me that this is one of the great days in the history of the American Indians. This council is one of a series of meetings being held throughout the United States. I think it is the first time in the history of the United States, that Government officials have come to the Indians and asked them for advice on their problems.

Before we discuss any more details of the proposed law I beg you to put out of your minds any fixed ideas that you may have brought here based on any reports about our policies and this proposed legislation. I hope that you will keep your minds open. The questions to be discussed at this meeting are of big importance to each Indian. There should be no hurried, careless thinking or action. It is the policy of the present Indian administration not to do things even if they are going to act unless the Indians are willing to go with us. It is also true that in the last 4 or 5 years the members of the House Committee and of the Senate Committee on Indian Affairs have taken the view that they are representatives of Indians in all Indian matters. These members of Congress want to know the views of Indians. It is on their behalf, the behalf of these committees and these members as well as the Indian Administration, that we have gathered this morning to meet with you. I am convinced that there are some things which all the Indians need and that they know they need them. They need them in order to prosper, in order that their children and their grandchildren will prosper, and that in order that their children and their grandchildren will prosper, and that in order that they may be free men. Therefore I shall talk first about the fundamental conditions of your lives as I understand it.

VOICE FROM THE AUDIENCE: Mr. Chairman, will you please be a little more louder. Please speak louder, because I can't hear. You are far.

MR. ZIMMERMAN: All right. I shall first talk about the fundamental conditions of your life, as I understand it. What are those fundamental conditions? Some of those conditions, we think, are wrong and we want to put them right. First, that the Indians of the U.S. have for two generations been steadily losing their property. They have grown poorer and poorer. If you take the U.S. as a whole, the wealth of the people has been increasing year by year. During those same years the wealth of the Indians has melted away. So much for property.

The second fundamental condition is this: that the Indians of the U.S. are living under conditions which put them at the mercy of the Indian Bureau. The guardianship of the Federal Government of Indian life which was intended to be the means of making the Indians both prosperous and free has been having the opposite effect. It has been making them poorer while they were also being deprived of their freedom. Therefore, many people including some Indians have arisen and have said that the only hope for Indians is to put an end to the guardianship of the Federal Government. I do not hesitate to say that if the guardianship of the U.S. is to continue to do some of the things it has been doing, if it has to go on in the old way, then I think it had better be stopped and thrown aside and the Indians will do better without it. But that is not the answer.

The cure of evils done by the Government is not to abolish but to reform. Make the government do good things instead of doing bad things and that is exactly true of guardianship over the Indian. The answer to the evils of the past and the present is not to abolish the guardianship, not to end the responsibility of the Federal Government but to change it so that it will build up the property of the Indians instead of taking it away. Across a century of time, the U.S. has interfered too profoundly with Indian life; has stamped its mark too deeply for it now to withdraw all responsibility. The guardianship should not come to an end. It is still possible for the U.S. to do the right thing and I think it is fair to say that the present Secretary of the Interior Ickes, and the present Commissioner hold the positions that they do because they are expected to bring about changes in the Federal guardianship. The U.S. is not making a mess of Indian guardianship because its employees are either wicked or stupid. That is not the reason. They are not wicked and they are not stupid, but the guardianship now maintained by the U.S. is carried out under a body of laws which are wicked and stupid. They make slaves out of government employees who are there to carry them out. There was a time when it was the policy of the U.S. Government to crush Indian life. It isn't now the policy of the Government to rob the Indian or to crush the Indian. But these old laws are still in force. The problem of deciding what new laws to get is a fundamental matter to the Indians.

I may repeat what Mr. Marshall has already said but I will go on with it just as it was written. Now I would like to talk about provisions of the allotment act for just a moment. If we can go back to the year 1887, the Indians were the owners of 138,000,000 acres of land. That means all the Indians of the U.S. Its acres included some of the best land in the U.S., some of the larger farming lands, the best grazing lands. It included most of the land best suited to irrigation. And it also included great mining lands: oil, lead, zinc, metal, and other minerals before the surface. In that year 1887 Congress, against the protests of many Indians, enacted the allotment act. That is the backbone of Indian law, the great basic law of Indian Affairs. Now if we come from 1887 to the present day, we find that the amount of land now owned by the Indians is 47,000,000 still owned. About 20,000,000 acres is desert or semi-desert land. All of you know that the allotment law wasn't applied to all tribes.

The great Navajo tribes were spared, the Pueblos in New Mexico and Arizona were spared. Those tribes that were spared have nearly doubled their holdings since 1887. Every one of the tribes which was spared from the allotment act has more land now than in 1887. In other words, the losses of land have all been those lands that were allotted. If you take the value of land lost it would be more than 80% or 4/5 of the total value of all the lands held in 1887. The problem now is: How can the allotment system be changed. First, to stop the loss of land by Indians. Second, to give new land to landless Indians. And third, to protest the rights and equities of those Indians who have not yet lost their lands. Let me say what we think is necessary to do under some law to be enacted.

First, the further sale or loss of lands, of Indian lands, must be stopped. Second, land must be procured in order to take care of the Indians who have lost all of their land. New land must also be procured to supplement the land that is so poor. Third, we may say what we want about the bad results of the allotment system, but the fact is, that the allotment system had created (valid and rightful) property rights and those rights must be protected. As a result of the allotment act, thousands of Indians live on or are owners of individual parcels of land. They own that land. It is their right not only to continue to own but they have the right to transmit, to pass on what they own to their children. This right should not be taken away from them. Therefore, in addition to stopping the loss of land and getting more land, any change in the law must protect these individual property rights of living allottees.

There are many kinds of organizations in the modern world.

VOICE FROM AUDIENCE: (*interrupting*) Read that over please!

MR. ZIMMERMAN: There are many kinds of organizations in the modern world. For example, there are corporations organized to take care of various kinds of business. There are associations of cattlemen. There are cooperative societies. For example, to run creameries. There are cooperative societies organized to buy in large quantities so as to cut out the middle-man's profit. The white man has all kinds of cooperative economic organizations. But the word "Indian" is shut out from all these phases of organization. We're proposing that Indians shall be allowed and helped to organize. To organize for mutual benefit and for local self-government, and for business in a modern way. We are proposing that there shall be set-up a new credit system through which the government will extend financial credit to these organized groups of Indians. Remember, the Indians will only organize if they want to do so. When and if they organize, their organization will be instruments of the Federal Government. This must be clear when the Indians organize. It will be under federal law enacted by Congress.

Such an organized group may be very small. There are tribes in the U.S. with fewer than 100 members or a whole reservation might decide to organize or, again, a large jurisdiction might be broken up, might be divided into three or four groups. Still again, a group might organize for a special purpose such as, for instance, as a cattle association. Such a group would not assume all the responsibility of local self-government. Back many years ago when the Indians were still at war, when the U.S. was overrided to treaties with some of the tribes; in those days, the government adopted a policy of forfeit to Indians who organized in any way. At that time for Indians to organize was an illegal act. That *word* has come down to the present.

The laws passed in those days are still the law. Is it not strange that there should be anybody in the U.S. who would want to forfeit organizing of Indians when everybody else is organizing? It has come to pass that the only way they can get power to organize, the only way they could get power to make contracts, power to borrow money, power to do business was to pass out of the guardianship of the Federal Government. Indians have been taught that they had to choose between remaining like so many slaves, being taken care of by the Indian Bureau or else be thrown to the wolves.

VOICE FROM AUDIENCE: What was that?

MR. ZIMMERMAN: I say that Indians have been taught that they had to choose between remaining like so many slaves, being taken care of by the Indian Bureau or risk being thrown to the wolves. At least, that is what many Indians thought. Perhaps that was a natural understanding. In any case, that misunderstanding will pass away. Everybody understands that the Indian who progresses under this plan, will progress under federal law, federal guardianship. In other words, within the framework of guardianship it is possible to build up for the Indians freedom as an individual, freedom as a human being, with power that goes with organization. I think that there will be more federal protection in the end than there is now.

For just a moment I want to remind you what is going on in the country as a whole. Under the leadership of President Roosevelt, fundamental changes have taken place swiftly at Washington, and from Washington they will spread all over the country. The time will come when these changes will be ended as far as laws in Washington are concerned. The country will settle into a new mold. That may be one year, two years, three years, nobody knows. But the chance for the Indians is now. It is the chance of all times for you to get whatever it is that you are entitled to have. Now is the time of destiny, for you Indians. You must use your best brains in deadly earnest. You must face your problems, you must determine what you need and you must ask for it clearly. Perhaps, you understand now why we have come here to discuss with you these problems of your own lives.

MR. MARSHALL: I will now introduce the permanent chairman of this meeting, Mr. Woehlke, who is Mr. Collier's field representative of the entire Indian Bureau.

MR. WOEHLKE: My friends, I do not like this arrangement, I do not like to have anything between me and you so I will come in front.

Moves to front.

Now, I would like to have you clearly understand the purpose of this meeting. Mr. Collier called this Congress and a number of other Congresses of the Indian people throughout the country for a very definite purpose. He called you together because he wanted to tell you, either through his own words or through the members of his staff, of the Wheeler-Howard Bill—what this bill is going to accomplish. After having problems and the meaning of this proposition, of this new law explained to you, then he wanted to hear from you as to what you thought of it and of its various provisions.

But in order to discuss the bill intelligently, you must first know what its intention is and what its various provisions mean. Therefore, we propose now, very briefly to have some of the experts on the Commissioner's staff take up the bill, title by title, and explain to you briefly, shortly, what each section means, what it does and what it doesn't do. Commissioner Collier was very anxious to talk to you himself. Just before we left Rapid City, he spoke of various individual problems that confronted the Yakimas, Umatillas, and the Colvilles, and various other reservations and said he would like to be here and speak to you himself. But he was worn out.

During the four days of the Great Plains Congress, the Siouxs gave him a name. They called him the "Iron Man" because for 14 hours he kept going and wore out four of their interpreters. And I would like to have you understand that the time is short and the subject is very large and most important not only to you, but to us and to all the people in the various agencies, the federal employees. It is important to all of us. In order to get through and cover the ground thoroughly, we must proceed in an orderly manner. We cannot transform this congress into a mob; therefore I hope you will understand if I am compelled, in order to preserve the orderly proceedings, to shut off someone or refuse to recognize someone, it is because we must have an orderly proceeding in order to get through within the limited time.

And now I want to introduce the members of the staff with whom you will come in frequent contact within the next two days. I would like to have the members of the staff stand up as I introduce them so that you may meet them. Mr. Ward Shepard of the Indian Office who is in charge of land policies. Next we have Mr. Cohen who is the Assistant Solicitor of the Department of the Interior. I believe you met Mr. Siegel, Asst. Solicitor of the Department of the Interior. And I know you have met Mr. Marshall who is in charge of forestry for the Indian Service. Next we have Mr. Roy Nash, will you stand up. I believe most of you have met Mr. Nash and you know that you can rely upon his judgment and upon his complete sympathy. After these few words I want to ask one of the members of the staff to go right into a brief explanation of the land question of the Wheeler-Howard Bill. The gentleman who will make the explanation has been working on land policies and timber policies for many years and he was responsible for the lumber code which has been accepted by the lumber industry throughout the country. Mr. Ward Shepard.

MARKISHTUM (delegate from Taholah): Mr. Chairman: Will it be possible for any of the delegates to secure records or transcripts of the minutes of the meeting.

MR. WOEHLKE: We are making stenographic or mimeographed records so that there will be enough copies for everybody. And before our next speaker, Mr. Shepard, starts, I want to ask you again to put your questions (and I know you are boiling over with them) and see to it that they reach this table here before the beginning of the afternoon session so that we may start answering your questions as early as possible.

MR. SHEPARD: My friends, I have a very difficult job, to attempt to explain in a few moments the most difficult and complicated part of the bill. I am going to begin by giving the first four objects of this bill and then to build the explanations around these four purposes.

The first purpose, the fundamental purpose of this legislation is to prevent the further loss of Indian lands. The second great purpose, and here we come to the greatest difficulties of the bill—the second great purpose of the bill is to put into tribal or community ownership those lands and only those lands that can best be managed in tribal or community ownership. The third great purpose of the bill is to acquire additional lands either for the Indians who have no land and for Indians who have not enough land or to consolidate Indian lands where they have been checker-boarded so that they can be readily used by the Indians. The fourth great purpose of this bill is to give the Indians what they have never had before and without which they can have not economic and that is, to provide a great credit system by which Indian land can be developed for Indian use. Now I want to go back and review as briefly as possible the methods by which the bill seeks to adjust each of these four purposes and I want to ask you to make careful notes in writing as I go along on any questions that you may have that I do not make clear and especially criticisms of the provisions of the bill.

Now to go back to the question of preventing the further loss of Indian lands: First of all, the bill provides that henceforth no Indian lands shall be allotted in severalty—I think that is perfectly clear and plain—no more land will be allotted in severalty. The second step to prevent the loss of Indian lands provides that the so-called surplus Indian lands, the lands that remained after the allotments were made, and were offered for sale or homestead entry, that none of these surplus lands needed by the Indians will henceforth be opened to entry or sale to white citizens.

VOICE FROM THE AUDIENCE: Please repeat that last sentence.

MR. SHEPARD: The existing legislation provides that after allotments were made, the so-called surplus lands were opened to homestead entry or to sale to white settlers. This bill provides that if all the surplus lands are needed by Indians, they will permanently be withdrawn for sale or entry by white settlers and will henceforth have the status of tribal lands held permanently under trust. If the Secretary advises that there are certain surplus lands that are not needed by all the Indians, then he may reopen those to entry. The third step in preventing the further loss of Indian lands is to extend the trust patents on all Indian lands, tribal or otherwise, extending them indefinitely until Congress otherwise directs. In other words, all present and future tribal or trust-patented lands will be held permanently in trust. The bill further provides that no Indian land held under trust owned by the individual or by the tribe can be sold outside of the tribe or the Indian community. It can be sold within the community, but not outside.

During the hearings in the House Committee of Indian Affairs, when the provision had been explained to the committee, one of the members of that committee said, "Isn't it a great pity that the same system can not be applied to the white man's property?" As a matter of fact under the modern administration of property there is an increasing tendency throughout the white community and white property owners to put their money in trust for the benefit of their families so that it can not be wasted in Wall Street, so that the money is there for the permanent benefit of their families.

Now I come to the second fundamental purpose of this bill and it is here that there is misunderstanding of what we are really driving at. That second step, you will recall, has for its purpose to put back into tribal ownership the land which can best be managed in tribal or community ownership. The problem of putting these lands back into tribal ownership is to get all kinds of land especially the forest lands, the timber lands and the grazing land and put it all into one piece so that it will be useful. The criticism has been made by some Indians and by some white men who don't understand the bill, that it is communism. If this is communism then the U.S. Government, which is *not* communistic, is practicing communism on an immense scale.

VOICE FROM THE AUDIENCE: What is communism?

MR. SHEPARD: Communism is a system under which everybody throws his money into the pot. It means no more individual enterprises, the individual bossed by the community and the complete loss of property rights and of freedom. It has been said that this provision is communistic. If this is communism, then one-fifth of the entire U.S. is also communism because one-fifth of the U.S. is owned in common by the people. First of all, there are the National Forests, with 160,000,000 acres of land, three-tenths the total area, owned for the benefit of all the people of the United States, and operated for their benefit. There is now before Congress the so-called Taylor Bill which seeks to apply to 180,000,000 acres of grazing lands of the public domain precisely the system of management that we want to apply to the Indian grazing lands and Indian timber lands. But the government has been trying to allot the public domain for the last 50 years. They tried every possible inducement to get white men to go in and take up homesteads on the public domain and they still have 180,000,000 acres left.

VOICE FROM THE AUDIENCE: There a net profit on managing National Forests?

MR. SHEPARD: It depends on what you call profit. In the National Forests the principal charges for a great many years had to go to building roads, telephone lines, and other improvements to make the forest accessible for use. Also the National Forests in general have the least accessible timber in the United States. Many of them are on top of the mountains where the timber is difficult to get. The Taylor Grazing Bill recognizes that grazing lands, in order to be managed successfully, must be held in large continuous areas. We are going to have the same system of land management that we proposed in this bill. The chairman tells me that I have ten minutes, but I have just gotten started.

I want to try now to correct the provision of the bill which puts back into tribal ownership all Indian lands. It is not going to apply to all Indian land, it is going to apply to those lands which the Secretary determines must be consolidated into blocks in order to be economically operated by the Indians. I am going to explain how we propose to do that, but first of all, I want to explain one very important change which we propose to make in this bill. Title Three, Section Eight of the Bill as it now stands says that the Secretary may require the living allottees to relinquish his title to the tribe if that relinquishment is needed in order to consolidate the land into economic units. We decided to take that compulsory feature out of the Bill and we are going to change it to make it absolutely voluntary on the part of the Indian allottees. In regard to living allottees the Bill will be amended to read that their lands will be relinquished only voluntarily, if they wish to do so.

VOICE FROM THE AUDIENCE: Then the word "otherwise" may mean condemnation later?

MR. SHEPARD: That means that voluntary relinquishment in place of compulsory relinquishment, and applies also to the present heirship lands; that no present heirship land will be put into a community without the consent of the owners of that land. Now we come to another extremely important provision on which we invite your careful thought: What are we going to do with these heirship lands that Mr. Marshall described, where you have one hundred heirs to a hundred and sixty acres of land, and in the next generation you will probably have a thousand heirs. Do we want that system to continue? What will be the results? This bill seeks to solve the problem that now exists. If the owner dies and it has been determined that his or her land is needed for consolidation for economic use, hen the allotment shall pass to the tribe, or community but with full safeguards of the equities of the heirs.

VOICE FROM THE AUDIENCE: I want to ask if the inheritance law concerning the Indian is different from the laws concerning the white people?

MR. SHEPARD: Yes, it is different. In the case of white people it is customary that they leave a will and then you avoid this breaking up of farms into small parcels. If a farmer has 160 acres of land, he will probably leave it to his oldest sons. If he has ten children, he does not split it up into ten pieces with 16 acres to each child. The result is that throughout the United States you find that farming lands are held in useable units. We shall continue this discussion immediately on resuming the session at 1:30. You are requested to meet on the step outside here for a picture to be taken for the *Oregonian.* The following people call at the Main Office for messages.

Minutes of the Northwest Indian Congress

March 8, 1934, Thursday P.M.

MR. WOEHLKE: The session is now in order. I have just had a question concerning the seating of the delegations. There seems to be quite a number of delegates here, to use an Irish bull, who are not delegates. They should come up further in front to hear better; it seems to me that the official delegations would not object if those non-official delegates in the back would come around on the sides and front here. Any of the non-official delegates who would like to come up further in front here are perfectly welcome, thanks to the official delegation.

I wonder if the family is all here. I see a lot of missing territory there. However, we are fifteen minutes behind schedule and we are going to start. Before we begin with the official program again, the chairman, who is supposed to keep quiet and just pound the table, desires the privilege of saying a few words. I will give myself that privilege.

I would like first to have all of you understand that neither Mr. Collier nor anyone connected with him is trying to slip something over on you. I would like to have all of you realize, completely realize that neither Mr. Collier nor any of his associates want to take from you something that you have and I want you especially to realize that Mr. Collier doesn't want to ram something down your throat or to force you to do anything that you do not want to do. I wish you would keep those thoughts in mind in the discussion of the details of this program.

Please remember throughout this discussion that Mr. Collier, Mr. Ickes and the Congressional Committee want to give you more than you have, not act to take away from you, to add to what you have both in your property and in your ability to run your own affairs. And I want you to remember that in this offer of self-government the Commissioner is not going to force you to take any of it.

Rather he is offering it to you and saying "Take as much of it as you can handle, when you can handle it; here it is, but you don't have to take any of it if you don't want it." After all in the forming of a community it will be entirely up to you to say whether you want a community at all; if you do want a community, it is entirely up to you to say under what conditions that community shall be formed, so the whole thing is merely permissive. The Commissioner reminds me that I talk too much, that I should give the interpreters a chance to do their dirty work. I am sorry, I forgot. Do the interpreters remember? Otherwise I will repeat briefly what I said.

VOICE FROM THE AUDIENCE: Would like to have you repeat some of that. We didn't get much.

MR. WOEHLKE: I will put it in very brief words. The Commissioner and Congress and Secretary of Interior do not want to take from any Indian that which he has. Is that plain? On the contrary they want to add something to his belongings, to his rights and privileges. They want to increase them. We have not yet discussed the self-government features of the bill. We will in a very short time. But what I want to tell you right now is this: The Indian's house all over the country has been badly burned, the insides have been gutted by fire; not much is left. The fire that hurt this house was the allotment system. We propose to put out the fire, to put an end to the allotment system, but that alone is not enough. Your house is empty, very little is in it, so in this bill we provided a store and in that store you have furniture, and other things of all kinds. You have 2,000,000 dollars a year for buying land. You have a revolving fund of five or ten million dollars, whatever Congress says is all right, and credit so that we can help you put back into the house that which has been burnt up.

Once upon a time, you were self-governing in your old house. Now you have no self-government. The Secretary of the Interior and Commissioner, as the law is today, can tell all of you where you head in, they run your affairs and you have no say about it. But we do not want to have that power. We don't like it. So through this bill, we put up this store with credit machinery in it, with the land benefit feature in it, with the self-governing features in it, and there it stands. If you will patronize that store, it is there, but you have to do your own selecting. You have got to walk into the inside, you have got to help yourself to what there is in it. We are not going to force it on you.

VOICE FROM THE AUDIENCE: Excuse me for making a suggestion but knowing Indians like I do, I know it is going to complicate this idea, and if you just talk in straight-forward language, I am sure that they will understand it better.

MR. WOEHLKE: Anyway it is strictly up to you to take as much of the self-government and all the other things of the program as you want. Nobody is going to force them on you. In other words, you are going to have freedom of choice if this bill becomes law.

I want to surrender the chair to a man of your own race, a man who has spent his childhood right on a reservation, who grew up and became one of the great educators of the country, who is known from one part of the U.S. to the other. I have the pleasure of introducing to you a man who is 100% American, who is derived from the Winnebago race, Dr. Henry Roe Cloud.

MR. ROE CLOUD: Ladies and Gentlemen: I am very happy to be here because I have recognized a great many of my friends in several delegations. Now it is always good for a friend to meet friends and the fact that we have had fine associations in the years gone by makes my heart very glad to be with you today. I would like to make a little change in the proceedings right here, and I think it would help the speeches and program. The group that has the largest number speaking English, will the interpreter stand? Now which group is that? The Umatilla interpreter, will you stand up and interpret so we can hear plainly even if we don't understand you? Now when you cease speaking, I will begin to talk again.

Questions have been submitted here in writing and questions will be coming up all the while in written form. And this conference will be so conducted that when we get through, no one of you will feel "Well, my question wasn't answered," when we go away. In other words there should be perfect satisfaction before the Congress closes on any questions pertaining to this bill. Besides these questions there will be speeches from the floor from every delegation, also the older group of men. The first of this program is for these men here to explain to you one after the other the various parts of this bill. We will now proceed to do that. If someone rises and I do not recognize you, it is simply to give the speaker the fullest opportunity to explain.

This morning when the meeting was adjourned Mr. Ward Shepard was speaking and he didn't have an opportunity to finish, so I will call on him to continue.

MR. SHEPARD: As this lady down here in the front row suggested I am going to try to be simple and straight-forward and if anything that I say is not clear, please do not hesitate to interrupt. When we stopped for lunch we were talking about what would happen to the present allotments when the allottee dies. I was explaining that when the allottee died, his land would go to the tribe providing that land was needed in order to block out a unit such as grazing land, or timber land for economic use. (Refer to Title Three, Section 11.) If the allotment is not needed in order to block out an economic unit, then it will go to the heirs.

If the land goes to the tribe or community, there is a special protection for the rights of the heirs. In the first place, if the heirs are occupying and using this land they may continue to occupy and use it. If the heirs own a lot of small pieces of land, scattered in different parts, they may get the same amount of land all in one piece. Or if they don't wish to use that land, they will get the lease money either from the same land or the same amount of land. Or if they want to graze cattle and that land goes to the community, and that allotment is a grazing allotment, they will get a permanent right to graze in that community the same number of cattle or sheep that they could have grazed on their land. The heirs are also entitled to the ownership of any improvements on the land such as fences, barns, houses, etc. If they do not wish to continue to use those improvements they will be entitled to be paid for them. It is perfectly clear that when an heir or allottee surrenders the title to his land to the tribe, he loses absolutely nothing except the title. He either continues to use the land or he gets the use of just as much other land as he had. He has the choice.

I would like to say who will pay for these allotments and improvements: the government or the Indian community. Who is to furnish money to finance this purchase? The Government proposes in this bill to appropriate 2,000,000 dollars a year for improvements, but the bill also authorizes the Indian tribe to purchase land.

Before I leave this part of the subject, I want to speak about what will happen with farming lands on which Indians are living and which they are cultivating just as any white farm land. In my opinion this legislation in most cases does not affect those lands because the present owner will continue to use them and his heirs will continue to use them.

Now I come to the third problem. The bill directs the Secretary of the Interior to make a thorough investigation, a thorough study of the entire Indian land problem, in order to find out how much additional land the Indians need and to find out how much white-owned land should be purchased for the use of the Indians. Then the Secretary will go into a reservation that is badly checker-boarded, cut up with white ownership, and will start to buy up land in order that you may get your grazing units all in one solid piece, to get your timber land into one solid piece, or to get more farming land, if you haven't enough farming land.

VOICE FROM THE AUDIENCE: What about lands where there is not timber? I our community we have no farming lands as it is all fishing.

MR. SHEPARD: You mean will the government buy timber land? Well, that would be very easily possible. The government can buy any kind of land under this bill.

VOICE FROM THE AUDIENCE: You buy all kinds, all from the same community or would they be separate communities.

MR. SHEPARD: We could buy them all for the same communities. In many parts of the country there are Indians who have lost all of their land, in California and in parts of Oklahoma, for example. This purchase provision will permit the government to get land for those Indians so they can earn their own living. Now my time is getting short and I am going to explain briefly the credit system that we propose to set up, the loan system. The bill will set up a revolving fund of 10,000,000 dollars. This money will be given to the Indian communities which are organized for self-government under Title One of the bill. Each community will be given a sum of money in proportion to their needs. Each community will organize a credit association such as the white farmers organize.

VOICE FROM THE AUDIENCE: Mr. Chairman, we have a community within our immediate district whose main activity is fishing. We have no farming whatsoever. Would it be necessary to make a change in the bill to meet the needs of this community?

MR. SHEPARD: You mean about the credit system? No, I will explain it in just a minute. This credit association will make loans either to individuals or to Indian associations in the communities. No interest will be charged on these loans and they may be for as long as thirty years. These loans may be used by Indian farmers for building houses, or barns, or purchasing cattle or horses, or sheep or farming tools. Money will be lent to associations such as, for example, as a cattle association for the purpose of building fences and buying good bulls. Money would be lent to the community or an association to purchase a sawmill or logging equipment. To come to this question about fisheries: money would be lent to an association or a community to help you market your fish products; in other words, these loans will be available to individual Indians, to associations, to communities for the purpose of developing your economic life.

VOICE FROM THE AUDIENCE: On what security will these loans be based?

MR. SHEPARD: On moral security.

Applause.

Now this loan fund stays with your community. These loans remain in your community as a revolving fund. Therefore it is going to be up to each Indian community to help the Indians work out a good credit system so that the people will borrow money and pay it back to the funds. And when they pay it back you can lend it to somebody else.

MR. TOWNER: Suppose this program does not work out and the Indians had a local community that produced a lot of wheat, grain, corn, sheep, timber, or fish or all the produce that is derived from the community, will the United States government guarantee to buy that from the Indians?

MR. SHEPARD: I don't think we need to worry about that problem at the present moment. We know that the Indians as a whole are not producing really enough to enjoy a good standard of living. We want first of all, to have the Indians all over the country produce enough food so that they may live in comfort and security.

MR. TOWNER: My idea was this: The Indians living in this sort of a community, they are going to have more than they want because the idea behind the whole thing was to make the Indians prosperous, and if he is going to have a surplus from all of these industries, they have to sell some of these somehow. Will the American people buy it or will the U.S. government buy it.

MR. SHEPARD: I really can't see that this question pertains to the Indian Government at all.

(Interruption from Towner.)

DR. ROE CLOUD: Let's give the speaker a chance now.

MR. SHEPARD: I want to say just a few words in closing about what the land section of the bill doesn't do. I explained this morning that the bill is not communism.

INTERRUPTION FROM THE AUDIENCE: What?

MR. SHEPARD: It is not communistic. It is going to give to every Indian a better chance for individual effort than he has had in the past. It is going to give the individual Indian a chance to work, to cultivate his land with proper equipment. It is going to give the individual Indian a better chance to go into the livestock business than he has ever had before. It is going to give the Indian a chance to work his own timber, to manufacture his own timber, to get the wages and profits that now go to the white man. In other words, the purpose of this bill is to give real economic security to the Indian and give the Indian a chance to develop his own lands along modern lines.

MR. ADAMS: I just want to call the attention of the gentleman who just finished speaking that his entire talk was very good, I enjoyed it very much; there is just one place, the word "communism." There is no such word in the make-up of the Indian languages. That is something we know nothing about and I don't know how the interpreter interpreted such a thing to the Indians.

MR. ROE CLOUD: The following persons have not called for their messages: Mrs. Philips, J. L. Kirk.

The following subjects will be discussed this afternoon. The question of self-government and education, and before I call on the expert on self-government, Mr. Cohen, I would like to make a few remarks. You know we have been complaining as Indians that we do not have enough self-government ourselves. Even the word "slaves" has been used in the system of government of the Indian. If I understand the bill, the purpose is to instil in the Indians themselves a larger measure of authority and responsibility in governing their own affairs, and to reduce the power of the Secretary of the Interior over them. I think that is a wonderful feature of the bill where we can govern ourselves and settle our own problems and without all this red tape, waiting months and months before we can sell a cow or something of that sort.

Before Mr. Cohen speaks, that question of Mr. Towner's wasn't answered. I suppose that the U.S. government shall proceed to absorb the things that the Indians raise, but I will call on Mr. Marshall who is an expert and who can answer that.

MR. MARSHALL: I just wanted to answer Mr. Towner's question, to tell him what is already being done by the Indians. On the Menominee Reservation the Indians have been manufacturing their own lumber for 25 years. They have been making better lumber than the white men around them have made and they have been able to sell every bit of it which they manufacture. And they have gotten 1,600,000 dollars for it. At Red Lake the Indians have sold their fish on the regular market so the government doesn't have to buy their products. The people of the country, the private consumers want to buy them and they will buy them. Because the Indians have not had to pay taxes, they can produce lumber, cattle, sheep and farm products cheaper than their white neighbors. So I don't think you will find the least trouble selling them.

PARSONS (Nez Perce): You don't consider that the cattle industry or any other industry, the Indians have been under the same governmental regulations, the present agricultural administration, as the white man because on our reservation we are subject to the same laws concerning grazing and what effect would the proposed bill have on the future prospects of Indian farming and stock raising?

MR. MARSHALL: It is true that all of these Indian operations will be in exactly the same boat as your white neighbors, but you will have the great advantage of freedom from taxation which will put you ahead of him. Now Mr. Towner.

MR. TOWNER: My question was directed for this purpose. Possibly the Menominee Indians have a good trade of timber, but in covering the various industries around the country we are subject to certain restrictions and my idea was this: Suppose we do produce more than the white whether the government is going to guarantee to buy it or whether we are going to have to take our chance and sell it to the public if they will buy.

MR. MARSHALL: If we guarantee to buy all the Indian's produce that way all the white men would turn Indians as Mr. Zimmerman just said.

MR. ADAMS: Let an Indian answer an Indian: The question brought up by Mr. Markishtum of Neah Bay relative to the Salmon industry. Salmon is the most important industry in the State of Washington. No, logging is first, and salmon is second. Neah Bay is the world capital for the Chinook, the best salmon that ever swam in the water. There never will be enough Chinook salmon to give all the people in the country a taste. No one need ever be afraid of an overproduction of salmon that would come from Neah Bay section, so you need not have any fear about that. And speaking of timber, everyone has heard about the Douglas Fir. This timber will sell when other timber will not. So the State of Washington can take care of itself if the Indians were given a chance.

MR. ROE CLOUD: We are glad to see that this Congress is coming back to life. The point was this, Mr. Markishtum of Neah Bay raised the question and it was very properly answered relative to salmon and relative to lumber and their possibilities, giving you folks a picture of what can be done. It is up to you.

MR. WASSEN: Could the record show the amount of stumpage the Menominee Indians own or the amount of stumpage that was cut?

MR. ROE CLOUD: Was that a question?

MR. WASSEN: I want the record to show the amount of stumpage that was cut.

MR. ROE CLOUD: No, I haven't got it. That information is available and can be had. Now that talk about overproduction. I would like to see the day when any Indian, I for one, when the Indians have too much. Mr. Roy Nash, the man sitting here, is appointed by the Chairman as the permanent secretary of this Congress, and the Congress is honored by his presence. I have a very important message delivered to me by Mr. Woehlke and I would like to read it to you at this time.

> "To all the Indians of the Northwest, the tribal delegation and other Indians attending the Congress now in session. It is with sincere regrets that circumstances over which I have not control are not permitting me to attend your Congress and meet all of you individually and the delegations. As you all know this country of ours is very large. Hence much time is consumed in traveling and due to my returning to Washington as soon as possible it is absolutely necessary to limit my trip throughout the Indian coun-

try at this time. However, I realize the tremendous importance of this Congress and have the greatest personal interest in your welfare and in your deliberations. I have sent practically my entire staff to council with you. After the Plains Indian Congress was concluded at Rapid City, it was physically impossible for me to accompany my staff to your Congress although it was my desire to do so. Although, physically I am not with you I am in spirit and take this means of wishing you success in your deliberations and I assure you that your welfare is as close to my heart as any other Indians." John Collier, Commissioner.

A moment ago I announced that a speaker would get up and speak on the subject of self-government. I will appoint Mr. Cohen to speak on self-government.

MR. COHEN: I should like to explain the provision of the first part of the legislation. The first part of this bill deals with self-government. I have been told by some interpreters that some of the Indian languages do not have a word for "self-government." So I want to explain for the benefit of the old-timers what self-government means. For one thing, self-government means that the various rules and regulations that govern your property and affairs will not be made in Washington by the Bureau of Indian Affairs and will be made by yourselves. In the second place, self-government means that you will have power to choose all your own officials instead of having them chosen for you in Washington. In the third place self-government means that you will have control over all of your own funds instead of having all the control in Washington. To sum it all up, the idea of self-government means that the Indian Bureau is to become a purely advisory bureau to help the Indians instead of to rule them.

How do we propose to achieve this end of self-government. The first part of the legislation, the whole Title One dealing with self-government, is optional with the Indians concerned. This is a very peculiar law. It does not tell all the Indians what they have to do. It tells the Indian what they can do, if they want to do it. It is, in effect, a bill of rights for the Indians. Now this problem of bringing about Indian self-government is a very difficult thing and it can not be achieved in one day. The Provisions of this Title One show the various steps that will be necessary in order for any group of Indians that want self-government to get self-government.

This first part of the legislation refers to communities. I think probably some of the old-timers have not properly understood what a community means. A community is simply a group of people who have gotten together to do something. If they get together to raise cattle, as the Shoshones do at Fort Hall, then they have a community for raising cattle. If they should organize a corporation as they have been trying to do up at Klamath, then they would have a community for cutting and selling timber. When a number of white people who live near each other get together and form a township, well, that township is a community. And a white man's county is a community. And also the old Indian tribes are communities.

When this legislation enables the Indians to form a community, it does not mean that there is one kind of community that all of the Indians must form. Some of the Indians will form one kind and some another kind. Down in the Southwest, as many of you know, some of the old tribal organizations are still in effect. Those Indians down there may want their community to be like one of these old tribal organizations. Up here in the Northwest, most of you people have had more contact with white man's organizations, and your communities can be the most modern, the most up-to-date communities that you are able to manage. There is nothing in this bill that forces you to wear blankets or to elect chiefs.

If this legislation passes, the Commissioner will come to each reservation and he will discuss with the Indians on that reservation what kind of community they want. It may be that on that reservation he will find that the mixed bloods want one kind and the full bloods want another kind. In that case, there may be two communities, and that might happen on reservations where there are two tribes which don't like each other. Now when the Secretary of the Interior and any group of Indians get together and decide what kind of organization they want, this will explain the kind of organization that is to exist in that particular reservation or on that part of a reservation.

This charter will be, in effect, a contract between the United States and those Indians. And if the Secretary of the Interior or the Commissioner of Indian Affairs at some future time does not live up to that contract, then we are going to have a special Court of Indian Affairs into which the Indians can go and compel the Secretary of the Interior to live up to that contract. And that works both ways. If the Indians agree in this charter to do something—for instance, to spend their tribal funds in making a saw-mill—and then don't live up to their end of the bargain, the Secretary or the Commissioner can go to court and compel them to do what they agreed to do.

I won't go into a long list, but I will explain three kinds of things that a community may do under its charter. In the first place, an Indian community can, if it wants, have the powers of a village or a county. It can elect its own officials and have its own code of ordinance. In the second place, a community may be given power in its charter to do the ordinary things that a business corporation does. For instance, the Indian community may under its charter have power to manage its own grazing and other matters which are regulated by the Office of Indian Affairs. In the third place, this charter will give the Indian community the right to do many things that the Office of Indian Affairs now does. The charter might provide that the individual Indian community could lay down and enforce the rules about wills instead of having the Secretary of the Interior decide whether each individual Indian will is valid or invalid. At present Congress can spend your tribal money in any way it wishes. Once a charter has been made and given to a community, and this applies to all communities, Congress can't spend your funds without your consent. Congress can't appropriate for irrigation systems for white men and then charge it up to you as reimbursable loans.

Another thing that applies to all Indian communities—every Indian community has the right to remove federal employees. The Secretary of Interior may, however, lay down the conditions under which you can bring proceedings against any employee. The Secretary of the Interior must lay down a trial period and during that trial period you can't remove an employee because he hasn't yet shown what he is made of. Not only can an Indian community remove an employee, but it can also appoint one of its own members to a vacant position. That person need not go through with the regular Civil Service examinations, but the Indian Office will lay down the qualifications for the particular job whether it is the job of forester, or teacher, or anything else, and if an Indian can meet those specifications, that will get the position.

This charter, that deals with all these matters on which you and the Secretary agree, can be added to from time to time. You don't have to, you are not expected to, want all these powers at once. I doubt if there is any tribe that would want at the present time to run its own health service, but in the long run you will want to take over all of the services. And this bill provides for special training which will help you take over all your services. Our chairman will explain the provisions of this bill that deal with this special training for your young people. As your young people grow up and learn to do all sorts of things that your white employees are now doing, there will come a time when you will want additional fields, additional powers, to those in your charge. And if you are prepared to take over those additional fields, then you will get an amendment, a supplement to your charter. Furthermore the Secretary is directed by this bill to lay down the necessary qualifications for the various positions and various functions that the Indian Bureau is now performing; and when any community meets those qualifications and they can show they can meet them, that job will be turned over to the community.

There is one misunderstanding about this whole project that I want to make clear. Some people who don't want to see this bill passed have gone around saying "This is a relinquishment of federal guardianship." This is simply to continue. This bill specifically says that "Nothing in this bill shall be construed as rendering the property of any Indian community or any member of such community subject to taxation by any State subdivision thereof, or subject to attachment or sale under legal process, or as an expression of intent on the part of the United States, to abandon the duties and responsibilities of guardianship of any Indians becoming members of chartered communities." The Federal guardianship will be administered, not in Washington, but on your reservation. The government of your Indian community will be itself an instrumentality and agency of the Federal Government just as the Indian Bureau is an agency of Indian government. Your Indian Bureau now gets appropriations.

VOICE FROM THE AUDIENCE: We had orders today to ask questions.

DR. ROE CLOUD: The questions will come in due time. The administration wishes that the . . .

VOICE FROM THE AUDIENCE: You're out of order. You are out of order. We understood this morning that this afternoon was to be spent in answering questions that were presented on the table.

DR. ROE CLOUD: The chairman came in after the meeting had commenced. And I personally did not know what had gone on this morning. What I understand is that the present program is to get at the educational part of this bill and immediately proceed with the questions that have been asked. I am trying to get to them just as soon as possible. The order of the day should be followed. Well now the question has been raised as to whether or not we are going to hear further explanations of this bill or should we go on to the answering of questions?

MR. ADAMS: Let us hear something more first before we have questions.

DR. ROE CLOUD: The question is here and I am going to put it before the house. All those in favor of beginning the answering of questions without further examination of the bill, will you raise your right hand.

Very few hands raised.

Now all of those in favor of a further explanation of the bill before beginning the questions raise your right hand.

Majority of hands raised.

Now that settles it. That establishes the order of the day. We will have more explanation of the bill before we begin to ask questions.

MR. COHEN: There is just one more statement that I wish to make before I sit down, with regard to appropriations. In the first place, this bill provides a sum of 500,000 dollars which is to be given to the Indian communities to give them a start. That is in addition to the 2,000,000 appropriation which goes to land. When an Indian community takes over any job from the Indian Bureau, the money which Congress appropriates for the job will be given to the community. More than that, whenever a bill comes into Congress which authorizes the appropriation of money within any Indian community, the Indian will have a say about that bill. A copy of that bill and they will pass a resolution approving it or disapproving it or suggesting some other way in which to spend that money. And those remarks must be sent to Congress so that Congress can know where the Indian community disagrees with the Indian Bureau as to how that money should be spent.

DR. ROE CLOUD: I know that every division has a great many questions to ask and they are technical to that division. For instance, most of you probably don't know the Colville problems or the Tulalip problems. An arrangement has been made so that these particular problems can have due consideration. They will be discussed tonight within each group.

Proceeds to give directions as to where tribes are to meet.

Now this is going to be very brief indeed. I know you are getting rather tired and we want to get to those questions.

These special arrangements in this bill concerning the education of Indians are mighty interesting to me. The bill says that the Indian is going to be helped by the U.S. Government and for his or her education, he must be at least one-fourth Indian blood. This educational system is going to be put in practice for the purpose of putting Indians in jobs in the Indian Service for one thing. And in the second place, it will be education to fit Indians for the jobs that are going to be created by this bill. That will be educational jobs for education. That is to say, education to train Indians for Public Health Work. Education to teach how to live so they can get along nicely together, some people call it Social Service. Educating Indians to take care of law and order; Educating Indians for the management of forestry, and grazing, taking care of financial accounts, statistical records and public libraries. Here before you, right in front are these boys and girls being trained for just that sort of thing, bookkeepers, accountants, etc.

The Commissioner of Indian Affairs may use some of these school buildings or some other reservation for the training of these Indian people. For the education in the higher branches of learning, he will send them to universities, colleges, and schools of medicine, of law, engineering, agriculture, and other institutions and he will pay for that training. The money loaned to the Indian boy or girl, half of it need not be paid back. The other half that he does pay back is non–interest bearing. He doesn't pay interest on it. The Indian who has borrowed this money, as long as he or she is out of a job, need not pay it back until he is reemployed. For this purpose, this bill asked for $50,000 every year. If the Commissioner of Indian Affairs in looking around the various Indian tribes finds some outstanding boy or girl, he has an educational fund of $15,000 to educate that particular boy or girl.

This bill says that whatever good things the Indian has developed in this country a thousand years back to the present, things of his mind and of his heart—Indian civilization—they are going to study that, put them before the whole country. The bill recognizes that the Indian tribes of ancient time had a great many things they can give to the white man, but attempts have been made to destroy them. Now an attempt will be made to relight the spiritual fire that burned in the hearts of the Indian people in ancient times. Indian crafts, arts, schools and trades will have new dreams, new schools and a new deal.

I would like to say something on my own success on that point. I was talking to an acquaintance in the Dakotas and he said that this bill is going to segregate the Indians and put them all by themselves. On the contrary, this bill sends our own Indians to the white schools, sends them with white children where they want to be. And it brings back to life the culture that we used to have and will give you responsibility and we will begin to hold our heads up as we have never done before. The Indian and a white man walk down the road. The Indian doesn't know what is in the white man's mind. They may just as well be a thousand miles apart. But an Indian living under the conditions specified by this bill will begin to have his mind wide open so that he can see his own world and the white man's world. In other words he is not living only in his own world. He is in contact with his white neighbors in thoughts and in his heart more than he has ever been before.

(Recess is declared at 4:00 p.m.)

(The meeting came to order at 4:25.)

DR. ROE CLOUD: This meeting will now come to order. Will you please be quiet so that we can commence the meeting. This is the first question on education that I would like to read to you.

As a graduate of Chemawa Indian School in 1927 and Haskell Institute in Lawrence, Kansas, in 1931, and a student in Eastern Oregon Normal at LaGrande, I made an application to the Civil Service for a position as Boys' Advisor and on June 1, 1931, was rejected because I did not have the necessary experience. Also, I applied for an educational loan but because statistics were inadequate I was unable to receive one. This burden not only confronts me but many other Indian students throughout the country so I am voicing in behalf of the Indian Youth who are adjusting themselves to be benefactors to their fellow tribesmen. I want to ask, "How will one get the required experience, get required specifications, to get a job in the Indian Service?"

JACK ABRAHAM: One to get an educational loan must own property.

I think that is a very good question. The Indian Service in recent years has set up certain educational qualifications for most of its positions. There are many positions, as you know, that are classified as laborer positions and other positions as that the U.S. Government and the Indian Bureau are trying to put under Civil Service. Now the spirit and plan of the Civil Service is a wonderful thing. What it does to the whole country is to standardize the requirements all over the country and puts the youth of the country on a high plane. And the requirements for the Civil Service which the white man makes in many instances have been too high for Indian young people to pass. Civil Service is a high fence and you have to take a running high jump to get over and the fence has been too high for our young people to get over it. It is the duty of the Secretary to require a certain amount of teaching experience before they will accept anyone in these salaried positions. Now, as I understand this bill, the plan that will be worked out in the near future is to classify all the positions from so high to a higher one and then to the very high positions. Those with a fair training will receive the little jobs, those within a higher training will receive higher positions and those with professional training the highest. But as it is now the Indians have to compete with white people and in a very great many cases are shut out. Several years ago there were more Indians working in the Indian Service than there are today, and the reason for that is because they have raised the standards too high for the Indians to pass. But I do not see why a young man who finished Chemawa, Haskell and Normal School should not receive a position. I happen to know that many young men have been appointed advisors although they have not the educational qualifications required by the Civil Service. Now under this new bill arrangements will be made so that you will see a great many more Indians in the Service than you ever saw before. That is just to start things off. If I haven't answered that to your satisfaction, someone of the staff will supplement just what I have said. Now we are ready for the questions that involve the land. The land questions now will be taken up first and we have these questions now written down and Mr. Siegel will take that up.

MR. SIEGEL: I have a list of excellent questions from the Spokane group and I will begin my discussion on these questions by taking up the questions on the land subject one by one. Is there anyone going to interpret this? The first question is this: Will the government restore alienated Indian allotment lands to the tribes? The answer: The Secretary is authorized to spend $2,000,000 to purchase alienated lands. Those lands will be purchased for those Indians who need this land. In other words, land may be restored legally to tribal status and the landless Indians who need the land will be given certificates entitling them to use this land.

SECOND QUESTION: Will the government restore all alienated land to the tribe? Answer: The bill authorizes an appropriation of $2,000,000 a year. We would like to have more but the government budget must be pruned down. If you can do anything to help us by adding in the passage of this act we would be delighted to have you cooperate.

THE QUESTION IS: Will the government restore all other alienated land to the tribe? At this point I would like to emphasize again that we need the cooperation and assistance of the Indians and if they will petition Congress for the passage of this act it may be possible to get more than is asked for in the bill.

QUESTION: Will the Indian department stand behind the Indians in the securing of these lands to the extent that if it becomes necessary to condemn those lands, will they go into court on behalf of the Indians and the land for its real value instead of three or four times the sum.

MR. SIEGEL: Someone has already asked that question and I was going to answer it later, but since you brought it up, I will answer it now. One of the powers which may be granted to a chartered Indian community is the power to condemn land for any special purpose. The act, as now drafted does not give that power to the Secretary of the Interior but perhaps the Secretary should himself have that power until that community is organized. Perhaps the bill should be amended.

THE QUESTION IS: By what method will the alienated lands be restored. I expect what I just said in part answers that question—if we can't condemn, we will buy it.

QUESTION: Will this land which is going to be bought, will it be bought for all the members of the tribe?

MR. SIEGEL: The answer is that this land which is being bought is going to be bought for the use of the Indians who have no land to use now. I want to emphasize that point because one of the main objects is to restore lands to and colonize these Indians, who, through the allotment system, have lost everything they ever had. At the same time I want to make it plain that we are not going to take the present tribal land that has not been lost. That will be distributed equally as it is now.

MR. ADAMS: I wish you would repeat that again, particularly that point. It won't be bought back? I really don't know.

MR. SIEGEL: I will explain. First, the lands which we are going to buy back are going to be bought for the use of those who have no land to use now. Let me make it plain that we are not going to allot any of it. We are going to allot them the use of the lands which we are purchasing for them. Secondly, the lands which are still in tribal status which have not been allotted may be used equally among the members of the tribes.

COLVILLE DELEGATE: I wish to ask you a question in regard to this land system. I have been among the Indians and lived among them. It is a well-known fact that some of the officials in Washington have said that many have lost their allotments through the allotment system. If you will explain to our people what you really mean and intend to do. Perhaps it does not involve what is now in our possession and that you do not intend to take away the land given to us under this allotment system. Will you kindly explain?

MR. SIEGEL: I am very confident that no official of the Indian Bureau has misrepresented the plan we have submitted. However, even they may justly be confused by the information which was submitted to them some time ago. This bill is not meant to take the land from those who have it, whether it be allotted or inherited or their share in tribal property and give it to those who are landless. Under this plan each individual would be entitled to the use and rental of that same amount of land that he has now and his heirs would inherit that same right or an equivalent to the same. Any land which the landless Indian is going to get would be from the land which we are going to purchase for them.

QUESTION: Is it a fact that the first part of page 12, of this bill, down on line 22 of section 8, is it a fact that that portion is merely declaration of policy on the part of Congress, not on any future Congress, or any future Administration. Is it not merely a declaration of policy? Would it be too much trouble for the gentlemen connected with the bill to explain to these people fully regarding this?

MR. SIEGEL: I would answer your question this way: No part of this bill is binding on any future Congress, but a good part of it is intended to be binding on future administrations, that is, Commissioners and Secretaries of the Interior.

QUESTION: How would you construe line 3 to 6, on page 32 in the Senate Bill? The part referred to is "The Secretary of the Interior may sell and convey to an Indian or to an Indian tribe or community any restricted lands inherited by any member, whenever, in his opinion, the sale is necessary for the proper consolidation of Indian land."

MR. SIEGEL: I will say that there is a misprint and that should say "any Indian Tribes or community." Now in answer to the question directly, the present law as it now exists independent of this bill in the act of 1910 specifically authorizes the Secretary to sell any heirship land and we are merely adding to that power by allowing that community or tribe to use their funds to purchase them.

Now I have just said that this bill does not attempt to take any land and give it to those who do not have any. I want to explain in detail what it means. As originally written, this bill would allow the Secretary to transfer to the community or tribe any land which had been allotted to the individual allottee and would give him in exchange a certificate which would indicate the right to an equivalent value, or the right to get the value to rise from an equivalent amount of land. The Commissioner has decided that power should not be exercised without the consent of each individual owner of property. However, the present law authorizes the Secretary and he would have the power, independent of this bill, to sell heirship lands to a tribe or a community. At the death of the present owner any restricted allotment lands or heirship lands of the heir of the individual property owner will receive a certificate which will entitle him: first, to use and occupy the same land that his ancestors had before, the same land that his parents lived on. Let me repeat this. He will have the right to continue to occupy the same lands that that person who died occupied and used before his death. He will be entitled to keep the improvements on any land or else to receive adequate compensation to [*cannot read*] such improvements. I think I better restate that. There is no intention to take any improvements without the consent of the owner. He can hold them. He can sell them to the Government, tribe or community. Now the statements I am now making answer in part one of the questions which was submitted by the Spokane group and I will read.

QUESTION: Would the whole tribe or the individual be included in the community group? Can't the Indian farmer still live on it and still farm his land? Would the individual farmer lose control of his farm and improvement? Would the individual Indian lose the right to lease the land for his own benefit?

MR. SIEGEL: During the lifetime of the present farmer, the answer is that he would lose no right but I must frankly admit that under the terms of the bill as presently drafted, he would lose the right to lease that land.

However, while I cannot speak nor can any one of us speak with authority for the Commissioner, I see no reason why an individual farmer, why the heirs of a farmer cannot continue to have the right to lease that land and the bill might be amended to preserve that right. Mr Cohen calls my attention to the fact that farm lands might possibly be included in the area which is to be brought together into units. This provision would then not apply at all and the old law would continue to apply. Let me explain why there would be no objections to keep individual control of farm units. The reason is this: the reason for the heirs provision in this law is that under the conditions there are so many heirs to one piece of ground, to one particular allotment, that nobody can use it. The allotment is broken up into small unusable units. Now if any Indian is farming a farmland in a large enough unit so that he can make a living out of it, he will be entitled to make a will transmitting that property to his heirs, it will go to his heirs with one qualification.

QUESTION: Any number of acres?

MR. SIEGEL: The allottee may have the privilege to devise property, personal or otherwise, to his heirs.

PETER JAMES: What I wanted to know is the explanation of this Section on page 32, line 3 to 6, where the Secretary of the Interior may sell and convey to an Indian or to an Indian tribe or community any restricted lands inherited by any member, whenever in his opinion, the sale is necessary for the proper consolidation of Indian lands.

MR. ADAMS: I think those few lines are self-explanatory. The Secretary may sell and convey to an Indian or to an Indian tribe or community any restricted lands inherited by any member, whenever, in his opinion, the sale is necessary for the proper consolidation of Indian lands. I am surprised that a man as well-educated and as bright as you, Peter James, cannot understand it.

MR. SIEGEL: Any person who owns farm land may continue to keep it as his own for his lifetime, whether it be an original allotment or heirship land. If he has been using that land before, his heirs will be entitled to keep all allotments on that land and improvements. It is my opinion that there is some doubt whether or not his heirs will be entitled to lease that land. If there is such a doubt, although I can not speak without the authority of the Commissioner, I do not see why the heirs could not be entitled to lease that same land, or to inherit that same land.

All of you Indians know very well that through the operation of the heirship laws, your lands, including your farm lands, your lands have been broken up into such small parcels that nobody can use them. Therefore, the Secretary is given authority to make rules which will forbid heirs from inheriting in small pieces and will prevent or refuse to recognize any will which breaks up into small units farm land that nobody can use.

What are we going to do with those Indians who are entitled to heirship land? What are we going to do with those who are left out?

In the first place, we believe that many of the difficulties will solve themselves under this new plan. As you probably know, there are many cases where one heir has many little bits of land, pieces which are too small for anybody to use but if you put them together into one piece everybody can use it. One heir might have one piece of land on the north side of the reservation, another piece on the south side, another piece on the east side and another piece on the west side of the reservation. Some of them are so far away that many heirs probably have never seen their own lands. Now, with regard to farm land, all this bill would have to do is to bring those pieces together and thereafter prevent anybody breaking it up again.

Under the bill, does the Government purchase land for the tribe and make the tribe keep it? If so, would an individual Indian have the right to lease some of this land for his own benefit?

The Government has a limited amount of funds which it intends to use primarily to buy lands alienated from Indian heirship into white ownership. We have the authority to buy heirship lands and sell heirship lands and the tribe or community is given authority to buy such lands and the tribe or community has the right to use tribe or community funds to buy such lands. If the heirship land is not sold or purchased, the person will be entitled to keep it and lease it.

If the bill passes, will an Indian be compelled to sell his Indian lands to the tribe or community if he does not want to?

I have already answered that.

Will not the officers of the community have control of all lands belonging to the tribe?

The answer is that it depends upon whether or not they are given such authority by the charter and they do not have to accept the charter unless they want to.

As several of the delegates have tried to ask questions during the speech, Mr. Siegel adds the following:

I want to add again that I have no desire to cut anybody off from asking questions. It is only to save time, and they shall have a chance on another occasion.

CHAIRMAN: We have not finished the questions regarding land but will continue with them on meeting in this hall tomorrow morning at 8:30. The house is now open for adjournment.

VOICE FROM THE AUDIENCE: I move that we adjourn.

ANOTHER VOICE: I second the motion.

CHAIRMAN: It has been moved and seconded that we adjourn. All in favor specify by saying "Aye." (*Unanimous.*) The Congress is adjourned.

Friday, A.M., March 9, 1934

MR. WOEHLKE calls the meeting to order: The Congress of the Pacific Northwest Tribes is now called to order. I would like to ask the Reverend Dr. Roe Cloud to say the invocation now. Dr. Roe Cloud.

Dr. Roe Cloud gives the invocation.

MR. WOEHLKE: Before we proceed I would like to suggest a slight re-arrangement of the seating of the delegates. Our friends from Yakima and from Warm Springs have quite a large number of older men who do not speak English and need an interpreter. They are so far back in the room that it is difficult for them to hear and translate. I would, therefore, ask the three delegations on this side in front to make a little room for the Yakima and Warm Springs delegations to occupy this section so that they may hear better. Move the Yakima banner over here. If there isn't room on this side, I suggest that one of the delegations take seats on the front row on the other side. Perhaps the Warm Springs delegation would like to sit over here (*south side on the front row*). Is there any room?

ANNOUNCEMENTS: It has been suggested that we have an entertainment here this evening so that the delegates may see what their children can do. We would like to know whether the delegates would like to have such an entertainment this evening or if there is any objection. If I hear no objection, I shall assume that you would like to have the entertainment and that arrangements will be made for it and that the announcements as to the time will be made this afternoon. Is there any objection to the entertainment?

Applause for it.

It seems to be unanimous. I have an announcement to make: All the Haskell students, the institution of which Dr. Roe Cloud is Superintendent, are requested to have luncheon with Mr. and Mrs. Wade Crawford at 12:15 at the Club House. All Haskell students and graduates.

We were right in the midst of answering questions, and I believe that even though we answered many questions in the individual meetings last night, we should continue with that program until 11:00; then we should call upon the older people, those who do not speak English, to let us know through their interpreters what they think of their condition and receive their suggestions concerning the solution of the problems. If this meets with the approval of everyone, we shall proceed along those lines immediately; and I believe this afternoon we should give a certain amount of time to each delegation so that they, through spokesmen, selected by themselves, could tell us what we ought to know. We have been doing all of the talking up to this time, and we will show you that we can take it as well as dish it out. Will you interpret that?

Before we start in with the replies I would like to tell you about a most pleasant surprise which happened last night. We met with a group including three tribes of the Umatilla Reservation. Mr. Zimmerman was very pleased to learn that the three tribes of the Umatilla Reservation had no trouble at all, that they had practically no landless Indian people, that they were getting along beautifully with their superintendents, that they were happy and contented. And that the only effect of this proposed bill on them was to disturb them and make them fearful. So we were able to assure them that this bill was not written for tribes or reservations where these conditions, prosperity and contentment, prevailed. We wouldn't need any such bill if all of the reservations were like the Umatilla Reservation. We didn't mean it for those people; and when we framed the bill, we worked it out for the benefit of the 100,000 landless Indians and we were able to assure the Umatillas that if the bill passed or didn't pass, they wouldn't be affected.

The next group of questions will be answered by Mr. Siegel.

DELEGATE: Mr. Chairman, I would like to suggest that the Yakima tribe interpreter get up on his feet and interpret so that it could be understood by those who do not understand English.

MR. WOEHLKE: I think the Yakima interpreter should come up and stand and interpret so that we know when he is through. Will you do that?

DELEGATES: Yes.

MR. SIEGEL: The first question is this from the Yakima delegation: Supposing that in this checker-boarded area there was a parcel of land that had been transferred to white ownership. Can the Government purchase that parcel of land and return it to the Indian? The answer is "Yes." Another question from the same delegation: There has been also land that has gone into white ownership through fraud and has been purchased for a less amount than the actual appraised value. Can this land be returned to the tribe if proof of fraud can be furnished? The answer is: If you can prove that fraud was practiced a comparatively short time ago so that the statute of limitations has not run out the answer is "Yes." I will correct that a little and say that it would be returned to the person who owned it before. Even if we can prove fraud but the statute of limitations has expired and you can't bring suit, the Secretary of the Interior has authority to purchase that land.

NEXT QUESTION: The question has already been asked whether this bill will permit the purchase of lands now taxed and not on a reservation, with trust funds, and require such land to be free of taxation.

THE ANSWER IS: That section 16 of Title 3 in the Land section authorized the Secretary of the Interior to proclaim new Indian Reservations on land purchased for the purpose enumerated in this Act, or to add such purchased lands to the jurisdiction of existing reservations. Such lands will be free from taxation, so long as the title to them is held in trust by the United States or an Indian Community. I do not believe that the authority of this Act extends to permitting the tax exemption of lands purchased by a tribe with trust funds outside of the reservation, which are not now tax exempt. However, if the land were within the reservation boundaries and were purchased for the community it would be tax exempt.

NEXT QUESTION: Would the bill also permit land already purchased on which taxes are already paid to be taken from the tax rolls? The land is not on a reservation. Would there be any difference whether the purchase was from trust or unrestricted funds?

ANSWER: If the land is off a reservation and is not constructed into a new reservation for the landless Indians, I think the answer is NO, it would not be taken off the tax rolls and it makes no difference from whatever money it is purchased with. What the person probably has in mind is this: Under the old law, as courts have held, where restricted funds are used to purchase fee patented land which was formerly subject to taxation and is purchased by the Secretary of the Interior on behalf of the tribe, or to form a new reservation, that land will be exempted. I think it ought to be made plain, if it is not already plain, by amendment to the bill, that any lands purchased by the tribe within the reservation areas which were formerly not subject to taxation should similarly be made tax exempt. I am making a note of that now.

NEXT QUESTION: Can a tax payer live in a chartered community and still own their taxable property?

THE ANSWER IS, "Yes."

NEXT QUESTION: In case an Indian wants to buy improved farms outside of the reservation out of the proceeds from the sale of Indian property, will the Indian have to pay taxes?

THE ANSWER IS "Yes." But I think the law ought to be amended so if he bought land within the community area the land ought to be exempted from taxes if purchased with trust money.

NEXT QUESTION: (Tulalip Agency) What effect will the bill have on landless Indians known as non-reservation Indians, also those living on the Public Domain property?

ANSWER: As the chairman has already explained to the audience, one of the most important reasons of this legislation is to provide land for non-reservation Indians and that includes those living on the Public Domain, provided that such Indians have one-fourth Indian blood or more.

NEXT QUESTION: What will become of heirship land owned by Indians from another reservation? Will the tribe purchase such lands and will the proceeds go to the rightful heirs?

ANSWER: This is one of the most interesting questions which has been submitted to us. I must admit that we had not given this problem the careful consideration and attention which it deserves. I am informed that there are many cases where Indians on one reservation inherit land on another reservation. One of the first things that we can do is try to arrange a process of exchanging such lands on reservations for lands on which the individual lives.

If the problem cannot be solved that way, those lands may be included in the plan of purchasing the rights of the heirs on the reservation in which the heir does not live. However, we have not reached a definite conclusion as to how to solve this problem and we would welcome any suggestion from the Indians as to how the problem ought best to be handled.

But, let this be plain in your minds: Whatever solution is adopted under any scheme no land will be taken from any Indian under this Bill.

NEXT QUESTION: Why have we not had anything from the Government?

THE ANSWER IS: If this Bill passes you will get something from the Government.

Noise of train in the distance.

MR. WOEHLKE: The Southern Pacific has the floor. We will now ask Mr. Cohen to answer a large number of questions that he has been studying all night.

MR. COHEN: These questions are from the Spokane Delegation. The first question is this: What would be the first duty of officers selected? I think that question looks to the future and supposes that some community has been set up and asks what would be the duty of the community officers. That question is very complicated. As many of you know, there are two kinds of officers. On the one hand there are officers who make laws: Senators, Congressmen, and directors. On the other hand, there are special officers who have particular jobs under those laws. Let's think of these two kinds of officers in the Indian community that may have been chartered in the future. The first kind of officer is the one who makes laws, rules and regulations. These officers will deal with questions which the Indian Office now deals with, or that your superintendent now deals with. The Indian governing body will then deal with them. When these officers are first elected they will have difficulty and very important tasks. They will want to have their own laws and such special laws over wills; heirship; marriages; divorces; and so on. Or they may decide, since they live among people of the State, that they want the State laws to prevail, in matters of contracts and such things.

In addition if they want to make recommendations to Congress as to appropriations of funds, I'll ask you to remember what was said yesterday: Congress cannot appropriate tribal funds without the consent of the community. That means, for instance, that if any tribe will succeed, and I hope you will be successful, in prosecuting your tribal claims under treaty rights, Congress will not be authorized to take these funds and use them for other expenditures, provided the Indians have an organized community. The law-making officers of the community will consider any appropriation Congress will want to make. If that appropriation is out of tribal funds, then they have the final say, "yes" or "no." If it is appropriated, then they will make recommendations to Congress and the Secretary must send these recommendations to Congress.

Then in addition to making laws, rules, regulations, etc., and in addition to deciding matters of finance, there will be one more thing for them to do. They will have to deal with special officials on the reservation. They will require, for instance, the superintendent or principal to come before the council and explain his policy to the Indian community. If he is in charge of forestry, or allotment work, he will have to come before the Indian council and explain what he is trying to do and after he has explained to the council and to its officers, he will come back at a later time and tell them whether he has done his job according to his promise. These officers of the community will decide whether or not he is doing the right thing on the reservation. If any Government official is not following the right policy then the community can remove him from the Indian Service, and also wherever there is a vacancy in the Government service and the community has a person who is qualified to fill that vacancy, then the community can appoint that person to fill the vacancy.

So there are the three duties of the highest officers: First to make laws, rules and regulations; second, to deal with Federal appropriations; and third, to remove any government official who is not following the right policy. Now in addition to these law-making officers, councilmen, etc., there will be some special officers in your community. The community may elect or appoint its own judges and policemen. It might want to have a land commissioner to take care of all its lands and homesteads. You can see as you go through the list that there are a great many other jobs that such officers can fill.

There is a second question here that I think I have answered.

THE QUESTION: Would there be a certain amount of duties specified and by whom?

I have explained what these duties would be and you will find the various duties specified and listed in the bill.

QUESTION: Who would select the officers?

I think that is a question that the men of any reservation can answer for themselves. I suppose the reservations in this part of the country would want to have elections of your law-making officers and they would have these law-making officers appoint or select the special officers for the special jobs.

QUESTION FOUR: What pay would the officers receive? And I want to read—

QUESTION FIVE: Who will pay the officers?

Now let me ask you to bear in mind the two kinds of officers that I spoke of a moment ago: the law-making officers and the special officers. The law-making officers, if they receive any salary at all, would be paid by the community. The special officers would be paid with the funds which Congress appropriates for the special jobs that those officers do. For instance, Congress now appropriates money for so-called Indian judges and Indian policemen. These Indian judges and Indian policemen are hired by your superintendent. If any community is chartered it will naturally want the right to select its own judges and policemen, and the money which is being appropriated for the superintendent's judges and policemen will then be given to the community to pay the community and policemen. Similarly, if the community wants to have its own land clerk to take care of its own land leasing, the money these clerks now receive will be given to the community to pay its own officers who will be doing the same job.

Some of you may think it is unfair for the Federal government to pay the special officers of the community and not the law-making officers. I think you will see that there are some good reasons for that difference. If the Federal Government paid your law-making officers, your law-making officers would look to the Federal Government for guidance and not to your own people. Then you can see that when Congress is appropriating money for an Indian judge or an Indian policeman or a land clerk it can see the justice in transferring that money to the Indian community if the Indian community does the same job. But your law-making officers will be doing a new job that has never been done before. And as you want that job, and as you want to make your own laws, and to govern yourselves, you ought to be prepared to pay any necessary salaries for your law-making officers. I don't think the salaries should be high. I think any man worthwhile in his community would be willing to make the laws of that community without getting any salary or at least without getting a large salary, and the expenses of that position might be largely taken care of by the Government. This bill provides that the various kinds of property which the United States Government has on the reservation can be given to the Indian community. That means that buildings, furniture and such things that the council of the community may need and various clerical supplies, etc., can be given to the community and in addition to that this bill provides a fund of $500,000 each year for necessary expenses of organizing the communitics.

THIS NEXT QUESTION IS: Who will assign duties to the officers, the tribe, the Commissioner, of the Secretary of the Interior? The answer is that the community will assign the duties of its own officers in its charter and in its by-laws.

THE NEXT QUESTION IS: Would an Indian have to have any certain amount of Indian blood to hold office in a community group? The answer is that each community would have to decide for itself whether it wanted any blood qualifications for membership or holding office. There are some communities where they would not even want to have a half-blood in office, and there are other communities where there aren't any full-bloods. So you see we can not have a rule in the law governing such matters. Each community will have to decide that for itself.

THE NEXT QUESTION: What kind of Indian courts would be established on a reservation? The answer is: That this legislation provides for two different courts. First of all, there is the local court which is appointed by the Indians of the community. The second is a Federal Court of Indian Affairs which is appointed by the President of the United States. I shall try to explain the relation between these two courts when I answer the next question.

THE NEXT QUESTION IS: What questions would be handled by the local courts and what by the outside courts? The answer is that the local court of the community could deal with all the disputes between members of the community and all the misdemeanors committed by the members of the community. It could not fine anyone more than $500, or imprison anyone more than 6 months. If any community did not want their judges to have so much power, their power could be decreased. Now the community court could also deal with white people or non-members of the community who cam into the community and committed any misdemeanor there. That means that if any white cattle trespassed on the reservation the Indian local court could deal with that problem. But in any such case where the white man is involved or where an Indian who is a non-member of the community is involved, then either party can appeal to the Federal Court of Indian Affairs. This Federal Court of Indian Affairs will also deal with more serious crimes. This Federal Court of Indian Affairs will also deal with any disputes between the community and one of its officers. If the community shuts out one of its members and doesn't live up to its constitution and its charter, why then that member, or the Secretary or the Commissioner acting on his behalf, can go into the Federal Court and compel the community to act in accordance with its charter. And so, when there is any question of anyone being deprived of his constitutional rights. And as I said before, if the Secretary of the Interior doesn't live up to his promises in this charter, then the community can go into this Federal Court to get justice.

And if any member of a community has any rights in the community he could go into this court and get protection. Now this is something very peculiar as far as Indians are concerned. In the past the Secretary has been able to do almost anything he wanted with the Indians, and they haven't had any right to sue the Secretary of the Interior. But in the white world, you know, many officials are sued by private individuals, if these officials have done anything that is unconstitutional. And so the courts have very often prevented officials from doing certain things which the courts thought unconstitutional. Under this bill you would have the same rights.

I am going to answer a Nez Perce question on this subject: Upon conviction of guilty Indians, to what prison would they be sent, to a county jail, to a penitentiary, or would Indian imprisonment be used?

Interpreter asks the question to be read over.

MR. COHEN repeats question: If they are convicted by the local courts they will be sent to the local jail, and if they are convicted on a more serious offense, they will be convicted by the Federal Court and sent to the Federal Penitentiary.

Now the last Spokane question is this: Would special laws be made for the Indians or would County, State or Federal laws be effective on the reservation? The answer is: That each Federal law such as the law, enumerating crimes tried in Federal Courts, would continue to be tried in Federal Courts, but with respect to other matters the Indian Community would have its own ordinances.

May I ask the Spokane Delegation whether that answers their questions?

DELEGATION: Yes, thank you.

MR. COHEN: I have only one more question here. That question refers to Title 1, Section 2, of the Bill. It refers to the clause which says "No charter shall take effect until ratified by a 3/5 vote at a popular election open to all adult Indians resident within the territory covered by the charter."

And the question is: Doesn't this clause leave open a chance for a small minority to execute what the majority may be opposed to?

Now what the man who asked this question is thinking of, I suppose, is a situation in which most people simply don't vote, and just the few who do vote, vote in favor of accepting a charter. Of course, we have the same situation in elections for white officials, for President, and for Congress. Very often most of the people who are entitled to vote for an important office don't vote. There is nothing peculiar about the Indians in that respect. Ordinarily people who don't take the trouble to make their voice known, don't have any voice in what happens. I feel confident that when an important question, like the granting of a charter, comes before you, that really all of you will vote on that question. And that, of course, includes the women as well as the men. If however, you believe that a charter should not be issued without a larger vote, then I would suggest that you ask for an amendment to this effect: That if some percentage, say 2/5 of all persons eligible to vote, did not take the trouble to vote, then the Secretary should not be required to issue a charter. But you must remember that in some communities the women are very bashful and won't vote, and that means that if we required more than half the members of the community to approve a charter the charter could never get approved.

MR. WOEHLKE: Here is a brief announcement: Mr. Charles Larsen requests a meeting of all ex-Chemawa students on the north side of this building immediately after this session. He promises that this meeting will be short. I would like to have Commissioner Zimmerman state to you the provision of the new law and the effect on treaty rights and all your claims. We have had a large number of questions on that point and we can have them all answered by the Commissioner himself in a very short time.

Mr. Zimmerman?

MR. ZIMMERMAN: What I have to say will not take very long. Mr. Collier feels very strongly that there must be some change in the method of settling tribal claims. The lawyers of the Interior Department are working on a new bill which will make it possible to dispose of claims more promptly. Under the present system, it will take probably 100 years before all the claims are settled. I think 100 years is too long. We will ask Congress to take steps to pay the amount due each tribe. Mr. Collier thinks that it is important that each claim should be adjudicated, so that you will at least know how much money will be coming to the tribe.

You understand that we can't pay you this money. That must come from Congress. So far as this bill affects any change I can only say that we see no change. This bill does not change the status of any tribal claims. We are willing and will recommend to Congress one more amendment to this bill. It is the intention of the present administration that any money spent for the purchase of land under this bill will not be used as an offset to tribal claims. In order to make sure that that is understood we will recommend that such an amendment be placed in the bill. Then it would be impossible for the Government to state in 10 years from now that the two million dollars we spent for your land must be paid back and that unless it is paid back that your claim is settled.

MR. WOEHLKE: The Assistant Commissioner says many things in a few words. We have just about 12 minutes left and we have many questions to be answered, so I will ask Mr. Shepard to be very brief until we call on the delegations to speak.

MR. SHEPARD: These questions are from the Siletz delegation.

QUESTION ONE: How will the bill affect the people who don't accept self-government? The answer is that it will leave them very much as they are at present, although certain provisions of the land title of the bill would affect them.

QUESTION TWO: "Will those who accept self-government have the privilege immediately of changing those who have shown themselves incompetent such as Superintendents and agents." We expect that when the Indians organize self-government they will approach this and all other problems with a feeling of responsibility. I don't believe an Indian community when it got its charter of self-government would wish to turn out all of its white employees. There would have to be a regular procedure as in a court of law and the white employee would be entitled to the same kind of protection of his rights as any other citizen. I believe that once we get this new system into effect most of the causes of friction and disagreements between Indians and white employees will disappear. The Indians and white employees have both been trying to make a bad system work and it won't work. No one can make it work.

THE NEXT QUESTION: If we are formed into a community and accept self-government will that exclude our rights to vote on State Officials?

The answer is "No." It would not in any way affect your present rights to vote. The chairman says two minutes more.

I am going to take this further question: Will the Indian be subject to any form of taxes, income or any other form of tax on person or real property? This is a very complicated question. I shall not attempt to answer in full. In the first place, this bill would continue to exempt all restricted property from taxation. Under this bill restricted property will not be taxable. Nor would any money derived from restricted property be taxable. The Indian community may, however, levy assessments on its members to cover the cost of community work, or if the Indian does not want to pay in cash he must pay in work.

MR. WOEHLKE: We have now arrived at the period at which we will hear from the older members of the various delegations. But I would like to ask the Congress one question before we start: Would you like to take a recess for ten minutes?

(Recess declared.)

(After a period of twenty-five minutes the conference of the Northwest Tribal Councils met at 11:30 a.m. for the continuation of their meeting.)

MR. WOEHLKE: I have been requested to make some announcements. All Chemawa ex-students and employees are requested to meet in front or near the flag pole to be photographed before lunch. All old Carlisle students are requested to form a group immediately after the Chemawa picture is taken so you are going to be photographed instead of eating. I have also been requested to announce that a wrist watch has been lost. If found, please turn it over to the secretary here. We have now arrived at the time set aside for the expression of opinions from our friends of the older generations who speak through an interpreter. There are many delegations and time is very short; I would, therefore, suggest that some of the delegations combine and instead of each one having a speaker, let two or three agree on one speaker to speak for them. I shall call on the various delegations in alphabetical order but before I proceed with it, Dr. Roe Cloud asks the privilege of speaking for forty-two seconds on self-government.

DR. ROE CLOUD: I want to bring up that when you elect your officers, you elect all fat men, for fat men cannot stoop to anything.

MR. SHEPARD: I would like to have a speaker from the Colville Reservation take the floor. Who is the speaker for the Colville delegation?

CHRISTINE GALLER: Mr. Chairman, there is a group who asked me to speak for them, but there is another group who will speak for themselves, so we have two groups.

MR. SHEPARD: This is for the group of Indians who do not speak for themselves and will have to speak through an interpreter. Will you give us the speaker's name, please?

CHRISTINE GALLER: Jim James of the Nespelem tribe.

JIM JAMES: *(through interpreter, Christine Galler)* The Indian superintendent just told us to select our delegates. I am going to tell you about this bill and about your papers today. I am going to tell you that there are many people back home that are old people and women that must know. I understand all of this bill in full, I have listened in at this meeting and when I reach back home, I will tell it to my people and when they understand I will see that you hear about it at once. I want to know to whom may I write back in Washington. I want to know the address.

MR. WOEHLKE: To John Collier, Commissioner of Indian Affairs.

JIM JAMES: (*through interpreter, Christine Galler*) That is all.

MR. WOEHLKE: We will next call on the Coeur d'Alene delegation.

CHIEF PETER MOCKTUM: (*through interpreter, Basil Peon*) I am very much gratified to be with you at this council to offer my suggestions in this great meeting. A little better than forty years ago, you sent your representative to my tribe where we were given a treaty. He granted the Coeur d'Alenes that they should have a reservation permanently and forever. That was the law they gave me. At that time I thought that my reservation, my land, was forever. They advised me to go to work and improve my country, my reservation, and till the soil. It wasn't the Government that gave me this encouragement, it was the own chief of my tribe.

At this time my tribesmen went to work and they had great fields of wheat, grain, etc. At the time, I didn't get much encouragement from the Government but from my chief. The treaty that I have is on record in Washington and also in the Indian Office on the Indian reservation. What I have accomplished is also on the record in Washington, D.C., and also on my own reservation. I do not see where the Government of the United States has ever helped me. The white people have broken all of the prosperity I ever had. Right today I am very poor. My rules on my reservation at these times were very good and strong. I was living good. The white people have taken my own laws away from me up to this day. You surveyed and allotted my reservation by force. The Government promised me at the time of the allotment that this was to be my own individual allotment forever. Very few years after the allotments were made some delegation of yours informed me that the young people, the competent Indians could have their patent in fee.

Again the treaty was broken. My allotment and also my inherited lands belong to me. When these heirship administrations were settled, I was obliged to pay some fee on these certain inherited allotments. I did not refuse to pay these heirship costs at the time because it was according to law. It cost me about $50 for an allotment for the inherited land. My agent was supposed to have this on the record at the office of the Commissioner of Indian Affairs; another record of this is at my agency. We had to pay the cost of fixing these heirship lands and therefore, I believe these allotments should be mine forever. I did not fix these heirship laws myself. It was your own decision. It was fixed by your own officials. In my heart, I believe that these heirship lands should always belong to the owner of these lands. Have pity on me, on our Indians. The Government in my country has picked on our Indians. The white people have made me poor. Why do you not have pity and help me and give me justice. This is my suggestions to you.

MR. WOEHLKE: That is what we are trying to do. Thank you. The next delegation to be heard from is the Flathead delegation. They have been very quiet.

ENEAS CONSO: (*through interpreter, Steve Knapp*) He says he is very glad you came over and visited us, the red men. At the time of the treaty of 1885, you never have come before us this way. After that treaty you have been fooling the Indians ever since. They never given them the right to talk. Now you people are different. Maybe you people will help the Indians out. And maybe you are in earnest about it. I am glad for that reason. About the half-breeds on the Flathead reservation, a lot of them want to be turned loose—to get paid off and I see things here that most of the other tribes have got that same idea and that after a time they will be turned loose. And if you turn them loose and take them off the reservation—back to their old grandmothers and grandfathers because their old grandmothers and grandfathers might have a little something to eat yet. I have lots to say but the time is short, I will make my speech short. That is all.

MR. WOEHLKE: We thank you. The next delegation is to be heard from. The Fort Hall delegation.

JOHN BALLARD: (*through interpreter, Philip LaVatta*) At one time, we were but one nation—but one people, placed on this nation by our father and we were glad to have you come here to talk to us. The things that was placed here for us to enjoy are many, are numerous. I cannot tell you all of the things that was placed here for us, not only on top of the earth but under the earth also. For that reason I say we are just one people that was placed here upon this continent. That same great being created the white people on the other side of the ocean and they are one of us—one great nation.

After that, you people came over on to our land. You know things. We, as Indians, do not seem to know anything. That being the case, the Government has placed something good for us here. You people think that you can force us on a small piece of land—a small reservation. The things that you have promised me in the past have not been fulfilled. There are things we thought were good, turned out to be bad. To this day, I find that the new Commissioner we have made a new plan—something new for us to follow. His plan seems to run in the line exactly what I want. It seems that he has placed us in a condition that has made us poor. We are wanting many things and are trying to follow in the footsteps he is leading us in. There are two things that have made me poor and that is the act of trying to make a citizen of me and my children, some of them are mixed bloods.

Now, I wonder if you are trying to fool me, but I believe you are telling me the truth—telling me something that is good for me. This thing that we call "bill," I am glad to know you have got that and are presenting it to our people. The outcome of this bill, I cannot tell what will happen. For that reason I am telling you what is good for the Indians. This bill is good for me and that is all I have got to say to you.

MR. WOEHLKE: The next speaker will be from the Grand Ronde delegation.

GRANDE RONDE DELEGATE: We haven't any interpreters. Isn't this limited to only those who have to speak through interpreters?

MR. WOEHLKE: Yes, we will pass on to the Klamath delegation.

KLAMATH DELEGATE: We have no interpreter either.

MR. WOEHLKE: The next one will be the Kootenais.

CHIEF ISHADORE: (*through interpreter, Michael Francis*) When I first stepped in this hall, I can recognize that you do not quite approve of having an interpreter. I mean to say that first of all you should not like us to speak with an interpreter. I am an inhabitant of America and I will use my own language. To begin with, I can see that the whites had planted some time in the past and they had appointed a man to cultivate the plant, what you call superintendent.

In other words, we might say that you sent in a man in our country and here is a tree standing—a genuine tree, and you cut off one of the branches of this tree and you ask the man that you send out to me to break one of the branches off my branch and cultivate it. Now I believe you white people intend to get some results of this that you have grafted on my branch and I have tried my best to help you along. When the superintendent here cultivated this plant, as I stated before, I try my best to help him along and I can see today that you are pulling this man away from me and without your knowing whether I am going to bear any fruit from the other branch you grafted on my tree. I had been hoping that I would not be useless; therefore, I have been complying with the superintendent as much as I could along the line. It is not right—I feel that the one branch that you have grafted on me will die because you ask the man that is cultivating this branch to leave me and you ask me to go ahead and to make this one branch to bear fruit.

What I mean to say is this: You come along and here I was an Indian, uneducated Indian, and you ask me to go to school. That is your graft. In the meantime, we have become civilized. We have been going to school only but a few years and the highest grade my children went to in school is the fourth grade, and in a few years time we have attended what school attendance we have and that is the sixth grade. Now you can see for yourself—picture for yourself, what I have expressed today. Is it impossible to carry on the work that you have asked: I would to ask one of the members of the delegation from Washington.

Now we will turn the question the other way. Supposing I come along here and if you were in my place and me in your place, you can very well see just what I mean. I can see every one of you members from Washington went to college and graduated or you could not very well fill the position that you are now holding today. Now we will come back on the other side. Just a few years back and you will have presented a man to me to lead me along and I would be satisfied this way without complaining, walking side by side with the superintendent and now you want to put him out. I feel like a child who would get lost when his guide left him. I should say I would rather let things get ripe and not rush things. Should we not rather put another plant or graft another branch on to me and cultivate it some more and still have a good man to cultivate this branch and this tree shall bear fruit.

MR. WOEHLKE: We want to thank the delegate from the Kootenais and I am sure the Assistant Commissioner will pay attention to what he has said.

We will reconvene in this hall at 1:30.

Adjourned at 12:15 p.m.

MINUTES OF THE NORTHWEST INDIAN CONGRESS

March 9, 1934, Friday, P.M.

MR. WOEHLKE: Congress will please come to order. It seems to me a lot of the delegation are staying out in the bright sunshine and enjoying it, but from what I can see of the dust on the roads you seem to need more rain here. The Chair has been informed that the delegates representing the largest tribe on the Taholah Reservation desire to leave early so as to be able to return to their business and they have requested to be heard out of their turn, so I will now like to hear some of the comments of the Taholah Reservation and I would also like to remind each speaker that his time is limited to five minutes because time is getting short. What was the name please?

HARRY SHALE: A meeting has been held by the Quinaielt tribe regarding this self-government matter. They held this meeting on the 21st day of February. The meeting was called by Superintendent Nicholson, who is in charge of that reservation, and he read the proposed bill regarding this self-government and explained it all and looked into it thoroughly and have decided that they did not care to accept this self-government so would not do so, as we are already self-governing. Years ago the Indians of Taholah won a case from the government regarding their fishing which is their main industry and is handled entirely by them. Their case has been handled by the Indian Office but we took it to the Court and it was decided in the Indians' favor.

Since then, the Indians of Taholah have elected their officers, such as a President, Vice-president, Treasurer and the committees who are in power by the tribe to act in all fishing cases and so far we have made a success of that self-government. We are getting along nicely. Taholah is a self-supporting tribe and for that reason they object to your request to the people of Taholah. I have been represented here for them and to make the statement to you gentlemen who are here from Washington to confer with the Indians of the West. I merely state their opinion of the Quinaielt tribe and when I go back, I will also report to the tribe about these meetings, this conference, and will thank you good men from Washington for your aim to better the condition of the Indians in the West. Your problem for the Indians fits in many cases, but not in Taholah. For instance, I have heard a gentleman by the name of Williams who requested for some land and another gentleman has a reservation with nothing but gravel. Well, people like that are in need of this help and my request to you gentlemen who are here to better the conditions among the Indians is to recommend that strongly for them. I will admit the people of Taholah will not accept your offer but probably later on if we see other people make a success of that self-government, probably, we will. Thank you.

MR. WOEHLKE: I wish you would tell your people that if they are organized now and governing themselves that they are doing something illegal. They are not allowed to do it under the law as it is now and the Indian Commissioner can abrogate your Organization any time he wants to. You are not allowed, according to the law to organize and it is only by permission of the Secretary of the Interior and the Commissioner of Indian Affairs that the law permits you to organize now. What we want to do in this law is to get you the right to organize so that you do not have to depend on the Secretary or the Commissioner.

MR. SHALE: Our organization has been recognized at the Indian Office and all of the government officials have been advised by the Indian Office to have no voice in any of our fishing cases that may come upon the reservation.

MR. WOEHLKE: That may be, but the law of the tribe is still illegal. Now we will hear from the Nez Perce delegation. Are they ready? Is the speaker for the Nez Perce reservation ready? Please come up in front here.

MR. JOHN WILSON: I want to extend my greetings to you representatives of the Indian Department. It was very good for me to meet you personally and made me very happy at heart. I am a member of the Nez Perce delegation to this conference, to listen to the discussions of the problems in hand. I do not feel that I can ask any questions other than those that have been asked and to which you have replied. I did not come to decide what is the best thing for the Nez Perce reservation to do, but came as a representative to listen to the problems discussed and take back to my people for their consideration and explanation, to which the Nez Perce will seek a decision.

My personal opinion is that they are inclined to oppose the Bill. There is one big objection to the Bill: the reason is the Nez Perce claim 18,000,000 dollars in lieu of ceding the Montana hunting grounds to the government. The promises were extended as part of the Indian interests into the treaties with the government in 1855 and the promises that the mountains and rivers would be ours have never been kept. Now we find ourselves at a crossroads with the government who trespass on these places that were promised to us. I am just wondering now whether the State has precedence with the Federal Government over us in the promise of the free use of those places.

MR. WOEHLKE: We shall report what you have said to both the Commissioner and to Congress, but we also hope to hear later on from those of your people who have no land. We are now prepared to hear from sunny California. Perhaps they have elected their spokesman.

SACRAMENTO DELEGATE: The Sacramento delegation is very small, composed of only four men. We do not represent landed Indians like the others here, so really have nothing to say, more to listen.

MR. WOEHLKE: Then suppose you listen and speak later on if you so desire. Well, we can pass on to the Siletz delegation. Have they their spokesman selected? If so he may take the floor for five minutes.

MR. ABE LOGAN (*Mr. Hoxie Simmons, interpreter*): I thank God for the opportunity to meet with you gentlemen from Washington, for also the opportunity for you to see me. In the first place, along early [eighteen-] forties, the white people came to my country and that is what I want to talk about to you. The white people covers the Rogue River from mouth to end and kept on until they have removed my Indians far away. In 1855 they made Treaty with the Indian, made promises to build homes for them in this Willamette Valley, right here but they put them to the bottom road to Astoria, pushed them on over to the Coast range, clear to the ocean; and they gave them that land.

They surveyed the land and gave them the boundary line on top of the coast range. While the Indians were trying to hold their reservation they did these things without the consent of the Indians, without any consideration of us. They, the government, sent three commissioners to make agreements with the Indians and the Indians wanted $2.50 per acre paid them for their land. Then the government would pay them only 80¢ an acre, very valuable land. What I have heard from you gentlemen seems to please me. I am going home now to my mother who is over 90 years old and the younger people and tell them all that you have said. We will let you know by letter what we want to do about this.

MR. WOEHLKE: I want to thank you. I believe I can truthfully say that all of us here are thoroughly ashamed in the manner in which the Government of the United States has treated the Indians and I also believe that all of you agree with me when I say we want to do our very best to right part of the wrongs the Indians have been suffering in the hands of the government for the past 100 years. Now I hope the Spokane delegation has its spokesman ready.

SPOKANE DELEGATE: We have no speaker. The questions we asked were all we had to say and they were answered.

MR. ADAMS: I do not know if there are any other members of the Taholah Agency who are going to take advantage of this opportunity and I would suggest that you pass on and if you have a few moments to spare later on, then I would like to tell you a story or two.

MR. WOEHLKE: Then we will pass on to the Tulalip.

DELEGATE from Tulalip: Mr. Chairman, we are very fortunate in having one of our men with us and he would like to express himself in this Congress. Mr. Campbell and his interpreter is Sampson____?______.

MR. CAMPBELL: This land was all Indian at one time and the people of this land all had good hearts. Later on Governor Stevens came to the Yakima and gave us the same good will and the Indians in return gave him their good will and heart and the promises that was given them by Governor Stevens have none of them come true yet. That is all that he had done, is the land that has been taken away and now we are landless. That is the reason why I am glad you gentlemen from the Indian Bureau are saying you are going to return some of those lands to us. That is all I am here for today to hear about this bill and I want to thank you people. That is all.

MR. WOEHLKE: Next we have the Umatilla Reservation. Are you ready? Who will be your speaker?

JIM KANINE (*Wade Minthorn, interpreter*): I am not going to tell a long story. I shall speak the same words I spoke last night and I feel that we understand each others' words very thoroughly. I have in my heart and remember the promises you made me last night. All of the land that I own on the Umatilla Reservation, my life depends upon that ground. The living conditions under which I was raised, and I still maintain that I should live the same way. You come from Washington and we meet face to face to discuss this matter and I am very glad that I have had this opportunity to speak to you. I shall never forget your remarks and I hope you will remember mine. That is all. Thank you.

WADE MINTHORN: I suppose I can say a few words.

MR. WOEHLKE: Not in English now. The next delegation to be heard from is Southern Oregon.

MR. WASSON: Mr. Chairman, the Indians in Southern Oregon have lived so long without the allotment system which may have also deprived them of any tongue other than what God gave us. With the unanimous consent of the floor we will proceed for five minutes with the only language we know, that which the Great Father left us in place of what he took away.

MR. WASSON: Fellow tribesmen: The Public Domain Indian is not ashamed of his record, he is not afraid to stand up and look you in the face and he is not ashamed to go to Washington and look Congress and their officials in the face, therefore, I stand up before you so that you might look at me. I may not be very much to look at but that is all there is left of us. We gathered here this afternoon to have explained to us another form of legislation prepared in the Great White City. This comes to us very often, at long intervals I meant to say instead of very often, but right after each depression, we get it.

At the time of the establishment of Chemawa School and the establishment of another school at Carlisle, the allotment law on the Dawes Bill took effect. At that time the Great White Father sent our Commissioners. The Public opinion of the world at that time was that it was the greatest act that Congress ever passed for the Indian. It was to remove them from their present environment and place them in the environment of the civilization of the world so that the children could learn the habits of the white men and learn to be self-supporting. They left us under that law. They left us under that system and you have suffered by it and now these great men come out from the Seat of the government and tell us that

that is a failure. Now we must look back; consider your grandchildren and great-grandchildren. Will another commissioner come out from the seat of the government and tell them this community system is a failure?

You must consider what this is going to do to your children and grandchildren and great-grandchildren. It is going to create another environment for them, what they are raised up under at this time. You are going to be getting together on a confined piece of property, you are going to live in a community. You will have to make an environment. What is it going to be? Is it going to be an environment that will enlarge the character and broaden the minds of your children or will it get them back and narrow them down? There are very few of you old people that will ever receive the benefits that is proposed under this new bill as we will all be passed to the Happy Hunting Ground when this takes effect, so you must not think of yourself but think of your children. I am not here to mock this bill. I am not here to mock any legislation these people might propose. It might be good for some of your people who live on the East side of the mountains. If it isn't good for us we will get together and formulate an amendment and perhaps we will have it.

And one more thing. You talk about the Indian Commissioner, who is the Commissioner at the present time. Personally I have a great regard for your Commissioner, I believe he is sincere. I think that John Collier is just as sincere in his work as Major Pratt and Gen. Wilkinson was at the time the Carlisle School and Chemawa was established. You all know they were your friends and I assure you that John Collier is your friend.

MR. WOEHLKE: We will next hear from the spokesman for the Yakima delegation.

YAKIMA DELEGATE: Just a minute, Mr. Chairman, the Yakima are in council. Our speaker is Frank Seltice, our interpreter is Philip Orre.

MR. SELTICE: You gentlemen that are representing the Commissioner, I want to have you listen to me very attentively, so that when I am through speaking I hope you would not be hurt from the remarks that I am going to make. This bill that we have been discussing. I, myself, have been discussing it for the last three weeks, it seems. For an illustration I will say that it is just like putting a big pack on a small horse. The contents of that Bill is getting very heavy on my shoulders. For that reason I feel in behalf of the Yakima delegation that we are not in position to accept the Bill. I have my treaty that was given to me in 1855 and I want to live under that old treaty. I, myself, am personally acquainted with Commissioner Collier and I hope he will not be hurt by the remarks that I have made. That is all.

DELEGATE from Yakima: Can another man from Yakima speak now?

MR. WOEHLKE: The time assigned is now up. The Warm Springs delegation had requested that the time be divided into two parts. We will now hear from the first spokesman.

FRANK MEACHEM: (*Isaac McKinley, interpreter*) Since this great gathering has opened Thursday I have listened to all of the points brought out in regards to this new Bill. I did not bring anything much of importance to you, but came to listen to this gathering and the different viewpoints. As I always have been—and will be there—in my reservation that the Great White Father has given to me and which now exists from the time we selected that reservation.

That reservation remains as the selected place for my home but has never been legally established with the boundaries. I am always looking to my reservation where my father has pointed out as a proposed boundary line. I still remain under their promises of the Great White Father that I am supposed to keep the reservation without the establishment of the white people. I have not sold any land or leased my grazing land or sold any timber or either my individual allotment. I have not done this. I only hope that the Commissioner will fulfill the promises that he made during the Treaties of 1855 which still remain unsettled and I wish the Commissioner would uphold this immediate action and have it settled.

Chairman, MR. WOEHLKE: Time is up. Second Warm Springs Delegate will take the floor. Speak very briefly.

ROBERT SMITH: Friends, as you look at me here today, I am a delegate from the Warm Springs tribe.

As I stand here today, I imagine my feet have been cut up and there are scars all over them. The Government has given me land, it has been cut up and divided among the white people, and I imagine it is my feet that have been cut up. And when you talk of self-government today, I take in every word of it. The Government did make promises ever since the reservations have been started. My reservation has been unsteady ever since it has been under the treaty, on the south, the north, the east, and the west. I do not feel any want today, but I want the Government to make good and perform its duties. And especially, I want the government to make things good on the reservation. And I want my children and grandchildren to live on the reservation. And when you get back to Washington, I want you to tell them not to forget Warm Springs talk here today. I want you to listen to what I say today. The land that lies in the valley, the mountains, the whites have settled on it and have taken it up. At one time, under the treaty, we were given the right to hunt but we are no longer allowed to do so.

MR. WOEHLKE: Time is up. Thank you. With permission of the conference, I would like to extend a few minutes to a delegate from Yakima who wanted to say a few words a few minutes ago.

THOMAS SAM (Yakima delegate): We have quite a large number of Indians on our reservation and these so-called Yakima Indians, the adults and children, are not in want of any land. Speaking of this community plan, we are not in favor of it. We feel we have plenty of land of our own. As a spokesman of the Yakima Indians, I stand here before you and I say it seems we are not able to take care of ourselves yet. For that reason I object very strongly to the introduction of that bill into our reservation. What I have expressed, I have expressed for the general sentiment of the Yakima Tribe of Indians.

Speaking of purchasing land for the Indians, my suggestion to that would be this: purchase land for the landless Indians outside of our reservation and put them on that land that you buy for them. But these allotments that I have on my reservation, also the inherited lands, that certain described land, I want it to remain in the ownership of the Indians forever. It would be gratifying to me if our friend, Mr. Collier, would extend these trust patents indefinitely for us. Also to restore our Indian schools such as this school right here, as most of our children come to this school. What they have learned in this school they bring home with them and tell me right from wrong and help me to get along on this reservation. I am speaking in behalf of the delegation and I want them to say that we don't accept this bill. I am constructing a very large canal here. This bill will float on down to the other people and pass me up. If this speech I have made is approved by these fourteen councilmen, I would like for them to arise and show their approval.

All of them stood up

MR. WOEHLKE: I would just like to tell the delegation from Yakima that their spokesman asked for part of the bill when he asked to have the trust periods indefinitely extended and that their land be extended and preserved for their children and their grandchildren, and yet he says that the bill doesn't suit his reservation. That means that due to heirship and the splitting up of their allotments into smaller and smaller pieces, the Yakimas will lose their land as others have. As you will notice, he is thinking up a plan to keep their land for their children and grandchildren. The administration of this land at the present is costing more and more each year and if it keeps on, all the money for administration will have to be spent for heirship lands which, of course, is impossible. I am quite confident and I believe the Commissioner is convinced that if the Yakima delegation understood what the bill will do for them, for their children and for their grandchildren, they would reverse their stand and I hope they will go home and study this bill thoroughly before they make up their minds definitely to oppose it.

I would, also, like the interpreter to translate to the Yakima delegation that there came to the Assistant Commissioner this morning a group of young members of the Yakima Tribe with a request that $6,000,000 be spent on the reservation on some land which they have, on which there is no water for irrigation. So that the attitude of the younger delegation is a much different attitude than that of this delegation.

Now the chair would like to exercise its privileges and call upon a speaker of his own free will. I would like to hear from Mr. James Minard of the Colville Reservation.

JAMES MINARD: (*Christine Galler, interpreter*) I am going to speak a few words. The reason I have not spoken much, I have left this to the other delegates that came with me to represent my people. I may not have spoken, I may not have talked right as a delegate to come before my people; I would feel sorry that I should talk for nothing.

I am going to tell you a story that happened to me many years ago. This story was given me and I always have remembered it. I went to Washington, D.C., in the time of President McKinley, and Commissioner Jones was then in office. He told me this story. He foretold at that time what was to happen to the Indians. Now today we have reached that same thing said by Commissioner Jones. The prophecy that he made to me was the education of the children like those children in front of me taking notes, and the opportunities of the younger generation and what they know.

His prophecy has been fulfilled. When I returned back to my reservation I went to the different parts of my reservation. I went to Nespelem, to Omak, to Colville and other parts of the reservation to study conditions. I told the people what I have learned that only through forming one organization, that through one government as a people as a whole, we will be able to do anything. If we don't do like white people, adopt one chief or one leader, we never will be able to do what we should do. When I stop to think that the white government has one chief, has one president of all these states, and has one constitution which is over all the states, counties and cities, that is the reason we must have one head chief or leader. I have been accused of my people trying to be like a white man. They told me that if we did like white people, that our land will be taxed like white people. We will be able to lose all our land by acting by white people.

I am going to tell you, my friends, the officials and the Indian people. Why are they adopting the language of the white people and acting like them? You have let your children go to school and by letting your children go to school, you can see how you are gradually accepting the white people's customs and education. We are behind Collier, we are behind

Roosevelt, but that isn't to say that maybe another Republican, another Hoover, may not be in. For the benefit of those old people like myself, the old men of the tribe, perhaps if you accept this self-government, perhaps it will be to your benefit to hold this land and if the law is changed to take care of those things.

I want to tell you a little more on what Commissioner Jones told me. We asked in the time of Commissioner Jones to stop the south half of the reservation from being thrown open at that time. When I asked him for that extension of the south half of the Colville Indian Reservation, Commissioner Jones told me that he couldn't do anything for the Indian at that time according to the law at that time. He told me then it would be just in a few years that the Indians will be as neighbors to the white people and there would be a universal language between the Indians and the white people. Commissioner Jones told me whenever you have reached that time when the Indians have adopted the white man's ways of living, then we will be in a position to go under your own laws. He told me that whenever we come under that universal language then you will come back and it will be finished.

MR. WOEHLKE: I have a few announcements to make. There will be an entertainment in this building at seven o'clock and you are all invited to attend. And immediately after the entertainment, the Superintendents, officers and employees are requested to assemble at the Practice House. A dance in the gymnasium will take place immediately after the entertainment of the delegates and I hope you will attend.

Now let us proceed with the statements and the speeches in English from the various delegates. We have not time for the various delegations to have the speeches interpreted because time is getting short, exceedingly short. We will now proceed with the program and we will limit the time of each speaker to seven minutes and we will begin from the beginning again. The Colville Spokesman.

CHRISTINE GALLER: With your permission, may I use the stage to stand on? I thank you Mr. Chairman for the kind consideration you have given me and I thank you ladies and gentlemen. I have spoken many times before the white people; and I am sure I am going to speak to you, I suppose all that I have thought of and all that I have planned will be forgotten because I am self-conscious.

Everyone laughs.

Ladies and gentlemen: My education did not come to me on a silver spoon. I am one of seven children. We children were very, extremely poor. My mother and father were prejudiced against education. What I have learned was through the hard ways. I learned of my own free will and I am proud today to say that I learned the education of the white man's language and tongue. What little education I have I worked hard for it. And it was through the Indian school as a stepping stone. It was here that I first accomplished my education. I fought for 25 years for the cause of the Indian people. The reason I have fought for my people is this: I owe it to them, the old men and the old women of the Colville Indians. It is for their benefit that I speak for them today. I am a woman and you might think it funny that the Colvilles elect a woman for a delegate but the capacity of an Indian woman's head has the same amount as a man or a white man. Any woman can do what a man or a white man can do in any instance.

It is all up to you whether we will go back to the blanket. To those people who are not in favor of the bill, there is always a place for them. If they want to keep their allotments and their land they can ask the government for them. John Collier could take every foot of land, if they wish to, with the stroke of the pen according to law and we would lose every bit of ground we have. He has given us this privilege to find what kind of people we are. That is why he sent this Congress before you.

Someone said a while back that if it wasn't for the government we would be retarded back to an environment where our children would not have an opportunity like the white people. Due to them, all over the Indian reservations there are schools that your children could attend, like Chemawa. There are schools for your children to go to. There is always a place for you if you don't want to be self-government and to pay your obligations of taxes and being a citizen of the United States, to direct in any way what you want done.

We have been driven. We have been led by the white people for 122 years since the white people came into this country. We have never been given the choice of our leaders. We have no voice in anything. And now you are opposed to the bill of Collier's. He has worked for 15 years for the Indians cause. You want to be driven to it because you are not accustomed to lead your people. Your people as a people, industrious and self-governing, can do just what you want if you have the Federal Court to back you in your cause.

Ladies and gentlemen: I hope that you don't think that I am like Emma Goldman or any other woman, but as an Indian, my heart is with the Indians. Let us hope that with this new form of government will not be imposing on our old people, that you younger men and women will have a voice in the government of the U.S. Let us try a new deal. It can not be any worse than what it has been. You can say the government has stolen your land away from you. For the wagon, the implements, the government has given us direct compensation. That word "education" in exchange for the bow and arrow. That you can be thankful for. I thank you ladies and gentlemen.

MR. WOEHLKE: I think the speaker who has just finished spoke the truth. The thinking capacity of an Indian woman is equal to that of an Indian man's or a white man's. I would also like to say that a similar objection to this program was raised at the Great Plains Congress. When it was said "This will set the Indians back 50 years," a Pine Ridge Sioux delegate rose and said: "I went to school with Henry Roe Cloud. We went to school together. Look at him now. Do you think it will set him back 50 years? Do you think he will ever go back to the blanket." The next speaker will be from the Coeur d'Alene Reservation.

MORRIS ANTELOPE: (*Basil Peon, interpreter*) I wish to thank you, the delegation from Washington, D.C., and I wish to thank the honorable Assistant Commissioner for being with us and also you all that are with him. I would like to say a few words about the problems of all of these number of tribes. You officials in Washington only know us by our name. I am very pleased today that all of us can meet together, as many tribes as there are, face to face, and discuss our problems. That is a real good meeting when we meet this way in two parties—the white man's representation and a representation of each tribe. Let all concerned be satisfied. If we have a disorderly conference, it wouldn't be very polite.

It seems that our superintendents see people that look to be very incompetent. He seems to disregard those that show any progress. That is why most of our tribes are going backwards instead of progressing. We are in great hopes that from now on that those sorrows may diminish and be taken away from us. We hope that the whites and Indians will be in great relationship as brothers. We hope that we Indians and you white people will be friends or comrades; it is a custom among the Indian friends to give presents to one another as a token of friendship. We Indians, I believe in my heart, are giving you a whole lot of benefit. The way it looks now to the present administration, the Indians are coming to more sorrow and more poverty. Today I extend my hand to you representatives and also I extend and send my regards to the Commissioner in Washington, D.C. There is one thing I am going to say in regard to the Coeur d'Alene tribe and the Commissioner knows this one thing. On January 8th of this year, 1934, we went to the Department a statement written by the Coeur d'Alene tribe. We told a great deal of our business there. That is all I have to say. I wish to thank you.

MR. WOEHLKE: The next delegation to be heard from is that of the Flathead.

JOE BUCK: Well, I don't see much of an opportunity for me to make much of a speech. It seems like there has been pretty much said on this bill. I think though that the delegations here in general would go according to the speaker from the Colville Reservation. I think she gave them a piece of good advice. She is a much better speaker than I am. I am not a public speaker and I would like for you to know that. But the Indians will always be Indians in their way of thinking. If you put a bunch of twenty-dollar bills on the table there and told them to go up and get them, they would be afraid to go and get them. That is the way of the Indian. He is suspicious, but you can't blame him. It has been pounded into him. In our own home council we have democrats and republicans. I think our delegates here today are pretty much in favor of the bill. I do not think there is much more for me to say. I have a pretty good head on me but sometimes it won't work.

MR. WOEHLKE: I appreciate what the speaker has said and I know there are a lot of speakers who keep on talking when they haven't anything more to say, but he wasn't that kind. The next will be the Fort Hall delegation.

TOM COSGROVE: There are ten of us here from the Fort Hall Reservation. Before we left our home we had decided to accept this bill. We feel that we understand this bill pretty well. We know that there are ten thousand Indians who are homeless and we feel that if we accept this bill that we are going to help our Indians and have been told that the government is going to take care of us and going to educate our young people. We feel that the Commissioner of Indian Affairs is with the Indian people and we want him to help us. I am something like this fellow from Montana—sometimes my head don't work, so therefore I won't make a long story out of this. That is all I want to say.

MR. WOEHLKE: Next will be the speaker from Grand Ronde.

HARRY JONES: Ever since having come to this meeting and having heard some of the remarks of the various delegations, the Grand Ronde people feel this way about the bill: We are not going to divulge whether we accept or reject, but they have asked me to comment on this bill. The Commissioner can confer with our delegation and we guarantee our answer today. Since we have been asked to enter into a controversy this afternoon, I feel this way about it. I believe that if we had an older man and one who would speak, having to have an interpreter, he would speak in the terms that I speak now. Therefore, I shall just summarize the contents briefly, in a few statements. What assurance have we, as the people, that these gentlemen here assembled will declare to us a more firmer and surer bill, or contract, or agreement or treaty, whatever it may be, than Paul Palmer, the name that succeeded them and the man who stood before Congress and the Indians. That is the question.

I think every one of the older men who may speak, having to have an interpreter, want to be governed by the treaty rights. What assurance have we that this is a more genuine agreement than that of Paul Palmer? There are several things in this proposed agreement that could be utilized and used on our reservation; we want some way by which we can draw the good of this proposed bill. I believe there are those here that will benefit by this measure or bill. There are those of us who are still doubtful, still wondering if we are going to benefit by this bill or whether we will stand in the future as perhaps we have with the past treaties. How much better off will we be then if we accept it now?

There are many questions that have been asked and there are many questions that can be asked now, but because of time and because of other things and other members that must speak, I shall put them on paper if you so elect. We have formulated an answer to this question because we believe that when we accept or reject that we can still be considered a people that have attempted all along to cooperate with the government in its proposed plan. At one time there were twenty-three tribes on the Grand Ronde reservation. Now the reservation is comprised of an area of eight by twelve miles. Now it is immaterial to you other delegations what we have done—what we accept or reject. We will propose amendments that will fit our own environment and we know everyone will do the same.

MR. WOEHLKE: The next speaker will be from the Hoopa Valley delegation.

EDWARD MARSHALL: Chairman, ladies and gentlemen: In behalf of the people we represent, as members of the tribal council, we want to thank you for discussing the merits of the Wheeler-Howard bill. We also wish to thank you for the courtesy and patience you have shown in explaining the different parts of the bill. I will admit that we, as members of the tribes, are in a skeptical frame of mind as regards to the merits of the bill. If we would accept the bill, we, as members of the tribe, would have all to gain and nothing to lose; however, we cannot give the voice of our people until we have gone back and explained to them what we have learned here, and we wish to thank John Collier in his efforts to give the Indians a new deal.

MR. WOEHLKE: The next speaker will be from the Klamath delegation.

CLAYTON KIRK: Chairman, members of the Interior Department, and ladies and gentlemen: Having such a short time, I cannot go into this question this afternoon as I would like to, but in opening the short discussion, I would like to say that this bill is on trial today. On the one side you have the best talent that is in the Indian Office—four lawyers, a timber expert, an educationalist and I don't know what the chairman is. You have listened all day yesterday to these men who are learned in that line of work.

I would like to have seen the Indian side represented by a lawyer who would represent every delegation that is in this room. You know what a lawyer is capable of doing. Many of you have been in a courtroom. They can almost make you believe that black is white. All day yesterday and part of today you have listened to these men and they tell you that this is the best thing that the Indians can have. This bill, as I see it, will bring more trouble in the future than you will ever realize. I would advise that every Indian or every tribe of the Pacific Northwest not to accept this bill until you have a thorough understanding of how this bill will do the things that is told to you by the brains of the Interior Department.

I do not want to say too much this afternoon, but in closing I want to say this: I would like to advise you in this way, that it would be wise for you, upon leaving this place, to go home with the idea of talking to your people and explaining to them and seeking their advice. But never accept a bill of this kind before you go home. I wish to thank you for the many happy hours I spent here, day and night, and again I hope that you will never accept this bill unless you are thoroughly convinced that it will do for you what it represents.

MR. WOEHLKE: I want to assure Mr. Kirk that that was the very reason we are calling these conferences all over the country—to give you a chance to understand the bill and amend it. You don't have to accept the whole thing at once. The next speaker will be from the Kootenais delegation.

SIMON FRANCIS: Ladies and Gentlemen: We all know that these men are stepping out here to plant something that we should have to take care of for our benefit and that these transactions they are representing is for the benefit of the Indians of America. Now you heard some of those men make a remark some time that an Indian never will overproduce. That is a fact. The plants you sent out here for us to work on, that is when we go home, they will bring out just exactly what they have planted for us Indians. Are we going to carry on the work, and how are we going to do it? It takes experience to carry on the work. And remember some of us have bad habits that affects our work, so I believe this here plant is for us to give it a good consideration before we accept it. Examine ourselves and see if we believe we are able to take up this work upon our shoulders and carry it on.

There are no plants, no matter what kind it is that is planted, if he takes the plant and cultivates it and in this way you shall expect to get some results, and unless you do that this plant will go to waste and it will be full of weeds and you shall not get any production out of your plants and that is to say it happens this way to any nation. I shall not take up much time now. If my chief wants to accept this bill, he may do so and I will believe his expression myself and I shall accept and shall try my best to carry on.

MR. WOEHLKE: I am afraid that our friends from the Kootenais are still misunderstanding some of the objectives of this bill. I believe that you will all agree that at the present time the restricted Indians are not free. They cannot do anything for themselves without the consent of the Indian Office. We know that it is very difficult to learn to walk, but sometimes you have got to make an effort or you will never learn to walk. You may take a few bumps while you are learning, but it will be far better for any race to walk on its own power. You do not have to accept the whole plan at once, but take as little of it as you can digest. When you have gained strength by eating a plate of self-government soup you can eat the self-government roast. You can take it just as fast or just as slowly as you can handle it. Next we will hear from the Nez Perce delegation.

MR. PARSONS: Ladies and gentlemen: I am not going to say very much this afternoon. As regards to this bill, we have been discussing this matter for the last two days and I want to say for the Nez Perce delegation that I am not permitted to enter any decisions in regard to this bill. I will leave that matter to our own people when we go back. I want to make this plain. We are not in a position to advise any of you Indians or you delegates as to what to do because local conditions would govern a decision as regards to this bill. I think that is all.

MR. WOEHLKE: The next speaker will be from the Sacramento delegation.

STEPHEN KNIGHT: The Sacramento Indians are unanimously in support of this proposed bill. We have been in favor of it before it was ever drafted a bill. I have read on congressional reports in which it was stated that we have no reservations in California. Perhaps I wouldn't want to go on a reservation if I had a chance. I have always been independent and free and will always want to be that way. We find large reservations that are like a checker-board where the white men have gotten possession of the largest part of the reservation. Some reservations are composed mostly of inherited land; if this policy should continue for the next two or three generations, most of the Indians will be out on the road. About twenty years ago a man from Washington, from a department that is now abolished, said: "If I had the say, I would never grant an Indian a patent in fee, because they will lose their land, within 4 or 5 years over 50% of the Indians will be landless."

Five years from that time, in California, I found white men in possession of the cream of the land, while the Indians had rock piles, etc. Do you want to continue that policy? I, myself, say no. I have nothing to gain from this proposal. I know of the fight that the Commissioner of Indian Affairs has put up on behalf of the Indians. I have enough faith and confidence in that man that I would support any proposal he might put up for the welfare of the Indians of America.

MR. WOEHLKE: We will next hear from the Siletz delegation.

COQUELLE THOMPSON: With us the shoe fits perfectly and I will assure the delegation that when we explain it to our people they will give it due consideration. There is just one question I would like to ask: What will eventually become of the schools like Haskell, Chemawa and Sherman Institute?

MR. WOEHLKE: I think Dr. Roe Cloud might answer that question; as you know, he is Superintendent of Haskell Institute.

DR. ROE CLOUD: I honestly say to you that I have been apprehensive lest Haskell be closed, but I hope that it can become a national institution for all tribes for an indefinite period to come for our children and grandchildren. This bill encourages education most tremendously; perhaps if it is passed Haskell, Chemawa and Sherman Institute will be kept open indefinitely for this reason.

There are features in this bill which call for the technical training of our young Indian people to go out and learn and then come back and help us with our self-government. I think Haskell can play a large part here. If this bill is passed, I think it will be the means of keeping these schools; otherwise, if things take their natural course, these institutions will be closed. I am very much given to this bill from the standpoint of education and I hope those who want education for their children will become interested in this bill and will work hard for it.

MOSES PHILIPS (Spokane delegate): I have one more question to ask: If this bill is passed, will it give the Indian time to decide the answer?

MR. WOEHLKE: If this bill is passed, then every tribe on every reservation will be consulted and will be given a chance to decide what, if any, part of the former provision he wants to use.

MR. SIEGEL: I would like to limit that statement to the self-government future. If the bill passes, it would mean the eventual end of the allotment system.

MR. PHILIPS: All of you people have heard about the questions that we asked in writing and that were answered yesterday and today. We have those questions before we left the reservation. We have to tell our people that are at home waiting for us. So I cannot say whether we will accept or not. It is up to the people at home to decide that matter. But one thing that I can say is that I did not come here to advise you people what to do. I came here to bring the news to my people.

MR. WOEHLKE: There is another fellow from California who would like to say a few words, with your permission.

MR. RAY JOHNSON: I want to say that we have already handed our claim over to the chair or before your department members and it is for them to approve them. That is our procedure today. And about the bill we cannot guarantee an answer. We have no power to say. All of our power rests within our tribe. That is all.

JACK GEORGE (Taholah delegation): Friends, as we are here before the conference, we know what this conference or this meeting is for. The gentlemen here have been explaining many things and we have seen and heard what they have said. We have heard a word here and there which we surely know is good for us and which we surely know we will try to preserve for our grandchildren. I, myself, as a delegate from my tribe of Indians, I have been ordered by the tribe to come and listen to what is going on.

We have lived from time of my boyhood as self-supporting people. We haven't caused the so-called Indian government any trouble of any kind. We have been trying to uplift civilization among our people and I do pray that the delegations from all over the Northwest may take this in consideration to the very best of their knowledge. Furthermore, these men have said that we can receive loans from the so-called revolving fund and they have said that we can receive loans from the government without security. We must live honestly and live a moral life in our homes. I think these are good people from the Indian Office trying to save the poor drifting Indians. We do not know how long we are going to exist. That is all I want to say.

MR. WOEHLKE: The next speaker will be from the Tulalip delegation.

WILFRED STEVE: Chairman and the staff and fellow tribesmen: Some little while ago I was asked by one of the members of our organization to speak a few words in behalf of this organization. I am reminded of a little story I heard at one time about a young married couple. At the supper table, and after the marriage ceremony, the bridegroom was asked to give a little speech. He stood up and of course his bride was by his side and he leaned over and put his hand on her shoulder and said: "My dear friends, this thing has been thrust upon me." And that is what the organization wants of me this afternoon.

Now I wanted to say this one thing in reference to the proposed Bill that has been under discussion. The Indians of the Northwest comprise thirteen tribes with a population that will run into three thousand members. We saw the need of an organization in 1913; we went ahead and organized officers, board members representing each tribe, and went ahead and did work and tried to put over a program what they thought would benefit our own people and in doing so they used the best efforts to cooperate with men who were looking after them, even to the Indian Agent that was residing within their community. This self-government is not new to us as we have been working along that line for over 20 years. There are some things where we differ, but we have taken it up and discussed it with the Indians in Council.

The provision of self-government looks good to me, the provision on education looks good to me. The organization of the Northwestern Federation of Indians have been working along that line, trying to give some of the younger girls and boys jobs. I know the Government has been trying to set aside money to send these brighter young girls and boys on into the universities and colleges and the money they have set aside in the proposed Bill is for this purpose and for which we should be very grateful.

If these men will give us plenty of time to discuss the various measures and we can offer amendments to it, from what they have told us, they have given us that, but I feel this way: whenever a bill is introduced into Congress where it vitally affects so many people it is introduced for one Congress and in the other it lays and is discussed before it was passed, and then we were given so little time. The first paper sent us, our tribe at Tulalip, we took that thing and threw it into the waste basket. A few days later they sent us the Senate Bill which looked better and that was followed up a few days later with an explanation and it looked still better. If they had turned it around and sent it to us just vice versa, we might have considered it. I am representing the Tulalip Indians although we have taken the proposed Bill and threw it in the waste basket; we were given instructions that we should consider the Bill with an open mind and I surely have enjoyed listening to these other delegations accepting and rejecting. It is going to be very good news for our people and while I am talking along this line I have a resolution that I would like to read:

> Resolution: "Chemawa Indian School, March 9, 1934. We, the Indians of the Pacific Northwest in Congress assembled, do at this time express our sincere appreciation to the wonderful and courteous

manner in which the delegates have been treated by Superintendent Ryan, Superintendent of Chemawa, also to the wonderful staff of stenographers comprised of Indian girls in the front, for writing the minutes of the meeting so that our people at home can have a true report. Also to the staff of dining room girls for the wonderful manner and courtesy to the people being served, and also our young boys who have acted as escorts for the delegates, and we may add the entire student body of Chemawa Indian School who have made our stay at this conference pleasant."

Respectfully submitted by Wilfred Steve, Northwest Federation of American Indians.

Resolution was adopted.

WEBSTER HUDSON (Taholah delegate): The gentlemen from Washington, friends and visitors to this conference. I represent a small tribe of Indians known as the Quinaielts. I think you know that I am just as small as they are. You will notice that my head is so small that it is doubtful if I have anything behind me for talking, but I want to take this occasion in saying a few words in regard to the Bill and the discussions that have arisen out of the questions that have been brought to the men who are working under and with the Honorable John Collier, Commissioner of Indian Affairs. I merely want to say to you people that we have nothing to dictate to your minds. Coming from the rainy region of the State where the Pacific rolls every minute of the time, we don't go very far from home very often. I want to say that so far as it concerns our people that choose just two of us to come out here to listen to the discussions pro and con of this Senate Bill which is designed to change the status of all the Indian people.

I think it has been one of best moves ever made, but like some other delegations, we represent a group of young people that may be able to come out in the same order. We are going back to tell those people there what we have heard for and against the bill and the final decision lies with them. Thank you one and all for listening. This is bringing you one grand opportunity that may never happen again in your lives, to appear before you the body of men you can see here and being asked what you think of the new deal that was offered to the American people by President Roosevelt, and when he was in office, there came along John Collier promising the same to the Indian people.

I am forever looking for the five-minute period and this is what I am going to say and we want to think very carefully and thank John Collier and his staff the way that this is being taken before the Indian people for their earnest consideration to come here at the expense of the several Indian agencies that looks after our affairs. This is more consideration than we ever got for many, many years. Thank you.

MR. MCDOWELL: There are about seven small tribes under the Tulalip Agency, which prevents them from speaking at this meeting. You have heard from but one small band so this is submitted in writing to be included in the minutes of this Congress.

> The Muckleshoot Indians A few years ago a great power company built a great power dam on the river adjacent to their land. This dam has changed the once fine agriculture land to an arid rock pile: it is also done away with the fishing grounds used by our own tribe and the State of Washington game officials arrest our people for fishing in other rivers. We have never been paid.
>
> The Swinomish reservation is no more than a great gravel pit having little value as forest land and very little being farm land. Our children have been forced to leave the land of their people and in many cases are living in surroundings that do not do them any good. On this reservation are four tribes, any of which have enough people to absorb any income that may come from the land.
>
> The Puyallups are totally landless, none of that tribe having received any allotments for the past 45 years or more. Only the older Indians of said tribe ever received any land.
>
> The Duwamish Indians are also landless.
>
> The Nooksacks are living on homestead land that has been logged before the Indians got on it.
>
> The Upper Skagits are living on homestead land that is a little better than that of the Nooksacks.
>
> The Lummi reservation is a fertile one but far too small for the people residing on it.
>
> These Indians are as a whole, fishermen and loggers. The fishermen are continually harassed by State Officials who refuse to recognize the promises made to the Indian regarding fishing by the Gov-

ernment in their treaties. They feel the government should attempt to reach a solution to this problem with the State Officials instead of they being compelled to fight for their own rights, for the things they feel were guaranteed them by the Government.

We go home and make our reports to the various tribes on this meeting and do not intend to influence them either for or against the Bill, but with the hope that the officials will be awakened to the terrible conditions most of them live under.

Submitted by the Northwest Federation of American Indians composed of the tribes signing the Point-Elliott Treaty.

DR. ROE CLOUD: We will now hear from the Umatillas.

WADE MINTHORN: Mr. A. E. Towner will represent the Umatillas at this time.

MR. TOWNER: My friends, I have been delegated to speak for and in behalf of the Umatilla Indians from Pendleton. I feel like my friend Mr. Kirk when he made a statement that we are well fortified on the other side of the table. That is their privilege and they are friends and we all realize that Mr. John Collier and the present administration is trying to do something really constructive for the American Indians.

We also know that for the first time in 50 years or of 70 years that we have at least friends at the Indian Bureau, if they are going to carry out the policies that Mr. Collier has for us. I thought Mr. Collier was going to carry on right when he was carrying on the work of the Indian Defense Association for the past fifteen years, and any of you people in this audience that have not had any copies of the U.S. Senate report on conditions of the North American Indian, I insist that you write a letter to Senator B. K. Wheeler, Chairman of the U.S. Indian Investigation Committee at Washington, D.C., and they have published twenty-six volumes of a book that can be had for the asking. And if you read these volumes, it will make you boil when you think about the affairs of the Indians for the past seventy years.

Mr. Collier has fought tooth and nail against the old guard, and if I remember correctly one of our former Commissioners of Indian Affairs, Charles Burke, went so far as to call John Collier—what did he call him—anyway it is not fit to print. The Umatilla Indians, have turned this piece of legislation down in its entirety. But I would like to make a few suggestions on my own behalf. This morning we were informed, in speaking of the jurisdiction of various courts, that marriage and divorces would come under the jurisdiction of the Indian Courts and about five minutes later, the question that the representative from Washington answered was concerning contracts. He said, contracts, no doubt, would be handled in the state Courts but this is just a suggestion that there are many loopholes in this bill.

As far as I know the Federal Courts never have had jurisdiction over divorces and marriages; they have always been under the State institutions. Marriages and divorces are a civil contract and a government body that brought this into existence is the only body that can divorce that contract. Therefore, I suggest there is a discrepancy here. On one hand they inform us the Federal Courts is going to have jurisdiction over marriages and divorces. On the other hand they say contracts would be handled by State Courts. What are we going to do about it? Marriage, from my view point, has always been under the State institutions; marriages have always been a civil contract and it will always be so.

I am speaking for myself now. These various delegations may be for or against this proposed legislation. We know some tribes are not going to understand it and want to live exactly as they are doing now and have in the past, but don't forget, my friends, even though various members of the various tribes are not in favor of it and that we do owe a moral obligation to those who do not own land. Even though we do turn it down, we are not going to lose anything by passing of the Bill; we will be practically helping those that are practically destitute.

MR. ROE CLOUD: The Chair has been requested that a statement be made regarding Mr. Towner's statement relative to marriages and divorces.

MR. COHEN: It is a very short statement. I do not think that Mr. Towner represented accurately what I said this morning. What I said this morning was that if an Indian community wants to adopt a state rule for a contract it can do so.

INDIAN from Umatilla group: Please have an interpreter interpret.

MR. ROE CLOUD: We are under the rule of the day that English speaking prevails.

MR. COHEN: I have a very short statement. Take marriages and divorces. They have in the past been dealt with through the Indian tribes and they can, in the future, be dealt with through Indian communities.

MR. ROE CLOUD: If Mr. Whitlock, Superintendent of the Yakima Agency, is in the audience, I would like to have him come to the platform a minute. We will now hear from the spokesman for Southern Oregon.

DELEGATE from Southern Oregon: We will not take the time as we have nothing to say.

HENRY MARKISHTUM (Taholah): Mr. Chairman, ladies and gentlemen: I stand up here because of moral persuasion. I have so little to say myself. I come from the most extreme Northwest portion of the United States outside of Alaska, from the reservation called Makah, near Neah Bay. I was sent here as a spokesman for my people and I beg to differ with the gentleman who held the Chair before, although some of his remarks were elaborately done. I believe you should take this proposition that has been given you, and which you will probably take. I have nothing particular to say only that this new deal is on and there are certain geographical centers that differ in the way they should be handled as there are reservations, just as a friend of mine said from Nez Perce, you cannot apply the same rules to each individual reservation but amendments can be made according to each.

We have a little forest on our reservation, live in a village and have to live on our own efforts. It is different on all of the different Indian reservations according to the conditions as they may be in various localities. For myself I am in favor of parts of this legislation. I do not want to say that for my people though. I am sent only as spokesman and to bring back word so I cannot say what their attitude would be. You can get this charter by a 25% vote but you can turn it down later. I want to thank the people who have been considering all our troubles and they have had some difficulty in trying to explain it to us. They are all legal talent and they understand things better than we can. Thank you.

PETER J. JAMES (Tulalip): I want to thank you, the staff from Washington, for giving me this privilege of talking for two minutes, being that I have been delegated, through the jurisdiction of our Superintendent, Mr. Upchurch. I wish to say this in hearing all these questions and the answers, that on my return to the people that delegated me, I will inform them fully as to what is my understanding as well as the understanding of others that is now on the Bill that is being introduced by Senator Wheeler. Neither will I accept or reject same at this time, even though I was instructed to come here. I will return and give all of the Indians just what has been said by the different delegations, at this Congress. I may have a few more words to say but being very limited to two minutes I will only say, to clarify the gentlemen talking about marriages, that I suppose it is about the old custom marriages and it might be a nice policy if it can be adopted.

MR. TOWNER: The State of Oregon does not recognize commonlaw marriages.

MR. ROE CLOUD: The Chair is informed that the Federal Government does recognize commonlaw marriages.

MR. JAMES: Well you gentlemen from Washington that are sitting there, I hope you are going to give us a fair deal on your return there.

DR. ROE CLOUD: We will now hear from Nealty Olney of Yakima.

NEALTY OLNEY (Yakima): This is a great day for our people—a day which will bring back the memories of like gatherings of our forefathers many years ago. It is another episode in the history of our once great race, who roamed the vast valleys and mountains of this great country, as a free and independent people. Now we are gathered again, after many years, under the white man's civilization and education, to plan a new deal for our people, so a great responsibility rests upon us. I do not know whether we can do any better than our untutored forefathers, but we are here face to face with our problems and we must act. We must not shirk this great responsibility for the government believes the time has come that some changes must be made in the management of our affairs, and so we are faced with one of the greatest responsibilities ever given our people since the time of the treaties and so we must act and help right some of these wrongs.

Today we have a great friend, John Collier, as Commissioner of Indian Affairs, who is familiar with the wrongs and mistakes of the system of the Old Indian Bureau, and he is now making every effort to right these wrongs and mistakes. He has called this conference and many like conferences in other parts of the United States to ask Indians to help him work out some new deal. Commissioner Collier is aware of the fact that in the past many laws, rules, and regulations were made for our people whereby our people suffered untold losses and misery without a voice. Today he is giving us an opportunity to help him make some future new plan for the welfare of our people. Therefore, I beseech you most earnestly to think and work with him for the future welfare of the remnants of our race.

The time has come when we must choose between a new plan and the Old Indian Bureau System. You are all aware of the wrongs of the old Indian Bureau System and you know that our people must have a new square deal if we must survive and hold our remaining properties and save our people from becoming paupers and a burden upon the States and Government. This is Commissioner Collier's affair of which he has gathered from his long experience among our people. If we will work with him and our present Superintendents, most of whom are our friends, I believe we can work out some workable plan which will save our remaining properties and be a self-supporting people. We would not have had this opportunity if it were not for the great friendship and desire of Commissioner Collier. We must not fail him now for after three years we may have a new Commissioner and new superintendents and we may never have another opportunity to help the destiny of our people. Our Indian matters and problems are becoming more serious each year and I sincerely plead and urge you to help the present officials to plan for our future welfare and destiny. Many of you have been selected to represent your people at home at this conference and you should not shirk the duty you owe them. Do not think only of yourself, but think of the future generation; it is for them you are now planning, so plan well.

I have attended many councils of the Yakima Tribe and heard them complain, that the old Indian Bureau never consulted them in any of their matters as promised their forefathers, when the treaty was made, that no laws, rules or regulations would be made unless they were first consulted, and this was never done until the last few years. Under any new plan which may be adopted, I would urge that this should be stressed very strongly; that in the new plan, no laws, rules, or regulations be passed, regarding any Indian matter, without first giving the Indians an opportunity to voice their wishes.

Commissioner Collier is giving you this very opportunity, are you going to help. It is the question today. Commissioner Collier, or the government, do not plan to make a complete sudden change in Indian Affairs, but plan to work slowly, carefully and earnestly in order to safeguard the Indians and their remaining properties during the completion of any new plan, because they are aware of the many phases and problems to be worked out and this is going to take time. In any self-government plan which may be adopted, I believe the Government will first select deserving Indians and place them in different departments of the Indian Service and train them carefully in the fundamentals and management of Indian affairs, and each year this will be continued until sufficient numbers are trained and qualified to take over any self-government plan which may be adopted, and during all of this training the Government will have strict supervision of such training and will continue until the government and the Indians believe they are qualified to take over such a plan.

This matter is too serious for the Government to make any haphazard plan, and the Government is going to be very careful in working out any self-government plan, because of the many angles, phases and problems to be worked out hurriedly.

I again urge you not to fail to grasp this opportunity to help Commissioner Collier now, while he is in a position to help you. Don't delay too long and allow the white man, who is not posted in your needs and welfare as you are, to work out some plan which may rob you of your remaining properties. You must help him plan the destiny of your people while you have an opportunity to do so. We have many friends in the Indian Service and they can see the handwriting on the wall, and that is the reason they are urging you to make your wishes known as to how you want to handle your affairs and remaining properties to the best advantage of the greatest majority of our remaining race. The Indians are marked for a change, as are other people of the United States, so you must act and act wisely for the future welfare of our people.

MR. ROE CLOUD: Is the Warm Springs delegate ready?

Warm Springs did not speak.

MR. ROE CLOUD: The Chair would like to take this opportunity to say just a word. In summing up the advantages of the Bill, I should like to remind you that there will be $500,000 to organize with, two million a year for land purchases, ten million a year credit system for capital purposes to start what we call industry. Industry is composed of three parts: land, labor and capital. This Bill brings into possession the Indian land and the capital; all it asks the Indians to do is supply the labor. When you have those three things industry will begin among the Indians themselves under the further provision that they will have their own self-government to direct these activities that are to be started.

Then another thing we are told today, that any future tribal claims that are won after this Bill is passed that is going to be amended; that whatever the Government has spent in dollars and cents will not be used as an off-set. For instance, if my tribe has a claim of two million dollars the money the Government has been advancing under the present law can be put up as an off-set of said claim. If I were to vote on this representing my tribe, I would go in for this adventure on the sole reason of this off-set being amended. There will be millions and millions of dollars saved on these claims. You must give that your very earnest consideration. Let me repeat to you again today that we used to have great Chiefs among the Indian people: Black Hawk, Tecumseh, Rain-in-the Face, Red Cloud, and you can name your own chiefs. Where are our great men today? Our great men are not in evidence because the Indian Bureau has been running our affairs and we have not had a chance to develop. I see in the future a rising of great Indian people under this new Bill so that we should consider all the great advantages offered us.

If those tribes who feel so comfortable, the Yakimas and the Umatillas, feel that the system of government under which you are now living is the best for your children on the one hand, don't forget that on the other hand this Bill is going to help many, many thousands of other Indian people. Times are bringing adversity and if there is going to be suffering then you certainly will be glad to come in under this bill.

Let me repeat again on this note, in the consideration of this Bill and the passage thereof: no one is going to lose anything by this Bill if the Bill passes now. The only thing is to stop allotments.

You can reject the land feature and merely select the self-government feature, or vice versa, until they (meaning the Indian department) come back to help you today or next year or the next year. You can take your time to begin.

Our time is just up so Mr. Whitlock, Superintendent of the Yakima reservation, will lead us in singing "America."

This concludes one of the greatest conferences the Indians have ever had. The Congress of the Indians of the Northwest is now adjourned.

Exhibits

March 9, 1934

We, the Indians of the Pacific Northwest in Congress assembled, do at this time express our sincere appreciation to the wonderful and courteous manner in which the delegates have been treated by Mr. Ryan, Superintendent of the Chemawa School.

Also to the wonderful staff of stenographers comprised of Indian girls in recording the minutes of the meeting whereby giving an accurate report to our people at home.

Also to the staff of dining room girls for the wonderful manner and courteous treatment to the people being served.

And also our young boys who have acted as escorts for the delegates, and we may add the entire staff and student body of the Chemawa Indian School who have made the stay at this conference so pleasant.

Respectfully submitted,
For the Northwest Congress
By The Northwest Federation of American Indians

CHEMAWA, OREGON
March 9, 1934

We, the undersigned, heads of the various delegations represented at the Northwest Indian Congress, wish to express our grateful appreciation of the sincere efforts of the Commissioner, John Collier, to better the conditions of our people, to preserve and increase our lands and to restore to us a greater measure of control over our own affairs.

We appreciate the invitation extended to us to take part in framing the legislation that may secure these great purposes.

CHRISTINE GALLER,	Colville, Washington
G. N. ADAMS,	Taholah Agency, Washington
A. E. TOWNER,	Umatilla, Oregon
CLAYTON KIRK,	Klamath, Oregon
DON McDOWELL,	President N.W. Federation of American Inds.
P. J. JAMES,	Tulalip, Washington
SILAS D. WHITMAN	Lapwai, Idaho
JULIUS MERCIER,	Grand Ronde, Oregon
NEALTY N. OLNEY,	Yakima Indian
HOWARD BARRETT,	Suislaw Tribe, Glenada, Oregon
PETER MONETELMO,	Coeur d'Alene, Idaho.

We, the undersigned the Business Committee of the various tribesmen of the Warm Springs Indian Reservation do hereby protest any move toward self-government until such time as all boundary disputes have been settled and until the United States Government has made proper settlement with the

Indians for all of the lands that rightfully belong within the boundaries of the said Reservation as originally defined in our treaty with the U.S. Government, said treaty being the one of 1855.

WM. McCORKLE
HARRY MILLER
SAM WEWA
BIG FRANK QUEAHPAMA (+ his mark)
JOHN D. POWYOWIT
Business Committee
O. B. NALAMA, Sec.

PAUL QUEAHPAMA
JERRY BRUNOR
CORBET HATE

CHAPTER 5

MINUTES OF THE SPECIAL SESSION OF NAVAJO TRIBAL COUNCIL HELD AT FORT DEFIANCE, ARIZONA MARCH 12 AND 13, 1934

EDITOR'S NOTE: The following is the index published with the text of these minutes. The page numbers refer to the original documents. For the reader's convenience the approximate page numbers are provided in brackets at the beginning of each new session of the council.

INDEX

Minutes of the Special Session of
Navajo Tribal Council
Held at Fort Defiance, Arizona
March 12 and 13, 1934

[(a)–(b)]

The Navajo Tribal Council was convened in special session at Fort Defiance, Arizona, on Monday March 12, 1934, with the following officials, delegates and alternates present:

Honorable John Collier, Commissioner of Indian Affairs.
Wm. Zimmerman, Assistant Commissioner.
Mr. Thomas Dodge, Chairman of the Council.
J. M. Stewart, Chief of the Land Division.
A. C. Monahan, Assistant to the Commissioner (Property).
Wm. H. Zeh, Acting Director of Forestry.
Robert Marshall, Director of Forestry.
Felix Cohen, Assistant to Solicitor, Interior Department.
Ward Shepard, Land Division, Washington, D.C.
W. V. Woehlke, Personal Representative of the Commissioner.
J. D. Lamont, Co-Ordinator, E.C.W.
Hugh Calkins, Regional Director, Soil Erosion Service.
Louis C. Mueller, Chief Special Officer.
H. C. Neuffer, Supervising Engineer.
Mark Radcliffe, Field Agent.
Oliver LaFarge, President National Association of Indian Affairs.
Dr. C. J. Whitfield, Director of Research.

R. V. Boyle, Erosion Service.
Dewey Rierdon, Assistant District Road Supervisor.
A. H. Womack, Irrigation Foreman at Large.
Supt. Henry Roe Cloud, Superintendent Haskell Institute.
Charles Collier, Erosion Service.
R. M. Tisinger, State Supervisor of Indian Education, Arizona.
H. F. Patterson, Asst. State Supervisor of Indian Education, Arizona.
Miss Dorothy Ellis, Assistant Supervisor of Home Economics.
John G. Hunter, Superintendent, Southern Navajo Agency.
S. F. Stacher, Superintendent, Eastern Navajo Agency.
E. R. McCray, Superintendent, Northern Navajo Agency.
J. E. Balmer, Superintendent, Western Navajo Agency.
E. N. Hammond, Superintendent, Hopi Indian Agency.
Theodore Hall, Superintendent, Leupp Indian Agency.
C. E. Faris, Superintendent U.S. Indian School, Santa Fe, New Mexico.
Guy Nobgood, Superintendent, Truxton Canyon Indian Agency.
D. E. Harbison, Forest Supervisor, Fort Defiance, Arizona.
A. G. Hutton, Extension Agent, Fort Defiance, Arizona.
Chee Dodge, Ex-Chairman of the Council.
Deschna Clahcheschillige, Ex-Chairman of the Council.
Avena M. Wade, Stenographer, Fort Defiance, Arizona.

DELEGATES	ALTERNATES
Northern Navajo Jurisdiction, Shiprock, New Mexico.	
J. C. Morgan	Boyd Peshlakai
Robert Martin	Bob Bekis
Allen Neshki	Sam Manuelito
Eastern Navajo Jurisdiction, Crown Point, New Mexico.	
Becenti Bega	John Ferry
Southern Navajo Jurisdiction, Fort Defiance, Arizona.	
Henry Taliman	Jim Shirley
Albert Sandoval	Toadechenia Cheschillie
Frank Cadman	Denet Tso
Black Mustache	Lee Parker
Western Navajo Jurisdiction, Tuba City, Arizona.	
Lee Bradley	Scott Preston
Geo. Bancroft	Billy Sawyer
Hopi Jurisdiction, Keams Canyon, Arizona.	
Fred Nelson	Billy Pete
Leupp Jurisdiction, Leupp, Arizona.	
Marcus Kanuho	Nal Nishi

Interpreters: Howard German and Alfred Bowman

[1]

CHAIRMAN: The meeting will come to order. We will have the roll call.

All delegates and alternates responded except Henry Taliman, Albert Sandoval and Marcus Kanuho.

Members of the Council: The purpose of this meeting is several-fold. We all have heard of the new policy that is being set afoot by the new administration as far as the Indians are concerned and this new policy is embodied in what is termed the Wheeler-Howard Bill. The Commissioner is here to explain this bill to us and after he has explained it to us then we will discuss it. Mr. Collier:

MR. COLLIER: Friends, of the Council, and others here: As your Chairman has stated, there are a number of subjects to be dealt with at this meeting of the Tribal Council. There are important matters that just have to do with the Navajo Tribe, and then there is an important matter that is being laid before all the Indians, the Wheeler-Howard Bill. Your chairman has decided that the meeting will first deal with this Wheeler-Howard Bill, the bill that concerns all of the Indians.

I shall try to tell you about this bill, not giving too many details and not using up too much time. You all know the importance of the Constitution of the United States, which is the fundamental law of the life of the United States. This bill, which is being laid before the Indians, will be as important to them as the Constitution of the United States is to all of the people of this country. We believe that all of the Indians, when they understand the bill, will not only endorse it but will want it and will work and fight for it. It is our belief that even a thing as good as this is, as we believe it is, should not simply be put through Congress because we think it is good, but only because the Indians want it. And for that reason we have called great meetings of the Indians, or congresses, in many parts of the country, and I am going there, and the Assistant Commissioner and other members of the Indian Bureau Staff, are going to the meetings in Oklahoma and the northwest, the Dakotas and California, and all over.

The Navajo tribe is the largest of all the tribes with the largest area of land owned by any tribe and the bill will have an important bearing on the welfare of the Navajos, and therefore, we are laying it before you, as before the other Indians.

I want you first to understand that the bill represents the policy not only of the Indian Office, but of the Interior Department and of the Secretary of the Interior, Mr. Ickes, and in addition, the policy of the President, Mr. Roosevelt.

I have here a letter, which I shall not read at this time, from the Chairman of the House Committee on Indian Affairs, Chairman Howard. I shall place this letter in the record to be printed along with the proceedings. He states that he is sorry he cannot be here himself. And he says that if he could be here—I will read his words here: "I know that if I could be there I could prove to them that the bill, as a whole, will be for the welfare of the Indians in greater measure than any piece of legislation ever presented to Congress."

The bill is a long bill. It is 48 printed pages long. So you understand that we cannot take time at this meeting to read all of the bill out loud. The Department has prepared a long discussion of the bill with an explanation of each section and part. And this entire document, prepared by the Interior Department, has been printed in the *Gallup Independent*. The publishers of the *Gallup Independent* are going to send out to you 200 copies so all of you will have this statement in printed form. And I want to say here that I think this action by the *Gallup Independent* in printing all of this material that you need is a very generous one, and we are grateful to them for it.

Now, I am going to tell you about this bill, those things which I believe you would want to know; the important things which connect with your own life, and your own needs.

The first thing I want to tell you refers to a question in your minds and is this—that this bill does not change or affect your Treaty in any way. Your Treaty of 1868 stands unchanged in every respect and in all its effects. The bill gives you additional protections and additional advantages which are not in the Treaty, but it does not change the treaty.

I will first show what the bill does in relation to your land, to your reservation, and to your property and land. To begin with you know your land is under the trust or guardianship of the United States and is not taxed. The bill contains a new declaration by Congress, looking toward the future, which says that the trust period over your land shall be continued; the guardianship of the United States shall be continued and the freedom of your land from taxation shall be continued. There is another thing which the bill does which is of even greater importance to the Navajos, and to all of the other tribes of Indians.

As most of you know, there is a law, passed in 1887, which is called the General Allotment Law, and which applies to all Indians, including all Indians in practice, but as a matter of law it does apply to all of them, including the Navajos, and this General Allotment Law has been put into practice for most of the Indians, for more than two-thirds of all the Indians, and it has ruined and destroyed a great many tribes.

You may not think this is important to you but it is because the law could be applied to you any time that any Secretary of the Interior wanted to do it. And this General Allotment Law directs that the Government shall break up each reservation so that every man and every woman and even child gets one little piece of land all by himself. And then after a certain number of years, the government takes away the protection from that land so the Indian has to pay taxes on it and can sell it, and if the man (what we call the allottee) dies, that is, when the man or the woman or the child who gets a little piece of land, dies, then the land is sold by the government to the white people. Under that law, since 1887, the white people have taken possession of 91,000,000 acres of the best Indian land—have taken it away from the Indians. In other words, under that law, the Indians have lost an amount of land about five times as large as the entire Navajo reservation. I know that some of you may think, "why are you telling us this, because what has it to do with us," but I am telling it to you as it has everything to do with you, as you will see in a minute. In order to show you just what it has to do with you, I will tell you about the Oklahoma tribes, which are called the Five Civilized Tribes of eastern Oklahoma.

The Five Civilized Tribes hold their land under Treaties, just like your Treaty of 1868. They owned about 16,000,000 acres of the best farm land of Oklahoma, which is a greater area than the area of the Navajo reservation, and they thought that they were secure and they had treaties just like yours, guaranteeing them the ownership of this land. But there were white people who wanted to get possession of this land, and there were white people who wanted to collect taxes from this land, and so this allotment law was brought into operation against those tribes. Those tribes know what it was going to do to them and they said, "You cannot do this to us because we have treaties and this would violate the treaties." They said, "We have the strongest treaties and the clearest titles of any Indians," (and that is true) and they said "You cannot apply this plan to us which will take away our land." And they took their case into court and fought it clear up to the Supreme Court. A very famous lawsuit, known as the Lone Wolf Case.

The court ruled (I mean the Supreme Court of the United States ruled) that they had no protection; that the law could be applied to them; that the Secretary of the Interior had the power and that their treaties could not help them. What is the result to-day in those Five Civilized Tribes? One hundred and one thousand men, women, and children, of these tribes, received each one, a little piece of land. Today, 72,000 of that number are landless. They have not a grain of sand or a square foot of land. They are homeless on the face of the earth. They had nearly 16,000,000 acres and they now have less then 3,000,000. All the rest has passed into white ownership. And of the land that they still have, the little remnant, half is subject to taxation. It is being taxed and taken away through taxation. Now you might think, "Surely they could not do this to our lands because how can you break up our grazing land, and give each person a little separate piece?"

"You cannot do that to grazing land," you will say. "They cannot do such a thing to us." Well, you all know about the Crow Indians and their reservation. That is a grazing reservation just like yours. This law has been applied to them and their land has been broken up just as I have been telling you. All the land of the Blackfeet tribe is grazing land. That has been broken up just as I have described. And the land of all the Sioux Indians in North and South Dakota is grazing land like yours. And the land of the Jicarilla Apaches just over to the east, grazing land, has all been broken up this way—allotted.

I will put it this way. Ever since 1887, whenever the government or politicians wanted to take away Indian lands but the Indians were protected by ownership, or by treaty, the method was not to break the treaty but to allot the land and the Supreme Court has held that they can do that. Any Secretary of the Interior could say: "The law directs me to allot the Navajo lands, and the courts have upheld my power. It is my duty under the law." And he could proceed to do it and nobody could criticize him and the Indians could not do a thing.

Now, this Wheeler-Howard Bill repeals the allotment law, and that is the most important thing in it to you, and to all the other Indians. It forbids the allotment of any Indian land anywhere from now on. And by so doing, it protects all of those Indians who still hold their land as tribes, and it takes away the only method which white men can use to rob you of your lands.

Much of the bill deals with how to save those Indians who have already been allotted; how to get land back to them and prevent them from being ruined further by what has been done to them. You are not concerned with that part of the bill. You are just concerned with the repeal of the allotment law which would forbid any future Secretary of the Interior from allotting your land.

Now the next thing in this bill that you are concerned with is the subject of financial credit to Indians. As all of you know, the Indians, you and all other Indians, are discriminated against. You cannot borrow money under conditions as favorable as white people. The government extends to the Indians, to all the Indians, a financial credit that amounts to about $300,000 in any one year. Three hundred thousand dollars for about two hundred thousand Indians. That credit is extended in the form of seed and implements, etc., which you get from the Agent and which the Indian pays back after awhile. Of course, that is so little credit that it is almost nothing. It does not help you much. For the rest, the Indians are dependent upon stores, upon traders, for their credit. Any credit that they have is what the trader lets them have in the shape of goods for which he pays the trader later. Of course, the trader himself has to borrow the money to carry the Indian. He pays interest on it and the result is he has to charge a good deal more for what he sells the Indians.

Now we propose to institute a new system of financial credit for Indians. At the time the bill was introduced, the part dealing with credit had not been perfected and was still being worked over by the different departments of the Government. So the credit feature of the bill was put in by amendment in the House and the Senate. The full text of that credit item is found on Page 108 of the printed hearings of the House Indian Committee.

The proposal is that to begin with the government shall donate to the Indian tribes $5,000,000; not lend it to them but give it to them. This gift of $5,000,000 is to be used as a loan fund to lend money to individual members of the tribe or to stock associations of the Indians. Any money that the borrower pays back does not go to the government but goes back into the loan fund to be loaned again. The members of the House Committee on Indian Affairs thought that the $5,000,000 was too small; that they ought to start with $10,000,000 and of course we agree with them. Ten million dollars is better than five million.

Now, that is the second feature of the bill important to you. It sets up a credit system and provides the necessary money for all proper uses, all business purposes by Indians.

Now the third thing in the bill which is of importance to you, as Navajos. The bill broadens the educational program for Indians. It directs the Commissioner of Indian Affairs to go ahead and furnish all of the education that will equip an Indian to hold any position in the Indian Service. For example, it directs the Commissioner that if there is an Indian who wants to qualify as a forester or as an irrigation engineer, or as a stockman, or as an agency clerk, or as a nurse or a doctor, or a teacher, then that education shall be furnished that Indian. And if it cannot be furnished him in the schools of that state, or the colleges, the schools of medicine, nursing or engineering, there is a broad provision for loaning funds to help Indians go through any education they want to. Of these funds that are advanced to individual Indians, one-half shall be a gift, according to the bill, not repayable at all. The other half shall be repayable without interest, but shall not be repaid except when the Indian is earning and can afford to pay it. I do not need to discuss this part of the bill because it is as clear as day and by merely reading it, you will see what it means to you.

I will merely mention the fourth feature of the bill, which concerns all the Indians, including you, which is the feature of the court. The bill sets up a court of Indian Affairs, whose judges will be appointed by the President and confirmed by the Senate, just as the regular judges of the Federal Courts are appointed and confirmed. You know the way it is, at present, where an Indian is charged with an important crime, the kind that goes to the Federal Court, he has to go away off to wherever the Federal Court is sitting; way off from the reservation. He has to find some lawyer and pay him, and he has no way of knowing he is going to get a good lawyer and no means of paying him.

He is likely to be tried before a white jury, drawn from some distant place, that has no sympathy with him and no interest in his peculiar problems. The same way when the Indian has what is called a civil case, a litigation or suit. He has to go to a distant court and go through all these strange proceedings or practices. The result of that condition practically is to deny to Indians the equal protection of the laws. This court of Indian Affairs created by the bill would come to the reservation and do its work right here where you are. The judges would be men selected by the President because of their interest in the Indians, their sympathy and fitness for this peculiar kind of court work dealing with Indians. And in addition, the bill creates special attorneys responsible to the court, attorneys who would represent the Indians before the court. These attorneys would be paid by the government to assist and represent the Indians who appear before the court.

This court, of course, would not deal with the little things that belong to the local courts. They deal with the big things, any disputes between the Indians and the white men, and any time when the Indians are charged with big crimes, like murder, arson or larceny, or anything of that kind. And incidentally, these courts will be given a power of review over anything which the Secretary of the Interior does; things which he does now with no court reviewing him. This court would review him and correct him if he made an error.

The final part which concerns you is the part dealing with what we call self-government. That is Title One of the bill. It is the only part of the bill that requires a detailed explanation so far as you are concerned. I had hoped to finish this explanation before twelve o'clock. It may be I cannot finish it but I will go ahead until twelve. But before coming down to the details of this Title One, let me talk with you about the condition at present.

The Navajo Tribe has a Tribal Council and that Council meets and works in a regular way. And you all know that it is the policy of Secretary Ickes and myself for the Tribal Council to have all the power and build itself up in a great freedom. But if we had a different policy and wanted to smash your Tribal Council, destroy it, we could do it in one day. We could take away every bit of your authority and we could do it in one day. We could take away every bit of your authority and we could deny every one of you to sit in the council and do it as arbitrarily as we wanted to. If your present Council were in disagreement with us, we could abolish that Council and appoint a new Council, hand picked, so every member of it would be our rubber stamp and do exactly as we told him. We could, if we wanted to, adopt a rule that prohibited you from meeting more than once every five years and you would have to obey it. Or if we wanted to be real devilish, we could adopt a rule that to be a member of the Tribal Council, you had to attend a meeting every day at Fort Defiance, otherwise you were not a member.

In other words, your self-government in the most important matters is simply a matter of what the Secretary of the Interior wants you to have. He can take it away whenever he gets ready. If I wanted, myself, to dispose of your oil property in some way you did not like, I could tell you that either you would be abolished or you were going to give me unlimited power to sign away your oil property and I would have the power to do it.

Now, that is the condition under which practically all of the Indians are living now, at the mercy of the Secretary and the Commissioner. There are a few exceptions, as in the case of most of the New Mexico Pueblos and the Osages of Oklahoma. They have certain rights under statute law, but otherwise the Indians are all situated like you are. Now what we are seeking in this Title One is to cure that situation and to place you where you will not be at the mercy of the Secretary of the Interior and the Commissioner of Indian Affairs. And by that I mean we want to give you the power so if you do not want to be at our mercy you won't have to be. If you want to stay at our mercy, you can stay there, but if you don't want to, you don't have to.

The most important fact about this Title One is that no part of it would be compulsory on any Indian tribe. No part of it. It would all be something they could do if they wanted, but if they wanted to, only.

Now what is it that a tribe, let us say the Navajo tribe, could do under this bill, if it wanted to, and only if it wanted to. Let us see what it could do. It could take out a charter of self-government. Under that charter it could have power to do just a few things or a large number of things, entirely according to its own wish. For example, the Navajo Tribe might want simply to charter itself in order to maintain the Tribal Council, just as the council now is, under its existing laws and regulations. That might be what the Navajo tribe would want to do; no more than that. In that case it would receive the charter simply to run as it is running now through the Tribal Council, the way it is, and after the charter was issued, the Secretary of the Interior could not take the charter away. Only the tribe itself could take its own charter away or Congress could do it, but not the Secretary of the Interior or the Commissioner of Indian Affairs.

Now, let us be clear about this charter; just about the issuing of the charter in the first place. Under this bill either the Secretary could offer a charter to you or you could ask for it, the initiative to come, let us say either from me or from you. Suppose he did not want to issue you a charter, what then? You would petition for a charter. The petition would have to be signed, the way the bill now reads, by one-fourth of the adult members of the tribe. And on receipt of that petition then the Secretary of the Interior and the Commissioner would either have to grant it or else make a written statement why they won't grant it and what has to be done by the tribe in order to get a charter. And that written report of findings would go to Congress. In other words, if we did not want to issue the charter we would have to justify our action to the Congress of the United States, which would not be easy.

After the charter was issued, it would still have to be ratified by you. It would have to be ratified by election, and three-fifths of those who voted at the election would have to vote for it. And as I say, once the charter was issued and ratified, then the Secretary of the Interior could not take it away. He could not revoke it any more than he could cancel your treaty so that you would be saved from being at the mercy of the Secretary of the Interior and the Commissioner. Within a short time after this bill was passed, Secretary Ickes and I would then proceed to issue the charter, and no one who comes after us could take it away from you.

Now, there is more to tell you about this self-government feature which is so important that I will have to go on after lunch. It is so fundamental and important to you that I will have to go on, but it is 12 o'clock now, so I will have to stop at this point. (*Applause.*)

CHAIRMAN: I just want to announce for the visitors that lunch will be at 12:00, dinner at 5:30, and breakfast from 7:00 to 8:00. If there is no objection, the meeting will adjourn until 1:30 p.m.

Noon Recess

[9]

CHAIRMAN: Meeting will come to order. The Commissioner will continue with the presentation of the Wheeler-Howard Bill.

COMMISSIONER: You are going to hear a great deal from me in the next day and a half on other things beside this bill, and I am going to ask another member of our staff from Washington to finish the presentation of the self-government part of this bill. After he has finished, I may have some more things to say, myself. The member whom I am going to call on is Mr. Felix Cohen, who is an Assistant to the Solicitor of the Interior Department.

MR. FELIX COHEN: Friends: This is a very peculiar bill, and many people have misunderstood it. Most laws that deal with Indians say that the Indians must do this or that. This law does not give a single command to any Indian insofar as the self-government part of the law is concerned. If this law of self-government is passed by Congress and your people don't want to take advantage of it, you can leave the law written on the paper and it will have no life. This law, when it passes Congress, is only the beginning of things. In order to mean something, you will have to take advantage of it, and if you don't accept it, after it is passed, then it will mean nothing to you. You will understand that I am talking merely about the first part of the bill, which deals with self-government.

Now, let us imagine that this bill is passed by Congress. What advantages will you be able to get from this bill? You will have your meetings and discuss the many difficult problems that are involved in this bill and then you will ask for a charter. And this charter will be like a contract between your people and the United States Government. And in this charter, or contract, the United States Government will guarantee to you many powers which you have not had before. And if at some time in the future the Secretary of the Interior does not live up to this contract, or charter, you will be able to bring suit in the Federal Court of Indian Affairs and compel him to live up to this charter, or contract. And this contract works both ways. If you agree in your charter to do certain things, for instance, to use tribal funds in a certain way, and then do not do this, then the Secretary of the Interior can compel you to live up to the charter which you have accepted.

But it will be entirely up to you whether you want any charter and you need not accept any charter that does not please you. And it will also be for you to decide whether you want one charter for all the Navajo people, or many charters for different Navajo communities or villages.

Now there are three kinds of rights which you may secure by this charter. In the first place, you may want and receive the right to have your local government like a white village or county. And if you have your own local government, this means that you can have your own ordinances and your own courts to enforce these ordinances, and anyone in your community, whether he is an Indian or a white man, must live up to those ordinances. And if there are disputes they can be taken care of in your own courts. And then, above your own courts will be the Federal Court of Indian Affairs, appointed by the president, and when a dispute arises between an Indian and a white man, either party may appeal to that court, if the community court does not do justice. Now, that is the first power which you may have under this charter, if you desire it. The power to have your own local government as white people have their own local government.

There is a second great power which you may receive under this charter. And that is the power to do business like a white man's corporation, or partnership. You will be able to organize your own company, in which your people will be the members, and this company can do the various kinds of business that you would like to do. This company could buy and sell sheep and rugs and silverware, and anything else. In this way you would naturally get the profits of your own work. And this company could borrow money from the United States under this new bill under the credit provision of the bill that has been explained to you. And it is my belief that with your organization, you could sell your arts and crafts work over the United States.

Now, there is a third great power which you can receive under this charter. And that is the power to do many things which the Indian Office, the Secretary of the Interior, or the Indian Commissioner now do for you. Self-government means that the various things which the Secretary of the Interior and the Indian Office now do in the way of governing your lives may be done by you, yourselves. At the present time the Secretary of the Interior has power to make many harsh rules and regulations over you. Commissioner Collier has explained to you this morning some of the harsh rules and regulations which the Indian Office has made for other Indians in recent years and as a result they have lost their land. And even if you believe that the present Secretary of the Interior is a good man, who has your interests at heart, and that the Commissioner is a good man, who has your interests at heart, it is a bad thing to leave that power with the Secretary of the Interior for the future and with the Commissioner of Indian Affairs for the future, and not to have your say as to how that power will be exercised. And under this charter, the Secretary can give over to you the many problems, the many rules and regulations, the many fields of activity which you, instead of he, may thereafter exercise. So that the many questions which affect your lives will be decided in your own Councils and not in Washington, D.C.

Now, what are the other things that are now done in Washington that you might do yourselves under this new bill? One of these things is the choice of your employees. If any community receives a charter under this bill it will have the right to look to its employees who are chosen in Washington, and require them to serve the community in a proper way. Each employee who is selected for you in Washington will be required to come to you and tell his plans and his purpose. And you will tell him what you think ought to be done in the way of education or in the way of health or in the way of the general superintendent's jobs, and so on. You will discuss these things together so that the Federal employees will be your employees and not Washington's employees. And then if these employees do not serve you in the proper way, you will have the right to remove such employees. But you cannot remove these employees until they have had a fair chance to show you what they are made of. You cannot remove them until they have had a fair chance to explain their policies and to try to work them out. And your charter may lay down how long a trial period should be allowed to the Federal employees before they can be removed. And it also can be provided in the charter what kind of a procedure and what kind of a vote are necessary to remove a Federal employee.

Not only will you have the power to remove employees, you will also have the power to appoint your own people to positions in the Government service when your own young people have learned to work these positions. When you have a man or a woman in your community who is qualified to do a Federal job and there is a vacancy in that job, your own community can locate that person in that office. And that person will not have to meet present civil service tests and examinations. And Commissioner Collier has already explained to you that under this bill, we will offer your young people the training which is necessary to qualify them for these various positions.

And just as one of your people can take a Federal job when he is qualified for it, so your whole community can take over a service, can take over many jobs, when the community is qualified. When many of your young people have learned to be teachers and when your community is able to run the whole educational system, why then you will be given the right to run that system and the funds will continue to be appropriated to you instead of the Indian Bureau. These are two of the things which the Indian Office does for you: make your rules and regulations, and chooses your employees. And these things, as I have explained, can be turned over to you if this bill passes, and if you ask for these things.

There is a third thing which is now done in Washington which you might be able to do. And that is to have some say as to how the money which Congress appropriates for you is to be spent. At present, the present Commissioner may come to you and discuss these financial matters, but in the past, most Commissioners have not done this and in the future, they may not do this. And all over the country, many Indian tribes have found that the Indian Bureau and Congress has spent their money for purposes that did not do them any good.

Now, under this bill, Congress can no longer appropriate your money, money out of your tribal funds, and spend that money as it pleases. And likewise, Congress cannot appropriate money for some purpose and then some day later, make you re-pay that money on the grounds that it is reimbursable. Under this bill, Congress cannot take any money out of your treasury without your consent, if you have obtained a charter. And with respect to gratuity appropriations that Congress may make to you—gifts of money that Congress may make to you—to build roads or to build schools or to dig water holes, or for any such purposes, as soon as any law is introduced in Congress for such things, a copy of that law is passed, you will have the right to consider it in your Councils and to send your recommendation. And you may say this is a good expenditure of money, or this is a bad expenditure of money. And these recommendations will be sent to Congress at the same time that the Department of the Interior makes its recommendation and Congress will know what you think about this proposed law before it passes it.

There is one more money matter that I would like to speak of. When Congress is appropriating money for some special service, like education, and the Indian community wants to take over and run it, itself, Congress will give the appropriations to the Indian community, rather than to the Indian Bureau. Under this bill, your community will be something like what the Indian Office now is. Where the Indian Office has power to make rules and laws, now your community may have that power in the future.

Where the Indian Office has power to select all your officials and employees, your community may have that power in the future. Where the Indian Office has power now over all your appropriations, your community may have that power in the future. In effect, we will be breaking up the Indian Office and giving a part of its powers to each of the Indian tribes. And in the end, the Indian Office will no longer be a Bureau that governs your people, because you will be doing the governing yourselves. Rather, the Indian Office will be an adviser to you. The Indian Bureau will be like the Weather Bureau. The Weather Bureau gives the farmers good advice, and sometimes it gives them bad advice, but it does not compel them to take the advice if they don't want to. And that will be the future of the Indian Bureau if this bill is passed. But this future will not come tomorrow. It will take some time before your people will be ready and willing to run the various functions and services that the United States Government is now running for you. This bill merely lays down a new road. And it will be up to you to decide how fast and how far you will travel along this road.

CHAIRMAN: Before we turn this bill over for the general discussion, I just want to express a few facts. I don't want you to accept or approve this bill unless you thoroughly understand what it means, and I believe that the Commissioner is of the same opinion. He is not going to force you to accept this bill or reject it. He is leaving it up to you to decide for yourselves and here are the suggestions I would like to make. If, after a general discussion that we are going to have, still you do not understand the bill, the thing to do is to ask for more time, say a month from now, or two months. We will have another Council meeting whenever it is convenient, and within that time, we will probably arrive at some conclusion.

J. C. MORGAN, Delegate from Northern Navajo: May I ask the Commissioner how long it took to write this bill?

COMMISSIONER: A good many months.

J. C. MORGAN: Then it will take us a good many more months to study it out.

COMMISSIONER: Mr. Chairman, while they are thinking about things to say or questions to ask, I might give you a little more information about the situation in Congress. Congress may be in session until the beginning of June, which means three months, or a little over three months from now. Probably this bill ought to be acted on by the present Congress. Otherwise, action would be delayed for a full year. And we, and the Committees of Congress, are hoping for some expression from the different tribes soon enough to be of use this year.

It is my belief that any Indian tribe would be able to decide about this bill in a month, to study and discuss it, or at least any Indian tribe could decide about some parts of this bill without taking a very long time. Especially, when you remember that all of this part of the bill which Mr. Cohen explained to you is merely something that you could have if you wanted it. If you wanted to wait ten years before deciding whether to have any self-government you could wait ten years to decide, under this bill.

There are parts of this bill, on which I expect that you can reach a decision quickly. For example, it ought not to take very long for the Navajo Tribe to decide whether it would like to be able to borrow money at no interest out of a fund which the government would give the Indians. And I don't think it will take the tribe long to decide whether it wants its land permanently kept out of taxation or would rather have it taxed. It probably would not take the tribe long to decide either, that it did or did not want the allotment system applied to its lands. As a matter of fact, everybody knows in advance just what the tribe would decide on points just like this. And again, it would not take long to decide about that part of the bill which gives a larger educational opportunity to the young people. The part of the bill which may seem hard to understand and that may require discussion and debate is Part One, dealing with what we call self-government. Because that part of the bill is, if you like, a complicated thing and it requires close thinking and the asking and answering of many questions before it is clear. But even that Part One, which is complicated, that is the very part which is simply offered to an Indian tribe and the tribe does not have to take it either now or hereafter. Therefore, it seems to us reasonable to hope that the Navajos can reach a conclusion in less time than it took us to write the bill.

We have explained to the tribes everywhere else that any tribe which desired to be left out of the operation of this bill by language that would be put into the bill, or language left out of the bill, that tribe could be left out. I don't believe there will be any such tribes after the thing is all understood.

Actually, the situation is this, that the bill may not pass at all unless the Indians work for it, not merely consent to it, but work and fight for it. Because in other parts of the country, there are very powerful forces which will work against the bill, not Indians at all, but white forces. For example, the greater part of the land belonging to the Indians in states like Dakota and Montana and Wyoming, the greater part of that land is even now in the possession of whites; they are renting that land. And even in the state of Arizona there are some reservations where most of the lands are being rented by white cattlemen and not being used by Indians. These cattlemen pay a smaller rent than they would pay for other land, that is the Indian lands, free from taxation, is what gives a lower rent than the other lands. Now this bill proposes to provide the money which will enable these tribes, all, to get their own cattle and sheep, and operate their own land, and, of course, the white lessees don't want it and will fight it with all their power.

Again, there are more than seventeen million acres of Indian land and the best farm land, which are allotted in severalty, and which will be sold to whites, sooner or later, and much of it very soon. The white people will get this land and they will pay very little for it. And, of course, these white interests are going to be fighting against this bill, which would stop the sale of these lands for all time.

And a great many different states would like to be able to tax the Indian lands—states and counties. And these white states and counties don't want a bill passed which makes the tax exemption permanent for Indian lands. In other words, this bill has got a multitude of enemies. Its friends are the administration, and the friends of the Indians, and the Indians. And to actually pass the bill, we need the active, enthusiastic help of the Indian tribes. At the same time, we have no desire to stampede any Indian Tribe into a decision about the bill as a whole, or any part of the bill. We only hope that the tribes will put their minds on the question without delay and will study it out and reach their decision as soon as they really can do it.

ALBERT SANDOVAL, Delegate from Southern Navajo: On Title Three, Section 17, we would like a little more explanation.

COMMISSIONER: Mr. Stewart can best explain that to you.

JAMES M. STEWART, Chief of Land Division: As Mr. Collier pointed out this morning, largely Title Three will be effective only where the allotment system has prevailed. Now, on those reservations where allotments have been made, we propose to purchase many of the allotments. We also propose to exchange those allotments. And also to purchase what we call dead allotments, where the Indian is dead, and the heirs hold his allotment. This Section 17 is part of Title Three, and under that Title, we propose to remedy, to put back in solid areas, the lands of those Indians of the northern, and other reservations, where the allotment system has prevailed. However, realizing that the Navajos have approximately six thousand allotments on the domain, that Indians in California have public domain allotments, and other Indians elsewhere have public domain allotments, and who have no tribal connection like the Navajos do, we deliberately put in this Section 17 so as to protect those Indians having their public domain allotments or homesteads, and not disturb them in any way. We don't want to give them the idea that we are going to disturb their allotments in any way. Now, this Section 17 will not disturb any Navajo allotments or any Navajo public domain Indian homestead.

MARK RADCLIFFE, Field Agent: Mr. Stewart, I believe if you would explain the difference between allotments that the bill speaks about and the public domain allotments, I don't believe the Indians understand the difference between an allotted reservation and a public domain allotment.

MR. STEWART: Reservation allotments and public domain allotments are very much different. In order to be entitled to a reservation allotment, an Indian has to be enrolled with that tribe. And so, all over the country, where tribes had reservations like this reservation here, under the law, all the enrolled Indians, as a rule, were given a small piece, or an allotment, of land within that reservation. That is the main difference between what we term a reservation allotment and a public domain allotment. The reservation allotment is within or inside the boundaries of the reservation, the public domain allotment is outside the reservation.

Mr. Collier will also make a few remarks.

COMMISSIONER: I know that among some white people there is some confusion about this matter of public domain allotments and there may be in your own minds, and I'd like to, myself, make it clear to you. As you know, when a Navajo Indian receives a public domain allotment, it means that the government gives him a piece of the public domain for his own home. Now, that has no connection with the allotment system which I've been talking about this morning, except the unfortunate fact that the word allotment is used in both cases. The allotment system which the Indians have suffered from works this way. I'll describe just how it works.

A tribe owns a reservation just like the Navajo Tribe owns its reservations. The title is in the tribe. Then the government comes in under the allotment law and says that each Indian of the tribe shall have, let's say twenty acres of land belonging to the tribe, twenty acres shall be taken away from the tribe and given to each individual Indian. And then after that division has been made there is nearly always a good deal of tribal land left over, sometimes millions of acres. And that land, the government then calls surplus land, in other words, lands that the Indians do not need. And that surplus land is thrown open for white settlement. Now, it's that thing that our bill proposes to change, and to save the Navajo Tribe from. But the matter of homesteading on the public domain or of what we would say allotting an Indian on the public domain, is a different matter and is not touched by this bill. Except that this bill would make the trust period permanent wherever an Indian has an allotment on the public domain.

I think the difficulty centers around the meaning of the term community as applied to the ownership of reservation lands.

ALBERT SANDOVAL, Delegate from Southern Navajo: Does that mean that the tribal laws of inheritance will be done away with?

CHAIRMAN: I think the difficulty in the minds of most of the Navajos, is centered around the meaning of the term community as applied to the ownership of reservation lands, that they understand this to mean the laws of inheritance will be abolished.

COMMISSIONER: First, let me say clearly that the laws of tribal inheritance will not be abolished and then I'll explain how they will not.

Now, the word community is used in this bill to describe a tribe after that tribe has taken out a charter, then it becomes a tribal community, which is the same thing as saying a chartered tribe. Now, it is established in the bill that when a tribe takes out a charter, and thereby becomes a chartered community, then all of the property and rights and claims of the tribe shall also be the property and rights and claims of the chartered community. In other words the tribe takes on the powers that belong to a chartered community, without surrendering anything it has now under treaty or ancient custom, in the nature of claims against the government or anything else that it has now.

I might add at this point that when we speak of a chartered community, if you read the bill closely, you will see that it does not say just how that community shall govern itself. That is not stated in the bill at all. A tribe obtaining a charter could carry over into the charter any peculiarity of its ancient life or government that it wanted to carry over.

Undoubtedly, in the minds of some tribal Indians, there will be a confusion if they try to apply to themselves the part of the bill which applies to allotted Indians, whose condition is entirely different. But the best way, I think, to answer the question that I think must be in your minds would be if we turned our thought away from the Navajo for a moment and look at the Pueblo. Let us say, the Pueblo of Taos, or say of San Domingo.

As you all know, the Pueblo, let us say, of Taos, has a body of land that belongs to the tribe, the Pueblo tribe, and it holds its land according to ancient custom. Now, such a Pueblo, let us say Taos, could become a chartered community without changing its ancient way at all. That is entirely up to the tribe, as to what it wants. And in the case of the Navajos, if the Navajos decided to become a chartered community, they would carry over their existing system of inheritance and everything else as it is now, until they got ready to change it. And when they got ready to change anything they would change it by amending their charter. It is required by the bill that any chartered community must protect the rights of minorities.

And, of course, any charter would have to do that, protect the rights of minorities, but those are rights under the Constitution, anyhow, and they exist already.

ALBERT SANDOVAL, Delegate from Southern Navajo: Well, I still don't quite understand this Section 17. What I am trying to find out is whether the Indians that are allotted off the reservation, if this bill passes, have to relinquish their titles.

COMMISSIONER: That is just what they don't have to do. They keep their title and remain just like they are, except that their trust period becomes permanent. That is the meaning of Section 17.

ALBERT SANDOVAL: Another question, if this bill passes, would you still allow Indians to be allotted on the public domain.

COMMISSIONER: This bill does not affect that at all. The right to allot Indians on the public domain is not touched by this bill. In fact, I did not explain that when I was telling you about the way the Indians have lost their land. There are a hundred thousand Indians who have lost all their land. The government must get them land. There will be a very large problem of acquiring land, but the Navajo land problems do not come under this bill, but under the Boundary Bills, as you know.

MR. STEWART: Mr. Chairman, I just want to bring out the fact that we have plenty of copies of this bill here. Copies of memoranda, copies of the Gallup newspaper, with a full set-up there. They are available here for distribution to the Indians as far as they will go around. Some of the Council appears to be without even copies of the bill. I suggest that you get copies now, of the bill, and the other.

CHAIRMAN: I think the Chair will declare recess until four o'clock.

LEE BRADLEY, Delegate from Western Navajo: May I suggest that we have someone read the bill to us, and explain it paragraph by paragraph. It seems that some of them here do not seem to understand the bill.

30 minute recess

[19]

CHAIRMAN: I want to present at this time the Assistant Commissioner, Mr. Zimmerman. I think most of you do not know him. (Applause as Mr. Zimmerman acknowledges introduction.)

COMMISSIONER: Mr. Chairman, regarding this question about Section 17 of Title Three. On examining that Section after the question of awhile ago, we find that it needs to be amended. Section Four of Title Three extends the trust period on all Indian owned lands, including public domain allotments. But the language of Section 17 is such as to cast doubt upon the meaning of Section 4. Therefore the language of Section 17 will be amended so as to make it clear that the trust period is extended on public domain allotments.

Now, another word about Title One, self-government. Mr. Oliver LaFarge, who is here, President of the National Association of Indian Affairs, has made a suggestion; which is, that we state again, and make clear that the development of self-government would be a slow, gradual process, that would take years and years, before it was finished. And further, that if a tribe moved faster, if a tribe found out that it had gone ahead too fast and had taken on too much power, then the tribe could surrender that power and go back to where it started from if it wanted to. If a tribe became too enthusiastic about self-government, and, as we say, should bite off more than it could chew, take on more than it could manage, then the tribe could change its mind and go back to something easier, and begin all over again.

And the bill expressly provides that where a tribe surrenders some power that it has taken on under the charter, gives it up, then the Secretary of the Interior must take it on again in the old way. And it is very important to grasp this fact, that the bill extends not only the trust period over the land, but the guardianship by the government over Indians reaches far out into the future for all Indians. So that the government would go on exercising its guardianship, it might exercise it through the Secretary of the Interior or it might exercise it through the chartered Indian community and in any case, the government would go on exercising its guardianship.

It is this way, if you picture the Indian Bureau as being a house, not very comfortable, not very nice, and a place where the Indians are kept behind bars, if you like to picture it as a house with barred doors and barred windows, now. And this bill just takes down the bars and throws open the doors and says to the Indian, you can go out if you want to, but you can come back and use the house all the time. If you want to go out and try building your own house and don't like it, if it falls down on you, you can always come back here and live if you want to. So that it is even possible to say that the bill is of such a character that the Indians cannot be made victims of their own mistakes, if they made them.

I think another way to put it is one that was used with the Plains Tribes at the big Congress last week, by Mr. Woehlke, whom many of you know. Mr. Woehlke said about this self-government plan, that it is like putting before the Indian a big table, a table loaded with food. And on the table there is beefsteak and sausage, and there is also weak tea and soup, and easy foods like that. And if a tribe of Indians has plenty to eat, they may not want to take anything from the table. They may say, "We don't want that food." Or they may say, "We'll just try something that is easy, like soup or tea, and see how it works." Or if they want, they can take the beefsteak or the buffalo meat, but they don't have to.

BLACK MUSTACHE, Delegate from Southern Navajo: There is a question in regard to the public domain allotments. How would you work it out in case of the private allottees owning the allotment? Should that be supplied to the tribe, to those on the reservation?

COMMISSIONER: A public domain allotment belongs to the allottee, doesn't it? He owns the surface and also the oil, doesn't he? This bill would not change that. My understanding is that when a Navajo Indian has been allotted on the public domain, he has obtained title to that land and to anything in that land. I am told that there are actually some allotments over in Mr. Stacher's area, in the Eastern Navajo, where oil has been developed, and the royalties are being paid to the individual allottee who owns that allotment. And that is not changed at all by this bill, it is not affected by it.

Mr. Hunter says maybe there is another question in your minds. Maybe you are wondering, when an Indian with an allotment on the public domain dies, what becomes of his allotment? Does it go to the tribe, or does it go to his heirs?

It goes to his heirs, to his own heirs. But the Bill provides on Page 30, in Section 7, that the Indian who has a public domain allotment inside the reservation, may surrender that title to the tribe if he wants to. He is not required to surrender it but if he wants to, he can turn it back into the tribal reservation.

MR. STEWART: In order to correct probable erroneous impressions given out while we were discussing the extension of the trust periods on these allotments, I want to point out that our Navajo Boundary Bill is distinct from the Wheeler-Howard Bill. It is entirely separate. Under the Boundary Bill, we are not proposing to extend the reservation boundaries and leave these non-taxable Indian allotments outside that extended line. As a matter of fact, the lines have been designed to bring into, or cover into, the reservation the bulk of these public domain allotments. By throwing the line out around those allotments, where they are especially heavy, and also by bringing inside of that line, through exchange, allotments that are outside, so that there will actually be very little material tax less locally through this Bill.

DESCHNA CLAHCHESCHILLIGE, Former Chairman of the Council: Mr. Stewart, some of the Indians asked me to bring out a question for them concerning the Eastern Navajo jurisdiction under Mr. Stacher. Suppose some Indians have relinquished their holding of their allotments on the public domain and when they relinquished their holdings and went into the consolidation, when they get there, the other Indians are all on it and they are afraid that they will not gain anything by it. That is the question.

MR. STEWART: These Indians that relinquished have the right to make selection or get new land or new holdings within the government areas. They have that right and could assert it. However, I understand Mr. Dodge, Chairman, here, has something to say about discussing these various land situations, and rather than go into detail now, I think we ought to wait Mr. Dodge's pleasure on that situation.

CHEE DODGE: In Navajo, I have been giving an explanation of the whole bill, as you might say, in a nutshell, and I believe the people understood. I have presented it to my own people as I, myself, understand it applying to the Navajo people, also to the Indians.

I told them what the allotment law is, and the way the northern Indians got rid of their allotments. They were given title to the allotments and then sold everything, now there they are, with nothing. They are on the Government's shoulders again. For that reason they do not want the Indians to get in the same fix again; that is what this new bill calls for, protection of the Indian from getting in the same fix again. That when the government gets this new land for them, they cannot sell it and be with nothing again. This law is for us, so that we will keep our land always, so we won't get into this trouble that the northern Indians have.

JIM SHIRLEY, Alternate from Southern Navajo: We are not subject to loss of our lands like the other tribes that the Commissioner has told us about. Every year in our Council we propose that new lands be given us, for the enlargement of our reservation. That should convince the public.

CHAIRMAN: There is just a little time left before suppertime. I believe we should adjourn and take this up again tomorrow. Before we adjourn, we want to announce that there will be a night session at 7:30. It will be a closed session; only Indians will be allowed to attend. The Commissioner and his staff will be the only ones who will be admitted. If there is no objection at this time, the Chair will declare recess until tonight.

[22]

Night Session (Closed) 7:30 P.M.

CHAIRMAN: The meeting will come to order. Tonight we will take up the general problems of erosion and I understand there are several things that are connected with this problem of erosion, and the first topic will be the Boundary Bills, New Mexico and Arizona Boundary Bill, and I understand that Mr. Stewart is going to present the land question.

MR. STEWART: At the last Council meeting, over at Tuba City last November, we, at an executive session, discussed the land matter. At that Council, or at that executive session, rather, we attempted to give you a historical picture starting with your treaty reservation, leading up to your present extended area. We also told you of plans with respect to enlarging the existing reservation. We tried to show you the difficulties we were meeting with locally from the white people in regard to extending your boundaries.

CHAIRMAN: I understand that reporters wish to attend this session, and I want to say that they are welcome to attend the session.

MR. STEWART: *(continuing)* At Tuba City, we told you that we were immediately leaving for Farmington and Aztec, New Mexico, to confer with the local white people about the extension of your boundary in San Juan County. We did go there, and made an adjustment, which at that time was satisfactory to the local white people, and which I believe is still satisfactory. About ten days ago we went down to Holbrook, Arizona. Objection had flared up again down there against extending your boundary in Arizona. We quieted that objection, and, in fact, got a resolution by the County Board to Senator Hayden favoring the Boundary Bill in Arizona. We are reminding you of these objections that keep cropping up from time to time, to illustrate to you the difficulties we have met with in increasing your reservation. These local objections and flare-ups, and so on, that we meet, are very small compared with the battle that we are going to have, to get your boundary bills through Congress. We have a man in Washington, who is over us, whom we have no control over. He holds the strings, you might say, to the money-bag of the government. His title is the Director of the Budget. And that is where our biggest battle is going to come. However, we feel sure we can win, with your co-operation.

There are two Boundary Bills involved, one covering the extension in Arizona and one in New Mexico. These bills ask of the government almost $500,000 apiece, which the Federal government will give for use in buying certain privately owned white lands within these proposed extended reservation lines. It will not be a burden on the Navajo people. It is free. Tribal funds will not be involved. We repeat, we have got to have your co-operation to get this money and get this land.

Now, to go back to Tuba City for a minute. Over there last November, the Council passed a Resolution approving the great program whereby the government will spend more than a million dollars to stop the washing away of soil and saving the grass. This is the Resolution:

"BE IT FURTHER RESOLVED, That we approve of the great program whereby the government will spend more than a million dollars to stop the washing away of our soil and bring back the grass. We promise the Government the help and assistance of the Navajo people in this great undertaking to save our homeland from destruction through erosion, and we will submit to all of our people that part of the erosion-control program which has to do with overgrazing and stock reduction, urging our people to follow the counsel of the wise men who urge this step."

Now, that resolution of the Council at Tuba City gave us great courage in going forward with drafting and initiating these two bills. So we wrote up these boundary bills as we promised you we would and attached to each of them a report and have written letters to Congress, to the Committee in Congress, recommending that they be approved. In that letter which the Secretary of the Interior will sign, and which is to go to this man who holds the strings to the Government's money bag, we said this:

"This proposed boundary extension represents the ultimate line to which the Indians can hope to extend their reservation. This fact is realized by the Indians themselves, as evidenced at their Tribal Council at Tuba City, Arizona, last November. They are aware that they must reduce the number of their sheep and goats to prevent overgrazing. That erosion and range control must be conducted continuously if they are to survive and make substantial progress."

Now, by ultimate boundary, we mean this, that it is the end of further extending the reservation. These bills will add large areas of land which we have explained to you in the last two Council meetings, to the present reservation. Now, we are in this position. We have drafted these bills, written these bills enlarging your reservation. We have written letters to the committees of Congress justifying this legislation and the million dollar appropriation, feeling that the Navajo Tribe, as a whole, would co-operate and back us up. If the Navajo Tribe does not back us up in this, we will be forced to go back to Washington and tell those people that what we said in our letter was wrong. And, personally, I am sure that these boundary bills will not be enacted if the program of soil erosion and range control is not carried forward, because it would be throwing good money after bad. We will have to show Congress that if these additional lands are given to the Navajo Tribe and this large sum of money is given to purchase these lands, that the lands we get, the additions we obtain, will not be overgrazed, and that soil erosion will not take place. We cannot show that soil erosion, overgrazing, will not take place on those additional lands without your backing and co-operation. We feel sure that if we can go back to Congress and tell them that the Navajo Tribe is behind this soil erosion control, range control, and stock reduction, we will get this additional land, and money to buy that land.

You put in a program of stock reduction within the last twelve months in a wonderful spirit and it has helped the range tremendously but in order to get this additional land for you and money to buy land, we have got to go back to Congress and say that the Navajo Tribe is willing to reduce their stock a little bit more. Now at Tuba you were told of the work that would be given you in order to compensate for loss of income due to any stock reduction.

Now, as to our plans of estimated extra work for the Navajos for the coming four years. I'll tell you later as to the amount of money involved. For 1934, next year, and that is very low, a conservative statement, there will be about a million and a half available. This money will be spent within the reservation, giving employment to Indians. Building roads, irrigation projects, schools, erosion control, and for the years 1935–36–37–38, there will be almost that amount available each year. It is anticipated that there will be more work on this reservation for Indians than there will be Indians to fill the jobs. At least for the next year, 1934. So, except for a case here and a case there, of old people, there will be no need of any Indian going hungry or lacking any foodstuffs because he can always get work on these various projects. No one will need to be left out, unless it may be some old people who are not able to work.

Now, to get back to our goal of having you back us up to get this additional land and this additional dollars to buy land. First, we have got to tell Congress that the Navajo Indians want this land, want this money, and are willing to make an additional sacrifice over what they made this past year in stock reduction. We have got to go back and say that the Navajo people want us to continue erosion and range control. But we feel that that is something for you people to work out after this meeting, when you get home. We will submit to you what we think must be done and we have got to have the Council go on record as being in favor of that being done. The plan which you are to consider when you go home, but which the Council must approve in principle, I'll read:

"We should like you to consider when you go home after this Council, a reduction during the next twelve months of 150,000 head of grown stock, of which all or at least a hundred thousand (100,000) head, should be goats. We are convinced that we will not ask again of you to reduce your stock. It won't be necessary.

"The next thing to be done would be to castrate within the next year all remaining male goats and substitute, therefor, in the future such a number of milch goats as may be needed for home use, based upon a study to be made later.

"And the last would be to maintain and keep up the yearly or annual sale of all wether lambs and any percentage of ewe lambs not needed to maintain the youth of the herd, at least 80% each year."

Naturally you are wondering, in addition to the other benefits which we have mentioned, what other benefits are to be gained from giving up any of these goats. We believe that they should be purchased but with all of this work money that we are getting to spend on the reservation, together with this million dollars we are to get to buy land for you, and other money we are getting for you, it is hopeless to ask Congress to appropriate money to buy these goats. There are only two plans that we have been able to think out, after hours of study and talking, and I'll read them to you.

"Plan No. 1 is to obtain legislation loaning the Navajo Tribe $225,000, or the amount necessary for the purpose of purchasing the 150,000 head of goats, the tribe to reimburse the government from its future oil royalties and also from the proceeds of the sale made of the stock, goats to be purchased at $1.50 per head, sheep at market price.

"The other plan would be a stock and wage tax. Now, it is proposed to tax stock at dipping time at the rate of 10¢ per head, 2½¢ of that going for dipping, and 7½¢ going for stock purchase. Also to tax wages of those employed on these works being carried on, on the reservation, at the rate of 10% of their pay."

Now those plans are for your consideration, if we are to purchase that number of goats. We would have to have money to make the purchase and this is the only apparent painless way we can raise it. So we want or would like to have you go back to your chapter organizations and back home, and discuss this whole matter and work out one of these plans or some other plan that is acceptable to you, whereby we can get the money to buy these goats. And in closing, I want to again remind you that it is necessary for this Council to give us written assurance that the Navajo people will go forward with range and erosion control and this number of stock reduction, as soon as they can possibly do so. If we do not get that assurance, it is almost certain that we will not get this additional land and additional money to buy land that is called for in these two bills.

Mr. Collier would like to add to these remarks, I believe.

COMMISSIONER: I, first, want to give you a fact about the past year, what has happened since last July 1st. It was about that time, at the Wingate meeting that we first talked about the erosion problem and the need of stock reduction and all these questions. From July 1, last year, to now, the amount of extra money paid out in wages on the Navajo reservation has been $1,600,000; that amount in a little less than a year. I remind you of this just in order to convince you that we are not merely making promises. I think the record of the last ten months shows that we are fulfilling our promises.

Now, if we take these figures which Mr. Stewart read you about the five years ahead, about the wages which can be paid out here in the five years from now forward, the total, which is a very low estimate, far below the facts, I believe, is $5,080,000 to be paid out in wages in the next five years. And in addition to that $400,000 of new earning from the irrigated land that is too, to be brought into use under the new irrigation work. I want to emphasize that there are no other Indians who are receiving anything like as large a grant from the government of money to be spent on wages through these new kinds of work.

Now, I have got to strengthen what Mr. Stewart said about the seriousness of the present situation. It is very serious. I shall not go over the subject of destruction of soil and the deterioration of your range because that, I believe, is now understood by everybody. I just remind you that for a number of years, due to overgrazing, the Navajo reservation has been falling off in its productivity year by year, and the falling off has been more rapid as each year went by. That great areas of the reservation have been injured almost beyond repair already. That with respect to much more than half of the reservation, the soil is deteriorated so that it will take years to build it up again. And the condition in the years ahead will grow very rapidly worse unless something is done. So that in fifteen years or twenty years, if things go on the way they are, the Navajo reservation will have become largely a desert and no place to sustain human life.

Now, these facts are known to you but what we are talking about tonight is, these facts are known to Congress and they are known to the President. The reason why extra money is being spent on the Navajo last year and the year ahead is because Congress and the President and Secretary Ickes know that your condition is serious and dangerous. That is why the money is being spent here. They will continue to spend the necessary money if they are convinced that the spending of the money is going to accomplish the result of saving your soil. But if they believe that in spite of all this money spent here, nevertheless, the soil is continuing to wash away through overgrazing, they will stop spending the money. That is absolutely certain.

For example, this paper that Mr. Stewart was reading about the expenditures to be made down here, about the wages to be paid in the next five years, contains one item of $2,000,000 to be paid in wages for work on erosion control. Now this erosion control work is being done by another department of the government, not by the Indian Bureau. It is being done by the Soil Erosion Service. I believe, as a matter of fact, that the amount of money which they should spend, and which I hope they will spend on wages, is more than $2,000,000 in the next five years, and I point this out to you, and if I err, if I make a mistake, I want the Director of the Erosion Work, Mr. Calkins, who is up here now, to correct me.

The Soil Erosion Service is doing work in many parts of the United States, not only here, but in twelve or fourteen places besides the Navajo reservation. There is a great competition to get the money of the Soil Erosion Service, and to get the help of that organization, competition all over the country. Wherever they go in and spend their money and do their work, they do it upon the condition that the local people co-operate and control the range and stop overgrazing on the range. Otherwise, they don't go in. Of course, that is their rule, because what is the use of going into a countryside and spending great sums of money on erosion control unless they procure erosion control. What's the use of doing it if all the time the soil's going to be washed away faster than they can save it. Dr. Calkins, will you confirm or correct me on this, that the Soil Erosion Service, when it works in other parts of the country, requires the range control and agreement to stop overgrazing.

MR. CALKINS, Regional Director of Soil Erosion: That is correct.

COMMISSIONER: Now, I am not telling this to you because I like to tell it to you, nor as a threat, I am just telling you as a fact I cannot change. That unless we can obtain range control here and stop overgrazing, then the Soil Erosion Service will withdraw their money and their work here and spend it where they can obtain range control. The same is true of the other big expenditures that are going on and that are planned for the Navajo Reservation.

I believe that Mr. Stewart spoke correctly about your Boundary Bill when he said that unless Congress can be assured that you are going to control your range, Congress will not pass that bill. I think he spoke the truth. And even when it comes to these new schools that we have talked about and which are going to be built, these schools where we will pay out $800,000 in wages to Indians, in order to build the schools, even in that the same thing holds good. There is no sense in putting nearly $2,000,000 into new school buildings in places where a few years from now the soil will be all gone, and, therefore there will be no goats, and no sheep, and therefore, no people.

This is not a thing which I have control over, nor even a thing which Secretary Ickes has control over. It is beyond us. The money comes from Congress on the recommendation of the President of the United States. And it is certain that they, that is Congress and the President are going to take the view that I have stated. They are not going to pour money in here unless overgrazing is stopped. They won't do it.

Now, I point out to you what a million dollars represents, a million dollars in wages, or in any other thing. A million dollars represents the income from 400,000 sheep in a year. If you figure that each sheep yields a dollar for wool and $1.50 for lambs, then 400,000 sheep produce a million dollars a year. The 1,600,000 paid out in wages to you in the last ten months is the same as the income from more than 600,000 sheep in a year. And 600,000 sheep is half of all the sheep on the Navajo reservation. So we don't feel that it is asking you to do anything very hard to ask you to reduce your stock in the way Mr. Stewart described when you are being compensated two or three times as much as you give up year by year. And when, at the same time, the reduction of the sheep and the erosion control work are saving your range and building up and increasing the wealth that will belong to our children.

Now, we perfectly understand the nature of the difficulty about stock reduction. We understand pretty well why it is so difficult. We know that very often the man who is being asked to reduce his stock is not the man who wants to take a job and earn wages, and we understand that you are in agreement with all that we say but the difficulty is to find out how to reduce. That is the real problem.

But we also know that reduction is possible. People reduce their stock in other places and you can do it here if you want to. I agree with Mr. Stewart that it is important and even necessary for the Tribal Council, at this meeting, to take some action now, and not at some later date. It is necessary in connection with the Boundary Bill, which is so important, and it is necessary in order that the Soil Erosion Service can go forward with their plans and can request the additional money from public works which is needed here. It also is necessary because we are now at the point where we have to plan the Emergency Conservation Work for the next year, for the year ahead. We believe that the President is going to allow us to go forward until April of 1935 with the Emergency Conservation Work, but that work, most of that work here on the Navajo reservation, will not be worth doing unless we are going to get erosion control, which means range control.

We understand perfectly that the Council gets its power from the people here on the Navajo reservation. Its power grows out of the fact that it has the confidence of the people and that the people go along with it. And so we don't expect the Council to make undertakings beyond its power to fulfill. But we also believe, and it is believed at Washington, that the Navajo Tribal Council is a truly representative body, and that when it speaks, that is the views of the Tribe. And we are confident that if the Council is giving to Congress and the President its assurance that it is going to back up the range control and the stock reduction, if it does that, we are confident that without help, with the authority of the government behind it, the Council can do the thing it undertakes.

Now, I think I have said enough. I have said everything two or three times and I am going to yield the floor. It might be of help if you had a few words connecting what we mean by range control from Mr. Marshall, Director of Forestry or [cannot read], Forester for the Southwest District, and I suggest that to your Chairman.

CHAIRMAN: Now, it is necessary to get the meaning of range control, and before we can proceed with our discussion we should get some idea of range control, so I will call upon Mr. Marshall.

MR. ROBERT MARSHALL, Director of Forestry: There have been about two thousand books written on range control. And I could talk about sixty-nine hours about range control, if any of you were strong enough to listen, but I think I will follow the example of Mr. Dodge this afternoon, and tell you about it in a nutshell, as he has told you about the bill.

When the grass and bushes grow faster than the sheep and goats eat them, then you have range control. And when the sheep and goats eat the grass and bushes faster than they grow, then you have overgrazing.

When the Navajos first came into this country, the grass and bushes were growing a lot faster than their sheep and goats were eating them. And, so they tell me, you had deep grass, and lots of bushes, lots for the animals to feed on almost all over this country. But, to-day, as all of you know, the grass and bushes are getting less and less because the sheep and goats are so many that they eat them faster than they can grow. And, although you may do a lot of work and the Erosion Service may do a lot of work to build up your soil and build up your range, it does not do much good if there are still too many sheep and goats. Because your grass and bushes will keep getting less and less.

It would be as if you went down to Gallup some night about when the night train passed through town and as the train started to pull out of the station you started to run a race with the train. You might work awful hard and you might run harder than you ever ran before in your life, but you would keep dropping farther and farther behind the train, no matter how hard you ran.

Well, that is the way with your grass to-day. It will keep dropping farther and farther behind what the sheep need, no matter how hard you work. And there is nothing you can do to stop it unless you make the sheep less and give the grass a chance to get more. That is the nutshell, and Mr. Zeh will tell you a few of the things that can be done.

MR. ZEH, Forester for the Southwest District: Mr. Marshall has told you in such a good way what we mean by overgrazing and what we mean by proper grazing that I will not attempt to repeat or enlarge upon his explanation. But I want to get back to the point, to say that if you have a grass area, or range area, with a large number of stock, you all know that the stock eats the grass and the bushes as fast as they can grow. We all know that any plant, in order to multiply itself, must have a chance to make seed. Now, if your sheep and goats and other stock eat the range down so it can't have a chance to make seed, you know that your range will be getting less and less each year. That is not any secret or any technical statement. It is something that you all know, yourselves. You are on the range every day. You all know these things yourselves.

Now, men coming in from outside, who make range studies their lifework, tell you and tell us that there is by far too much stock on the range to give the grass a chance to multiply and give you better grass. Now, you have heard our several men from this platform about range control or controlled grazing. Now, one of the simple ways in which we can bring back a range so it will produce more feed for the stock is just by letting it rest, while letting the stock graze on another part of the reservation. In that manner we give the grass growing on the area which we are resting a chance to make seed and become stronger and produce more grass. And to do this, you can easily see that we must have less stock than we have at the present time.

One other simple method that is used is called rotation grazing. When we practice rotation grazing, we start in one section of the range and start feeding from place to place, each day in a different place, until perhaps after a week or ten days, or a certain other period, we are back again. By the time we come back to a starting point, the grass will have had a chance again to put on some growth and by going over practically the same area, we can have some fresh feed for the stock. But if we have a small area or an area which is not growing much feed, we cannot do this with a large number of stock. With just these two simple methods, after we have reduced the stock to such a number that we know the range can carry, we can have a perpetual pasture, which will always be in good shape and gradually getting better.

I think with Mr. Marshall's very excellent description, you will readily see why a reduction in number is necessary, and after we have a reduction of numbers, I have tried to show you, by two simple methods, how it is fairly easy to have the range in a continually productive condition.

CHAIRMAN: We would like to hear the expression of your reaction to the program that has been outlined to us.

ALBERT SANDOVAL, Delegate from Southern Navajo: I think it would be advisable to take a recess on this and see what the organization's opinion is on the whole program, because I am pretty sure that most of these delegates are just like myself, don't know just what to say on the subject, and besides it is getting late and we are getting sleepy.

CHAIRMAN: Motion has been made and seconded that we adjourn until tomorrow morning. If there is no objection, we will adjourn until tomorrow morning at 9:30.

* * *

[32]

The morning session was open only to Navajos. Continuing at 4:00 P.M., afternoon of March 13, 1934, the Chairman asked that the following resolution be inserted in the Minutes.

> "BE IT RESOLVED, By the Tribal Council: That final action should be deferred on the Wheeler-Howard Bill until the 9th day of April, at which time another Council should be held."

(Unanimously carried.)

CHAIRMAN: The meeting will come to order.

> RESOLUTION
>
> WHEREAS, It is realized by a great number of Navajos that with the advent of money into the reservation from Emergency Conservation Work, and other National Recovery projects, the vices of drinking, gambling, and prostitution have appeared and have become so widely spread and flagrant on the reservation, that unless some very drastic measures are immediately taken to suppress and eradicate these vices, the very life of the tribe, as a whole, will be impaired to a point beyond redemption.
>
> WHEREAS, It is also realized that the evil of drinking, gambling, and prostitution, has become such a great problem, that the local chapter authorities cannot effectively deal with it, and that is now and questionable whether the whole tribe will be able to meet the problem through the Council and other tribal authorities.
>
> THEREFORE, Be it Resolved by the Tribal Council, in council assembled, that the Honorable Commissioner of Indian Affairs be, and he is, hereby, respectfully requested for a specific authority whereby a police force of fifty or more Navajos under the direction and supervision of one or more able law enforcement officers, may be created and for the purpose of suppressing and stamping out this great evil of drinking, gambling, and prostitution is found to be impractical, then by all means some other solution should be attempted without any delay.

HENRY TALIMAN, Delegate from Southern Navajo: I would like to suggest that since it is for the good of the people to know what is going on at the Council, that every speaker come before the loudspeaker so that everybody listening outside can know what is going on before the Council.

CHAIRMAN: The Chair accepts the suggestion.

ALBERT SANDOVAL, Delegate from Southern Navajo: I believe what Mr. Chairman read is similar to what we sent in to the Commissioner several weeks ago and I would suggest that we hear from Mr. Commissioner, since the resolution is adopted.

COMMISSIONER: We have been very much concerned about the condition which is stated in the resolution. It has been very much on our minds. And we are entirely in accord with the resolution, in agreement with it. We believe that the plan would do a great deal to help the situation. We do not believe that we can control the drinking and gambling and the prostitution unless you help in the way that the resolution states. We have the authority to deputize your men as policemen. We can do that and will. And furthermore, we have the authority to put rules and regulations back of any reasonable plan that you adopt in the way of punishment for drinking and so on.

Now, when it comes to paying these fifty mounted policemen, that may be difficult. If we pay fifty policemen at $30 a month each, that is $1500 a month. We have not got that money in our appropriation for the suppression of liquor traffic. That appropriation has been cut by Congress and we just haven't got the money in that appropriation. Possibly we can get authority to pay these men out of the Emergency Conservation funds.

Undoubtedly, we can get the authority to pay some of them out of these emergency funds. Mr. Monahan, who is here, is directly in charge of our Emergency Conservation Work at Washington. He thinks that we can surely get authority for a reasonable number, perhaps twenty-five, to be paid out of the Emergency Conservation money. Under existing law, as you know, your tribal funds could not be used. It is all obligated for land purchase. The tribal balance at this time is only about $20,000. But we will promptly go ahead and arrange to pay as many as we can get the money for and I am sure that at least twenty-five can be hired.

Now, we would like this force of mounted policemen to represent both the Commissioner of Indian Affairs, and the Navajo Tribal Council. But we want it clearly understood that if this resolution is passed—I understand it has not generally passed—then we would want it clearly understood that this plan is the Navajo's own plan. We would want the Chapters and the Council to find the men and vouch for them, the men who were to be put on the payroll. And we would want the Council to help work out the plan of making the whole thing succeed. In other words, we want this to be your liquor suppression plan, carried out by your representatives, with our advice. We will put the government back of your men and back of the Council and back of any ordinances it adopts.

I know that this is a matter which very deeply interests Mrs. and Secretary Ickes and that they'll want, as much as I do, to go along with you, to go the limit with you. And as Mr. Zimmerman, the Assistant Commissioner, is here, as well as I, we can give you our full action right here and now. I would like to ask Mr. Zimmerman right now whether he finds these remarks in accordance with his views.

MR. ZIMMERMAN: It seems to me it is absolutely important that every one of these men be picked out by the Navajo himself and that they have your confidence and that you know they're the right men for that job.

COMMISSIONER: Mr. Monahan has raised an important question which I will repeat to you. The government has the authority to imprison or fine for offenses of this kind. It can both put a man in jail and it can fine him. Now, this is a technical question that I cannot answer but I should think that the government could give the Tribal Council authority to fine as well as imprison offenders. And that the money collected might be put in a fund that would not be under the control of Congress but under your own control.

If that were legally possible, then the fines could be used toward paying the salaries of the policemen or toward hiring additional policemen, if you need them. This could absolutely be done under this bill we have been discussing. I am not sure whether we can do it under existing law but if we can, we will arrange it that way. Now, Mr. Monahan is afraid that the present law does not allow the fines to be paid into your own control. But this much I will assure you, that the Department has very broad powers in the matter of imposing penalties and we can put all of these powers back of the Council. That I know. So, leaving aside that technical question about whether the fines can be paid to you or would have to go into the Treasury, I can assure you that all the rest can and will be done.

Our people have been consulted, and they have talked with the Chief Clerk at the Agency. Our conclusion is this, that under existing law, fines collected would have to go into the treasury of the United States. But under this new bill they could be paid to the Tribal Council. Therefore, all of the payment of these policemen must come out of the Treasury and the fines cannot be used to pay their salaries.

BOYD PESHLAKAI, Alternate from Northern Navajo: A lot of people have come from a long way to gather here and when I look at the audience here, I see a lot of good prospects. You all look like beautiful flowers. Why are we accused of a lot of evils. There are, however, a lot of these evils existing. I am a policeman from the Shiprock community. It is our purpose to keep up the standards there. We are a people with high standards. Why should we have a lot of evils of this kind?

Mr. Commissioner, what would you think the right penalty would be for a man that drank only once? Also what would the penalty be for the second offense?

COMMISSIONER: I would rather have the Navajos decide that.

BOYD PESHLAKAI, Alternate from Northern Navajo: I wish also to say a word in connection with playing cards. There card games come from our white people and they don't seem to think it is very much of an evil when they get together in groups and play, such as, we say, in society. But when the Navajos get together and play they put down money and it gets to be a big thing. When it comes to that, something should be done about it. Also about liquor. We wish that law and order could be more enforced in connection with these things.

JIM SHIRLEY, Alternate from Southern Navajo: I wish to comment on what the speakers preceding me have said in connection with liquor and all those evils. I am very much in favor of doing what we can against the evils that have more or less pulled the Tribe down. It seems like a lot of us don't seem to realize the evils of it but if we are going to get anywhere we must start now. All of that money has not been appropriated with the intention that we should buy liquor with it. It was appropriated with the intention that we should help ourselves and that we might buy food with it. Very little has been said about this. I am very sorry that the Commissioner has been away and our letter probably is in Washington now. He favors the resolution and we hope that everyone will study the thing out and thoroughly understand the evil of liquor and all the other vices.

J. C. MORGAN, Delegate from Northern Navajo: I want to tell a little story first about house-cleaning. There is a school in the east where everybody has a chance. Everybody has an equal chance to learn something that is useful. One day a boy came to that school. He did not have any money, only 50¢ in his pocket. This boy applied to enter that school. He had never been to school in his life, but the principal of that school said, "All right, I will give you an examination. If you pass the examination, then you will be enrolled." The teacher gave him a broom and dust-pan and a dust broom. She told him to start in and sweep the room. Then the teacher left the room.

The boy began to sweep that room. He swept that room carefully, every corner, but as he went around he saw some dirt left. So he went around the second time and swept that floor, and again the third time, but was not satisfied. He swept that room four times. He got down on his knees with the dust rag, he wiped the windows, window casings, everything, until everything was clean. Pretty soon the teacher came back. She had on a very clean white glove, a very clean handkerchief. She came into the room and looked around and touched the floor with her white glove and looked at it. There was not any dirt on the white glove. Then she went around the window frames but the dirt was gone. She dropped her clean handkerchief on the floor to see if it would gather some dirt, but it did not.

That boy passed the examination and was admitted. He became a very great leader among his people. That black man was Booker T. Washington. That story is a good example.

Our reservation is a great big room and we all keep that room. We have got to sweep it out. In order to do that we have to have a good broom. We have got to have a dust pan, a dust-rag of some kind, and that broom, or the dust broom, must be our own example. The example of the Navajo Indian leaders. We should begin right here in our own Council. Each Council member must be an example before his people. If he likes to drink, he must quit. Otherwise, he cannot sweep that room. And he must do a good job. If he does not succeed the first time he must try and try again, according to the old saying.

And then another thing. There are a great many things going on in our institutions. We must protect our young boys and girls as they grow up. Too frequently, they learn those things there. Those tender minds begin to grow, begin to harden as they grow, and when they leave school, they cannot get away from those things. That is what the Chairman brought up awhile ago, the liquor and the immoral life among our people. The immoral life among our people is a menace to the health of the tribe. If we are going to do a good job of house-cleaning, we must begin with ourselves, as Indian Navajo leaders.

I want to say to our government employees, our friends, they should be an example before our people. Sometimes they get together in their homes, sit down together and play these games. I do not know anything about these games. Away into midnight, the Indian passing by, sees the white man playing and says "I guess we can play." The Navajos are a great people to imitate things. As long as they do it, the Navajos will do it, too.

These are only some of the things I want to bring out, once and for all. Because I feel it in my heart, that if you want to save our people, we must begin right now. We talk about self-government. We are not ready for that as long as we do these things. What kind of a government will we have if our people cannot keep away from these evils. Let us clean the house first and then we would not need such a big force of policemen.

What the Commissioner has said is that it takes money to have a big force of police and I hate to see a jail, and I hate to see an Indian go to jail. Let us keep out of it. So, let us be an example for our people, so they can follow it. But, remember, so long as we have a large number of policemen and expect them to stop these things alone, the people will say, "We will follow our leaders." There is where the danger lies. I am sorry to say these things but it must be said. There is no use beating around the bush about what we have to say.

CHAIRMAN: I think everybody is agreed as to the merits of the resolution as submitted, and I suggest that we take a vote on that resolution.

(Motion made, seconded and adopted unanimously.)

CHAIRMAN: Now, we will turn back to the resolution on range control and the goat question.

ALBERT SANDOVAL, Delegate from Southern Navajo: Mr. Chairman, just a question. I want to ask the Commissioner how we are going to dispose of these goats. Now, the way we are to do, as we understand it, is to raise money and buy these goats. The question is now, after we raise the money to buy our own goats, what are we going to do with them.

COMMISSIONER: That is a big question and that would be a long story if I tried to answer it fully. We'd have to find out a way to get rid of these goats, and to sell them. Undoubtedly, the Indian Bureau, itself, could use a large number, and slaughter them and feed them to the children in the schools. And we have discussed a great many other possible ways of marketing them.

They might be turned into jerky and sold to other people, to the Mexicans. There will be a market for all of the skins of the goat. They will bring in some money. It is possible that we can get the government to buy some of them and feed to the white people and Mexicans who are getting relief from the government, the poor people. There are a number of other possibilities but we cannot tell you for sure that we'll be able to get a good price for all the goats. There will be some loss, unquestionably. There is even talk about one possibility that I will tell you about for your interest and amusement.

Down in Old Mexico, the government of Mexico is supplying land to Indians who haven't got any land, the Indians living down in Old Mexico. And it is supplying these Indians with stock. There are a great many of these landless Indians down there, maybe a million of them. Now the Indian in Mexico likes a goat better than he likes anything in the world. And the idea is that maybe we can get the government of Mexico to buy these goats and give them to the Indians of Mexico. All of these are possibilities but the disposal of the goats will be the job of the Indian Bureau. We'll have to work it out.

Mr. Monahan has something to tell you.

MR. MONAHAN: Mr. Collier would not tell you this story. He wanted me to do it. Last winter we sent some of the mutton from your stock into the plains country where some of the Indians have been starving. They had never eaten mutton before, had always eaten beef. They've eaten all the mutton and one Indian sent to the Indian Office and said: "Send us another carload of Navajo turkey."

CHAIRMAN: The Chair would like to present a question. In case the Council turns down this resolution, is it probable that Congress will not pass the Boundary Bills, and is it also probable that the different works that are now going on will stop?

COMMISSIONER: Does this mean the resolution about stock reduction? My answer can only be what I, myself, told you last night. I do not speak about this resolution so much, but if Congress and the President thinks that the Navajo tribe is not going to carry out reduction, I believe that the Boundary Bills will not be passed and I believe that the expenditures here will not be continued. Does that answer it?

CHAIRMAN: I would like to call on Mr. Stewart for a few more words.

MR. STEWART: As I told you last night, I have had to go up before the various Congressmen and Senators from the Southwest on these Boundary Bills. These visits have been informal but invariably they would ask me, individually, what is the end. Where is it going to end? You come up and tell us that these lines represent the end. That if the Navajos get these additional lands, it means they won't look to expand further and go on and on. My answer has always been that the Navajo Indians want this land and they need it so badly that we must expect sacrifices from them. And that I, personally, was sure that the Navajos would do a little more sacrificing in addition to what they've already done. Also that they would agree to put in range control and erosion control.

By telling those Congressmen and Senators just what I've mentioned, we have been able to break down a very violent opposition to this enlargement, on their part, until now we have their sympathy, and they'll go forward with it, I am sure, if we can keep our word that the Navajo people will sacrifice once more on their stock, as I pointed out last night, and let us go forward with the range and erosion control. Otherwise, my personal belief is that if these things are not done, these bills will not be enacted.

CHEE DODGE: We have brought this legislation on ourselves. Regarding self-government, every time we hold a Tribal Council, complaints are brought in about this and that, and they say why do you not do this thing or the other thing. We say what is the use of our children getting an education and come back home and find there nothing they are fitted to do. That simply makes loafers of them. We go to the government and say we want jobs for them, and they say they are not qualified. Now, they have a chance to hire these people. The people who have the most sheep and stock are the ones who kick most. They ought to pay a tax, a feed tax on stock on foot. They ought to have a certain number exempt and pay a tax on each head above that number. Now, if the government introduces that, you have no kick coming; we have brought it on ourselves.

And another thing, you just put in a complaint that when you pass so late in the night and you see the teacher, maybe the superintendent, playing cards. Well, that is the power the government is trying to give you. If you want to come to that place, you have that power, and can go up there and play cards too, if you want to.

CHAIRMAN: It is practically suppertime and with the permission of the Council, the Chair will declare a recess until seven o'clock to-night.

Recess until 7:00 P.M.

[40]

CHAIRMAN: The meeting will come to order.

We still have the goat resolution under consideration. Before we proceed with this discussion, we want to hear from our former chairman, Mr. Deschna.

DESCHNA CLAHCHESCHILLIGE, Ex-Chairman of the Council: This morning I gave a little talk on things that have led us step by step, up to where we are to-day. Shall we take another step or shall we stand still. I am going into detail but I just want to read here, by permission of the community of Shiprock, which held a meeting several days ago, a report which we would like to insert in the minutes of the Tribal Council, which they wish to have inserted by me as President of All Officers, chapter officers or community officers, whatever you want to call it, on the Northern Navajo jurisdiction, the same relating to self-government. We call ourselves over around Shiprock the Indian Farmers Association.

REPORT OF INDIAN FARMERS ASSOCIATION, SHIPROCK, N. MEX.

"The Indian Farmers Association was organized in 1929 by the present Hogback Irrigation Project Manager, to promote better co-operation in irrigation and farming work, and also to promote the welfare of the Indian. The officers are the President, Vice-president and Secretary, and the elections are held once a year.

"Meetings are held once a month, at which time all business of the organization is transacted. This includes seeing that all land assigned is cultivated and planted, keeping of stray stock from fields, calling upon all members for work when needed, and any other question for the good of the community. Talks are given on the use of water, soil, and farming methods.

"Farm machinery is bought by the association for the farmers under this project and used as community property. At present we have a large Case threshing machine, for wheat, oats, and beans, which has been paid for in cash. Also rakes, mowing machines, corn planters, hay-balers, and reapers, on which payments are now being made. Machinery has encouraged the Indian to cultivate a larger acreage and has produced a larger yield per acre. Plans for a community house are under way.

"Money paid out for machinery, and other purposes, is collected by an assessment on the members, and also when a member does not do his proportionate share of ditch work, a certain amount is paid into the treasury by him. Money thus collected is put on deposit in the bank, checks are then issued for the payment of bills. This month $49.26 has been collected, making our present bank balance $316.01.

"Since being organized, there has been $23,140.00 worth of labor performed on this project without pay, or an average of $4,448.00 a year. This labor has been on wash-outs on the canal line, work on the temporary diversion dam, rock jetties along the river bank for land protection, cleaning the canal each spring, and many other jobs.

"During the five years of organization, great headway has been made in our working and living conditions. With the new improvements and extension of the Hogback Project, we expect to make this the garden spot of the Navajo Reservation.

Signed:
Natoni G. Nez, President.
Deschna Clahcheschillige,
President of all Officers.

Things like this lead up to the self-government, as being discussed to-day. I am not going to discuss anything about boundary extension yet, but I believe whatever is proposed for the extension of our reservation, which we all know, and which our government officials have been telling us, are being created, something must be done about it tonight. I do believe whatever the legislation is in Congress concerning this land extension, I believe we should favor the whole program. I think it is best for our people where there is self-government, erosion control, range control, and stock reduction. It is for our benefit.

ALBERT SANDOVAL, Delegate from Southern Navajo: The speakers ahead of me have given little stories when they started their talks. When I was in school I read a little story. When the white people first came across the ocean and first came in contact with us, the Indians, they began to push the Indian back. Finally, a general and an Indian Chief had a meeting. They sat on a log together. The Chief kept telling the General to move over and give him more room. He kept pushing him over and pushing him over. Well, finally, the General said, "There is no more space left for me to move on." He was on the end of the log. Then the Chief said, "That is just the way you people are doing us. You are pushing us back and pushing us back, until we are on the end of the log."

That is the situation now with us, the Navajos. The white man gave us a little space, of [grants?]. We found out right away that wasn't big enough and we asked for extensions. The white man was beginning to say "No more room for me to move back." But we know there is plenty of room, plenty of land back there. The only way I see to get enough land is to adopt the resolution that has been prepared here. That is the only thing, I think, that will help us out, because we have been fighting for this for years. I am much in sympathy with that resolution, although it is going to bring on a lot of harsh talk and scolding back home, but I do not see any other way out, except to take it the way the resolution reads.

FRED NELSON, Delegate from Hopi Jurisdiction: Friends, Commissioner, and Staff from Washington: There have been a lot of things brought out in this Council, and before going on and adopting this new resolution that is afoot, we would like to refute a proposal that we made at the Tuba City Council, the resolution at the Council to reduce our sheep a hundred thousand. I think we should refute that resolution before we go ahead with this new proposal. At the time, when we passed that resolution that we were to reduce our sheep 100,000 head, most of you here, if not all, were present at that meeting.

Now, at that time, we tried to propose that this reduction of sheep be left until our next meeting. Our argument at that time was that we would like to consult our people back home before going on with the proposal to reduce our sheep. In spite of the fact that we tried to carry over this proposal plan at the time, we were asked to make our resolution to reduce our sheep.

Now, the government, at that time gave us an outline of a program that we were to be compensated for, in this proposal. That we were to be given employment, and things in that line. It seems the program, as it was outlined at that time, is not fully carried out, and for our part, we have carried it out. We think it not fair to do our part and the government does not meet us half-way. I think we have done our part, and now the proposal that is afoot, that we were to be taxed at dipping time 10¢ per head for all the sheep and goats that we were to dip this summer, or that we were to be taxed 10% of the wages we were to earn from this E.C.W. work.

Now, that is something complicated to us. It seems to us the wages are not sufficient for us, as wage earners, and it seems we should not be taxed, at that. We are only getting $42.00 a month on the E.C.W., at most. Out of this amount, $4.20 is to be taxed, out of the sum of money we are to earn in a month. If we were to get a loan from the Federal government in order to purchase these surplus goats, instead of using that money for purchasing our stock, is there any way that we could use that money for leasing land outside of the reservation. Would that save our goats? Is it possible that we could get a loan and lease some ranges in order to transfer what surplus stock we have, to control our range here on the reservation.

For the white people, the good old dollar is where they get their sustenance of life and the Navajos get their sustenance of life from the goats and the sheep, so it would not be fair to the Navajo to give up their goats and not the white people part of their dollars. We depend upon the goats and sheep for our life, our income, everything, the same as you depend upon your American dollar for your sustenance of life. That is what is puzzling us. We are wondering, having gone twice as far, and you have gone half way back, which doesn't seem to appeal to the Navajo.

COMMISSIONER: It has been stated that the government made undertakings at the last meeting and did not fulfill those undertakings. Now, I am anxious to know what these undertakings were that were not fulfilled, what promises were broken.

FRED NELSON, Delegate from Hopi Jurisdiction: One of the undertakings that they decided on at the Tribal Council was to undertake the erosion control. The erosion control plan was to be carried out throughout the reservation. There is only a little place where they are working. We understand it was to be undertaken all over the reservation.

COMMISSIONER: I think that this will be clear to you all. The erosion work is a thing that will have to go on across many years of time. At the Mexican Springs place there is one experimental and demonstration area. There will be many more, and it will be at least five years before the entire reservation is covered by the engineering works and the new planting of grass. Most of that cannot be done at all in the winter, as will be clear to all of you.

But I want to say this, if you look at the record of the Tuba City meeting, you will find we gave certain figures about how much the government was going to spend in wages and in every way. If you take those figures and the figures given here, you will find the government has spent a good deal more than it said it was going to spend, not less.

In addition, at the Tuba City meeting, we told you the E.C.W. work would have to stop April 1st. Now, we can tell you it will go on another year. The only thing I want to make clear here is that we have not made promises we did not fulfill. It would be a very bad thing to have you think we made promises and did not fulfill them. You will find we have done more than we promised. In the matter of erosion, at Tuba City, we told you there would be a million dollars spent. I have told you since you came here that if we are able to get range control and go ahead with the erosion work, the amount to be spent will not be one million, but possibly three or four million. Therefore, the government's work is more than we told you we would do. We have tried to be conservative. We have understated, and we are now understating, not overstating the facts.

There is one other thing I would like to say, and that is about the wages. We must remember that all of the work that is being done, for which you are being paid wages, is being put on your own land, it is work for the improvement of your own land, the development of your own water, the protection of your own soil. Not a bit of it is being given to anybody else, so you should not only think of the wages, but you should remember, you are improving your own land. You are not working for somebody else and being paid, you are working for yourself and the government is paying you to do it.

I want to say something else, which is a confession, and which puts me in agreement with our friend, who has just been speaking about something that he feels. He feels it hurts him and it hurts you, this idea of giving up sheep and goats. It just *hurts*. Two years ago, at the beginning of the great storm that descended upon the Navajo reservation, I was going through the Navajo reservation and saw the terrible things it was doing to your stock.

I saw the cattle standing with icicles hanging clear to the ground, of their frozen breath and I saw sheep dead, frozen in the cold. And it hurt me just like it hurt you and I hurried back to Washington. I was not then the Commissioner, I was the Secretary of the Indian Defense Organization, and I started a very intense campaign back in Washington. A campaign to get money to save your goats and sheep and we get from Congress, as I recall, $150,000 to help get feed to your stock. And it was not enough and so I kept on fighting, I was so anxious to save the sheep and the goats, and the cattle. And there were people back in Washington who said: "You are making a mistake because there are too many sheep and goats. The range is overgrazed and the blizzard is sent by God to cut down the sheep and goats and save the range from overgrazing." And that made me very mad when they said that. I wrote statements and the papers published them and members of Congress put them in the record and there was a very great to-do about it.

Well, later on, I have found that I was mistaken. That there were too many stock. That I was not really doing the right thing. But I tell you, I felt it just as strongly as any of you do about your sheep and goats. I had to learn that bitter fact which you all know now, that the range is overgrazed and has been very greatly damaged, and is going down fast so that if we go on the present way, there will be no food there for the goats or the sheep or the people in a few years.

That is a hard fact and I have had to learn it and have had to admit my error of two years ago. And then having learned that, which is the truth, I went to work along with all of your other friends, to see if there was a way to save your soil and build it up again and restore your prosperity, and, therefore, all these millions of dollars are being spent because we know it is possible to save your range and restore your range, and to add enormously to your well being, but it does require a temporary reduction of stock.

The other question is, could not the money be used to rent land outside the reservation and move that many stock off and get them off the reservation in that way. We have gone into that rather carefully and the answer we get is that on the whole it cannot be done. Some help can be had from renting land off the reservation, but not enough. I think Mr. Stewart had better give you the details.

FRED NELSON, Delegate from Hopi Jurisdiction: There is still another question. In regard to the land, also reduction of sheep, at the Tribal Council gathering at Tuba City, it was the understanding that we made, that if we reduce our sheep we would be entitled to some of that land that is in question now. That was our understanding.

COMMISSIONER: I am very glad this was brought up because it may be a misunderstanding in other minds as well. I think it is a misunderstanding. Many of you have copies of the minutes of that meeting. I see a copy down here. Many copies were made. If you read the record and refresh your memories, you will find that we told you that the necessary reduction was very much more than 100,000.

We gave you figures five times that large as the total amount of reduction that would be necessary in the long run. We spent hours of time at a blackboard and we put all the figures down as to the reduction that would be necessary before you had reduced enough. Now, just at the time of that meeting we had an opportunity to get the money from Mr. Harry Hopkins, enough money to buy a hundred thousand sheep. We were to buy these sheep in order to feed the unemployed, you will recall. But we never told you that a hundred thousand taken away from the number you had last fall was all you needed to reduce. We told you the opposite of that.

This was merely a first step and there were other steps that must follow that first step. And what we told you about your boundary bill and all these other things at Tuba City is something we are telling you now. I'd like to repeat it in one, two, three, order. Before doing that I want to read you exactly what we did tell you at the Tuba meeting. It comes on page 37 of the record.

"Let me say that you are going to need to cut down your goats by at least 200,000 head. Your *goats*. And you are going to need to cut down your sheep by at least 200,000 head."—And many pages more, giving the details. Now what we told you at Tuba was the thing you already know, just as we know it now. And it was:

1. That the government was prepared to spend very large sums of money on your reservation, if the money would do good, but not if it would not do any good.
2. And we told you that the government was convinced that unless erosion was stopped then it would not do any good to spend money on your reservation. Unless erosion was stopped, the government might as well get out. That is what we told you.
3. And we told you that erosion could not be stopped unless the number of stock was reduced, overgrazing checked, and range control instituted. We told you that was the position in the mind of Congress, of Secretary Ickes, of the other members of the cabinet interested in your affairs, and of all of the authorities in Washington. That was their position, and we could not change it. And that was the fact and it is the fact now, except that it is more true now than it was then.

Because since your Tuba meeting, a great many more facts about erosion have become known and the government has become more deeply interested in the erosion question. Since then the Soil Erosion Service has been set up to work all over the country, and Dr. Bennett has been made the head of that erosion—Dr. Bennett was the man who made the erosion survey of your lands last July. Since that meeting in Tuba, as I personally can tell you, the very Congressmen upon whom you depend to pass your boundary bill have learned a great deal more about the erosion problem. Mrs. Greenway, Senator Hayden, the New Mexican Senators, and particularly Senator Cutting, now know all about the facts; as much as we know. If you read the hearings of the House Committee on Appropriations, the committee that appropriates the money, the hearings held in December, you will find that that committee knows all the facts and knows that unless erosion can be stopped there is no use in doing anything more down here. Your friends like Mr. Stewart and like me, we could not hide the facts from Congress. We could not deceive Congress and the President, even if we wanted to, because they know as much as we know. And neither Mr. Stewart nor I have spoken as strongly as the facts are. We have spoken as though we merely had an opinion as to what was going to happen, if we cannot stop soil erosion. We could tell you that we know what is going to happen if we do not stop soil erosion. We do know.

MR. STEWART: The remaining question as to why we could not use the loan money spoken of last night for leasing additional land instead of buying the goats. We, at the present time, have under lease for the Navajos close to a half million acres. I believe there are more under lease but I am not sure. I am sure of that, however. We would lease more land to-day if you can show us where it is. We have money available that we could use for leasing land but all the land that we have not leased for you is leased by white stockmen who will not give up their leases or else is owned by white people. So, if you know of any land that can be leased, take it up with your superintendents and we will lease it for you. But we have been unable to find any additional land that we could lease for you. This has been our experience.

Now, apart from that question, I would just like to make this remark, that you have before you tonight the biggest and most important question ever confronting a Navajo Council. To you, individually, the biggest thing probably appears the matter of us buying a certain number of your goats, 150,000. You are looking at the matter through your eyes and not through the eyes of your living children and the hundreds of unborn children that will follow. I will put it to you in the form of a question, rather than trying to state it in another way. It is this. Do you want to leave land that your children can use and raise sheep on, like you do, or do you want to leave them piles of sand and rocks?

FRANK CADMAN, Delegate from Southern Navajo: There is a question in regard to the price of these goats. In regard to what the rate would be for a one year old goat, or a kid or a wether. What would be the prices on that?

COMMISSIONER: I will refer that question to Mr. Stewart.

MR. STEWART: I don't believe that has been worked out in detail at all. The plans that we left with you to take home and consider and work it out was the reduction of 150,000 head. A maximum of $1.50 would be paid for the goats, however, and it would be up to you to consider and graduate the scale after you consider the matter.

FRANK CADMAN, Delegate from Southern Navajo: Graduate down or up?

MR. STEWART: Down.

FRANK CADMAN: I thought it was $2.00, up. When we get very sick, when we need a physician, we go and look for the best physician and the best medicine we can find and when we find that medicine, we are satisfied.

Now, in regard to our land—our land seems to be very sick. And the plan that is put out so that it can be brought back to normal state, I favor. That is the land erosion control. And the proposed plan to re-establish our reservation or bring back the soil that is in a state of deterioration, is the erosion control plan. That is the only thing that would solve it and bring back the soil. I favor it, and we should be willing to accept it.

We have been hearing about this plan for a long time, until they have actually come out here and actually brought with them an exhibition of what the erosion control really is and they have an experimental station at Mexican Springs now, so we may look at what is meant by erosion control. And another reason why I favor the erosion control plan, is that I would not fall out or be offended if these people did not succeed after they have put forth every effort to bring back the soil and bring back the range, if I neglected the seed, and let the seed fail; when I look at the soil, that is all patched, that if we lose it by putting forth every effort, then I would not feel bad. But when there is a solution that will solve the problem, we ought to be able to take it. The erosion plan is the remedy and solution for that thing. That is the main thing that I came up here for, and I wish now to ask you a few other small questions.

The other little thing that I referred to is the Superintendent at Fort Defiance, Mr. Hunter. What business have the people in Gallup to try to put him out? We need him. If he is to be put out we ought to have our say-so and not the people at Gallup. Another thing I forgot to mention, what did Mr. Hunter do that they try to put him out? We would like to have an understanding, would like to know about those things. When anyone is going out we would like to have our say-so about it. Another man that they know is really doing his work, is Mr. Parker, and they are also after him, the people at Gallup. We'd like to have our say-so about him too.

The last thing I wish to speak about is, the Catholics would like to have their instructions over at Naschiti just the same as the Protestants and would like to see them have that right, because they favor both sides there.

JIM SHIRLEY, Alternate from Southern Navajo: There are two sources of life, of living, I wish to convey to you. The two forces are the land and the livestock. One force is the land, from which we get mineral, from which we raise crops, from which we get our sustenance of life, and the other source is the livestock, and for the livestock, we cannot get by, we cannot profit by having livestock when our range is deteriorated. Therefore, we need to develop our soil that we may be able to take care of our livestock, and, therefore, we cannot put the livestock before land. We have to have the range before we can have livestock and for that reason, people may criticize and they may have the opinion that we are more or less deciding to handicap them in having reduction, in cutting off that source of living that we get from livestock, but the bigger question is the land question. If we have the land, we have everything.

HENRY TALIMAN, Delegate from Southern Navajo: I would like to suggest to the people a resolution which has been presented to the Navajo Tribal Council, and also presented to the people in general here this afternoon. It is very well understood in the resolution, how this Boundary Bill can be approved by the Navajo Tribal Council, where there is a million dollars involved for such purpose. It is my suggestion that we vote on this subject. It is my suggestion that we approve this resolution and then go back to our people, back home, and tell them about it, the meaning of this Boundary Bill, which has to do also with reduction of the stock on the Navajo reservation.

A great deal has been said about the livestock and the overgrazing and the land problem. One thing I would like to ask concerning this bill. What are the people going to do who are living off the reservation if this bill does go through? It is my opinion that this exchanging of land bill pending before Congress, if we approve this resolution, that will go through without any difficulty. We all know how much depends on the overgrazing of the country, so I say that we should vote on this resolution, then at the next meeting, we can act upon how the livestock can be reduced to the best satisfaction of the people.

My friends, I would like to say a few words concerning another matter, which was brought out by the delegate from Tohatchi. It is about the personnel of this community and the man in Gallup. If we are going to have any power or any say in the matter, in anything, that the Navajo people ought to have it. It is my opinion that we have a man who knows the Navajo people, and has been among us for many years, Forrest Parker. Mr. Parker is very well qualified among the Navajo people. No matter how much some people think that he has done in his younger days, as a whole, I think he is pretty well qualified for the place he is now holding. I don't believe that the people in Gallup have done so much for Forrest Parker as Mr. Collier has done for him.

Just because Mr. Parker has made an open statement, which we do not know, that he is guilty of a certain crime, just the same, I think he has opened the way to something of greater importance to the Navajo people, and has made an open statement to try to protect the Navajo people, to keep other people from getting the best of them. He has opened something that is true, but at the same time, he has done some good for the Navajo people. Whereas, the Gallup people were getting all they could from the Navajo people, still they are never satisfied. I feel sure that the Commissioner has knowledge of this fact about Mr. Parker and Superintendent Hunter.

It is my suggestion that we adopt a resolution by the Council that we keep these two men as long as we can, on the Navajo reservation, because Mr. Hunter has done so much all these years for the best interest of the Navajo people, and other people. He has accomplished something, to the best of his ability. Just because some people may think they should not have done what they did, it should not be taken seriously by the Commissioner, or other officials in Washington, for I know that we will not take it seriously among the Navajo people, because no matter what we do, no matter how hard we think we can do, we always get into some mischief; no matter how hard we try to protect ourselves from evil things, it always comes our way. I think these two men ought to be considered just the same as we feel about it.

J. C. MORGAN, Delegate from Northern Navajo: Just a few words. I believe we are going to follow too much out of our way. I want to quote a statement made by the Chairman at Tuba City, which I think very good, and I am going to abide by those words as long as I am a member of the Council. He said this to the Council: "You should avoid all political complications."

That is enough. We are going to look to him as our leader. What he says we are going to abide by. This is something out of our line. If we go into these things, I am afraid we are going to get out of our way. Let me repeat again, "You should avoid all political complications." So I think I shall not go beyond this statement here.

ROBERT MARTIN, Delegate from Northern Navajo: I'd like to ask this question. How much is there lacking of filling the contract agreed to at Tuba City, the 100,000 sheep? Mr. Collier, here, knows, I guess.

COMMISSIONER: We have got about 90,000 of the 100,000. I do not remember which jurisdictions fell short. I believe that Leupp almost went over the top. I believe that Northern Navajo went clear over the top. I am not clear as to which ones did fall short. The superintendents could answer that, each for his own jurisdiction. They are all here except Mr. Stacher, who went home early.

SUPT. BALMER, Western Navajo Agency: Taking into consideration the sheep we sold to the moving picture companies, and those sold to the camps, we are over the top, but if we only take into consideration those actually shipped out on the contract, we are under about 5,000.

SUPT. HALL, Leupp Agency: We lacked 22% of having our full quota of 8,000 sheep. However, the Indians sold, in addition to that, 5,000 to traders and 440 consumed by Indian camps and schools.

SUPT. HUNTER, Southern Navajo Agency: Our quota was 32,000. We purchased under this program, something over 27,000, in addition to which we used a great many in schools and camps.

SUPT. HAMMOND, Hopi and Keams Canyon: We shipped off 9,115, but we got rid of 10,000 on the reservation.

SUPT. MCCRAY, Northern Navajo Agency: We went nearly 2,000 over the 20,000.

HENRY TALIMAN, Delegate from Southern Navajo: Mr. Chairman, this is a puzzle to the Indians. If we are going to have it printed 100,000 sheep, we must go ahead and do it. And we are puzzled again. As you said yesterday, if the government has the authority, why doesn't it put it in the regulations and enforce the reduction of the sheep, as they did about matters sixty years ago.

COMMISSIONER: It is 150,000 goats, not sheep.

ROBERT MARTIN, Delegate from Northern Navajo: Goats are the same as sheep.

COMMISSIONER: The other question, you say why doesn't the government come and take them. The answer is, we could do that as far as the law is concerned. We don't think we ought to do it. We think it is the problem of the Navajo Tribe and the Tribe, itself, should decide and act.

MARCUS KANUHO, Delegate from Leupp: We have talked a great deal, most of the afternoon, about this matter. Therefore, I make a motion that this resolution be adopted.

ALBERT SANDOVAL, Delegate from Southern Navajo: I second the motion.

J. C. MORGAN, Delegate from Northern Navajo: I want to ask a question. There was a little difficulty, I understand, at Pine River, last fall, when the question came up, some of the people having a very small bunch of sheep, and having a family of maybe five or six to support, while they do not oppose it, but are willing to help go over the top, I have been wondering if it would not be possible in some way to think of these people. While they are willing to help, I wonder if there is not some way that Congress would consider giving them something for the sale of their sheep, because it is the only living they have. They may have only twenty-five or thirty sheep and they depend upon the wool of those sheep for blanket weaving, and the goats for mutton. I don't want to say this in opposition to the passing of the resolution, but I want to think of those people. They are willing to do their part, but I think we ought to think of their circumstances.

COMMISSIONER: Of course the question of method is not settled in the resolution. Surely it will be clear to everybody that it is the man with a large number who ought to give up the most. The man with a small number ought not to make so great a sacrifice. I should think that could be taken care of when the procedure is worked out. That ought to be done.

J. C. MORGAN, Delegate from Northern Navajo: There is one family I knew of. A young woman, whose husband is sick and unable to work. This young woman gave up out of her herd of twenty-five, five head. This is taking away their mutton.

CHEE DODGE: Perhaps it could be worked out this way, that those families not give up any stock, to a hundred. Those having more than a hundred, let them give up the goats, but from a hundred down, not touch their flocks.

CHAIRMAN: If this is the feeling of the people, I think this resolution needs to be amended.

J. C. MORGAN, Delegate from Northern Navajo: Mr. Chairman, I would favor amending the resolution according to what has been suggested.

COMMISSIONER: Suppose there is a man who has a hundred head, but of the hundred head, fifty or more are goats. If such is the case, would it be a hardship to give up the goats?

LEE BRADLEY, Delegate from Western Navajo: In that case, say for instance, a family owns a hundred head of animals, and fifty are goats, fifty are sheep. Rather than take the goats from them, why not take the money and buy the goats from them and replace them with sheep.

MARCUS KANUHO, Delegate from Leupp: Mr. Chairman, this reduction is to get the stock off the reservation, isn't it? That way we would have to keep them on the reservation.

LEE BRADLEY, Delegate from Western Navajo: That would be protecting our poor people. By taking their animals, we would send them to the poorhouse.

COMMISSIONER: I think our friend is right. You see, the goats would be taken off the reservation. Then that money would be taken to buy sheep from one Navajo and given to another. So, there would not be any increase in the number of sheep on the reservation, and the goats would go.

BECENTI BEGA, Delegate from Eastern Navajo: We could give them the right, if they wanted to, to sell some goats, if they have one hundred head, half of them goats and half sheep.

NAL NISHI, Alternate from Leupp: I would like to say for Leupp jurisdiction, we might not be able to meet the requirements on the goats. We met the requirements on the sheep but we do not have many goats on our reservation. We would try to meet the number but with regard to the lambs used, we might not be able to handle that part of it and keep on sending the wethers. Regarding the fine advice in regard to the goat question, why not sell some of these goats over to where they do not have them. Those people can give them up better than those who have so few. The point is, if you give me five goats, I would take care of and use them. Why not take some of that money and pay the people up above who have charge of the rain?

HENRY TALIMAN, Delegate from Southern Navajo: What are these people going to do who are off the range, when this bill is approved. As I understand it, as long as these people who are off the reservation do not have a title to the land, they will stay where they are now, otherwise, they will have to come back in the reservation.

Another question, regarding the people off the reservation, about reducing their sheep. The Council at Tuba City approved the reduction of sheep and that if they reduce, they will get work on E.C.W. Now a lot of the people feel that they are not getting a square deal because they are off the reservation.

COMMISSIONER: From now on there will be more E.C.W. The people off the reservation will be entitled to get work in the E.C.W. The E.C.W., and other projects, building schools, etc.

BECENTI BEGA, Delegate from Eastern Navajo: Probably there will not be a chance to get any more appropriations for erosion control off the reservation. They are off the reservation over there in Eastern Navajo. They managed to get some of that money for E.C.W., and they got several reservoirs and several water ways developed. They got that but as has been stated, they have no chance of getting any of the money for erosion.

COMMISSIONER: With respect to those who are clear outside the east boundary who cannot be brought into the reservation, and the present erosion service cannot be extended to them, many of those who are now outside, will be brought in. There will not be many left out. Mr. Stewart had better explain this.

MR. STEWART: The Boundary Bill in New Mexico adds to the present reservation. And in addition, we worked it so that if the bill goes through and is passed, four areas: Star Lake, Cannoncito, Puerticito, and Ramah, will be taken in. Outside of that, we are taking in the main reservation addition, so that on passage of the Boundary Bill, money can be spent in those areas, also, for those Indians.

BECENTI BEGA, Delegate from Eastern Navajo: The reason we brought this question up is that they are suffering. They are compelled to reduce their herds just as much as people on the reservation, and they feel they were entitled to the erosion control plan as much as anybody else. Since there is a chance in the new bill for some of this work, as they are put under the same plan in reducing goats and are under the same ruling as those people living on the reservation, they feel they should be entitled to have money appropriated for them the same as the people living on the reservation. We have been suffering the afflictions put on us by cattlemen over there. They are continually pestering us, everlastingly have their foot on us. If we could join the people living on the reservation, we could be entitled to some relief and some money that is being appropriated to help save them on the reservation.

All the Northern Navajos live along a certain piece of land that not a tribe of Indians has ever used. It is always leased to the white cattlemen. The tribe there probably only gets the benefit from the lease rentals. Why not the Indians of the United States, instead of renting to outsiders, lease the surplus lands to each other, the Indians, instead of leasing to outsiders.

Also, along the boundary line, just across the State of Colorado, the Agency meets our reservation. Our people, the Navajos, live along the Mancos Creek. These Indians have always lived there, also the Utes. In olden times they used to kind of hate each other, but since a few years ago they have begun to like each other and have lived there peacefully and haven't been on the warpath with each other.

So the Navajos have used the water from the stream for their livestock. At this time of year it is hard for sheep to go ten or twelve miles for water. This is the question, should the sheep be fenced out from the stream or should net gates be established so we can get to the water for our livestock.

Another question, why is it stated in the bill, when the bed of the river is a natural boundary line for our reservation, why should not the middle of the stream be the boundary line?

CHAIRMAN: I will read the resolution, with the proviso attached to it.

RESOLUTION

WHEREAS, the Navajo Tribal Council has heard and carefully considered the program of future employment of Navajo Indians on reservation improvement work and especially is impressed with, and is appreciative of the proposed reservation boundary extension which involves a total appropriation of approximately $1,000,000.

THEREFORE, Be it Resolved, that the Navajo Council agrees that it is imperative that the Boundary Bills be enacted at the earliest possible date, and in order that Congress may be assured that the Navajo people realize that in appreciation of the large grants of free or gratuity money involved therein;

Be it Further Resolved, That the Navajo Tribal Council agrees that erosion control and range control should be carried on as explained by the Commissioner and his staff; and further that stock reduction as explained by the Commissioner and his staff should take place, with the understanding that the Council delegates will return to their people in order to explain the proposals so that the Navajo people may consider the matter and devise ways and means of effecting consummation of the stock, or goat, reduction plan.

AMENDMENT: Provided that any family having one hundred sheep or less number, shall be exempt from any reduction; but this provision shall not apply to those having a total head of one hundred, a majority of which are goats. In such cases, the goats shall be purchased and in return sheep of equal value shall also be purchased from large stock owners and given to the family whose total head was one hundred, but who sells his goats; provided further that large stock owners shall sell such goats, so purchased, from small herds.

ALBERT SANDOVAL, Delegate from Southern Navajo: I don't know whether I understand that clearly. Do you mean that big sheep owners would exchange the same number of sheep for goats, and then sell the goats?

CHAIRMAN: No, not the same number, but equal value.

ALBERT SANDOVAl, Delegate from Southern Navajo: I move that this resolution, as amended, be voted on now.

LEE BRADLEY, Delegate from Western Navajo: I second the motion.

CHAIRMAN: It has been moved and seconded that the resolution, as amended, be adopted. Are you ready to vote on it? If so, those who favor the resolution, as amended, will signify their votes by standing.

(Unanimously adopted.)

COMMISSIONER: I will answer Mr. Becenti's question about the Ute lands. Mr. Wattson, Superintendent of the Utes, states that as soon as the permit expires, the permit under which the white men are on the land now, the Utes are going to stock it with their own sheep and use the lands themselves, and, therefore, they are not willing to rent it, either to Indians or whites, heretofore. If it should not be that way, and if the Utes should want to continue to rent their lands, then we could negotiate with them in behalf of the Navajos and we might even bring into play the claim of Indian preference, but we understand the land will not be rented any more, but used by the Utes.

Now about that question, why the bill reads to the South boundary of the river, instead of the middle of the river, the answer is this. The Supreme Court has ruled that the San Juan River and the Colorado River are navigable. That is, the Supreme Court has ruled that boats can go up those rivers. And the stream bed of all navigable rivers belongs to the state, and no title can pass to any party; therefore, your boundary has to stop at the boundary of the river instead of the middle of the river.

Now, I feel that I ought to answer, as far as possible, the question of two delegates who spoke about certain officials of the Indian Bureau who have been under attack or were said to have been under attack. Whenever charges are made against an employee or official of the Indian Bureau, or allegations are made about such an employee, then it is the duty of the Commissioner of Indian Affairs and the Secretary of the Interior to investigate the charges or allegations. It is our duty to sit as judges in the case and to perform our duty as judges, impartially.

I say this in general, regardless of who the person is. It is always our duty, no matter what we personally may think. It is our duty not to be influenced by politics in any way.

Now, with reference to the two officials mentioned; that is, Mr. Hunter and Mr. Parker, I can only tell you, and I want to speak carefully, that I do not know of any present plan to remove either of them from office. I don't know of any such plan. Whenever any charges are preferred, I repeat, it is always our duty to investigate, and to sit as judges, and to act accordingly to the facts we find, after investigation. It is always our duty. Now, I will say this much more. That, while I don't consider Mr. Hunter or Mr. Parker perfect men—I don't know any perfect men—but I do consider that they have been faithful servants and friends of the Indians and of the government. That they are exceptionally able and faithful men, have done good work, and are doing good work, and I think that's saying enough. But, what I say is no undertaking with respect to things that might come to us in the future, which it might be our duty to investigate, and that is true of all employees in the Service, without exception.

I just want to say, and I am speaking for all of your friends here, that you have made us very happy by the action you have taken tonight, your unanimous action on this erosion matter. As I told one of the reporters today who asked me what I thought, I am never worried about what the Navajo Tribe is going to do in the long run. I know they will always act with wisdom and good sense. I never know them to fail and I know they never will fail. And speaking for all of us from Washington, I can promise you that we will do our very best to help you through all of this difficulty and to deserve your confidence.

CHAIRMAN:

RESOLUTION.

WHEREAS, the Navajo Tribal Council, in regular meeting assembled, duly authorized, realizes that it may be to the benefit of the Navajo people, as a whole, to have a livestock association of their own;

> THEREFORE, Be it Resolved, that the Chairman of the Navajo Tribal Council, be, and he is, hereby, authorized to appoint a committee from the assembled Navajo Tribal Council, or Alternates, for the purpose of investigating the matter, which committee will report back to the Council at its next regular session.

I would like to have this adopted without further debate if possible.

J. C. MORGAN, Delegate from Northern Navajo: I make such motion.

ALBERT SANDOVAL, Delegate from Southern Navajo: I second the motion.

(Resolution adopted unanimously.)

CHAIRMAN: One more resolution:

RESOLUTION

> Be it Resolved, By the Tribal Council, that no tribal law or custom has ever existed or exists now, by which anyone can ever become a Navajo, either by adoption, or otherwise, except by birth.
>
> Be it Further Resolved, That all those individuals who claim to be a member of the Tribe by adoption, are hereby declared to be in no possible way an adopted or honorary member of the Navajo people.

J. C. MORGAN, Delegate from Northern Navajo: I move that we table that until the next meeting. That will give us a chance to tell our people about it.

CHAIRMAN: Our reason for the resolution is that every time a movie star happens to pass through the reservation and returns to Hollywood, he claims that he is a Navajo, and every time an ex-mayor of New York happens to go to Gallup, he returns and says he is an adopted member of the Navajo tribe.

HENRY TALIMAN, Delegate from Southern Navajo: I think this resolution will also stop the movie actors or the Mayor of New York from saying they are Navajos, but other people will be stopped from that also. Mr. B. L. Staples is claiming he has only one more degree to go to be in the Navajo Tribe. I think that will cure a lot of people like that, too. But I want to ask, that no matter who is married, of any other nationality, into the Navajo Tribe, they should always have the right to live within the reservation, or if the Navajos marry into other nationalities, he will still have the right to be off the reservation, and to be away from these people if he wants to.

I move that this resolution be adopted by the Council at this time.

MARCUS KANUHO, Delegate from Leupp Jurisdiction: I want to ask a question. In case that a moving picture outfit should want to come on the reservation, like on the Tuba Reservation (Western Navajo), would that exempt them from coming on the reservation.

CHAIRMAN: No, but it would prevent them from claiming they are Navajos.

ALBERT SANDOVAL, Delegate from Southern Navajo: I move that this resolution be adopted.

(Motion seconded, and unanimously adopted.)

ALBERT SANDOVAL, Delegate from Southern Navajo: Where is the next Council meeting to be?

CHAIRMAN: At Crown Point, April 9th.

If there is no objection, the Council will adjourn.

The council adjourned at 11:15 P.M., March 13, 1934.

CHAPTER 6

MINUTES OF ALL-PUEBLO COUNCIL
SANTO DOMINGO PUEBLO
MARCH 15, 1934

The meeting was called to order by the Chairman of the All-Pueblo Council, Sotero Ortiz (San Juan), with Pablo Abeita (Isleta) acting as Secretary, and Antonio Tapia (Pojoaque) as Interpreter, at 10:30 A.M., March 15, 1934, in the Council Hall of the Santo Domingo Pueblo.

The following pueblos answered to the roll call, giving the number of delegates present:

Northern Pueblos:	Taos	6	Delegates
	Picuris	5	"
	San Juan	6	"
	Santa Clara	5	"
	San Ildefonso	6	"
	Pojoaque	3	"
	Nambe	4	"
	Tesuque	4	"
Southern Pueblos:	Cochiti	5	"
	San Felipe	10	"
	Santa Ana	4	"
	Jemez	5	"
	Sia	6	"
	Sandia	5	"
	Isleta	5	"
	Laguna	7	"
	Acoma	10	"
Zuni:	Zuni	7	"
Hopi:	Hopi	14	"

The following officials and others were also present:

Honorable John Collier, Commissioner of Indian Affairs; Wm. Zimmerman, Assistant Commissioner of Indian Affairs; Felix Cohen, Assistant Solicitor, Interior Department; Charles de Y. Elkus, San Francisco, Mrs. Wm. Denman, San Francisco, Oliver LaFarge, Judge Hanna, Fred Wilson, Attorney, Albuquerque, Mr. and Mrs. Burge of National Association on Indian Affairs; Elizabeth Sergeant; Ruth M. Bronson, Asst. Guidance and Placement Officer; Burton I.

Staples, Indian Trader, Coolidge, N.M., James W. Young, University of Chicago, Chairman, Committee on Indian Arts and Crafts; Walter Cochrane, Pueblo Attorney; Geo. A. Trotter, Supt., Zuni Agency; L. A. Towers, Supt., Southern Pueblos; C. E. Faris, Supt., Northern Pueblos.

SOTERO ORTIZ (Chairman): Friends and gentlemen, now we have this meeting so we can say what we have to say in regards to this Bill that we have before us. This Bill and its explanation has been sent some time ago for us to study, and I believe each pueblo has studied it and must be more or less familiar with it. You may not understand it all but perhaps the principal points which affect us Indians, I mean the Pueblo Indians. It is true that this bill deals with all the Indians as well as with the reservation Indians and the Pueblo Indians. Its main points are with our lands, the form of Government, the schools, and some other things. Now this morning we have our high official, the Commissioner of Indian Affairs, who is Mr. John Collier. You all know Mr. Collier very well; he is one of our best friends; he fought for us for many years and he is still trying to help us. I know very well and have confidence in him and I hope that you will be the same way as I feel. He will do the best he can. Of course, he won't be able to do all that we ask, but he will do his best. Then besides, there are the superintendents, the Superintendent of the Northern Pueblos, Mr. Faris; the Southern Pueblos Superintendent, Mr. Towers; and Mr. Trotter from Zuni. Of course I don't know who they are, all of them, but I know that they are friends of the Indians and are trying to help us Indians. Besides our superintendents we have our Attorney here, Mr. Cochrane, and some other Service men.

Now yesterday we went through this Bill, discussing it among ourselves. Some of us did understand and some of us didn't and were in doubt. It must be because we didn't understand it. Now we have here Mr. Collier and he will explain for us, at least the places where this Bill deals with us Pueblo Indians especially, read it for us paragraph by paragraph and explain to us, and after he explains it to us I think we will all adopt it. I thank you.

MR. COLLIER: Mr. Chairman, friends of the Pueblo, and friends of the Hopi Pueblo, whom I am glad to see here. I am not here alone and I want first of all to introduce to you the Assistant Commissioner of Indian Affairs, Mr. Zimmerman

Applause.

and the Assistant Solicitor of the Interior Department, Mr. Cohen.

Applause.

In addition, I wish to remind you that you have here Mr. Fred Wilson, Judge Hanna's partner; you have our old and tried friends, Charles Elkus from San Francisco; you have Mr. LaFarge; Mr. and Mrs. Burge of the National Association on Indian Affairs; Miss Sergeant, whom most of you know; and all of your own local officials of the Indian Bureau whom all of you do know. I do not need to introduce them.

Now, as we go forward with our discussion, I think it is important for anybody to raise the question that is in his mind, when it is there, so that we may know what is in his mind. Any of your friends who are here should raise questions that they think should be raised as we go forward.

It was more than 14 years ago when here at Santo Domingo I first met with your All-Pueblo Council. During all of those years the Pueblos, through their Council, have worked for themselves, and they have also worked on behalf of the Indians. The New Mexico Pueblos have always felt that they had a responsibility for all of the Indians and not only for themselves. We now come to you with a Bill which we may say is the result of all these years of work and study, a Bill which does affect all the Indians and also you. I am not going to start reading the Bill, page by page, but I want to tell you in simple language some of the main things about the Bill. You understand that we are laying the Bill before the Indians in every part of the country. This is one of the great congresses of Indians that have been called for consideration of the Bill. Although the Bill is an administrative measure, and the administration probably has power to pass legislation if it wants to, we didn't want to do it that way. We wanted the Indians to know about the Bill and pass on it. We would rather go more slowly and go along faster without their understanding. I myself have just come from many days of meeting with other Indian tribes and I have almost lost my voice, as you will notice, by now. Part of the day other people have got to do the talking.

Now I want to begin on the matter of land. As you all know, the Pueblo lands fall in two classes. You have your land grants along with your purchase grants, and then you have large areas of reservation created by Presidential Order, Executive Order reservations. These Executive Order reservations are just like Indian reservations anywhere in the country. As for the Hopis, their land is all of the reservation character. If you take the area of the Pueblo lands in New Mexico, at least four out of every five acres are reservation lands of the Executive Order kind. Certainly three-fourths of all your land is Executive Order reservation. I emphasize this to show that your land problems are not entirely different from the land problems of other Indians. You are concerned with the same land problems that concern the Indians everywhere else.

Now, there is a law called the Allotment Law; that is a law according to which Indian lands that belong to an Indian tribe are taken away from the tribe and then each person gets a little piece of land; each man, each woman, and each child gets a little piece. That law has been applied to most of the Indians in the United States. After they make this law apply, then each man, woman and child gets a little piece of land, and then after a certain length of time, a certain number of years, the Government takes away its guardianship from that land and taxes are put on that land.

May I stop at this point? Mr. LaFarge reminds me that the Hopis do not speak Spanish, and I better find out if all the Hopis here know English. There are fourteen Hopis here. Do they all understand English? What are we going to do about their understanding this talk? Who can interpret to the Hopis?

DELEGATE: There is a man there that is very competent.

MR. COLLIER: Then we will have as many as two interpretations going on at one time.

HOPI DELEGATES: Most of us understand English; one or two don't understand English and we will explain the meeting to them.

MR. COLLIER: All right then, we will go on. Now I come back to what happens when a piece of land is taken from the tribe and given to the individual Indian. After a while the man dies, the one that owns that piece of land, and then his land is sold. The government sells it to a white man. I will not explain this very much in detail because you do not need to know the details. Since that law began to be applied to Indians the Indians have lost their lands at great speed. Ten times the number of all the Pueblo Indians have lost all of their land. They have lost their last acre, their last bit of land. Those Indians who have been allotted have lost something like four-fifths of all of their land in the whole country. They have lost their best lands, so that the law has been a most dreadful thing in its effect upon the Indians.

Our starting point is to try to help those Indians who have been destroyed or ruined by the Allotment Act, including those who have still got some land but who are going to lose it unless we can change that arrangement, and also to prevent the same thing from happening to the Indians who have not yet suffered. In other words, we want to stop the allotment system—to repeal the Allotment Act. We want to forbid the Secretary of the Interior from ever allotting any more land in the future anywhere.

GEORGE K. PRADT (Laguna): Can I interrupt a minute? I am not an official representative of the pueblo. I have just come as a member. I do not believe that the tribe can fully realize the importance of this Bill from the fact that they do not seem to be asking any questions.

MR. COLLIER: I think you will find that they will ask them.

GEORGE K. PRADT: This is pretty important and they should ask questions. Furthermore, I believe, from what the newspapers say, it will be to the Indians what the Constitution of the United States is to the people. To get the true significance of this it should be discussed. Because of the Allotment law you say that the pueblos have lost land. Most of the land that the Indians have lost is through litigation.

MR. COLLIER: You are mistaken. You mean most of the land that the Pueblos have lost. To continue, what he said is good but I want you to follow my thought. We are not talking about everything in the world now. We are talking about the Wheeler-Howard Bill and what I want to get to your minds is that the Wheeler-Howard Bill repeals the Allotment law, and that fact is of great importance to you Pueblos because at any time the Allotment Law could be applied to all of your reservation lands.

GEORGE K. PRADT: Does that mean the land grants?

MR. COLLIER: I am talking about your reservation lands. It applies to the Executive Order reservations of Laguna, of Zuni, of Santo Domingo, of San Felipe, and so on, including all of the Hopi lands. The Allotment law could be applied tomorrow to all of your Executive Order reservations, and unless that law is repealed some Secretary of the Interior will apply it and your reservation lands will be quickly lost. I am not talking about something in a storybook at all. The grazing lands of Indians in many parts of the country have been allotted, lands just like your Executive Order lands, and when they have been allotted they have been lost; the white men have gotten them. The Pueblo Indians are not only concerned with this year and next year. Secretary Ickes is not going to allot your lands.

We are putting this bill forward to safeguard you for all time to come. Now, as for your Grants, it is not settled whether the Allotment Law could be applied to your Grants or not. Nobody knows. There is no treaty against it. This is not a debate. I am not answering questions now. There is no treaty guaranteeing that the Allotment Law shall not be applied to your

Grants. There is no guarantee in any statute. There is no prohibition law against allotting any of your Grant lands and the Supreme Court has not decided whether they can or cannot be allotted. The Indians of the Five Civilized Tribes of Oklahoma possessed their lands under tribal title, communal title just like yours. They thought the Allotment Law could not be applied to them. The Secretary of the Interior went ahead and did apply it and allotted their lands. They went into Court; they went clear up to the Supreme Court, and the Court held that regardless of their belief their lands could be allotted and their lands were allotted. Where they had 16 acres, they now have less than 2 acres for each man. There are 72,000 Indians of the Five Civilized Tribes today entirely landless.

If the Allotment Law were applied to the Pueblos it would not only result in their losing their land, it would promptly destroy their tribal governments and would wreck them. It would be the end. Therefore, I say, you are greatly interested in the part of this Bill that deals with allotted lands. It stops the allotment system forever. It forbids any more lands to be allotted anywhere, and it forbids any Secretary of the Interior hereafter from removing the Government guardianship from any Indian land. It makes the guardianship permanent and continues the freedom from taxes on Indian lands. Now at this point I would like to pause because we better understand things, one main point at a time. This is the point for questions or for any Indian or white friend to disagree with what I have said.

PETE VIGIL (Nambe): Honorable John Collier, Chairman, Secretary, and friends here. I am a delegate from Nambe.

ANTONIO TAPIA (Interpreter): You are a delegate from Pojoaque. How can you be from Nambe?

PAUL JOHNSON (Governor of Laguna): Ladies and gentlemen. This Bill that is going to be explained to us this morning here, do not start to talk or ask any questions if you do not understand. We all know that we are not lawyers. Mr. Collier is well acquainted with the Bill and he should explain. If we are to have a full understanding of the Bill we should patiently listen when Mr. Collier is explaining, and Mr. Cochrane should at the same time explain to us, assist Mr. Collier. If all of us don't quite understand the Bill why should we start in and talk before things are understood. Let us wait until things have been explained, then it is time to give your opinion. If we all or some of us understand the allotment policy, then those that don't understand it will have time to ask Mr. Collier. This is the way at Laguna. It isn't quite understood yet but we have confidence in Mr. Collier that he can give us a full definite answer. So here I say to you Lagunas, don't start to talk before we get a full explanation, and the man that is not delegated from Laguna should quiet down. You should let me know if you are going to talk. Some of you are not delegated. This is all I have to say, so listen patiently to what Mr. Collier has to say. I thank you.

MR. COLLIER: Concerning this land question, you understand; those who have the Bill, the land title of the Bill is Title III beginning on page 25. Questions always bring out valuable ideas. Therefore, I shall go on for a minute answering the questions from Laguna. The question was about losing land inside the grants. For twelve years this Pueblo group, along with myself and others, have been fighting to protect your Grants, to get back land that the "squatters" have taken away, to get compensation where you didn't own the land. No squatter hereafter can get any land by squatting on your Grants. No pueblo, or individual in it, can sell grant land. That long battle is in the minds of all of you and it came to an end last May when the Pueblo Relief Bill was passed.

I am talking now about another thing. The fact that you have been saved from the "squatter" does not mean that you have been saved from the Allotment Law, which is ten times worse than all the "squatters." The Allotment Law has been worse for the Indians than the "squatters" ever were for the Pueblos. We now propose to save you from the Allotment Law and save all of the other Indians from it. Now if there are any Indians in the Pueblo country who possess individual allotments, and I believe there are some at Laguna, they don't have to worry about this Bill as this Bill will not take their allotments away from them. It does not cancel their allotments. It does not give their individual allotments back to the tribe, but perpetuates the trust patent and makes those allotments permanently safe from taxation. Before going on, I want to ask different people who are here, whom you know and in whose judgment you have confidence, to just arise and indicate whether they disagree with me. Mr. Elkus, do you understand the matter as I have stated it?

MR. ELKUS: Yes, I understand it exactly as you have stated it. I would say further, that they have lost land. They should not have lost any land through the "squatters" but they lost some land. Even though they may have been compensated for it they have lost the land. Now, with this Allotment Act, it is like a loaded pistol. Nobody has used it yet, but somebody may, and why leave it lying around loose where someone may get it. It can do you no good and may do you a lot of harm. The best way is to get rid of the Allotment Law.

MR. COLLIER: Mr. LaFarge, do you understand the situation as I have stated it?

MR. LAFARGE: Yes, I do. As far as the land part of this Bill is concerned, I think it necessary protection which the Pueblos, as well as all other Indians, should have. I think your presentation of it is exact.

MR. COLLIER: Judge Hanna has just telegraphed that he will be here this afternoon, arriving from Washington.

INDIAN from Minnesota: Mr. Collier, I am not a member of this tribe. I am entirely a foreigner here. I am a northern Indian from Minnesota, Red Lake. You are probably well acquainted with it. Those Indians are treaty Indians and are subject to allotment, as you are aware. They still have their reservation intact and they have one of the newest things, probably something that has never happened in the United States. They have created an Indian forest. I am a government employee in the Forest Branch at Mescalero. A number of the Indians conceived the idea of preserving it as an Indian forest. Of course, this allotment treaty which was made in '89 is still in danger. I have seen a lot of Indian allotments; have worked on Indian allotments all my life. In 1900, along about in there, or 1906, the law enacted by Congress alloted those lands. How long did it last? About five years. All of those mixed bloods were given authority to sell their allotments and they did sell them, and the result of it is we are scattered all over the country. Now that would be the result of the Allotment Act, although they say from that source we acquired what is called citizenship. They done everything to us. We were citizens under that Act and some of the boys were on the front during the war. Now, whether that law will still apply or be eliminated by this bill, I ask that.

MR. COLLIER: This Bill would correct the law for you too, to safeguard your Red Lake against allotment.

INDIAN from Minnesota: Mr. Collier, there is a delegation here from the Mescalero reservation where I am employed. There are five members here from Mescalero.

MR. COLLIER: The Mescalero reservation has been allotted, as you all know. Any Indians who have an interest in allotted lands will want to know some details about this Bill that do not concern the other Indians. Let them, during the day, meet separately about their allotment problems with me, or with Assistant Commissioner Zimmerman, or with Solicitor Cohen from Washington.

DELEGATE from Mescalero: Our reservation is not allotted.

MR. COLLIER: I was thinking you said Jicarilla. Mescalero is not allotted so all that I will say applies to you. Superintendent Towers says that some of you are asking whether this Bill would prevent your getting allotments out on the Public Domain. No, it would not.

Now, we come to the second thing in the Bill, which is also contained in Title III, the Land Title.

Interpreter is asked to speak louder.

MR. COLLIER: The second part, which is a part of the land title, I have explained—how a great many Indians have lost their land. There are more than 100,000 Indians that have lost all of their lands and a great many others who have lost so much that they haven't enough to make a living. Something must be done to give land back to the Indians who have lost their land. In the main that means that the Government must buy land and give it to the Indians who have lost their land. The Bill sets up an arrangement for buying land for Indians who need land. It directs the Secretary of the Interior to find out the situation of all these Indians, to examine the lands that they need and to go ahead and buy land for them and to help them to set up their life on that land. The Bill authorizes an expenditure of Two Million Dollars each year in buying land for these Indians. Now you can see the importance of that Bill to the homeless, landless Indians, but you also know something about your own condition. Let me speak of the condition of Sia Pueblo. Sia Pueblo has got very little land, not enough farm land and not enough grazing land. It is terribly poor. Sia did not get any compensation award from the Pueblo Lands Board or from the Pueblo Relief Bill. Therefore, Sia has no money with which to buy grazing or farming land. If this Bill passed, a part of that two million dollars a year could and would be used to provide the additional land which Sia needs in order to keep on living; and there are other pueblos that will need land which they cannot buy with compensation money. I don't think this feature of the Bill needs to be argued. You will all want it.

Now I will pause and explain what I am trying to do. I am trying to explain this Bill, dealing first with the part that will be hard to understand. We can forget about the other part that we have understood already. But I pause now on this matter of the two million dollar a year grant for land purchase to see if there is anything anybody wants to say on that.

Now, we come to the third thing in the Bill. This third feature deals with financial loans to Indians, and it is not found in the printed Bill as you have it. It was put into the Bill by amendment and is found on page 108 of the printed Hearings of the House Indian Committee on this Bill. The amendment in brief does this. It establishes a loan fund for the Indians. The amount of this money to start with is five million dollars, but the members of the House Committee all thought it ought to be raised to ten million dollars to begin with.

This money, be it five million or ten million dollars, is not to be loaned to the Indians by the Government, but to be given to them. It will never have to be paid back to the Government. It is to be set up as a bank, a loan fund that will be kept and loaned out according to need of the Indians. Under the arrangement, a pueblo could borrow from this fund. The Navajo tribe could borrow from this fund. Also an individual Indian could borrow from it, or an organization of Indians to run their cattle in common. Or, if the Indians wanted to start a grist mill they could borrow the money out of this fund, or for any other purpose that was right. A tribe could borrow from this fund in order to put stock on its land; to buy a threshing machine; if a group of Indians wanted to organize and run their own store, run their own trading post, they could borrow the necessary capital from this fund. When repayments were made the money would not go back to the Treasury, but would go back into this fund to be loaned again. Now all of you know better than I how much trouble the Indians have about credit, about borrowing money.

The only loans that you can get now are seeds, plows, and implements, reimbursable loans, and the entire appropriation for the whole country is $300,000 a year, more or less, or about $1.50 for each Indian. Well that is no credit system at all. And for the rest you have to go to the stores and get goods on credit. The result is you often pay very high prices, and we consider that it is fundamental that there must be a modern credit system for Indians: that the amount put into the fund must be sufficient and the five million dollars is only the beginning. Now that is the third feature of the Bill. I now pause, as I will on each topic, to see if there are any questions or remarks.

Assistant Commissioner Zimmerman thinks I may not have been clear about one point. The money to be appropriated by Congress will not have to be repaid to the Government, but it will be put into a loan fund and when a Pueblo or an Indian borrows from that loan fund then, of course, he will have to pay back to that loan fund so that the money can be used to lend another man or to lend him again.

DELEGATE from Mescalero: We would like to ask a question on that. With our case over on the Mescalero reservation, we are indebted and we cannot borrow money. How could that be remedied?

MR. COLLIER: Shall I explain your situation? Whom are you indebted to?

DELEGATE from Mescalero: We are indebted to a trader and the Government. That is what holds us down from borrowing money, and in that case how can we have a way to get a loan?

MR. COLLIER: You could borrow from this loan fund to pay off your indebtedness, or you could borrow from this loan fund for anything else.

DELEGATE from Mescalero: But it might be that the Mescaleros are not the only ones that owe money.

MR. COLLIER: They are not by a long shot.

DELEGATE from Mescalero: I just want to ask if it can be remedied some way.

MR. COLLIER: Of course, if you owe money you want to pay it back. This is not a scheme so that you won't have to pay back your debts. A debt is a debt. You could borrow from this fund to pay the debt if you wanted to, and we hope that you would want to if they are honest debts.

DELEGATE from Mescalero: It would be debts yet.

ELI BEARDSLEY (Laguna): In the event that a community or any individual borrows money, would there be any interest charges on the money. That is the first thing that the Indians would ask, whether there would be any interest charged on the loan.

MR. COLLIER: Suppose Laguna Pueblo comes and asks for, let us say $100,000 to be taken out of this loan fund, the pueblo would have that money to lend to its members. If the Pueblo of Laguna wants to make a charge to cover the cost of investigating who ought to get a loan, or the cost of collections, that would be entirely up to the Pueblo of Laguna, and they probably would do that because they would want to make this thing self-supporting. I should make this clear—that these money loans will be loaned to organizations and committees and they will then lend them.

ROLAND DURAN (Picuris): May I ask this question. Suppose a pueblo or an Individual Indian wishes to borrow money? Would he be required to give security?

MR. COLLIER: That is not required, but there might be given cases where it ought to be required, where the loan fund would need to be protected by requiring security. The Bill itself does not provide that, but if I had the management of this money there are some cases where I would require security.

FRED TENORIO (San Felipe): Could an Indian put up his land for security?

MR. COLLIER: The Bill provides that land can never be taken in payment of any judgment or anything else, but there is no reason why an Indian tribe could not pledge its future income from oil or sale of timber against that loan. That could be done.

JOSEPH TAFOYA (Santa Clara): Suppose now, you borrow that money individually, if you die before you pay it, who is going to pay it back?

MR. COLLIER: Ordinarily, you would be borrowing this money from your local council, or your organization fund where you are, for credit purposes. This local council could require that you not only agree to pay it back, but that your heirs would be required to pay it back in case you died, very much as you work it out now. Those are details that would be worked out by the local community.

ROLAND DURAN (Picuris): How about the length of time on a loan?

MR. COLLIER: That has not been worked out yet. It would depend entirely on the kind and purpose of the loan. There is a maximum period of thirty years, but if a man is borrowing for some purpose that is going to be finished right away, or for the purpose of carrying his crops over until next year, he will want it for only a short time and he would not be given thirty years to pay it back. It would be like it is with banks now. Or, if a man is known to be honest and his credit is good he can carry a loan for a lifetime.

ROSENDO VARGAS (Picuris): When will this money be available?

MR. COLLIER: The money will be available as soon as Congress appropriates it after passing the Bill. Our friend from Mescalero has spoken truly. The needs for credit are very great among the Indians. I don't want you to think that I believe that five million dollars is enough, or that ten million dollars is enough. What we are trying to do is to establish the policy of making credit available to Indians and then get enough to start on. It is all we can do in the first Bill.

FRED TENORIO (San Felipe): If the Indians have no property what will they take for security?

MR. COLLIER: Reputation—like banks do. They could take his right to future income as security, or the reputation of the man who is borrowing and of his relatives.

ANTONIO MIRABAL (Taos): I want to speak a few words. The question about the loan money, we have to realize what it means. We raise too many questions before we have the money. It is more or less my understanding that it is up to the council of each pueblo with the Governor. If they want to borrow the money I think it is up to them to settle the whole question, charge interest, or decide what kind of a person he is and so on, because it is almost same thing like with our community money, the little we have at each pueblo. We lend out a little money and it depends on the people. It is almost the same thing, and the best thing for us to do is to wait and see if we get that money and then we can discuss this matter.

ROLAND DURAN (Picuris): This meeting is to ask questions. What are we going to do about it? I think it is right to find out while Mr. Collier is present.

ELI BEARDSLEY (Laguna): I would like to suggest to the council too that there are important things that we have to discuss and so many of these things that concern each individual tribe ought to be left out. Those things we can work out ourselves. We would like to get as much of this as we possibly can.

MR. COLLIER: When we get to discussing self-government you are going to find that many of the questions are going to be answered by that part of the discussion, so suppose I go on now and try to get rid of the easy things first.

The next easy thing is education, which is dealt with in Title II of this Bill, beginning on page 22. You know the Government does a great educational work already—day schools, boarding schools, and extension work—but all Indian tribes need to have their young people educated for leadership. It ought to be possible for an Indian who has ambition and ability to go and get the education he needs, whether it be engineering, forestry, or animal husbandry, or to be a nurse or a doctor, or a lawyer, or to know how to handle books and accounts and be a treasurer. You all know how very hard it is for the Indians to get this education now. The educational title lays it down that it is the policy of the Government to help every ambitious Indian boy or girl to go on and get the special education needed in order to have a career. In other words, to hold an important position. He might hold that important position right among his own people. He might hold that important position in Albuquerque or in New York. He might hold that position in the Indian Service or anywhere else. It would be for him to decide. But it is the Government's duty to provide the education.

Then the Bill goes on and gives certain details. It provides that the Government shall furnish the tuition money to enable a boy or girl to go into a nursing school, a medical school, a college of agriculture, or anything like that; the money that pays the fee of the school and the cost of living too. And where any boy or girl takes advantage of that grant, half of it is a gift and half of it he pays back, without interest, but he shall not pay it back if he hasn't got employment. To start with, the appropriation is modest. It is only $50,000 for the first year. It will be increased according to need. In addition to that it is provided that where a boy or girl has extraordinary talent they can be put through all the education that they need and it is entirely free, no loan at all—all gift.

In addition, Section II of this Title directs the Commissioner of Indian Affairs to go to work so that every school run by the Indian Bureau shall do practical work, shall help the Indians in the ways that they need it where they are. It directs that in our Government schools we shall have courses which will give the Indians understanding of their own problems, their problems of law and land, and proper knowledge of their own history, so that the schools will, under this law, be built up into something better than they are. If you read the Title carefully you will get the whole meaning without any more explanation. Again, it is something about which there would be no dispute, but from our point of view it is very important to get this title because it would give to us the legal authority through which we could go to Congress and obtain the money necessary not only for these scholarships but also for improving all the schools. Now I will stop at that point.

PABLO ABEITA (Isleta): I made a mistake or I may not understand. I will read from Section 2, line 17, of this Bill. "The Commissioner is authorized to employ individuals familiar with Indian culture and with the contemporary social and economic problems of the Indians to instruct in schools maintained for Indians." It seems to me that this "individuals" should be "Indian individuals." A white person goes to the Indians and gets acquainted with these things and then turns around and tries to teach it to the children. I think it should be an Indian who already knows those crafts instead of employing a white person who has to first learn it from the Indians and turn around and teach the Indians.

MR. COLLIER: You are right and it says that the Indian community will decide this. The pueblo would have to decide this. The Pueblo would have to decide whether it wanted to put an Indian or a white person to teach pottery making or blanket weaving. This is very important and we will have much more to say about it in the self-government section.

Now the last Title is the Indian Court, and because you will be getting tired of me pretty soon I am going to ask Mr. Cohen to talk about the Indian Court—I will change what I said. Mr. Cohen thinks we ought to talk about the Court in connection with the self-government part, so I will only say now that this Indian Court title would establish it permanently that your affairs would not be under the State Courts but under the Federal Courts. I mean that any of your affairs that are not under the local community would be under the Federal Court and not under the State Courts.

I guess we are ready to tackle the big problem of self-government or home rule. Now, let one thing be clear at the start. If you read Title I, which is called Indian Self-Government, which goes from page 1 of the Bill to page 22, you will find that if this Bill be passed each pueblo or tribe, or group of Indians, would decide whether it wanted to take advantage of this part of the law or whether it wanted to go on the same way it is going on now. It would be entirely for the Indians to decide in that pueblo, or that tribe, and they wouldn't have to decide that day after the Bill was passed. They could go on like they are now for five years, or for ten years, and then they could decide that they would like to take advantage of this self-government, so that it is entirely permissive or optional. It merely extends something to the Indians, offers something to them which each pueblo or tribe would take or not take, just as they thought best. If a tribe or pueblo decided to take advantage of this self-government thing and took out a charter under this title, and after they tried it decided it wasn't a good thing and wanted to go back to the old way, then the tribe could go back to the old way whenever it got ready, so that things would be as they had been before. I am anxious to get this into your minds fundamental to everything else, to free you of worry or fear about this part of the Bill, and now I want to talk about your conditions of government and life as they are now. Let us forget this Bill for a few minutes. At present the pueblos of New Mexico have more control over their own affairs than any other Indians. You have practiced self-government ever since the Spaniards came and for an infinite time before the Spaniards came, and, as you know, we, your friends, Judge Hanna and others have always contended that it was not within the authority of the Secretary of the Interior to take away your self-government. We have held that if the Department or anybody else tried to take away your self-government, you would be able to go into Court and forbid it. We have held that we could do that partly through the Treaty of Guadalupe Hidalgo, and partly through the fact that the Territory of New Mexico made your pueblos corporations, and partly because there is a statement made by the Supreme Court that you are municipal corporation.

The subject has never been tested as to whether the Secretary of the Interior could force you to change your self-government or take it away from you, and we have always wanted to avoid a showdown in Court because we might not win. Of course, when it comes to the Hopis, they have not such freedom. They are at the mercy of the Interior Department and of the Indian Commissioner. We are not talking about this Bill at all. For a great many years your friends, including myself before I became Commissioner, have been anxious to get some declaration by Congress which would protect your self-governments and which would make it impossible for a Secretary of the Interior to disrupt them or forbid them. One of the things that we will get, if we get this Bill, is that protection. If a pueblo decided to qualify under Title I and take out a charter, then thereafter the Secretary of the Interior could never take away the charter, and if he violated the charter the pueblo could take the case right into Federal Court. I mean that pueblo could which took out a charter. When you look at the Indians in other parts of the country, practically all of the Indians are entirely at the mercy of the Secretary and Commissioner. We can forbid them to organize at all or we can say how they are to organize. We can ride roughshod over their local customs or their local conditions and they are quite helpless. They can't be expected to build up their life as long as any Commissioner of Indian Affairs can come in and knock it down, and in the past Secretaries of the Interior and Commissioners have spent a good deal of their time knocking down things that the Indians have been trying to build up.

Secretary Ickes and I are not doing that, but we are only temporary. Pretty soon we won't be here any more, and we want before we get out of office, to procure safety for the Indians in this matter of their self-government, as well as the matter of their lands. That is why we are promoting this self-government Bill.

Now, what do we mean by self-government? What are we talking about? It may mean a great many different things. Self-government may mean nothing but this; that the pueblo can decide about punishments for fist-fights or wife beating, etc. It can have its own court to keep peace. It might mean no more than that. But self-government might mean a great deal more than that. Suppose a pueblo borrows $100,000 for a loan fund. I mean, suppose the pueblo gets a gift from the Government of $100,000 to be used as a loan fund, and then the pueblo authorities begin to administer that $100,000 so as to make it do good, so as to be fair to everybody and so as not to lose the money but get it back and loan it again. That is self-government too. You can see that that is a great deal more than just having a police court. Now again, if a pueblo chartered, as it might be, under this Bill is concerned about the appropriation of money by Congress for schools and hospitals and everything else, thinks the money is being spent in the wrong way and would like to have it spent in some other way and do something different; if that was the case, then under this Bill the Secretary of the Interior would have to come to the pueblo and show the pueblo what he was going to do with all the money he was asking from Congress for that pueblo, exactly how he was going to spend it, and the pueblo would consider this whole matter and vote on it. They would or wouldn't want this, or they would like something else done with that money. Then the action of the pueblo would go to the Director of the Budget and to Congress, printed right alongside the recommendations of the Secretary of the Interior.

You would have exactly the same weight in law as the Secretary of the Interior, and you can see that that's a considerable amount of self-government. Again, suppose the Government has got some plan for building a big public works and is going to appropriate the money and put a reimbursable loan against the pueblo lands—the Government has that power you know—the Government can decide to build roads or irrigation systems and the cost is made a reimbursable debt against the Indian lands. The Indians haven't any voice. They can make a noise, raise an outcry, but they haven't any voice beyond that. Now, under this Bill, if anybody had a scheme to build a road or an irrigation system, or anything else, on or through your land and was going to make the cost a debt on you, they would have to come to you, convince, persuade you, get your consent; otherwise it would be forbidden by law to do this. It is put entirely up to you. You are given an absolute veto power. You can say "no" and that is the end of it.

In the past more than forty million dollars of reimbursable debt has been put on Indian lands either without the consent of the Indians or over their protest. Under this self-government arrangement that could never be done any more. You can see that the government of a pueblo which became chartered under this Bill could take on large power if it wanted to, only if it wanted to. It could take on powers beyond those I have stated, and once it took that power on under a charter the Secretary of the Interior and Commissioner of Indian Affairs could never take it away. The Indians themselves could give it up if they wanted to, and Congress always has power to take it away, but not the Department. Now some tribes would like to have a good deal of power; some tribes would not want but a little power. Under this arrangement the tribe that wanted much power could have it; the tribe that only wanted a little power could have just that much; the tribe that didn't want any power wouldn't have to take any. A tribe might want only a little power now to try it out. If you can imagine a river and its shores that are just shallow, you can wade in. If you imagine that river is self-government a tribe could get a charter that would allow it to wade just up to its ankles.

Some tribes would want to begin to learn to swim, and when they got ready to get a charter they could swim out to the deep water. But they wouldn't even drown if they got out there and found they couldn't swim because the Bill directs the Secretary of the Interior to stay on the edge of the water and if a fellow starts drowning to go out and get him.

Now, I will quickly state some of the other powers of self-government that a pueblo could take on if it wanted to, and then I think you will want to consider this title, section by section. You all know that many Indians are very capable of doing Government work, but they can't be employed because of Civil Service. They haven't got the academic, the college education, and so they can't qualify under the Civil Service and they can't get good jobs. It will interest you to know that the Indian Service has been going backward in this matter, not forward. The ideal of the Indian Service is to have all the jobs held by Indians, right up to the Commissioner. Actually, if you go back to the year 1900, 34 years ago, there were more Indians in the regular employ of the Indian Bureau than there are now, in comparison to the number of employees. I am not talking about the E.C.W., I mean the regular Indian Service. That is due primarily to the Civil Service. Now what does this Bill do? It directs the Secretary of the Interior to set out the qualifications that are necessary for an Indian to be a good workman in any of the Government jobs done in his community. In other words, the Secretary is directed to set up tests. Only Indians can take these tests, not white people, and the Indian can then show whether he is capable of being a good stockman, a good Government farmer, a teacher, a nurse, or a doctor, a school inspector, or a superintendent. Now, when the Indian has qualified and is found fit by the Secretary—the Civil Service Commission has nothing to do with it—then whenever there is a vacancy his pueblo can demand that he be appointed to that vacancy and the Secretary and the Commissioner have got to appoint him.

What this means is the setting up of a special Civil Service for Indians, made up in such a way that Indians can qualify under its tests, and then too the pueblo and the local community are given the power to elect, to appoint its own members to the Government jobs.

Now, one more power. At present the Secretary of the Interior appoints all of the officials of the Indian Bureau, and the regular employees have Civil Service protection. It has sometimes happened in the past that an employee was not satisfactory to the Indians. Any employee might be unsatisfactory, from the farmer up to the superintendent, but the Indians have not had anything to say about it. All they could do was to complain. Under this Bill, if an Indian tribe or pueblo took out a charter, then the pueblo or community could compel the Secretary and the Commissioner to move out any objectionable employee; of course, after due hearing and consideration and all that. This is a very important power to give an Indian community, and in some places it would lead to hardships, and it might lead to injustices to Government employees. Nevertheless, we feel that the Indian Service exists for the Indians, that in the long run we are the agents and servants of the Indians, and if we don't satisfy the people that we are working for, the Indians, then the Indians ought to decide whether they are going to keep us or get somebody else. We feel that that is a fundamental principle. We know that it might result in injustice sometimes. We know that the present arrangement results in injustices sometimes. Anyhow, that is in the law, in the Bill. The Indians, in a chartered community, are given the power to remove undesirable Government employees.

I think I have given you the main things in this self-government arrangement and either now or after you have recessed for lunch you will want to know the thing with more exactitude. I just give you my own opinion, that under this title, under this arrangement, the Pueblos can have every protection and power that they have now, can have them in a much more secure way than they now have them and, if they desire, can take on more power which, if wisely used, would be of tremendous benefit to all the Pueblos.

Recess of One Hour for Lunch

The meeting was called to order after recess by Chairman Sotero Ortiz. Interpreter Antonio Tapia to be assisted by Tony Abeita (Isleta). Delegates seated together by pueblos.

SOTERO ORTIZ: During recess time I believe you have consulted what has been explained to us this morning by our Commissioner. If there are any questions that you want to bring out we would like to hear from you, and the Commissioner and our friends here will be glad to answer you. From there on the Commissioner will proceed from where he left off this morning.

A. B. ORTIZ (San Juan): Mr. Chairman, you could call the members of the delegates of each pueblo, starting with Taos, or else begin from the lower end, and maybe in that way we will get a little better session.

SOTERO ORTIZ: Pueblo of Taos. If there is any question that you want to ask you can ask it now.

ANTONIO MIRABAL (Taos): I don't know of any questions to ask. I think that the Commissioner has given us a thorough explanation, from what I understand.

TELESFOR ROMERO (Taos): There is one other thing that I would like to have clear in mind, according to the line of education. When we come to this borrowing money proposition this morning, in order to have a thorough understanding and more education among the Indians. Now that is the very point I wanted to ask and I want to be clear on that line for the reason, according to this Bill, in the line of education most of us, in fact amongst the Pueblos, we come part way of education. That is where, like us, it is hard to understand a Bill like this. For the continuation of our education, I would very much like to know if this Bill passes, and then if there is a place where we can borrow money and pay for our education. That is the point I do not understand, whether the Government will help us to go to colleges, universities after finishing our high school course, by having a higher education than what we are standing for now. Then if there is any such thing as a Bill like this coming up we can read it and understand it. This is the point I would like for someone to make it clear. I am in favor very much for my people to have their education because right today we want a man with a full understanding in our public. That is the question I wanted to ask. I thank you very much.

MR. COLLIER: As I explained before, Title II of the Bill deals with education. That is on page 22. It provides that the boys and girls shall be given higher education in whatever school is best for them. Where they borrow in order to go into these schools, half of the amount will be a gift by the Government; the other half will be a loan, not bearing interest, to be paid back gradually, but not to be paid back if the student is not employed. Furthermore, the Bill provides various things for improving the schools that the Indian Bureau is running. The Indian Bureau schools ought to be much better than they are. This Bill will help make them better.

TELESFOR ROMERO (Taos): I understand. I thank you, Mr. Collier.

SOTERO ORTIZ (Chairman): Pueblo of Picuris. Any questions?

ROSENDO VARGAS (Picuris): We are not prepared to ask any questions right now but might be a little later on.

SOTERO ORTIZ (Chairman): Pueblo of San Juan is next. I am one of the delegates from San Juan. We have been studying the Bill and its explanation for about a month and we think that all its contents are satisfactory to us, but there are some words, maybe because we don't understand them very well or maybe understand them the way they are. That is why we are going to ask now, and, if we are right we would like to have it changed or corrected. Now, first, the terms used in this Bill are "reservation" and "Indian community," but don't say "Pueblo Grants." Of course we understand that the meaning of this Bill covers all that, but we would like to add "Pueblo Grants," if it can be done.

MR. COLLIER: We think that the word "reservation" fully includes the word "Pueblo Grants," but in order to make it very clear and to satisfy you we have already arranged to propose an amendment suggested by Mr. LaFarge, which reads: "any Indian reservation, including any Pueblo Grants."

SOTERO ORTIZ: Second. All matters of business (social and economic) having to do with the sale of land; the gift of land; the lease of land; granting of surface or mining rights; the transfer of land; the removal of restriction of all types; land patents and the distribution of land must originate with the chartered Indian government and, secondly, be approved by the Secretary of the Interior.

MR. COLLIER: The Secretary may transfer his authority to the community in the charter, and if the community accepts that charter then the community has the authority of the Secretary in that particular thing. In Title III of the Bill it may be we do need to change the language at some places. Title III dealing chiefly, as it does, with allotted lands may leave a wider discretion with the Secretary than we want, and where there is a chartered community the Secretary should be required to get the consent of the community, just the same way as at one point we found we had given the Secretary too much power over an allotment and we are going to change that.

These questions are fundamental and have come from other Indian tribes too, and I think I will cover them by saying in respect to the Pueblos; first, that we are seeking a condition by which the Secretary can give the greatest possible power to the public in its charter; second, that in any case we do not want the Secretary to be able to take away from a pueblo any power that it has got now; third, we will make sure that nothing is done under any charter which will have the effect of injuring the religious or customary life of the Indians and, in fact, the Bill provides on page 9 that (this is put in for the Pueblos primarily) if a pueblo takes out a charter for self-government, then the governing body as set up under that charter cannot be given any power now possessed by the ancient native organization or tribe unless the authorities in charge of the ancient native life want it to. This means—let me give you a particular case—if Zuni Pueblo wanted to take out a charter, as no doubt it would want to do, the authority possessed by the High Priests at Zuni could not be taken away from them under that charter, but they, if they wanted to, could confer some of their own authority upon the officers, which of course they can do now. And you all know, Mr. Ickes and myself have always been deeply interested in the ancient life of the Pueblos.

There would not be time this afternoon to discuss all the complexities of how the ancient life could be protected. I can just state, for both him and for me, that you can rely on us, that there shall be absolute and complete protection for the ancient life. This will in part be a thing where you will have to trust Secretary Ickes and me, along with your friends like Judge Hanna, but I think you feel you can trust us in this matter because of the long record that we have.

SOTERO ORTIZ: Here's another question. On page 9, line 8, 9, 10, and 11 provides that "the United States Government is not liable for any act done, suffered to be done, or omitted to be done by the chartered Indian government." Those lines should be removed from the Bill and new lines stating definitely that the United States Government will support and back the established Chartered Indian Government in its court.

MR. COLLIER: These lines relate only to these suits, only to paragraph 1 on page 9, nothing else. What it means is this. If a pueblo should enter into a contract; it might enter into a contract to buy some land or any other contract with a private party or a corporation and fail to live up to the contract, so that the court brings judgment against the pueblo. They can't make the United States Government pay the loss. They can't collect against the Government. They can't collect against the pueblo either as far as its lands are concerned; they can't be touched by a judgment. This has been much discussed in Congress—this very language, and the amendment which has been proposed in the House Committee is this—"Nothing in this provision shall forbid any person injured by an act or omission on the part of an Indian community, nothing shall prohibit him from seeking or obtaining appropriate redress from Congress." But he can't sue the Government. Now, for the rest the United States keeps full responsibility. It is only in this matter of suit. That really just carries on existing laws.

SOTERO ORTIZ: There's another thing. Should one of the seven judges prove unsatisfactory, what provision is made in this Bill for his removal. What section, page and line? State this.

MR. COLLIER: Page 44, Section 14. These judges do not have to be impeached. The language is "they may be removed by the President, with the consent of the Senate, for any cause."

A. B. ORTIZ (San Juan): I would like to ask a few more questions. As Sotero says, we read the Bill and we more or less tried to understand what was in the Bill, but what we didn't understand we thought we would ask you. On page 9, line 16 to 23, it does not state whether the local San Juan Court of Indian Affairs will have the legal right and obligation to interpret the terms health, welfare and security. We would like to have that explained.

MR. COLLIER: That's a very good question. The community when it is organized is given the power to exclude any nonmember whose presence there endangers the health, security, or welfare of the community. The question is, will the community be the judge? It will in the first instance. However, it would be a matter which could be carried up to the Court of Indian Affairs. It would have to go to the Secretary of the Interior; he would have to agree with you, and the act guarantees the constitutional rights of everybody and the rights of the minority, so that if a person was being excluded in such a way as to violate his constitutional rights, or in such a way as to violate his minority in a community; if he claims that these rights were being violated then there would be a review by the Court of Indian Affairs and from there clear up to the Supreme Court.

A. B. ORTIZ (San Juan): Again, if the future land is to be entirely community property, how will the younger landless generation establish homes. What stimulus will they have to better the land which is only lent to use and not own?

MR. COLLIER: How do they do it now in a pueblo?

A. B. ORTIZ: Most of the land is community and individuals just have pieces, but I am asking about the land coming to us now.

MR. COLLIER: What happens if a man at San Juan builds a house on it and uses it?

A. B. ORTIZ (San Juan): It is his.

MR. COLLIER: He can exchange it within the tribe and sell it, can't he? His children inherit it, don't they? So you have private ownership already; you've got it without this allotment scheme. Your land holding system is not changed by this bill. My understanding is that in all the pueblos the man who is using land, who has improved it, owns it according to the community law, and that is unaltered by this Bill.

A. B. ORTIZ (San Juan): Now again. What employees of the chartered Indian government would the community have to pay for salaries, etc.?

MR. COLLIER: That's a good question. The money would be transferred to the community treasury by the Government, the money to pay for those services. That is all made clear on page 14, line 15.

EULOGIO CATA (San Juan): On page 24, lines 18, 21 and 25, there should be more definite wording as to the race of the individual to receive training and then placement in a position. It should say "Indian Individual."

MR. COLLIER: You do not want to say that for this one thing we shall employ Indians only. You have to go back to the self-government part where it states the Indian who qualifies has the preference. Where he can qualify under the examinations, then he has the preference, if his people want him for an employee. Then there might not be any qualified Indian in a given place at a certain time and you wouldn't want the place left open. My answer is that the Bill as a whole covers your point and a great deal more.

EULOGIO CATA: The Bill should state in plain wording the classes of cases to be tried within the reservation, grant or community and before the Indian jury, such as murder, felony, etc.

MR. COLLIER: Do you mean by court, the Indian court or Federal court. There are two courts. There is the local court in the community and the special Federal Court. Are you speaking of the local court or the Federal court?

EULOGIO CATA: I am speaking of what is in this Bill, the Federal court.

MR. COLLIER: The Federal Court has jurisdiction over the eight major crimes which are listed in other laws, so we haven't repeated them here. You probably are familiar with them—murder, larceny, felony, arson, etc. There is a Federal law of that sort making it a crime to do certain things on the reservation. This federal court has jurisdiction over that, whether an Indian or a white man is involved, and this court also has certain other jurisdictions, which you will find, listed on page 39 of the Bill. This other jurisdiction includes all cases where a pueblo or tribe, or chartered community is a party. It is clear that if the tribe or the pueblo were a party it should not be sued in its own court, so that case would come before this special Federal Court. Then another kind of case that would come before the Federal Court is this. If a white man commits an offense on an Indian reservation or community; if he violates one of the rules of the community; suppose he takes pictures in Santo Domingo. Then he might be brought before the Santo Domingo Court, if that is a chartered community, and he might be punished, but in any case where a person who isn't a member of the community is involved then there can be appeal from the community court to this Federal Court.

There is one more kind of case in which this Federal court would have jurisdiction. Where a charter is granted to a community, it will guarantee to the community and to the members of the community certain rights. Now, if those rights are violated either by the Secretary of the Interior or by the community, or by the officials of the community, then the person who is injured can find redress in this special Federal Court and, if necessary, he can bring his action even against the Secretary of the Interior to compel the Secretary of the Interior to live up to the terms of the charter. There are the various cases that would come before this special Federal Court.

EULOGIO CATA (San Juan): Now, on page 20. Change to 3/5 of all the adult voters, not just those who come to vote. Suppose five of us come to vote and three voted. It should be three-fifths of the community or the pueblo.

MR. COLLIER: This is about adopting the charter. The way it reads now, the charter would go back to a referendum, a regular vote. Some people think that we ought to require that there be an affirmative vote by three-fifths of the qualified voters. The way it is now, an election is called and maybe only half of the people will vote. Now of those who do vote, three-fifths must vote for the charter. San Juan is asking the question—if the vote should be three-fifths of the total who could vote. I think the answer is the answer we have from our long experience with the white elections in the United States. The biggest elections we ever have are elections for President. You would think that most everybody would be interested enough to vote for President, yet the truth is that not half of the voters vote at the Presidential elections. Even with the political parties spending millions of dollars, they can't get our half of the voters. That is true generally. You most always never get 100% of the voting population, and if we required that the charter be adopted by three-fifths of those eligible to vote it might have the effect of making it practically impossible for a community to adopt a charter. We don't want to do that. Maybe the Indians are going to be better than the white people.

I think it is safe because the procedure would be such that there would be a very long discussion going on before the charter was presented. The charter would largely be worked out by the people themselves by calling many successive meetings, and everybody who had any interest in his people would turn out. There would be a thorough education of the people before they would vote.

VICTORIANO SISNEROS (Santa Clara): I am a delegate from Santa Clara. I haven't got a question to ask about this Bill, only whether the water rights are attached to this Bill. If one of the settlers lose their claims and the lands come back to the pueblo again, who is going to pay the water rights on any such project as we are having at Espanola?

MR. COLLIER: That is a question about Pueblo lands. That part is not touched by this Bill at all. The water goes with the land, as you know. Mr. Cochrane has more clearly in mind the question and he will answer it.

MR. COCHRANE (Pueblo Attorney): You have reference to the lands you got back under the Chimayo District. This Bill doesn't touch that at all; it is separate and apart from this Bill. It is out of the District now. They thought at the time it was in it, but successful court action has brought it back to you, and it will be worked out as a separate matter.

DESIDERIO NARANJO (Santa Clara): About this bill, we don't quite fully understand it. We have to study it over and now we are understanding it as Mr. Collier is explaining to us, but the way we feel right now we have to go back to our pueblo and have a meeting with the rest of the members of the pueblo and then we could decide about the Bill. Another thing, we have some children at Espanola high school and we have been asking for transportation for these children from Santa Clara to Espanola, and now as Mr. Collier is here I want to ask if you could give the children this transportation.

MR. COLLIER: That is a question of money. We are already paying the tuition of those children in the high school. Whether we can also supply transportation, I cannot say. After all, it is only two miles, and in many other parts of the country the children have to go ten or fifteen miles and we haven't got enough money to provide even for the long hauls. It wouldn't come ahead of everything else. All over this country children are walking two miles to public schools and more. I don't say that we won't do it; it is a question of money.

SOTERO ORTIZ (Chairman): San Ildefonso, have you any questions to ask?

EDMOND TRACY (San Ildefonso): I want to ask a few questions about the bill. Does that Bill give the same privileges to non-chartered pueblos?

MR. COLLIER: It will have some of the privileges, but not all. It gets all the protection in the matter of lands, but it does not get these different new powers of self-government.

EDMOND TRACY: How about borrowing money?

MR. COLLIER: I should say, a preference to handle the loan.

EDMOND TRACY: About voting, the Bill says that three-fifths of the adults that come and vote—but does that include women?

MR. COLLIER: As the Bill is drawn, it includes women. If the women don't come, they won't vote.

EDMOND TRACY: Suppose the vote was so even that they would have to come?

MR. COLLIER: You might have a vote where you would be just one short of three-fifths, then a crazy man could cast that vote.

EDMOND TRACY: About the jurisdiction of this new Federal Court, you stated that there were eight major crimes that come under that. We'd like to know just what they are.

MR. COCHRANE: They are murder, manslaughter, larceny, arson, assault with intent to kill, rape, assault with a deadly weapon, and felony.

MR. COLLIER: About these loans, preference would be given to chartered communities. The language of the amendment as introduced makes these loans, this five million dollar loan fund, for chartered Indian communities or its members. The community would have to take out a charter in order to get this loan fund.

SOTERO ORTIZ (Chairman): Pojoaque is next. Do you have any questions?

VICENTE PORTER (Pojoaque): I do not believe there are any questions. All questions have been brought out, and one question I had has been answered by Mr. Collier a few minutes ago, unless the rest of the delegates have anything to ask.

SOTERO ORTIZ (Chairman): Nambe. Have you any questions?

DELEGATE from Nambe: I have no questions to ask.

SOTERO ORTIZ (Chairman): Has Tesuque any questions?

MARTIN VIGIL (Tesuque): Awhile ago the Commissioner mentioned about land after this bill passed, that the government would buy us more land in case we are in need of it. Now, are they going to buy land for Tesuque? If the land is going to be bought for the Tesuque Indians and they are not satisfied with it, would the Indians of Tesuque have the right to decide what land they want? The reason I ask this question is because we have land for cultivating and what we want is forest land. The Government should buy us forest land.

MR. COLLIER: The Government would buy what the Indians wanted, of course, and the purchase would be a gift. There would be no reimbursable loan features. It is my belief that Tesuque is a pueblo where we must get more land.

SOTERO ORTIZ (Chairman): Cochiti is next.

DELEGATE from Cochiti: No questions to ask just now.

ANTONIO LUJAN (Taos): Mr. Ortiz raised the question a while ago about land. We from the Pueblo of Taos, we are accustomed to, when a man has a large family; he has a right to give land to his family. What I want to ask is this. If a man dies and leaves his heirs what he has, leaves it in writing; what I want to ask is, from what I have heard, that when a man dies the property returns to the community. For many years we are accustomed to when a man dies, or his wife dies, the property is left to the heirs. I don't think it is right that the property should return to the community. That's what I wanted to ask.

MR. COLLIER: The matter that Antonio Lujan refers to is on page 33, Section 7. It says that when an Indian who has been allotted land dies, then the title goes to the tribe although the heirs may continue to live on the property and use the improvements. This does not relate to tribal lands at all and does not touch the Pueblos. The ownership of land, the use of land, and the inheritance of land in the pueblos is controlled by the pueblo custom law and this Bill would not change that.

SOTERO ORTIZ (Chairman): Santo Domingo. Any questions?

JIM CORIZ (Santo Domingo): We don't have anything in mind now. Mr. Collier explained everything this morning. The same questions over and over again take up time. I think he should explain where he left off this morning.

ANTONIO LUJAN (Taos): It is very necessary that we should take time in discussing these matters; we shouldn't be in a big hurry.

SOTERO ORTIZ (Chairman): I think we must be a little bit more patient. It makes no difference if we take a little longer time. It is important that this matter be discussed and we want a thorough understanding before we take action on it. San Felipe, next.

FRED TENORIO (San Felipe): Is there any provision in the Bill whereas the Indians are guaranteed to secure jobs outside the Government Service, to be recognized equally as our white brothers on the outside. In my past experience I have seen two Indian boys who were well educated in the capacity of bookkeeping and they were working as such, but because they were Indians they were paid under wages and through false accusations of some kind by their white brothers they were discharged.

MR. COLLIER: The Bill cannot compel white persons to hire Indians. All we can do is to provide more and better training so that the Indian is better equipped for competition in the white world. But beyond that we can't go under any law. We can't break down race prejudice by a law. The Bill could not require white persons to employ Indians outside of the Government Service.

SOTERO ORTIZ (Chairman): Has Santa Ana anything to say?

PORFIRIO MONTOYA (Santa Ana): I will go back to the charter again. You are tired of speaking about that but I have to go back again. I have heard talks on various things; that where a community has been chartered they are given the advantage of all the money questions, educations, etc. I'd like to ask about that again. The answer that I think I heard is this—that the chartered community has that advantage, and the unchartered, whether I failed to hear it or not, seems like there is no answer to that yet. Of course, at noon times I heard various pueblos say they are in a position to accept the charter, and if they do it will give them the key to all these advantages. Without that charter they seem to understand that they won't be able to get the loans, or get the money to buy lands with. Suppose an unchartered community wanted to have some kind of money loan to its community members, like to use in the line of education, will it be necessary to have a charter or not?

MR. COLLIER: That's a very good question. I'm glad you asked it now. On matters about getting new land, those advantages are for all Indians whether they get a charter or not. All the advantages of these educational loans, to give higher education to boys and girls, are for all Indians. All the advantages that will come from the Court of Indian Affairs are for all Indians. The lawyers who are to be paid by the Government to assist them and represent them will be for all Indians. The reimbursable loans that are now being granted year after year will go right on for everybody. All that is for all Indians. Now, a tribe that wants to borrow from that five million dollars loan fund, according to the way the Bill is framed now, would have to take out a charter. A tribe that wanted to have a voice as to who should be employed by the Government would have to take out a charter. The various new powers in the way of self-government provided in the Bill would go to chartered communities.

I think there may be some here who exaggerate the difficulty of becoming a chartered community. It would not be difficult. As I explained before, the community can be chartered for little things or for big things. This Bill gives a long list of all things a community might want to be chartered for, now or 25 years from now. But it doesn't say that to be chartered you have to do all those things at once. No tribe could begin them all at once; so there would be no difficulty about getting a charter, except in the case of a tribe that was split very wide open by factions, where you couldn't get any agreement on anything. Such a tribe couldn't get a charter until it patched up its differences and got together, but that tribe would have all it has now, nothing would be taken away from it. Let me make the thing still clearer.

Let us take a pueblo like the one we are in right now—Santo Domingo. Santo Domingo has a very efficient local government right now. It has got already its customary law and everybody knows what it is; at least all Santo Domingo know. It is a very well organized community right now. There would be no trouble for Santo Domingo to get one of these charters. It wouldn't cost them anything and nobody would make you take a paper. If it didn't, it would keep all it has got now and get the additional advantage of protection in the matter of land. It would get all those new things that go to all Indians, but it wouldn't get the increased power in self-government which this Bill gives. I do not mind saying that I think it is a pretty good thing for that five million dollar loan fund to go to only chartered communities because that will be a strong motive for the tribes that are split to get together again and adjust their differences and organize for self-help. I think any pueblo, with enough reason to get together and be united, would be united. During the long fight over the Bursum Bill and the land legislation, each pueblo did get together, and I think under this new plan the advantages of uniting would be so great that many of them would unite.

SOTERO ORTIZ (Chairman): Has Jemez anything to say?

AVELINO CASIQUITO (Governor) through Fred Baca, Interpreter (Jemez): We rejoice to see you. We have the honor, dear sir, to be with you today. It gives me the greatest of pleasure as a spokesman of the Pueblo of Jemez to extend a sincere greeting from my people. It interests the Jemez Council and individuals and they are very much enthused of your progress of your administration. Realizing that you have been and are giving us things which are necessary and educational for the pueblo communities of the southwest with the suggested problems and possible solutions which are connected within the Bill now pending. It is the most far-reaching measure of legislation probably in the whole history, since our great father took us by the hands to guide us. There are some dark pages in this history of the white man's dealings with the Indians and many parts of the records are stained with greed and avarice of those who have thought only of their own profit, but it is also true that the purposes and motives of the great Government and our nation as a whole toward the red man have been wise, just and beneficent. The remarkable progress of the Pueblo Indians toward civilization is proof of it and open to all to see.

In 1887 when this so-called Allotment Act came into existence and became law, most all of our most beloved country had been lost. Take for instance, the Jemez Indians are shut up in a small grant, cooped up, considering the number of ruins in which they had lived and called their very own. The ruins can still be seen on the San Diego Grant and some of the Santa Fe National Forest. Realizing all these difficulties, doesn't it give you heart burning sensation of what had happened in old times. Jemez Indians had been given an opportunity to homestead the eastern part, from the present grant, before the Santa Fe National Forest, but lost the opportunity through lack of knowledge in land tenure. Probably the interpreters of that time failed to translate rules and regulations in homestead and perhaps was not that far advanced in education, and through these disadvantages we lost our rights.

The Jemez Indian community is greatly in need of grazing and timberland and cultivated land is limited. It is a matter of life and death. Our present grant and reservation is not sufficient to care for, to graze our livestock. With the number of sheep, cattle and horses, we have now, it is over-grazed many times. We can go just so far in stock raising, no means of an advancement or to forge ahead to an agricultural achievement. We are in a sad predicament, my friends, thinking of the future. What will the next generation live for, live by, live with, as the population is increasing. We number 670.

The Jemez Council at large has gone through a special study of this Bill and circular, to the best of their knowledge, and found it necessary for the possible means of the reimbursement of land we once owned, through this legislation. We urge that action be taken to repeal the Allotment Act. We had lost the land on the east portion, T. 16 N. R. 3 E.–T. 17 N. R. 3 E.–T. 18 N. R. 3 R., through our neglect and misunderstanding as to the homestead law or rules. Also the Jemez, Sia, and Santa Ana Grant. The Chief, his staff, Governor and headmen of the Pueblo of Jemez had set their minds to purchase on this Grant, if we had lost the deal through the Supreme Court of the United States again through some expert lawyer who knew our weakness and through the language of the deed. We had discovered a deed similar to this, and with this we had lost the Canon de San Diego Grant. We lost one of the Grants legally but we still must claim the other for we could not have lost the two grants legally, for two deeds speak the same language. Now friends, we are in a place where we can reach for but find none.

SOTERO ORTIZ (Chairman): Sia, next.

LORENZO MEDINA (Sia): I will not ask anything. Sia only asks for more grazing land. We want the Government to give us more grazing land. The information has been taken by some of our friends who are here in this meeting today and they will prove what kind of land we have. We need this land very bad. We hope to get this land back some time. We thank Mr. Collier for speaking this morning about our land.

ANTONIO MIRABAL (Taos): I will make it as short as possible, my statement about the Sia Pueblo. I was sent down there to see their land, their cultivated and grazing land, and it is true, just as he said. I also think that the Southern Pueblos officials—they are familiar with that land there. I have been on horseback as I didn't want to see just the village. The first day I went to the southwest corner of their boundary and there is nothing but sand dunes. I don't think there is ten pounds of hay to the acre, and I understand that they refuse to fence up their reservation because there is nothing that can pay. Also on the southeastern corner, as well as the northeastern part, it is just about the same as I saw on the southwest corner. Part of it has got some grass but it is overgrazed. There is a good piece of land about from two miles beyond, up to 17 miles, that is good land all right, but more or less my understanding is that part of it is school section land, some coal sections, taken up by people for coal mines and railroad sections as well. It seems to me from what I understand, that it is pretty hard for the Government to get that land for these people.

There is one Grant called the Borrego Grant. I think if the Government gets that piece of land, including one township between their Grant and the Borrego Grant, that's one place looks to me like they might do something. But, from what I saw, I don't see no reason why in the world the Southern Agency didn't look after these people. They got cattle and a few sheep and they are scattered out 17 miles from the pueblo to a place called the Armijo Lake. It is here they get their water. I would be very much pleased if the Government would do something for these people without much delay, and also concerning their farming land. They don't have hardly any farming land, that is, that amounts to anything, because some of the land what I saw is kind of red clay where no kind of crops grow, and also some of it has got more sand than anything else. For that reason I would be very glad for the Government to do something for these people without much delay. Thank you.

MR. COLLIER: That's one reason why we want to pass this Bill. We have no money now to buy land for Sia.

FRED BACA (Jemez): They have no pasture in which they can put their cattle and sheep, and their timber land is limited.

MR. COLLIER: You all understand that at the present time the Government has no money with which to buy any land. Only the money that was paid as compensation to the pueblos, they can use that to buy land. But for any more money we have got to wait for an appropriation such as we get in this Bill.

ELI BEARDSLEY (Laguna): I would like to make a statement while we are talking about the pending bill. We Indians should understand that it is not that we want to make any appeals today for anything. We are not appealing for these things now. The Bill is pending and we must understand that all these things are going to be had as soon as the Bill is passed. I think that we are wasting time in presenting our personal wants. We are putting up our individual wants—too many of them. I don't think this is time for it and we should go on with other things.

SOTERO ORTIZ (Chairman): Has Sandia any questions?

DOMINGO MONTOYA (Sandia): Sandia does not seem to have any questions to ask. All questions we were in doubt about seem to have been answered.

SOTERO ORTIZ (Chairman): Isleta is next.

PABLO ABEITA (Isleta): We do not have much to say. It seems that everything that we could say has already been said time and again. I would only ask that we be given time to present this matter before our community and advise or rather inform the Indians of the contents of this Bill. After they have heard and fully understand what the contents of the Bill are, if their answer is "no" my answer would be "yes." I mean that as far as I am concerned, I see nothing that would be detrimental or injurious to the Pueblo Indians. On the other hand, I rather believe that the Bill gives us more right than we ever had before. However, I have to be guided by what my people say. If my people say "go ahead and fight Mr. Collier" I'll do it, but I will do my best to have the Bill adopted as it is.

ANTONIO ABEITA (Isleta): I am a member of the Isleta Pueblo. I am not a delegate but nevertheless I take this opportunity of asking a question or two. Mr. Collier, will there be any similarity between the Indian Courts that are proposed to be established and the "kangaroo" courts that were established years ago by the Indian Office?

MR. COLLIER: No, there will be no similarity.

ANTONIO ABEITA: Will the judges in these courts be paid from \$7 to \$10 a day each?

MR. COLLIER: That would depend entirely upon the community. The community would form its own court, elect its own judges, and enforce its own ordinances.

ANTONIO ABEITA (Isleta): In regards to the yearly elections that we have, will the people have a voice in their government or will we be as we have been for a decade or so?

MR. COLLIER: That will be up the people. That cannot be done from the outside.

ANTONIO ABEITA: I believe there are some other Isletas that should express themselves as to what they have in mind.

DIEGO ABEITA (Isleta): I guess the reference is made to me. For many years the Council's action, as you know, has been concentrated on a fight for more land and water; that is, as long as I have been a member—that is about five years on and off. It used to be pretty near a crime to express one's aesthetic feeling. We have been engaged in one land fight after another and in the past years, fortunately, we have won most of the efforts that we have gone into. A large part of the credit should be given to our Commissioner, Mr. Collier, and our friends, Judge Hanna and some loyal friends that have stuck by us all these years. Today it seems to me that we are discussing another phase of our problem; that is, a recognition of our cultural existence, a recognition of our rights, of our form of government, of our system of land ownership and property ownership. This Bill, as I see it, does not affect so much the Pueblos with respect to property rights because our property is already held in community. Our community governments are organized much after the fashion that is indicated in the Bill. The Pueblos have tried that system for a long time without recognition and help from the Government, and in this Bill the Government proposes to recognize that form of existence and help the Pueblos to a great extent. The Bill embodies many policies that have been advocated and voiced by the All-Pueblo Council for a great many years.

All that the Pueblos should say, the way I see it, is that we have tried the system advocated by the Bill for a good long time and they have got it on a nearly workable basis, and with the help that is proposed in this Bill it will be put on a workable basis. It seems to me that the Pueblos ought to get behind it and approve of it, and I hope that it will get by. Thank you.

MR. COLLIER: Resting upon what Diego Abeita has just said, it is not going to be easy to pass this Bill. In the first place, it is not easy to pass any bill that appropriates about eight million dollars and undertakes to appropriate as much more each year, more or less. It is a hard thing to get that money. In the second place, all over this country there are powerful white groups who want to get possession of the Indian lands. They are getting them very fast under the old law. They will fight against this bill because the Bill will prevent them from getting possession of Indian lands. Wherever the Indians have large land holdings there are powerful white interests that want to put taxes on those lands. They will not want this bill because the Bill continues the freedom of the Indian lands from taxation.

With respect to the life of your great tribes down here in the southwest, you who have kept your old languages, your old way of life, and your ancient religions, there are many interests that want to take away from you those things. The Pueblos know that well. They have fought many a battle for religious liberty and freedom, for their ancient religion, and for equal rights between their religion and all other religions, and for the preservation of their old culture and ideals. There are some quite powerful interests among the white people who are opposed to anything like this Bill or to any policy that Secretary Ickes and I might advocate because they think we are too sympathetic for the old Indian life and because this Bill would give to the Indians who like the old way, the freedom to live the old way, just as it would give to the Indians who might like the new way to freedom to live the new way.

So, even though it be true that this Bill has the endorsement of the administration and of the President, yet it is true it is going to be hard to enact this Bill. We are not going to be able to enact it unless the Indians speak out loud and bold and make it their Bill. They can't expect Secretary Ickes and me to do all the fighting. Furthermore, we do not want to lose too much time. The needs of many Indians are desperate. We have heard about the condition of the Sias. Their condition is terrible, shocking, and heartbreaking, but bad as it is, they are rich men compared to other Indians in many parts of the country who have no land at all, who are simply tramps on the face of the earth. Time is very precious now. We don't want to stampede any Indians. Whenever we have gone to meet the Indians we have said, "take just as much time as you really think you need to take, but for goodness sake don't put off your decisions." We have come out here to learn your wishes. We have told Congress that we are going to do what the Indians want and are not going to do it unless the Indians want it.

Therefore, don't force us to wait until Congress has adjourned before we find out what you want. Possibly the next Congress will not be as friendly as the present Congress. Possibly the financial condition of the Government will be much worse next year than it is this year. If the Indians hesitate and delay too long it might even give the President the idea that maybe they don't want this Bill very much. I am not urging you to act today or any one day, and I certainly am not asking you to endorse this Bill but only to express your thoughts. I am suggesting that the time is very precious; that if we could hear from the Indians promptly all over the country, then it is practically certain that we could pass this Bill before Congress adjourns; whereas, if the Indians delay too long it will be thrown over into the next Congress a year from now.

ROSENDO VARGAS (Picuris): Since our Commissioner is here we would like to ask this question. On the 17th of December, 1931, one of our tribesmen, Reyes Mermejo, was shot and killed by a Mexican while hunting up in the mountains, and what my people would like to know, because there has been nothing done, and our attorney, Mr. Cochrane—he's supposed to be our attorney—he hasn't done a thing up to this time. We would like to have Mr. Cochrane explain to us what is his reason for not prosecuting this case. If he is going to let this go the way it is we might all of us be killed like dogs.

MR. COCHRANE (Pueblo attorney): I have explained to you several times that that offense occurred outside your pueblo lands, that the jurisdiction over it was in the State of New Mexico. The Prosecuting Attorney for that district had a hearing and dismissed the case. There was no proof that he was murdered. I have told you people that many times. I have told it to your pueblo officials. They presented what they had; there was a hearing on it and it was dismissed. There is nothing more that we can do.

EDMOND TRACY (San Ildefonso): When does Congress adjourn?

MR. COLLIER: I wish we knew. It might adjourn in May and maybe not until June, but the longer we delay the greater will be the danger of not passing it. The Pueblo Indians know, it took us three years to get the Pueblo Relief Bill out of Congress.

PAUL JOHNSON (Governor of Laguna): The Governor of the Laguna Pueblo wishes to express himself in behalf of the whole tribe. I have told my interpreter to talk for me and he will give you my ideas on these things. Honorable Commissioner, ladies and gentlemen: This is the second time we have heard Mr. Collier in this Council hall since he has become the Commissioner of Indian Affairs. We wish to say that when he first came here last year he came to notify us that he had been empowered, as much as to say that the Indian had been liberated. This, I say, has been one of the emancipations for the whole Indian race. Mr. Collier has championed our cause. He has proven himself a true friend of the Indians, a real acid test. We must understand that while this Bill has been framed the greater part of it has been Mr. Collier's idea, and if we are to make him our champion what must we do? Must we not stand solid behind the cause because it has been promoted for our livelihood and for our benefit. This has been a great cause, the things that we have heard this morning, the explanation of this Bill.

Previous to this time we had the idea that we were safe and secure in all our land holdings under our grants and our purchases. We had not realized that they were in jeopardy. In this matter we will say that this Bill is not intended for Mr. Collier or anybody else, except for us Pueblos. With this idea in view we shall form a solid mass behind this purpose. There are things in the Bill perhaps that we may look at in a way that will work hardships on us, but are we going to fail him? There are none of us that would be willing to do so. Therefore it is up to us, although perhaps we may not understand the whole Bill, but all these things that are in the Bill are to preserve our future religious liberties and everything that goes along. It is very important, as Mr. Collier has said, that we act and not simply fight over it. Instead of that we ought to try and work these things out, whether we will accept all the powers that this Bill is going to give us. We ought to take at least a portion, one at a time if necessary.

ANTONIO TAPIA (Interpreter): I would like to speak for myself on this matter.

MR. COLLIER: We'd better let the Lagunas finish.

PAUL JOHNSON (Governor of Laguna)—By interpreter Eli Beardsley: My pueblo has expressed themselves as approving of the Bill and its form because it has not been out of line with what the Indians have been accustomed to for time immemorial, time back, except with the incoming new power that is going to be given them. These things we will have to take gradually, if the Bill passes. We have certainly appreciated the efforts that have been done by our present Commissioner and his forces. We can not express ourselves with the present feeling that we have over all that he had done and all that he is trying to do for us. The thing is for us to stand behind. If it is to be a success we must stand united and push this thing ahead. Mr. Collier's success depends on our aid and our response to these things, and it will be our success too. I thank you folk for listening and I think the Lagunas perhaps have one or two questions to ask after I am through with my talk. I thank you.

CHAS. KIE (Laguna): Mr. Collier, as we sit in this room here, 14 years ago the majority of the young men that spoke today were mere boys then, they are able to talk now. We had a council of old men here then, with war paint, to fight the Bursum Bill, and that is what we will be up against. We don't want to destroy the 14 years of work that Mr. Collier has led on with the good lawyer friends of ours. There are a good many white loyal friends that have helped us fight through. We can not condemn all of them. This is the way the Lagunas feel. We are standing behind Mr. Collier.

ULYSSES PAISANO (Laguna): I want to ask a question. We want an explanation about our personal holdings, about the trust patents, and the homesteads that have been held in some places inside of the Executive Order.

MR. COLLIER: These are homesteads, are they not? They would not be changed in any way except that the Trust Patent would be made permanent. You could turn the title over to the tribe in exchange for land, but you don't have to. The titleholders are not to be persuaded to do this. If they do not want to make a change they can stay as they are.

SOTERO ORTIZ (Chairman): Acoma, do you have any questions?

BAUTISTO PINO (Governor of Acoma): I come here to listen to the talks of the meeting and now I will ask the interpreter to go ahead and say what the pueblo wishes to say.

ALBERT PAYTIAMO (Interpreter): Friends and Commissioner Collier. This is a pretty long tiresome meeting and it seems like we never come to anything that we should. I think the majority has asked many questions and I don't think there is anything else to be asked. It seems like this is the only Commissioner of Indian Affairs up to this time, the only man that has done something for the Indians, and I believe that Mr. Collier ought to get credit. He has worked, has been a friend of the Indians for many years, and if we can all back him up, all stand behind him, we might do something and help each other if we help Mr. Collier. But if we start to go in different directions we will get nowhere.

There are many here who have been educated and I don't see why that many of these Indians here, they ought to have gone on with the English language right through instead of having two interpreters and wasting our time. I agree with my friends here, the Lagunas, what they have said and it is true. Some of us might think we understand the Bill, but might not. I think the Bill as a whole is pretty good, but there are some things in the Bill that are kind of hard to understand. We have been having our self-government right along many years back and it is just about the same. What I want to ask, Mr. Collier, is about the Exchange Bill which has been before Congress. What has become of it? We have been paying seven years, leasing the land on those two townships. It seems to me that Congress ought to pass this Bill right away. I wish you would tell us, Mr. Collier, just how it is.

MR. COLLIER: That Bill is pending in Congress now. It has been endorsed by the Secretary of the Interior and the Budget Director says it is all right. I should think the bill would pass without doubt.

BAUTISTO PINO—Interpreted by Albert Paytiamo: Another thing I would like to ask Mr. Collier. There are some homesteads in that township. My friend the Lagunas homestead it and they try to sell the land to us, which amounts to $8,000, more or less. I wish to ask if the Congress or Government would buy those lands in order to consolidate that area.

MR. COLLIER: That would be exactly the kind of thing that would be done with this two million dollars.

BAUTISTO PINO—By Albert Paytiamo: Well, we have been here all day and feel like going home, so I think I better stop talking and maybe all of you feel the same way. All of you thank Mr. Collier and his staff for what they have done, especially for the schools, and the Superintendents. Many of you have been educated and ought to appreciate it. I thank you all, each one of you from each pueblo, for your attention.

SOTERO ORTIZ (Chairman): Zuni, have you any questions to ask?

DELEGATE from Zuni: I am a delegate from Zuni. All this talk that we hear about this Bill, all the Zunis favor this Bill. There is only one thing we wish to ask Mr. Collier in regards to this land title. There are about, maybe half a dozen Navajos allotted right inside of our reservation. We wish to know if there is any chance that we could move these Navajo families outside of this reservation when this Bill is passed.

MR. COLLIER: If the Navajos' Boundary Bill passes it is probable that that can be taken care of by exchanging those Navajo lands for other lands of the Navajo area. Otherwise, the appropriation contained in this Bill could and would be used to buy them out so as to get a solid area of land.

SOTERO ORTIZ (Chairman): Has the Hopi delegation any questions to ask?

OTTO LEMITOVI (Hopi delegate): My name is Otto Lemitovi, a Hopi Indian from Oraibi, Arizona. I have a question or two to ask pertaining to the Bill before us. Is there any provision made in this Bill whereby the governor of each village can be authorized by the community to pardon criminals in that locality, people convicted in the Indian courts.

MR. COLLIER: The Charter could be drawn that way, just as the Governor of a state has that power. That would be entirely up to the community.

OTTO LEMITOVI: I have questions to ask which probably would not be of much interest to the rest of the people here, but have a momentous effect upon us Hopi Indians. The first question I wish to ask is this. Did the Spanish Government, the Mexican Government, and the United States Government recognize the Hopi form as a community government? Was the Hopi form of government recognized by the Treaty of Guadalupe Hidalgo in 1848.

MR. COLLIER: As I remember the Treaty, it does not recognize any community government. It recognizes the religious liberty and guarantees that, and it likewise guarantees any property rights they had before that time, but I have no doubt that you could carry over the remarks of the Supreme Court to the Hopis. The Supreme Court recognized the Pueblo of Santa Rosa down in the Papago country as a corporation and I believe that same would carry to the Hopis too.

OTTO LEMITOVI (Hopi delegate): Now, inasmuch as Mr. Commissioner made a remark this morning to the effect that the Hopi Indians of Arizona, formerly of New Mexico, were entirely at the mercy of the Commissioner of Indian Affairs and the Secretary of the Interior, I should like to ask this question. Inasmuch as the Treaty of Guadalupe Hidalgo, a copy of which I have in this note book, recognizes property rights and titles to the area occupied by the Pueblo Indians at that time, then are the Hopi Indians of Arizona, Pueblo Indians, considered as reservation Indians in the legal sense of the word? Are the Hopi Indians in Arizona, formerly of New Mexico, being Pueblos, considered as reservation Indians in the legal sense?

MR. COLLIER: Yes, the Pueblos are all reservation Indians, all of the Pueblos.

OTTO LEMITOVI: The title and right to occupancy to the areas has been recognized by the Government of the United States and the previous governments. I should like to ask another question. The Executive Order of December 16, 1882 by President Arthur was supposedly to have created a reservation for the Hopi Indians. After designating the area to be set aside, it goes on to say "for the use and occupancy of the Moqui and such other Indians as the Secretary of the Interior may see fit to settle thereon." I should like to know, Mr. Commissioner, if it is necessary for any person, before settling thereon, to have an official act from the Indian Office.

MR. COLLIER: No, but you have to recognize the ownership of land through a Spanish Grant and the ownership of land through the right of occupation. They are not the same, and unless the Hopis can find evidence of a grant, then they can't make the same claim of ownership to a specific area as the Pueblos have successfully made. The area set aside by President Arthur contained at that time Hopis and other Indians, and had at various times in the past contained other Indians besides the Hopis, so that the right of occupancy was a mere right asserted by more than one group of Indians. I don't think the courts could hold that they violated the right of occupancy. I think that the answer to the whole problem is one of arbitration between the Navajos and Hopis and the determination of boundaries, bearing in mind that the Navajo area is being increased.

OTTO LEMITOVI: Then the right of occupancy is recognized. But a few Navajos and Indians were very much removed from our occupied lands; they have been drifting toward our settlements within the last 15 and 20 years. The reason for asking is this. We all know that before Christopher Columbus' grandmother was born we had our government probably in existence precisely as it is today, and our rights by the former governments have been fully respected with regard to the area we were actually using, perhaps not so much by farming, but by stock raising and hunting purposes by which we derived our living at that time. Consequently the areas are large.

The Bill now before us, as I understand it, gives us these things that it recognizes—our form of government. It revises it and gives it added power to meet conditions in the particular area in which we are living. It seems this way to me. I will illustrate it this way. We were living in a nice house as Pueblo Indians. Our house was crude but substantial. It was satisfactory to us. We were happy and everybody was engaged in something. The white man came one day and says, "that house of yours looks crude to me. I will offer you a better one in its place. I will set that house on fire." We remonstrated but he set fire to it; we lived in it anyway and to his consternation the thing hasn't burned for the last three hundred years. The foundation is firm and still present.

Now the Government, through our Honorable Commissioner, Mr. Collier, a true friend of the Indians, has voiced its decisions and says, "we have failed to find a satisfactory substitute for your form of government. Therefore, we are going to pass a law and the effect of it will be this—we will help you to build up that house we tried to destroy." We only wish to say that it took a mighty long time for that house to burn down to its foundation and it is going to take a mighty long time to build it up. It holds out to the Indians security for the future, it holds out a strong hand for an Indian whereby he can be enabled to cope with the situation, by offering him unlimited education with means. As to his land rights, it guarantees that to him with a promise of more additional land. As to religious affairs, that is fully protected under the Constitution of the United States. The Bill does not touch that. As to law and peace, it provides a way whereby it can be handled and carried on.

It appears to me, speaking for the Hopis from our pueblo and other pueblos that the Bill should pass. There are some things to which I take exception, perhaps because I have not fully comprehended its meaning. Perhaps after a full understanding it will be all right, but in order to expedite these matters and help our Commissioner and the men who have labored for our welfare, realizing the fine vision they have for the Indians' welfare, we must have something given us to govern in the way of land matters. Therefore, I suggest that perhaps at this time delegates from various pueblos in New Mexico and Arizona, whom I judge are authorized to act on behalf of their people, should take a vote at this time on whether we should have the Bill passed or not.

ANTONIO MIRABAL (Taos): I want to say a few words. We have been here speaking about this Bill all day. We haven't taken any important action yet and I think that now is the time for us to take action. If we want to throw away what we have worked for fourteen years, it is up to you people here to say whether we should vote about this Bill because we have talked all day to understand every point, and we from Taos feel that we can't go against ourselves and we are willing to vote that we are in favor of the Bill.

OTTO LEMITOVI (Hopi): As I understand it, the Bill does not force us to seek a way backwards out of the solution. It gives us full liberty to solve our problems in the way we think that it should be solved. We appreciate Senators Wheeler and Frazier, and Mr. Ickes, who have drawn up this Bill are not ignorant of Indian conditions in the United States. They are men who have given much of their time and life to the study of our conditions. Therefore, I cannot conceive the idea that the Bill was drawn up in such way as to catch the Indians. I do not see that there is any tendency or anything in the Bill to make us want to go back to the old form of life. No person with common sense today would want to do that. We are looking forward. But education or civilization does not consist of the white man's form of civilization. We Indians have always had our own government and civilization composed of progress in arts and crafts and contentment.

Perhaps the Government might have adopted what I term an indirect form of Government rather than direct in working through our government. In 1924 we were declared citizens of the United States, but how many of us are citizens? Our lands are being taken away notwithstanding. We have no access to courts. I do not see that the Bill would have any tendency to drive us back into the old form of government, and if it does I don't think any Indian would want to do it. We will progress ahead. Thank you.

PAUL JOHNSON (Governor of Laguna)—by Eli Beardsley, Interpreter: One or two more words from the Laguna Pueblo. It is true that my land is under consideration. This whole United States was once my own, and later the white settlers have come into our lands and settled. At this time the red men and the white men are here to discuss the common needs of my people. You realize that this whole island that was once mine, after the white man has taken possession of it, you in turn today have given your greatest and utmost thoughts in considering my present condition. Today I have to buy everything, which in previous times I had the right to take to make my living from this land of mine. In previous time I had the right to take the game of this land, and my forefathers had made their livelihood from this occupation. For this reason we are here and you have given your greatest thoughts in considering us.

INTERPRETER: He is taking all the Indians in. He is giving his ideas and he appreciates what in turn you are trying to do for us today.

PAUL JOHNSON: If Congress wants to know the truth of this whole matter, they should send for us and we will explain the full situation, our whole condition as it is today, so that they will believe and realize that they owe us something. I am ready and willing to explain things that I know, which concern me, although in my condition, not being educated, yet willing to give the truth of my condition. You brothers that are here should realize what this means. We ought to give everything. We ought to consider ourselves. We ought to give our consent today as to what is before us. John Collier has given us these things, and in all these years that he has worked among us he has taught us our needs and he has worked for our needs. This is all. Thank you.

ROLAND DURAN (Picuris): Before saying yes or no on this Bill, I wish that our Commissioner would explain further the appointment of judges and the probate attorneys.

MR. COLLIER: The judges of the Court of Indian Affairs would be appointed by the President, confirmed by the Senate, and removed by the President if not satisfactory. He would search for very able men who are sympathetic with the Indians and know about Indian life, and they would be appointed for long terms and paid by the Government. The Probate matter does not concern you here because your lands are not allotted, but, in brief, where they are allotted the Government has a big job of determining heirs. There wouldn't be any need for the Probate attorneys. I think I mentioned already the appointment in the Bill of ten special attorneys who would represent the Indians in contests that might arise to be carried before the court. Your pueblos are the only Indians outside of Oklahoma who have a Special Attorney to represent you. The other Indians are not represented and are quite defenseless.

ANTONIO TAPIA (Pojoaque): We all have spoken something in this meeting now in general form. I am not going to take a side; I am going to try to state why this Bill is a need of all the tribes. My reason is this. Looking back when the Spaniards came to this country and the Indians of New Mexico expelled the Spaniards out of here and gave them these Grants; now on the 25th of September, 1689, the statement was given expressed in these words: "each pueblo shall be considered." The Crown, in order to reduce these Indians, he went and established what we call an aristocratic government which was transferred to these Indians, the way I see it, and this sort of government was exercised by the Nobility of Europe.

Now this government, according to the way we understand it, is just the right kind of government that the Indian pueblos can handle because the best men of the pueblo or tribe are in authority. And I say "yes," this Bill should be passed in Congress for the very reason that the Indian as a whole is not recognized as a citizen, neither as a voter, but is recognized as a dependent nation. That's the way I understand it, and that is the reason I think it is necessary for the Pueblo Indians in general, we of all the Indian tribes, to accept it, so that we can make our claims before the Federal government. Now you see here is a man from Picuris who says that if the Government doesn't do something his people could be shot like dogs. Our government was established by Spain and our forefathers took the oath; therefore I think it is very well because we can not combat with the democracy government. That's the form of government we have in the United States. We need it to sustain and support our claims, and that's the very reason I say that all we need is power to function. Our Commissioner is the man that is trying to put it through Congress to safeguard our rights and I think it is a necessity for us to accept it. That's the way I look at it.

EULOGIO CATA (San Juan): I make a motion that this Bill be approved as it stands.

MR. COLLIER: The way the Bill is drawn now; the power of the local community over these local matters is final. There are some people in Congress that think we should amend the Bill and allow a review if the penalty is made too large. In other words, it might be an abuse of power and they ought to have an appeal from any large decision.

PABLO ABEITA (Isleta): Mr. Collier, ladies and gentlemen: I wish to state just one more thing. A motion has been made here that we should adopt this Bill as it is. I object to it, not that I don't like the Bill, but it is up to my pueblo, my people. I cannot go ahead and give my people something that they don't want. We must consider what our friend from the Hopi country said, that we had the same form of government that we have today long before Christopher Columbus' grandmother was born. Our form of government was functioning before the birth of the United States of America. The King of Spain recognized it, and we have a cane which was supposed to have been sent by the King of Spain, confirming authority on the governors of the pueblos. Isleta was one of them.

When the Mexican government was formed during the war in 1812 and the change was made, we have another cane that was sent by the Mexican government recognizing the pueblo authorities and their governors. When we came within the United States Mr. Abraham Lincoln gave us another cane as a symbol of our authority, recognizing the authority of the different pueblos at that time. Up to this time we have the same form of government. At that time the Europeans were pillaging, murdering, and massacring each other, and the Indians were living in peace. I can say, without hesitation, that when it comes to pure meanness, the white people take the first prize, the blue ribbon, because when the Indians have killed one, they already have killed thousands. When the Indians steal or rob 15¢ the white man has already stolen fifteen million or more. And that is not all; when the Indian is caught doing these things he is either jailed or hanged, and when the white man is caught he is given a good lecture, told to be careful so that he won't be caught the next time.

However, the Bill before us is not for me. I may live a few years, but it is for the next generation. I would very gladly accept it as it is because it safeguards my people, but what if my people ask me "Why did you do that? We sent you over there to hear and tell us what it is all about." We have read it over time and time again, and when we finished we were just as much in the dark as when we started. Now we have a little better understanding. I hope that I will be able, or my governor and delegates will be able to convince my people that it is for their best interests, but I don't want Mr. Collier, the Commissioner, and the Secretary to get peeved if my people say "no." They don't know, they haven't learned enough. The old people want their old customs, because we have lived by it, through it, and we want the old people to live through the same form of government that we have lived.

When the new generation comes I'll be down in the ground, so for that reason I don't want to tie my people. The first thing that was decided at the meeting we had yesterday here was that we should not be guided by the majority of the people in this meeting. Formerly when the thing was brought up and a vote taken, if the majority of the pueblos voted for a certain thing it went. In this matter we reserved the right that we should be allowed to present this Bill to our people, and if they want to say "yes," I will say "yes" with all my heart. I thank you.

MR. COLLIER: This has come up in years past. Some delegates have come authorized to act, some only to report. On many occasions those who came authorized to act have proceeded to record their vote, and those not authorized to act have later sent it on to Washington. On every important Bill that has come up, some are prepared to act and they act, and those that are not, they wait. I have a record of nearly all of your meetings and find that that is the way you have generally done. Each pueblo has stated its own position and that has been transmitted to Washington. Now why couldn't the same thing be done. Those free to act now, act, and those not free to act, go back and write to us in Washington.

FRED TENORIO (San Felipe): It is agreed among the delegates of San Felipe that they should be given a little more time to go back home and explain what we have learned here from Mr. Collier himself.

SOTERO ORTIZ (Chairman): Friends and gentlemen. We have been discussing this Bill all day, and for years and years we have been asking for help from the Government, more power to our form of government, protection for ourselves and our property and our religious affairs. Never before did we have such a Bill drawn like the one we have before us. I believe, but don't want you to think or have in mind that I am trying to force you to do what you should not do, but I want to tell you, more or less, and make it clear, that now is the time for us to take the protection we have been asking for a long time. Now, while our friends are holding office, while the Congressmen, as we heard our Commissioner say, are more friendly and favor us Indians, it is easier for a Bill like the one we have to go through and become a law. If we wait longer we do not know if we will ever have that chance again. Maybe we will lose entirely forever the chance we are having right now before us, and I believe with a clear conscience that if we want to help ourselves, if we want to protect ourselves and our form of government and our religious affairs, now is the time for us to adopt the Bill that is before us. We do not know yet and we can't be sure that the Bill will go through. Maybe there will be plenty that will be objecting to its passage without our objections, and for that reason I think that for us Indians we must be united and work for the betterment of ourselves and for our children to come, and vote for this Bill. I mean those delegates who came from their homes with full authority to act on what takes place in this meeting. Those who have not full authority, they can go back and report what they have learned today and later on can send a report to Washington of what you think of this Bill. I don't want you fellows and friends to feel any hardship about the way I talk. I want to be friends with all and we all have the liberty to say what we want. That is all. Now, we will have a roll-call from each pueblo, and those who have full authority, you can say "yes," and those that haven't full authority, you can say what you have to say.

PABLO ABEITA (Isleta): You have heard what our chairman has said. We are going to call on all pueblos, taking a vote as to whether you accept the Bill as it is, or whether you are going to wait and send in a report later. Taos, first.

TAOS: We already told you from that that we are not going to fight against ourselves. We are in favor of the Bill.

PICURIS: We are in doubt yet. We want to take this matter up with the Council up there, and as soon as the Council decides we will write to Washington.

SAN JUAN: I guess San Juan is authorized to answer. We are in favor.

SANTA CLARA: Santa Clara is in doubt of the Bill yet, but we will notify the Office later on. We have to notify the Council first.

SAN ILDEFONSO: San Ildefonso will also wait and have a council with the rest of the tribe.

POJOAQUE: Pojoaque favors passage of the Bill.

NAMBE: Nambe will wait until we let the Council know about it.

TESUQUE: As I told you, Tesuque is a small group but we are united. We have heard all what the Commissioner and all the brothers from all the different pueblos have to say and it seems to us that my governor here authorized me to speak for the pueblo of Tesuque. We are standing right in the middle of the Bill and we are in favor of it.

COCHITI: The Governor of Cochiti wishes to explain that he will take the matter back to Cochiti and notify his Council.

SANTO DOMINGO: Santo Domingo will not vote until further discussion among themselves.

SAN FELIPE: San Felipe will not vote until it is discussed and then we will give a definite answer.

SANTA ANA: Santa Ana is also not authorized to act now.

JEMEZ: Jemez is in favor of the passage of the Bill.

SIA: Sia is in favor of the Bill and will follow the others.

SANDIA: The governor wishes to state that he has not been authorized to vote against or for this bill so we will take this up with the people and report later.

ISLETA: Will not vote yet.

LAGUNA: Laguna doesn't want to take this matter back to the pueblo. We have been authorized to give approval. We are in favor.

ACOMA: Acoma wishes to say this. According to what the rest have said, we think this Bill is pretty good, but it has been said by the Councilmen of Acoma to take it back until they discuss it among themselves, the way they told us.

ZUNI: Zuni is in favor of the Bill.

HOPI: As stated a while ago, there are nine villages among the Hopi people and they are not all represented here, so, while I advocated its passage personally, I cannot speak for the whole tribe, but I can safely say our pueblo of Oraibi, that we are in favor of it. However, we will take this matter up out there because we can not form any intelligent conclusion until it is taken up.

ULYSSES PAISANO (Laguna): Please do not lose this great opportunity. That's all.

PABLO ABEITA: There are 20 pueblos represented here. Out of the 20 there are 9 who are voting "yes" and the rest, as I understand it, will take the matter up with their council and the people and will advise Mr. Collier later.

SOTERO ORTIZ (Chairman): As I have said before, when I ask you to vote on this Bill, to adopt this Bill, some of the pueblos say they have come with full authority of their pueblo to act on what was going on in this meeting. Many times before the delegates from the different pueblos have been authorized that in the next meeting they would come with authority. The pueblos must select their best men as delegates with full authority so that they can act and have the full power to say what they have to say. Because in this meeting that we have we are supposed to work for the welfare of our pueblos, for our people, for ourselves and for our children. For that reason you have been asked several times to send your best men with full authority. Now, after you go back home, please tell your councilmen that at another meeting that may be necessary to be called, please come with full authority from your own pueblo so that we may know what we are doing. You have the free privilege to say what is good for you and for your people and what is not good for you and for your people.

Now, the Bill before us, we don't see anything that may be a detriment to us Indians. It has been worked out or drafted by men, not only one man but by various men, and men who have fought for our rights. They have already been mentioned and we must have full confidence in them because in the past they have worked for us and they are still working for our benefit, and they want to protect our rights, our property, as well as in other matters. Now these delegates that come without full authority, I wish that when you go back home you would consult with your people what the real meaning or explanation has been in regards to this Bill and how it affects us and after you get a thorough understanding I hope you will adopt it too. Send your reports to Washington. Now, I want to express my sincere thanks from the Pueblo of San Juan to all the gentlemen, our Commissioner, and all the men that have worked for the benefit of us, all those men who have assisted in helping us. Thank you.

PABLO ABEITA: We wish to thank our Commissioner, Mr. Collier, the Assistant Commissioner, Mr. Zimmerman, and all the rest of our friends, even though they took no part, but it seems that they have the welfare of the Indians in their heart or they wouldn't be here this late. I wish to thank you.

MR. COLLIER: I have a little piece of business to bring up; it has no connection with what has gone before and it will only take a minute.

Secretary Ickes has instructed me to find out the wishes of Pueblos in this thing I am going to speak of. He keeps getting letters from people asking him when he is going to be removing certain names from some buildings up here at Santa Fe. He asked me what the Indians thought about it. I got out the stenographic record of the last All-Pueblo meeting and found therein nothing but a speech by one of the Taos delegates which called on the Government to remove those names from those buildings, chop them off. There was no vote taken and Secretary Ickes instructed me to find out what the Pueblos wanted, whether they wanted the names kept on those buildings or taken off. Secretary Ickes has adopted a general rule that they are not going to put the names of living men on the buildings, but he is reluctant to destroy what a past administration has done, unless the Indians want him to. Now, I am leaving that with you and you can either answer it with a rising vote now or any way you wish. The names in question are "Cramton" on the hospital, "Meritt" on the boys' dormitory, and "Burke" on the Wingate School. Those are the only three that Secretary Ickes has asked me about.

Vote taken by pueblos—All in favor of removing above names from the buildings mentioned.

MR. COLLIER: I will transmit this to the Secretary of the Interior.

I wish to mention two men who have done you great service in the years gone by. Your first Indian Agent, Calhoun, gave his life to save your lands and establish your governments; he is the greatest Indian Agent assigned to the southwest. Another man who fought for you and did much to tell the whole world about you was Charles F. Lummis. Someone suggests a third—Bandelier.

DIEGO ABEITA: May I suggest the name of an Indian, unheralded, who gave up his life—Popé, the great Pueblo [leader].

MR. COLLIER: Mr. Zimmerman points out that the name of "Burke" School has been put into an appropriation bill, so it may be difficult to change that.

ANTONIO TAPIA: Just another name—Ca-ti-ti of Picuris. He got up the scheme for the expulsion of the Spaniards.

JUDGE HANNA: I just want to say one thing. I have been in Washington for two weeks and I want to say to you that all of your friends there are very much interested in the passage of this Bill. Those of you that have to report to the governors and councils, please be prompt about it because I know that you will lose the opportunity to express your views unless you act promptly. The Bill is all right, it is in the interest of the Pueblos, and there is nothing you have to take if you don't like it. There is nothing objectionable in it and you'll find that out I am sure if you study it, but act promptly.

MR. COLLIER: One final word. Regardless of what you do, as your Chairman pointed out, we can't promise to pass the Bill this year. Before the Bill is passed, you may be sure that anything that isn't exactly right in it will be made right. We are going to continue to fight for the fundamental principles in this Bill until we get them. If it takes two years we will go on for two years, but I predict that before we are finished we are going to get the things that this Bill is trying to get.

SOTERO ORTIZ (Chairman): I believe that this is about all that we have to discuss and you all must be tired.

The meeting is adjourned. (7:00 P.M.)

CHAPTER 7

REPORT OF SOUTHERN ARIZONA INDIAN CONFERENCE HELD AT PHOENIX, ARIZONA, MARCH 15–16, 1934 FOR THE PURPOSE OF EXPLAINING THE HOWARD-WHEELER BILL TO THE ASSEMBLED INDIANS

PHOENIX INDIAN SCHOOL PRINT SHOP
PHOENIX, ARIZONA
SOUTHERN ARIZONA INDIAN CONFERENCE

Officials present: A. C. Monahan, Assistant to the Commissioner, Walter V. Woehlke, Ward Shepard, James Stewart, Melvin Siegel, and Mark Radcliff.

Delegations: San Carlos, White River, Sells, Sacaton, Colorado River, Truxton Canyon.

March 15, 1934, 9:27 o'clock A.M.

Meeting called to order—Mr. Monahan, chairman.

MR. MONAHAN: Friends, I am very sorry that Mr. Collier could not be here. He has many meetings in different parts of the country. He had to go east because Congress is in session and he must be back or many things will fail without his presence. But he asked me to say to you that he was very sorry he could not be here and to ask you to consider the Wheeler-Howard Bill very carefully and then write to him and ask anything that you want to know about it. Mr. Ickes, Secretary of the Interior, asked me as I left Saturday to give his very best regards to you delegates that attend this meeting.

This meeting today and tomorrow is to discuss this proposed legislation which is now before the Congress, and on which hearings are being held by the Senate and House Committees on Indian Affairs, but Congress wants to know what the Indians themselves think of this, so that what you have to say here in this meeting or after you go back home and your people tell you what they want to say or what any one of you as a single person has to say, will be taken up with the committees in Congress so that they will know what you want.

As this meeting is for this particular purpose, we will not take time for any other matters that have to do with local questions that some of you from different reservations want to discuss. Strictly tribal matters will be taken up at some other time. If you have some other matters that you want to discuss, we will save time in answering them. When we are through with that, those who have something to say will have an opportunity to do so.

MR. MONAHAN introduced Mr. Woehlke: First I present Mr. Woehlke, of California, who is a field representative of the Commissioner of Indian Affairs.

MR. WOEHLKE: Mr. Chairman, Friends: Before I proceed I would like to have you know the various officials of Washington who have come here to consult with you. They have not been mentioned so far, but I believe it would be a good thing if you knew who they are and what they are doing. This distinguished gentleman in front here is Mr. Ward Shepard, specialist in land policies for the Washington Office. Of course, you all know Mr. Monahan, assistant to the Commissioner.

Behind him is Mr. Stewart, chief of the Land Division in Washington and far in the background is Mr. Siegel, the assistant to the Solicitor of the Interior Department.

This legislation which is presented to you for your consideration is the most important law in the history of the Indian people for at least a century. It means a turning point, a change in the direction of the current of Indian rights.

For fifty years the basic law, the law which dominated all Indian rights, was the allotment of 1887. Although Arizona tribes have not been very much affected by this act, it was the theory of the allotment law that if you could attach a piece of individually owned land to each member of a tribe instead of having them own their land in common one could thereby almost overnight turn the Indian into a white man, able and willing to compete with the white man and live the white man's life.

It was the belief of the men who framed the allotment act that through its workings the Indian reservations would be broken up; that the tribal life, the community life of the Indian tribes would be broken up and that through the individual ownership of property the Indian would, with the utmost speed become completely what we call civilized, and be absorbed into the white life of the Nation. That was the theory. But it did not work out that way. Here in the Southwest you do not know the full effect of this splitting up of the land into small pieces and of attaching ownership of each piece to an individual. You have not had that system in general here; but elsewhere, up among the Sioux, in Oklahoma, in Oregon, and in Washington, where this system has been working now for thirty or forty years, the principal effect has been to take the land away from the Indian and leave him landless and less able to compete with the white people.

Discussing the allotment system with the Assiniboines in Montana a month ago in their community house—it was six below zero and the community house was not heated, but there were a lot of them there. They were very much interested because the allotment act had been applied to them twenty-five years ago and they knew what it had done to them. One young Assiniboine of about thirty years of age, got up and said, "Some ten years ago I thought I was smart; I had an allotment of three hundred and twenty acres of land and I asked for a fee patent. I thought I was smart. I got my fee patent and turned around and sold it and with the purchase price I bought an automobile. And then I wrecked the automobile. And now I have nothing except the clothes in which I stand and what I have in my pockets—and I have nothing in my pockets but my hands." And that reminds me of Charles Davis, a Navajo whom we met a few months ago when we gave him a lift to a trader's store. We asked him about his family. He said he had three girls and two boys, and that both boys were grown up. We asked him what they were doing now. He said one lives over here and one over there, and then we said, "But what do they do?" And he said, "Not very much; you see, they both bought an automobile now and they are broke."

Through the working of the allotment act the land estate of the Indian as a whole has been constantly shrinking. Back in 1887 at the time this allotment act was adopted the Indian estate consisted of one hundred thirty-three million acres of land; in 1933 that shrunk to forty-seven million acres and it was still going down. Yet the main loss, practically the entire loss, of land had occurred in those regions where the allotment act was applied. In the regions and on the reservations where there was no allotment there was no loss of land. In fact, in several instances Indians who were not allotted have today more land than they had in 1887.

This legislation which is placed before you puts a stop to allotment. It ends that source of loss of land for the Indians. That source will be plugged up, and that is the principal reason, the basic feature of the bill before you. At the time when the allotment act was passed it was the idea that for just a little while the owners, the Indian owners of these individual pieces of property would need the protection of the Federal government against this loss, so in the beginning Congress provided a trust period of only five years. It was the idea that in five years the Indian who received a piece of land would learn how to handle it, how to protect himself and become a white business man. After five years the average Indian would be a good business man so that he could take care of himself and he would be able to pay taxes and become a member of the white community without any special privileges, but they found it didn't work. Five years wasn't enough so in many instances they extended the tax period to 25 years. It was found that the five-year period was not enough, no, not even a 25-year period was enough, so under this policy the Government's guardianship over the Indians was extended while at the same time the basis of their economic life, the thing from which they could make a living, was slipping out from underneath them; the land was going away very fast, and with the loss of the land the need for protection, for Federal guardianship was greater and greater.

Now what this legislation proposes to do is: first, to build a firm foundation on which all the Indian tribes can stand and continue to stand and make their own living, in other words it proposes to save the land, to enlarge the land holdings where necessary, to put this land in condition for the best possible use by the Indians themselves and to provide the necessary credit and capital so that as far as it is humanly possible every Indian tribe and every Indian individual who wants to remain on the land can become self-supporting.

You can be free only if you are self-supporting. Most of you who have had anything to do with bankers know that if you owe the banker money, you are no longer free. He tells you where to head in, he regulates your activities. It is the same way with the Government, just so long as the Secretary of the Interior will have to regulate your lives. It is only by becoming self-supporting that you will become free. You are not free now; the Secretary of the Interior, through the Commissioner, can regulate you until the cows come home. Under the law as it now is, it is illegal for you to organize a tribe or council. You can only select a delegate or organize a council if the Commissioner of Indian Affairs will kindly allow you to do it. But the present Secretary and the present Commissioner have no desire to rule your lives, so they propose to abolish all those old laws and make it possible for you to run your own affairs as fast as you demonstrate that you are capable of doing it.

These then are the main purposes of this legislation: on the one hand to save your land, to increase your land where needed, to put that land in condition so that you can make a living on it and to supply the credit and capital facilities with which to make a living on that land and become self-supporting. On the other hand it wants to extend to all Indian tribes the right of every American citizen to run his own affairs and in order to do that a system of transferring the government services which are now rendered by the Indian Bureau to the various tribes has been worked out in this bill so that those tribes which become self-supporting can at the same time become self-governing. There will now be more detailed explanations of the different parts of the bill by other members of the Washington staff.

MR. SHEPARD: My Friends: I am going to talk very briefly about the first bill—the title dealing with self-government.

The purpose of this title of the bill is to bring to an end the absolute power of the Indian Bureau over the lives and affairs of the Indians. This part of the bill is a rather peculiar type of legislation. It merely says that if any tribe wishes to have self-government, the Secretary of the Interior will grant it a charter of self-government; but if an Indian tribe does not wish to have self-government no effort will be made to force that tribe to accept it.

As Mr. Woehlke has just said, any power that you now have of self-government, such as electing a tribal council or sending delegates to this conference, is done by the permission of the Secretary of the Interior, who might if he wished refuse you that power. What we wish to do under this bill is give you definite, legal rights of self-government just as the members of the white community have definite legal rights of self-government. If a tribe wishes to have self-government, it will petition to the Secretary of the Interior, who is authorized by this bill to issue to that tribe a charter which will define the powers of government to that tribe. You have probably all read the first part of this bill and have probably found it long and complicated. The reason for that is this; we give in this section a list of all the powers that may be conferred on an Indian tribe, but that does not mean that all of those powers will necessarily be conferred on any one tribe. When an Indian tribe gets ready for self-government, the Secretary of the Interior will send out expert advisors who will help you to frame the kind of charter that you would like to have with the powers that you feel ready to undertake.

You might, for example, want to undertake the ordinary powers of a county, or of a village, such as appointing your police officers, appointing Indian judges, issuing your local laws and ordinances and enforcing those laws and ordinances. In that case a charter would be worked out which would define those kinds of powers. Or you might wish to have another kind of power, for instance the power of going into business like a white man's corporation. You might, for example, wish to go into the saw mill and lumbering business, you might wish to develop the cattle business among the individual members of your tribe, and so the charter would give you powers to carry on business as a legal group just as the white man's corporation is given power to do business.

I want to repeat and make it completely clear, first, that you do not have to accept a charter if you do not wish it. If you do not feel ready to undertake the powers of a charter, you do not have to accept a charter; second, that you do not need to take on any more power than you wish to. You can gradually build up your experience and then get more power instead of trying to undertake everything at one time.

There is another point that I want to make clear. This bill does not set up any particular form of self-government. That again it is going to leave to the Indian tribe to determine. As you know, among the Pueblo tribes of New Mexico there are very ancient forms of government which go back far beyond the time when the white man came to this country, and this bill would not in the least disturb those types of government. On the other hand, there are many Indian tribes who are living very close to white communities or inter-mingled with white communities who would like to have the white man's kind of government, and this bill would also permit that. So you see as far as the Indians are concerned this whole question of self-government is absolutely voluntary; if this bill passes it means that you will only have self-government if you want it.

I want now to come to a second important part of the self-government idea, and that is that in the future under this bill the powers now exercised by the Indian Service over the lives and property of the Indians will be on a different basis and that basis will be that of cooperation so that the Indian Service will become the cooperator and advisor of the organized, self-governing Indian tribes. We plan, for example, that the Indian communities, these organized communities that receive a charter, will become capable of gradually taking over the functions and services now performed by the Indian office and that your own young people will be trained to undertake that work and will be given jobs and will be paid by the Federal Government. That means, for example, that gradually Indians will be trained as teachers, farmers, foresters, range managers, administrators, police or as agricultural extension workers, and Indian girls will be trained as nurses, domestic science workers, teachers, office workers, and as you have qualified workers to take over these services, they will be transferred to your community. Congress will give you the right to hire these people and Congress will pay for it. You know that at the present time all these local jobs in the Indian Service are under the Federal civil service and that as a rule the Indian can't get those jobs. There are fewer Indians in the Indian Service today than there were twenty years ago. We believe that the Indian young people can be trained to do this work just as well as the white young people, but we do not want to force you to compete with all the millions of white people that want to get these jobs. We think that these jobs should be kept for the Indians because they are in your own community and they are for your own advancement.

Under this bill these jobs which are to be filled by Indians will not be under the civil service, but the Commissioner of Indian Affairs will lay down certain qualifications and requirements for these jobs and Indians who wish to get these jobs must meet these requirements. We feel it is necessary to help your young people to get the right kind of training so that they can carry on these services and therefore this bill provides an appropriation which will be loaned without interest to help the young people to get the right kind of training at our regular universities or in special schools. The government will pay half of the cost of the education and the student will pay back gradually the other half when he gets a job. If he doesn't get a job, he doesn't pay it back.

There is another provision in this bill which is designed to remove the absolute powers of the Indian Bureau over the Indians, and that is the provision which empowers an Indian community to require the transfer of an unsatisfactory Federal employee away from the community. That, of course, is a very broad power but it must be clearly understood that there are two sides to a question and that the white employee, the Federal employee, has got to have his rights safe-guarded just as much as the Indians have to have their rights safe-guarded in such a case. It doesn't mean, for example, that a regular legal procedure must be set up and a clear cut case made out against the efficiency or character of a Federal employee before he could be transferred.

I cannot go too much into detail, but there is one other highly important point that I want to mention that I know will appeal to every Indian here today, and that is if this bill passes, the Federal Government can no longer spend tribal funds without the consent of the tribe. Is that clear? That your tribal money in the future cannot be spent by Congress or by the Secretary of the Interior or by the Commissioner of Indian Affairs unless you agree to have him spend it. As you know during the past 30 years or more, hundreds of millions of dollars in tribal funds have been spent by the government without the consent of the Indians and much of that money has been used for the administration of the office of Indian Affairs.

Another important point is that in the future no federal appropriation spent for the benefit of the Indians or spent on the Indian reservation can become a reimbursable debt against that tribe without the consent of the tribe. In other words you are not going to have debts fastened on your shoulders unless you want to have them. Moreover, under this system of self-government in the future the Indian community that is chartered, is going to have a part in making the budget estimates for Congress. Before an estimate is sent to Congress for an appropriation to spend on your reservation, you are going to have a right to make your recommendations to your Congressman, to the Secretary of the Interior, to the Director of the Budget, and to the Congress so that the money can be spent more in accordance with your desires than it has been spent in the past.

I want to say just a word in closing. Don't be afraid of this self-government. It doesn't mean that the Federal government will take anything away from you; it doesn't mean that the Federal government is trying to get away from its responsibilities. The Federal government will do just as much as it ever has done in the past, it will do more than it ever has done in the past, and it will do it more intelligently because you will have a part in determining what is to de done.

You know you can't learn to swim without getting in the water and you can't learn self-government without beginning. The Indians have the choice of going on perpetually as they are now, dominated by a Federal bureau, or they have a chance to come in and take a part in running their own affairs in a way that is absolutely essential to their own progress. I want to end by saying something that Commissioner Collier has been emphasizing at many of the tribal councils we have been holding in various parts of the country, that this legislation that we have put up is a part of the "New Deal." This happens to be a time when it is possible to do big things, but we don't know how long that time is going to last. Therefore Commissioner Collier has urged the Indians in considering this legislation not to take the attitude that we may wait two years or ten years. This chance may not come again.

MR. MONAHAN: You have said, "must we have self-government, must we change our system under the provision of the bill?" You need not. You may go on exactly as you are. If a tribe desires to have self-government, 25 per cent or 25 out of every hundred adult Indians residing on any reservation shall ask for it in a petition for the issuance of a charter. Then the Federal government will help prepare the charter, or constitution or by-laws, but before the Secretary of the Interior is authorized to put this into operation, three-fifths of the adult Indians on that reservation must vote for it; so that on 25 per cent of them sending in a petition it can be prepared, but unless on a vote three-fifths of the adult Indians vote that they want it, it cannot be put into operation.

I want to correct a mis-statement that Mr. Shepard made unintentionally. He stated that there were fewer Indians in the Federal employ now than twenty years ago. He meant to say proportionately, as there are very many more in the Federal employ today than twenty years ago. I want now to ask Mr. Stewart, chief of the land division in the Washington office, to speak—the division that has to do with buying land or selling land or anything to do with land and with much of the business of having to do with the disposal of the resources of the land, such as coal, oil, and other things produced on the land.

MR. STEWART: Mr. Chairman, assembled Indians, and white friends: I shall try and be as brief as possible because our reactions to these other Indian councils have been that they got more out of asking us questions if we gave them a general outline as to what it was all about. First of all I don't believe all of you know what we mean by an allotment. By an allotment of land, stripping it of all technical description, it merely means this, that at one time or another various Indian tribes had very large, solidly blocked out areas of land all their own. Then certain laws were prepared by which and under which little pieces within this large reservation area were carved out, surveyed and listed in some one Indian's name for which he was given a piece of paper saying that the Government would hold that for him—the land in the paper—for twenty-five years free of taxation. After that twenty-five year period, which we call the trust period, had expired, a fee patent or complete title could be had by the Indian under the existing law, or cast upon an Indian, and thereafter the individual Indian would have to pay taxes upon that individual allotment.

The Apaches, Hualapais, and others have never been visited with this allotment system, but the Pimas, Yumas, and Colorado River Indians have. The fact that those reservations mentioned have not been visited with this allotment system is no reason to assume that under the existing law they cannot or may not be visited with that system. We can, under the existing law, allot tribal lands of any reservation. Under the existing law the allottees of the various reservations, Pimas, Colorado River, and so on, can sell those allotments to white people and thus bring in white people within the reservation as has already happened up in the Sioux country where the lands are almost all under white ownership. The Sioux Indians now have the very poorest land that was within the reservation.

What I am trying to drive at is this: because of this allotment law, the Indians of the country have lost ninety-one million acres of land. How have they lost it? I will trace down a little of the history of it. In 1887 an act was passed called the general allotment act. Under the terms of that act, the Secretary of the Interior can always continue to allot the surplus land of any reservation. Once those allotments were made out of the tribal lands, then the white people of the northern states got behind a political movement to have what was unallotted, what remained after these allotments had been made, opened to homestead entry and settlement by the white people, the Indian people of the reservation to get the net proceeds of the sale of those lands to the white entrymen. In that manner the Indians, particularly of the northern part of the country, have lost approximately ninety-one million acres of lands which would never have been opened had they not been given allotments. That was the foundation upon which their surplus allotment was based. That can happen to any reservation here in Arizona under the existing law. Now this legislation, title three of this bill, will guarantee that there will be no more allotments made on any reservation; that the trust period on any allotments heretofore made will be continued indefinitely; that there shall be no more sales of Indian lands.

Now the situation is not as acute in this part of the country as it is in the Northern States, so that instead of going into technical details as we had to up there, I am just going to give you an idea of what this bill will do for you and be as brief as possible. It will keep your lands in tribal ownership, that is, the tribal land that is still left, it will keep your allotment under restriction and untaxable indefinitely, and it will prevent any further sales of allotted lands to white people or to Indians unless it is necessary in connection with a chartered community. So in order that the rest of the bill may be explained to you with as much time as possible left to you to ask questions of us, I am going to stop now and be on hand the rest of the day and tomorrow to answer your questions.

MR. MONAHAN: (*introducing Mr. Siegel*) Mr. Siegel is from the solicitor's office of the Department of the Interior, which is the office that handles all the legal work for the Department of the Interior.

MR. SIEGEL: The reason for establishing a special Indian court and providing for appointment of special attorneys is very simple. The Indians have not had their fair day in court. Nor have they been given a very fair representation by the district attorney. We feel that for the most part the district attorneys have refused to be bothered by the majority of Indian cases and that therefore it is necessary to employ special counsel in order that the Indians would have adequate representation.

The same is true with regard to the court. We feel that the Federal district courts have often been unwilling to consider the kind of Indian case that is frequently presented to them. Many of them are small, petty matters which the Federal court does not handle and it is therefore desirable to get a Federal court that has all of its time to devote to Indian matters.

I want to make a few general remarks with regard to the entire bill. I have heard this bill described as a "back to the blanket movement." Some people say that it is "socialism." Well, this bill is not a back to the blanket movement and it is not socialistic. We want to put an end to the allotment system of which the evil effects have not been felt here. We want to prevent the further loss of Indian lands, that is one reason. We want to put an end to the allotment system because through the heirship problem it has broken up the land into such small pieces nobody can use them. The allotment system was honestly intended to give the Indian a chance to improve his own economic system. We approve of that idea, but we want to put the land into such a condition and to provide such credit opportunity for such organization that the Indian will be given an opportunity to improve his own economic condition.

No Indian will be compelled to stay at an Indian reservation if he doesn't want to. We are not going to build a wall around the reservation and close the Indians inside. The educational features of this bill will undoubtedly aid many Indians to compete in the white world as they never had an opportunity to compete before. This bill continues the present policy of attempting to train the Indian to live in a new and changed environment. Any Indian who is so trained so that he may leave the reservation and live in the outside world may do so and may be compensated therefore.

There are some very important questions relating to the heirship settlement of the land system about which we would like to speak later. There are so few reservations which are affected by the problem that probably we had better discuss it with them in small groups or in response to their own questions. We wanted to get through with our general program remarks as quickly as possible as this meeting was not arranged so that we could talk to you, it may be news to you, but this meeting was arranged so that you would have an opportunity to question us. I think that if you will lend us a hand and your aid we can learn something with the cooperation of the Indian. We have not come here to praise this bill, but we do not want to bury it either—we would genuinely appreciate it if you would make suggestions as to how this bill could be improved to gain its object. We would also be interested to know if you think its objects are ill-conceived. This is the opportunity for the Indians to get the legislation that they want if they want any. I don't have to tell you that you at least have a friend in the office of Commissioner of Indian Affairs. He has sent us here to present our idea of what should be done and if you do not approve you tell us what you do want. Already in some of the conferences that have been held we have been given valuable suggestions wherein this bill can be improved, and I want to repeat that this is your chance to tell us wherein this bill can be improved or whether you think this bill should be adopted at all. I am going to stop talking so that you can make up your minds about that question.

Afternoon Session

MR. SIEGEL: We have quite a collection of questions and I think some of you have some questions that you have not passed in so we will ask Mr. Hall to go around and bring them in.

QUESTION BY F. BONAVENTURE: The Papago country is an aggregation of independent ranching or farming communities, living within definite boundaries. There is no union between the villages, so close as to make one tribe, that could be ruled as one community.

Could one of these Papago communities organize and form its own charter, based on the laws which governed that community before the forming of the reservation in 1917, without the other communities organizing? Could such a community have a charter which would give the local place self-government, with its own court and police force and at the same time have the agency continue to care for Federal improvements such as deep wells?

ANSWER BY MR. SIEGEL: This bill uses the term communities very carefully as distinguished from the present reservation so that if within the reservation parts want to become chartered as a unit they may do so. The parts of the Papago reservation that would want to have a charter and become separate communities could do so. (I think that answers the second question also.) Yes, the community may have a charter which would permit it to have self-government.

QUESTION: Will the Federal government continue to operate the schools or will it turn them over to the communities?

ANSWER: At the present it is the intention of the Federal government to operate the schools, but with the active aid and leadership of the Indian community.

QUESTION: Will the communities be under the county, or state or under Federal jurisdiction?

ANSWER: They will be under the Federal jurisdiction—not under county or state.

QUESTION: An Indian charter is revocable, without the consent of the Indians. The Federal Court of Indian Affairs should make it a duty to hear pleadings and pass judgment on whether a charter should be revoked or not. Indians should be given a voice at such hearing.

ANSWER: I suppose you mean that Congress could revoke a charter; the Secretary of the Interior would not have authority to revoke a charter. There is no valid reason why the Federal court of Indian Affairs should not judge whether they have lived up to their charter or not.

QUESTION: Why should the Secretary of the Interior have the sole power to determine what lands are not needed by the Indians, and such lands to be reopened to sale, entry settlement, etc. Powers should be granted Indians to consent to such.

ANSWER: I agree with you. I think that perhaps the bill should be modified so that the leasing and reopening of lands should be done with authority of the chartered community.

QUESTION: Why is the leasing or permitting the use of the Indian lands vested solely with the Secretary of the Interior? The bill should grant the Indians powers to consent or otherwise determine when such actions are necessary.

ANSWER: I agree that the Indians should have more to say on this point.

QUESTION: Will this bill's acceptance cancel any old claims tribes may have against the government or against other tribes? Will it cancel claims of the government against any tribes?

ANSWER: It is not our intention that any treaty rights should be cancelled by this act nor should any claims against the United States be lost by this act, and in order to make this perfectly clear we are going to amend the bill so that all treaty rights would be respected.

QUESTION: Does this bill cancel previous treaties between the government and tribes?

ANSWER: No, it is not our intention that any treaty rights should be cancelled by this act.

QUESTION: Under this bill will it be possible for a tribe or Indian community which so desires to have a charter of self-government on any other than a communistic basis; for instance, suppose the Pimas should want to maintain a form of individual ownership of land under certain community regulations as to sale, inheritance, subdivision, etc. Could they be granted a charter under this bill providing for such restricted individual ownership. In other words is the communistic land basis an unavoidable part of a self-government charter?

ANSWER: With regard to the Pimas' lands, farm lands, the answer is that this bill will perpetuate individual ownership in any real sense. The only evil we are trying to get at on any Pima reservation is the inheritance question of scattered small pieces of land that no one can use. The only object of the land bill with regard to farm lands is to consolidate those small pieces into units which are large enough to support a person and that land will continue to be inheritable as before, but cannot be subdivided into uneconomical units.

QUESTION: Will there be an effort made to force Indians to organize a community and get a charter? What about the provisions of the bill where it provides that there shall be no valid will made, no allotments, and what will happen to the allotted lands at the end of the trust period?

ANSWER: Any land which any individual owns now he may keep unless he wishes voluntarily to transfer it.

QUESTION: Is the bill in question final or is it subject to amendments? Is it subject to amendments after Mr. Collier is through conferring with the Indians throughout the country?

ANSWER: The purpose of this meeting and the other meetings was not merely to explain the bill but to get suggestions from Indians as to what amendments should be made and if we can agree we will suggest such amendments as we have so that Congress can change it, but it will not be changed unless there is something seriously wrong and the Indians would want the bill changed.

QUESTION: Why is the water rights or guarantee of any water rights not mentioned in the bill? Agricultural land is valueless without water.

ANSWER: I suppose that you are right. A question like that merely reveals the misfortune of having somebody in Washington who doesn't know as much as he should to draft the bill. I would have appreciated it if you people out here could have been in Washington to help us. We had no intention of taking away the water rights now attached to the land which you are using. We will put something in the bill to take care of such rights.

QUESTION: In the development of surplus lands as irrigable lands, how can the government provide for the obtaining of the water rights to these lands?

ANSWER: I think you will purchase them just as you have to purchase lands. We are authorized to spend two million dollars a year to purchase lands. I will make it clear now that that includes the purchase of water rights.

QUESTION: In the light of what is now being said and done in this meeting, if someone should see fit to attack this as violating a rule of Indian Affairs, would not this hold the bill if passed to be null and void?

ANSWER: I think we made the statement that through the graciousness of someone in Washington we are permitted to gather here today, that you have no right to organize without the consent of the Secretary and that this meeting is here held with the consent of the Secretary.

MISS ROSS: I think I understand what the difficulty is. May I explain please. Whether this bill is passed or not, or if it is passed, will the procedure of the Indian Office have precedence in Indian affairs? Will the bill be constitutional?

ANSWER: If this bill is passed there is no doubt as to its constitutionality.

QUESTION: In the election of community leaders, who will pay the salary, the community or the Federal government?

ANSWER: Here you have to distinguish between two kinds of positions. Many jobs which the community takes over which are now being performed by the Federal government will continue to be paid by the Federal government—jobs which Congress will continue to appropriate for. In regard to the other jobs which the community establishes for themselves I do not think that Congress will appropriate for those jobs. However, there is a five hundred thousand dollars appropriation in this bill to get the communities started, and as to any other officials the community elects the answer would be that the community would have to support them themselves unless Congress makes an appropriation for that purpose. Any function that the Federal government is now performing, the Federal government would of course continue to perform so long as Congress made the necessary appropriations.

QUESTION: How long is this good news going to continue. Is there a period of this aid from our government?

ANSWER: The answer is that we cannot bind the future Congresses, that is very true. But we can't bind the Congress right now, even if this bill is not passed, and nothing we can do will prevent Congress from appropriating nothing at all if it wishes not to appropriate. If we get a declaration from Congress declaring that it desires such policy and desires to promote self-government by Indians, I think that we can reasonably be sure that those appropriations will be continued. I would suggest that there is more hope for the Federal government continuing them under this law than under the old law, and for this reason, it was the old idea, and that was the mistake on which the allotment system rested, that after a brief period of time the Indian could be turned loose; that has been proven wrong and that in any Indian community it will be impossible for them—at least at the start—to make enough money to support all divisions of their government by themselves. We have recognized the necessity of continuing the Federal guardianship much longer than was ordered under the allotment act. If you want this aid to continue longer, I think the best thing for you to do is to organize and make your wishes and feelings known.

QUESTION: We would like to know if we hold positions as government employees, would we have the same privileges as the Federal employees have as to drawing pensions after thirty years in the service?

ANSWER: Plainly, yes.

QUESTION: Will any individual leaving the reservation or community to live among the white race and should fail in his or her efforts, will he or she return to his or her people and enjoy the same privileges as before his or her leaving the reservation or community?

ANSWER: There is nothing in this bill to prevent you from leaving the Indian community and going out in the white world. There is nothing in this bill which deprives you of any citizenship rights or anything that you might have had before; on the contrary, it will give you more rights than you have ever had. Of course, that will depend upon what the community says. If no community is organized the existing law would persist. Under this bill, the chartered community can be given the power to determine membership and terms of readmittance to membership.

QUESTION: I have one hundred acres of inheritance land in Oklahoma. Would I have to sacrifice it to benefit those who have sold theirs and blown the money?

ANSWER: No.

QUESTION: The Papago communities have their own old laws regarding inheritances and heirs. Would the bill abrogate these?

ANSWER: I do not think that the bill would have anything to do with that, even if it were an allotted reservation over which the Secretary of the Interior now has some jurisdiction. The charter could be given authority to take care of matters of this kind.

QUESTION: How much government would an Indian have in regarding laws regulating business matters?

ANSWER: Section 4 of Title I allows the Secretary to give a community authority to regulate business matters, or to regulate commerce between the whites and Indians. There is a provision in the bill that the Secretary cannot compel the Indians to take a charter if they do not want one. If you don't like the conditions, you can protest to Congress. If you think that the bill in that respect gives the Secretary too much power, you can make suggestions as to how that power might be curbed. But I would like to mention this, that the bill must be sufficiently flexible so that it may vary from reservation to reservation. The desert lands all differ and there must be sufficient power in the bill to allow us to draw charters which will meet the needs of different reservations.

QUESTION: Mr. Stewart stated that a trust period could be made to expire any time. In other words the Government could refuse to renew or extend the trust period.

ANSWER: As I have said before, the Secretary under existing law can force the issuance of a fee patent, but under the new bill this power would be revoked.

Mr. Santeo passed in something that I will read to you. "Your talk sounds all right, but what is all in the bill? I am sure it is not all what you have said this morning. It will take months before we can thoroughly understand the bill. So give us time because many of our people do not know a thing about this bill. Furthermore, this country was ours and when the Spaniards came here in the early days they claimed part of our country and our people and made a treaty with us and gave us grants. We want you to show our grants if any before we can talk on self-government and land ownership, etc."

ANSWER: You are speaking of the old Mexican grants. There is no conflict. This bill isn't going to pass tomorrow or the next day. It will be some time before the bill goes through Congress and you will have time to read it and discuss it. We don't want you to be hasty in your action, but be assured that nothing in this bill will hurt you. The white cattlemen don't want to let it get through. They are afraid of this bill because they are afraid the special privileges that have been given them will be lost and that you would have as many rights as they have.

MISS ROSS: I think that there is one thing that will help to answer that question. Does this bill give the Indians, every Indian, the right to hire his own attorney? Some attorneys who would have given good service have been turned down and some who have been in there are not so good. It has been almost impossible to get good representation. I believe that the Indians should back this bill, even if they object to every part of it, if it gives them the right to have their own attorneys; and their day in court.

MR. SIEGEL: Although not a part of this bill, Mr. Margold drafted, some time ago, a court of claims bill which would expedite the hearing of the Indian claims. Now if you had to wait to have the Federal court of claims, you would have to wait a long time. Along these lines, Mr. Santeo, we expect to recommend this bill for a special Indian court of claims which will consider all these cases of Indian claims so that even it may be included in your charter.

QUESTION: Suppose we were to throw our allotments back into the pot, how about the improvements we have placed thereon?

ANSWER: I have already indicated to you that under the plans stated you get as much back as you put in, furthermore you keep all improvements.

QUESTION: Whether a group of Indians that are ready to adopt self-government and charter will not be held back by the illiterate Indians who are not ready to progress?

ANSWER: The act authorizes us to divide reservations into communities and to give a charter to any group which wants to form a community, and to withhold it from those who do not.

QUESTION: What will be the outcome of Indians not taking or adopting the so called "New Deal" self-government?

ANSWER: I don't know. The way they are going now they will probably be extinguished. There are many indications from the other parts of the country to this effect. In the future they will lose all their lands and will gradually lose everything.

QUESTION: If the Indians are allowed to vote, will they be required to pay taxes?

ANSWER: I would say that there is nothing in the law that would require you to pay taxes if you got the right to vote.

QUESTION: Is there some way that you can invent some system whereby we could get in Fort Apache our copies of what goes on more quickly? We wonder if you can't manage to get us literature more quickly.

MR. SIEGEL: When did you get your first copy of this bill?

ANSWER: About a week ago.

MR. SIEGEL: We will try to see you get your literature as quickly as possible.

SAN CARLOS delegation asked the following questions:

San Carlos Apache individual cattle amount to a value of $750,000. If this amount comes back community ownership, who is going to pay for the cattle, how much and when?

ANSWER: This bill applies only to land and not to cattle. You retain your cattle.

QUESTION: If any Indian leaves the reservation, does he lose his share in the community property? Can he be reinstated and who is going to pay for his share in the community property if he loses and how much?

ANSWER: That would depend entirely upon the community rule. The community could buy his land if he so desired or if that was in the community charter.

QUESTION: If an Indian is one-fourth blood how much share has he in the community property? Has he as much share as a full blood?

ANSWER: If he is a member of the community and is one-fourth blood, he has as large a share in the community property as a full blood.

QUESTION: How will the community cattle be divided into shares of the Indian? In other words if one man has twenty, one man fifty, and one man none, we want to know?

ANSWER: We are not going to turn cattle into the community at all, only land. Tribal herds will be tribal property just as they are now.

QUESTION: How can the community force the Indian to do the community cattle work?

ANSWER: Well, the community could be given authority to levy an assessment on an individual member if he doesn't want to work.

QUESTION: Why is it that some of the people vote and some of them cannot vote, why is that?

ANSWER: In the state of Arizona, an Indian that is living off the reservation can vote.

QUESTION, JAMES STEVENS: It says in this bill that a chartered community can sue. What can they sue for?

ANSWER: Heretofore no Indian tribe could bring suit or be sued without the consent of the United States. However, the Indian community is fully protected because it is provided that Indian property cannot be taken away by legal process even though the community is subject to suit.

QUESTION: Can they sue an Indian for libel?

ANSWER: I don't see why not. There is no reason why you couldn't sue him.

QUESTION: We have a dam on our reservation, what we call the Coolidge Dam. Suppose we have a big rain and it breaks and goes all over Casa Grande Valley, could they sue us?

ANSWER: Probably not.

CHARLES PETTUS, JR., Ft. Apache, Arizona: In case of suit, if they were organized, could the land be sold to answer to the judgement of this suit?

ANSWER: No.

QUESTION: Could their property be attached?

ANSWER: No.

QUESTION: How could these suits be paid then?

ANSWER: At present there is no way of satisfying judgment against an Indian or Indian tribe which has nothing but restricted property. Suit would be worthless.

MR. STEWART: Not quite. If an Indian is sued, sometimes thereafter acts of Congress give the Secretary of the Interior the right to remove the restrictions in order to satisfy such claims. Congress could do that.

JAMES STEVENS: I have money in the bank, that bank went broke, what redress have the Indians against that bank? He is a ward of the government, he puts his money in there innocently, and the bank went broke?

ANSWER: No redress. No more than anybody else. Did he put the money in there individually or did his superintendent put it in there for him?

MR. STEVENS: Individually.

ANSWER: If those had been restricted funds, and the superintendent had deposited them on your behalf, and if the bank went broke, it wouldn't have bothered. You would have a preference, and the deposit would have been covered by bonds.

MR. H. O. DAVIDSON: If the bill passed, would the federal employees known to us as the Indian Bureau still remain on the job?

MR. SIEGEL: We hope that the Indians will be trained to take the places of the men in the Federal Bureau.

QUESTION: It is provided in the bill that any community can dispose of any employee in this office, can compel their transfer to another reservation. They can't fire them because they are so organized?

MR. SIEGEL: No, but because he may be very efficient and yet be very unfit to you. He would be transferred somewhere else, or if the charges are serious enough he would be fired completely.

DIRK LAY: In regard to the San Carlos Irrigation project, what effect will the bill have on that? Some of us say that the Pimas have the first right to the water, but we have heard rumors of a ruling that we do not have the first right. Will this bill have any effect?

MR. SIEGEL: I don't think this bill will affect that.

H. O. DAVIDSON: I wish you would make it plainer as to the transfer of the white employees.

MR. SIEGEL: I think it should be made plain that the employees as stated this morning are going to be given a very fair opportunity to demonstrate their efficiency and would be given a fair opportunity to be heard before being transferred anywhere else.

MR. JUAN KISTO: Does an Indian trader have to pay taxes to the state?

MR. MONAHAN: This bill would not subject him to taxes.

MR. TRUMAN JONES: Was there an amendment to Title I, Section 13, whereby a system of financial credit was proposed?

MR. MONAHAN: It ought to be stated right now that this bill will be amended. The credit amendment has already been made. Congress would authorize the appropriation of ten million dollars to be loaned on long payment terms to the Indians and which loans would be non–interest bearing. Those loans will be made for any purpose involving the economic improvement of individual or tribal lands and property, such as cattle, etc. We not only ought to change the land system but we also ought to provide the credit so that the Indians will be able to use their land. That fund will be a revolving fund so that the amount that is loaned out can be used again as soon as it is repaid.

MR. H. O. DAVIDSON: Suppose we borrow money. The Secretary of the Interior has looked our land over and we organize. We fix papers and everything that allow us so much money out of that revolving fund, then we lose, don't operate right. Will that money be charged to us?

MR. MONAHAN: Not until you can pay it.

QUESTION: If an Indian is a citizen can he go off of the reservation and locate a mine and locate it as a citizen?

ANSWER: Yes.

MR. MONAHAN: Are there any more questions that you would like to ask? It is getting late and I have some meetings with some of you after this meeting and if you do not have any more questions to ask this afternoon, I suggest that we adjourn and meet tomorrow morning.

It was regularly moved and seconded that the meeting adjourn until 9 o'clock A.M. *March 16, 1934.*

March 16, 1934, Morning Session

Meeting called to order at 9:26 and the business of the day proceeded.

Mr. Monahan called the meeting to order and Mr. Stewart explained chart showing what is happening to lands in allotted reservations in north. After this was done Mr. Monahan told the assembled Indians that they were ready for questions.

QUESTION: What effect if any would this bill have on an Indian who has his patent and is paying taxes on his land?

MR. MONAHAN: It wouldn't have any more effect on it than it would on a lot that I hold in Washington, D.C. If an Indian holds that land and pays taxes on it, it can't be affected by the Wheeler-Howard Bill.

QUESTION: Would his land ever go back to the tribal tracts?

MR. MONAHAN: Absolutely not, unless the tribe bought it and paid for it. That land is no different from any other land. It is owned by him and can't be touched except by purchase or by voluntary sale.

MR. JAMES STEVENS: Can an Indian own a store on an Indian reservation without a trader's license?

MR. MONAHAN: I don't know of any reason why not. All traders' licenses, as I understand it, are to take care of white persons desiring to have a store on an Indian reservation.

MR. STEVENS: What I want to know is what degree of blood he would have to have to run a store?

MR. MONAHAN: Any blood at all.

MR. STEVENS: Suppose he was one-quarter blood?

MR. MONAHAN: It doesn't make any difference.

MR. STEVENS: Can a superintendent of a reservation administer an oath for a person if something comes up?

ANSWER: If he is notary public.

QUESTION: Would he have to be a notary public? Wouldn't being superintendent take care of that and give him a right?

MR. KNEALE: Yes, on all official papers. On anything pertaining to the Department of the Interior, or Federal government. On other matters, no, unless he is a notary public.

QUESTION: Suppose a question arises on a reservation and in swearing this person in it is found out that he swore to a lie. What can you do to him? Can you try him for perjury? Can he be tried by the Indian court or tried outside?

ANSWER: It all depends what he swore to. If it were Indian matters, it would probably be an Indian court matter; if something outside, he probably would be tried outside.

QUESTION: Would he be subject to a perjury charge if it concerned a white community?

ANSWER: Certainly.

MR. H. O. DAVIDSON, delegate from the Mohave reservation: I believe that you have brought that picture (referring to the chart showing the loss of lands up north) along so that the assembly here might see for themselves what the allotment act has done for the Indians up north. I believe that the picture there can be stronger if 1492 is put up there and the Indians owning the whole land.

MR. DANIEL (Indian delegate): Mr. Chairman: Under the title of education we have all heard the explanation of that, but I just want a little more explanation regarding paragraph (a) under Title II, Special Education for Indians. I shall read it:

> (a) The Commissioner shall extend financial aid and assistance on the basis of financial need to qualified Indians for the payment of tuition and other costs of education, including necessary costs of support. One-half of the amount so expended shall be a non-interest-bearing, reimbursable loan to be repaid in installments whenever the beneficiary shall have received employment anywhere, but the obligation shall be temporarily suspended during any period of unemployment.

Now further on it says that notwithstanding the provisions of this section the Commissioner may grant scholarships to any qualified Indian of special promise, no part of which shall be reimbursable. I would like to be enlightened as to why the first part should be required to pay-back with interest and this other part is gratuitous.

MR. WOEHLKE: If you look you will see that there are two appropriations, one fifty thousand dollars a year in paragraph (a) and the other of fifteen thousand a year in paragraph (b). If you will refer back to Section I, it says, "and he may provide for the training and education of Indian students in universities, colleges, schools of medicine, law, engineering, or agriculture, or other institutions of recognized standing and may subsidize such training and education under the following conditions." This fifty thousand dollars, part of which is reimbursable, is to be applied to the large number of students who may wish to qualify for the minor positions; then the additional grant of fifteen thousand dollars is for scholarships for those students who have unusual ability to go on to universities and colleges and qualify for complete technical or other training, and for these especially gifted ones these scholarships may be granted on a non-reimbursable basis.

MR. PETTUS, JR.: Would that give these Indians the right to go to law schools and still hold their Indian rights, the right to take up tribal matters?

MR. WOEHLKE: Certainly, if the bill is adopted and appropriations are made and the regulations under which these scholarships are granted are made out, you will find that they will cover that particular field as well as any other training. The whole purpose of this bill is not to defeat any tribal rights of anyone possessing them under any circumstances.

MR. PETTUS, JR.: It has been my experience here in the Southwest—and I have been to many reservations—that we have people qualified for every branch of training except law, and I find that the different departments have in the past neglected this very important piece of training. We have no lawyers to protect our own interests or we would be very much better represented.

MR. MADISON handed in the following suggestions: You stated yesterday that there is need for haste in the enactment of this bill (Wheeler-Howard Bill) because of the present favorable attitude of Congress which might not long continue. Also that no community or tribe of Indians need come under the law until they are ready. But this Bill when enacted should be in such a form that when the Indians do wish to function under it, it will be satisfactory and pertinent to their needs. Hence I am offering a few suggestions that will help to this end.

MR. WOEHLKE: Now before I read any further I am going to say, that the favorable attitude of Congress might continue, but Congress may not continue very long. I think Mr. Stewart made the statement to you that Congress is going to try to get through by the 15th of May and go home. Whenever they adjourn to go home unless they come back in an extra session later in the year, this Congress will be through. We elect a new Congress in November to take office in January, and we would like to have this Congress who are now considering it to act on it. Now I will read the suggestions for amendments to the bill by Mr. Madison:

Senate Bill 2755, page 3, line 13 after the words "adult Indians" strike out the word "residing" and insert "holding membership." Page 10, line 21, beginning at the words "provided however" strike out "the powers given the Commissioner of Indian Affairs" and insert therefor "the right of the employee concerned to have a hearing or trial before the Court of Indian Affairs of the community where he is employed."

Page 26, lines 12–18. Strike out entirely. Page 47, lines beginning Sec. 23. "The Indian Tribe or community should have the sole rights to choose their attorney to represent them before the Court of Indian Affairs, Court of Claims, and the Supreme Court of the United States and in all Government Bureaus."

MR. WOEHLKE: These are very good suggestions and we will hand them to Mr. Siegel to be considered in the rewriting of the bill.

QUESTION: What the Pimas are talking about among themselves is how this proposed bill will affect these four things:
1. Subsurface rights, minerals, etc.?

MR. STEWART: All existing rights will be unaffected by this bill.

2. Water and irrigation rights?

MR. STEWART: Water and irrigation rights will not be affected.

3. Personal property?

MR. STEWART: Personal property will be unaffected by this bill.

4. The provision which gives the Secretary of the Interior the right to determine surplus lands and to dispose of them as he pleases.

ANSWER: That surplus land angle is not particularly applicable in this part of the country. That means that the bill provides that there will be no further disposal of surplus lands, that they will be returned to the tribe.

MR. KNEALE: I heard a gentleman say this morning that he was not particularly interested in the bill inasmuch as his reservation had not been allotted. I want to ask you this question: Under the existing law is there anything to prevent the Washington authorities from allotting the San Carlos reservation tomorrow, if they saw fit so to do?

MR. STEWART: As I understand it, there is nothing to prevent us from going in and allotting the San Carlos reservation tomorrow.

MR. MADISON: I was a party to lobbying at the time of the act of June 2, 1924 giving full citizen rights to the Indians. At that time I held an office as secretary and it was my business to find the Indians who were interested in citizens rights and we went into the matter quite thoroughly. The Indian office had eight or ten provisions in that bill on what would happen if the Indians were given full citizenship rights. We asked this question of the Committee at that time, whether this would give us a day in court, and they said "Yes, you can't get anything stronger than that and it is up to the Indians to enforce this Act." Now I don't believe that it is possible to force any tribe to accept patent fees without giving them their day in court. I don't believe that you can allot any reservation today without going to court to take care of it. I want to say this, that under that act we are protected by the constitution of the United States just like these Indians were prior to the Gadsden Purchase. They came here and afterwards became wards of the government; then they had no rights to say anything, they had no citizenship rights, and if we haven't anything to say in the court, well then, we ought to enact such a law or sponsor such a bill that will do that. I don't understand why this bill should be hastened to be put through at this session. We are told that maybe in May the Congress will adjourn. Well, you have another session to which you may take this bill for enactment.

MR. MONAHAN: This question about the allotment, whether they have authority or not, I want Mr. Stewart to say another word to you on that subject.

MR. STEWART: You are mistaken when you think that we cannot allot this reservation. The general allotment act of 1887 gives the Secretary of the Interior the right to allot the land of tribal reservations when he thinks it is best for the Indians. You have no right to stop him when he thinks it is best. This bill takes that right away from him.

MR. MADISON: Then as I take it, the citizenship bill of 1924 does not affect us in the way the white man has his citizenship. He is protected by the laws of the United States. Don't this law passed in 1924 apply to the white man's citizenship law?

ANSWER: It does not exceed the power of the Secretary as guardian over ward—no.

MR. JAMES STEVENS: In other words, the citizenship law that we have is only a name.

ANSWER: Just about.

QUESTION: If this bill went through, would we become full fledged citizens?

MR. STEWART: Probably when you pay taxes on your lands.

MR. MADISON, Chippewa Indian from Minnesota: When the law was enacted in 1924, it provided that it shall not affect tribal or other property. What does that mean?

MR. MONAHAN: Have you got that act of 1924 with you? I am not familiar with it.

(Dr. Skinner went to get a copy of the act from files of the Indian School Office.)

MR. MADISON: A lot of Indians haven't voted because they think they will be taxed. Right here is a chance where we ought to get some help in the interpretation of that act.

MR. MONAHAN: I can state very definitely that allotments can be made and have been made until very recently. Mr. Collier is absolutely against them and if this act is passed no more allotments will be made.

MR. PETTUS, JR.: You made the statement that allotments have been made without the Indians' consent. My superintendent informed me that they never have been made without the Indians' consent.

MR. MONAHAN: Who is your superintendent?

MR. PETTUS, JR.: Mr. Donner.

MR. MONAHAN: Mr. Donner, would you tell us what you meant by the statement?

MR. DONNER: I don't know where they have not had Indian consent before making an allotment, at least before they allotted a reservation.

MR. STEWART: You are right, Mr. Donner, but that consent, as you and I well know, doesn't amount to much. The point that I am bringing out is that when the local politicians wanted reservation lands allotted, they saw to it that the Indian delegation came into Washington previously hand-picked for allotments.

MR. DONNER: I would like to know if this bill directly and thoroughly excludes these people who are responsible for the hand-picking.

MR. STEWART: It prevents further allotment, so that naturally prevents any activity at all along those lines.

F. BONAVENTURE: I know that allotments were attempted in 1909 against the protests of nearly every Papago Indian living on the reservation. We know that allotments have been attempted against the consent of the Indians.

MR. PETTUS, JR.: Would it be possible for this bill to include qualifications of members of all Indian delegations through giving their organized bodies power to exclude illiterate and more backward Indians so that we could get good representation?

MR. STEWART: That is a matter that could be handled in the charter that would be given to your community. The community can suggest their qualifications.

MR. WOEHLKE: It would all depend on the character of the individual case. We would have to guard very carefully against discrimination. If you attempt to exclude anyone from the general franchise that charter would never be accepted because it is specifically stated that there must be protection for the minority. On the other hand, you could well state in your charter the qualifications which would have to be met by those who are running for the tribal councils or to act on any delegations, and in those qualifications you could very well demand moral character, clean records, and various other things so that on your delegations and your tribal councils you would have men and perhaps women of high character, of intelligence and wisdom, but I doubt whether the ability to read and write would be as important in those offices as the character of the person. All too frequently the people who do not read and write have greater wisdom and more common sense than those who are skilled in the different arts, and you certainly would not want to exclude wisdom and experience even if it were illiterate, but this you can put into your charter defining qualifications for the various offices.

MR. JAMES STEVENS: Can a group of Indians on a reservation get together, hold secret meetings with an outsider, make a formal treaty, and then go off the reservation and make that agreement binding on the rest of the tribe that are not aware of it?

MR. MONAHAN: That can't bind the rest of the tribe.

MR. STEVENS: In holding elections, suppose a bunch of them gets on a spree, gets drunk, would they be allowed to vote under the conditions thereof?

MR. WOEHLKE: There was a bunch of doctors held a meeting recently and said it wasn't possible to tell whether a man was drunk or not—how are you going to tell?

MR. STEVENS: If he wobbles.

MR. WOEHLKE: You might set up your charter with a provision defining drunkness by its outward visibility—by the unsteady gait. Define what drunkness is in your charter and then provide that anyone who shows those symptoms shall not be allowed to cast his vote but shall be cast into jail.

MR. SANTEO: On page 6 lines 11, 12, and 13, if you will read it, it says: "To elect or appoint officers, agents and employees, to define the qualifications for office, to fix the salaries of officials to be paid by the community, to—

Does that mean that the Indians have to pay the salaries for these officials or will the government pay the salaries?

MR. WOEHLKE: The community will pay the salaries of those who are its own officials. As you know for instance, the Pueblos already have a form of self-government in which they elect their own officials and those officials do not hold positions that are considered as political plums; as something that is to be fished for, for the sake of a salary attached to it, but rather as an opportunity to render real service to the community, and where the official would serve the community free of charge rather as an honor. The moment you attach a sizeable salary to any position you attract the politicians, who go out not for the sake of serving the community but for the salary. Therefore, these positions should be honorary positions with only a minimum salary or expense money attached to them, and these salaries for elected officials will have to be paid by the community, whereas, the salaries of the employees such as policemen, teachers, or in positions taken over from the Indian Service by the community, the salaries will then of course be paid by the Federal government. Is that clear?

QUESTION: In other words, if we are to be like the Pueblos, some of them will serve for $30 a year.

MR. WOEHLKE: That is right.

MR. KNEALE: How long do you suppose it will be that the Government will be willing to pay the salaries of teachers and farmers, how long is this going to exist?

MR. WOEHLKE: Do you want to know how long the government will continue to pay the salaries of people who render service to the community or under the present system?

MR. KNEALE: Under the present system.

MR. WOEHLKE: Under the present system, it is getting more and more difficult to obtain appropriation because under this system such a huge part of the money that Congress appropriates for the Indian Service does not produce any constructive results, it is wasted in a system of futile land administration. When you think of this chart here which showed the conditions of the land on the Pine Ridge reservation and multiply that condition by fifty or sixty, then you will see that the Indian Service is running a huge and enormous real estate business in which every year the receipts of this business go down and the amount of land goes down and the amount of work that needs to be done increases constantly, so that within a comparatively short time you can figure out that the cost of running the Indian Service real estate business will be greater than the total receipts from it. Under the condition you can see that Congress will be in no mood to continue the appropriation on the present scale. As you already know Congress has made an enormous slash in the appropriation to the Indian Service for 1934–35; there will be available to the administration and the relief and help of the school work of the Indian Service twelve million dollars less than two years ago.

That gives you an indication of the mood Congress is in. It is not going to continue large appropriations to be thrown down the rathole of the present system of enormous real estate operations, which defeat themselves and get nobody anywhere. That is why this bill which brings about a constructive system, which endeavors to lay a foundation, which endeavors to rebuild your life, that is why this bill is so important. It builds new hope for the Indians as well as for the whites. If this bill is adopted you will find that these enormous administrative expenses based on meaningless real estate operations will gradually diminish; that the economic level of the Indian community due to the credit machinery to be set up and the annual appropriation for constructive purposes that is made in this bill, will rise; and that Congress will be more likely to make larger appropriations when those appropriations place the entire Indian Service and the Indians themselves in a position to do constructive work and where the Indians will be in a position to help themselves and to go ahead on their own. As soon as Congress sees the evidence of the fruits of the new policy, you can rest assured that it will be glad and willing to make ample appropriations in order that they can keep the work going in the right direction. But under conditions as they are, if these conditions are to continue, you will have to figure on a diminishing amount of Congressional appropriations probably accompanied in the future, under some future Secretary of the Interior, by a new outbreak of patents in fee. That is the only way that the load on the United States Treasury can be lightened, and it is to avoid this possibility of the return to the old methods that this bill has been introduced.

I would like to answer Mr. Madison as to the matter of considering this bill. As you probably know Mr. Collier only has four years in which to set in motion the policy which has been in his mind for a good many years, and one year of that has gone. It has taken him this one year to get in motion all this civil works program and all other emergency measures that were necessary to give the Indians jobs through this past year. On top of that he has used that year to make and formulate the policy which would probably be glad to pass this bill and the authorizing of the appropriations if there comes from the Indian an expression of support and sympathy for this general policy. As you have all seen through a study of this act, it is largely an enabling act which provides ways and means of instituting these various rebuilding policies, but which makes none of them mandatory. The only mandatory things in that bill are the absolute stoppage of the allotment system and the taking away from the Secretary of the Interior of a number of discriminatory powers, including the one now where he can by force allot a reservation. That is the fundamental principle of this bill. If you approve of that you needn't worry about the rest of the bill, because the rest of the bill is up to you to decide how you want to handle it. Furthermore, you can always, in the future, amend the act in these minor matters to suit your general needs and requirements, but what is necessary is to establish the general policy and to do it right now. If you wait until next year, heaven knows whether it will be possible to establish the kind of policy you want. The time to act is now, not to wait and quibble over line 2 paragraph 3, and so on. Once you have that policy established, you can still go ahead and go over the details and whenever they need amendments you can and should suggest the amendments and the Commissioner will be only too glad to amend it wherever reasonable and feasible, but get busy now and put it over while you have the chance.

MR. PETTUS, JR.: Mr. Woehlke has just said that now is the time to act. I thoroughly agree that now is the time to act, and my support is with the bill, but I believe that Title IV in regard to Indian Affairs, or Court of Indian Affairs, Sec. 14, where it says:

> "Sec. 14. The Judges of the Court of Indian Affairs shall hold office for a period of ten years; they may be removed prior to the expiration of their term by the President of the United States with the consent of the Senate, for any cause."

Why should the president appoint these judges for ten years? Suppose we get the wrong officials in these jobs and they put their feet on the Indians' necks and push them in the mud, or will we be given some say about who these judges will be and how long a period they will be appointed for?

MR. SIEGEL: The bill provides that the judges shall be appointed for ten years. The reason it was not made for life was that we wanted not to place them beyond control for the reasons that have just been suggested. On the other hand it is desirable to appoint them for not less than ten years, in order that they may become expert in Indian affairs and to give them some power to review what they done, and to give the Indians a chance to go into court in confidence that their case will be heard by experienced and competent judges.

MR. PETTUS, JR.: I would suggest that these organized Indian councils from all the different reservations each year have a representative member sent from the reservation to meet, say in Washington, to discuss this matter of the court, and when they find that some particular judge is being unfair to the Indians throughout the United States that they may be permitted to bring charges against this judge and have him removed from office.

MR. SIEGEL: I think that you will find the provision on page 44 of the Senate Bill, Section 14, where it says:

> "Sec. 14. The Judges of the Court of IndianAffairs shall hold office for a period of ten years; they may be removed prior to the expiration of their term by the President of the United States, with the consent of the Senate, for any cause."

It may be desirable to strike out that clause "with the consent of the Senate."

MR. PETTUS, JR.: I believe that would leave the power to the Secretary of the Interior.

MR. SIEGEL: Is this section 14 satisfactory to you?

MR. PETTUS, JR.: It is satisfactory to me if the Indians can in some way be provided so that they can bring charges against a judge.

MR. SIEGEL: This gives them the right to bring charges.

MR. PETTUS, JR.: They can bring them, but how?

MR. SIEGEL: You could always protest in an official capacity and the President could act on your suggestion.

MR. PETTUS, JR.: Our protest to be made to the President of the United States?

MR. SIEGEL: Yes.

MR. PETTUS, JR.: What steps would we take?

MR. SIEGEL: Prepare a protest at your council meeting and forward to the President or Commissioner of Indian Affairs, and request that it be submitted to the President.

MRS. GOULETTE, a member of the Pottawatomie tribe of Oklahoma: I would like to give a little experience that will probably be of assistance. I am a member of the Pottawatomie tribe in Oklahoma. I have gone through all of the trials that the allotted members have experienced. I and my people have gone through all the trials of allotments. What you have heard here, the information you have been given, has been absolutely correct. We have suffered a great deal by it and especially because of the courts, of our local courts giving the Indian nothing and giving it all to the white man. When I heard of this plan whereby the Indians could have a community by themselves where they could govern themselves like a city has its own government, but yet have access to the outside influence and help to the extent that they would wish to take it, I said then and there, this is the best thing I have heard of for the Indian and his property. Our older Indians were compelled to take deeds, often at the poor judgment of a few members of a family and it was up to the Indians.

Those who were capable of holding on to the property were in the minority. The courts were for those who didn't understand the business and so they got the property away from the older Indians. This is a question that is very vital and it is a question that the Indians should consider earnestly now while they have the opportunity to consider it. The white man's laws have taken everything that the majority of the Pottawatomies have had and I believe that this court of Indian Affairs should have on its benches Indian attorneys, Indian blooded attorneys, whom the Indians know, and have confidence in—not all Indians, that would be too much the other way, there should be an even balance, but somebody at the head of it who could cast his vote for the deciding vote, whatever they were divided on, and the Secretary of the Interior might be able to cast his vote to swing it over to the right side. I believe that in justice this court of judges should have Indian attorneys. You can't expect the Indian to have confidence in a court where it is all white people when they have brains to look back and see that it has been the white men that have had the rule in their hands all these years, and the Indians that have suffered. I would not only recommend that the Indian be represented in this proposed court but the Indian would also, as suggested a while ago, be permitted to have his representatives confer on the appointment of judges. I taught in Indian schools, I have gone through everything that an Indian could have a chance to go through. Our present Secretary of the Interior, our President and Commissioner are the best ones we have had. If we can judge by their actions, I think they are in sympathy with the Indians and that they want to do justice and they want to right those wrongs that have been made by the others in the past.

For all I can see or reason out there are very few things that will restore confidence unless there is somebody they have confidence in connection with the higher chance to find out whether they are selling merely land or valuable minerals. The whites are fighting for that mineral land, they are pulling every string in Congress and everywhere else to get rights to the mineral on the Papago reservation and everywhere else. Well, I had mineral, oil, and by political pull got that land, and in the end they came near getting every bit of it.

I am for helping the Indian and I am for getting justice for the whites who are friends and who are trying to do justice for the Indians as well as the whites, but I see where these loopholes have been and I know what will happen to our lands and our Indians if the higher ups have everything in their lands. We were told about the Assiniboine Indian who said that he sold his land and bought an automobile and then wrecked his automobile and so had nothing left but what was in his pockets and in his pockets he had his hands. Well, the whites will do the same thing to you. It is done all over the country. People who have had any land will remember that if they should give up their lands for an automobile, when the automobile is gone there is nothing on which to make a living. I have gone through everything myself, I know the Indian school work from A to Z. I know how our Indians are trained by the supervisors, I know all our superintendents.

I know all this, and what we want to do is to take the advantage from the hands of the whites whose only idea is to get what they want. The only thing I say is to get the President to appoint some well versed man on that "court of affairs," and when they have a mixed court with the proper judges, then the Indians themselves will get together and they can have justice. We want the white people to live, and we want the Indians to live. We don't want the mineral right taken away from those who have not had a chance to use the mineral that belongs to them. I know that the Indians have gone through, the only remedy I see is to take the absolute power out of the hands of the higher ups and at least give the Indian a chance to have a voice in these things that would be done. Whether the mineral rights are to be sold on the land should be for the whole tribe to decide, not of the individual. If it is grazing, let the tribe get the benefit of it. That is my idea. On this court, I suggest that half of them be Indians, not one Indian, but at least half of them.

MR. SIEGEL: If you want your question considered when we make over this bill, you may put it in writing. We are in sympathy with your views under the educational program. Under that title in the bill the Commissioner is charged with the duty of training Indians for the various administrative and technical services, which includes legal work; and as soon as we could train Indians so that they would be competent to do these things and go into these courts, I am sure we would do so. But it would be unwise to appoint an Indian on this court simply because he is an Indian unless he is qualified to do that work.

MRS. GOULETTE: I am acquainted with several men of Indian blood, I have worked with them, who are just as competent to be a member of this court today as any white man is. Not a full blood, but of Indian blood. If we are looking for the Indians, we can find Indians who are capable enough that they can fill almost any job that is filled in the Indian service. This training has been going on for fifty years. Not all of them have shown their talent in the same line, some of them have shown their talent in the legal line. There are Indians who are capable of taking charge of an Indian school and keep it up with the times and carry it through. I have noticed in the past that the white man has had friends to put in these places and they have kept them and the white man has not let the Indian have the job. You will find on your records in Washington, D.C., opposite the names of the different employees of service, excellent, good, and so on. Look at the names, then see which of those did the excellent work, who was above the average, who was to be depended on. Find out who shirked their work, and then see if they got the high salary. I have taught, I know all these things. I have been out of the service for over twenty years, I know I gave ten of the best years of my life to the Indian service; I was transferred to one school and then to another. What we want is for the white people, those of you who are in sympathy with the Indian right now, to get to work and find those Indians who are competent and then show us what you can do by putting those competent Indians in places so that the rest of the Indians will see that you mean what you say.

MR. SIEGEL: I may say that the educational program and self-government program is designed to train the Indians and give the jobs to them and if they don't need the training it will be that much saved for us. We are all very pleased in the progress the Indians have made.

MRS. GOULETTE: The thing to do is to take advantage of the education offered them, but take advantage of it by getting down to business and get everything out of the course that is offered in the schools that you can so that they will have to send their instructors away to get more to teach you.

MR. MONAHAN: Dr. Skinner has just brought me a copy of the Act of 1924 which Mr. Monahan referred to awhile ago, and I will read it to you.

Mr. Monahan read the act to the assembled Indians.

> An Act, approved June 2, 1924 (Public Law No. 175, 68th Congress), as follows:
>
> "Be it enacted by the Senate and House of Representatives of the United States of America in Congress assembled. That all noncitizen Indians born within the territorial limits of the United States be, and they are hereby, declared to be citizens of the United States: Provided, That the granting of such citizenship shall not in any manner impair or otherwise affect the right of any Indian to tribal or other property."

MR. H. O. DAVIDSON (Mohave): May I ask you who proposed that bill?

MR. MONAHAN: I don't know who proposed that, it doesn't give it here.

MR. DAVIDSON: There was a difficulty came up in the Indians who were seeking to ratify the 18 treaties made back in 1852, whereby twenty thousand Indians organized to get together and see if they could go to court. We have no law, no right. We just sat down and listened when that bill was made by the Indians themselves, and in making that bill they made it so that it would not interfere with the government holding our property and we sent it to Washington and it came back. We sent it from the state of California, then Congress says: "There are forty thousand California Indians, we want a majority vote on it." The twenty thousand Indians didn't care if they had land or not, they were not looking for it. We had to go to women's clubs, welfare associations and work through them to make a majority vote on this bill. It went to Washington, then was presented to the House, then was passed. On that day I was in the Chamber of Commerce in Los Angeles when John Collier arrived, they were anxious about this bill. He read that bill and said that Congress passed on it aimlessly, they knew it didn't mean anything, but it does mean a whole lot to the Indian. Now they say we can become a chartered community, and have full rights if the Indian make it pay and work out right. But that is the law of 1924, of June 2, 1924.

MR. MONAHAN: I am glad to know that. Now it is getting toward the time when we adjourn for lunch. Do you want to finish this up before noon or have an afternoon session? I have to meet with several delegations and I would like to have a little time.

It was regularly moved and seconded that the meeting stand adjourned until 1:45 p.m.

Afternoon Session

The meeting was reconvened at 2:00 p.m.

Mr. Woehlke presiding as chairman of the afternoon session.

MR. MONAHAN: (*Holding a pamphlet in his hand, speaks to the assembled Indians in the audience.*) The man who wrote and circulated this and hasn't got the honesty to put his name on it certainly isn't honorable enough that we should pay any attention to what he has printed and circulated. These unsigned letters that come into our office—if a man can't sign a letter we stick it in the waste basket. The people that wrote this if they are honest will sign their names and tell who they are. If there are objections to this bill, they have a right to express themselves; but they have no right to do it in an underhanded way. They can do it just as you are doing it here on the floor publicly.

MR. WOEHLKE: This afternoon we are going to hear a delegate from each different delegation sent to this meeting. First we will have a very rare thing among the Indians, a woman speaker. Mrs. Waterman, representing the Fort McDowell Apaches, will come forward and tell us what she and her folks think of this bill.

MRS. WATERMAN: I will try to tell you what our people think. Our people do not object to this bill. For many years our people have wished they could have a say in what has been done on our reservation and now it comes to us that there is a way, and we are all glad and are supporting the bill. Of course our reservation is a small reservation and of course the older Indians are dead, but the younger people are living on. I am not young, but I feel that I must help hold on to that reservation, and we always have wanted to have a say on our reservation on what they are going to do. As I say we would like to have a say in what they do. We want to say whether they can or can't do it, and now when this bill comes before us and it gives us a chance to have a voice in this business we are very glad and we will support it, and that is all I can say for my side.

Mr. John Rice, Apache Indian, San Carlos, spoke in his native tongue, interpreted by Mrs. Waterman.

MR. JOHN RICE: You gentlemen are sent by the government and I am also a ward of the government, but this is a chance to have a say and I will cooperate with you and I am glad of it. You told us that if we can't have a charter we can hold our reservation and we can run our own business and I am glad to hear of that. As long as I remember we never had that chance offered to us, but now we are having a chance in our affairs and I am glad to hear it. Whatever I may do for it down on our reservation we are willing to cooperate with you. Whatever water rights I have had before or this bill will give me, I am glad. Some of us have starved and we need a little more land and we have small reservation. I don't want any white man to come in and help himself even to brushes and wood on our reservation without we tell him to. Long ago the government told us not to say anything, just put your head down, don't even look around. Many years back they said that to us. Now I may have a voice in all things pertaining to my reservation and I think it is a good thing.

The water pipe that extends on our reservation, we never gave consent to the city to do that. I just want to mention that. If a white man has land and he is living on it and somebody comes along and would do the things that they do on our reservation, I am sure you would say something about it. You don't just keep quiet and let them do those things. And now a bill is before us telling us that they are going to do away with that and I can say what I want to say. I feel this way, that there is a God and I believe that he gave this land to us Indians; if he gave it to us, I feel that it is mine and mine alone. I am saying this to show you that I am just living on a little spot of land, and now you give me a chance to have my voice in its business, in the business on my reservation. That is all I have to say.

DAVID MILES, Fort Apache: We Apaches come before you and say that we are very much pleased to hear of the bill and what Congress is going to do for us, and by us I mean all the tribes of the United States. What you tell the men here, what the men from Washington tell us here sounds good to us and you say that this bill will guard our interests and give us self-government, but we Apaches from Fort Apache have not had time to study this bill and discuss it, therefore we plan that we can hold a general council when we go home and discuss this bill and then let the Commissioner know our decision as soon as possible.

CHIEF BAJA, of Whiteriver reservation, in native Apache; George Warren interpreting: For two days I tried to find someone to speak for me as I don't understand the English language. I have been waiting and looking up to this time when I could speak to you. There is a line around his home (he means the reservation line) and in this line or reservation there are quite a number of Apaches living, which is Oak Creek, White River, and the others, and we feel that we are all of one blood and we are here today to defend our lands which have been allotted to us by the Government, and if you have anything to say let us have our say about the land. Just leave the reservation land just where it is, don't have anything to say about it.

Just before we started out we had a council and most of the Indians have already decided to keep their reservation as it is, and this breaking up our allotment business is no good for us and for our families. This allotment to individuals will only cause a loss of our land which is chiefly our main occupation. I am old all right, maybe you think I shouldn't have anything to say about the land but then I am only talking for the good of the future generations who will need their land very much. We have some young men who turned students and who will undertake this business and will attend to it when we are gone, and we will try very hard to improve our schools in every way.

We want to retain the schools and then the government will give us some more maybe, then we will have more English delegates like these people here who are all able to speak the English language. Maybe I was only one that was afraid of the white man when the white man started school. This is shown by the fact that I do not speak English. He had the right idea in going to school and learning something. I want to say once more that we are to retain our schools and do not turn the boys and girls out to us and tell us to send them off to school at our own expense, because we are still reservation Indians and then again we have no money, and only by having money can we do something. There is a school but it is too small, then there is a big building and it is just like nothing, it is useless now. Try to make something out of that for us. From that these future generations will say then that it was through the help of the white man and Indians that they have retained this education. I am pretty sure that everybody here who understands English is pretty thankful to the white man for bringing this education to him and I am very thankful that it is that way, that the Government has given an education to them which I don't have. That is all I have to say.

STEVE SMITH, talking for Chief Pete Lambert of Fort Mohave, native tongue; Mr. H. O. Davidson interpreting: I am introducing some papers at the same time I talk. We have come here and we sit here and we have a meeting here of all tribes of people, all kinds of people to listen to the men from Washington. We listen here, we heard the argument to phrases and clauses contained in the bill, we understand some of it and some of it we don't understand. I want everybody to understand that I am not the chief, that I am just talking for the chief at this time. He is sitting here by me but I have represented him in many cases and he asked me to say that we are disappointed that Mr. Collier could not pay us a visit. We happen to know him personally. We are sorry the Indian commissioner cannot be here because business permits him not to do so. When we came here we introduced ourselves and we explained ourselves as to how the government's promises pertaining to land do not assure us.

I can produce the charter that was once issued to our tribe—that is why we are asking your committee when we come in here, "Are they going to give us a charter to keep?" The white government has the same proposition that we have, they had to live up to the new ruling during the administration of President Roosevelt. Mr. John Collier is the man appointed as Indian Commissioner who will give some rights to the Indians and we are glad to come here and have the privilege to talk before you.

We came here and we listened to that bill. You know we have made researches of our conditions and it was very dark, but now a light has shown through that bill. This bill itself is explanatory, what it will do for the Indian, to form communities by charter and use their laws as a corporate body in law and everything of that kind. In reference to the bill there are two particular points that are explained by the Government officials, one is the reducing or taking away the power of the Secretary of the Interior, or the Indian Bureau who have such powers invested in them that they will act as advisor and will be better prepared to act—they have power over us sometimes pretty dangerous. Here is one thing, reducing the powers of the ruling element that rules us, and another point the allotting system. A good many of you have allotments who are attending this meeting and you have more to say about it for this reason, you know what the allotment is, but I agree with the bill that this should be passed and be adopted. This is about all I am going to say of the bill. Those two points are all we are prepared to talk about and we are going back home and tell the people there about it, what action is taken here and it is up to them if they want to form and organize, they have this privilege, but I am sure it is a good policy to be adopted as it stands.

MR. DAVIDSON speaks for the Mohave delegation in English: May I proceed. I am going to tell you I am not a chief either, I am just an interpreter, but I have the privilege to talk for Chief Goodman who is plenty smart in an Indian way. I shall tell you that he wanted me to speak on the Federal court to be instituted for the Indians. Mr. Goodman is a great war chief. In times of war they created a system or a law by which they elect him district United States marshall, and he is a boy scout. He did not happen to have his old paper to show at this time but I can show the people here the official paper of the War department. His father's name was Chief Askin. Of course Mr. Goodman here does not take an active part in the Indian Bureau administration. He can't do it because they have the power to run it, and this bill came up and he came down here to represent them and he said "I would like the officials to know my history." Then he said that in this bill there are some parts to be scratched out and some recommendations have been made here, and Chief Goodman said why don't those Indians go back to the reservations and make it according to their knowledge, that is what he said. Another matter is about the school system. He said that if what these men say is true, the bill can be adopted, as it stands and then can be amended and changed as they go on and the Indian learns more about it. That is all Mr. Goodman said for me to say for him at this meeting, and I have great pleasure in having the honor to speak for him.

Colorado River Delegation, RANDALL BOOTH, spokesman: Ladies and Gentlemen of the House: I have the pleasure to be spokesman of the Colorado River delegation from the Colorado River Indian reservation. I want to present to you briefly and pointedly in regard to Indian self-government. Now the Indian who lived along the Colorado River has always thought that he was self-governed before any white people arrived on the scene, and when the Mexicans came over and so called discovered this land, they found some human beings there and when they recognized that they were human beings they made an agreement with the Indians that where they lived that was their land. That was the grant which the Mexican Government granted to these Mohaves about eighty miles below Parker and to the Black Canyon where the dam now is today, and afterwards when the United States bought this country of ours they bought this country with all animals and human beings in it. Of course the Mexican Government tried to show the United States Government that they recognized these human beings as Indians, and that they had inhabited this land long before the Spaniards came and the United States must honor that grant. With that agreement the United States bought this land. But when the United States got this country they ignored such lands and grants, and when this was taken up with the War department they passed a law and set aside this little piece of land, this executive order and they are kept there. So the people went to Washington, the chief of the people, and he was presented with this medal (shows a medal to the audience) and when the chief went to Washington he wanted to know why, when they risked their lives in behalf of their country, they should be allotted this land when actually it belonged to them already. So our organization of self-government extends away back over one hundred years ago, and the Indians of today have a record and they have a constitution and by-laws to carry out the best they can, the condition that existed away back there, and this is one of the main things that bill brings up, self-government.

Now the allotment act of 1887—why didn't we know at the time that would be a detriment to the Indian, why didn't we know that it would not get us anywhere? Where was the voice of the Indians then? That is for you to answer. Now another law stands before us and we see that it not only deals with the Indians here but it deals with all the other tribes of Indians, and therefore that is why you must decide seriously. If we decide in favor of a bill or if we are opposed, probably we are doing an injury to some of our fellowmen, therefore we must think twice before we leap. I believe that this self-government is the only government and we know that we want to revise this allotment act, so that we can have the whole land to ourselves. Now the most important thing to the Colorado River delegation is that we have land over there and they are building a dam right above us to give us water, as land without water is useless. If we have this land, more land, the point is this, the Secretary or the bill says that we want to have more land and then turns around and puts his hand in the pie and says if you don't need all of this land the Secretary has the right to sell what he thinks you don't need, that is our only objection to this bill. I believe now that it is up to you to oppose or support this bill.

This delegation says that we simply come here to understand fully and some kind of figure that this bill ought to be explained paragraph by paragraph. The first thing that this session took up and the bill read that has been the understanding of our people in a general way, but now they want to go back with this thought that they will go back and present this down among their own people and then voice the opinion of all their people to the Secretary. That is the wish of this delegation. This is my personal talk.

MR. HARVEY CAWKER (representing Pima delegation): Friends and assembled Indians: I am glad I have the privilege of saying these words to you this afternoon. We gather here for a great cause. During the two days that we have met we have heard discussed and I believe that we have been shown as a whole, what is before us, and I am sure that the rest of your tribes and you delegates feel as we do. The Pima delegation feels that the matter of the bill before us is a bill that we must back up. Say that we ought to see it go through, with the amendments if possible, and so that what appears before you can be changed. We had the privilege of listening to a man here this morning who knows and has shown to you what the result is in the past years, and they want to change that so as to prevent it from further depriving the Indians of the land that they possessed.

We were told that in 1887 a law was introduced, an allotment act. I will say to you that when this law went into effect, it was like a game of football, and those laws were the rules and regulations that the game is to be played by, and the Indians were to play against the government at that time, and there were few Indians that understood English or could read and write, therefore they did not know what the rules and regulations were and the result was that they lost. You can see for yourselves what the loss is. It is up to you, brothers, if you want to keep them for the generations in the future of our own people. And if you do, it is up to you as I see it to accept this new plan, these new rules and regulations that we are to play this game by, and from the way you conduct yourselves in the meetings here, I will say that I am proud of you all, and you can bet that this meeting has been conducted in such a way that it has been pleasing, and I am sure that the officials are pleased in knowing and seeing the way the meeting is conducted.

We are here and given a chance from men who, during all these years, have seen the game played by the Indians and the white man and the result always, the Indians lose. Maybe the Indians have come to the time when they will no longer be deprived of the properties that they have. It goes back to the President of the United States and on down to all the officials in Washington and the Commissioner and the men who are here today with us. They are interested in you; if they were not, do you think they would take the trouble to come away out here to give us this hearing?

I am telling you that to do that is to show you what that bill means to us, it shows that they are interested for your protection and I tell you that it means nothing to them but it means everything to you. If you feel as I do toward the government and the people who are the spokesmen of the bill, I am sure you will back them up. Now under the new rules and regulations of this game we are playing you will have a better understanding, you will have a part just as we are here today to understand the rules and regulations of that game, you will play that game knowing the rules and regulation of that game, you will want to do the same on them. You can feel assured that you will play that game knowing the rules and regulations, knowing the loopholes and you can avoid those loopholes and not lose out as you have been doing, as shown on that map that Mr. Stewart showed this morning. I say that his game will be played as the games are played today, I refer to the games that this school played with the white schools. What was the result of the last game? The Indians won that game, and I am sure now that we are through losing. If we know the new rules and regulations, we will win out every game that we play, and if you know the rules and regulations of the white man's game that we play, and I say that the games we have been playing are the white man's games and if you know the rules and regulations of the white man's game you can beat the white man at his own game. It is true that there are in this bill loopholes and we are trying to plug those loopholes, but I doubt if we could do it, I doubt if anybody can plug all the loopholes.

I want to say another word on something which applies to us Pima Indians. There was a bill introduced in Congress years ago and we were told that bill was leak proof, but there was something wrong with that bill and that is why the government is not living up to the law and that proves, I say, that you cannot produce a bill leak proof and beyond loopholes. For that reason if you see it the way we do you will accept this bill even though there are loopholes.

If we can prevent any further loss of our land and play the game more fairly, give the Indians an equal chance to win, we ought to be satisfied to adopt that bill and later on we can plug up those loopholes and that is why I say to the Pima Indians that we can plug up those loopholes and that is why I say to the Pima Indians that we should vote for that and I challenge also a statement made yesterday that this bill is nothing but a change from one coat to another. If that is so, are you willing to throw away the good coat that you are offered when it is better than the one you have on?

The Pima delegates are willing to make the exchange so that it would be better than what they have today. The delegation feels that they are speaking in fact for the tribe. Long before this meeting the people on the reservation have gathered and have discussed this and with this understanding the delegation feels that when they go back from this meeting they can inform the people back home and enlighten them and they will be more anxious to support this bill. So I hope that my Indian people will take that attitude and I hope that all you people will take that attitude. But don't take that attitude because the Pima delegation says so; use your own minds, study the bill and you will find that it is for your protection.

Now as was stated awhile ago from the platform in regard to a paper which you have all heard, that came from some source other than from the Indians, perhaps it may be something good, but any man that will not sign his name is no good and this paper did not come from the Indians, but you Indians are capable of using your own judgment and when you do that, when you use your own judgment on this kind of matter and you have nobody to blame but yourselves when you listen to anything that is put around without a signature, and further by using your own judgment you will learn to depend upon yourselves and stop depending upon someone else. You are intelligent enough to do it yourselves. Before this pamphlet we refer to there was another pamphlet passed around indicating that the Pimas had nothing to do with that, so you must guard yourselves and when you find out that you have accepted something not important, this is for the Indians and the Indian people alone to decide for themselves. I thank you.

San Carlos Delegation, OLIVER BELLVILLE, native tongue, interpreted: Dear friends and Arizona Indians. I wish to say very few words. I belong to the San Carlos reservation. The only thing that I have to say pertains to those who live on the San Carlos reservation. To begin with I wish to say that in the old days the San Carlos were situated where they are today. I will say that we are concerned as to the matters of our land and everything else on our reservation. These men sit up here, what do they know about our reservation? What I want to say here will not be very much but it will cover all that I have to say so that I don't have to tell you all of it. I was to tell you that all of the San Carlos Indian reservation is my own reservation and if anyone has anything to do with the land or anything to say about it I want him to show me a paper that will give him the right to say anything about my reservation.

I was born on my reservation, I do not come from any other place. This is what I had in mind. I will say that the San Carlos reservation is mine and these representatives of the Government sitting up here that came a long ways I am glad to see them and glad to say this to them. The Apaches were on our reservation in the year 1871 and those that were on our reservation at that time are no longer living and now a younger generation have taken their places on our reservation, and I want to say to these gentlemen up here that I want them to know that the reservation is mine and I want to keep it. A very small portion of the Indian reservation has been cut off and it runs almost inside the reservation and I feel that the part that has been taken away from me belongs to me and I want to reclaim that and there is another place just below the Coolidge Dam that has been cut away from my reservation that I want to reclaim. In years gone by this is the only place we have to live on, but we were forced to fight, we fought different tribes in order to hold this reservation of our own.

All of that has gone past. I am not talking of this, and I am not taking into consideration the other reservations concerned. I only want my own reservation. That is all I ask of you gentlemen, that the San Carlos reservation is my own.

MR. WOEHLKE: That is just what we want to do, we want to see that he keeps it.

MR. MARTIN MORISTO, representing the Papago reservation, speaks in English: Ladies and Gentlemen: We are in a new era now. We are for this country whether we accept this bill or not, but we should accept this bill. We have been told that our chance is now. We are not young any more. In olden times we were young just like young people here but we have grown now and we begin to realize and think for ourselves what this Wheeler-Howard Bill means to the Indians of Southern Arizona, and I would suggest to my tribe that they back up this bill. They say they are going to back up this bill by groups, as fast as the Indians become acquainted with this bill and begin to realize what it means, we will back it up in groups, not as a whole tribe. I think we can all easily realize and think for ourselves, that the old Indians are not going to hold you down when it comes to the education of the Indians. This government had spent thousand of dollars to educate the Indian children to learn to stand up for themselves, yes, they are spending millions of dollars to educate our children, and let the illiterate learn from you and show him how to live a white man's life and a white man's way, that is what education means. I will not take much time because all of the other members have stated the same thing and I don't want to say the same thing so I will quit here.

JOSE PABLO speaks in native tongue for the same delegation: Ladies and Gentlemen: I am just one of the Papago Indians who live on the farthest side of the reservation. Sixty years ago or more my ancestors were enemies of the Apaches and here I am a descendant of one of them. It was a law that if any Apache showed up on our lands he was not to go out alive. So it was similar in our case, we were not to go to the Apache reservation, and if we did we could not come out alive. Now everything is all gone, that war has passed away, and all the people are today gathered here as friends, as people who are willing to help each other. Now I say this, that if we get together we can accomplish more by standing together as one person.

This new bill that has come up before the Indians is a bill that is going to open up more opportunities for the Indians. It is up to the Indians to push this bill through; it will open up new opportunities. In some cases our people are afraid of it, but we can't get anyplace by being afraid of it. Some of our Papago Indians are now ready to accept this bill, but it doesn't mean that it is that way as a whole. I am going home and try to talk to the other Indians and when they learn that it is for their benefit we will let the Commissioner know.

CHARLES MCGEE, of the Hualapai delegation: Ladies and Gentlemen: We thank the government for sending these men here and we thank you for explaining this bill. I do not think that I will take much of your time but we are thankful for having these men here to explain this bill and they are friends of the Indians. And our Indians have gone over the matter point by point and I think a whole lot of our tribe have thought about it, but we, this delegation, were not sent down here to say whether this tribe accepted this bill or not, but this delegation was sent down here to understand this bill, and hear the explanations. There are some things in the bill that will benefit us, and we will go back to our people and explain just what is in this bill more fully and a whole lot of us do not understand very many parts of it. But when we go back to our people again we will explain just what has been gone over down here and we will send our decision in to the Commissioner of Indian Affairs after awhile. I thank you.

MR. SANDHUT of the Maricopa Indians: Friends: We have come here to listen to the Government officials explain the bill which was to be passed in Congress, and I have listened all these two days. The bill itself is all right according to the self-government, but as I sat here and studied it over I find that there was a question that I want to bring up that concerns every one of us along the Gila and the Salt River reservation. That is this: It doesn't mention any prior water rights in this bill, and my opinion is that this bill should mention land and water both, because we make our living on these two important things, that is land and water. Land without water is worthless so for that reason the bill should mention land and water so we will know where we stand. If the land is provided with water then we know where we stand and then is the time that we have the bill to act on. I thank you.

VICTOR MANUEL, representing Salt River delegation: Members of the Committee, Fellow Tribesmen, and Members of this Assembly and Friends: I don't know just what has been taking place here, I just heard a few remarks from the last speaker and I will say this, that the last speaker was right. Even though we have been assured by the speakers on the platform and I think they are our friends, that everything pertaining to anything that was not covered by this bill would be added so that it would be taken care of, that certain portion of the bill which has just been spoken about is the most important part to us because I believe we ought to go a little slower and not rush into the adoption of this bill at the present time. We are convinced however, that a great part of that bill is to our liking, and it sounds well and good, and I know that perhaps the authors of that bill are sincere and want to remedy some of the policy that has been in effect for the past years and I am sure that the Commissioner is sincere in his efforts to help us out. But it will be just a matter of time when the older people are gone and we want to take them into consideration. They were the ones that have made the supreme sacrifice in a great many cases in order to hold the present land which we are supposed to have. I think it won't be long perhaps until there will be a shortage of water over there and the white man is going to have the preference first before the Indians will get what they are supposed to get and so I believe in going a little slower in this matter.

MR. SIEGEL: Would they approve this bill if they have their water rights protected?

VICTOR MANUEL: I think so.

MR. SIEGEL: Maybe we can add a part like that to the bill.

MR. MANUEL: If you can add a part to the bill to protect our water rights and if you guarantee us additional water, then we can go ahead and plan what we can realize from our allotment.

MR. SIEGEL: We can't guarantee it, but we will do our best.

MR. MANUEL: What about the mineral rights?

MR. SIEGEL: The fact is that the mineral rights were withdrawn a long time ago. Those rights have been withdrawn a long time.

MR. MANUEL: A long time ago?

MR. SIEGEL: Yes, those are protected without this bill and this bill doesn't take it away from you.

MR. THOMAS VALENZUELA (representing Lehi): I want to say this much. When we had our meeting, I said to our people that this is a step for the betterment of the Indians. We need self-government, we have had it before the white man came. Of course our ancestors understood it but we didn't because they took it away from us. We need it because the time is coming when the government shouldn't tie us up without giving us that chance. This land question is the biggest. It has been promised through this bill that the government or the Secretary of the Interior in whose hands it was left to say if you need more land, we have got those promises today that they will get it for you just as the gentlemen has said, but also just as this last speaker and the one before him has said, the land is no good without water.

Of course we realize that when this bill was made those people were born and raised where they don't need any irrigation water, that is why they forgot to put it in this bill, but here in the Salt River Valley we have been fighting for water and we have been fighting on the Salt River reservation for a good many years. Now the promises through this bill are so good I don't see any reason why they couldn't give us water. Give it to us now just to prove how much good they can do us. Just show us where we are and what we can expect.

MR. LANCISCO HILL (representing Salt River, Lehi): I want to say just a few words in regard to what was said yesterday in regard to having an organization to discuss these matters once a year. There is an organization of the Southwest Indians right here in Phoenix and everybody and all those that belong in the Southwest are welcome to come and discuss with us as we do all these matters. We were formed a year ago. We are not very strong but I am just saying this as an invitation for this organization.

Mrs. Goulette suggested that there was someone in the assemblage that was trying to poison the minds of the Indians into believing that what she had stated in her talk was not true and she also stated that she could prove that every word she said was true.

MR. MONAHAN: This has been a very splendid meeting. I will tell Mr. Collier the very fair attitude that you have taken about this bill and will give him, as you state, your honest opinions, that you will send these opinions to him after you have general council meetings and tell your people about what you have heard and understood here.

QUESTION: What about the water rights on our land?

MR. SIEGEL: We will all discuss this later at our meetings after this general meeting is over.

QUESTION: We want to have a public expression here before this assembly.

MR. SIEGEL: It is my personal opinion that this irrigation act that you speak of was ambiguously drawn and that you should have first rights to the water.

Meeting adjourned at 5:02 o'clock, p.m. Friday, March 16, 1934.

Representatives from the Washington Office who were present:

Walter Woehlke	Melvin H. Siegel	Ward Shepard
A. C. Monahan	James Stewart	

DELEGATES

From the Pima Agency, Sacaton, Arizona.

Employees:

A. H. Kneale, Superintendent

Delegates from the Salt River Reservation:

Burgess Burke	Dan King	Vernon Smith
Herbert Shurz	Harvier Enos	Charley Chough
Ambrose Johnson	Lancisco Hill	Victor Manuel

Delegates from Gila River Reservation:

Anton Jackson	John E. Johnson	Frank Stanley
Alfred Jackson	Rudolph Johnson	G. Truman Jones
Henry Johnson	Xavier Cawker	Paul Azule

Delegates from Laveen, Arizona:

Herbert Grant	Howard Sanderson	Walter Rhoades
Leeds Soatike	Harry Lanes	Ambrose Jackson
Tony Breckenridge		

Other delegates from the Sacaton jurisdiction:

Santiago Johns	Juan Kisto	
Antone Nomane	Joe Manuel	Harry Sundust
Francis Patton	Alex Cannon	Joseph Sneed
Vincent Nelson	San T. White	Hirman Carlisle

From the Colorado River Agency, Parker, Arizona.

Employees:

C.H. Gensler, Superintendent	P.B.E. Skiff
Norwood Cox	Mr. Burns
J. B. Brooks	W. L. Buck

Delegates from Colorado River Reservation:

Charley Paddock	Aran Patch	Henry Welch
Winfield Scott	Dan Lamote	William Eddy
Kenneth Stoddard	Billy Sands	Jay Gould
Daniel Eddy	James Spam	Roger Stoddard

Delegates from Fort Mohave Reservation:

H. O. Davidson	Albert Davidson
Pete Lambert	Capt. Geo. Harrison
Chief Anyarre Goodman	Leo Kornes
Steve Smith	Joe Courtright

From the Sells Agency, Sells, Arizona.

Employees:

J. W. Elliott, Superintendent	Jose X. Pablo
V. D. Smith	Frank Rios

Delegates from the Sells Reservation:

Frank Vasque	Juan Harvey	Joe Thomas
Juan Joaquin	Jose Cruez	Francisco Salcido
Narcho Felix	Nesto Lancisco	Bernard Manuel
Jose Listo	Juan Jesus	Carlo Santos
John Louis	Alonzo Marina	Esperito Adams
Joaquin Lopez	Frank Rios	

From the Fort Apache Agency, Whiteriver, Arizona.

Employees:

William Donner, Superintendent
P. E. Arterberry
A. C. Baldwin

Delegates from the White River Reservation:

Chief Baha Alchesay	Charles Shipp	Silas Tenyieth
Jack Keep	Roe Clark	D. Pettis
Wallace Altaha	Floyd Loggie	Carter Johnson
John Taylor	David Miles	

From the San Carlos Agency, San Carlos, Arizona.

Employees:

James B. Kitch, Superintendent
Mr. Allen

Delegates from the San Carlos Reservation:

Thomas Dosela	Richard Baylish	Rankin Rogers
William Stevens	James Smiley	Victor Kinderley
George Cassadore	Roy Harney	

From the Truxton Canon Agency, Valentine Arizona.

Employees:

Guy Hobgood, Superintendent	N. Seippel
Mrs. Kate Smith	H. G. Ramsey
J. H. Crickenberger	

Delegates from Truxton Canon Reservation:

Bill Andrews	Lee Marshall	Chief Manakajo
Charles McGee	Fred Mahoney	Clark Jack

From the Mescalero Apache Reservation, Mescalero, New Mexico:
J. C. Cavill, Superintendent

Camp Verde Sub-Agency, under jurisdiction of Phoenix Indian School.
Employees:
Emory Frailey, Farmer
Delegates:

Jack Kinsey	George Hunt
Don Juan	George Williams
George Hamalay	Charley Pattea

Phoenix Indian School—April 30, 1934—1M

CHAPTER 8

PROCEEDINGS OF SOUTHERN CALIFORNIA INDIAN CONGRESS HELD AT RIVERSIDE, CALIFORNIA, MARCH 17 AND 18, 1934

SUPERINTENDENT BIERY: We of Sherman Institute are very happy indeed to have a meeting of the delegates and visitors here and we hope that your stay at Sherman will be very happy. We hope also that your conference today will be most interesting and fruitful to you. We have seated here on this side the leaders of the Mission Indians, on this side here the delegates from the Navajo District and in the next row we have delegates from the Yuma Agency. In the third row on this side are the delegates of the southern section of the Sacramento Valley.

I wish to introduce to you Mr. A. C. Monahan, the special representative from the Commissioner of Indian Affairs, Washington, D.C., who will have charge of the conference.

MR. MONAHAN: Friends, I have a telegram from Mr. Collier that I want to read to you. Before I read that, I want to say also that the Secretary of the Interior Ickes asked that his greetings be extended to you. Mr. Ickes is very well acquainted with Indian Affairs, spending a good deal of his time in Indian country, and he is exceedingly interested in what is being done by the Indian Office; I want to say also that President Roosevelt has shown himself deeply interested in Indian matters. He is giving more time to Indian matters than has been done by any President for many years past. Before I read this telegram, I want to know how many need interpreters.

Do you all understand? Do you want interpreters?

I now want to read to you the Commissioner's message:

Albuquerque New Mexico
March 18 1934

To all Indians of California—the tribal delegates and other Indians attending the Indian congress now in session. It is with sincere regret that circumstances, over which I have no control, will not permit me to attend your congress and meet all of you individually and by delegations. As you all know this country of ours is very large hence much time is consumed in traveling and due to the need of my returning to Washington as soon as possible it was absolutely necessary for me to limit my trip throughout the Indian country at this time. However realizing the tremendous importance of your congress and having the greatest personal interest in your welfare and in your deliberations I have sent members of my staff to counsel with you. After the Plains Indian Congress at Rapid City, South Dakota and at Fort Defiance it was physically impossible for me to accompany my staff to your congress although it was in my heart to do so. Although physically I am not with you I am in spirit and take this means of greeting you. Wishing you success in your deliberations and assuring you that your welfare is as close to my heart as any other Indians.

John Collier
Commissioner

MR. MONAHAN: This meeting has been called for one purpose and that is to discuss this so-called Wheeler-Howard Bill, named from Sen. Wheeler, Chairman of the Committee of Indian Affairs of the Senate; and Congressman Edgar Howard, Chairman of the Indian Committee of the House. It has been prepared after many months of Mr. Collier's leadership. He has brought into it the results of his ten or twelve years of very close study of Indian matters. You are familiar with the work he has done so that you know it is not a thing of a few months but of ten years' acquaintance with Indian matters.

This conference is for the discussion of the bill only, therefore discussion of other matters will not be in order at this meeting. Some of you may have other matters that you would like to discuss relative to things on your own reservations. I would be glad to take time with the delegates of the reservations sometime later today or tomorrow, but this meeting will be devoted only to the discussion of this bill.

Now those of you in these front seats are official delegates of this meeting, therefore it is for you to discuss the bill. All the time necessary will be taken to discuss the matter. There are many others who are not official delegates who will be helpful to us in clearing up matters. Questions they wish to ask should be written and handed to one of the stenographers at the table, and they will be answered. All of the rest of you that are here, we would be very glad to have written questions and we will be glad to answer them as soon as possible.

The general understanding is that we will limit our session here to the discussion of the matters in this proposed legislation.

Now before I ask Mr. Woehlke to explain the bill, I want to emphasize one thing. There is practically nothing compulsory in this bill. The bill gives an opportunity to form tribal organizations if the Indians wish to do so. If they do not wish to do so conditions will remain as they are. It is not expected that all of the tribes favor it. There will be many that will go on just as they have been in the past. Tribes that wish to take up the provisions of this opportunity may do so if it passes Congress. The movement must start with you, not with us. If you decide that you want to take up the provisions of this act then at least 25% of any group on any reservation must petition the Secretary of the Interior or Commissioner for a charter. The charter must be prepared by you and the Commissioner. No charter need be the same. The Yuma charter will not suit the Walker River Indians. The by-laws, which must be worked out by the Indians concerned and the Indian Office, before they can become effective or put into operation, must be accepted by 3/5 of the adult Indian members so that out of an adult Indian population of 1000, at least 250 must sign the petition before we do anything, and 600 must vote in favor of it before it can be put into operation.

The matter of allotment is definite. If the bill passes with the provision, there will be no further allotments to individual Indians, but they will retain trust patents as they are doing at the present time.

I will take no more time now, as it is going to take most of this morning's session to discuss the general features of the bill. We will put this before you and give you as clear an idea as possible and if Mr. Woehlke is willing, you may interrupt him if he does not make himself clear. This afternoon's session we will devote entirely to the questions you may raise relative to the bill.

10:27 to 10:45 a.m. Saturday

March 17, 1934

MR. WOEHLKE: I hope you realize that it is an historic occasion, that in this year of grace 1934 there is happening a reversal of the policy under which the Indians of the United States have been living for the past fifty years. During that half-century the entire Indian policy was based on the general allotment Act of 1887. Prior to 1887 most of the Indian land throughout the United States was held in common by the various tribes. After the allotment Act it was broken up into small pieces, and the ownership of an individual piece was transferred to individual members of the tribe. That General Allotment Act was sponsored by two different groups of people. One of the strongest advocates of general allotment was Carl Schurz, Secretary of the Interior at that time, who was responsible for the introduction of Civil Service in the United States Government—a very able man—a man who was sincerely a friend of the Indians—and who endeavored to do them a good turn.

It was his belief and the belief of a good many others that the tribal relationship and the tribal ownership of land maintained the Indians in a state of savagery—that if these tribal relationships could be broken up and if the Indians could be made individual property owners with all of the responsibilities of self-respecting citizens, the civilization of the Indians would be speeded up, and that within a very short time the Indian would become a self-supporting, self-respecting free agent, a complete citizen and a member of the white community.

This was one theory. On the other hand, and with motives not quite as high-minded, there were a lot of white people in and around the reservations who regretted the fact that they could not get their hands on Indian property. It was impossible for them to obtain title so long as it remained in Indian tribal ownership, so from their standpoint the great motive of the allotment was not civilization, but a break-up of the land in such a way that white people could get it, and would get it.

In 1887 the Indians' ownership totaled 137,000,000 acres. As a result of the allotment system, that body of land, that marvelous estate, shrank continuously, until last year the total had gone down to 37,000,000 acres, and it was still going down at such an alarming rate that within a very short time practically all land on allotted reservations will pass out of Indian ownership. The selfish motives of the greedy whites and the splendid motives of Schurz and his associates produced this result: impoverishment of the Indians. It became apparent within ten years that the high-minded purpose for which the Allotment Act was passed did not materialize. It was found that if at the expiration of the usual trust period the allotted Indian was treated as a full-fledged citizen, with full control over his property, his land went out from under him with great speed, and in exchange for his land and other property the Indian received so little or it was spent so fast that in a very short time, the Indian became a public charge. Therefore, the Allotment Act had this result: That the Government, contrary to expectation, proceeded to extend the guardianship of the Indians, and to prolong the restrictions on his freedom of action ten years, twenty-five years, for another renewal of twenty-five years, thereby admitting that the idealistic purpose of the allotment policy has failed. Yet, having acknowledged the fact, in spite of the fact that the allotment policy had failed, it continued in effect.

The proposed legislation is to put a complete stop to any further allotments, and through cessation of allotment, preserve the remainder of Indian lands.

Now the Commissioner proposes to try another way to reach the ideal of those who passed the Allotment Act in good faith. He believes that through the gradual extension of self-government to all the Indian tribes as fast as they are able and willing to accept responsibility for their own government, it will be possible to build up within the framework of the federal guardianship a body of self-supporting self-governing Indian citizens who will then be ready to be assimilated into the white body politic on a plane of social equality. He proposes a general uplift of the economic plan through the land act, through the credit machinery that he will set up, and through the suggested educational subsidies the Commissioner proposes to lift the general level of Indian education, of Indian income, of Indian culture, and of Indian character within the framework of the federal guardianship to such a point that the barriers which now exist will be broken down, and assimilation will be able to take place at a normal rate. That is the general purpose of the program which is placed before you.

As Mr. Monahan has told you, the Wheeler-Howard bill is largely an enabling act, a declaration of policy, and a system of methods, of legal methods through which the Indian can in future so operate for the self-government. As he—Mr. Monahan—told you, most of this legislation is permissive, rather than mandatory. There is a very good reason for this, but there are in this bill several provisions that are mandatory. For instance, the keystone of the arch, the declaration by Congress that the allotment policy is dead, and shall not be revived, that is a compulsory feature. There is furthermore the provision concerning heirship of lands. In many of your Southern California reservations where no allotment has taken place there is no trouble about heirship of lands, but I believe on the Yuma Reservation and especially some of the northwestern and eastern reservations the heirship problem is exceedingly pressing and important, because through its operation the Indian land is constantly being drained out of Indian possession and into white hands. Under the present system there is no other way of solving the complicated heirship situation except by final sale into white hands.

I shall ask Mr. Siegel in a moment to go into details of the land title and especially of the heirship provisions of this title.

The bill rightly starts with a long section prescribing ways and means and methods by which an Indian tribe may obtain self-government, may reach in the course of time the right to run its own affairs in its own way. I don't want to go into the technical provisions of the title extensively except as to the reason why the method of reaching self-government is through community organization. This title prescribes in detail how a tribe or how a part of a tribe may apply for a Federal charter, what this charter may contain, what powers it confers upon the Indian community organized under such a charter. It also prescribes the regulations and the procedure through which those communities may be organized. You will notice, if you will look through this section, that the rights to be granted, the functions of the Indian Service to be transferred to a community, that all these things are optional and are based on the ability of the Indian community and of its members to perform the services and exercise the authority in a competent manner. In other words this title does not mean that under the provisions of the bill the government will turn over to a tribe, as it exists now, all the appropriations which are now being made for its benefit and say: "Here it is: go to it." There is no such possibility. If you will look thru that title carefully you will see that every grant of power and funds is conditioned, is based on the ability of the members of the tribe to organize, to render service and exercise authority competently. You will also notice that this title provides for the protection of any minority within the chartered community so as to forestall a condition under which the ruling group might oppress and suppress the minority and deprive them of the rights which the constitution guarantees to every American.

The process of transferring power, authority, functions, and appropriations to organized or re-organized Indian communities must necessarily be a slow and gradual one. In order to speed up this process, in order to make it possible for the various Indian tribes to organize chartered communities, for these chartered communities to take over various functions at a higher speed, this legislation provides for special educational subsidies. The Commissioner and his advisors realize that the great crying need of the various Indian tribes is leadership, competent leadership. So the educational title of this bill was written for the special purpose of training your young men and young women not only in technical professions and for the administrative positions which you will have a chance to take over, but also, in character and leadership.

The educational title as it is drafted now, provides only for an annual appropriation of $50,000 to be used for special training of young man and women for administrative places on the basis of reimbursable loans to the extent of one-half the cost of this education. This half is to be returned over a term of years, but the payments are to be suspended whenever the person who has had the educational benefits is out of a job. In addition, it provides $15,000 for scholarships for training and education in universities and colleges for those qualified and able to go thru with professional education. You see that these two titles—self-government and education, are closely connected. The educational provision has been inserted for the special purpose of speeding up the process of Indian self-government by the creation of qualified persons who can take over positions and go into the administrative end of the Indian Service or of the new community.

MR. MONAHAN: I shall interrupt Mr. Woehlke for a moment because I have forgotten, to say that I want to meet the employees of the Indian Service. Mr. Biery has arranged for us to have our noon meal together.

MR. WOEHLKE: Before we leave the self-government title of this Wheeler-Howard bill, I would like to point out to you that I believe this is the first time in history that the Commissioner of Indian Affairs has taken an important piece of Indian legislation and consulted with his Indian constituents to find out from them what they thought of it and ask for suggestions concerning changes. I believe that is the first time that the Indians have been asked to take a hand in forming basic legislation affecting them. Under the present Commissioner the policy is to hear from those affected by this act. He also wants to point out how little control, over your own lives and your own property and homes, over your own persons, you Indians really have. As you know, Congress has through a long line of decisions been given plenary power to do with the Indians as it pleases. To all intents and purposes under the present law you are still prisoners of war; there is still in effect a law, going back to old wartime days, which makes it illegal and seditious for an Indian tribe to organize. The Secretary of Interior still has almost complete arbitrary power to regulate your life, your conduct and your property as he sees fit.

Now it is proposed to take all those old laws dating back to the days when the Indian was an enemy and prisoner of war, and to throw them on the scrap heap. That is what the Wheeler-Howard bill does. It takes arbitrary power away from the Secretary of Interior and turns this power and authority over to you. All these matters are covered in the various sections and clauses of the first title of the Wheeler-Howard bill. The technical aspect and procedures of the land title will be explained to you by the Assistant Solicitor of the Department of the Interior who had a hand in framing this title and putting it into proper legal language. It affects only a few reservations here but the credit part of the land title is of vital interest to all of you. If you own a piece of land, even if you have water on it, very little effective use of it can be made unless you have enough capital to build a house, buy plows, rakes, livestock and make this land productive.

Under the prevailing system the restrictions on your lands and various other circumstances have shut you off from the sources of credit open to the white people, with the result that you have had to rely on the government for your credit needs. This government credit has been so inadequate that the total amount of it available to an Indian in the United States has been about $1.50 per head per annum. Naturally you can't do very much with a credit restricted to such tiny sums. So in order to correct that feature of the situation, there was added to the bill during the hearings before the House Committee a credit section which sets up a revolving fund of $5,000,000, out of which to make loans not only to communities, but also to the individual members of the chartered communities for the purpose of developing their lands, for building homes, acquiring livestock and for other [purposes] which will enable the communities, or members of the communities, to make productive use of the land.

While this credit section was being discussed by the House Committee, one of the members said, "You have $5,000,000 here. That is wholly inadequate. We want to make it at least $10,000,000," which shows you the attitude of the members of Congress at the present time, both in the Senate and in the House. They are sincerely anxious to work out a constructive program which will fulfill the purposes of this proposed legislation, namely to make every Indian self-supporting and self-governing.

At the earliest possible moment this fund is to be loaned out without interest and the re-payments of the individual or community loans are to be extended over long periods of perhaps twenty-five or thirty years, so that if an individual should borrow any $2000 from this fund, his repayments would amount to less than $75.00 per year. This money, after its repayment, will go back into the fund to be loaned to others. I believe this credit provision, which is not in the bill before you, but which appears in the third part of the House Committee Hearings, is one of the most vital parts of the proposed law.

To sum up: We have in the first place provisions for the organization of self-governing communities, for the repeal of all the old statutes and laws, which kept the Indian in what we might call a jail—kept him still a prisoner of war. We have these provisions which should enable him to take on the obligations of a full-fledged citizen and to take over the functions and services which the Federal Government is rendering him now, to take them over as fast as he is able to handle them. You have that in the self-government title. In the educational phase of the bill you find methods and money for developing leaders and for training Indians to make wise use of government funds; in the credit section of the bill you find the provision for financing the operations of the Indians under the protection given their lands and their titles. And similarly in the title, which establishes a Court of Indian affairs, you will find provision for better and more sympathetic justice to the Indians.

Now, I am going to ask Mr. Siegel to speak to you about the land title of the bill and to set forth the benefits this provision seeks to establish.

MR. SIEGEL: I will try to explain to you in a few simple words what of course has been to the most of you a muddle. The land section has three objects: First, to reacquire some of the lands which were lost by the Indians. Although we cannot promise to buy the entire State of California, as there are white people who desire to come here to live during the winter months at least, we will try under the terms of this bill to get some of it back for you. This act authorizes $2,000,000 a year for land, a very small sum to be sure, but we will try to have that amount increased. If the Indians feel that this sum is insufficient, they should bring pressure on Congress to increase the amount.

The second object is to keep for the Indians the lands that still remain in Indian ownership. Therefore it is stated that there shall be no further allotment of lands which have not yet been allotted and the existing restrictions on alienation shall be continued indefinitely.

The third object is to meet what Mr. Woehlke has called the heirship problem. On the death of the first allottee, the land descended to many heirs, each one owning a small place. Sometimes one heir owns many small places in many allotments.

I will speak of the effect of this bill only on farm allotments, since only farm land has been allotted in this part of the country.

11:15 a.m. to 11:30 a.m. March 17th

In effect, all that the heirship provision and other provisions in Title 3 of this Act do to the farm lands which have been allotted in this area, is to gather together those small heirship places, put them into one piece and effect their assignment as one large unit; and thereafter it forbids further breaking up of that unit into small pieces that can't be used.

If there are any living allotments—that is to say allotments the original owner of which has not died, the only thing that will happen in substance will be that when the original owner dies, he can leave that land to his heirs, but cannot will it to so many heirs that it will be broken into such small pieces that nobody can use it. It keeps the original allotments in large enough farms so that they can be used economically.

I understand there are no grazing or timber allotments in this district so that we need not discuss such lands. With regard to farm land, this bill does really not end the evils of the allotment system. All it does is to prohibit subdivision of allotments into small units which are too small to be used to advantage; and secondly, where the land has been broken up and passed into heirship so that many people have many small pieces and no large piece, the Act brings small pieces together to be assigned in large enough farm units that can be used and will be ample to support a family, we hope, and thereafter prevents further subdivision into small units.

I do not think that very much more need be said about Title 3 save to add that all lands which are covered by this bill will be exempted from taxation indefinitely. Probably what I have said has not been very clear and if not, I should like all to write out questions and put them on that desk during the noon hour; we will devote the afternoon to answering these questions.

Furthermore I would like to say this with regard to the land title particularly. It was drafted by a few people in Washington who readily admit that their knowledge of the Indian land situation was not all that it should be. It would take a lifetime at least, to go around to all the reservations in this country, study their land situations thoroughly—enough at least to fully comprehend the problems peculiar to each reservation.

One of the main objects of our meeting here is to invite your criticisms of the bill as it stands and to get your suggestions as to how it might be improved. That is particularly important with regard to the land title. As soon as that title is passed, the heirship provisions of the bill automatically go into effect.

I want to say a few words relative to the Court of Indian Affairs. Briefly the reason that Title IV of this Bill is proposed is this: We have felt that at the present time, both the Federal Courts and State Courts as well as local District Attorneys, have been too busy with other matters or have not been very friendly to the Indian cause to pay much attention to the Indian cases. We, therefore, feel that it is first very necessary to provide adequate legal representation by appointing special attorneys and second, to establish a special Indian court which will devote all of its time to Indian matters and will be especially versed in Indian law and which we hope will be friendly to the Indian cause.

The Wheeler-Howard bill especially provides that the term of these judges shall be ten years. The reason that it was not made lifetime tenure was that we did not wish to turn over an absolute power to an Indian Court which might prove to be unresponsive to Indian wishes as the Indian Bureau has proven itself to be in the past.

I think the best way to conduct this meeting is not for the representatives of the Commissioner to take the time talking and saying their own say, but to spend their time answering questions which you are interested in. We are very anxious to find out what it is in this Bill which interests you or what problems this Bill attempts to deal with in which you are interested. I hope you will take the opportunity to write out your questions and as soon as we can get to them, we will try to answer them.

Mr. Monahan has asked me to clarify one problem with regard to the special Indian Court. There are two Courts which may be established under this Act. Two Indian Courts. One of them is a federal Indian Court and the other a Community Court. The officers of the local court may be appointed by a chartered community and will have jurisdiction to hear all petty cases involving the violation of local community ordinances such as drunkenness and like matters, the kind of cases which are now handled on some reservations by Indian judges appointed by the superintendent. The only difference will be that the judges will be appointed by the self-governing community if it so desires and the laws which it may enforce will be those which are enacted by the local Indian community. Over all violations of such laws, this Indian Court will have exclusive jurisdiction. There will be no appeal as the Act now reads. If it fines somebody for drunkenness, that will be the end of it. However, to avoid any danger of abuse of power, the extent of the fine or penalty which it may impose will be strictly limited to a small amount—$100.00 or three months in jail. I don't know whether this is a small amount or not. The amount can be made even smaller in the charter, which will be issued to the Indian Group, and if they don't want to face the danger of three months of jail during this nice weather, they can make one month the limit in their charter.

The special federal Indian court does not deal with the small petty criminal offenses with which the local community will deal. The special Indian Court will deal with all cases of controversy between Whites and Indians. Also all specific Indian cases which are now punishable in Federal Courts will be under the jurisdiction of the proposed special court which will also hear all cases brought to enforce any rights which are guaranteed by charter such as the privileges of a minority and the civil rights of all individuals. In other words the local community Indian Court will do the job which the Indian judge appointed by the Superintendent has done in the past, and, the special Indian Court will hear all other cases. Now if that still isn't clear, I will be glad to answer any questions about this part of the bill later.

One more word. As you all know, the California Indians for years have been interested in the Court of Claims. I suppose they have been interested in that more than anything else. At the speed the Indian Court of Claims cases are being settled now we won't be done with all of them for a hundred years or more. It would be a very nice thing if the Indians now living could enjoy the benefits of any judgments that are going to be obtained, and therefore a Bill has been drafted and was introduced some years ago. We expect to reintroduce it. It will provide the machinery for a very rapid and speedy decision of all Indian claims against the United States. This will be a special Indian Court of Claims which will devote all of its time to Indian claims against the United States. That bill, however, has nothing to do with this one and a special Court of Indian Claims has nothing to do with the Court proposed in this Bill. I should also add since you are undoubtedly interested and we are now talking about the Court of Claims matter that no money appropriated by this Act for the benefit of Indians will be set off against any claim which the Indians have against the United States. If that is not clear by the terms of this Bill, we will amend it so that it will be clear.

Secondly, any funds that the Indians will recover—any funds which an Indian chartered community recovers—will no longer be spent without the consent of the governing authorities of the Indian community. I think that is a very important matter because in the past the Indian Bureau has been in the habit of paying its way with Indian tribal funds and it is very important to provide that if any Indian moneys, any claims are settled in the future by a judgment award in the Court of Claims, the proceeds cannot be used for administrative expenses; that money should not be used to pay the salaries of Indian officials.

MR. MONAHAN: I think I will have to correct one statement that Mr. Siegel made. He said that the Indian Bureau was in the habit of using tribal funds to pay its expenses. In justice to the Indian Bureau I have protested against Congress appropriating money for that purpose. Congress insisted in using tribal money for administration of Indian affairs on the Indian reservations. I don't know that that money has been paid for salaries in the Indian Office in Washington, but it has been used constantly for the support of the Superintendent's office on some Indian reservations over the protest of the Commissioner of Indian Affairs for years back as far as I can remember.

MR. SIEGEL: There are two other sections in the Bill I want to bring up. There is one section in the Bill relative to special education. It is an additional type of special education in addition to the present type of schooling.

There is another matter that I want Mr. Woehlke to explain and that is relative to whom the charters will apply when they are granted so that there is no confusion between existing reservations and communities and new ones that might be established to take care of the 100,000 landless Indians scattered around the United States that may want to form communities.

Finally there is nothing in this Bill that would in any way affect any of the present treaty rights.

11:45 A.M. Till Noon

March 17, 1934

MR. WOEHLKE: We ought to bear down heavily on that point. This bill is aside from any treaty rights or from any claims which any of you, singly or collectively, may have against the Government. They are not affected one way or the other. As Mr. Siegel told you, there is a bill which aims to speed up the process of collecting money due the Indians under ancient treaty rights by first speeding up the bringing of those claims to trial and simplifying the procedure and by supplying special tribunals. As Mr. Siegel said, under the present procedure the five or six hundred claims and suits of various Indian tribes against the United States Government will take one hundred years to finish. The Commissioner would like to see them all given their day in Court, and to have treaty rights settled within ten years, instead of one hundred years. The expectation, the hope, or the promise of very large sums to be derived out of the U.S. Treasury at some future date is acting as a blight; it is paralyzing the people who harbor it. It is being used by white people to prevent them from helping themselves. In many tribes this pot at the end of the rainbow which is constantly being dangled under the noses of the Indians by frequently self-seeking persons is preventing them from doing the things now which are right before them, through which they can realize their ambitions and get somewhere.

That is the case all over the Indian country everywhere. There is a dream of $100,000,000, of $200,000,000, of $100,000,000 that is being dangled before them with the promise that they will all be wealthy some day, if we can only push these suits, but in the meantime cough up so that our attorneys may be paid, or so we may do this, that or the other thing. Yet at the present speed, it will take one hundred years to settle all claims, and after they are finally brought to judgment, it is still up to Congress to appropriate the money. Even after getting judgment, it is still up to Congress to say that they want to pay the judgment. The Commissioner of Indian Affairs is very anxious to see that justice is done to all tribes that have claims against the Government, so that the old ghost which is paralyzing present-day activities, this will-o'-the-wisp which is leading you into the swamp of helpless inertia, may be laid for good—that all claims may be settled once and for all, and the Indian people may set their hands to the plow right now to pull themselves out of the hole. It has nothing to do with the Wheeler-Howard Bill, which leaves them just where they are. This must be completely understood.

I was talking a little while ago about the special education section. I think I ought to go a little more deeply into the subject. Under the self-government title of the bill you will find that all the way through the Secretary of the Interior and the Commissioner of Indian Affairs are endeavoring to hand over to you certain powers, rights, privileges and appropriations. Almost every section of that bill deals with the transfer to the Indians of functions and authorities, but all these transfers are based upon a chartered community. A chartered community does not mean necessarily an entire tribe or a single reservation. It means that a certain territory is set aside, is delimited, and that the residents within that territory by their own initiative, under their own steam, and through the petition of 25% of the resident population for a charter and the vote of 3/5 of that population in favor of that charter may broach the matter to the Department. All of the enrolled members living within this territory which is proposed to organize into a community are eligible as members of the community, and are entitled to vote and say whether they want a community or not.

The enrolled members within the area must petition for a charter, and after they have decided by a majority for the charter, they must negotiate with the Secretary of the Interior for the powers, functions and kind of community organization they want to have. These negotiations as to the kind of powers they want, as to the services they may take on, all these negotiations must be carried on carefully because it is a most important step in the entire procedure to determine the character and quality of the charter, and of its various provisions.

That is where the special educational feature comes in. Suppose you organize a community and suppose you have a charter, and that charter gives power to take over the functions of the agricultural extension service. As soon as there are members of the tribe who wish to take over that work, the section on education provides ways and means whereby the young men may be sent to school, may be given special training that would qualify them for positions. Before you can take over that service you must have men qualified to perform the work, and that is where the educational provision comes in—to give a community the chance to develop men to do the job. That provision also applies to a number of other services which a chartered community may take over and do for itself.

There is a distinction between the services which such a community may take over and for which it will derive funds from the Government and the job created in the administration and organization of the community itself. If you have in a community a council, and a president of that council and a secretary and certain committees which run the business of the community, then it would be strictly up to the community to provide for any compensation that these officials may receive. It is purely a community matter. If you want to govern politically your own affairs, you must be prepared to accept the burden of responsibility that goes with authority.

Afternoon Session

March 17, at 1:50 p.m.

MR. SIEGEL: There are so many questions and so many difficult ones that I don't know which to begin with. I shall start with the hardest one. Here it is—"What becomes of the allottee's land in case of an allottee's death. What must he do to protect his family?" If an allottee dies, his land will go to his heirs, but there will be such restrictions as are necessary to prevent the breaking up of that allotment in many small pieces which cannot be used separately. The original owner may make a valid will, but the number of heirs or devisees under his will must be limited so that there will be no unnecessary breaking-up of land into many small pieces. What is true of land, also to improvements on the land. The improvements will go to the heirs, but the same restrictions as to land will prevail. In regard to land which has already passed into the heirship status and has been broken up into small pieces, the act will operate in this fashion: If an individual owns several small pieces, he will be enabled to turn them over to the community and receive in return the right to use a single piece of land big enough to make a living on. This assignment is no different from an allotment equal in amount of land to the total number of acres which he would have inherited in small pieces.

QUESTION: What steps does an allottee take to retain his rights on the reservation and at the same time be a non-resident?

ANSWER: The rights of a non-resident allottee are protected as much as the rights of an allottee residing on the reservation. In other words, no property is taken from an Indian whether he lives on or off the reservation.

QUESTION: What provision does the bill make to protect non-residents and other Indians enrolled in the reservation?

ANSWER: We are not going to take land of an allotted Indian and give it to an unallotted Indian. We will have to purchase land for that purpose. However, an unallotted Indian may not feel that he cares to spend his time working the soil, therefore the bill provides there education for Indians who do not care to work the soil, educates them for professional careers either in the Indian Service or in the white world.

QUESTION: Differentiate between effect of the bill on reservation and non-reservation Indians—non-ward Indians residents in California.

MR. SIEGEL: The bill does not differentiate between them. It holds out its benefits to both according to their needs.

QUESTION: Will the non-ward Indians of California be benefited by this bill?

ANSWER: Yes. If the person is 1/4 degree of Indian blood or more, we are authorized to spend two million dollars a year for the purchase of lands. These lands may be added to existing lands on reservations or may be used to start new communities for Indians without any land whatsoever.

MRS. MILLS: In other words, state ward is just another term meaning state citizen?

MR. SIEGEL: Yes, there is no such thing as a state "ward."

MRS. MILLS: The explanation is then, that persons who are not accepted as enrolled Indians would continue to be state wards.

MR. SIEGEL: With the possible exception of New York, no state has established guardianship over Indians.

First: "Is the authority of the Secretary of the Interior as exercised now in any way curtailed by this Bill?" I think the answer is yes and in some respects let me frankly say no. It will be a very large question to answer but I will try to make a general statement first with regard to the chartering of communities. There is no doubt that the Secretary is given very wide discretionary powers to charter a community. However, once that community is chartered, the Bill does provide that the Commissioner and the Secretary must establish standards and conditions on the fulfillment of which various functions now performed by the Secretary of the Interior and the Commissioner will be transferred to the community.

The only limitation on the Secretary's discretion in making the conditions is this, that any community or any group objecting to the Secretary's action, may through regular channels forward their protests to Congress, and the Secretary must forward that protest and his reasons. We believe that if the Indians are organized and are given established channels through which to lodge their protests, this will be a method of curtailing the Secretary's powers.

It may be possible that the discretionary authority which is given the Secretary under this Bill to establish self-governing communities and to determine the conditions under which functions should be transferred, should be limited and if there were a way to do it, I am reasonably confident it would be done. However, we must bear in mind that we are dealing with diverse conditions. The conditions in California widely differ from conditions in Oregon and Washington in Oklahoma and even the Pueblo Indians differ among themselves.

Therefore, it is absolutely necessary to have a bill sufficiently flexible so that it can be adjusted to meet the desires and needs of the various Indian groups. On the other hand, we do not recognize that the wide discretionary power given to the Secretary has been the source of grave abuse and we therefore attempt to establish a system for the transfer of function and we do provide that if he has established those conditions and others that are made, there is no further discretionary authority left. Although an unfavorable Secretary of the Interior or a Commissioner of Indian Affairs could frustrate Title I by refusing to issue charters, the bill authorizes an appeal to Congress by the Indians.

Second: If the Secretary of the Interior does transfer a function, he transfers a power to the Community which cannot be taken away from the Community unless the Community fails to live up to the condition under which the function is transferred. The Bill does not provide who is to judge whether or not those conditions have been lived up to. It has been suggested the Indian Court should have charge of this matter. The Bill might be accordingly amended but I do not think that the Bill in any event increases the discretionary authority of the Secretary of the Interior and it does tend to decrease it.

With regard to the Land Title: the Secretary of the Interior if the Bill is passed will have no discretionary authority to continue the allotment system. This will come to an end. There will be no future discretionary authority to issue a large number of forced patents on Indians. I will admit, however, that the Secretary of the Interior probably has at least as much authority over Indian tribal property as he has heretofore enjoyed.

It is impossible for me to go over the 4 titles of the bill and examine where the Secretary has been given discretion and where he has not. In brief the Secretary is given a very large discretion to determine whether he should charter a community or not. With regard to the land, the Secretary of the Interior is given no discretion in determining whether the allotment system shall come to an end, but he is given some discretion over the leasing of land which he did not have before, but I think that this feature of the bill could be amended so that it could not be abused.

QUESTION: If a group of Indians do not want to have self-government and do not accept the bill, would it affect them?

ANSWER: No. Self-government is purely voluntary. No charter will be issued unless 3/5 of the people residing in the territory in which the charter is granted approve it.

QUESTION: Will they get help like the rest?

ANSWER: The educational feature of the bill will no doubt apply to such people. As to the others, the allotment system will come to an end upon the passage of this act. Whether or not the community chooses to make use of the new powers will be left entirely to the people. If they share in the charter move they will share in its benefits.

QUESTION: If this bill passes will they automatically close the present boarding schools for Indians?

ANSWER: The answer is that this bill has nothing to do with the opening or closing of the Indian schools. That is a matter for the commissioner to decide on the individual merits of the boarding school. It will also depend upon whether or not Congress will furnish the appropriation.

QUESTION: What will become of the land that has been allotted to the Indians and which they have spent on in improving?

ANSWER: My answer to some other question has already answered that question. The use of such land would be retained by the owner; after his death it would go to the heirs, but with restrictions and could not be subdivided into such small units that it could not be used to advantage.

Before I go any further into this other list of questions, which I see have been carefully prepared, I would like to know if I have satisfactorily answered the questions already asked. If so I will continue.

QUESTION FROM WOMAN IN THE AUDIENCE: Seems that on one list of questions there were two questions and only one was answered.

QUESTION FROM THE AUDIENCE: Who will decide which Indians are to go to school on these reimbursable funds?

MR. SIEGEL: First of all let me say that only one-half of the sum which is given to the Indians is reimbursable and in some instances none of it will be reimbursable. The responsibility is placed on the Commissioner under the terms of this act. It may be a good suggestion that such responsibility be placed on some of the chartered Indian communities. The Commissioner is given the responsibility.

QUESTION FROM THE AUDIENCE: Who appoints the judges in the Indian court?

ANSWER: If memory serves me rightly the President, with the consent of the Senate.

QUESTION: Who will pay the educational expenses?

ANSWER: If students die before payment of such loans, the bill provides that the obligation to repay should be suspended temporarily during the period of unemployment, and I don't know whether the court would call it a period of unemployment in case of death or not. I would say that although such obligation, if any, is not a personal one, it would be taken out of the estate before passing on to the heirs. I would see no objection to eliminating that charge on the estate, and provide that the payment should terminate at death as well as during the period of unemployment.

QUESTION: How will the unallotted Indian on unallotted reservations be cared for?

ANSWER: Some persons say that the $2,000,000.00 to purchase land will not be adequate. Pressure then should be made on Congress to increase the amount. We would all appreciate it. What was your other question, please?

QUESTION: Well, it's the Howard Bill. Isn't that to be discussed this afternoon?

ANSWER: Yes, which bill is it?

QUESTION: Bill No. HR803.

ANSWER: What does it deal with?

QUESTION: It deals with Indian Affairs.

ANSWER: How interesting. What part? I don't know what the bill is. Have you a copy of it?

QUESTION: No, I haven't.

ANSWER: There are several bills before the House, some large, some small and I can't keep in mind what the bills are by number. If I had a copy I might answer that, but I don't know what it is about. Doesn't anyone have a copy? We can't answer the question without knowing what the bill is about.

QUESTION: Explain more definitely with regard to the 2/3 vote held on reservations?

ANSWER: It's a 3/5 vote. 3/5 of the people of the territory have to vote in favor before granting a charter to that community.

QUESTION: You made the statement 3/5 of the people in the community, and I would like to know what is the status of people owning land on reservation, but living in town. Have they voting rights?

ANSWER: The bill does not give them the right to vote with regard to a proposed charter, as non-residents are not eligible to vote. However, even if the individual is excluded from membership in the chartered community, they will have a right to their property—their property in that community cannot be taken away from them.

QUESTION: Who is a state ward?

ANSWER: As I understand it, the individual who breaks his tribal relationships and takes his place in the outside world is known as a non-ward Indian. I am not perfectly clear that an individual who has broken off his relations necessarily ceases to be a ward of the Government, but to all practical purposes he probably does.

QUESTION: In case of an allotment where there are more than ten heirs, how is the land to be divided?

ANSWER: You mean where there are too many heirs so that the land would be divided into small pieces. Where there are too many heirs to one allotment they would be limited to a number who could use the land economically. For the other heirs new land will be purchased. But the land will not be subdivided in such small pieces that it cannot be used to advantage. The bill expects to do away with dividing the land into small units.

QUESTION FROM WOMAN IN THE AUDIENCE: What will become of my land on the reservation. I don't belong on the reservation anymore.

ANSWER: That will remain your property and will go to your heirs for their use, the amount of land that you now own. Heirships and live allotments on the death of the owner will be kept—not divided into small pieces. The same amount of land will be given to the party entitled to it.

QUESTION: Where would land be given from—on that reservation?

ANSWER: Yes, on the same reservation.

QUESTION: What is the status of an Indian on the reservation so far as his citizenship is concerned? Are you considering him a citizen of the United States as yourself?

ANSWER: The Act of 1924 conferred citizenship on the Indian. This bill leaves that as it was.

2:30 P.M. Saturday,

March 17, 1934

QUESTION: Does this bill make the Secretary of the Interior final authority on matters pertaining to community charters?

ANSWER: No. The Secretary of the Interior has a wide authority in determining whether a community will be chartered and what powers will be granted, but once specific terms are fixed the Secretary has no final authority.

QUESTION: Will this bill make Indians competent witnesses in court?

ANSWER: Nothing could be done to add or detract from the character of Indian witnesses.

QUESTION: Is it not possible that benefits can be obtained under existing authority?

ANSWER: There is no authority to change or repeal the allotment system under existing legislation. No.

QUESTION: The California Indians are citizens of the United States by treaty with Mexico and by subsequent Acts of Congress. Does passage of this bill abridge citizenship?

ANSWER: No. There is no renunciation of citizenship. Although the Indian has been a citizen, he has also been a Federal ward, and the real genuine privileges of citizenship may be denied while the hollow core of citizenship remains.

QUESTION: When there are two factions on a reservation, may they be given charters as separate communities?

ANSWER: The Act gives authority to the Secretary of the Interior to charter those factions as separate communities, and gives authority to buy new lands for both factions.

QUESTION: What provisions are made for individual Indian water rights?

ANSWER: No adequate provision is made for water rights by the bill.

QUESTION: Can an Indian sell his lands to the Government and become a full citizen?

ANSWER: The Secretary is given authority to purchase allotments, but no authority to purchase personal property. It is impossible to deal with all situations alike.

QUESTION: Why is the present administration removing qualified Indians from the Service?

ANSWER: There has been no case where an Indian has been removed from the service where qualified. If you know of any instances, the matter will be remedied.

QUESTION: Will this bill have the right to infringe on constitutional rights of Indians?

ANSWER: No.

QUESTION: Is it not possible that any group of Indians in the State of California can incorporate their number, thus securing community rights?

ANSWER: No. However, if they can, there is of course nothing in the bill which would forbid them from doing so. We would encourage them to do so.

Saturday 2:30 p.m.

QUESTION: Is it not a legal fact that the bill entails legal disabilities?

ANSWER: I do not know. I certainly can see no legal disability.

MR. SIEGEL: I am confident there could have been a much more effective administration of Indian laws than there has been. This is the major purpose, and to provide a training system, and thus end the day when the Indian Bureau can arbitrarily control the life of the Indians without the possibility of court review. Mr. Collier worked many years in attacking the abuses, and the bill which is now proposed is an effort to provide some measure of self-government and self-determination which Indians have never had before. The process of starting self-governing communities is left largely discretionary, and must be left so. The bill, once begun, looks towards an increase rather than decrease of self-determination. The allotment system under which we have worked continued in effect ever since 1887, although its evolution meant complete destruction of Indian life. Nevertheless, the principle of inertia which somehow works in Indian affairs has managed to keep the system going for a long time, and will continue to do so. The difficulty is to make the change.

The way to be sure that there will not be any experiments you do not want is to organize into politically effective communities which can transmit their desires to Congress, and not remain as they are, wards without a voice in their own affairs. Of course, I cannot guarantee the next Congress will not change this act, but they will probably not do so. Congress does not very frequently change Indian policy even if the policy has bad results. If the new policy has good results, there will be no reason for Congress to change it—except to improve it.

QUESTION: Wherein has the Indian been given a voice? Will the Indians' approval or disapproval make any difference? Is it not a violation of all American principle?

ANSWER: I would suppose that this very extraordinary occasion—calling together a Congress of Indians from various parts of the country, not a very usual occurrence in Indian history, is plain evidence that we wish not only to explain the bill, but to get your impressions and desires, and shape the bill accordingly.

MR. SIEGEL: There is nothing in the Act which deprives the individual of his citizenship rights, but grants to a large number of ward Indians who have been controlled by the Secretary of the Interior the right to self-government.

Now the problem of segregation. There is no desire to put a closed wall around the Indian. We merely believe that the policy of forcing the Indian into the white community proceeded at much too fast a pace in the past. It was done much too rapidly. Indians were turned loose before they were able to compete in the white world. We recognize the problem of thc Indian has changed since the white man came and there is no desire to bring about racial segregation through the new communities. The Indians will be trained to perform all the functions that white people ordinarily performed, which the Indian Service is now performing, and we hope those standards will be high enough so that if the Indian chooses to enter the white world he may be able to compete with the white man. The Indian may leave the community, but we believe at the present time and for some time to come there will be a large group of Indians who will prefer to stay within the Indian community, or must stay because they cannot compete in the white world. We believe every effort should be made to raise the standard of living and that the group should not be deprived of a voice in its own affairs. They should be allowed to stay on the reservation and only so long as they want to stay. We believe those Indians who want to stay there should be given an opportunity.

That is all this policy means. It is not an attempt to segregate Indians. We will make a greater effort to bring the white man's civilization to the Indian, a greater opportunity for education than ever before—lift the group that remain on the reservation so that they may, if they choose to leave the group, be able to compete more easily in the white world than if they were forced out as in the past.

With regard to citizenship. This bill does not take away your right to vote or your right to exercise any right you might have as a citizen, but gives to Indians who have not been free some self-government, self-determination in their own community if he does not want to go into the white community.

With regard to bringing court action to restrict the Secretary of the Interior. Under the existing laws the Secretary of the Interior is frequently given authority to act in his discretion and unless he very gravely abuses that power, he acts within his rights either with or without your consent. The charter will be so worded that there will be no doubt as to the rights of the parties. It will take away discretionary authority, or transfer it from the Secretary to the Indians, and those two ways we believe are the ways out that this bill chooses.

MR. MONAHAN: The bill HR 803, discussed a few minutes ago—Mr. Dady and Mr. Biery are unable to find a copy of the bill in the office. I haven't the slightest idea what the bill is. I wonder if it could be the Howard Bill, which is identical with this bill.

QUESTION: If that is the bill you mean, here it is. I have a copy of it here in this report. (*Gives bill to lady.*)

Meeting turned over to Mr. Biery for entertainment during the intermission.

MR. MONAHAN: Now let us proceed and ask the delegates to raise questions and speak any way they wish. I am sure many of you will have something to say.

MR. SIEGEL: May I say that the only question in which you have to make some definite decision before this bill is passed is in regard to the land matter. As we have already explained, no group will be chartered unless a large majority of members of a proposed community approve of that charter. There is nothing here that I can see with regard to self-government, Title I, nor with regard to the educational features to which any of you could fairly object now. You might very well refuse to accept a charter and we would not object to your decision, but you will always have opportunity to draw that charter according to your wishes. But the heirship provision, which is a critical one in the land system, will go into effect immediately on the passage of this Act and I wish anyone here who does not understand Title 3 of the Land Bill will raise any objections and give any suggestions as to how to improve that Title. It is our opportunity now and we will try to answer the questions.

STEVEN KITCHEN (Mission Creek Res.): I want to ask, are you a personal representative of the Commissioner to investigate the rights and welfare of the Indians of the State of California?

MR. MONAHAN: No. I am here as an assistant to the Commissioner of Indian Affairs. Let us continue this meeting. If there are any other matters you want to take up outside of this let us do so.

MRS. R. C. BLOCH (Osage Indian of Oklahoma): If the direct heir to an heirship land is less than 1/4 blood and that would be the only direct heir, does that land go back to the tribe or is it held by that heir of less than 1/4?

MR. SIEGEL: There is nothing in that Bill imposing a blood requirement, but the Secretary of Interior is given authority to change the existing rules with regard to inheritance where they have worked what he considered evil results in the past. I am frank to say that the discretionary power in that section, much too great a power, should be curtailed before the bill is passed, if it is passed. In any event it was not intended to make a blood requirement as to inheritance; rather it was intended to give the Secretary of the Interior the authority to prevent subdivision of allotments into small unworkable units.

MRS. BLOCH: In the matter of final decisions left to the Secretary of the Interior, in case that these matters are left with the Probate Court and are in the State of Oklahoma, then what?

MR. SIEGEL: Mr. Woehlke says "There has been a Bill introduced to take from the Oklahoma courts the jurisdiction they now exercise in Indian Probate matters." Even if that jurisdiction remains or if it is taken away from them that has nothing to do with the question as to whether or not a blood degree will be established as a requirement for inheritance. The question is first, what is the law, and secondly what Court is to administer the law. Under existing law the state inheritance law applies. The Oklahoma Probate Court administers that law with regard to the Indian estate. With regard to most other Indian lands the Secretary of the Interior has authority to determine heirs. Under Section 10, Title 3, he is given power over existing laws of inheritance. And I would say that if the Bill is passed a blood test requirement would not be needed. However, the Secretary of the Interior, under this Act, may give to a chartered Indian community the authority to establish rules of inheritance and to administer their probate Indian estates. It is possible under that authority that the Indian community could establish a blood test for inheritance.

MR. MONAHAN: There is no mention in this bill of degrees of blood except in one place where it limits the purchase of land to persons with one-quarter or more of Indian blood.

MR. SIEGEL: There are large numbers of Indians in California scattered around who have no reservations. In other states there are thousands of Indians who have no reservation. This bill provides for the purchase of land which might be used for such Indians if they wish to go on these lands, and it provides that a person eligible to use such land if and when purchased must be at least 1/4 degree of blood.

SATURINO CALAC (Escondido, Calif.): My question is: Should this Bill become effective as a law, what effect would it have upon the present allotments that have been given and which allottees have trust patents. Would this prevent the Secretary of the Interior to refrain from giving further patents?

MR. SIEGEL: Did you mean would it prevent the Secretary of the Interior from issuing fee patents? It will definitely. First of all the Act forbids any further allotments. Secondly, it continues trust patents indefinitely—forever—unless Congress acts. The existing restrictions and trust periods extend and continue as tax exemption of the trust allotments. Now with regard to the other things which the Act does to trust-patented land, I will speak with regard to farm land only. The only effect that the bill will have on trust-patented land, aside from what I have already mentioned, will be this: If it is a living allotment which is still owned by the person to whom it was originally allotted, it will go to his heirs but there will be provisions, which will prevent the break-up of the land into small units. Secondly: If it is already in the heirship status and you have already inherited this land, then those small pieces can be put together into one unit and that will be given to the owner and to the heirs but not for subdivision.

CALAC: Ownership still continues?

MR. SIEGEL: Ownership in any sense you have now. Your right now as an owner is to occupy that land and receive a rental from it, to receive a fee patent and sell it. All those rights—except the right to sell—are guaranteed.

Where you have certain scattered pieces of land which you cannot possibly occupy as a whole now, the bill enables you to exchange the 4 small pieces for one large one.

MR. SIEGEL: It is necessary to bring small pieces together in one piece. The only purpose of the land inheritance feature is to prevent breaking up allotments into too small pieces for anyone to make a living on.

QUESTION: How long is this restraint to hold good insofar as it has to do with a piece of land under a restricted trust patent?

ANSWER: No further certificates of competency will be granted under this act. However, this might be done if the individual desires to abandon the community: He could abandon the community and the community would have to purchase his land. It would not have to pay for it all at once, but would have authority to purchase the interest of any person who left the community.

QUESTION: Is there a provision in this bill that has to do with the proposed policy of the Indian Office to institute higher standards among us that will enable us to be fit for citizenship? Is it reversing the present policy of civilizing the Indians and forcing him to revert to old conditions?

MR. SIEGEL: The Indian will be permitted to go in either direction that he chooses. If the Navajos wish to retain their ancient tradition, they may do so, but if the California Indian prefers to go with the white man, he will be given the opportunity to do so much greater than ever before, because we propose to begin a real thoroughgoing educational system which will train Indians to take their place in the white world as never before. Furthermore, even for those Indians who do not choose to go into the white world and nevertheless progress in the ways of the white man, this bill also provides that the Indians may have the advantages of white civilization without competing in the white world. The economic and financial aid are meant to bring all economic and educational advantages into the Indian reservation, if he chooses to have it there. If he chooses to remain in the Indian community he should have all the opportunities that white people have, and sufficient opportunity to raise his standard of living to that of whites.

QUESTION: I think that any policy that gives Indians opportunity of choosing for himself brings about danger of reverting to old conditions that might be a menace to Indian people. The policy should be to encourage our people to progress. That is personally my sentiment. I feel the question might be raised is the self-government and its policy to be under the supervision of the Indian Office? Are they to suggest what the self-government is to be?

MR. SIEGEL: The Indian Office intends to cooperate in every way and encourage the Indians to improve their standard. Even these Indians who prefer ancient traditions will be encouraged to take advantage of modern science. There is no intention of going back to the old days. I will say, however, that the present Indian administration does not share the view of most Indian administrations of the past that there was nothing in the Indian civilization worth saving. On the contrary it thinks there are certain things in Indian life that should be preserved if Indians wish to preserve them.

QUESTION: That is swell, but we must remember that the foundation of our nation was founded by its forefathers upon Christian principle, and I don't feel that there should be any opportunity given by which Indians may go back. There is that tendency to go back, because we see it.

MR. WOEHLKE: Go back of what?

INDIAN ANSWER: To the old tribal ceremonials and Indian religion.

MR. WOEHLKE: You do not believe in the constitutional principle which guaranties religious freedom?

JACK MEYERS, spokesman for the Santa Rosa Reservation: I have no questions to ask, but would like to comment a little and tell something about the Santa Rosa Reservation in regards to the inadequate appropriation of $2,000,000 which is far too insignificant for the work which it is proposed to carry on. The Santa Rosa Reservation is between five and six thousand feet high, in rocks. We cannot farm for a living, we cannot grow crops. We have to depend upon cattle grazing. The ground is all rocks, and with that inadequate $2,000,000, if they go along like they have, it will be one hundred years before they get any new land. I wish to go on record that the Santa Rosa Indians want more grazing land because that is the only way the people can subsist. I thank you.

MR. MONAHAN: I can testify you need the land. There is nothing left but a great gully that is washed out. At least $30,000,000 is needed for Indian land, but it is hopeless to get any money from Congress because Congress has many demands and many demands from groups better organized than the Indians of the United States.

RAMON AMES, spokesman, Barona Reservation: I am very glad about seeing laws for self-government, and I think self-government is coming back.

In regard to these people who are non-reservation people who have been coming from Mexico to this country and visiting our reservation and put on the census and becoming members of reservations, I protest against this.

MR. SIEGEL: Only members or descendants of members may have Indian rights. There are some reservations where the rolls have been closed.

WINSLOW CURE, Santa Ysabel Reservation: I would like to know what provisions are made for Indians who do not want to come under bill. Is there separate bill for them? Why are they excluded?

MR. MONAHAN: The Five Civilized Tribes and the New York Indians are under special legislation, and for diplomatic reasons it is not best to mix that with this. New York State takes care of the New York Indians.

DR. BARTLETT: I have learned to think that perhaps the white civilization is not the wisest, when there is so much failure among the whites. I feel that the Indians have something to teach the whites. I think something will come to them if they really recognize that the white man is recognizing their arts and crafts.

YUMA DELEGATES: I understand that trust patent on land is to be extended indefinitely. If it is that way, will the Indians of our reservation have to pay for water charges against these lands? I would like to know if they have to pay water charges on that land if it is leased out to white men?

MR. MONAHAN: The bill would not affect that particular matter. The point is this: That the land will be held in trust patent forever unless Congress changes the bill. Therefore, it remains, as Indian-owned land forever, and under the so-called Leavitt bill passed two years ago, water charges cannot be assessed so long as land is owned by Indians. Operating and maintenance costs must be paid for somehow. Someone has got to pay for it. It can be paid for in labor or in cash. The Government cannot be expected to continue paying irrigation charges. As long as the land stays in Indian ownership the operation cost cannot be assessed against land.

MR. SIEGEL: Hitherto the charges were assessed against the allottee. Under the new system the technical title to property will be in tribe or community. Charges will be assessed against the community.

Troup 4:16 Sat.

HARRY SAMSON (Reno, Nev.): I would like to ask on that question, the last word you spoke, in case a chartered community does not pay for the water right on that land, what will come if they fail to pay for the water?

MR. SIEGEL: The government will have the right just as now to turn off the water if O and M are not paid.

MR. SAMSON: Over at Reno we have something like 200 Paiutes and Washoes and the majority of us over there have nothing. We are living in a little colony, 20 to 30 acres. We have little lots and if this bill should be enacted as a law and if the community should recognize us and issue a charter and the majority preferred to purchase land elsewhere from Reno, will that segregate us from the whites in Reno?

MR. SIEGEL: Sorry, I do not get the connection.

MR. SAMSON: I mean, well say, if the community is chartered and the majority of Indians prefer to purchase land elsewhere from Reno, in that way I think this bill would segregate the Indian from the white community.

MR. SIEGEL: Are these Indians living on their own land? It is altogether possible that the Secretary could purchase land away from the place where they are living, but I wish to make this clear; even if the majority do want to live away, the minority do not have to go. It is purely voluntary and you would not have to follow them.

MR. SAMSON: Supposing a group of Indians in the city, would they be compensated for their land?

MR. SIEGEL: Yes.

JUANITA MACHADO: I am very sorry Commissioner Collier is not present here today to hear what I have to say. It seems every time that a government official is to be here, an excuse is made for him not being here.

MR. MONAHAN: Mr. Collier himself has never said that he would be here. The newspaper report was purely a newspaper story. It is impossible for him to go to every meeting in the country. This then is not a changed schedule.

MRS. MACHADO: Nevertheless, don't you think that the only way to give full justice to California Indians is first for our government to fulfill the promise of our treaties before we can consider any other bill?

MR. SIEGEL: The answer is, no. I do not think so. I do not see any reason why the two bills have to be considered together if we offer one advantage. I do not see any reason why it must be rejected. Let me call your attention to the fact we are also about to introduce another bill which will speed up the adjudication of Indian claims. You know that at the present rate it will take at least one hundred years to settle all of them. At the present the benefit would not come to you in your lifetime. Mr. Collier wants the judgments to benefit Indians now living. He also wants it understood that appropriations made for the benefit of Indians by this act can not be set off against any court of claims suit now pending. What

Mr. Collier offers the Indians, he offers to them only voluntarily. If you choose to wait until your claims are settled, you may do so even if the Howard-Wheeler bill becomes law.

MR. COSTO: Suppose a group of Indians live on wasteland reservations, what would become of these lands? Of course, I am speaking of reservations which are worthless and want something new. What would become of these lands?

MR. SIEGEL: What would you suggest.

COSTO: Throw them away, all them and get something better.

MR. SIEGEL: It would be possible to have other land. There is appropriated $2,000,000 a year to purchase land for those who need more land or have no land at all.

COSTO: But it is inadequate. How are we assured that we will get some of that out here? Nothing assured where it will be spent. No way for us to compel Congress to spend it for us. We cannot be assured that it will be spent for us. Congress will say how it will be spent. It will not do away with bureaucracy. Court of Indian Affairs will create seven new judges, attorneys. Is not that creating more offices for the citizens to pay for?

Saturday 4:16

MR. SIEGEL: What do you want, justice with judges or judges without justice?

COSTO: With us, we have had justice and will continue to do so.

MR. SIEGEL: I am delighted to learn that the citizens of California have had all the justice they need and deserve.

COSTO: Under this bill Indians will own no land, no personal property. It will all belong to the community.

MR. SIEGEL: The proposed certificate is in nature of an allotment title and will be a property right in every sense that a trust patent is. If you want it discussed in terms of jurisprudence, I will explain it to you later.

COSTO: We have nothing we can call our own.

MR. SIEGEL: I have said that you will have the same property rights as under the allotment system.

COSTO: That is quite communistic isn't it? Communism, socialism. Going right back to that, taking away all rights belonging to everyone. Can't own anything for ourselves. Isn't that right?

MR. SIEGEL: No.

ROBERT MIGUEL: I want to speak a little bit about the treaties. My father was a man who fought in the Mexican war. I know what he told me about it when I was a little boy. From what I understand Mexican government made treaty with United States and they have rights to lands. That is in this treaty with United States they were to be responsible.

Before that the Spanish government had control and the lands were ours and they are ours today if we are treated right by people who had hearts, but we are treated like animals. Made treaties with Mexico and today they do not respect those treaties.

MR. SIEGEL: They can pay your claims whenever you establish them in the Court of Claims.

MIGUEL: We were on this continent first and you took the wild fruits, the water and the lands we were living on. After American government got in this ward business, they promised us this and that and have fulfilled nothing on those promises. They forget rights our ancestors had, but now Indians get what is left and citizens get the best.

MR. SIEGEL: You do have the same rights as your ancestors.

MIGUEL: Way things are now they gave us schools and lands, but times have changed. Not paid a penny for anything: Settle it in Congress, not with Indian Bureau. I do not know about how the eastern Indians were treated, probably same as we are. I want you people to clearly understand about our rights.

MR. SIEGEL: Yes.

MR. WOEHLKE: I fully agree with you that the claims of all the Indian tribes throughout the country should be adjudicated and settled, the rights determined and money paid at the earliest possible moment. Mr. Collier agrees with you and has already taken steps. As we have repeated at least five times that a bill has been introduced to create a special court to consider nothing but your claims and the claims of Sioux and Chippewas, Pottawatomies and 60 or 70 other Indian tribes treated in the same way that you have been.

You are not the only ones who got it in the neck. The California Indian program was not the only Indian program we have outlined. Look at the history of the Five Civilized Tribes, how they have been persecuted—land taken away in Florida, Georgia, Alabama, Tennessee, how they were placed under state laws a hundred years ago and had their allotted land taken away by force, how they were taken down one river and up another over the Trail of Tears, how they were hunted down, forced to settle in a place and have their new homes taken from them by the same procedure 70 years later. Now 72,000 of them are facing starvation. If you were undergoing the same suffering as these people, you would not say: "We want our claims settled before we will agree to let you help other distressed Indians." We are thinking of those 72,000. We want to help them as well as you. You should be ashamed of your selfishness. We have told you again and again that we want to settle your claims, but give us a chance to help those who need help right now through this bill.

MR.MIGUEL: Just one word, answer in a nice way, do not get hot about it. I am an Indian as long as I am on the reservation.

MISS MACHADO: This bill is asking for the right to make us wait another eighty-two years for our rights.

MRS. COSTO: I am a member of the PTA at Perris and on Citizenship committee and proud of it. The other day Mr. Redwine had an article in the *Riverside Press* not favoring communism and socialism for us Indians. I am one hundred percent American. I tell you this bill preaches communism and socialism. We don't want none of it.

MR. COSTO: It is a very good sounding bill. Subtle in meaning. After delving into it I find we will always be under the Department of the Interior and the Commissioner. Self-government. But you will always be under the Commissioner and Department of Interior. Sounds good, but it is so good it takes away my personal rights, sends me back to reservation, keeps our children out of public school. I do not want to do that, I want to be as other people. Why segregate them on reservation and not be with white people. Is that the way to make American citizens of us? As far as I can see it isn't. Why shouldn't we go to court same as the white man? I have written my Congressman telling him to vote against this bill and some of my white friends are doing the same. Glad I am able to do this and a citizen of the state of California.

MR. JOSEPH L. WEAVER: I was born and raised in California. I am glad to be here; at the same time I ain't going to say much. Tell you why. I belong to a big body of Indians in California. We have a noble man down there and he got a head. He don't get excited like we do. He will talk to you. I want to tell you one thing and take this back to Washington, please. I have been driven away from my home. I raised a family. I raised some boys and soldier boys at that for an Indian father. And the way I have been treated—I am speaking for myself and I want every father to hear this talk. I just had two boys serve in the government, one in the Navy and one as a soldier. What can I do for the poor man? No place to raise them, no place to put them to work, no place to teach them. I worked for the Los Angeles Farm and Milling Company to educate those boys. Just as my brother said here about this school—getting the children back to the reservation. Brothers, I don't object to getting the children back to the reservation if we had the territory we had when the white man came. We were here a long, long time before you white men. If we had the land I could put that boy to running the threshing machine, working six mules, or driving a tractor, but I have nothing. So friends, take this to Washington and they will sympathize. They would talk nice to us. How many sons have you got? (*To men on platform.*)

MR. MONAHAN: Three.

MR. WEAVER: You boys come in here with that experience. It is right. We are glad to hear it. And we have been tormented. I went wandering when they chased my people away and I came down here and have been in the fight for fourteen years and I am going to continue until God calls me home. If my boys will take it up God bless them.

MR. MONAHAN: It is rather noticeable that we haven't heard from the official delegates. I announced this morning we would let the official delegates express themselves. I would like to hear from some of them.

QUESTION: Delegates, I would like more information about the communism. If this bill passes and an Indian community accepts the charter, will they automatically become communists, or socialists?

MR. SIEGEL: We don't know what communists or socialists are. Mr. Monahan, will you explain to them?

MR. MONAHAN: The Klamath Indians have about $20,000,000 worth of timber standing on the reservation. Every Indian on the reservation has an equal share they hold in common—we can't say they are reds because they do that. All property is community property in a sense, whether purchased property or inherited. All property you own at the present time is held by your community. The individual property, that was community property, that was given to the individual and has become an allotment, will remain with that individual. That is not to be taken away.

His belongings, his individual property, the improvements that he has made remain as his. The cattle he owns are his—no charter is going to take those things away from him. All his individual property will be his. But just to stop this process of when a man owns land as a trust allotment the government comes along and gives him his fee patent and he goes, or someone comes along and he sells it, spends the money and has nothing left. He is landless. Or he may die and his land goes to his eight children; if there is 160 acres at the beginning, divided among the eight heirs each would have only 20 acres. Not enough for any one to make a living on. Now, there are three things that might be done: first, the Superintendent lease it and divide the proceeds among the heirs; second, divide it into twenty-acre lots on which no one could make a living; or third, sell, probably to the highest bidder. If he is a white man he gets it, and divides the proceeds among the heirs. Because people are going to die and out of the 133,000,000 acres that was actually Indian owned only 47,000,000 acres are left with the government at the present time, and 20,000,000 acres of that is desert land in Arizona and worthless as far as earning a livelihood is concerned.

If the process continues as at present, all allottees are going to die—we are all going to die—it won't be but a few years until all the land has passed out of Indian ownership entirely. There's no communism in this, as some of you seem to think. Just read the bill—read it carefully and study it—find out for yourselves. I think you will be satisfied that it is not communistic or socialistic.

5:00 p.m. March 17, 1934

MR. MONAHAN: As a matter of fact, the number of landless and homeless Indians is great. There are hundreds of thousands of very poor people of Indian blood that are homeless but there are around 100,000 on the United States census reports living as squatters. I have just been in Florida. There are only 50 living on lands owned by the Government—the rest are scattered over a great territory of wasteland—railroad lands and etc. We want to buy land for them.

We are more or less running on schedule so we will try to stick pretty close to it. I want to ask the opinion of the delegates as to meeting tomorrow.

MIGUEL (Yuma Reservation): I think that by tomorrow morning we will meet here again and the delegates from my place from Yuma have a few things to say—a few questions to ask—rather—but they have been so interested in what is being said that they would rather listen than to exhibit their ignorance. I think that if we stay another day we will be changing our minds about this thing.

MR. DEWEY SAMPSON (Pyramid Lake Reservation, Nevada): Mr. Chairman, Mr. Wochlkc, and representatives of the United States Commissioner, delegates and friends. It is with great pleasure that I meet with you today and bring you greetings from Pyramid Lake Indian Reservation. There is no question but Indians are advancing and gradually coming into their own when one gazes about this convention hall and sees the great number of intelligent Indians representing the various localities.

We are principally to discuss the Wheeler-Howard Indian Bill—Senate Bill 3755—and other matters of vital importance to all Indians. I am glad of this opportunity to publicly express my sincere appreciation and approval of the Bill so far as I understand its purpose. But I feel this Bill should be thoroughly discussed at this Convention, especially as we have Mr. Woehlke here representing the Commissioner.

There is one question in connection with the money to be appropriated by the Bill for the Indians' use that I want to have definitely explained. Some of my council members at Pyramid Lake are sure that the $500,000 to be appropriated by Congress is only a loan and must be repaid. I am of the opinion that the money is placed at the demand of the various units for the purpose of defraying all expenses of the unit (by voucher) when wisely disbursed, and that such expenditure will be carefully supervised by the Indian Department and that all expenditures must be under direct vote of the members of the unit interested. I take it that his money is simply taken from salaries of employees of the Indian Bureau. In other words, the Indians are asked to spend this money, taking care of themselves instead of seeing it paid out to white employees who do not take very good care of us.

If this Bill passes and we come into the sum of two million dollars, which is not enough, expanded in advancement of the Indian race, we hope to carry out the following program:

Feed the Indians of my reservation out of this fund.
Housing them in homes with modern equipment—electricity, sanitation, etc.
Freedom of choice in medical attention and hospitalization.

And when and if the Government builds the proposed highway, we shall request that the Government fence its highway for the protection of our land against trespass, and we shall urge the use of Indian labor. But all other fences, including drift fences. will be financed by us out of the two million dollars or more.

We will continue to urge a new storage dam in place of the useless diversion dam now being used. It is almost impossible to raise a crop of any kind upon which the Indian or his stock may subsist.

In the event of the establishment of "upstream storage" on the Truckee River, the Indian shall insist upon his quota of water in keeping with prior water-right law.

We shall continue to ask the Government to recover all land formerly belonging to the Indians where acquired illegally or by default. I have here with me, a copy of the original map of Pyramid Lake Reservation drawn by Capt. Dave Numana, Paiute Indian, many years ago. I would be glad to show it to anyone interested. The original of this map is now filed in Washington, D.C. The map shows 3 distant lines of survey. We hope to establish and prove Indian ownership of this land because of its value for grazing and hunting.

Under the management of the old Indian Bureau system, the Indian has gradually been losing ground. The Indians have been kept in the dark concerning their affairs and will welcome the opportunity to manage their own affairs. Finally, we demand that this will guarantee to the Indian for all time, the right of holding their land without taxation. I thank you.

Morning Session

Sunday, March 18, at 10 a.m.

MR. MONAHAN: I want to answer the questions that were asked last evening on an entirely different matter. I was asked if the ECW was to be continued, the work under which you have been getting employment during the last year. We expect this to be continued until April 1, 1935. We have not received the money for the work yet, but we have been told to make our plans for the year and we have asked for the allotment of money that will be necessary to carry it out. We expect this year our present money will be gone the 1st of May, but we expect to have money given to continue until April 1, 1935. I am very pleased personally about it. We have been able to do a lot of work of very permanent value but the thing that has been so gratifying is in carrying out that program, we have been able to use Indians in the better jobs where Indians have never worked before. This Agency here has had as many as 617 Indians employed at one time and only 3 white men connected with the whole work. Indians have been employed as sub-foremen, tractor operators and etc.

We have one large Reservation where the Superintendent began by putting on some 30 white men, and said he did not have an Indian who could operate a grader or work of that sort and we told him that we would take the money away entirely if he could not find Indians to do it. That superintendent was able to find in a few days plenty of Indians able to do the work so that tractor work and all other work was done by Indians. We have had in the camps, where it was necessary to establish camps, white men as camp leaders. Mr. Collier signed an order to replace the white men with Indians when available. One hundred camps are practically led by Indians. Practically every sub-foreman is Indian and very many of the foremen and some engineers are also Indians. Roadwork is another part of the program I attended to personally. We are spending 4 million dollars on roads on Indian reservations. That does not include all roads—merely county roads. On practically all of that work we are using Indians.

Mr. Collier's idea is, and I am thoroughly in sympathy with it, that the Indians must be given a chance to learn to operate machinery and to become foremen even if the work is not quite as efficient as it might be at first. They must learn by handling the job. So ECW work, I think, will continue another year and I am very hopeful we are going to have another appropriation for the road work to continue another year. With the large number of Indians who are carrying out this work, I think there will be no question in the future but what there will be Indians trained to carry on that work with very little help from white engineers or any one else.

Now let's go back to the Wheeler-Howard Bill. We will confine our discussion to the Bill and kindly refrain from bringing in things that are too far from the subject. Congress is going to have many hearings on this soon and they want to know what you think about it. We do not want to fill records with things that have nothing to do with the Bill. Congress will not read it. This meeting is to be given over to the official delegates to talk, and we will be very glad to hear them speak. Most of the talking yesterday was done by non-delegates rather than by the delegates. So today I am going to recognize the delegates and want the delegates themselves to express themselves. We are not expecting that you will take any action on this question today.

You delegates were selected to come here and get the information concerning it and take it back to your own reservations and discuss it there at a council meeting on your own reservation and then have your council express themselves—for it, against it, for parts of it, etc. Be yourselves, decide what you want to do and write the Commissioner and tell him. We are not going to make any decisions here today that are final. Your delegates must report to your own people—so get all the information that you can. We want to answer all questions we can so that you will know as much about it as possible. We don't want you to express yourselves for or against it today. For instance if the Yuma delegates put themselves on record in favor of it that would not mean that the Yuma tribe is in favor of it—you can still go home and ask the tribe to pass on it. It is pretty difficult to understand; the Superintendents will be able to help to a certain extent—that is why we wanted them here. But you delegates have the difficult job of explaining to your people what it is all about so that they will have a clear picture to put before them and so they can act intelligently about it.

There is one thing I must emphasize that I want you to emphasize to them. That the legislation is permissible; it permits the tribe to do something in the future. If the tribe wants to organize under a constitution or a charter or a set of by-laws—called charter here—they will be able to do so if this legis-lation passes where they cannot do it now, without authority. If a tribe voluntarily wants to do that and the charter is prepared by you and by the Indian Office together, accepted by the Secretary of the Interior, before it can be put into effect, 60 out of every 100 adults must vote in favor of it.

Another thing I think is important is that there is no intention whatever if a tribe takes on this tribal organization to cut out the appropriation from Congress for the support of the tribe. It does not mean any decrease in the amount of money that Congress is going to appropriate for the ordinary expenses of the tribe. It will mean that more of you will occupy more positions just as rapidly as you have local people who can handle the job now held by white people and sent from the Washington office. The money will be spent by a bonded agent who might be a local Indian just as it is being spent now by bonded agents, some of whom are Indians already and some are white. You will have the same trouble with the Comptroller General's Office and Accounting Office that our Disbursing Agents have now, but they will inspect it anyway. You will find men competent to handle it just as some of the men who are handling it now. I cannot say how many Indians are now acting as Disbursing Agents on the Reservations but there are a large number. There are at least 8 superintendents of various reservations who are Indians. A full-blood Indian is superintendent at Haskell Institute in Kansas. There are very many competent Indians already in the Indian service but the proportionate number will be much larger as soon as they are trained. This Bill will permit among other things that present Civil Service regulations will be modified in such a way that Indians will stand a better chance to compete. Civil Service now gives examinations. Indians under the present regulations must compete with white people who have a better opportunity to qualify in that examination.

The white man may not be better suited for the job. The Indian knows the reservation but a white man in Maine who never saw an Indian or a reservation may be able to pass a better examination in stenography and typewriting than some Indian who has gone up on the Reservation and graduated from the school of this sort. But Civil Service is such a machine-like organization it isn't possible for us under the present situation to give the Indians a fair chance. One little provision here will break that down.

Now then, remember that you delegates want to get all the information you can and take up with the people at home. I will ask some of you delegates to speak. I will read this first. This is from the Morongo Reservation, Banning, California. "The Bill put before must be put up before our people before we can give our decision and pass upon it. I would like to say that Superintendent Dady has done a whole lot for us. Our Reservation is also very scattered and we would like to get consolidated and we think our Superintendent will help us. Also on page 26, Section 3, we would like to have that explained more fully."

MR. SIEGEL: That is a section dealing with the closing of surplus lands to the Indians.

MR. MONAHAN: I would like to have the superintendents help with Page 26, Section 3. I would like to have it explained more fully.

MR. SIEGEL: That is the section dealing with surplus lands.

MR. MONAHAN: We are here to get information and take it back to Congress.

MR. SIEGEL: In many cases—I do not know whether it is true on your reservation or not—the Government decided there were many lands Indians did not need. So these surplus lands were opened to entry by white people. These white people were supposed to pay a certain amount, and were then entitled to a fee patent to land. Through that method much land formerly owned by Indians has passed into white ownership. This section provides that surplus lands which were formerly declared not needed for Indian use shall no longer be opened to settlement by whites. However, the Secretary of the Interior, in his discretion, may determine himself which of these lands the Indians do not need and may after such determination reopen the lands not needed by the Indians to settlement by whites.

Many Indians have objected to the second paragraph which provides the reopening to settlement of such lands as he may determine. I am not sure but that this objection is a very good one and if they will voice it loudly enough, possibly we could strike that clause out entirely, and provide that surplus lands will no longer be opened to settlement at all.

MR. MONAHAN: I have a letter to give you the opinion of the Indians of said reservation. If he is here now will he get up and express himself.

MR. GRAND: I will endeavor to give you the opinion of the Indians of said reservation. The bill is not satisfactory. It seems to appear it would take away the rights of the Indians. It is the desire of these Indians not to favor the bill. In regards to education whether it be public or boarding school, should be opened up to Indians such as Sherman Institute, this is greatest training place for Indians.

MR. MONAHAN: Mr. Grand thinks this is too sudden. They have not had ample time to learn all about it, but you are going to have ample time and we want to give you all information so that you will have time to think it over. I wish Mr. Grand would state why the bill is not satisfactory.

MR. GRAND: It is too complicated, and we do not understand it. We are going to have meeting on it for suggestions by my people. There is a college boy that is supposed to be here now and express himself, and then we shall follow him, Chief Newman.

MR. MONAHAN: We do not want to do anything that is not right, until you do understand. This is the attitude we want you to assume, and not be in favor of or against it until you do understand. We have heard nothing from the Fort Yuma delegation.

MR. BLACK (Fort Yuma): The Indians on our Reservation have been putting in considerable time in studying the bill. We have had the bill before us for two months. We did not intend to make a decision on it, but proposed to keep working on it until the older Indians understand it, as we see it. We have on our reservation longhaired old Indians still wearing the G-string. Some of these Indians who have been to school, who are supposed to be intelligent, but who cannot see daylight. Personally, I have seen different reservations and foreign countries and have been around a good deal.

I was fortunate enough to talk to several white neighbors, some of them up in big organizations and brought the bill to them to discuss. We did not decide whether we would carry this bill through or not. The bill looks all right in a way, but we have never accepted it. We intend to go through the matter thoroughly and work on it some more.

We think several revisions should be made. One favorable provision is the two-million-dollar appropriation—but is a drop in the bucket. I have written up a few little articles on recent tribal conventions which were held 10 days last month. Much thought and study has been given to the tribal allotment situation, as we realize it is one of the most vital questions before the tribe. However it is a question that will require much more study and investigation. We do not intend to let it pass until we make thorough investigation. With reference to land already allotted we feel conditions are different than any other reservation and will require a different treatment in order to bring the most good to the Indian people. We recognize the matter of heirship as an intricate and difficult problem. Particularly in regard to a small reservation with limited available acreage such as our own reservation. The ten-acre unit is being cut up into heirship, as many as 16, and 16 pieces which creates allotments of only one-fourth acre, sometimes one acre amongst different heirs. There is considerable squabble over such places and in some cases where the allotments are fenced off, it looks like a jig-saw puzzle. We are fighting this and are trying to keep the land intact. We are trying to teach the Indians to go ahead and make a will to some particular heir in the family so it can be kept intact. This is a difficult thing to do as we do not like to force any Indian to do something he doesn't want to do.

We have other problems that do not concern the bill which we do not intend to present at this time. The delegate here is representing the educated element of the Cochan tribe of the Yuma Reservation. We fell back to our original name. Yuma is not correct. The Cochan tribe has had considerable trouble ever since allotment and we are looking forward to ways of keeping land intact and acquiring more land if possible. The Indians on the reservation at the present time favor the bill—I mean the educated Indians. Few of the old Indians favor it. We came here for the sole purpose of listening and not putting out anything and find out what Washington had to say.

MR. SIEGEL: I was very much interested in that report. The allotment problem on the Yuma reservation is a peculiar one and I would appreciate it very much if you would see me after the meeting.

MR. MONAHAN: On the Yuma reservation there is a problem that some of the others do not understand. You have white squatters on Indian land. The Indian Office has been trying to get them off. The whites have been demanding that the land be sold to them because they have improved the land, digging wells, building homes, etc. Of course, they had no right there and should be put off.

JOHN A. KERN: We do not understand these matters. I represent 273 old Indians on the Yuma Reservation who cannot read and write. The educated Indians would not let them understand what it was all about. We are afraid the Bill will tie us down. We question the authority of the delegates.

Sun. 10:35 [a.m.]

MR. MONAHAN: Both factions should discuss it. Get together if you possibly can. One of the greatest difficulties is that the Indians have two or more factions. We do not know what to do when one group wants one thing and another wants something else. The entire group should get together and let everybody have a chance to say something. One thing you both ask is that no action be taken on this until you have time to take it home and discuss it.

MR. SIEGEL: The Bill takes care of the factions because the reservation can be divided into more than one group. Any constitution made by the Indians is not valid unless a charter is made and the Secretary of the Interior approves it. That constitution which you speak of is not in force as a charter until the Secretary approves it and 60 percent of the Indians approve of it. Furthermore, if you have two factions that do not get along, this bill takes care of this and provides for the dividing the people into more than one group.

MR. MIGUEL (Yuma): We have two factions which I want to explain. The reason for this is selfish interest of some whites who are living off the Indians' nickels and dimes. A statement was made that we did not invite others to the meetings. I can show you where we invited every Indian on the Fort Yuma reservation to the convention where we talked over the bill. They did not invite us to their meeting. Why, I do not know. We have never contributed any nickels and dimes to white men and we do not intend to, but put them in our own pocket. We are not trying to interfere with any other organization at all. We are not looking for something better to advance ourselves. We do not intend to go back to the blanket. I was born and raised on the reservation among the old Indians. I know all the traditions. I know many old stories. Personally I cannot express it. This faction that they are talking about, we do not propose it at all. We would like to see them go ahead and do something. That is absolutely false. We studied on the bill and organized one second of February. From then on we picked out, through the convention, educated Indians we could get hold of and all old Indians in sympathy with us to discuss the bill. Our first convention lasted two days, after that we had an election, all were invited.

The opposite faction turned us down. Mr. Kern was also appointed to act as committeeman to help draw up constitution and by-laws and he refused to serve at the time. Now he says he was not invited. He was, but turned the invitation down. The idea of inviting these Indians was to give them a chance to see more what this bill would do for them. We made several canvasses later on. But these Indians who give their money to white schemers would not take part.

We have asked help from several whites in order to draw up the bill in a technical form. We drew up constitution and by-laws in outline and showed them what we wanted, but they had no say about it, not even the Indian agent had anything to say about it. Later on we canvassed the whole reservation including the members of the opposite faction which a number of them turned us down. We were also two days in interpreting the constitution and by-laws. This is only proposed and I personally asked them if any Indians had ideas we would like to have them present [at that] time. So far none have been presented.

There was a subcommittee and some white friends who helped us out on this. We have not donated to white people; they donated their services and time and we did not intend to go to the old Indians and collect any money off them. We are willing to split our loaf of bread with them.

KERN: Now they said something about a constitution. It is true they drew up constitution and by-laws. These delegates could not understand this constitution, what was in it, they had to ask the white man.

MR. MONAHAN: I have a question I would like to read—"If this new bill is passed will it close the Sherman Indian school?" The answer is no. As far as I know it would not close any Indian school. There is nothing in the bill which would mean the closing of any particular school and I know of no desire to close this school. This is supposed to be a pretty good school.

HUNTER (Tule River): On behalf of the Indians of Tule River I wish to say that we have not had ample time to study this bill. We have had only two days. We came here with the intention of learning about the bill and not to say anything about it. We came here to hear the delegates from Washington explain the bill to us and we do not wish to say whether we are for the bill or not. Our reservation is unallotted and for that reason we cannot say anything more about the bill.

MR. MONAHAN: Is there anyone else from the California delegation who wishes to speak. If not, I will call upon the Nevada delegates.

HARRY LAWSON: Mr. Chairman and fellow delegates and friends. I bring to you greetings from Fort McDermott, Nevada. I am glad to be with you and express my people's view on this bill. I am glad to tell you we are in favor of this bill so far as we know after reading this bill. There is no question that we all know as to the laws of our land thru the old Indian Affairs Bureau. I have with me statements of two old Indians telling of how their land has passed to white men without the Indian's knowledge. I wish this statement to go on record.

This statement is from Buckaroo Jack, an old Indian chief. He says: "In the year 1869 the Paiute tribe of Indians were first gathered here and were stationed here under Capt. Bernard. Through an interpreter, J. Long, he told Indians that this military reservation was 10 miles by 25 miles and that Indians should have it all. When they left, strayed away and met nine miles from the post he was arrested and told to leave because this was all in the military reservation. Now Buckaroo Jack thinks that since he heard all these agreements and he is still living, all this land should be given back to us."

The next statement is from Little Johnny and John Brigham: "During the time the soldiers were stationed here, Ft. McDermott, a school was started. The Captain's wife was the first teacher. The Captain and other officials called a meeting and told the Indians they were leaving soon and the reservation would be theirs and suggested Indians work north and south sides of the ditch and have it for their use if they furnished all the supplies. Captain Horse and his band of Indians took the south side of the ditch and took up all the land that was irrigable and Captain Long fix the north for the band of Indians.

"A verbal agreement had taken place at this meeting whereby Indians were to have the soldiers' possessions which was outlined as follows: North to Oregon line, east to the watershed of Twin River, on the south all the hay land and a few hundred acres which extends in Oregon. The first allotment was 80 acres, then it was reallotted and was 40 acres, then it was 5 acres. The old reservation changes as it is today. The Indians claim that they have no definite knowledge of how these changes came about. They claim that they were allotted 40 acres along the valley. The whites stole their property and forced them to leave their allotments telling them they were on the white man's land. The Indians today believe this is the reason it was open to homestead. Because Indians not there a survey of allotments made and whites claim Indians have no water rights, only supply water."

MR. MONAHAN: Now, the Nevada group, is there anyone else who wishes to speak?

HARRY SAMPSON (Reno): In the conditions at Reno, we study this bill and we find that it seems to us we do not know how it feels to receive compensation from the government. We have no land, therefore, if the bill is rejected or if it goes thru it does not matter because we have been thru this hardship, so it is up to this meeting to decide and I am here as representative from Reno to take in and get more information. In that way I believe I could go back and tell those people what I have learned. So far as the bill is concerned, I believe I am in favor of it, if it goes through we gain something; if not, we are in the same position we are in.

MR. MONAHAN: I want to say in regard to the Reno group, there are several groups living near cities—Needles, California, Burns, Oregon, living under the same conditions. We are trying to get money for subsistence from the Public Works Administration to be able to buy land, build new homes to improve these conditions. But in some of these cities, such as Needles, the Indians work in town and live nearby. Some of the women work in homes, the men in the shops and railroads. Some of the women sell beads and pottery at the railroad station and live in little houses on lands they do not own or the government does not own. Some live on railroad land on which they cannot build permanent homes. We hope to get money to take care of those groups. There are 30 or 40 similar groups in the U.S. in various places. They have the same problem that you have at Reno.

SAMPSON: I believe I brought my statement up last evening in the last meeting. As it is over there we haven't got practically anything at all. We are in favor of this bill. Why? Because we believe everything is in our favor and we cannot lose anything. We have everything to gain.

RAY FILLMORE (Dresslerville): Just a few days ago before I came down here to this meeting the Washoe Indians had a barbeque to discuss this new deal taking place among the Indians all over the U.S. While there we had attendance of at least 300 Indians and out of those most of them were in favor of this bill and just five families were against the bill and that gives the councilmen of the Washoe Indians inspiration to go ahead and try to take the things they have given us. This is all I have to say.

MR. MONAHAN: Any other from the Nevada delegation?

TED JAMES: I would like to ask a question in regard to others living on the reservation. We were supposed to be paid for lands on the reservation, but at the present time and during the depression they have not met their payments and I would like to know what could be done about that. That is all.

MR. MONAHAN: You are referring to the white men who have leased places and are unable to pay their rent.

TED JAMES: Yes.

MR. MONAHAN: Of course, under the law, the superintendent of your agency should throw them off, but during these hard times if we went to the limit of the law and threw out everybody who was unable to pay his debts, there would be a lot of us out of homes. If times get a little better they will be able to pay their bills and I think that will settle that question.

TED JAMES: Referring to that just said, a lot of those fellows have stock grazing on the land—for years they have all kinds of privileges to pay for the stock they got, but they just left it so long that when we tried to go and collect they said "Hard times now; we can't do a thing." They have had all kinds of chances. We don't know the procedure necessary to prosecute these men.

MR. MONAHAN: Have you discussed this with your Superintendent?

TED JAMES: The Superintendent told us he did not know who was holding the mortgage on the stock.

MR. MONAHAN: Now that of course is something that is a problem of yours. We will give you the information later.

MR. NASH of the Indian Office: I have just one criticism to offer about this meeting. I felt the same at Salem. We have men here like Mr. Holst; men like Mr. Julley who have spent their lifetime in the Indian service. Terry was here yesterday—one old Superintendent, retired, was here. At the Salem meeting they didn't take any part in the discussions, and they are not here at this meeting. I think we should hear from some of these men and see if they are for this bill or against it. Sometime before this meeting adjourns I would like to hear from these men. Whether they were against this bill or not would make no difference to Mr. Collier or the Secretary of the Interior, but they have a fund of information we ought to have.

MR. MONAHAN: Mr. Collier has extended an invitation to employees in the Indian service to express their opinions regarding this Bill and stated that he wanted their honest opinion. We have found in the office that Mr. Collier likes to have people disagree with him. I have heard one of them say to him (one of the assistants) "Mr. Collier, you are all wrong on this." Mr. Collier just smiled and said, "Let's talk it over." Mr. Collier was convinced on that little thing after talking. Mr. Collier likes to hear the other side of every story. He wants it to be as perfect as it can be made. Every suggestion will be given full consideration.

JACK MEYERS: I understand this meeting is for Indians and you want the opinion of Indians. Let us hold to that.

MR. MONAHAN: Mr. Nash, that is what these people were called for, to hear the opinion of the official delegates and have them express their opinion and get their information to take back to their people. I will not recognize anyone but delegates.

RUPERT COSTO: Is this an open meeting?

MR. MONAHAN: You took up far too much time yesterday. If you are an official delegate, sit with your delegation—if you have anything to say special, talk it over together with your delegates but do not interfere with this meeting. If you are not a delegate, sit down. This is not an open meeting—it is a meeting of official delegates, and I have recognized Mr. Meyers to speak for the Mission Indians.

JACK MEYERS: That is rather a large order to speak for all the Mission Indians—I prefer to speak for my own people. I cannot speak for the other tribes, but I would say—practically repeat what I said yesterday. We had a little meeting this morning and elected me their temporary chairman to discuss the bill. There was practically nothing accomplished as it takes all night with a little dancing for Indians to hold a meeting. There was a motion put to get the opinion of the delegates as to how they stood on the matter—for or against the Bill. The motion was out of order. However, I let it go through. We did not do anything as we decided we needed more time to take it back to our people and discuss and mull it over a little bit. We need plenty of time to do it, as I am in a hurry and my people are in a hurry. We have no houses, just a bunch of rocks so the only thing is we are all in favor and the thing that we all seemed to agree on is that the two million dollars appropriation is far too small.

MR. MONAHAN: I misunderstood Mr. Meyers. I understood that you were elected to speak for all the Missions who were sent here as delegates of the different groups.

WINSLOW CURE (Santa Ysabel Reservation): I understand you to say that you will not let any other Indian speak besides the delegates?

MR. MONAHAN: Word was sent to the Indian tribes on the Indian reservations to elect official delegates to come to this meeting and invite others if they wanted to come. Yesterday I stated that we were to hear from them. The result was that others in the hall took the entire day and the official delegates had no chance to talk. Today's meeting is for official delegates. Those other people had time to talk yesterday. This meeting is not an open meeting; it is for the official delegates.

WINSLOW CURE: I think most of these delegates were not elected by the people to come here.

MIGUEL (Yuma Reservation): It may be that the gentleman is correct and it may be that he is not correct. In my country along about the 2nd of February we received the circulars pertaining to this bill. An invitation was sent out to all the Yuma Indians on the reservation and they came on the day that this meeting was to take place. It took about one day to read the circular and the Bill. We took the whole of the next day to give the Indians, the Yuma Indians, a chance to ask questions. It happened that they appointed me as the interpreter to interpret the circular and the Bill. It isn't because I could do justice to it, but because I have such a boisterous voice that everybody could hear me.

In that meeting, particular emphasis was made that every Indian was allowed to say what he had to say, and present his views on the matter. The old Indians, quite a few of them, had expressed themselves and quite a number of the educated element have expressed themselves. A committee was appointed after the second-day meeting with a view of making further study of the circular and the bill and to draft a constitution. There was no line drawn on anybody.

The Federation Indians were invited to take part in it, but they absolutely refused to take any part in it. The leader or captains, as they are called, even refused to come to the meetings. It happened though that the non-Federation Indians on my reservation were in the majority, so we went right ahead anyway and drafted a constitution and set of by-laws. There are 19 articles in the constitution and 19 articles in the by-laws. We have a copy of it here. Then the constitution and the by-laws were read and interpreted to the Indians of the whole tribe. At that time several chipped in and were had a big food. There were about 400 Indians turned out that day. After the matter was thoroughly gone over, there was a vote taken and it passed almost unanimously. There was only one dissenting vote. Then immediately after, the question was put to the Indians as to who should attend this meeting? I suggested that the Indians nominate whom they wished to nominate. The Indians did not make any nomination. They didn't seem to know what to do, so one of the educated Indians got up and said he suggested that the committee which had drafted this constitution be appointed as delegates to this convention. The matter was put to the house and it passed unanimously. That is the reason why we are here. The gentlemen may be right so far as to the delegates are concerned, but so far as the Yuma delegates, I think we are representing the Yuma Indians.

MR. MONAHAN: I think you are representing the Yuma Indians. You were duly elected by your people. I am not inquiring and going back to find out the details of the election, but you were sent here by your people and therefore you are the official delegates.

JACK MEYERS: Quite some time ago our Superintendent, Mr. Dady, sent out to all the reservations to have an election and elect spokesmen and committee members. That was done on most of the reservations. We have most of our delegates and committee here. There was no special election held for this meeting. There was no time for it and brother Cure has labored under some pressure. You are representing your people. See that you listen and take it back to your people. I am spokesman for the Santa Rosa Indians and we were all duly elected. I don't understand why you say anything of that sort.

MR. SIEGEL: Yesterday the entire day was devoted to unofficial delegates and it is only fair that the other delegates, official delegates should be heard from. There is nothing but an hour or so left.

MR. CURE: Give the rest of the Indians a chance to talk.

MR. SIEGEL: Today is to be devoted to the delegates who should also be heard from.

MR. MONAHAN: I will recognize delegates.

LEON PALAWASH (Spokesman of the Pauma Reservation): I am speaking for the Indians of the State of California. Congress should endorse any legislation. Congress and the Senate have asked the Indians to endorse the legislation. Why does Congress ask the Indians to adopt the resolution and why does not Congress endorse that policy instead of the Indians? The bill does not give the Indians any independence. We will not endorse the Wheeler-Howard Bill. We have a committee at Washington who are now introducing all claims of Indians of the State of California for just settlement. Therefore you gentlemen may return to Washington and expedite the just settlement to the Indians of the State of California of claims in Washington.

REMEJIO ROBLES (Spokesman of the Pala Reservation): I had a meeting before I came up here with my people. I see now things that all the people could not see, because we only have had very little time to study the bill. When I had the bill, I looked it over and I think about my people. What are they going to do now, what are they going to say? It seems it was a very big thing for them to understand.

So I went and had a meeting. Some of them came up—they heard what it was, but did not understand. So I had another meeting, so they said it seems to me that in Washington, the same way as we are here now—all messed up. Before we can go into any of these big problems, we must open our eyes—all of us. It is a big thing for us Indians. We are over 21 years—we want our right! We do not want to be Government charges. This is what I am bringing from my people for you to hear. We cannot settle anything here; we came here to listen. The bill should be modified in many places.

MR. MONAHAN: It was rather difficult for Mr. Collier, in preparing the bill, to satisfy everybody. He has put in there what has come to him in 10 years' experience in meetings with the Indians all through the United States. He has tried to express the Indians' wants. It is pretty hard for any one group to know something applying to another group. Mr. Collier wants every suggestion that you can make.

VIVIAN BANKS (Girl from Pala): My people are opposed to this bill. They do not think it is fair. No other bill should be brought before them until the Court of Claims bill is settled if it takes 100 years to settle it. My people do not understand the bill. I do not understand it fully, myself. It is too complicated. We have had it only two weeks and it would take anybody longer than that to understand it.

MR. MONAHAN: The claim of the California Indians is before the Court of Claims and it rests with the court. What they do with that has nothing to do with what Congress does on this. There are 98 Indian cases before the court and literally thousands of other cases, so it will be slow to get the court to act. The Secretary and the Commissioner cannot have one particle of influence on the court. The Court of Claims case is entirely independent of the bill. This should not block progress on the Wheeler-Howard Bill.

MR. AMES for Barona: Gentlemen, friends, brothers, I am going to say a few words about our affairs. I am not well educated like most of you people here. I have not been to college. I went to an Indian school about three years. But I have had experience among my white brothers. I have listened to what they have said. The bill is pretty good in some places, but I cannot say whether it is good or not. I would like to take more time to study it. I could not favor this bill just now. Mr. Collier, the Commissioner of Indian Affairs, has worked on the Indian Defense Association long enough to know the Indians' ways. He worked with what you call the Mission Federation. He has studied the same things I have. He knows because he went with us and was not told by anybody. He got the job of being Commissioner and he is doing everything he can for the Indians in Southern California. I believe the bill will give us Indians a chance. Why should we protest against it? What should we lose by the bill? My father had 20 head of cattle. He told them to fight the Government, give the money to the fighters. Brothers, we cannot fight the Government. But now the Government has given us a chance.

Why should we protest the bill on account of the Court of Claims case not being settled yet? Are we going to wait another eighty years? Some of the people protesting against the bill have good places to live—they don't care. Other Indians have no place to go, no homes—thrown out of reservations. Why don't we Indians help our brothers and put them back on the reservations if we can? Why throw them out? We are of one blood. We used to own this whole country—now the white people have taken it. They have promised to pay and we can demand this claim. The Government is giving us one point to go forward. Why not take it? We cannot accomplish anything by being two or three groups. I do not know anything about those people going to Washington to hurry things up. I can say these gentlemen are giving us a chance. We must have one solid foundation if we are to accomplish anything.

Question brought up if bill would close boarding schools.

MR. MONAHAN: This bill would not have any effect on whether boarding schools would be left open or not. There is a bill for closing boarding schools to smaller children. The Boarding schools would take care of orphans and older children. There are twenty thousand children that have no school to go to. If we can build day schools near their homes where they can attend, it would cost only one-third as much to educate them as in a boarding school. Our boarding schools would be for advanced grades and special training. The Government is building 70 day schools for the children of the Navajo.

MR. CURE: Here is a point I would like to bring up. In some schools they are segregating the Indians by themselves. If it is going to be a public school why not let the Indian children mix with the whites, then they will be able to compete with the white man like anybody else.

MR. MONAHAN: You are absolutely right on that and wherever it is possible, children are being sent to the public schools. One-third of the Indian children who are in school at the present time are going to public schools and the United States is paying the tuition. Some states will not let Indians go to public schools for whites. The Indian office will not let Indian children go to public schools under such circumstances.

JOHN BLACK (Yuma delegate): I would like to make a statement concerning the educated element on our reservation. We have taken steps among ourselves, the educated element, organizing for the benefit of all Indians on this particular reservation. We have made some progress in doing this. We have been able to consolidate our voices in getting appropriations so that the Indians would be able to work on the reservation. The county of Imperial, California, has helped us a good deal. They have used their influence in conjunction with ours and a few people in the state of Arizona in securing for us appropriations from the PWA, CWA, keeping the Indians from begging, giving them work, road work, Johnson-grass work and that has helped us a great deal. No individual Indian can claim these appropriations. It was thru the work of consolidation of several whites.

The Indian Agent on our reservation has been tied down thru the department and never able to do very much for us under certain rulings. We have broken these rulings regardless of whether they liked it or not in going ahead instead of looking backwards. We have also taken steps in sanitation matters and also in educational matters and in land tenure. We are fortunate to have with us here a good man by the name of Mr. Strahorn who surveyed the reservation to investigate how the land tenure has turned out. The river bottom land in some places is very good; in some places, not. When the allotment system was opened, there were practically 7,000 acres tillable. Today not quite half of that. The water table on the river bottom has risen to certain heights that it is making an alkaline sediment all over the reservation. Reclamation Service has promised to put in drainage. They have only put in one. We are going ahead regardless whether they like it or not, asking for another drainage system on the reservation. We do not intend to be held up. We are looking to the coming generations, we are not looking backward. If Indians would organize and work that way I think they would be much better off. Thank you.

MR. MONAHAN: Now we will hear from the Mission delegates.

TOM ARVISO (Rincon): We come up here invited to attend this meeting as delegates and I will speak for the Rincon reservation. First, I must say I am not acquainted with the bill just received the past few days. I am not in a position to make a decision here, only to get instruction on what is said by the delegates from Washington. We will go back and study the bill thoroughly with our people. In order to do so I will have to ask a few questions here so as to know what I am talking about when I get back. In regard to the allotment question—our reservation has been allotted recently and about 60 percent of the people have accepted allotments holding a trust patent for same. I do not understand very well and I am going to ask, does the Secretary of the Interior still have the power to issue patents in fee for land allotted now?

MR. SIEGEL: Yes, he has that power, he can still issue patents in fee or certificates of competency which means the same thing.

ARVISO: With regard to people living on reservations that are not allotted I would like to have an idea as to how we are to handle the affairs of people not allotted. Some have applied for a place to establish a home and since we had more allotments made we have problems to contend with. What are we going to do with the people who want to establish homes and have no way to support themselves?

MR. WOEHLKE: Have they homes on the reservation?

ARVISO: Some have and some haven't.

MR. WOEHLKE: In that case the one thing would be to apply as soon as this bill passes for an appropriation or an assignment out of the appropriation to acquire enough additional land to provide homes for all those who are unallotted and for whom there is no room on the present tribal lands. You are now assigning unallotted members to locations on your tribal lands, aren't you?

ARVISO: Yes.

MR. WOEHLKE: When they have made selection you recognize it is theirs to have and to hold while they make use of it. You will continue this system except that we will have to ask for sufficient money to acquire additional lands to take care of all.

ARVISO: We will go back and study the bill altogether and make our decision accordingly.

MR. MONAHAN: Any other Mission Indians wish to speak?

DELEGATE: I understand little English, I have not much to say regarding the bill. Copies of the bill have been sent, but I received a letter from John W. Dady stating I must come to attend the conference so I am here. I understand many things going on here and there is much talk. It seems as though you must go in one track all the time to get there, and some people say this has to be settled here, others say back to their own home. About this bill here, I have absolutely nothing to say about it. All I know is I was appointed as delegate to come and understand these matters and hear. We have been working 14 years for our rights and we have sent delegates to Washington to look into this matter. I think the best way for you fellows is to have a good group sent from southern California. They got all the Indian boys in Washington and us here, we are appointed by the Indian to come up and understand these conferences, so we are here.

WOLFE (Soboba): I was sent over here to learn more about the bill and go back and explain and give my opinion to the people, in favor or turn it down.

VENTURO PAIPA (Captain, Grando): I got the bill late and I never go over it. I know just one part of it. It was for me to come here and hear what the delegates from Washington say, so I am reporting here but I cannot say any more, but go back home and explain what I have heard here. That is all.

MR. MARCUS (San Manuel): Mr. Chairman, as spokesman for my reservation I have tried to explain this bill to my people. They have objections to certain parts. Of course this is hard to explain. Indian self-government has been too sudden on the Indian. The bill is too complicated for interpretation in Indian dialect. But I came here just the same telling you the same thing and it is just as hard as ever. Therefore, I prefer that until such time as all the Indians are educated, then we will compete with the white race. While this system is still in effect, I would like to have the U.S. Government make Sherman Institute the Carlisle of the West. Speaking of schools, I have thought the idea of teaching primary and secondary schools on the reservations according to the bill good. Community or reservation schools as stated in this bill to my understanding will take away the privilege of the students to mingle with the white people. Therefore, they will not grasp the ways of the white people. They will be slow. Therefore, try to educate the Indians in public schools wherever it is possible. Most of the reservations are not alike. A person has to live on them to know the cause and effect. I wish to thank the white people for giving us education, learning through the Indian schools.

MR. WOEHLKE: I believe you are under a misapprehension when you believe that the bill would bring about the compulsory education of the smaller children in reservation schools. That is a mistake. It does not change the present system at all. And the present policy as you know is to place as many Indian children as possible in the public schools. We are doing that so far and we are going to continue that policy. The only reservation schools that are being established are those where no public schools exist, where none are available, where children do not go to school at all. The only thing that could be done was to catch them and put them in boarding schools. So now we are building them day schools so that they may have an education. There isn't anything of the kind in the bill at all. It just means that where there are no schools of any kind we want to put in day schools. And on top of that we have added the proposition for taking the specially gifted ones, the bright and ambitious ones and give them schooling following their earlier training that they may become engineers, even lawyers if they want to. That is the meaning of the educational program.

MR. FLORES (Pechanga): As I have been here the second day I have been paying attention to what has been said. This question of self-government is causing confusion to the minds of our people because it is so sudden. It comes to us so suddenly we cannot decide. This much I will take to my people. I cannot say that the people will say yes or no, for I don't know. So there is one question that I would like to ask. It has been answered in some ways and some ways not. It is this: This proposed bill, will it change the present system of governing the Indians here or not?

MR. MONAHAN: Not at present. Not until the particular tribe asks for change and it is approved. Otherwise it will go on as now without change.

MR. FLORES: Will it prove a benefit toward the welfare and forward the progress of our people?

MR. MONAHAN: We think it will.

MR. FLORES: You think it will?

MR. MONAHAN: Yes.

MR. FLORES: You just think it will but we will try it and see? That is all I want to say. We are going to try to do our best to explain it to our people what we have gotten from you.

11:55 a.m.

March 18th

MR. MONAHAN: There are some other Mission Indians representing some other groups who wish to speak.

TOM ARVISO (interpreter) for ROSCENCIO ARDILLA (Pauma Reservation): Before coming up here I called a meeting. I am Spokesman from Pauma regarding this Bill that is here. My committee read it. They are not in favor of it and neither am I. We have sent some delegates to Washington to arrange our affairs. We have signed up and that is the reason we cannot do otherwise.

MR. MONAHAN: Others to be heard from of the Mission Indians?

BASQUET CHIHUAHUA (Torres-Martinez Reservation): I am going to say one point. I am here at this meeting to hear you fellows and listen to you what you are advising us and I am going to take this matter over my folks and tell them about it and study about the Bill. Later on we will see and decide.

MR. MONAHAN: We want to close this morning's session and we also want to see that everyone who wants to be heard is heard from. Any other Mission delegates?

ROBERT CHUTNICUT (Los Coyotes Reservation): I understand that all those who have time to study this Bill, but where shall we send the decision?

MR. MONAHAN: Send it direct to the Congress addressed to Senator Wheeler or Congressman Howard, Chairman of the House Committee, or send it to Mr. Collier and he will see that they get it. It will receive consideration in any case.

Now if there are any more of the Mission Indians I want to say just one word. I want to make this perfectly clear. Most of you have said this—you want to take this matter home and then study it—that is just what we want you to do. Take it home, discuss it with your people and let us know what your opinion is—for it or against it. I want you to be sure of this, however—do not want you to make up your minds from some other letters circulating around the country—many written by white lawyers in Washington, D.C., because it would cut their little business out with the Indians. I have in my possession a three-page circular typewritten and mimeographed and sent out all over the country. The men who wrote it did not have bravery or honesty enough to sign their names to it. And they say John Collier's ideas are communistic and socialistic and they said that under this Bill all your cattle and all you had would be taken away from you and given to the whole tribe and divided equally among you all. One thousand copies were sent all around the country—they were not honest enough to sign their names. Any man whose opinion is worth anything is ready to put his name down and say who he is.

You are going to find lots of people opposed to it for selfish reasons. Congressman Howard, when the Bill was introduced in Congress, asked if any man has any objection. Sitting right beside me was a lawyer in Washington whose firm represents half a dozen tribes in the United States. I said this is the time for you to put your opposition in. He said he hadn't any. A day or two later one of the Indians from a tribe that lawyer represents brought to me a carbon copy of a letter which that lawyer wrote and which that Indian signed, and which he told me he didn't know that he was signing. He did not want to sign and did not mean to sign it at all. That lawyer also wrote a letter back to the tribe in which that Indian did not understand that he was opposed to the bill. I have his written statement that he did not want to sign the complaint.

Congressman Howard asked if there was any opposition, but this party waited until he went home and then wrote those letters. In that particular case he said in his letters all Indian oil rights would be taken away from them. He knew that he was lying and that if that Bill passed he would lose his little job in representing those Indians. These lawyers in Washington whose principal job is to represent you are trying to make you pay a little money for their expenses. They will never get anything for you. I haven't any sympathy for these shyster lawyers who prepare claims for various personal reasons.

So when you study this matter study the bill itself. Get advice of disinterested people, not interested people, and interested in something for themselves that this might interfere with. Get all the opinions you can. Ask some of your good lawyers near you who are not interested in your land, but interested in you and your welfare and who will give you what they think this means. Get all the help you can on it, but beware of these unsigned letters that are being circulated or even those signed by those who have a personal interest for defeating the bill for the sake of their own pocketbook.

Now let me repeat once more that Mr. Collier and Senator Wheeler and Congressman Howard want your honest opinion whether you agree with them or whether you disagree with them. Think it over and send your honest opinion and every word you write to them will be given consideration.

QUESTION BY AN INDIAN: What is the extent of time before the bill takes action?

MR. MONAHAN: There is no possibility of stating what the time is. Congress is in session now. There was an item in the newspaper a few days ago in Washington that they hoped to adjourn by the 15th of May. I doubt it. But you must remember this is election year and some of these men are anxious to get home for the primary elections, so I think they will close some time in June. This Congress that is meeting now will be replaced by the Congress that is elected in November. They meet in January. This Bill will have to be reintroduced in January if it is not passed by the present Congress. I do not know whether it will be passed by the present Congress or not, but the Congressmen are not going to be forced into hasty action. They want to be sure they are right. They want to wait for your opinion. We do not know whether it is getting all the consideration that it needs with all the other bills pressing Congress. I urge you to take all the time that is necessary to think this matter out for yourselves—get your opinion in as soon as possible. Do not take too long—it might be too late.

MR. SIEGEL: At any rate what we said has been taken down and there will be a printed copy of everything that has gone on at this meeting and I think if you do not remember all we said or what it represented, you will be able to get a written copy of this meeting within a week or so. Moreover we prepared a very detailed explanation section by section of this law before Congress and have had copies sent out to Indians together with the Bill. If you will go over that carefully and consult with your Superintendents and your copy of the record of this meeting and also the hearing in the House and the Senate, gradually some light may be shed on this matter.

MR. MONAHAN: I want to thank you all for your personal attention and your suggestions. It has been a very delightful meeting in every way.

CHAPTER 9

MEETING OF THE COMMISSIONER OF INDIAN AFFAIRS, HON. JOHN COLLIER, WITH THE INDIANS OF WESTERN OKLAHOMA AT ANADARKO, OKLAHOMA MARCH 20, 1934 FOR THE PURPOSE OF DISCUSSING AND EXPLAINING THE WHEELER-HOWARD BILL

MR. MCCOWN: My friends, I know this is going to be a happy day for all of you. I am glad to see so many present to meet the Commissioner. I understand that some of our delegates who have seats reserved for them in the front of the building have been unable to get the seats due to the other people crowding in. Those who are not delegates will please vacate these seats in order that the delegates may have the seats reserved for them. At this time I will introduce Mr. Ross Hume who will make the address of welcome.

MR. HUME: Mr. Commissioner, ladies and gentlemen, Anadarko is glad this morning to welcome the Hon. John Collier, Commissioner of Indian Affairs, the tribes of this reservation and the guests from the other reservations in Oklahoma. One hundred years ago, in 1834, the Government first came in contact with the Indians of the plains in Oklahoma. Since that time your ancestors have been in more or less continuous contact with the Government. For seventy-five years there has been an agency and headquarters for the Indians in and around Anadarko. We have watched for many years your development and your improvement. We are interested in your social, economic and political affairs. We believe that the visits of the Commissioner with you, where he can see what your condition is, will benefit you. We believe that it will benefit him in his work for you and now, Mr. Commissioner; I wish to present you to the Indians of Western Oklahoma.

COMMISSIONER COLLIER: I am glad to be with this great gathering of the many tribes from the State of Oklahoma. I bring you the greetings of Secretary Ickes of the Interior Department. I shall later in the day read you a communication from Congressman Howard, Chairman of the Indian committee of the House. I shall read you later a communication from President Roosevelt. Before we get going—I don't know anything about how the voice carries in this hall—I want to be heard by everybody but don't want to talk any louder than is necessary. Am I being heard now? Let us have as much quiet as we can. As some of you know, I have come here from a series of meetings with other Indians. Meetings are being held among the Indians all over parts of the country and more will be held. I have gone out, and most of the staff of the Indian Office in Washington, has gone out to talk with the Indians. This is a very busy time in Washington and not an easy time for the Commissioner and his staff to go into the field but we have gone because we are determined that the Indians themselves shall know about the administration program and bill and shall themselves pass on that program and that bill.

There are in this hall now Indians whose memory goes back a long way; whose memory goes back across a great many acts of legislation, and I do not believe these old men can remember any time when the administration and any of the friends of the Indians in Washington, came to the Indians themselves and asked them whether they wanted a proposed new law. Laws have been passed not only by hundreds but by thousands. There are thousands of laws dealing with Indians and whether they be good laws or bad laws they have been passed because people in Washington thought they ought to be passed. We at Washington believe that we are proposing a law of great advantage to the Indians but we do not want that law to be considered by Congress until Congress knows the views of the Indians and we not only want the Indians to study that bill and criticize it, we are determined that the Indians shall do that and shall take the responsibility for deciding about this legislation which affects them.

Now before going further I am anxious to know whether everybody who can hear me also understands me. Aren't there a good many Indians here who do not understand English? How are we going to arrange it so that they shall understand as we go forward? Let us get interpreters in every group. Can't the non-English speaking members of the delegation get close around the interpreters so the interpreters can talk in a low voice right along? There is no use in my speaking to you unless you understand.

Interpreters designated by the various tribes.

MR. MCCOWN: On account of the large crowd we will have to be just as quiet as possible. The Commissioner has been making speeches for the last three weeks. If there are any crying babies in the auditorium please take them out as they cause confusion.

MR. COLLIER: If we are really going to accomplish anything today; if this meeting is going to do any good, then we are going to spend many hours talking to each other. If necessary the meeting will go on, not only this afternoon, but tonight, because the object is that we arrive at an understanding. The meeting must not consist merely of my talking with you. You must talk to me. You may be sure that any question that one of you think of or any remark you make will be valuable to all the others and will throw light on the subject. But you first will want a general statement from me explaining what it is we are trying to do. I shall also in this first talk tell you a lot of things we are not trying to do and do not propose to do, because there are some misunderstandings—extreme misunderstandings—about this Wheeler-Howard Bill and about what the administration is proposing to do. I also want to get out of your minds any feeling of hurry; any feeling that anybody is trying to stampede you because there are some groups of Indians in Oklahoma, and other places, who seem to feel the house was on fire and they had to do something very quickly, and they have gone and passed resolutions before I could meet with them. I wish we could understand clearly the reason why this meeting and all these meetings of Indian congresses, are being held. You know that at the present time President Roosevelt controls both houses of Congress. When President Roosevelt wants a piece of legislation he gets it from Congress. The bill we are going to discuss today is an administration measure—it is a President Roosevelt measure. The majority of the members of Congress do not pretend to understand the Indian question in detail at all. The majority of the members of Congress have nothing to gain or lose by any Indian legislation.

In other words, if the administration had wanted to put this bill through quietly and quickly, understand they had the power and they have the power to do it. The administration, as I stated before, has adopted a new policy which is the policy of bringing all the Indians into consultation on the bill, even though it entails, or may entail delay; even though it may slow things down, therefore, every Indian should realize that the administration is not trying to put something over on them or stampede them or steamroller them. Because if that were the purpose of the administration these meetings would never have been called; the administration would simply have gone quietly ahead and put the bill through Congress. I am saying this in order to ease your minds and get them open so we may think together about the problem.

Already in other parts of the country we have obtained the most important new ideas from different Indian gatherings. Suggestions of how to improve this bill, which are fundamental, have been made and have been accepted. The meetings already held have proved worthwhile, if only to consider the new ideas the Indians have given us, the criticisms and further ideas they have given us for improving the bill.

I want to tell you a little about the first of these Indian congresses held up in South Dakota two weeks ago. That was the meeting of all the plains Indian tribes of the North—from North and South Dakota, Nebraska, Wyoming and Montana. The first day of that meeting—this meeting held on four and one-half days—it was clear that a great many of the delegates' minds were closed like a trap—they were shut. They were full of distrust, fear, suspicion. Their minds were closed and at the beginning we did not get much help out of them in the way of new ideas and criticisms. Then after they came to understand what you will understand before the day is over, their minds opened up and they went to work and furnished more valuable criticism and new ideas, more suggestions for needed changes in the bill, than we had gotten out of the House Indian Committee in a week of hearings. I do not care whether you agree with me or not. I don't care whether you endorse this bill or propose it, and the administration does not care. What I want and what the administration wants is your thoughts, your ideas and your criticism—that is what we are here for and not to get your endorsement of this bill.

Short recess for the installation of a loudspeaker.

MR. COLLIER: There is just one more preliminary statement I want to make. All that goes on in this meeting is being taken down by stenographers and copies are going to be made of the proceedings. The proceedings are going to be furnished to Congress and will be just the same as if they were statements made before the House Committee or Senate Committee on Indian Affairs. Any suggestions that are made by delegates will appear in the proceedings.

You may therefore be confident that neither I nor any other representative of the party are going to say things to you that we cannot back up later. It is all going to be of record and if we make mistakes, if we make misrepresentations we will be confronted by it later.

There are good and sufficient reasons why Indians, any Indians anywhere, ought to be watchful and even suspicious. There are good reasons why you ought to be. Now in all of the years, for one hundred years, people have been coming to the different Indian tribes, including your tribes, and telling them things that sound good and getting the tribes to agree to those things which sound good. Again and again you have found afterward that you had not been told the truth, that you had been misled and tricked. That explains a great many things in the history of the Indian tribes. Therefore, it is necessary for you to not only hear what I say to you but remember it and check it against the records and do your own independent thinking and follow the Government blindly in nothing at all. At the same time action is necessary; a change is necessary and new legislation is necessary and therefore you cannot merely refuse to act. You have got to use your heads, decide and then act. Whether you come under this bill or whether you decide to stay out of it, either decision is important and serious.

It is you, yourselves—tribe by tribe, who must decide whether you are to come into the bill or be excluded from it and stay out of it. You must decide that. At least that is the position which I take and which the Indian Office takes and that will be the arrangement as far as we have power to persuade Congress, that you, yourselves, are to decide whether you are to come in or stay out. But that is not a decision in which you will have to hurry or be stampeded. You are to take your time about it.

And now I can go ahead and tell you about the bill. First I will tell you the reasons why the bill has been drawn by the Administration and put before Congress. There are Indians in a great many different parts of the country. There are Indians all the way from North Carolina and Michigan up to the State of Washington, down to Southern California and in nearly all of the states between. Oklahoma is one of more than twenty states that have important Indian populations. The Government is the guardian over all of these Indians, in all parts of the country, except the State of New York. And even in the State of New York, the Federal Government has an important responsibility toward those Indians too. Now the greater number of all of the Indians for many years have been getting poorer and poorer, not richer and richer. The rest of the country taken as a whole, the United States taken as a whole, has been increasing its prosperity and wealth year by year, while the Indians have been losing their property and getting poorer and poorer year by year. I do not refer to the temporary setback that came with the depression that came in 1929. I am talking about the country as a whole and the wealth that has been increasing enormously year by year taken as a whole.

Furthermore, if you break up the United States into groups of races, if you look at the Italians, the Germans and if you look at the Negroes, you find that these groups have been getting more prosperous as the years went on. Their condition has been improved year by year, but the condition of the Indians has been going backward year by year, and they have been getting poorer year by year. This fact must be of importance to each Indian and each Indian must want to know why it is the way I have said. There are some people who would say that the Indian has been getting poorer and losing ground because the Indian is inferior, incapable of helping himself and is doomed to perish. There are many people who would say that, and I believe there are even some people who think that way. I shall give you my reasons for thinking that that is not true and my explanation of why the Indian has been losing ground while other people have been gaining ground. But first I want to bring to your mind this important fact. There is a country north of here, Canada, and Canada has one-third as many Indians as there are in the United States. In Canada the Indians' property is increasing both in money and in land and the Indians are going forward along with the rest of the population. That is the way it is in Canada. The very same tribes, for example the Blackfeet, live in Canada and have land in Canada that live in the United States and have land in the United States. In Canada they are holding on to their land, but in the United States they are losing their land and getting poorer and poorer. Now why is it?

There is another country south of us, Mexico. In Mexico there are millions of Indians and thirty years ago those Indians were practically slaves and they had no land thirty years ago. Now with each year the landholdings of those Indians grow larger. All over Mexico the Indians' landholdings are increasing, the Indians' wealth is increasing and the Indians are coming into more and more power. Why is that? Are the Indians of the United States weaker and inferior as compared to the Indians of Canada and Mexico? They certainly are not, and the explanation is different from that, as you are to see in a few minutes. You can see that it is bound to interest the President of the United States and Congress to know why the Indians of the United States are losing ground when all of the other people are gaining ground and why the Indians of the

United States are losing ground when the Indians of Canada and Mexico are gaining ground. This is a very interesting question, an important question.

Now before discussing why the Indians of the United States are losing ground, let me remind you of the facts so you can see how much ground you are losing. I will first give you facts about all Indians of the country because that explains why we have to have legislation for all Indians and then I will give you facts about Oklahoma Indians, about yourselves. In the year 1887, the Government adopted a new Indian Policy. That was in the year 1887. In that year the Indians were the owners of 138,000,000 acres of land and the land, which they owned, was the best land in the country, the most fertile. In the year 1887 Congress enacted the new policy, as it was then, that is the General Allotment Law. What is the area of land owned by the Indians now after these intervening years? The total area now owned by the Indians is 47,000,000 and the amount of land the Indians have lost is 91,000,000. Let's get that.

Since 1887 the Indians have lost title to 91,000,000 acres of land and they now have only 47,000,000 acres remaining in the whole United States and out of the 47,000,000—20,000,000 acres is desert land that no white man wants. So the good Indian land has been reduced to not more than 27,000,000 acres out of the 138,000,000 acres of good land which they had in 1887.

Now if this were just a thing of the past, if it were just a matter of history, there would be no reason for talking about it now. We would be wasting time on things which were mere history. That is not why I am speaking of it at all. The point is the Indians are continuing to lose land, the land is going right away, melting away, just as it has been for the last forty years. The same cause and the same laws which have deprived the Indians of 91,000,000 acres since 1887 are going ahead and will deprive the Indians of the remaining land within a few years. It is not only the land which has been lost but which is being lost by the Indians; it is not only the land, it is something else.

Since the year 1887 nearly a billion dollars, nearly one thousand million dollars, has been paid into tribal funds of Indian tribes. Nearly one thousand million dollars, and do you know how much is left, if you take all of the tribes' funds and put together, how much of that amount, nearly one thousand million dollars, how much is left? I will answer it. Nearly twenty million dollars. I am anxious for these facts to sink into your minds because they are sensational, extraordinary, terrible facts and every Indian must know them.

Now I will just break into my story right here and say that this Wheeler-Howard Bill is first of all put forward in order to stop the loss of land by the Indians and to increase the amount of land owned by the Indians, and to stop the misappropriation of the Indians' tribal funds. If the bill does not accomplish the purpose then let's get something that does accomplish it, but let's get something and stop the loss of Indian land and stop the misappropriation of Indian moneys. My own statement would be this. That for the United States to go on as guardian over the Indians in the way it has been going, with the results that I have been describing, is intolerable. The Government cannot and must not go on in that way which is taking away all of the land, misappropriating all of the money of the Indians and reducing them to a lower and lower economic standard. It cannot and must not go on in that way. If that is the only thing the Government as guardian of the Indians can do then the Government had better wash its hands of the whole subject and quit as far as the Indians are concerned. Now of course the thing does not have to go on the way it is going. It can be changed and that is what we are here to talk about today.

Now let us come right here to Oklahoma and see what has been happening and what is happening. Oklahoma Indians, like the other Indians, were brought under the Policy of 1887, the policy represented by the General Allotment Law. That law was forced upon the Oklahoma Indians against their protest and they even went into court and appealed clear up to the Supreme Court for protection against it but they could not get protection. The white people, the Government, had grown tired of breaking treaties, were tired of taking their land by that method because the breaking of treaties had resulted in a great many Indian wars. And wars were distasteful and expensive and we didn't want to do that any more. But the Indians had a great deal of land the white people wanted and a way had to be found to get that land away from the Indians without breaking treaties and without having more wars—and a way was found.

You all know what that way was, how the allotment plan was worked, but I am going to tell you in order to refresh your memories. And again I am not talking about the past in order to talk about the past, I am talking about the past only because it is the present. The allotment law as you know parceled out to each living enrolled Indian a piece of land, one piece of land out of the tribal estate. When each living enrolled Indian had been assigned his piece of land then all of the rest of the land was called "surplus," that is, something the Indians didn't need and never would need, and it was thrown open to white entry. The Indian tribes were paid the nominal sum, as a rule it was a dollar and a quarter an acre for this surplus land, as it was called, and the Government took it and turned it over to whites. It seemed to be the theory of Congress that there wouldn't be any more children born among the Indians—there were not going to be any more children so they didn't have to worry about them. Now at this point I won't go into any more detail about how the allotment plan was worked and is working because I now try to paint the picture in large lines. We will talk about the allotment system more during the day.

If we forget about what they call the "surplus land" bought at $1.25 an acre, which really means confiscation; let us forget about that for a moment. We will talk about the land that was allotted to the Indians, the land allotted to the living enrolled members of the tribes, about twenty-three million acres of land taken out of the tribal estate was allotted to the Indians of Oklahoma, about twenty-three million acres. And of that total all but a little more than three million acres has passed to white ownership. Twenty-three million acres allotted and the whites got twenty million acres of it. Just in order to give a picture to the eye we have brought here a map of one of your Oklahoma reservations, the Comanche, Kiowa, Wichita, and Apache. This, I am told, is the most fortunate in Western Oklahoma, that is, the loss of land by the Indians has been smaller here than on the other reservations of Western Oklahoma. The reservation contained at the time of allotment two and one-half million acres, two million five hundred thousand acres. You Indians here about are now the owners of 590,000 acres, in other words, you have lost nine-tenths of your land. Those of you who are close up can see this part (indicating the Wichita National Forest), the National Forest area—the white land minus that, just this little area.

In the total reservation there are 5846 Kiowas, Comanches, and Apaches, the total Indians are 5846 in number, and of that total 3742 were born since allotment and have received no allotment. In other words about four out of every six of the Indians are without land, about four out of every six. Of this total 3742, who are landless, a certain proportion have some interest in heirship land, between fifteen and twenty per cent. The others haven't even got an equity in a deed allotment. Now the condition among the other tribes of the west, such as the Pawnees, is worse than it is here.

Oklahoma Indians, as I stated, received allotments to the total area of twenty million acres. They have now got about three million acres, and half of that is being taxed. If you take the Five Civilized Tribes, just take them alone, the number of Indians who are totally landless, is seventy-two thousand. Seventy-two thousand of the Five Civilized Tribes are totally landless.

Right here let me turn aside from the story to explain clearly to you. Some people have thought that the administration has a plan of taking the land which the Indians still own and dividing that up so that the Indians who have lost their land would get a part of the land which the Indians still own. In other words, some people thought the Wheeler-Howard bill would take the land of an allottee, who has kept his land, and divide it to allottees who have lost their land. Without going into detail at this point I will just say that.

Of course, the Administration has no such idea and, of course, there is nothing like that in the bill; of course, Congress would never pass a law doing anything of the sort, but if we had a ridiculous idea like that and if Congress passed a crazy law like that, then the courts would immediately declare it unconstitutional because it would be unconstitutional and it would be null and void. I want to dislodge that erroneous idea from your minds if it is there because if you think that is what we are aiming at you are going to be worried and you are going to fight us.

I want to repeat because this is fundamental. You understand what I think of the allotment system, which has been a means of the Indian under the law. You know what I think of it. Nevertheless, allotment once it is carried out creates a vested property right in the allottee, a property right vested in law. That property right is protected by the Constitution. By the Constitution of the United States, just as the property right of the man who owns a town lot in Anadarko is protected by the Constitution. If Congress should pass a law to take one man's allotment from him and give it to another man that would be confiscation, would be violative of the Constitution and would immediately be thrown out by the court and would be null and void. It couldn't be done. This is an elementary fact of law that any honest lawyer could assure you of; which anybody who has studied the Constitution in high school knows and could assure you of. Furthermore, suppose that Congress has the power to take the land belonging to the allottee who has kept his land and to distribute it among the landless Indians, what would be accomplished by doing that. What good would it do?

The basic fact is that there is not enough land belonging to the Indians, that we have got to get more land to supply the landless Indians, new land. It would do no good to take the insufficient land from one Indian and give it to another. The whole problem is for more land, for new land. I will come back to this point later on when we are examining the details of the bill. I merely want to give you the assurance at this time that these bugaboos are merely creations, that they are not in the bill and never will be in the bill, they are just bugaboos. Now I come to a point, which is absolutely essential, and I am anxious for you to understand it as I go along. I have told you that Congress, itself, cannot take a man's allotment from him, an Indian's allotment, and give it to another Indian. I have told you that, but there are other ways than confiscation to get an Indian's land away from him. There is a way to take your land away from you which is entirely constitutional and legal. There are two ways and they are both carefully provided for in this General Allotment Act which we have been discussing.

One of these ways is to declare the Indian competent, issue him a fee patent and thereby compel him to pay taxes and allow him to mortgage his land. That is one way. You all know about that method, the method of fee patenting and putting the land under taxes, you all know about that. Perhaps you do not all know that the allotment law contains that, that fee patenting of the land is one of its essential parts, that the allotment law intended for Indian allotted land to be fee patented. That is part of the law so that the Secretary of the Interior at any time may lift the restrictions, terminate the trust period and thereby force the Indians to lose their lands. As you all know the period of restriction, the trust period, is so many years. It is either 25 years after allotment or some date in the future which Congress has fixed after which there will be no more trust period on the land for the particular tribe. But the time set for the end of the trust period is merely an outside limit and at any time the Secretary of the Interior may shorten that period by issuing a Certificate of Competency or fee patent just the way that Secretary Lane did in 1917, which resulted in many thousands of Indians losing their land quickly.

That danger always hangs over the head of the allotted Indian whose property is still held under a trust patent. For example, tomorrow the Secretary, if he wanted to, can force a fee patent on you with all of the consequences that you know. Secretary Ickes is not going to do it but he could, but the next Secretary of the Interior could and he might. Right here I will mention one feature of the Wheeler-Howard bill, which is to take away from the Secretary of the Interior and the President the authority to terminate the trust period on any Indian land, which makes the trust period permanent until Congress shall otherwise declare. Legislation cannot go any further than that. It is impossible to take away from Congress its power to terminate the trust period. What we can do is to take it away from the executive and direct him not to do it and thereby make the trust period practically permanent, which this bill does.

Now there is a second way of forcing the Indians to lose their allotted land which is more important than the fee-patenting way, and I want to remind you of that and explain it to you. The man, or woman, or child who gets an allotment dies—after a while the allottee's life comes to an end. He is dead. Then the heirs have to be determined—the heirs who share in that allotment have to be determined. They are determined. Then it becomes the duty, under the law, of the Secretary of the Interior either to partition that allotment among the heirs—break it up among the heirs—or to sell it.

Now if there are only two or three heirs, then it is possible to partition the land in such a way it can be used when broken up. However, you can't partition an allotment among 15 or 20 or 50 heirs. It is impossible. Still less can you partition it among 250 heirs and a great many of our heirship allotments belong to 250 or more heirs. In fact, we have cases where an allotment has passed down through two generations, that is, the heirs have died and their heirs have inherited it and we have as many as a thousand heirs to a single allotment.

Now the government has a choice to make each time; it can't partition the land and so it can sell the land and divide the money among the heirs or it can hold onto it and lease it, collect the rental and divide it among the heirs. But if there is one heir who has been declared competent, the intent of the law is clear, if he demands that the allotment be sold, the intent of the law is that his demand shall be recognized regardless of the wishes of the non-competent heirs. I can summarize the thing this way: Through the death of the allottee and the multiplication of heirs, it becomes an administrative and financial necessity to sell the heirship land. It has been done down the years and must continue. Selling the land, of course, means usually selling it to a white man, it means that the heirship land is all marked down to pass to whites, so that it is entirely correct as we have stated in the Department's memorandum prepared for Congress. It is correct to say that the allotment system intends for all Indian allotted lands to pass to whites, in the second generation or at the latest in the third generation. In other words, the grandchild is intended to be disinherited of his land and he is or will be, under the allotment law and system.

Now that is the problem which we have to solve. We have got to find a way to save the lands, especially the heirship lands, while still completely protecting the vested property rights of each Indian who still owns an allotment or who has an interest in a dead allotment.

After lunch we are going to see how the Wheeler-Howard Bill will do the things I am describing. We are not dismissed yet. I still have got to give you one other fact before we stop for lunch because I want you to be thinking about it during lunch. I want to get this clear to you. The government's administration of your allotted lands does not save them from being lost. They are lost in spite of what the government does, through heirship sales. The government can't stop that, I mean that under existing law the government can't stop it under the present system of law, but with every year that goes by the cost of administering your heirship land increases until it now amounts to millions of dollars a year; a cost to the government now if that tremendous yearly expense of the government's were saving your lands or getting you new lands. It is merely like taking care of a dying man on his sickbed, knowing that he is going to die anyhow.

Let me show you in relation to the agency where we now are—the Kiowa agency, right here—the yearly cost to this agency including health work and extension work, is about eighty thousand dollars—eighty thousand dollars a year is spent by this agency and of that eighty thousand dollars, sixty-five thousand dollars is used up in these real estate operations connected with your allotments, chiefly your heirship lands, the leasing of land, the collection of rent money, the banking and paying out. All this real estate work does not save your land and does not build up your land. Sixty-five thousand dollars out of eighty thousand dollars is used up that way.

This agency, in my judgment, is efficiently conducted. It is doing as good as it can on the money and what is happening here is just what is happening in all the other allotted areas. Seventy percent of all the expenditures goes on this fruitless operation connected with your allotted lands, the leasing of your allotted lands, and therefore, the government hasn't got money for health work; hasn't got money needed for educational work—schooling—hasn't got the money that is needed to provide loans to Indians. The real estate operation connected with your allotments eats up all the money we can get from the government and so you don't get service and the four out of six Indians here who have not allotments, get no benefit at all. The money is used up on this allotment leasing and collecting and etc.

Now I want to put the thing to you this way. The government is not going to continue wasting several million dollars a year on this unsuccessful administration of the Indian allotment system. It is not going to continue doing it. Now that the President and the Director of the Budget and the Committees of Congress know the facts, they are not going to go on wasting money on this allotment administration, especially the heirship part of it; not when there are still 15,000 Indians out of school for lack of money and when the Indians are dying at the rate twice as fast as the white people for the lack of good medical attention. The needs of money are too great to waste the money in the way I have been describing.

What I am going to say to you is not an announcement of policy but a mere statement of fact concerning what I know is ahead. It is not my policy and it is not something I could change if I wanted to, but I have got to say it to you; unless some way can be found to cut down the costs of administering the allotment system and to save the land from passing to whites, unless that can be done, then the government will do one of two things. It either will throw the cost of the administration of allotments upon the allottees, or it will sell the heirship lands and thereby save the cost of administering them.

Later, I will explain why I know this is going to happen and will happen even if I and Secretary Ickes try to keep it from happening. Now we at Washington not only believe but we know that there is a way to meet these evils and difficulties—a way which, when you understand it, it is not going to be forced on you either as tribes or as individuals—not even as individuals though your tribe votes for it. The Wheeler-Howard Bill is the first step toward the solution, the first step toward the goal that you are all seeking.

Now I know that you are all getting restless and it is lunch time and we had better stop.

Telegram read by Judge Lawrence from Jed Johnston:

> "Please convey my best wishes to your distinguished visitor, John Collier, Commissioner of Indian Affairs, and accept my sincere regrets that I am unable to join my neighbors and friends in Anadarko in extending our cordial good wishes."

Afternoon Session

MR. COLLIER: I think the best way now is to start right in explaining the bill and to try and do that quickly, perhaps finishing in one hour so that then you can start the discussion. I would like to know whether all the delegates have copies of the bill with them. Those who have please hold up your hands. Seems like a good many have not copies of the bill. We distributed 125 copies this morning. Where are they all? I will go ahead and remind you again that a record is being made of all I say here—all anybody says. We shall not be able to dispose of every detail in the 48 pages of the bill now. We can't do that in the time we have. Those of you who are not accustomed to legal language in legislation will find a complete description of the bill in this memorandum dated February 19, of which copies are on the stage. Likewise, the printed hearings on the House Committee on Indian Affairs, gives the fullest details on all parts of the bill. The bill, of course, is going to be amended and improved by the Committees of Congress before they report it for a vote and I think what you want from me is a simple and honest statement of all that the Department believes the bill will accomplish and how it will accomplish it. I think you may be confident that if the bill should be changed in undesirable ways, so that it is not like the thing I am going to tell you about, then it would not be signed by the President. He would veto it.

Now I believe that the side of the whole question that most of you care most about is the land question and, therefore, I will begin with that, which is Title III of the bill and then after dealing with the land, take the self-government, education and the court features of the bill. The land feature, Title III, is designed first to put an end to the loss of the land which you still have and second, to get new land for those Indians who have lost their land or have not enough land. Title III looks forward to a large land purchase program by the Government—a program of acquiring new land for Indians all over the country but the Government will not spend millions of dollars buying new land for Indians only to have it lost again under the allotment system. We must rectify the existing land holding arrangements before the Government can be asked to spend money getting still more land for the Indians. So we will begin, not talking about the new land but talking about saving the land you have. Then we will talk about getting more land. Now I shall not repeat what I said this morning about how the allotment arrangement forces the Indians to lose their land. I will ask you to bear that in mind so I will not have to repeat it.

We begin with, the bill on page 25 says that there shall not be any future allotment—no more land shall be allotted in the old way. Then it says on page 26 that the trust period on all Indian land is extended indefinitely until otherwise directed by Congress—is carried forward into the future indefinitely. And it adds that the lands shall be continued exempt from taxation. Then the bill, on page 28, directs the Secretary of the Interior to take certain steps which I will describe to you. It directs him to examine each Indian reservation—each area where the Indians own land—and to select what area he shall try to make into solid Indian land. He is to study the reservations over all of the country and select those areas where the Government will help the Indians consolidate their land into solid blocks. He is to make maps and show on those maps what areas should hereafter be made into a solid Indian ownership. Merely to illustrate to you I go back to the map of the Cheyenne and Apache reservation. You see how the Indian land, which is the white, is scattered all around a large area among the white lands. And remember that the Indians who own land at all number about 2000–2100 own this land.

There are about 3700 Indians here who do not own any land but live here. Now if the Comanches and Apaches here wanted to be included in the bill, according to section 6, the Secretary of the Interior would determine how much land is needed so there would be enough land for every member of the tribe. Then he would proclaim the area to be consolidated through acquiring additional lands—the area to be made a solid Indian-owned area. Let us just say—I am merely using this as an example—let us suppose he finds the Indians require a million acres of this land altogether—they have got 496,000 acres. Then according to this section he would determine what should be the boundary of that million acres, which is to be Indian land. Now what would happen to the land inside that boundary—that boundary surrounding the million acres—what would happen to that? There would be three times the land obviously. In the first place there would be land not owned by the Indians but by the white people in that million acres. That land—the only way to get it would be through purchase from the white owners through buying it and adding it to the Indian land.

The bill authorizes an expenditure of $2,000,000 each year for buying such land from the whites for the Indians. Next we come to the allotments within that area—that area that has been selected for consolidation—the allotments belonging to individual Indian allottees. What would be done with respect to those allotments belonging to individual Indians? What would happen to them? The answer is this: The individual who owns an allotment could keep it just like it is if he wanted to—just like it is if he preferred. Or he could transfer his title to the community or the tribe in exchange for advantages or benefits that I will now describe. I may say that where the land is farming land the allottee might not want to exchange it for a tribal title but would want to keep it as it is.

Now let us see what would happen in the case of the allottee who did want to surrender his individual title to the community or tribe. Let us see what would happen in his case. What would he get in exchange for his surrendering his individual title to this allotment? First, he would get a guarantee from the Government that he could continue to occupy and use the same piece of land during his lifetime. That is number one. Second, he would get a guarantee that his children, his heirs, could continue to occupy and use the same land through their lifetime and so on down through all the generations. Third, he would get a guarantee that if he did not want to stay on that piece of land and use it but wanted to go somewhere else within the tribal area, then he would be entitled to the use of an equal amount of value of land within the area owned by the tribe. Fourth, he would get a guarantee of the complete ownership of any improvements which he had already put on the land, or might in the future put on the land so if he took another piece of land in place of the one he got he would be entitled to a cash value for the improvements. And finally this same ownership of improvements would descend to his heirs. They would have that too. In other words, the man who did relinquish his individual title to the tribe would keep just what the man would keep who did not relinquish it. You would not know the difference except the man who did relinquish it would get certain advantages over the man who didn't.

I want to make it clear at this point that all I have been describing is optional and voluntary and not compulsory. Those of you who have the bill and will turn to page 31, line 6, will see that the bill—the way it is printed here—reads as follows: "The Secretary of the Interior is authorized to transfer the title of the individual allottee to the tribe in exchange for all these things." That is the way the bill reads. It gives him power regardless of the consent of the Indians. I am anxious to have this translated clearly.

At the Congress of the Plains Indians two weeks ago we discussed that point for many hours and I found that the Indians didn't like that feature of the bill. Many of them did not like it. They were afraid the Secretary of the Interior might be reckless, unwise and might abuse his discretion and do things the Indians would not want under that language. We agreed with them that there was a possibility of abuse in the language and further that it was not necessary to accomplish the purpose of the bill and, therefore, the language should be changed so as to have this transfer take place only with the consent or upon the request of the individual allottees, and that is the way it will be when the second printing of the bill comes out. That amendment will be introduced. So much for the allotment belonging to an allottee now alive.

Now what about the future of the Indian lands after the present generation dies? In the case of allottees who die after this bill is enacted, then the title would in all cases pass to the tribe. The heirs would inherit first the right to continue to live on and use the same piece of land. They would inherit it and their children and their children, would inherit that right but the title would be passed to the tribe. They would inherit also what is called in the bill, the rental value of the particular land in question. In other words, they would be entitled through the heirs to payment equal to the amount of money obtained in rent from the allotment in question. They would inherit the improvements unconditionally, to either use or sell as they chose.

You will want to know what is the practical value of this arrangement contained in Section 11, about the title of heirship lands passing to the tribe, why it is necessary, etc. I shall explain that to you. It is necessary to prevent the thing we were talking about before lunch, that is, to make unnecessary the sale of this land to the whites. I shall explain just why. You are all fairly familiar with the way heirship rights work out at present. Each inherited allotment will belong to a considerable number of individual heirs, six, twelve, twenty, fifty, or more, and each Indian heir is likely to have some interest in a number of inherited allotments. A man or child may have a small interest in each of twenty or thirty, or even fifty dead allotments. We actually have cases where an Indian will have a rental interest in an allotment as low as 1/2¢ a year; he may have an interest in a hundred allotments—1 1/2¢ from those; 5¢ from another; 12¢ from another; and $3.00 from still another. Mr. McCown says that here they have allotments that yield 3¢ and 5¢ a year. For the Government or anybody else to be the real estate agent, the banker, etc., for these heirship lands under these conditions, is impossible. The administrative cost is too great—so great that often it is more than the whole income from the land. Therefore, the bill provides—and this is the practical effect—that all the heirship interests of each Indian will be lumped so that if a man is entitled to a rental income of let us say, $250 a year, which now comes in from six, twelve, or twenty heirship allotments, hereafter he will be entitled to that same rental income paid out from the rent received from all the land rented. The matter will be as simple as the payment of dividends by a corporation. If a man owns $100 worth of stock in a corporation and the corporation is paying 5% dividends he gets $5.00. It would be very much like that in this case. I am speaking of only the land being rented.

By dealing with that as a whole it will be possible to get better rent in a more steady way for all of it than by dealing with land broken up in parcels as at present. That would be true whether it be the Indian Bureau that goes out and finds the customer and executes the lease, the Tribal Council, or whatever authority. He deals with the owner in a business-like way. This will be clearer to those of you who have grazing land than to those who have farming land. The problem of grazing land is far more difficult. Farming land is much easier. The existing arrangement is not so bad for farming land. Now I want to go further about this matter and explain that as far as the heirs are concerned the change which is compulsory is only that change which requires them to take equal rental value and to receive that instead of compelling the Government to collect rentals from thirty or forty little parcels of land that they would be getting the same rental from the Government.

Now I want to go further and say that any tribe which holds back, which is still afraid of this thing and does not want to come in at all, that tribe can be omitted by putting in a proviso that they are omitted, that they are not affected by the thing at all. I think that when the advantages are understood and after I explain the rest of the plan there will not be any tribe that will want to be excluded. I think they will all be clamoring to get in, including some of you here who think you are not going to want to. There are some people very powerful in the Government who would be very glad if a large number of tribes decided not to come in. There are some people, I will explain who they are and why, there are some people who would be very glad if some of the Oklahoma tribes would not come in on this. They are people who want to keep down the expenditure of the Government, the Budget Director, the people who hold the purse strings of the Government. They would like to see some of the tribes stay out for the present.

For example, just take this matter of land purchase, take the matter of buying land for the landless Indians, take that matter by itself. The number of Indians with no land at all under their management amount to about one hundred thousand and they are all over the country. More than one hundred thousand Indians without any land. It is going to cost a large number of millions to buy the land for those Indians—many, many millions. If one-half of the tribes should decide that they do not want to come in on this plan at all that will cut down the necessary expenditures for land purchase by one-half and would save the Government that much money and that would please the Director of the Budget very much, I imagine.

Again, we have amended the bill to provide a further amount of five million dollars which is a grant by the Government, a gift, to Indian tribes to be used as a loan from the tribe, to its members. It will be used as a loan to the members for buying tools, seeds, building homes and in the conduct of business operations. The members of the House Committee asked us whether we thought that was enough to establish a loan fund and we replied, it was only a beginning as you will see by the printed hearings; they agreed it should be made ten million instead of five million. There is a terrible need among Indians for financial credit and it is going to be very hard to get enough money to establish adequate banks for Indians and therefore if one-half of the tribes stayed out it would be much easier for the one-half that came in and it would also save Uncle Sam lots of money.

Again, the Government, even next year will take from the tribal funds of the Indians more than two million dollars for the support of the Indian Bureau. It has been taking four million, five million a year, until, it has used up the funds of the Indians but even next year it is going to take more than two million from the dwindling tribal funds for Bureau support. This is important enough to repeat.

I spoke to you this morning about the misappropriation of the Indian tribal funds. Most of you have no tribal funds because they have been misappropriated, cleaned out, but the time will come when some of you will have funds again, as you know. Since the year 1900, the Government has diverted more than one hundred million dollars to pay the salaries and upkeep of the Indian Bureau. Now when the appropriations for the coming year were under consideration before the Budget Committee, we went before the Budget Committee and denounced this practice as wrong and indefensible, this taking Indian trust money to pay the cost of the Government. We said that these costs ought to be met out of gratuity appropriations, that is, ought to be made by the taxpayers of the United States and not taken out of trust funds. Our plea did no good and the Budget transmitted the appropriations to Congress in the old way, charging about two million dollars of the Indian Bureau costs against tribal funds of the Indians. We carried the fight to Congress and in the printed hearings of the House Appropriations Committee dealing with the coming fiscal year you will find that we denounced this practice as being immoral and abusive of the Government's trusteeship. So we are meeting that situation by putting into this bill that hereafter no Indian tribal funds can be spent in any way that the tribe itself does not want and approve. In other words, the bill gives the tribe the power to protect themselves absolutely, which would mean that that two million dollars a year would not any longer be taken out of trust funds but would be taken out of the Treasury where the taxpayers provide the money. And we have obtained the endorsement of the President to this bill, including this feature—we have obtained the endorsement of President Roosevelt, including this protection.

Obviously, the watchdogs of the Treasury will be very glad to see the Indian tribes not come in, because then their trust money can be and will be used in the future as in the past to take the place of money—will be used in the future as in the past to support the Indian Bureau. Now I want and hope for all tribes to come in, but you can see why many people do not want them to come in, good people. I mean, I am not talking about the people who want to get your land, I am talking about people who want to save the Government money. They will be very glad if one-half of the tribes do not come in and you can even see why such tribes as the Pueblos and others who certainly are coming in, why they would be very glad if other tribes did not come in because the amount of money for land purchases, the amount of money for loans, is never going to be enough anyhow and every tribe that stays out means more money for those that go in. So you will understand that other tribes are not going to beg anybody to go in, and nobody is going to be terribly cast down if this or that tribe stays out. Those of us who care about all Indians will be cast down because we do want to see your land saved and we do want to give new land to you landless Indians.

Now I will go on to the other features of the bill, which are not equally important with the land, but are very important, nevertheless. There was a time and you old men all remember it, when the Indians governed their own lives and did it successfully. They were not managed by someone else. They governed themselves and they were happy and successful and prosperous. Those times are gone away into the past and at present you are governed by the Secretary of the Interior and the Commissioner of Indian Affairs. We may govern you wisely, well and good, or we may govern you unwisely. We may govern you honestly or dishonestly, but we are the kings, we are the czars over the lives of the Indians, and if you have a wise and devoted Indian Commissioner and Secretary of the Interior and they set up a policy which is wise and good, their successors, and they always change pretty fast, are free to completely upset anything they have done and revise any policies they have instituted. It is a condition hostile to your past lives. You are entitled to govern yourselves and to be free. I am not saying that any tribe or group of Indians must govern itself, only that a tribe which wants to, and a group that wants to, should have that right.

Now that government by the Indian tribe, that home rule by the Indian tribe is possible inside the guardianship of the Federal Government. You do not have to go out from under the Government protection and aid to have freedom. You can have it inside the Federal protection. This bill strengthens and assists the Federal guardianship over the Indians, not only over their land but over their lives. It gives back to the landless Indians the Federal protection and guardianship of which they have been deprived through losing their land, while at the same time it extends the power of local self-government to those Indians who want it, but only to those who want it. It provides that a group of Indians or a tribe may take out a charter under the self-government, issued by the Federal Government and that charter would make that group of Indians or that tribe an instrumentality of the Federal Government itself, clothed with all the protection of the Federal Government.

No tribe or group would have to ask for this charter. It could ask for it if it wanted it and if they got the charter and did not like it, it could give it back whenever it got ready. But once a charter of self-government was issued the Commissioner of Indian Affairs and the Secretary of the Interior could not revoke it, could not take it away; only the Indians could take it away themselves, or Congress could take it away, but not the Department. Now under such a charter an Indian tribe or community could take over just as little power as it preferred, just a little bit, or it could take over a great deal, entirely according to what it was ready for. A tribe which took on very little power and found that it was satisfactory and worked well, next year could take on more power, and next year more power. If it took on too much power and things did not go right it could give it up again. It is left with the tribe.

We recognize that there are enormous differences in the situation of different tribes of Indians and in the situation of individuals within each tribe. There are tremendous differences and they have to be taken into account. There are some tribes made up entirely of pure bloods and who speak almost entirely their native language. There are other tribes whose blood is very much mixed and they all talk English. The conditions are not the same in those two kinds of tribes. There are tribes like the Navajoes who have escaped allotment and whose land holdings have doubled in the last thirty years. They have 25 thousand square miles of land, as big as one of the big states along the Atlantic seaboard. You can see they might want to set up a complete government within their solid area where there are not whites. There are more than 30 tribes situated like the Navajoes but again there are tribes where the members are scattered all about among the whites and are taking part in the general life of the country and state. You can see their situation is different from the Navajoes or Pueblos or Eastern Cherokees. This bill provides that each group can take on the form of organization fitted to it and can experiment and change whenever it wants to or it can decide to take on no organization at all, no self-government and just go on as a general community under the Indian Bureau. All of the tribes want to be assured that the protection and guardianship and financial help of the United States Government will be continued. They all want that and all who come into this bill get that.

QUESTION FROM THE CROWD: Will you please explain the other side, what will become of those who don't come in?

MR. COLLIER: The question was would I tell about those who do not accept the bill and I said I would answer that a little later, but I will answer it to this extent right away: That the tribe which does not want to come into this bill at all will go on just the way it is now until all of the land is lost and then I suppose it will come back and ask for a charter and some new land.

Now there are two things which I am very anxious for you to get about this self-government plan because they are of importance to every individual tribe without exception. There are two things which are important. The first thing has to do with the expenditure of money in the Indian Service, both of the Government's money and of the tribe's money. Whenever a tribe or community of Indians accepts this bill and takes out a charter then each year the Indian Bureau must come to that tribe and state in detail how it is going to spend the money next year: How much is going for schools, how much for agency, how much for hospitals, how much for extension and for all other purposes. They must present a budget to the tribe for the ensuing year, not just what it did with your money last year but what it is going to do with your money next year.

Now if the money in question is tribal funds, then you have the final voice. What you say goes. The money is spent the way you direct and not a penny can be spent except as you direct it. Where the money in question is Government money, gratuity money, then your recommendations are transmitted to the Bureau of the Budget and to Congress right alongside any recommendations by the Indian Bureau, and they have equal weight and importance. I don't think I need to argue why this will be important to every tribe. You know how your money is being spent and can control the expenditure of your own money and you have an equal position with the Indian Bureau about the expenditure of Government money.

Now the next thing which is important to all Indian tribes has to do with the future and employment of your Indian young people. In the first place the bill has a title dealing with education for Indians and it provides a very much broader education than you have at the present for your young people. This is Title Two of the bill and if you simply read it you will understand it. I hardly need to spend any time on it. Title Two of the bill. It directs the Secretary of the Interior, through his subordinates, to find the Indian young men and women with energy and ambition and talent; to find them and then put them through whatever schools are needed in order to give them the best training, whether as engineers or stockmen or nurses or doctors or lawyers or any trade or profession. He is directed that if there are not schools run by the Indian Bureau that meet the needs then he is to provide them with scholarships in the state college or college of agriculture or engineering or for whatever instruction will thoroughly equip them for life.

There are two kinds of scholarships arranged, or set up in the bill. One kind, half of the money is a gift to the Indian young man or woman and the other half is a loan to be repaid without interest, but not to be repaid unless the young person has a job. The other kind of scholarship is an outright gift in its totality to be made to Indian young men and women who show great ability, who ought to become leaders. They are to be financed through college or technical schools at no cost to them or their families.

Now connected with what I have just told you is a matter of employing Indians in the Indian Service which is dealt with in the bill. I would like for you to think over that fact. If you go back to the year 1900, that is 34 years ago, and compare with last year you will find more Indians employed regularly by the Indian Bureau in the Indian Service in 1900 than in 1933 in comparison to the total number of employees. The proportion of white employees in the Indian Service is higher in 1933 than it was in 1900 and the proportion of Indians is lower. The reason is Civil Service. The Civil Service law requires qualification of college training, academic training, and of special experience, which very few Indians can meet and, therefore, the white people qualify and get the jobs. We are constantly faced with the condition that there are Indians perfectly qualified to hold positions, they have ability, they have character, they have the practical training, but we can't put them in the position because they can't pass the Civil Service Examinations. I want to make clear that the trouble is not any willful discrimination against Indians in favor of whites. The trouble is the Civil Service requirements.

Secretary Ickes and I are more anxious to put Indians in responsible positions than we are for anything else. I don't think that anybody can doubt that we really want to do it and are trying, but we are not making much progress and can not under Civil Service. Therefore, we have put in the bill, and the President has endorsed, a new plan which I will describe to you. This will make it the duty of the Secretary of the Interior to set down in writing the practical qualifications which ought to be met by an Indian in order to qualify for any job in the Indian Service, such as farmer, extension agent, nurse, clerk, superintendent, and so on. He is to describe qualifications which, if an Indian can meet, will qualify that Indian for that job. When an Indian man or woman meets those qualifications then his or her community can require the Secretary of the Interior to give the job to that man or that women; can nominate its Indian boy or girl for the job and if there is a vacancy the Secretary has to give that job to that boy or girl.

Coupled with that provision is the other provision by which the Indians in an organized community, a chartered community, can require the removal of a white employee whom they find unsatisfactory. We have some experience to go on in this matter, gained in the last year in our Emergency Conservation Work which is not under Civil Service. There we have been able to place the Indians in the responsible positions. More than half of the supervisor jobs in the Emergency Conservation Work all over the country are held by Indians, not by whites. It has been completely successful. The Indian Conservation Camps are universally admitted to have outstripped the white camps, better than two to one all over the country.

During the coming summer we are going to be putting up a lot of buildings especially down in Arizona and New Mexico, principally day schools and high schools for Indians. Many of these buildings will not have a single white man on the job and every man from superintendent down to day laborer will be Indian. Everybody will be Indians.

Down in the Southwest we are carrying out some very difficult, scientific, complicated engineering work aiming at the control of soil erosion—the washing away of soil—and some of that work has been held up as a model for the whole United States because of the engineering ability used in carrying it out and all of the work has been done by Indians. This has been possible because under the Public Works law we do not have to apply the Civil Service requirements. If we did have to, this emergency work would be just like our regular work and we couldn't let the Indians in much.

Now if somebody says all these arrangements will cause the Indians to compete with each other and all that and will bring politics into the tribe, the answer is that no tribe has to take up any of them. No tribe has to take out a charter under the bill. It is entirely a local matter, whether the tribe wants it.

Now I shall not talk but about a minute about the court, the Court of Indian Affairs, because I don't think that will interest you much. That is Title Four of the bill. This bill will simply bring together under a special Court of Indian Affairs the matters that are now under the various United States District Courts, put them under a court which the President would appoint and would be made up of men selected because of their understanding and sympathy with Indians. And it appoints and authorizes the appointment by the President of ten special attorneys who would be public defenders for the Indians, that is, they would serve without pay and would represent Indians in cases that came before this court. This court would be given the authority to review the acts of the Secretary of the Interior and the Indian Commissioner so that we would not be any longer arbitrary, but subject to review by this special Court of Indian Affairs.

I am going to stop now so that you can begin with your remarks and questions. Before doing so I want to read you the President's statement about this bill. He says:

> "Opportunity for self-determination for the Indians in handling their property by providing for modern corporate management participation in local government, a more liberal educational system through day schools and advanced health measures are provided in the bill.
>
> "Adequate provision is made for his training in management, the protection of his property and the conservation of his health during the period that must intervene before the Indian may be entrusted with the complete management of his own affairs. In offering the Indian these natural rights of man, we will more nearly discharge the federal responsibility for his welfare than through compulsory guardianship that has destroyed initiative and the liberty to develop his own culture."
>
> (Signed) Franklin D. Roosevelt,
> President.

Now I am going to ask Dr. Henry Roe Cloud, the head of Haskell Institute who you all know, to take charge during this time of questions and remarks and we will answer your questions, if we can. When you arise to give your question or to make your remarks, please state your name clearly and your tribe or jurisdiction, for the record and your question will be repeated back so everybody will hear it before it is answered.

HENRY ROE CLOUD: The first thing we will do will be to have a ten-minute recess and as soon as we come back we will have these questions. We will have a ten-minute recess right away.

(10 minute intermission.)

MR. ROE CLOUD: Will the meeting now come to order. The meeting will now come to order and if everybody will be quiet we will proceed.

Now there are many delegations and many Indians who want to meet the Commissioner, to speak to him as delegations and individuals. We wish that the Commissioner could divide himself into ten or twenty parts and that every part would be equally effective in addressing these groups and individuals, but he is only one person—one unit—and he has asked that those who have some particular problems and urgent matters to take up with him personally, that they arrange to meet Mr. Reeves and I will ask Mr. Reeves to stand up at the present time so that you can see him. He is legal advisor of the Indian Bureau and this evening sometime, he will be very glad to meet this delegation and answer any technical questions that you may have.

Now that we have arrived at the hour when we are to ask questions and have them answered as best they may and you realize that there are a great many of you in this audience and there will be many hundreds of questions which need to be answered in your mind, but you see how impossible it is to answer all of them in the short time we have to answer them in; therefore, I hope that none of you when you ask questions, will make a long speech on your question that will take up the time of maybe ten or twelve other fellows who want to ask questions, and those other questions that are to be asked may be far more important than your remarks. So, let us rush this thing as far as we can.

Now, at the end of this meeting if we find that we are not satisfied and the delegates want another meeting tonight, I will take a vote of the house, as chairman, and we will decide to have another big assembly like this this evening, if you want it. If you do not want it, that settles the matter now. When anyone gets up to ask a question, will you kindly give your name and your tribe in every case so that it may be put in the record and everyone will know who it is that is speaking.

Now I do not propose to answer all these questions but there are experts and men who know on the platform here who I will call upon to answer the various questions that may come up in your minds. We are now ready for the questions and let's begin. Who is the first one?

ADELL DENNISON of the Kaw tribe: I want to know what effect this bill will have on Indian claims now pending in the Court of Claims?

MR. COLLIER: No effect at all. It will not have any effect. It will not disturb or alter any treaty or any claim arising under a treaty or anything being dealt with in the Court of Claims. Its only effect would be that once a tribe gets a judgment in the Court of Claims then this bill would protect that money from being misappropriated. At this point, I may say that another bill is going to be introduced—a Departmental measure—for the purpose of speeding up your claims and giving you a broader basis for asserted claims for violated treaties, but that will be another bill and probably will not come before Congress in an active way until next year.

MR. ROE CLOUD: That question about the claims which has just been asked, is an exceedingly important question. At the Northwestern Tribes' conference among officiating Indians, the question was raised so strongly and became an issue at that conference—one of the great issues—and we were delighted to hear Assistant Commissioner Zimmerman get up in the meeting and say that for those tribes who entered under the provisions of this bill, the bill will protect those tribes in their tribal claims so that no off-sets to the Indian claims will be permitted under this bill. If you are having a claim before the United States government in the Court of Claims and are liable or probably might get ten million dollars and the government has spent for educational purposes, health, and one thing and another, five million dollars of that in the years gone by, it will prevent the government from setting forth that five million dollars as an off-set to your ten million dollar claim leaving you therefrom only five million dollars when you should have ten million dollars. It will be in the form of an amendment, as I understand Mr. Zimmerman to say.

MR. COLLIER: More probably it will be a separate bill which I speak of—a bill that will be extremely difficult to enact because if we enact it, it will result in the government paying probably hundreds of millions of dollars to the tribes which otherwise it would not pay. I am inclined to think that would not come as an amendment to the bill but as a separate measure.

One thing this bill does clearly do, it will give an Indian tribe control over its own choice of legal counsel, not leaving that to be dictated by the Commissioner of Indian Affairs.

MR. CLOUD: Adding to the announcement about Mr. Reeves who arose a moment ago, the place to see him will be on the first door to the left back in the hall. Any personal questions or any tribal questions, delegates can see him there. I am now ready for the next question.

WALTER MCGLASLIN, an Otoe Indian: While here on this question of the Court of Claims, I want to ask the Commissioner why this Bill of Rights has preference over the Indian claims when the Indians' claims have been for years in Congress. Why was that pushed aside and this new bill, the Bill of Rights, put in and have preference over the old Indian claims?

MR. COLLIER: They have not been set aside at all. These claims either are being litigated in the Court of Claims now or are awaiting the Jurisdictional Act which will permit them to be litigated. The delay of one or two or three years in getting an Indian tribal claim in the Courts is undesirable but it is not fatal. The delay of an equal number of years protecting the Indian lands from being lost to whites is fatal. There is no absolute barrier now against the assertion of any Indian claim. Merely, we hold that new laws should be adopted making it possible to get into court more quickly and more advantageously than it is under existing law.

MR. ROE CLOUD: The next one.

MORRIS BEDOKA, a Kiowa Agency Indian: I am on the rolls as a Caddo-Delaware-Wichita. I have a set of questions here and I will start from the top and on down.

If an Indian joins the Colony and at a later date or time, he finds that the colony, or his own individual state within the colony is a failure how would it be possible for him to be reimbursed for the amount of capital that he had invested in the colony or corporation, when he gets out?

MR. COLLIER: It is a very good question. There are two answers. Suppose a man moves into Anadarko and he invests in real estate or puts up a building but decides that the city government of Anadarko is a failure. I am just illustrating. And he would rather move somewhere else. He goes somewhere else but that doesn't take away his real estate or his building. His investment is not affected by the fact that he moves to Oklahoma City. But suppose an Indian also wants to move away and take his capital with him because he doesn't like the town. What is going to happen then? The answer is, first, he can move away and collect his rent, but also, the community will buy him out if he wants it to and if the community has not the cash, he gets out any way he wants to.

MR. BEDOKA: If I sold a piece of land on the outside of the government block, that is the block that was designated for an Indian colony, would I retain the oil and mineral rights as the homesteaders will, within the Indian block, if they sold their homestead?

MR. COLLIER: I imagine you mean also in general, if a man transfers his title to the community, will he lose his oil and mineral rights? I am very glad that you brought that up. That has been brought up at different councils and the answer is "No." This bill is concerned only with surface land but in order to make that clear, up at the Plains Indian conference we undertook to insert an amendment expressly stating that the ownership of oil, minerals, and everything under the surface, would remain entirely with the individual under all conditions.

MR. BEDOKA: Could the government make homesteaders within the proposed block sell their homesteads?

MR. COLLIER: White or anybody? There is a provision that when a community becomes organized and chartered, it has the same powers of condemnation that rights-of-way, roads, and otherwise, it is a matter of purchase.

MR. BEDOKA: Suppose a homesteader, a white man, sells land to the community and that land has oil and mineral rights, what happens to that?

MR. COLLIER: He would reserve them unless the community wanted to buy the mineral rights and he wanted to sell and the community would pay accordingly but ordinarily he would reserve his mineral rights.

MR. BEDOKA: Can an Indian living within this block belong to some national, cooperative marketing association?

MR. COLLIER: Yes. Just as much as if he were living in Anadarko. An Indian can live in this community and none of his other liberties would be interfered with, whether in business, church, secret societies, or anything of that kind. I had better make that clear through an example that came up last week. The Navajo tribe—we just came from there—are going to organize a livestock association. The Navajo tribe will take out a charter under this bill but that livestock association of the Navajos will affiliate with the Arizona Livestock Association and also the New Mexico Livestock Association, so no freedom of association is curtailed by this bill.

MR. ROE CLOUD: The question has been raised by one of the Indians outdoors that he objected to this bill because it would segregate the Indians—put them all by themselves—and he had a sort of conception that after the Indians went into this community, they would have nothing to do with the white people surrounding them. They would be by themselves—"Jim Crowed." The Commissioner tells me just now that all the associations that the Indians now enjoy will continue. Any Indians belonging to outside associations with white people, will not be prohibited under the Bill, freedom and exercise of all those privileges under this new chartered community, so that it isn't a curtailment of anyone's freedom or liberty to do anything that he wants to and that he has in the past.

MR. BEDOKA: Would the State Stock Inspector have jurisdiction over the colony?

MR. COLLIER: That would depend on the arrangements in the particular case. He would have jurisdiction by courtesy. The colony itself could contract with the State to do its inspection for it, and as a matter of fact, in a place like Oklahoma, it would have jurisdiction. There might be some big reservation where the federal government would provide inspection service because the state was not providing it. That would be as it is now.

MR. ROE CLOUD: This young man has some very fine questions. If there is no objection I will ask him to continue some more. I know you are interested. If he takes too much time we will cut him off.

MR. BEDOKA: Will these buildings within the colony be government owned buildings and if not, who will do the insuring of these buildings?

MR. COLLIER: The buildings will remain as they are now. If the government built them and owns them, it will continue to be responsible for them. But suppose a chartered community took up a collection and built a community house, of course the community would insure it. The Bill does provide that the government, upon request by the community, transfer to the community the title of property. It may do that if the community wants it. But even if an Indian community took over a government building, like a school, the community, itself, is an instrumentality of the federal government so that the government insures its own building, and this would carry over to the community building.

MR. BEDOKA: If Indians were not members of those different units, would they still come under the jurisdiction of the appointed Circuit judges or would they come into the civil courts on all crimes?

MR. COLLIER: I think the question is a little different. An Indian who was not a member of the chartered community, was still a ward of the government, would he come under the jurisdiction of the state courts or of the federal court? The way the bill is now worded, he would come under the jurisdiction of the federal court, not of the state court. He couldn't be tried in both courts. The jurisdiction over Indians is definitely placed in this federal court. Now before the thing is finished that item may be amended, with respect to Oklahoma it could be so amended that Oklahoma Indians would remain under the state courts if they so desired. But the way it reads now, all Indians would come under the Federal Court.

At this point, it is well to remind you that in cases between white people, where the white people happen to live in different states, those cases may go under the federal court. Indians are not the only litigants who go exclusively under the federal court.

MR. BEDOKA: What would be the jurisdiction of the Court of Indian Affairs where crimes are committed outside of the community where the fellow that does the committing, commits it within a city. Say he committed it out here and committed it in Anadarko?

MR. COLLIER: Title IV, Section 3 would still give exclusive jurisdiction to the Federal Court in matters where the Indian was involved. Those of you who have the bill will find that a clear statement on what this new court would do is found on page 39. I think it is well to read it because as a matter of fact, I overstated the amount of jurisdiction this court of Indian Affairs would have and I think this had better be translated. I will read what the bill says:

> "Section 3. The Court of Indian Affairs shall have original jurisdiction as follows:
> (1) Of all prosecution for crimes against the United States committed within the territory of any Indian reservation or chartered Indian community, whether or not committed by an Indian;
> (2) Of all cases to which any Indian tribe or chartered Indian community is a party;
> (3) Of all cases at law or in equity arising out of commerce with any Indian tribe or community or members thereof, wherein a real party in interest is not a member of such tribe or community."

That means where a member of a community got into trouble somewhere else he would still be under the jurisdiction of the Court of Indian Affairs.

MORRIS BEDOKA: If he committed the crime in Anadarko and the officers of this town arrested him, he could not be tried here?

MR. COLLIER: The bill does not say that but the bill says the Court of Indian Affairs could take jurisdiction. In many white communities the Indian does not get a square deal before the local court. I quote further:

> "(4) Of all cases, civil or criminal, arising under the laws or ordinances of a chartered Indian community, wherein a real party in interest is not a member of such community."

It is quite clear that an Indian who committed larceny or murder, or some other crime in Anadarko, and was a member of an Indian community, the Federal Court could assert jurisdiction and take the case away from the local court if it wanted to.

MORRIS BEDOKA: Now what if the Indian was not a member of the community?

MR. COLLIER: He does not come under the Federal Court unless he is a member of the chartered community or is in some way involved with the affairs of the chartered community. He might come under it by transfer of his case from the Federal District Court to the Court of Indian Affairs. For Indians who are not members of a community—their status would remain what it is now. They are under the Federal Court.

MR. ROE CLOUD: The jurisdiction of the Indians is the most confused thing we have to deal with. Sometimes the State Courts have jurisdiction over the Indians because they are citizens. Therefore, the State has jurisdiction over him as to his person. When he commits an offense on trust land the Government has jurisdiction over him as to place and not as to person. This new bill will do away with all that sort of confusion.

MORRIS BEDOKA: If an Indian allottee were situated within a definite block to be colonized and did not want to get out or sell his acreage and turn it over to the colony, would he be objected the same as a white homesteader?

MR. COLLIER: They could not do it either with a white man or an Indian. The only way they could get it would be to buy it. If a community was organized as a municipal government everyone in it would be subject to its laws. As far as a man's property is concerned, that could not be taken from him except by purchase unless the community wanted to get it by condemnation the same as any town.

MR. ROE CLOUD: This gentleman has asked this question. If a man wanted to leave the chartered community and wanted to go somewhere else how would he cash out?

MR. COLLIER: That would depend on the deal he made with the community. Some communities would have the necessary money to pay him in cash. Some would have to pay him on the installment plan. Some communities might decide they didn't want his property at all. Then he would be out of luck. If his property had a rental value he would continue to collect that rent no matter where he went. The bill, as I say, permits any kind of arrangement that the individual and the community may want to make but it specifically looks forward to this: that if an Indian wants to get out of the community in a permanent way, sever his connections from the tribe, then the tribe shall buy him out but they don't have to pay him cash. They may buy him out on the installment plan or they might not do any more than pay the rental value of the property abandoned. The whole effort is to make it easy for an Indian to get out if he wants to.

MORRIS BEDOKA: If an individual Indian held several allotments could he transfer one or two of his allotments to the colony and retain the other allotments on the outside of the colony as individual holdings?

MR. COLLIER: Yes.

MORRIS BEDOKA: Now in order to secure a charter, as I understand it, you would have to have the recommendation of the local agent with the approval of the Secretary of the Interior. Is that correct?

MR. COLLIER: The bill provides that the thing shall take place this way. If a community wants a charter it submits a petition for a charter and upon receipt of that petition the Secretary of the Interior must do one of two things. He must either issue the charter or he must put out a public statement of why he will not do it, and what conditions must be met before he will do it. That statement he transmits to Congress. That is the first part. This petition has to be signed by 1/4 of the adult Indians residing in the community. That is stated on page 3 of the bill. Then on page 5 you will find the rest. Then after the Secretary of the Interior gives the charter to the tribes that charter has to be ratified by a 3/5 vote of the adult Indians voting at the election. After the charter has been ratified by the 3/5 vote of the adult Indians then the Secretary of the Interior cannot change or take it away.

At this time it was suggested that the interpreters be dispensed with on account of the time involved. Voted by the house to keep the interpreters.

MR. ROE CLOUD: The Chair will allow one more question from this gentleman. Then the other tribes will have a chance to ask questions.

MORRIS BEDOKA: If the Indians within this community at some future time find the plan is a failure could they reserve the right to have this community reallotted to those who live within that community?

MR. COLLIER: That is a question which the bill, as drawn, does not answer. I believe that they could, as a matter of fact, stipulate that under the terms of the bill but the bill does not touch on that question. It could be arranged in the charter of the community if the Indians so desire. They could do it that way. I want to say I think that question really is more theoretical than practical because the bill is so drawn that the individual's property right is fully protected anyhow so there would be no desire to take it out even though the community became nothing more than a name, but the charter could provide that if the Indians wanted it. You have to remember this, that the community as soon as it was formed would be the owner of land in addition to the allotments relinquished to it—the purchased land—so that I think the condition, if a community went to pieces, would be the way it is now with tribal land. Every member would have his share in the tribal land until such time as Congress might break it up into individual holdings.

MR. ROE CLOUD: The next question is by a member of the Comanche delegation who has been issued a patent in fee but still has his land. Can he be admitted to the community as a ward and will his land be placed in trust?

MR. COLLIER: There are two questions there. (1) Can a patent in fee Indian be admitted to the community? (2) Can he transfer his land back to the community? I think not except by having the community buy it. You are there in difficulty with the State law. After the community buys it it would cease to be taxable. A patent in fee Indian could transfer his fee patent land into the community and get in exchange that same right of exclusive use, ownership of improvements and the right to leave it to his heirs as an Indian having a trust patent would have. If issued under protest it would be the same. The patent in fee Indian deeding his land to the community would thereby acquire a right to an equal amount of land in the community and he could keep that patented piece of land if he wanted to and the land would no longer be taxable. Any existing lien or back taxes would have to be paid off before the community got it. I want to be sure this answer is clear. How many of you here are the owners of patent in fee land? Hold up your hands. You still own the land but have fee patents to it? There are not many here but there may be more out in the State so I will answer this again. If an Indian is the owner of patented land he can put that land into the community. The land will then be free from taxes and he will have exactly the same thing that another Indian would have who surrendered his trust patent land to the community.

HENRY INKANISH: How about paying taxes back four or five years on such land?

MR. COLLIER: The back taxes would have to be paid off by the community.

MR. ROE CLOUD: This question is asked: In case of a tribe of people who are not very well educated in the white man's language and have to use interpreters to understand the white man's way—they are not quite as capable of taking on this community and self-government idea as others. What provision does the bill make for their protection?

MR. COLLIER: Complete protection. Such a tribe could form a community and have a charter without taking on any more responsibility than they wanted to. The Federal Government would be the guardian of the property the same as it is now over trust property and the tribe would not take on any more responsibility than it wanted to or was ready for.

MR. ROE CLOUD: It is my understanding we can hold back the self-government feature of this bill until we are ready for it. Is that correct?

MR. COLLIER: That is correct.

MR. ROE CLOUD: This question is asked by Jasper Saunkeah: The Commissioner stated there were about 5800 Indians under this agency, 2100 of whom were allotted, the remainder unallotted. If the unallotted Indians joined the community and took up the land what would the allottees get if they joined the community.

MR. COLLIER: This is an important question and a great deal of opposition to the bill is due to the fact that the answer is not understood. I want to make it clear. When there is not enough land the only way to meet that condition is to buy more land. The allotted Indian who goes into the community will not surrender his land to the landless Indians. He will keep his land. The landless Indians have to be provided for by buying new land. That is why we have this appropriation of $2,000,000 in the bill—to buy new land. But at present, as you know, a great deal of the Indian-owned land has gone into the class of dead allotments, or heirship lands. The bill provides that the community using this Government money would buy the heirship lands from the heirs and would distribute them among the landless Indians. Be very clear that the allottee who goes into the community would not surrender his property rights to any one. He would keep them himself.

MR. ROE CLOUD: The Chair observes that it is now 5:45 and before I ask the next question I want to put before the house the question of whether or not this meeting shall be continued this evening.

After a vote was taken it was decided to meet again at 8:15 to continue the meeting.

JAMES OTIPPOBY, Comanche: After a person has his patent in fee and becomes an heir to property of a certain community what settlement will the community make with him?

MR. COLLIER: In the first place he would be entitled to the rental value of that property he inherited in the community. Just like he is now. In the second place the community when it got the money would buy him out if he wanted to be bought out. Such an Indian would either get the rental value or sell out as he preferred.

MR. ROE CLOUD: From the Comanche come this question: If any tribe does not wish to go under this bill will their trust period be extended in the future?

MR. COLLIER: In my judgment the answer is, no, for this reason. I do not mean their existing trust period would be brought to an end but I do not think it would be made permanent, as it would be if they came under this bill and I will tell you why. You can answer it yourselves by just fixing your mind on the heirship lands and on the conditions I described this morning—with the heirship lands broken up in small parcels with many heirs, which creates the conditions that neither Congress or the President would be willing to make the trust period permanent under those conditions, where the cost keeps on increasing and the conditions get more and more unsatisfactory.

I think that Congress and the President will take the same view that the Department takes, which is this: that a tribe can come under this bill without any disturbance of the property rights of any of its members. It doesn't sacrifice anything by coming in but if they are not willing to make a little adjustment then why should the Government go on spending million of dollars in vain?

MR. ROE CLOUD: Here is a question from Alfred Wilson of the Cheyenne and Arapaho reservation: Certain members of the Cheyenne and Arapaho tribes purchased land out of restricted funds, which land has been declared taxable on a decision of the Circuit Court of Appeals. Has this bill any provision to pay off back taxes due on said land?

MR. COLLIER: Only if the community is willing to use money to pay off those taxes. When legal taxes have accrued they have to be paid. The way the land would be taken out of taxation under the new plan would be by placing the title in the Government. In that way it could be taken safely out of taxation but for taxes that have already accrued legally—they would have to be paid. Now the community taking that land over could pay those taxes just like any man would pay a mortgage.

MR. ROE CLOUD: (*Reads Sec. 4.*) Now then suppose a community becomes self-supporting, or is on a self-supporting basis in a few years. What would happen?

MR. COLLIER: Of course, we can't control the action of Congress in the future. The community would continue to be free from taxation. Congress will always have, and nobody can take away from Congress, the power to end the trust period but let us look at certain tribes now. The Menominee Indians of Wisconsin and the Klamath of Oregon—they have been prosperous for years. They are unallotted and they are prosperous. Nobody is trying to remove their trust period. It is my judgment that the successful Indian community that uses its land well and builds up its wealth will continue to be freed from taxation for a very long time, but, of course, no one can say what Congress will do in the year 2000.

The bill provides that the Federal Government shall pay for the maintenance of roads, bridges and public service in these tax exempt lands. That means there will not be any pressure by the local communities to bring the lands under taxation. They will remain free from taxation.

Meeting adjourned until 8:15.

MR. HENRY ROE CLOUD: Now the meeting will come to order. We are a little bit late and while they are waiting for the Commissioner, if the house is willing, I would like to express my ideas of this bill before any questions are introduced because I know I can't answer a lot of those questions myself, you can stick me any day.

I would like to give my personal opinion on this whole bill and it might be interesting to some of you. What do you say?

Audience consents.

This is rather informal and it is my personal opinion on the bill. I am not speaking officially for the United States government in any sense of the word. I am just talking as one Indian to another. Now I happen to be in favor of this bill for the following reasons: I think I have had ample opportunity to study it and hear it explained when I tell you that I have been chairman of all Indian Congresses over the United States and have heard all Indians ask questions and the answers propounded by legal experts and John Collier, Commissioner, himself and all the other members of the staff who have been traveling with him and from that advantage point and understanding, I have come to regard the bill as a wonderful thing for the Indian people and here are my reasons.

In the first place for the organization of those chartered communities that we have been hearing about, there will be allowed five hundred thousand dollars for the purpose of purchasing additional lands for the Indian people. There will be an annual sum of two million dollars to enlarge the territory of these chartered communities and that sum of two million dollars a year will be an annual affair so far as I understand it now. There are one hundred thousand Indians who have land leased and some Indians have felt that it was rather an injustice to those who are still holding onto their lands to give those Indians who have squandered their inheritance and their lands, and turn around and give them some more land. But the Commissioner feels very strongly this way about it.

The issuing of the patent in fees at the time they did when Secretary Lane and Commissioner Cato Sells sent competency commissioners all over the United States declaring a great number of Indians as competent to become fee patent Indians, that was one of the gravest and most serious errors that the United States government ever committed against the Indians. The Indians' lack of the sense of the value of his holdings and lands, as all of you know, is notorious. Suppose that we as Indians require three or four more generations of training and experience before we shall come to a proper realization of the value of lands such as the white man has today by thousands of years of experience and in the handling of those kinds of values; the white people have been struggling for the possession of their small acres across the seas for centuries and they developed a strong sense of ownership in land when they first landed on these shores. Because the Indian had so many acres of this whole community to roam over, he did not value the land that he had.

If I had a million dollars in my pocket, it isn't worth anything to me to hand you one dollar of it. I wouldn't miss that one dollar because I have a million dollars, less one, in my other pocket. If I have millions of acres what do I care for one single acre. Not until the Indian had lost all his lands did he begin to realize the value of his own lands.

Now in the meantime, the white people have used every artifice and means and even trickery, to get a hold of these lands that the Indians owned, and these figures that the Commissioner gave today are appalling, indeed, very, very appalling to me that from something like one hundred thirty-eight million of acres, we have dropped down to forty-seven million of acres in the hands of Indians with ninety-one million acres lost. Just think of the terrible loss that is to the Indians of America. Now the loss of lands causes certain following things: It makes a people poor, without resources, and consequently, they cannot build houses and comfortable places in which to live and by and by they do not have enough to eat and the consequences of unsanitary housing conditions and lack of proper food bring on all kinds of diseases. And that is why the Commissioner today stated that the death rate among the Indians is twice as that among the whites. Now where there are white people living and Indian people living alongside of them, every time a white man dies, two Indians die and it would not be so very long before the Indian race would perish from the earth. If that condition of affairs continues, it all harks back to the loss of our lands. We don't have any estate to give us the production and the income to provide us with a wherewithal to live.

In the first place, the Indian, when the white man came to this country, lost his buffalo; and in the second place, he lost the elk and deer; and in the third place, he finds himself hard pressed for a place to hunt even small game; and in the fourth place, he has lost this vast territory of land involving his health and bringing about a high death rate and therefore a future that is mighty gloomy, indeed.

Now if the present allotment law of 1887 is going to continue, it will mean that these dark consequences that the Indian is suffering today will continue and the future of our race, no one can guess but in the most gloomy terms; I for one would like to see all Indian tribes brought back into such a condition where they begin to increase and increase.

The Navajo tribe of Indians who have their land in tribal holdings and have never lost a foot of their land but have gained more and more, have increased from six thousand in the day of Kit Carson to forty-five thousand—possibly fifty thousand—today, whereas our tribes in the middle west here are having a great struggle to even maintain their own population.

I never, for myself, have seen a Commissioner of Indian Affairs study the whole Indian problem in the large, and reduce it to certain definite, accurate, and mathematical conclusions as to the consequences of those kinds of conditions upon the future of the Indian race, and I have never seen a Commissioner of Indian Affairs evaluate these things and then interpret them in such a concrete and workable program, and great planning for the future, as to gain the ear of Congress and the ear and heart of the President of the United States, to listen to a great New Deal for the American Indian. Now in addition to these advances, bringing back lands to the Indian people so that their health may be restored and that they have a brighter future, there is a credit system provided whereby the Indians who are not able to go to a bank or trust company or to anybody else, can go to this credit organization that is to be set up according to the terms of this bill, and borrow from a fund of ten million dollars.

In one of the great gatherings of Indian Congresses, Commissioner Collier stood up and told them that everything in this country is organized except the Indian people. He told them that in organization there is strength and that as long as the Indian remains an undivided unit, pure and simple, and not willing to organize with his fellow tribesmen and put in an intertribal organization for the putting through of things that require national attention or even state attention, so long as that situation exists he is going to be pushed to the wall and the white man is going to get the best of him every time.

No Commissioner has ever come out among the Indian people and told them to organize into a great national body and unitedly make their demands upon the Congress of the United States and the conscience of the people as this Commissioner has done. Just think of the tremendous power that would come to the Indian people and the opportunity now offered to every one of us that we might get in power of direct action in favor of our welfare. Now in this system of organization, there will be safe to the Indian race something that has never been mentioned in those Congresses which I think is worth a very great deal. They will get lands and money by means of this credit system and organize ourselves into powerful units after the organization is got up and the self-government begins to function, then the Indian race will begin to gain up to its undetermined strength by the exercise of its power of mind and heart and will call forth all the energy at its command, and I know of no scheme of things that will develop the capacity of the Indian more than that opportunity.

The reason that we as Indian people, do not progress and forge ahead very fast is because we are looking to Washington and the Secretary of the Interior and Superintendents on each reservation to do the things for us that are necessary. What will happen if we take those powers and functions into ourselves and begin to exercise them on our own behalf?

The reaction to that sort of a program will be such tremendous development among the Indians as that we will begin to see the most wonderful and wonderful Indian leaders among both men and women and that is the secret of the meaning of self-government which this bill is seeking to bring back to the Indian people everywhere.

Now some tribes may not feel they are ready to begin that thing because the responsibilities are tremendous and great. When you consider that the budget estimates and the expenditure of those moneys is left to the initial judgment of the American Indian people themselves and to be considered by the Budget Bureau and Congress, and finally adopted according to the well considered planning and thinking of the Indian people, you can realize that is a great responsibility. How else can you develop the sense of finance and business among the Indians, two of the weakest parts of our racial character, because we have never had experience along those lines. How else can you develop those two things in the line of character unless you give the Indians a chance to do those things? Now one of the reasons why the Indian race has not developed the way it should is because of the white influence surrounding every Indian reservation. If the Indians had been left alone by themselves, left to their own best judgement and had been free from the untold influence of designing white people around the reservations in getting those lands and working upon them for political purposes and etc., the Indian would have been much further advanced than he is today.

I merely refer you to the Navajos where that influence is absent nearly one hundred percent, and look at the marvelous progress they are making down here. We are pulled by those influences every which way and we listen to those counselors on one hand and the other and never realize that they are designers upon our property and the things we possess, in their hearts.

And now this bill provides that there will be no temptation for those white people surrounding every Indian reservation, to practice this graft upon the Indian tribes because whereas these chartered communities are not taxed, the Commissioner explained this afternoon that in lieu of the taxes the county and state might receive from the Indians, the government will pass those expenses of building roads, bridges, day schools, and etc., for which a community is taxed in order that it may be a public benefit. The government will supply those things according to this bill and therefore the pleasure of the white people to tax Indian lands, will cease and because they can't purchase a foot of land under this chartered community plan, there will be no temptation by Indians to sell out for a "song" the lands that they have held in their possession.

The feature about tribal claims where if an amendment is provided and no set-off is made to these claims by the United States government, that alone means millions and millions in savings to the Indian people if they should listen to the voice of this bill and I want to say emphatically, if such a bill were brought to any group of white people from across the seas, these Bohemians, the Czechoslovakians, Romanians, and Russian communities in the United States, if any man came out of Washington and offered them a bill of this kind, they wouldn't hesitate two seconds and they would grab it. Never such a wonderful thing came out of Washington to the Indian people such as we have been offered in this day. Now I want to emphasize one thing that is this: This thing would go over big in Congress if the Indian people go behind it themselves and that is what the President is expecting to see. That is what Congress is expecting to see and that is what the Secretary of the Interior is hoping for and that is what Mr. Collier, Commissioner of Indian Affairs, has come out to ask you to give. Now in view of all those benefits, of all those wonderful provisions about the gift of moneys, of organization proposal and self-government in order to put a rainbow in the Sky for us Indian people instead of a stormy, black future, I think that every tribe ought to think very seriously, indeed, before they cast this thing to the ground.

Whatever feature of the bill that you do not want and want to postpone and wait and see some other tribe try it out for three, four, or five years before you decide to take it, that is your privilege. You don't have to come in if you don't want to. The whole thing is voluntary. It is not going to be forced upon any tribe of Indians but wait and see some tribe right next to you getting this credit system. I want to be a farmer. I have no money. I have no land. All right, the government comes to me and says: "I will start you out in industry." There are three things that make industry: Land, labor, and capital. The Indian does not have the land or capital but the Indian can give labor, the government today says: "I will give you the land and I will let you have the capital. You supply the labor." And you have industry among the Indian people. Whenever has such a chance presented itself to the Indian race.

The Commissioner, today pointed out there would be many jobs in the Indian Service as it is now constituted but he is going to open up jobs by the thousands in these chartered Indian communities that are being set up.

And the last word I want to say is on the educational feature. I happen to be a man dealing in education of young, Indian people. All my life I have been interested in education. Fifty thousand dollars is the initial sum offered for the education of the bright, young Indians of every tribe. Now there is no reason why the Commissioner of Indian Affairs could not increase that amount to two hundred thousand dollars a year if the Indian people showed him that that amount was necessary to take care of the higher education and professional education of the Indians. But you must begin somewhere, so he puts it down to fifty thousand dollars. He has to be diplomatical and tactful and he has to be wise in the presence of this bill and put it in a way that will appeal and finally get passage. It is far easier to ask for more money by presenting the increased need in that respect, of Congress than if he asked fifteen thousand dollars, in addition, that he would like to use in picking out a Comanche, Cheyenne, Arapahoe, a Kiowa, Wichita or Apache Indian who shows a special promise. Here is $15,000 for that purpose.

We have seen Indians in our travels, without any training; paint a canvas like out-of-doors nature in bounty and trueness to the laws of painting and the laws of nature. He would like to pick up one Indian like that and say: "You deserve special treatment. You have a great monument to your race and we want to give your natural and great ability to the world—to America"—and he says: "I want some money to do that."

And the closing of these institutions everywhere, if he sees that one school is needed for particular training of Indians and it happens to be located strategically in the Indian country, he will re-open it and put the Indians in there. He is asking for discretion and power to do that sort of thing and on these loans, only one-half is to be paid back for your education, and the other half, you pay a little interest on that. You don't even sign a formal contract and whenever you are unemployed, the government is not going to ask you to pay it back. I wish I had had that opportunity when I was a young lad and had to work my way. I sold cigars, cigarettes and chewing tobacco and Navajo rugs, and crawled on my hands and knees planting flowers for rich people back East in order to earn my way through school. No government, nor friend ever rose up and said: "I will lend you this money. You don't need to pay one-half of it back. You can pay a small amount of interest on the other half and I won't ask you to go into a contract and whenever you go into a job and pay it back." I wish somebody would have offered me that opportunity. But you have it now. You children, your sons and daughters, have it now provided in this bill. This whole thing means the rehabilitation of our family life and new self-respect.

We may have in our hearts the fires that have been low for centuries will be burning again and become bright and brighter because of the scheme of this bill. It means that your agriculture, the things you have built up for over a thousand years as a race of people, will be re-evaluated and re-established and you can look upon your people and my people as again a proud race of people instead of having this thing Mr. Collier, the Commissioner, calls an inferiority complex. Everybody up high but the Indian down here. He tries to restore the Indian race so that the Indian may be on a par in his mind and heart. That is the great objective that he is striving for and the Indian race, if it really understood the spirit and the contents and the accomplishment that this bill is aiming at, would become very friendly, indeed, toward the whole proposition.

We make mistakes all along our lives. The white people make mistakes. Every Commissioner comes in here and has a new policy and experiments with us, and now this Commissioner comes in here and says "Experiment with yourselves and see where you get," and in an experimentation of that kind I know of no better cause; no race of people has ever been known on the face of the earth to progress and go forward unless they experimented on themselves, by themselves, and for themselves.

Now I said I wasn't going to make a long talk but the Commissioner has come in and I will cut off my remarks here and give him an opportunity to answer some of these questions. I have a whole raft of them here.

By the way, I forgot to say that this bill, whether it passes or not, does not make any difference to me. I don't get any benefit or lose my job on the thing. I have just been reminded that the interpreters are now having a rest and can begin to interpret again. Will you interpret these questions and answers to your people?

LOUIS MCDONALD: Before you start on the question here, an old Indian wants to talk to you.

HORSE CHIEF EAGLE, Principal Chief of the Ponca Tribe: I wish to say a few words to the Commissioner. I am a man well in years and I have seen and experienced a great many things. Our old people used to roam these prairies. The United States Government has moved my people some distance and has settled them in Oklahoma. Since coming to Oklahoma from Nebraska we have located in Oklahoma, living in communities. The land in which my people have located, they have bought themselves from the Cherokees, fifty thousand dollars. After living in communities for twenty years in Oklahoma, the Commissioner have waited on the Ponca Indians and urged them to take the land in severalty. I see Commissioners have created a school building for educating our children. In doing these things they have special agreement of the Ponca Indians, but the last Commissioner that went out of office have broken the agreement with the Ponca Indians.

After living in communities the United States Government have passed laws issuing patents to my people. He also gives my people the right to dispose of their land, calling them competent. One thing I have forgot to mention I want to speak of. The Government made my people take land in severalty whereby we can settle upon these divided tracts. After the Government have made provisions for my people to settle up these divided tracts during the World War they compelled him to take his patent in fee whereby he can dispose of it.

In conclusion I wish to say that we have been treated unjustly by the United States Government all these years. Now here they come along and make propositions for me and for my people that if any of these Indians have any lands left he wants me to provide part of it and give to somebody else that the United States Government pronounced him competent.

MR. COLLIER: Our friend, the Chief of the Poncas, has not clearly understood. I refer to his last remark. Because as I explained to you several times today, there is not any proposal to take land from any Indian that has got land and give to landless Indians. That is not in the bill and it could not be done under the law.

MR. HENRY ROE CLOUD: Now we come to a great many questions which I hold in my hand and I will read one question after another so we can get through and if there are no more questions we may possibly hear from some of the older Indians.

Question No. 1—AMOS KOMAH: If Tom and Dick and Harry own a piece of land, inherited land which lies outside of the proposed community and Tom and Dick become members of the community, just how will Harry's interest be protected provided he did not wish to join or sell his interest.

MR. COLLIER: Harry's interest will be protected in just the way it is now. He would keep his interest, collect his rent and when he got ready to sell his land he would sell it. As a matter of fact the question deals with Tom and Dick and Harry, all of whose land is said to lie outside of the consolidated area. That land would not be affected in any way except that the trust period would be made permanent on it.

MR. ROE CLOUD: The next question is, if an Indian sells out can he still be restricted after he leaves the colony and buys other land, can that land become trust land again?

MR. COLLIER: This question means, suppose an Indian goes into a community and after a while he decides to quit that community and he gives up, he parts with his holdings and the community buys him out, suppose that Indian goes off and lives in St. Louis and after a while he changes his mind and wants to come back and hold land. Can he? The answer is, yes. He can either come back into the Community if they will let him or he can go into one of the communities for landless Indians. He can acquire land, deed it to the Government and in that way get it off the tax rolls while he will also continue to occupy it.

MR. ROE CLOUD: When can the Indians move into these colonies?

MR. COLLIER: Just as soon as the colonies become organized then he can move in. Many communities are already organized, the Indian is already there, but where new colonies are being created the Indian can move in as soon as created, or when he gets ready to move in.

MR. ROE CLOUD: Indian tribes who refuse to accept the Wheeler-Howard bill, but are subject to the old allotment act of 1887 in spite of its passage, will the Indian who is allotted many miles outside of the community sell his allotment to the Government for exchange?

MR. COLLIER: These are two separate questions. I have already answered the first one. I would say that if the Indian tribe which decides to stay out from the new plan, if it does not apply to you, then existing laws do apply, that means the old allotment system. You cannot be in and out at the same time. Either you take the bill or you do not take it and if you do not take it it cannot apply to you. If it does not apply to you then the old law does. The other question is about an Indian who has an allotment, trust allotment, but it is located outside of any area that is selected for consolidation, any area brought into consolidation. What is going to happen to this land? His land would remain just the way it is except that the trust period would be continued, made permanent. It would remain under Government trust. Otherwise it would not be affected by this bill, but if there were a white man who had land inside the community, the consolidated area, the Indian outside of the area might exchange his land with the white man and then he would have his land inside the community.

MR. ROE CLOUD: (*Repeating the question of CARL J. REID DUSSOME*) In the future after the establishment of those colonies, supposing a great calamity should befall us, such as disease, sickness, poverty, etc., would we be made to suffer these consequences for accepting this new deal, or would the Government come to our aid freely and not be charged to the colony.

MR. COLLIER: The answer is the Government would not only come to their aid if they had these calamities, it would come to their aid if it did not have. The Indian communities under this bill, all of the Government services now being preferred would be kept up and paid by the Government and if the communities did have calamities it would be the duty of the Government to step in and help just as now. All Government services to the Indians, all Government appropriations for the Indians will go right on for the communities and in addition there will be other services and additional expenditures for the communities.

MR. ROE CLOUD: There are a few Indians of the Kiowa Reservation who have patent in fee land which is encumbered. The Indians still have some equity but the property is on the verge of being foreclosed. Can the Government take immediate steps to protect the equity of the Indian in order that they might be protected?

MR. COLLIER: There is not any authority at present and there is not any money to relieve those Indians. We depend on the new bill for money and authority. There is none now.

MR. ROE CLOUD: (*Repeating the question of JOHN HAYES of the Cheyenne and Arapaho Tribes*). Supposing an Indian has three quarters of land. Can he join the community without taking any of these quarters into the community? If not, why will they take one who has squandered all of his land into the community without the land and not the other with land. If yes, who will approve the leases of that land outside of the community?

MR. COLLIER: That is an interesting question. That really contains a number of questions and I will answer the last part first. An Indian who owns land held under trust and that land is not in the community, as I have said before, that land will be just as before. It will be held under trust and the leases will be approved by the Superintendent just as at present. Now the other question is this. Supposing an Indian has three quarters of land and he does not want to put that land into the community, but he wants to be a part of the community. The question is, can he be? The answer is yes, he can be. He can keep his land outside and still be a voting, participating member in the community but he will not have as large share in the ownership in the community as he would have if he turned his land in.

Naturally you cannot eat your cake and have it too. But understand what a community is. A community is a group of Indians organized for mutual aid, receiving a charter from the Government and getting various kinds of help from the Government. A landless Indian can go into the community. An Indian who has land and keeps it off yonder, he can go in, both can go in. The Indian who goes in and takes his land with him will be entitled to an equal amount of land inside the community and to all property rights of ownership, rights of inheritance of that amount of land. Now the question keeps coming up about doing something for these landless Indians, on the grounds that they do not deserve any mercy because they have squandered their land. Remember this, under the allotment system thirty years from now you who have still got land will be gone, your children will not have the land, it will be gone. It will not be gone because they squandered it, but because of the way the allotment system works. Some Indians have been thriftless, have lost their land unnecessarily, but as a rule the Indian lost his land because he could not help it, because the allotment system was made to cause him to lose his land and he just could not help it.

The landless Indian is simply the Indian who suffered worse from the allotment system and the Government owes him more than it owes the Indian who has got his land. It owes guardianship and protection to both, but the landless Indian has been the worse victim and is entitled to Government aid. We must also remember that the children born since the allotment are landless. It was not their fault that they were born after allotment instead of before allotment. They could not help it and they are entitled to have land.

MR. ROE CLOUD: If the allotment law continues to work upon us in the future there will be just a very few Indians that have land left. It might be none will have any land and everybody will be landless. In this new deal the plan is, everybody is to have land.

JOHN YELLOW BULL: As an Indian I ask this question. What effect would the Howard-Wheeler bill have on the community? In case of a civil world war, I would not feel like going out to fight for only the reservation.

MR. COLLIER: We would hope that after the Indians got—were being treated right, had enough land and were getting not only a new deal but a square deal from the Government, that they would be even more patriotic than now, so when an emergency came they would be even more willing to respond than in the last world war.

JASPER SAUNKEAH: I want to ask this question. Would this bill take away the voting privilege we have in state and national affairs?

MR. COLLIER: No, in no way.

ERNEST THOMPSON, a Kaw Indian from Kaw, Oklahoma: What about the agricultural land owned by the old Indians who are not able to farm and depend on leasing it. What benefits are they going to derive, only taxation?

MR. COLLIER: The answer is this, that those old Indians depending on rental from their lands would continue to get the rentals from their lands, exactly as they do now. The benefits they would get would be the consciousness that their land would not be lost under the operation of the heirship feature of the allotment system but would be preserved for their children.

ERNEST THOMPSON: Mr. Commissioner, this morning you mentioned the certificates of guarantee. Who is going to back them up?

MR. COLLIER: This refers to the certificates which the Indian receives when he relinquishes his allotment, his title to the tribe or to the community and the question is, who is going to back up that certificate? The answer is, the same power that now backs up your allotment system, the United States Government. The same power that guarantees any property right you have now is the power that would guarantee these certificates. These certificates would be exactly the same as papers showing ownership of property and evidence of ownership, evidence of title; and not only would have Congress back them up but they would be enforceable through the courts.

ERNEST THOMPSON: In the northern part of Oklahoma we have what is called the Inter-tribal Council and that is the reason these questions were [cannot read top of pg. 44] here follows [cannot read] here said we have had things like the [cannot read] certificates of guarantee. We have gone through these trials before in the form of treaties and we want to know where there was one ever fulfilled.

MR. ROE CLOUD: May I say a word just here in that respect. You will note the bill is headed by the words it is the national policy of the United States Government to do thus and so in establishing these new communities and giving the Indians a new deal. Before that took place all treaties which the United States Government has violated has come about largely by the result of lack of the proper kind of public opinion opposing the Indian race. You must realize that the United States Government has taken one hundred fifty years or so to form into a strong unit and various factions and fighting each other. Some were for exterminating or killing off the Indians and others were to save them. Those who wanted to do right were friends to the Indians and wanted to save them. Therefore all broken treaties now coming up tending to turn him loose, probably will create thousands of friends of the Indians who can rally to their support and bring about much opinion to support the new policy declared into his new day and age.

MR. COLLIER: While I agree with Mr. Roe Cloud that this subject is not only reasonable but important, I would like to speak about it a little more, this question, about who would back up those certificates. My answer will be most clear to those who know something about law but I think I can make it clear to all of you. I explained this morning that if the Government wanted to confiscate your allotments it would not have the power, because your allotments represent property rights, which could not be taken away from you. If the Government should try to step in and take your allotments away from you without your consent, without compensation, the courts would enjoin the Government from taking your allotments and would protect your property rights which could not be taken away from you. Under the Constitution they could not be taken from you. They can be taken from you in the way you know, in an indirect method, by terminating the trust period and throwing the burden of taxation upon you but they cannot be confiscated.

These certificates Mr. Thompson speaks about are referred to on page 34 of the bill. When an Indian surrenders, that is, relinquishes his allotment to the community, he gets in exchange one of these certificates which is a matter of property rights just the same as the allotment was a matter of property right. If anybody, the President or Congress were to try to violate that certificate or take it away, the Indian would simply go into court and the court would enjoin the President or Congress exactly as it would do if they tried to take your allotment away. So that these certificates are protected as completely as any property right can be under the Constitution. They cannot be any more protected than that. With treaties the situation is entirely different. When the United States began to break its treaties with the Indians, and it began just one hundred years ago, the cases were taken to the Supreme Court and the court ruled that it was in the power of Congress to change or violate treaties whenever it wanted to, that the Indian could not seek protection in the court. He had no protection in the matter of treaty pledges. The record of the Government in the matter of Indian treaties is one of the most outrageous records in the world. There is hardly an Indian treaty which has not been violated to the injury of the Indian. Hardly one, but with respect to a vested property right such as an allotment is, or such as this certificate would be. It would not be in the power of Congress, it would not be in the power of the Government to take it away or violate it or change it without the consent of the Indian and you have the protection of the Constitution and the protection of the courts in the land and no one in the United States can have any more protection about any property than that.

MR. ERNEST THOMPSON: Are the Indian boarding schools going to be kept open until the community form of Government is set up. What will become of the Indian boarding schools in relation to the communities?

MR. COLLIER: What is going to be done with respect to the boarding schools has nothing to do with this bill. I would answer the general question this way, that a large number of boarding schools will be kept for an indefinite number of years, perhaps always. Some of them will not be kept, others will be kept and new schools will be started. The only bearing this bill would have on the boarding schools would be this, that when an Indian community becomes chartered then if the community wanted to spend the additional money which boarding schools cost it would be entirely up to the community to decide whether it were day schools or boarding schools.

ERNEST THOMPSON: Under this bill can you take Indians in regardless of the degree of Indian blood, who have had allotments and been recognized as Indians?

MR. COLLIER: The bill does not attempt to define an Indian. Any Indian who is a recognized member of his tribe is entitled to proceed under this bill. The only limitation placed is one where an entirely new community is being formed, homeless Indians are being gathered up and colonized, Indians who are members of no recognized tribes; in that case the bill says that they must be one-fourth or more Indian blood but with respect to Indians who are members of recognized tribes or bands they are simply included by virtue of their membership.

MR. E. E. THOMPSON: If an Indian bought a piece of land from another Indian, he being a patent in fee Indian, how can the title be transferred from the State to the Community making the land again tax-free.

MR. COLLIER: The answer is that he would do it by transferring land to the community and then the land would become tax exempt, and take in exchange a certificate which gives him ownership of an equal amount in value of land in the community and the right to transmit land and improvements to his heirs just the same as it were bought for the community, it goes off the tax rolls because it passes under guardianship of the United States.

MR. THOMPSON: Would not the separation produced by organization of the Indian Community not tend to reduce the influence of Indians in the larger activities of the State and Nation?

MR. COLLIER: That is a question deserving of much thought which has been asked many times. Would organizing of Indians into communities reduce their power as citizens and their influence in the outside world. It is a question to think about. I will give you my answer. When we talk about communities what we really mean is just organizations, Indian organizations. They might organize for any of a great number of different purposes and get charters for any number of purposes and when we say "community" we just mean organization. Now to be a member of any organization doesn't mean that you have to quit being a member of everything else. You can be a member of many organizations at the same time and most white people who have power in the world are members of many organizations. If you come into the life of any famous white man in the United States today, who has great influence, you will find that he is a member of organizations and his influence rests largely upon that fact. In the same way the Indians who organize into these communities and have gained power, become more prosperous, it is my judgment that they would have increased influence in the world at large, much more than they have now.

These Indian communities would not shut the world out from the Indian but would open the doors of the world to him. They would unlock the doors which are locked now. I think I can say a fundamental fact of American life is that the unorganized man is the helpless man, the man who has everything put over on him, the man who is low down on the social scale, and that in the American life, it is only organization which produces wealth or power, and this must be true of the Indians the same as of white people.

MR. ROE CLOUD: Among many tribes the son-in-law does not speak to his mother-in-law, they just won't do it. In cases where a man or woman is married and the wife passes away, who becomes heir of the household goods if there is no issue? Has the mother-in-law the right to take charge of the household goods, etc?

MR. COLLIER: I refuse to answer. That is beyond me.

MR. THOMPSON: Would not this bill be class legislation and be unconstitutional since money is appropriated for a given class of people?

MR. COLLIER: If this bill were class legislation in that the appropriated money is for Indians, then all the appropriations for Indians are class legislation. The answer is this. The guardianship of the United States over the Indians is a fundamental fact of our constitution. The constitution places upon Congress the responsibility relating to what is called intercourse with Indians.

The Supreme Court in a long series of decisions has definitely opened a doctrine that the Government owes a special and peculiar duty to the Indians, the duty of guardianship, so that to give special aid to the Indians has been held by the Court not to be class legislation. This bill merely carries forward that guardianship and that special aid which has long since been declared to be proper and the duty of the government.

MR. THOMPSON: Has there been an alien or foreigner employed in the Indian Educational Bureau or promised such employment under this bill?

MR. COLLIER: The question is: Has there been a foreigner, not an American employed as Superintendent of Indian Education or head of educational work? I am glad to answer that. The answer is "No." But I would like to say something else. I spoke this morning about that down in Mexico how the Indians' prosperity was being built up and land holdings were on the increase, down in Old Mexico. The way they do the thing down in Old Mexico is very interesting to us up here and connects with this bill so I will tell you a little about it. Mexico is now doing the thing we want to do in this bill, that is, Mexico is restoring great quantities of land to the landless Indians down there. Long ago, down there, almost a hundred years ago, Mexico tried the allotment system very much like ours and it had terrible results in the loss of land by Indians. They tried it once and they are not going to try it again, so what Mexico is doing now is trying to put Indians back on land. It requires Indians first of all to organize into a community. They must first organize and then they get the land. These organizations are called Ejidos which is the same thing as the Indian community as we describe in this bill. The title in the community, or as we would say the tribe which is the individual Indian, has complete possession of the land. He uses it and it is inherited by his children just as we propose in this bill.

The Indian Service down in Mexico is operated the way I hope for here. The Indians, themselves, hold nearly all of the positions right up to the top. The man who has had the most to do with the development of this very successful Mexican Indian program is a man named Sions, a Mexican Indian. Dr. Sions is at present the Minister to Ecuador from the Republic of Mexico. Last autumn our American Government invited Dr. Sions to come up here as its guest and to advise us about Indian matters and he came. It was very interesting to me, there in Washington, after he had finished going around the Indian country, to see Dr. Sions meeting with the high officials, including the members of the cabinet at Washington, Dr. Sions himself an Indian, and telling our own highest officials the story of how the Indians of Old Mexico are recapturing their lands, are getting schools for the first time, are being trained for all of the professions and technical arts and are taking over control of the government.

This was a very interesting thing to watch and hear him tell about. Dr. Sions who was loaned to us by Mexico has now gone back and is not here anymore but I wish it were possible to take one of you Indians down to Mexico and enable you to see that the Indians are capable of doing anything and of holding positions up to the very top of the profession and of being President of a great country and of running their own Indian Service.

MR. ROE CLOUD: The next question is will the Superintendent, being the guardian of children who have land, force their land into the community without the consent of their parents.

MR. COLLIER: No, not under this bill. I can only say in general that there can't be any forcing of any land into the community, neither the child's land nor the adult's, but it must be by voluntary relinquishment in exchange for the things I have told you about, or by purchase.

MR. ROE CLOUD: Now there are very many more questions and it looks as though we can't answer them all and the Commissioner has some few things to say to us, so I will read off one or two more questions and then give the rest of the time to the Commissioner. Suppose an Indian joins a chartered community and surrenders his land holdings to said community. At some later time he sells his interest to the community and invests the proceeds in property outside of the community. Then through misfortune he loses his property thus purchased, can he rejoin the community as a landless Indian and be supplied with land in the community and can he be reinstated?

MR. COLLIER: Yes, but he will come in as a landless Indian and won't have as large a share as he would have if he hadn't sold out.

MR. ROE CLOUD: If an Indian has been paying taxes since 1917 on land for which a patent was forced upon him, how can he join the community? This land has never been mortgaged; will the Secretary of the Interior make some kind of provider (*this question submitted by Theodore Howry, Arapaho*)?

MR. COLLIER: That simply means an Indian which has a fee patent can turn his fee patented land into the community and he can be tax exempt and he is a member of the community.

MR. ROE CLOUD: Can an Indian surrender title to the community and later want to move out? Can he get his title back on the outside (*this question submitted by Albert Whiteman, Cheyenne & Arapaho Agency*)?

MR. COLLIER: That is a question of an Indian who wants to abandon his community. He keeps his property interest in the community unless he can persuade the community to buy him out. If the community buys him out then he can take the money and buy land elsewhere, if he wants to spend it that way.

JASPER SAUNKEAH: Will the Honorable Commissioner give us a chance to give our view on the bill tonight?

MR. COLLIER: Yes, I would prefer to hear views of others on the bill.

JAMES OTIPPOBY: Our permission for five minutes' time has been placed in your hands, may we have it?

MR. ROE CLOUD: The question is whether we will have questions and answers or hear the views of various members. We are going into a very late period of the night and you have to have that in consideration. Shall we have some of these questions and answers or shall we listen to questions from the floor? All those in favor of listening to discussions in the next few minutes raise your hand. Now I am going to give two minutes to each person to speak. I will put another question.

All those in favor of dispensing with interpreters to gain time raise their right hand. All those in favor of continuing the interpreters raise their right hand.

Those in favor of dispensing with interpreters win.

JASPER SAUNKEAH: I am speaking for the Kiowa Tribe. My people have instructed me to say, I am only speaking as a representative of the Kiowa Tribe, that we are opposed to the two bills as a whole. The Kiowa Tribe is opposed to the two bills as a whole as presented by the Commissioner.

JAMES OTIPPOBY, as interpreter for HOY-KOY-BITTY or MILLOTT, a Comanche: Regarding our land, I for one value my allotment and speak for the rest of my people. I know they feel the same way. We love our allotments and we value them and we want to hold to them. That is all.

JAMES OTIPPOBY: Will you, if we reject to come under this new deal, without prejudice still continue to serve us as you have in the past. If not we shall shake hands.

MR. COLLIER: Surely we will go on serving you the same way. How well that is I don't know. I have made it very clear today that we are not urging you to endorse this bill or to accept it. It is up to you and it will not prejudice me at all if you do not accept it. However, do not exaggerate. Do not think too much about the power of the Commissioner of Indian Affairs. I told you this morning and I will tell you again this afternoon what I expect will happen if the Indian tribes insist on going on under the existing allotment arrangement. I predict for the tribes that go on that way and won't take advantage of that bill, I predict that within a very few years either your land will be fee patented to you or the Government will throw upon you the whole financial burden of administering your heirship land. That will happen regardless of John Collier. Don't exaggerate the power of the Commissioner; don't dream that Congress or the President is going to go on wasting money in the administration of a land system which can only end in no land and which grows more expensive to the Government while the land grows less and less. I can't make Congress do that. Mr. Ickes can't.

It is a serious decision to decide and to decide even in advance of this meeting as I am told the Kiowas have done that you will just have nothing to do with this effort by the Government to save your land, to restore your landless Indians to new land and to give you capital. It is a dangerous thing for a tribe to do. It certainly won't antagonize anybody but if that position were adhered to by an Indian tribe the result sooner or later would be in the undoing of that tribe. I wouldn't be honest with you if I didn't tell you what I know. Certainly it will not affect me. I am going on working for you as Commissioner but I will certainly tell you what will come to pass if you reject this bill and at the same time don't come forward with some better idea of getting yourselves out of your difficulties.

JAMES OTIPPOBY: I have expressed the sentiment of my Comanche people. The Comanches are utterly opposed to those things. They desire to maintain their allotments and their property and not relinquish in favor of the community plan but yet continue in this same old way. In so saying I speak the sentiment of the Tribe—not personally because I have no right, I have nothing to lose but much to gain. But after all as citizens of the United States we people wish to maintain our property and continue in this system. Therefore, I submit two resolutions, which the tribe has given to me, and we thank the Commissioner for all his efforts in order that we may be better people. We believe we will make better progress in our business affairs in the years to come and in so saying I speak the sentiment of my tribe.

MR. COLLIER: It would help us if we had a certain piece of information. I am asking this of the delegates who are here. I am anxious to know and you have as a part of the record this information. What proportion of the delegates are themselves owners of allotted land held in trust? I wonder if those who are the owners of allotted land held under Government trust would raise their hands. I would like to have that translated. Will the delegates who have no trust land hold up their hands?

No count announced to stenographers.

My reason for asking that question I will state to you. I have said that the concern of the Government as this Administration views it is the Indian whether he has got land or whether he hasn't got land, the landless Indian and the Indian who has still got land. I make that very clear, that is the policy of the administration. The Wheeler-Howard bill is intended for all of the Indians, including those who have no land. It is intended for all of the Indians, including those who have no land. I want you to get that clearly. Was it the opinion out on your reservation among the Indians who have not got land and whose only chance to get land by this and did they authorize you to vote against this bill.

JAMES OTIPPOBY: Yes, we were authorized by them.

MR. COLLIER: What is their idea? Is it they don't want the bill?

JAMES OTIPPOBY: They oppose community life and would just as soon stay without land and don't want to be segregated.

MR. COLLIER: Are you sure that is the majority opinion of the landless Indians?

JAMES OTIPPOBY: They want land but not under that sacrifice and going into a communal life.

MR. COLLIER: Then they don't want land if they have to stay where they are in order to have it?

JAMES OTIPPOBY: According to the bill we do not wish to have land.

MR. COLLIER: It is my judgment that ultimately this thing is so important to the majority of allotted Indians who have no land that the case will have to be carried back to the entire voting population of each reservation for them to say whether they want the bill. The landless Indian must directly vote as well as the landed Indian. The opinion of the tribal council will be transmitted to Congress and made a part of the record but it is my judgment that Congress and the President will say that they want the vote of the entire Indian population upon the measure.

JAMES OTIPPOBY: Commissioner, two resolutions have been placed upon the table. One of the general vote of the tribe. The other resolution is drawn up by the younger members. The majority do not have land.

MR. COLLIER: When a majority of the tribe decides that it does not want to come in that will certainly end it for that tribe, but a matter as weighty as this, affecting the whole future of the Indians, should not be passed upon except by all of the Indians. If they reject it well and good. The resolution presented by your Council will have full weight, will have great weight, but I doubt now whether Congress will be satisfied with anything short of a referendum in which the entire adult Indian population will be asked to cast a ballot, not now, but later on after they understand the bill. I think Congress will take this position because the President understands and the Committee of Congress understand that this bill does not take away the private property of any Indian. It does not take away the rights of any allotted Indian. It does not force any Indian to live in any segregated community. It does not contain these things which your resolution recites. This resolution must refer to some other bill. It is not in this bill and therefore I think Congress will insist that after due deliberation, after time for the facts to become known to them, the Indians as a whole, tribe by tribe, they shall be invited to vote.

If the bill had the effect, if it contained those things which are stated in your resolution, we would all be opposed to it from the President down. The bill does not contain these things, and therefore, I think that Congress will rightly say that there should be a second thought, that all Indians should register and certainly all Indians who are without land, because they more than any others will depend upon this bill to give them new land, but you may be sure your resolution will be placed in the records in toto, carried back to Congress, and made a part of the records of the House and Senate Committees. They may conclude your understanding of the bill is correct. I do not think they will because that is not the bill. The bill is something else than the thing you are talking about. Either it is or else I have been standing here all day telling you one gigantic farce, which I have not been doing and I urge that if this bill is not the kind of thing you want you search your own brain and find the thing you do want, find something that will stop this loss of your land. Find something that will restore the land to your landless brothers and children.

MR. ROE CLOUD: I would like to ask this question. How will the landless Indian solve his economic problem? Will the Indian have land to take care of the landless Indian say ten years from now, when there will be more Indians who have no land. The chair will recognize two speakers. This man and the man who arose here (pointing).

JOHN OTTERBY: I am a delegate sent here from the Clinton District. We require more information regarding this bill. I think I have acquired pretty near sufficient information to understand. I believe that delegations came here to hear the bill explained in detail and to report to our tribes and I think that it is the best thing that any Commissioner of Indian Affairs ever understood to do because just think of the condition that this Allotment Act put us today. It has not been more than one-half century since the Cheyennes and Arapahoes were allotted and today over two-thirds of the land is gone. This provision that the Commissioner proposed to use to extend restrictions on what land is left and provide land for the landless and the Government furnish money to educate our children—now I think that is one of the greatest things we have ever been offered. Cheyennes and Arapahoes are in a critical condition—we have no oil and are not educated as you people here. I am talking just for the Cheyennes alone and I want to thank the Commissioner for his efforts and to shake hands and bid him goodbye.

KISH HAWKINS: My name is Kish Hawkins, a Cheyenne Indian. I have seen both sides of life, wild life and civilized. We Cheyennes and Arapahoes have been sitting on the fence watching the procession go by. I believe this question has already been explained to them before by our superintendent and other officials of the Cheyenne and Arapaho Agency. I am pretty well sure, my friends, that they, the Cheyennes, are about convinced to take a step forward for their own good, for the benefit of themselves and their children and they are ready to back the bill. I am ready to vote "Yes." Let us go ahead, push it ahead and let it become law. My friends, I have been on the warpath and have been one of the prisoners. Then I went to school when I was 15 years old and that is why I am not able to speak good English like the others have.

I have been a Government employee and have been retired and am thankful for that. Now, my friends, Kiowas, Comanches, Apaches, and Arapahoes, some of you don't know but I want to refer back to you the Treaty of 1867, the Medicine Lodge Treaty. You tribes were ready to say "Yes" to the Commissioners that were sent out by the United States Government but the Cheyennes were holding back. They didn't want to say, you led us into it. We didn't know what instructions the Government gave the Commissioners how to proceed to get the consent to cede our lands away—the best lands out this way. We have heard read what the President has said to our Commissioner and I don't think any other President has said what Franklin D. Roosevelt has said in regard to this bill. I don't think you understood the provisions of the treaty and we should study over this bill and you follow us like we did. We were forced to sign the Medicine Lodge Treaty in 1867 but now we want you to come on.

MORRIS BEDOKA: I have been honored by representing the Caddos, Wichitas, and Delawares of this agency. We have called a meeting for next Saturday at 1:00 P.M. in the County Court House for the purpose of discussing this bill some more after we have heard the side of the Commissioner. We have discussed it before. Our Superintendent, Mr. McCown, has explained the bill to us but I don't think anyone could fully explain the bill as it has been explained by the Commissioner but yet at the same time as a parting goodbye to our Honorable Commissioner, we showed him the respect of listening to his side of the question. Then after he is gone we will discuss it among ourselves and after we decide at the Court House meeting next Saturday afternoon, we will then take a final vote as to whether we will accept or reject the policy outlined in it. It has been a fact that all Indian Commissioners who have served under the different administrations have had some pet policy that they wanted to get over. I am not referring to this with the intention of slandering the Hon. Mr. Collier—I am talking of past Commissioners. This is the first Commissioner who has come out and spoken a good word for the Indians. Along with that, do any of you Indians remember whenever a President of the United States has sanctioned a bill of any kind that was favorable to the Indians as our Hon. Franklin D. Roosevelt has?

Now after this bill has passed and become a law could there be another Commissioner under a different administration, come in and ask the Congress to revoke everything that takes place under this administration? It has seemed the Indian has always served as the guinea pig in an experiment and the experiment has always been done with the Indians' money.

Henry Chapman of the Pawnee Agency read the following resolution submitted by the Pawnee, Ponca, Kaw, Otoe and Tonkawa tribes:

Pawnee, Oklahoma,
March 17th, 1934

"We, the undersigned chairmen of the Tribal Business Committees for the Pawnee, Ponca, Kaw, Otoe, and Tonkawa tribes of Indians in Oklahoma, represent that our committees, after receiving Indian Office Circular dated January 20th, 1934, relative to a proposed so-called "Indian Self-Government" immediately called our tribes together for the purpose of considering the proposed program.

"We represent that at each of these tribal meetings the Indians in council assembled unanimously opposed the said program as outlined by our Commissioner of Indian Affairs, Mr. John Collier.

"We represent that these meetings were well attended by representative numbers of our Indian tribes, the educated and uneducated, and after a full discussion of the program, the opposition is unanimous.

"We represent that on March 16th, 1934 a general council of all five of the above tribes was held at the White Eagle Agency for the purpose of a joint discussion of the program referred to above, and of the bill which has been introduced in both Houses of Congress, title, Indian Self-Government, by Senator Wheeler and Congressman Howard. Several hundred representative Indians from the five tribes attended this joint council and it was unanimously voted that the sentiment of the various tribes was opposed to this program and to the bill now before both Houses of Congress.

"Therefore, we the chairmen of the five Tribal Councils under the jurisdiction of the Pawnee Indian Agency, and the chairman of the Inter-tribal Council representing the five aforesaid tribes, hereby express our protest against the program outlined by the Honorable Commissioner of Indian Affairs in his letter of January 20th, 1934, and further express our unanimous opposition to the aforesaid bill, "Indian Self-Government."

"The sentiment expressed at the various tribal meetings indicates that our Indian people do not feel that they are capable of handling such a large undertaking and it was pointed out that practically all of the so-called competent Indians have demonstrated their lack of business ability in handling their own individual matters. It is admitted that the Indians have lost too much of their land which was due to a lack of their business ability and a mistake by the Department in permitting them, and in many instances compelling them, to take patents in fee for their homesteads.

"We further represent that our people are opposed to the proposed change in our educational system. Facts will show that our children who have had the advantages of our splendid boarding schools are more advanced and better prepared to take their place in the white community than children who have missed a great deal of educational training by the attempt to have them attend the Reservation public schools. We recommend that the boarding schools be continued that Indians may have the advantage of our splendid Indian educational institutions.

"We recommend that the trust period on our trust land be extended for a period of fifty years and carry with it a non-saleable land provision. We recommend that the land be purchased for Indians who have disposed of their homesteads and that these homesteads purchased be protected with a restricted period of not less than fifty years.

"We recommend what we understand to be one of the Commissioner's policies of giving to qualified Indians preference to positions in the Indian Service. We commend the present policy of the non-sale of Indian land and the non-issuance of fee patents.

"We recommend the removal of all employees in the Indian Service now holding key positions who oppose the employment of Indians in the Indian Service.

"Resolved, that a copy of this protest be filed with the Honorable Commissioner of Indian Affairs and the members of the entire Oklahoma delegation now in the House and Senate."

THOMAS W. ALFORD, Shawnee: I have very few words to say representing my people, the Absentee Shawnee Indians. I am compelled to come down here to say a few words but I have been hesitating. I wanted to learn what I could through the questions discussed here today. We have been holding councils on different matters for the last three for four months—to get all the evidence we could and the most intelligent people of our race have appointed us to represent them here and say we are ready to accept this new program—a great program as you know. We are willing to take anything that we believe to be for the best interest of our people. This is a program that is a puzzle to us. Yet I have no questions to ask because I do not fully analyze it. But we have been told time and time again that we can take this matter to ourselves, discuss it and reject or accept it. So far as we are able to comprehend it, we are willing as Absentee Shawnee Indians, to accept this new program for the good of our people. This is all I have to say.

SAC & FOX REPRESENTATIVE: My Indian friends, I feel that it is necessary to give some kind of an expression to this gathering of Indian people as a representative of the Sac and Fox Indians of this State and also the delegation from the Shawnee Indian Agency. We have instructions—or rather we have no instructions—from our Indians at home to either reject or accept the proposition that has been discussed today. We came with open minds to learn about this bill so that we can go back to our people and give them a better understanding, but I want to say just a word to express my personal ideas in reference to this bill and what I am about to say is not the sentiment of the people at home—it is my own personal idea. I believe that a long sought opportunity has come to the Indian people through this bill. The Honorable Commissioner made the statement—rather referred to the misunderstanding that a great many Indians had about this bill, and that is true with my people at home. They think that if they accept this bill and go into a charter community they would have to give up or relinquish all of their rights on individual land holdings to the landless Indians; that they would be deprived of the benefits of their present holdings and, of course, naturally for that reason they are not in favor of the bill but I am confident in saying that had they been here today to listen to the discussions and the explanation given by our Honorable Commissioner, their minds would have been changed and they would be in favor of this bill.

One feature of this bill that I like is that one providing employment for our Indian people. What is the use of the Government spending thousands of dollars in the education of our Indian people and after they have completed their schooling they come back with nothing to do. This bill provides that when they can qualify for work among their people they are to be given the preference. I think that is a splendid provision. I think it is an opportunity that will lead to the development of our Indian people. At one time I had large holdings of land. I fell heir to nearly 1000 acres of land. The Competency Board declared I was competent and able to take care of my affairs. They gave me patents to my land. I disposed of the land by sale and today I have very little land left. I wish something of this kind had been brought to us while I had that land. Today

I would be in better financial circumstances if we had had something like this years ago. I think the measure is good and that it will be helpful to the Indians.

MR. MATTHEWS of Pawnee: I wish to speak to the Commissioner. He has been taking up all the time talking. I want to talk to him. You (*the Commissioner*) say you come here not to scare me but you scare me. You have given me a limited time to speak and I am going to speak a little about the allotment plans carried out by former Commissioners. The old Chiefs, when treaties were drawn up with the United States Government, were not educated to understand the stipulations in the treaties. Mr. Commissioner, you tell the truth when you say they misrepresented the things drawn up in the treaties to the older Indians.

The Great Spirit made me an Indian. As an Indian I am incompetent to carry on the white ways. When you took office I was in hopes you would fix matters for us in carrying on our Indian Affairs. Seems as though you are pushing me off the bank. I would much rather, as far as the Pawnees are concerned, that you make some provision where our homesteads would be secure from taxation and sale. I realize the fact that when you stipulate anything for us we are helpless to do anything. An Indian like me has no chance as I am incompetent to compete with the white men. I am incompetent and poor because the white people have taken all my lands by sale and other sources. I would much rather you would make some provision whereby our lands would be secure from taxation. I wish to make this statement: When the Pawnees were allotted they were not allotted right. Some got 60, 80, and 160 acres. The reason why my brother is stopping me from talking is he is working for the bill. The present administration should make some amends whereby the Government could right the evil of the Pawnees being allotted as they were. I am against the bill and would much rather the present land holdings be carried on.

With reference to Mr. Collier, the Indians where he is from are under a different environment. The conditions are different from those in Oklahoma. I am glad to speak to the Commissioner and from what remarks I have made I hope he carries that out.

MR. ROE CLOUD: The hour is late now and the Chair is going to call on the Commissioner to say a few words. Before the Commissioner speaks I will read the resolutions presented by the Arapaho Tribe of Indians from the Cheyenne and Arapaho reservation.

"Cantonment District,
Canton, Oklahoma,
March 17th, 1934.

"BE IT RESOLVED, By the Arapaho tribe of the Cheyenne and Arapaho reservation, residing in the Cantonment district, gathered on this day, March 17th, 1934 in a general conference to discuss the Honorable John Collier's plan of reorganization of the United States Indian Service.

"In our general discussion our conclusion to the new policy, and our best judgment for the best interest and welfare of the tribes concerned and that we have voted as follows:

(a) The Arapaho council on this day rejects the plan of abolishing the allotment act, giving land to Indians in severalty, was strongly opposed.

(b) The Arapaho council on this day rejects the plan of SELF-GOVERNMENT; Privileges of protection taken away from the State and Federal courts of this land was strongly opposed.

"We, therefore, on this day, formulated this resolution for our delegates to carry along for their presentation to the Honorable Commissioner, Mr. John Collier, and to be acted on at the general gathering and council of the Oklahoma Indians to convene on the 20th day of March, 1934 at Anadarko, Oklahoma.

"BE IT RESOLVED, also at this time we are appealing to the Honorable Commissioner of Indian Affairs, Mr. John Collier, to retain the present status of rights and privileges given the Indians comprising the Cheyenne and Arapaho reservation.

"And that our wishes be embedded with other officials of the Indian Affairs yet to come, that our Indians enjoy absolute competency with the civilized world before any governmental aid be abolished."

The following resolutions were also submitted and handed to Commissioner Collier:

Carnegie, Oklahoma,
March 5, 1934.

Minutes of Kiowa Council, called for the purpose of discussing the bills S-2755 and HR 7902 sponsored by Commissioner of Indian Affairs, John Collier.

Invocation by Albert Horse. Meeting opened for business by Chairman Jasper Saunkeah.

The bills were discussed pro and con for several hours in talks made by Delos K. Lonewolf, Chas. Apekaum, Guy Quoetone, James Daugomah, Ned Brace and others and then a motion was made by Delos K. Lonewolf, seconded by Ned E. Brace that the tribe reject the two bills as a whole. The motion was voted on and the vote was 280 against and 2 for. A motion was made by Jasper Saunkeah, seconded by James Daugomah to wire Senators Thomas, Gore, Congressmen Jed Johnson, J. V. McClintic, Will Rogers and W. W. Hasting requesting them to file our protest in the Senate Indian Affairs Committee and the House Indian Affairs Committee, on action taken by the council. Telegrams were sent to the above members of Congress.

The Tribal Business Committee was elected to represent the tribe at the meeting with Commissioner in Anadarko, Okla., March 20, 1934. An alternate was selected for each member of the council.

Motion was made and carried to adjourn at 5:50 P.M.

Jasper Saunkeah
Chairman

Secretary: James Daugomah

Carnegie, Oklahoma,
March 17, 1934.

The above minutes of the Council held on March 5, was adopted to be presented to the Commissioner of Indian Affairs on his visit here March 20, to show the present feeling of the tribe toward these two bills. All the members of the Tribal Council signed the resolution to adopt the March 5 minutes.

Jasper Saunkeah
James Daugomah
Robert Once
Joe Kaulaity
Charles Toyobo
D. K. Lonewolf
Goomdo

RESOLUTIONS

We, the younger members of the Comanche Indian Tribe, gathered together at the Reformed Church Mission on Monday, March 5, 1934, adopt the following resolutions;

We desire to express our appreciation to the Commissioner of Indian Affairs, John Collier, and to the Secretary of the Interior for the interest that they are taking in behalf of all the Indians of the United States and particularly for the interest they are taking in the members of our Tribe.

We appreciate and greatly sympathize with all landless Indians and respectfully petition and ask the Government to do something for the landless Indians to the end that they may be well and better taken care of and provided for.

We, however, would much prefer to have our affairs looked after in the future as they have been in the past, rather than to have enacted the proposed legislation, Senate Bill 2755, as we cannot see that it would be to our advantage or welfare to have said bill become a law.

Respectfully submitted:
Robert Coffey
Robert Chaat.

PROTEST OF COMANCHE INDIANS AGAINST THE PASSAGE OF THE WHEELER-HOWARD BILL
(S. 2755, H.R. 7902)

To the Honorable Members of the Senate and House Committees on Indian Affairs and the Honorable Commissioner of Indian Affairs:

We, the Comanches, gathered in council at the Ft. Sill Indian School, March 12, 1934, adopt the following resolution protesting against the passage of the Wheeler-Howard [bill,] S. 2755, H.R. 7902, and bringing the Comanches under its provisions.

We feel that the Comanches have made such progress in civilization that to bring them under the provisions of this bill, if passed, would be detrimental to their continued advancement, both economical and social. We are satisfied with the protection afforded by present law and feel that the passage of this bill would eventually return the Comanches and their descendants to reservation life instead of fitting them to take their places in the present advanced civilization. We are opposed to any legislation which would require us to give up our allotments or relinquish any interests that we have in any property that we have acquired. We do not feel that it would be equitable for us to enter into a community organization or to pool our lands and have undivided interests in tribal or reservation lands.

There is no need of any Indian towns or villages in our section of the United States as the Indians in Oklahoma exercise the right of suffrage and vote in state and county elections and if living in cities and towns, vote in such municipal affairs. We protest against the change of the laws of inheritance and the right to make and execute wills and the taking away of individual and property rights guaranteed by treaties and acts of Congress.

We do not see how this bill, if it becomes law, would help the Comanches to more quickly merge into the white civilization which we must do if we are to take our place in the affairs of our land. We feel that segregation which seems the intent of the bill would be a backward step for us.

We feel that it would take away initiative and endeavor on our part and the part of our children who have made great progress in their contacts and developments.

(SGD) Robert Coffey,
Chairman.

This is with reference to S. 2755 and H.R. 7902, bill sponsored by the Commissioner of Indian Affairs, pertaining to all Indians in the United States, "Indian Self-Government."

Realizing that no two tribes in the United States are the same in every respect, we are certain that no standard rules will benefit each materially.

Our Indians no longer reside on a reservation, and for that reason, a plan for a revision of the existing allotment laws will be very unpopular with our tribe, the Kiowas. The allotments of the Kiowa tribe are scattered over five counties, over an area of about eighty miles square, the allotments being from one to twenty miles apart. Although the present land holdings of our Indians are not satisfactory in every respect, the Kiowa tribe, as a whole, are against the new proposed laws sponsored by the Commissioner of Indian Affairs. Our tribe is satisfied with the present laws governing Indian allotments. They are making one request, and that is the legislation be enacted to forbid the sale of any land, tribal or allotment, except to Indians, and that all land be held under Federal jurisdiction.

There has been little or no encouragement extended to qualified Indians of the Kiowa tribe for Government positions in the Indian Service. We have Indians who are qualified to fill many of the positions now held by the white people. Educated and experienced Indians who are interested in the welfare of their own people can carry on the work more satisfactorily than white employees who are holding the positions only for the salary, and where Indians do hold positions they are given little consideration for promotions for their qualification and hard work which is unappreciated and credit for it going to someone else.

After having lived now for more than thirty-five years among the white people, we do not think it is just and fair to our Indian race to be segregated or isolated from the white people; many of those white people have assisted us in farming, stock raising, etc., and have helped us in many other useful things as good neighbors.

Education is the most important thing for our children. Training our children to apply the teaching received at Government schools to everyday life will enable them to cope with the problems of today and with the white neighbors. It is the only salvation for their future. We favor our Indian boarding schools and we believe a great injustice is done our children where Indian schools are closed and help, etc., is curtailed in others in order to save a few dollars. Our children in the Government Boarding Schools are always under strict discipline and receive the best attention and care, physically, morally and mentally and receive proper food and clothing.

If it is the real intention of the Government to help the needy, unallotted and landless Indians, some plan other than the Self-Government plan should be provided. Some of these Indians were made landless by the action of the Government when Patent in Fees to their allotments were forced on them. These Indians should be reimbursed by the Government for the loss of their lands.

The question of law enforcement regulation should not be seriously considered so far as our tribe is concerned, as we are familiar with the most important Federal and State laws and abide by them. I believe that many unfair and unjust decisions will be rendered by inexperienced Indian Courts, where the Federal and State Courts will be impartial and fair.

The determination of heirs for our Indians, the Kiowa, should continue to be conducted as heretofore by the Examiner of Inheritance under the supervision of the Federal Government.

The Congress of the United States should give legislative authority and power to the Tribal Councils, in order that they may be better recognized to present tribal business matters before Congress and other Departments in Washington. Authority and power should be given to Tribal Councils to remove or transfer Government employees when charges of negligence of their responsibilities are made by three or more complaints by reputable persons.

In conclusion I want to say that the Indians expect assistance from the Government. They have a right to expect it since everything the Indians ever owned, land, money, etc., has been taken away from them by treaties, legislation and otherwise, and has left him now on a few acres of land to live on. The Kiowa tribe now strenuously insists that common justice and rights be given them by permitting them to present their just claims to Congress, the Court of Claims and other departments in Washington to correct the wrongs that have been done to the Indians by recommending and approving such legislation.

(SGD) Jasper Saunkeah.

MR. COLLIER: I will now answer my friend who says I have been talking too much. I am sure I have. My excuse is that I am with you now and it will be a good long time before I can come back here. Our Pawnee friend refers to the fact that the Indian I know best lives under conditions unlike yours. That is true. They are the Indians of the Southwest, whose lands have not been allotted; whose holdings are on the increase; whose wealth is on the increase. What he said brought to my mind something that happened 13 years ago among the Indians whom I do know best of all. The Pueblo tribe of Taos. There was a meeting of that tribe to consider a bill. The Bill intended to enable those tribes in New Mexico to recover various lands which had been taken from them by white squatters and likewise to provide them compensation for other lands which were irrecoverable.

The bill was technical and could not be fully understood except by lawyers, and I remember that meeting 13 years ago when this bill had been presented to the tribal council, who, almost to a man, rejected it. They turned it down and they turned it down in a fierce way like our friend the spokesman of the Pawnees who just spoke. They would not have anything to do with it. I remember the years that went on, there was intermediate legislation. Year after year passed and finally, it was not until last May, that bill in its fullness was enacted by Congress and become a law.

When the Pueblos in 1923 voted down this bill, I said, "If you persist in your opposition it means you won't recover your land. You won't get compensation and the squatters will continue to take your land from you." It made me feel very sad and they asked me the same question that our friend did tonight. Whether it was going to make me their enemy. I said, "Not at all." I saw years go by and saw, one by one, those tribes line up behind the bill which has restored their land and has obtained for them a million three hundred thousand dollars' compensation and complete control over their tribal money. They are the only Indians who do have such control.

I have worked at Indian matters and with the Indians a long time. About fourteen years, I have done nothing else. Long enough to see many things rise and fall and see many changes of opinion among Indians and in Congress.

I began this morning by stating what I mean, and what we mean at Washington, that we do not want you to follow us blindly. We do not want you to endorse a bill because we say it is good, we want you to use your own judgment. That is why I came out here. If the Indians of Western Oklahoma and every tribe and every individual of every tribe went against this bill and against the whole plan of the administration, it would not discourage me because I know that in the long run, after the bill is understood, though it may take years, and after the bill is corrected if there is anything wrong in it, the time will come when the Indians of Western Oklahoma will want it and will fight for it.

If I had only been working at Indian matters a year, I might feel differently, but I have working at them 14 years and I have seen many things happen in that 14 years. And while the Indians I know best are those in the Southwest and the California Indians, and some others, it also is true that I have examined the Indian land system and all its history since the beginning of the American policy. I expect that I am one of the very few men who have read every report of the Commissioner of Indian Affairs, published since 1851. And a long time ago it became clear to me why the Indians were losing their land and why they must continue to lose it, because they had a fatal land holding system. Long ago that became clear to me; that there could not be any successful Indian Bureau administration until the Indians were given a voice in their government. That you cannot manage a race of men in an arbitrary way thousands of miles away from their homes. I don't have to know you intimately to know those things which every observer of Indian Affairs knows full well.

I am confident that before we are done we are going to be united, and if it is not on this bill, it will be on some improvement of this bill. I do want to get this across to you if I can. You have at Washington now a President who cares about the Indian and who wants to do the fair and generous thing by the Indian. You have at Washington now a Secretary of the Interior who for many years has fought for Indians' rights, long before he became Secretary of the Interior, a man of great power in the government and great courage.

You have at Washington now another man, head of the Department of Agriculture, Secretary Wallace, who is in a position to do things enormously important for the Indian. He, for example, will be in control of the millions of acres of sub-marginal land which the government is buying, and which could be turned over to the Indians as their land. And you have at Washington, in myself, at least a person who does care about your problems. And you have a Congress ready to follow the President. And a Congress well disposed toward Indians.

If there ever will be a time when the Indians of the United States can get what they need, now is the time. Now is the time when the government is doing big things in a generous way, making fundamental changes all through the country. Three or four years from now conditions may have changed. There may not be the same spirit at work. There may not be the same men there at Washington anymore, and the financial condition of the government may be such that we can't get appropriations for the purchase of land, for establishing credit. It may prove a case of now or never, and surely it is a time for every Indian to think seriously. Surely it is a time for every Indian to think of his children as well as of himself.

We are going to go on. Certainly we are not going to force anything on you. Every tribe that wants to be shut out, if I have any influence with Congress to get them to do it, will be shut out, but I beg you to continue to study the subject, not to close your minds, not to run a risk of throwing away the Indians' first chance, because it might be their last chance, to really establish themselves in safety and prosperity.

After a few remarks by Mr. Henry Roe Cloud, Chairman, expressing appreciation on behalf of the Indians for the privilege of meeting with the Honorable Commissioner of Indian Affairs, and thanking him for his courtesy and kindness, the meeting was adjourned.

CHAPTER 10

MEETING AT CITY HALL, MUSKOGEE, OKLAHOMA, MARCH 22, 1934

MR. LANDMAN, Superintendent, Five Civilized Tribes: I wish to call the meeting to order. We have gathered here today, as you know, representatives of the Five Civilized Tribes, to meet with the Commissioner of Indian Affairs, to discuss with him, to hear his explanation of the legislation which so vitally affects not only the Five Tribes, but the entire Indian population of the country. I wish to open this meeting first with an invocation by our friend, Mr. Green.

Invocation by Mr. Green.

MR. LANDMAN: I wish at this time to make some announcements. We have opened the doors this morning to the various Indian delegations and the tribes to which they belong, but we have not had an opportunity to register all those who have come. It will, therefore, be necessary to allow all those who have come to be admitted at the present time, but I would request that those who have not registered to do so. I trust that you will follow this request. We have our program outlined here this morning in order that we might carry forward in an orderly manner, and it will be necessary that we adjourn promptly at 12 o'clock. At 2 o'clock we will reconvene for another general session in this building, so that at 2 o'clock we will resume where we left off this morning. It is assumed that this morning will be occupied by the Commissioner in a general exposition of the bill. The legislation which we have come here to hear and discuss. It will also be necessary that that explanation be extended for some time in the afternoon.

After that time the meeting will be open for those who wish to speak on the bill, and for interrogation. However, that time will be necessarily limited, and as the meeting proceeds we will be able to advise you as to the time that will be allowed for questions and answers. It may be necessary for us to alter this program to some extent, but this is the tentative program. At the afternoon session it may be advisable to extend on into the evening, and there will be another session held at 8 o'clock, if we are not able to complete business during the afternoon. I believe this will cover the announcements.

I have thought it fitting that for a meeting of this kind, a meeting which so vitally interests the Indian, that we should have as chairman of this meeting an Indian, so that I requested our dear friend, a man whom we all know, one whom you all respect, the Hon. Houston B. Teehee, as the chairman of this meeting. It gives me great honor and great pleasure at this time to turn this meeting and its conduct over to the Hon. [Houston] B. Teehee of Tahlequah.

MR. TEEHEE: I appreciate the words of the introduction of Superintendent Landman. Now, ladies and gentlemen, whenever a stranger comes into our midst, it is proper that we give him a welcome to Muskogee, one of the best cities of the Southwest. It is my pleasure to call upon our friends to give us brief welcome addresses, which are to be limited to three minutes. At this time it is proper for me to present the Mayor of Muskogee, Mr. E. J. Phelps.

E. J. PHELPS: Muskogee has been the seat of Indian administration since 1876. We are pioneers in government, education, and progress. These words that are inscribed over the door to this building, were suggested by Mr. Grant Foreman, as being suitable to be above the entrance to this Auditorium. In my mind they show as briefly as could be the position that Muskogee occupies in this section of the country. We who live here are proud of Muskogee. We are proud to be numbered as the pioneers in government, education and progress. We are proud of the progress that we have made; not only in commerce, but all those things that go to make a place livable and pleasant in which to live. Our schools, churches, libraries and hospitals are all these things that go to make up an agreeable, happy community. We are proud of our history, which extends back over a hundred years, at the time the government was established at Ft. Gibson. We are proud of the men who have gone to make up our history, and I only wish this morning that I had time to dwell upon them and their accomplishments. Without further remarks, Mr. Commissioner and visitors, on behalf of the City of Muskogee, as its chief executive, I bid each of you a hearty welcome.

CHILI FISH, Representative of the Seminoles: We are glad to welcome you here among us, and are anxious to hear what you are going to say.

JOHN MOORE, Creek Representative: It is my privilege to extend to the Commissioner the welcome and greetings of the Creek Nation, on behalf of W. A. Sapulpa. We want to impress upon the mind of the Commissioner the fact that certain individuals have stated that the Creeks are opposed to the proposed legislation. Approximately 90% of the Creeks are poor. We feel that this condition has been brought about by the present method of Government supervision. We want the Commissioner to understand that the Creeks are not generally opposed to this bill, but we are more generally in favor of any legislation that is for the benefit of not only the Creeks, but of all the Indians collectively. This morning, Mr. Commissioner, we bid you welcome, and we appreciate the fact that you have come here to give the Indians a voice in their own affairs. We want you to feel welcome, and that we are more than willing to cooperate in any plan to help the Indian.

MR. BEN DWIGHT, Choctaw Representative: It is an exceedingly great pleasure, and a high honor to me to welcome the Commissioner here today. When the State of Oklahoma was formed the Choctaw people made a great sacrifice. They had to give up the institution that had served their people so well and so long, but they did that in the hope of bettering the conditions among their people. I think in a great measure that that hope has been fulfilled, but during the transition period there have arisen many new problems and, my friends, it is with deep appreciation that I welcome here today, on behalf of the Choctaws, the Commissioner of Indian Affairs, who comes among us to help to work out the solution of those problems. If I understand the spirit in which he comes, he asks us to participate in the solution and in the approach to the solution of those problems. In that spirit we welcome him from the bottom of our hearts. Mr. Commissioner, it is not in the customary way that we welcome you here, but it is in deep appreciation of the manner in which you come to us from the seat of our Government to help alleviate the sufferings and hardships and to help work out the problems that confront the Indians as a whole.

MR. JOSEPH W. HAYES, Chickasaw Representative: On behalf of the Chickasaws, I welcome the Commissioner in a candid, unbiased, mutual consideration of the legislation that is before us. For only through this means, by suspending judgment, and by waiting for all the facts before we come to a conclusion or commit ourselves, the Chickasaws are in this spirit, and the Commissioner, with his mutual feeling in his attempt by the very fact that this trip is being carried, we know that from this consideration will come mutual understanding and helpfulness, so I say in the words of our forefathers, "As the sun darts its perpendicular rays, we extend our pure hands in peace."

MR. TEEHEE, Cherokee Representative: Mr. Commissioner, you well know that Oklahoma was intended which it was first organized as the Indian Territory, as the Last Round Up. Peculiar circumstances arose in due course of time, which changed the situation slightly, and that idea which obtained in the mind of Congress when the original Indian Territory bill was passed, did not fully materialize. At any rate, we have at this time about one-third of the Indian population of the United States within the confines of Oklahoma.

Mr. Commissioner, heretofore I have occasion to say that Oklahoma is a splendid state. You already know that it is a land of oil and gas, a land of lead and zinc, coal and asphalt, corn and wine, schools and churches, homes, and kings and queens. This splendid citizenship of Oklahoma—we think it is a land where the smile dwells just a little bit longer, as someone said in poetry; where there is more of singing and less of sighing, and where you make friends without half trying; a land where the sunshine and the shadow chase each other across hill and plain. We are glad that you have come into our midst, and we hope that this brief association will be fruitful of the promotion of the welfare of the Indians of the United States, for whom you stand as sponsor, and for the Government of the United States.

This occasion has been brought about by the desire of him whom you shall presently hear, to consider with us the operative effect of certain legislation pending before the Congress of the United States, which we now commonly know as the Wheeler-Howard Bill. This bill concerns chiefly, as I understand it, those of our Indian citizenship who are yet classified as wards of the Federal Government, with its privileges extended to those who may be without classification, or rather to a certain part of that element. For a long time it has been the policy of the United States to assimilate the Indians; to make what we know as the allotment system; that is to say, lands have been allotted among the owners, and each individual

Indian took his allotment either in fee without restrictions, or without certain restrictions against alienation. The bill under consideration does not change this policy; that is to say, changing the policy of making the Indian a happy, industrious citizen of the United States, but only changes the method to that end. It is based on the principle of self-determination, as I understand it. In other words, it tends to encourage the class of people whom it will affect to work out their salvation in a much better way than they have heretofore.

The measure is sponsored by those who have the responsibility of administration of Indian affairs, and particularly it has been given careful, earnest, sincere and thoughtful consideration by the Honorable Commissioner of Indian Affairs himself, who for many years has devoted his best efforts to betterment and improvement in that administration. This bill merits our thoughtful consideration, and I trust that we will give our careful attention to what will be said. With that suggestion to you, ladies and gentlemen, it is now my happy privilege, and I regard it as a distinct honor, to present to you the Honorable, the Commissioner of Indian Affairs, Mr. John Collier.

Speech of Mr. John Collier, Commissioner of Indian Affairs, at the City Hall, Muskogee, Oklahoma, March 22, 1934.

Here at the Indian Capitol, which is to be the Capitol of the Indians in the years to come as well as years gone by, I feel peculiarly the difficulty of the thing which we from Washington have come out to do. Because of the pressure of the time, we are compelled to try, in one day, to reconsider the problem of the Indian and to discuss a bill containing more than forty-seven pages of technical language, and here more than in most places the situation of the Indians is complicated by a peculiar, special, local history and local laws. I want to say that before the meeting ends, we shall hope that every question may be answered and especially we wish that criticisms and all opposition may find a voice.

For the answering of questions, I suggest that those having questions in their minds shall write them out and send them to the platform because that will make a reasonably rapid procedure possible. I want to read a single paragraph from the President's communication to Congress dealing with the Wheeler-Howard Bill. I selected it because I believe it strikes the keynote of the whole plan. Under date of March 13, he said: "In offering the Indian these natural rights of man we will more nearly discharge the Federal responsibility for his welfare than through compulsory guardianship that has destroyed initiative and the liberty to develop his own culture." Through offering to the Indians in an effective way the natural rights of man, the Government will better discharge its obligations than through compulsory guardianship. I shall later present the entire letter of the President in the record.

Now from time to time in years gone by, important legislative changes have been enacted by Congress. Again and again far-reaching legislation has been passed making a sharp change from all preceding legislation and redirecting the whole policy of the Government toward Indians. There is no evidence from the record that these far-reaching legislative proposals of the past were carried back to the Indians themselves. Had they been carried back to the Indians, had the Indians been listened to and been given power in the decision, some of the terrible blunders embodied in the past legislative action would not have been. There is no reason to believe that the blunders of past legislation were criminal blunders. They were due to lack of understanding. Above all, they were due to hasty legislation and the failure of the Washington authorities to consult the Indians themselves and to change the legislation so that it would meet the real conditions, as the Indians themselves knew the conditions. Some of the results of past legislation have been as hurtful as any crime could be, but the intentions were not criminal.

THE WHITE HOUSE
WASHINGTON, D. C.

(copy) (copy)

March 13, 1934.

My dear Mr. Howard:

My interest has been attracted to your bill, H.R. 7902, because of the virile American principles on which it is based. Opportunities for self determination for the Indians in handling their property by providing modern corporate management, participation in local government, a more liberal education system through day schools and advanced health measures are provided in the bill.

Adequate provision is made for his training in the management and protection of his property, and the conservation of his health during the period that must intervene before the Indian may be intrusted with the complete management of his own affairs. In offering the Indian these natural rights of man we will more nearly discharge guardianship that has destroyed initiative and the liberty to develop his own culture.

Sincerely yours,
(Signed) FRANKLIN D. ROOSEVELT
President

(COPY)
Hon. Edgar Howard,
Chairman, House Committee on Indian Affairs.

We do not want to repeat that legislative record. We do not want, at Washington now, to go ahead and enact far-reaching legislation and change the Government's policy just because we think it is the thing to do. We believe we know what the right thing is but the people who sponsored these earlier laws believed the same thing. They were just as sincere and just as able as we are. Therefore, we decided to carry this new proposal back to the Indians throughout the country not in order to procure support for the bill, but in order to have the bill studied, criticized, improved by the Indians. That has been our purpose, and is our purpose; we are in good faith in bringing the measure to you. We have no intention of stampeding you or of steamrollering the measure through Congress. It is true that the bill has presidential endorsement and you know as well as I the line-up in Congress and the power of the President and Congress. Had we merely desired to enact a bill, we would never have called these conferences, of which this is one of many.

We are more anxious to have the bill right than we are to have it enacted and we would rather have it changed even in ways we would not like than to have it passed without the knowledge and consent of Indians. We are determined that when this bill shall be enacted, that it shall be the Indians' bill. In the previous Congresses a number of searching and fundamental criticisms and suggestions have been made by the tribal delegates. Unquestionably many more will come in as a result of the thinking that will take place after the conferences.

I am anxious for you to realize that this meeting is being recorded as it proceeds, that we preserve every word spoken; that the record made will go to the Committees of Congress, which means the Indian Committees and the judiciary committees; that what is said here will have a weight equal to what it would have if it were said at Washington to the committee. That anything that I say to you or the other departmental men here will be of record and will be as binding as if it were said to the committees. We cannot talk recklessly to you under those conditions.

I shall not begin by reading or commenting on the detailed parts and sections of the bill. I shall not begin that way and I shall not begin by dealing with criticisms and objections which have been raised. It is better to begin with an effort to spread before your mind the conditions and the facts which caused the administration to draw the plan up, because when those conditions and facts are understood, then the reasons for everything in the bill, or for nearly everything in the bill, become clear and yet I am going to change what I just said and make one or two dogmatic statements in order, perhaps, to open up the minds of some of you. I am just going to say some of the things that the bill does not do, is not intended to do and could not do. The bill does not take the land belonging to those Indians who have kept their lands and divide it among those who have lost their land. It does not do that, could not do that.

The bill is not intended to deal with the ownership of oil, zinc, lead and other minerals. In order to make that clear to everybody, language will be put in expressly so declaring. It is not concerned with your ownership of oil and gas, or other minerals. The bill does not compel Indians to organize into tribes, communities or anything else. There is nothing compulsory about organizing communities. The bill is not connected in any way with communism, socialism, paganism, and so on. The bill is what the President says it is: A scheme for extending to you Indians what he calls the natural rights of man; what he might have called rights equal to those enjoyed by the white man. At the same time the bill does not bring the guardianship of the Government to an end, but on the contrary continues it. The bill does not free the Government from any obligation or responsibility toward any. On the contrary it nails the responsibility upon the Federal Government. The bill does not deal with Indian claims, and does not modify any treaty or any contract.

With respect to the Five Civilized Tribes, it is proper to say that the bill is for the most part, a matter of discretion and policy. It holds out to the Indians certain advantages which they may take or not as they choose. One of the compulsory features in the bill now as applied to the Five Civilized Tribes is the extension of the trust period on such lands as are still owned under trust or under restriction. It is extended and the power to designate restrictions is taken away from the President and given to Congress and it may be that that feature should be taken out. Then the bill would be 100% optional and not even 1% compulsory.

Finally, if every other tribe in the United States should want the bill and want to be included in it and one tribe, let us say the Creeks, the Seminoles, or any of them, should want to be omitted, by express provision the bill does not apply to them. That could be done. If they did not want to have anything to do with it, all they would have to do is to make that known. That will be done insofar as I have any influence with Congress and in the course of our consideration we will see why it would be very easy to do it. These are negative statements to remove fears and resistances from your minds.

Now I come to the situation that led us to draw the bill and I will ask you to bear with me while I first present the nation-wide situation of the Indians, the situation of the Indians in a great many States. You will later see that the conditions in those other States are equally true here and are then true some more here so what I am saying about the Indians generally applies to you. As you know, there was a time when the Indians owned great areas of land; as a rule they owned them under treaties between the Government and the tribes. In 1887, the amount of land the Indians owned was 138,000,000 acres. Now, previous to that time, there had been numerous reductions of the Indian land which had been carried out usually by the breaking of the treaty on the part of the Government. The Government would undertake by a treaty that a tribe was to have a certain amount of land. Later on the Government could decide that it had been too generous in its commitments and would either disregard the treaty or get the Indians and force them to sign an agreement reducing their rights. That happened again and again. It had the effect of causing the Indians to break out in perpetual rebellion.

Border warfare was smoldering throughout the West as a result of that policy of the Government of dealing with Indian treaties as scraps of paper. During the 70s a computation was made as to how much it was costing the Government to get hold of the Indian lands by this method and therefore causing the Indians to rise in rebellion. It cost a million dollars to kill an Indian: a very expensive method. All of this was spread into the record of Congress. Moreover people did not like this method. There was a growing sentiment against it. But the Indians had too much land according to the white folks. That was the situation in 1887.

The Indians still had 138,000,000 acres and it included much of the best land, forest, agriculture, grazing; no one knew about the minerals at that time. Now there went on for some ten years prior to 1887, investigation, examinations and that all revolved around this question of what to do about this 138,000,000 acres of Indian land and the result of these discussions appeared in the general allotment act of 1887. The allotment act became the foundation of Government policy. It was and is the backbone of Indian Law. What has happened to the Indian lands since 1887, within the allotted areas is due almost entirely to the application of allotment law and the allotment system. We have to dwell on this because the present bill is definitely attempting to modify the allotment law to ameliorate its effects and save the Indians from those effects.

You know how allotment has worked. Each man, woman and child then living received his or her parcel of land, and there were then unallotted areas left over after every individual of the tribe got his parcel. The unallotted areas were called surplus, meaning that they were lands the Indians did not need. That was the language of the law. That was the presumption of the law. The surplus lands were bought from the tribes, practically a forced sale at a price of $1.25 per acre, and thrown open to the whites. The consequence of the arrangement was that the children born after a certain date could not get allotments; they were out of luck. At this point I may say that we are continually hearing that the Indians who have no allotments are in the fix they are in because they have squandered their lands. I wonder how a child born one hour after allotment managed to squander his land, or one born one day, one year, or five years after allotment. The children born after allotment were simply born too late by this scheme and the surplus lands which should have been held for them were turned over to the whites.

The money received, at $1.25 per acre, had been used to pay salaries of Government employees, etc. The allotment act provided that the lands should be held in trust for a certain period of time and then the trust or the restriction should come to an end and the land would be subject to taxation and could not be mortgaged or sold. The allotment act definitely contemplated the bringing to an end the guardianship of the Government over Indian land. The ending of the Government guardianship over land is the logical and distinct purpose of the allotment law. Sometimes the restriction period has been only in part, as in your case where you procured an extension of the trust period.

Then the allottees commenced to die. The land had to be partitioned among the heirs or else something had to be done with it. Of course, as a rule it is not possible to partition an allotment of land physically among a great many heirs. It gets too small for use. Then, if it cannot be cut up physically, the other thing is to sell it. Millions and millions of acres have been sold. Selling means nearly always selling to whites. The Indians could not borrow money. That will be so until this bill is passed. The land was sold to whites. The results were so disastrous that the Indians began to try to hold all these lands. They could not be partitioned, but the sale was postponed.

Secretary Ickes has issued an order forbidding the sale of these lands. The situation is that each dead allotment will be the property of many Indians: in some cases five, in some ten, in some fifty, and in some cases two hundred and fifty separate heirs, and each heir is likely to have a tiny part in ownership of two, ten or twenty different dead allotments. You all know this. It works out that we have all over the country the situation where the Government is collecting rent for dead allotments and paying out to heirs one, three, five cents a year. An Indian will have twenty places from which he is drawing such amounts. It staggers the imagination as we try to follow the thing through, the complexity of bookkeeping, in administering these dead allotments. The inevitable result has been that these lands are dumped upon the white market and bought usually very cheap. In the meantime, the cost of administering them is very heavy and the results are very unsatisfactory and in the case of grazing lands, the situation becomes insoluble. They cannot split up tiny parts of land. These Indians are hopelessly handicapped. Let us see what has happened as a result of this allotment arrangement; this allotment scheme which even now by some people is declared to have been the perfect policy.

In 1887: 138,000,000 acres. In 1933: 47,000,000 acres. Amount of land lost: 91,000,000 acres lost since 1887. But that is only the beginning of it. There are some areas which escaped allotment. It would take too long to go into the reasons. Taking those areas you find a sharp increase in land holdings since 1887. In the Southwest the Indian land holdings have nearly doubled, so that 91,000,000 acres is all chargeable against these lands that were allotted. Going further, if you leave out the mineral, oil and such values, take the surface of the lands; it is the best lands which have been lost, sold to whites. I will add this, that of the remaining 47,000,000 acres, 20,000,000 is desert land, worth from ten cents to two dollars per acre; the good land, something over 27,000,000 acres. Of the remaining land, 7,000,000 acres is in the heirship class and is awaiting sale to the whites.

That is a record of absolute catastrophe. If it continues, a few more years, it means the end of the Indian except in those areas where lands have not been allotted. The temporary escape under the allotment system is the extension of the trust period which is only temporary. The Indians grasp at it as a drowning man grasps at a straw and the administration in the same way grasps at it as the only way to prevent loss of the lands. But extension of the trust period under the allotment system means an extension of the period of what the President calls compulsory guardianship. That is what is meant by the extension of the trust period. With the arrival of allotment, the guardianship of the Government which before that time had nearly enveloped tribes of Indians, now reached down and enveloped the individual Indians so that all decisions were made for him by a Government agent and as a rule were made at Washington just as I have to do in endless thousands of cases month by month. There is no escape from it if we are going to keep on extending the trust period and that is the only way to keep the land from being lost.

It is perfectly evident, from what I have said, that some changes have got to be made; that the Indians have been put into a dead-end passage by this allotment scheme. I am saying that we need a change. There may be some better way to do it than we have found in the Wheeler-Howard Bill, but we need some change.

One more item I am very anxious for you to get that will have a controlling influence on Indians' affairs. I have spoken of the cost to the Government of administering this trusteeship over individual allotments and particularly the trusteeship over the dead allotments. It is a cost which grows greater every year in almost exact proportion to the way the Indian owned land grows smaller. Always less land and more cost of administration. A lot of people have said that it was because the Government was building up jobs unnecessarily. I quit saying that at least ten years ago when I got an understanding of the situation. It was not the case.

If the Government is to continue to act as a real estate agent for the trust allotment and particularly the dead allotments, the costs have to go on because the number of infinitesimal equalities always grows greater when the thing passes over to the second generation. So the Government sees that it is loaded with an ever mounting cost while the land is dwindling. The Indians groan and curse over their situation. And well they might, and they will and must go on doing so.

Down at the Kiowa Agency the other day, where the land condition is best, they have only lost 9/10 of their lands. We figured out the cost of administering the Indian lands. We analyzed the distribution of agency expenditures. It turns out that in a total agency expenditure of $80,000,000 for health, agriculture extension, welfare relief and everything else, of that $80,000,000, $65,000,000 is used on real estate operations connected with these allotments and especially the heirship allotments. In the Muskogee Agency we spend $300,000.00 a year, covering everything except education, etc. We have not got the figures segregated, but I am informed that 80% is used on real estate operations.

Carry this out over the whole country and it is a staggering result. Money which is taken out of the mouths of hungry Indians, taken out of the medical service needed by Indians, taken out of the dental services needed by Indians, out of the Indian educational needs, that money is sucked away by this useless, hopeless real estate operation under the allotment system. In the last two months, we at Washington have been conducting long battles to get a little more money for medical service to Indians. We fought that battle clear up to the White House. What did we get? We got a petty increase of $75,000.00, because we cannot get a net increase of total Indian Bureau appropriations, and while we can talk to the Budget Director about the possible saving of two or three million dollars out of this real estate operation, they say, save the money first, then come back and talk, about these things. We cannot save it except by an amendment of law. We cannot stop this guardianship over your individual property affairs until we change the law. We cannot give any promise of permanency of land owning until we change the law. We can go on extending the trust periods, which is becoming harder and harder to do. After a while there won't be any more straws.

I have taken a long time, too long, giving you this picture but after all it is the meat of the subject. It is the reason, at least one of the reasons for the Wheeler-Howard Bill. It is these facts which are as big and high and heavy as a great mountain that must be considered. Those who do not want to cooperate in the matter of the bill, who are just trying to talk it down, let them not merely try to break down the only solution now pending.

Now I come to Oklahoma. Let us forget all about the surplus lands that were thrown open to whites and talk only about the allotment of lands. There were 23,000,000 acres in Oklahoma, 15,000,000 odd in the Five Civilized Tribes. How much remains of that land? About 3,000,000, insofar as you are a part of that total, is now under taxes. That is a terrible reduction and has taken place in a short time.

I have here a statement from a very prominent and public-spirited citizen of Oklahoma. He does not like this bill. He says: "Pauperized Indians; there are none in Oklahoma." During the last few months a very revealing study has been made under civil works. This study dealt with 3,983 families. It took all the families in certain areas. Those families contained 15,799 Indians. How many of them have still got some land? 3,163. 12,636 are landless. Have they gone to New York, Washington, Buffalo, San Francisco; have they established themselves in industry, business, in the professions? No. They are living on this remnant of land owned by the relatives. What about the income of these 15,799 members of the Five Civilized Tribes? Taken on a per capita basis, if you include the oil and other mineral incomes, the per capita income per year would be $82.00, but if you exclude the oil royalties which are not divided among everybody, $47.00 per year is the per capita. That is the yearly income of these 15,799 members of the Five Civilized Tribes if you deduct the oil royalty. How does that compare with the average income in the United States? Based on only $60,000,000,000 of national income, the depression income, if the United States as a whole had the same annual income as your tribe as a whole, and each one having the same annual income, instead of $60,000,000,000, there would be only $9,840,000,000. Five-sixths of the income of the United States would have to be wiped out to equalize the white people with the Five Civilized Tribes. Wipe out the oil income, and if the people of the United States had an identical income with that of you people, man by man, the total national income would be $5,640,000,000 as against $60,000,000,000. In other words, they would give up eleven-twelfths of their income. The situation holds good in every one of your Five Civilized Tribes, of 9/10 of the Indians living in the United States today. While the national wealth has been increased, the Indian wealth has been diminishing. Something has to be done about that.

For a great many years the Government has been using Indian trust moneys, tribal trust funds for Indian support. It has been using from $4,000,000 to 6,000,000 per year without the consent of the Indians on Government salaries. We have made an issue of that in vain. We have called it criminal—I mean ever since I have become Commissioner—but in the next fiscal year we are going to use up $2,000,000 more in spite of the effort of the Indian Bureau not to do it. Since 1900 more than $100,000,000 of your trust money has been used that way. Since 1900, more than $30,000,000 of liens, of debts, have been forced on Indians by the Government without their consent. There seems to be only one way to stop this misappropriation of the Indian trust funds which is a misappropriation not by any individual, but by the Government itself. Your trust funds are taken in order to relieve the taxpayers of the United States of some of their obligations, that is all. There is not but one way that I can see and that is to give you Indians the final power to say whether or not it shall be done. Give you the control of your own trust money. That is what the Wheeler-Howard Bill does. If the Indians control their own trust money, this eating up of the trust funds by the Government would stop the first year.

The life lived by people in the United States other than Indians is essentially an organized life. Organization in the modern world is the key of all power. Only organization gives to a man power, the ability to protect himself, influence in the world. That is the fundamental fact at least of modern life. It is the fundamental fact of human life. Power is in organization and in only that.

The United States enjoys many types of organization. It has the corporation, that instrument of power, which is a thing like a great giant but controlled by the men who own it, the corporation, the business corporation. It has again the municipal corporation. We have in addition numerous other types of organization. If you wiped out that organization, the United States would be in chaos and until you got a new organization, it would pass away. That organization by which the country lives was not something we learned from Russia or Karl Marx. We did not learn it from anywhere.

The United States has built up its type of organization through experience. It is strictly an American product. It is only the Indians who have been forbidden to organization. The ward Indians, I mean, and it includes you Oklahoma Indians where your property is concerned. That common organization except under the sufferance of a politically appointed Commissioner. I may encourage you to organization. My successor can smash anything I do. This bill does provide to the Indians who want to organize, the power to do so and Government aid in the organizing. It does not prescribe how they shall organize. They may use any form used by anybody in the United States in building up wealth, self-help; they can organize as they will and the Government stands to help them.

Even today I read in one of the Associated Press dispatches about Collier's scheme of communizing the Indians, making them Reds, Russianizing them. I don't understand this, unless the whole United States with its groups, and its municipal groups, and its partnerships, unless the United States has already gone Russian without knowing it. Otherwise there is nothing Russian in this bill, which extends power and help to you in organizing your life, your self defense, as the white men already do. If that be Russian, then blame it on the United States.

Adjourned at 12:00 for luncheon given by Five Tribes employees honoring Commissioner Collier and party.

Afternoon Session

2:00 P.M.

MR. TEEHEE: We will now resume the meeting where we left off at the noon hour.

MR. COLLIER: I am now going to describe the Bill to you. Before doing that though, I want to get your minds once more on the fact of responsibility of a great many of your tribesmen. The number of members of the Five Civilized Tribes, as you know, who have no land is about 72,000.

Right here I believe I should stop and have Interpreters called to the stand to interpret for those of you out there who do not speak the English language.

Jos. W. Hayes interpreted for the Choctaw and Chickasaw Indians; Richard Glory interpreted for the Cherokee Indians; Wesley Barnett (of FCT Office) interpreted for the Creeks and Seminoles.

Before discussing the Bill I want to bring to your mind that a great many of the members of the Five Civilized Tribes have lost all their lands and are very poor. It is the policy of this administration that the Federal Government owes a duty to the poor and landless Indian just as much as to the Indian who still has his land.

We do not say that every Indian ought to live on the land and farm it and use it, but we do say that if he wants to live on the land and use it, it is the duty of the Federal Government to supply him with the land and with the necessary money to develop the land.

This does not mean that those who still have some land are going to be asked or compelled to give their land to other Indians or to divide with other Indians. The Government does not intend to do that. It does not intend to take away land from those who have it and give it to those who have lost it. The Government could not do that if it wanted to; that would be against the Constitution of the United States and any law passed of that kind would be thrown out by the Courts.

So, this Wheeler-Howard Bill intends first to help those Indians who have still got land to help them to keep the land, and second to supply new land for those Indians who have lost their land. But, before the Government will supply millions of dollars in getting new land for the landless Indians, the Government must change the allotment arrangement so that the new land will not be lost the same way that the land was lost before. There will be no use in getting new land for the Indians if they are going to lose it again the way they lost other lands.

Now, the part of the Bill that deals with land is Title III of the Bill which begins on page 25. That part of the Bill deals with protecting the land you now have and getting new lands. The Bill provides and authorizes the expenditure of $2,000,000 each year of Government money in buying land for landless Indians.

In addition to buying land, the Indians must be supplied with the necessary equipment for developing the land, building houses, etc., and do the things necessary to put him in possession of the land, therefore the Bill provides for the creation of a system of financial credit for Indians. The Government supplies the money—the amount as stated in the Bill is $5,000,000, and that is only a beginning—and that money is given by the Government to the tribe or community of Indians and they rent to the individual Indian for the developing of his land and building up his business.

That part of the Bill which establishes this loan fund is not found in the Bill as printed. It was introduced by an amendment in the House and Senate and you will find it on page 108 of the printed hearing of the House Committee, and on page 108–110 the members of the House Committee appeared to think the amount should have been made $10,000,000 instead of $5,000,000.

At Anadarko we talked all day and I explained again and again that the Bill would not take the land away from those who have it and give to those who did not have it, but that it protects the land of those who have got it. I read the Bill and at the end of 14 hours of discussion the Chief of one of the Tribes arose and took the platform and in English he said, "I do not want the Bill because it takes my allotment from me and gives to the Indian who has lost his allotment, therefore, I am opposed to the Bill." I think a great many believe that, and I must convince you the Bill does not do that.

Now, during the time while they are interpreting, I am going to speak on the main points of the Bill and not try to give you a technical explanation, because if I try to do that we would be here at least four days. After giving you the main points of the Bill we will have to do away with the Interpreters and I will explain in English. All of the proceedings are going to be mimeographed so that all can read them.

As a matter of fact the Bill—as it applies to the Five Civilized Tribes—is something which each Indian can take advantage of if he wants to, but if he don't like it, if he is not ready for it, he can let it alone and not be affected by it. That is true of all of it, except the last part which deals with Courts, and several provisions of the land title.

Now we will turn away from the land part and deal with the educational part of the Bill. The educational part is Title II, and directs the Secretary of the Interior to find those Indian young men and women who have ability, ambition and talent and to give them whatever education they need, whether as a stockman, or engineer, or teacher, or nurse, or doctors, or anything they want to be put through, and they are to be put through the best schools wherever those schools are, whether government, state or private, and they are to be supplied with money for tuition and living expenses while they are getting this education. One half of the money supplied them will be a gift by the Government and this they will never pay back, and one-half is a loan which will not bear interest and can be paid back in installments whenever the Indian shall have received employment. Those who are very talented will have their way paid with no cost at all to them. It is a gift. This is in order to prepare young Indian men and women for leadership among their people and for business success in the white world.

The next thing in the Bill for all of you to know comes in Title I, the title dealing with Indian Self-government. It is provided in that Bill that when an Indian has the ability, the qualifications which fit him to hold a position in the Indian Bureau—any position from the Superintendent down—when a vacancy occurs in the service, then his people can put him forward as a candidate for the position, and when they put him forward then the Secretary of the Interior must appoint him. This means that the Indian will be able to get work in the Government Service without having to qualify through the Civil Service, therefore they do not get Government jobs. This arrangement would enable them to get Government jobs if the Indians have the ability, without meeting the Civil Service tests.

Another important part of Title I is that part which authorizes the Indians to organize for various purposes, if they want to. They can organize and take out what are called charters, grants of power from the Federal Government and when organized in this way their organizations become a part of the Government, as the Bill says, instruments of government, clothed with the protection and some of the power of the Federal Government. After this has been interpreted I will explain some of the things which these chartered organizations will do.

These chartered organizations would be entirely voluntary. The Indians could have them or not, as they want, and each individual Indian could be a member or not as he wants. Now, what kind of things could the Indians do if they organize? The Bill sets down a great number of different things. Let me give you a few examples of what they might be. Suppose—I am just giving examples—suppose the Choctaw Tribe desired to become a chartered organization. Then, if it wanted to, the Tribe could take over its coal deposits, could form a company to operate their own mines and could borrow money from the Government to provide for the operating of the land—of their own coal mines. That is an example of what a chartered community could do if it wanted to, but it would not have to.

Now, something else entirely different. Just an example of what a chartered organization could do. Suppose Indians have land which they are now renting out to white cattlemen—a great many Indians in the west have this kind of land and they do not get very much rental, and the rent they do get is used to support the Agency. A chartered group of Indians could organize and obtain from the Government the money necessary to buy their own cattle and put them on their own lands, then the chartered organization could run the cattle as cattle ranches and keep all the earnings themselves. The chartered group would have the spending of the money and the Government could not take it for Agency expenses.

Now to give you a picture of something else a chartered organization could do. I will tell you first about the two little colonies that are now being organized on Choctaw tribal lands—that is, coal lands located at McCurtain and Wilburton. Two little colonies are being built there. We are using Emergency Conservation funds and Civil Works money. Houses are being built, four-room houses. There will be a community house where they can have a library and hold entertainments, a meeting place, and that kind of thing, which will serve everybody. The people can come there, and they will come because they will want to. Each family will have farm land around its house, good land that will belong to that family or be assigned for the use of that family. These two colonies are being organized now in the Five Tribes jurisdiction and are very interesting.

Now under this Bill, as you already understand, the Government will buy new land for the landless Indians. It would be solid blocks of land—let us say 10,000 acres of good agricultural land and on that land it would settle—well—let us say Cherokee Indians, or Creek Indians. They would come and have a colony on this land which would be a gift from the Government. There might be a thousand of them located onto this land with their houses, with their stores, perhaps their own local bank. Now that colony under this Bill would be a chartered organization and it could do anything that an organization of white people could do if set up in the same way. It would have charge of the stores and the courts and could pass local ordinances, just like a white town. That organization of Indians living on this land would be a municipal group if it wanted to be, there is nothing compulsory.

It could borrow money from the Government to form its own local bank and then issue loans from that bank to its members for financing their business, whether land or in town, for building houses. If you are familiar with how white corporations are operated for the benefit of members, then you will see how these Indian organizations will operate for the benefit of their members, but there will be this difference. This land to be bought for the Indians would not be taxable—the title would be in the Government and no taxes would have to be paid. Their land cannot be sold to whites; it can only pass from one Indian to another. And this organization, which the Indians might form, would also have the power to call the Indian Bureau before it on any matter and to demand an accounting from the Indian Bureau. It would pass on all moneys to be spent by the Government for its benefit and would control its own Indian moneys. The Indian Bureau would no longer dominate them. That is my idea of the situation that would be set up under the self-government plan of this Bill.

I repeat that this organization will be entirely voluntary. The Indians could have it or not, as they choose, and can have any kind of organization that they prefer that is reasonable. If the organization was not a success, then the Indian could abandon it, but the Government Service would go on just the same, but it would all be under the Federal Government, the spending of Government money would continue, the responsibility of the Indian Bureau would continue, so that if an Indian group tried the experiment or organization and did not like it, then decided to break up the organization and surrender its charter, then the members would go back to its present status of wards of the government. It is very important for you to realize that this Bill could not result in bringing the Government guardianship over you to an end. On the contrary it extends government guardianship over those who can not claim government aid now and makes that guardianship permanent and all that takes the place under the Bill takes place in the guardianship of government, which are the fulfillment of the government's obligation to you.

Now it will not be possible to go on with the interpreting because our time is too short; but I want to say one thing more for interpretation.

The Indians have been wards of the United States since the beginning of this Government. There was one President who took strong interest in the Indians. That was the first President, George Washington. Then many years passed by before there was another President who took a strong interest in helping the Indians. Not until Abraham Lincoln's second term was there a President who cared deeply about the Indians. President Lincoln said, "If I live this accursed Indian system shall be revoked." He meant the robbing of the Indians would stop if he lived—taking away their lands—but he did not live, so his promise remained unfulfilled.

From that time, as you will see from reading the records, there has been no high official who has made the Indian subject an important one, who studied it and has had a program of help for the Indians, until now. President Roosevelt is the third President, so far as I know, that has a strong interest in the needs of the Indians. I shall not read his letter about this Bill, but will place it in the record. (*President's letter incorporated in earlier part of the record.*)

I will tell you though that for his Secretary of the Interior President Roosevelt picked a man who for many years has been fighting your battles, that is Secretary Ickes. For Commissioner of Indian Affairs he picked a man who has been fighting your battles for over fifteen years—myself. Neither Secretary Ickes nor I sought our appointments; neither of us went after our appointments politically. We were selected, more or less, because President Roosevelt wanted a strong Indian program and now after almost a year that program has been worked out into bills. This Wheeler-Howard Bill is most important and the President himself has personally endorsed it.

I think that you all appreciate the fact that President Roosevelt is not going to mislead you, or sell you out, or betray you. He has no motive for doing that; but he has for his purpose helping you, protecting you, getting you more land, setting you free. You can trust him. I do not say you can or should trust me—you do not know me down here. You do not know Secretary Ickes, but you do know about the President, and I am sure that you old men here who do not talk English, if you do not fully understand the Bill, you know you can trust the President not to promote anything to your injury. He wants to create a feeling of confidence in your minds. President Roosevelt is determined to help you and has given his personal endorsement to this Bill. He will help you. He will keep you from poverty. When people say this Bill contains crazy things, and foolish things, just remember that President Roosevelt does not endorse crazy foolish things.

After this has been interpreted I shall have to go ahead and speak in English, as our time is so short.

MR. COLLIER: Now I will go forward and try to finish my statement as I can. I am sure you are wanting to go on today and I shall be with you as late as you want to stay. At this point may I say this—I am getting a great many notes asking me to appoint a time to talk with individuals about all kinds of things, complaints, appointments, and so on. On this trip that will be impossible, because I am going to be in meeting every minute and those who want to see me about anything except this bill should either see one of the Indian Bureau Staff who are here with me, or talk with my Secretary at the Severs Hotel.

Now I am coming back to the Land Section of the Bill. That is the one hardest to explain and most of the misunderstanding about the bill grows out of Title 3—The Land Title—I am addressing myself now to those who have got copies of the bill—I am wondering how many of you here have a copy of this bill. Will you hold up your hands—A good many of you. Now will you turn, you who have the bill, to page 31—Section 8 of Title 3, page 31—Beginning with line 6. That paragraph as drawn means this—I will first state the meaning and I will then tell you an amendment that is to be made in it—The Secretary of the Interior is directed by the Bill to examine the land situation among all the Indian Tribes and he is to determine—put it on a map—what areas shall be treated as areas to be consolidated for the Indians. Allotment has worked out so that the areas which were once solid areas are now all broken up, checkerboarded with white owned land and sometimes the Indian land is a very small part of the checkerboard, white land all around it.

Now the Secretary is directed to make a determination concerning what areas shall in the future be consolidated so that the Indians will own all of the land within those areas—the consolidation will require the buying out of the whites who own land inside that consolidated area. They cannot be forced out, but will have to be bought out—bought out with this money, which is being appropriated. Within that area it is desired that the title, the titles to the allotments, to the Indian allotments shall be transferred to the Tribe, or to the community, as it is called in this bill. Let me get that clear—the individual who owns an allotment would, it is hoped, transfer his title to that allotment to the community. He would receive in exchange a whole series of advantages and I will tell you what they are later—they are so great that in fact the Indians would all want to transfer their title, but at present I am just directing your attention to line 6 of page 31, which says: "The Secretary of the Interior is authorized to make this transfer of the individual title to the community."

As the language there reads, he has the power to do it even without being asked to by the owner of the allotment. He has the power to do it without the consent of the owner of the allotment, of the allottee. Now at the first of the Congresses, the first of these many Congresses held at Rapid City, I told them that this grant of authority to the Secretary was in my judgment undesirable and unnecessary, that the transfer should be made entirely voluntarily so that the Indian, if he wanted to, could hold out his allotment, or go on just the way he is going on now.

I told them that the bill would be amended so that the Secretary of the Interior would make this transfer only upon the request, or with the consent of the allottee, making the entire transaction voluntary and optional. I want to get that lodged clear because that is an item in which the bill is being changed in the direction of making it entirely optional and taking away that authority from the Secretary of the Interior. Why do I say that the Indian would want to make the transfer? I will explain that because it is the most difficult part of the bill for Indians to grasp.

I will proceed by saying that as a matter of fact this hardly applies to Oklahoma at all, but it does apply in a few places and I, therefore, will explain it to you. Get a picture in your mind of an area that is going to be consolidated—that will be 10, 20 or 30 square miles, and the Indians will own all of it—it will be solid Indian owned land and inside that area there is an Indian who has an allotment, say 60 acres. What happens when he transfers the title to the community? He gets a whole series of things. First, he gets the right to stay on that land, on that allotment of his and to continue to use it until he dies. Second, he gets the rights for his children to stay on that land and continue to use it. He keeps the ownership of his improvements and passes it on to his heirs. All improvements and pass it to his heirs. Third, he gets the guarantee that if he desires to move off of that allotment onto some other place within the community, he shall be entitled to an equal amount of land where he selects it and shall be paid for the improvements which he leaves behind on the land which he abandons.

Next, if he is renting the land and not living on it, but is just getting a rent from it, he gets the rental value of that amount of land. That also passes to his children. So what really happens is simply that the title, the underlying title, passes to the community or the Government in such a way that the restrictions can be made permanent—the trust period permanent while the Indian keeps everything that the title represents—he keeps it and his children keep it.

He would still have all these things even if the Secretary of the Interior had the authority to compel him to transfer his title, but we do not think the Secretary needs that authority, or ought to have it, and we propose to make it a voluntary matter from start to finish. Now as for Oklahoma, the thing I am describing will take place within the area marked out for consolidation. Your land in the Five Civilized Tribes is, of course, widely scattered—is all over this part of the State. Usually your allotments would not fall within any area marked out for consolidation. They would not be within an area picked for consolidation and they would not be affected at all by this, except that the trust period is to be made permanent until Congress might other declare.

So that for most of your allotments in the Five Civilized Tribes there would be no exchange of title with the community at all—or it would remain as is with an extension of the trust period. But where your land fell within an area that might be selected for consolidation, then if you want you could make the transfer to the community in exchange for all those things which I have told you, and for other things of which I will tell you about later. But the Indian who would not see it this way, who just wanted to stand pat—he could stand pat now and hereafter. He merely would have the advantage that the trust period would go on until he did want to sell his land—that might be a disadvantage to him. He might want to sell his land. This bill as drawn does extend the trust period. He would have to come to Congress for authority to sell his land.

Now let us for the moment forget about the allotment, the existing allotment that lies outside a community that is going to be consolidated. Let's picture an area that the Secretary of the Interior, under this bill, selects for consolidation—say it is an area of 100,000 acres of the allotted land belonging to Indians. The rest of the area has to be bought in, bought from white people. What about the allotted Indian inside that area? Nothing, unless he wants to leave; he stays and he keeps his allotment. But suppose he turns his title over to the community, then he gets this freedom to use an equal area anywhere in the community, or to stay where he is. If he moves to another part of the community, he can sell his improvements to another Indian, or to the community. His heirs inherit all his right to stay on that land, or to share in the total area of the community. The more land he desires to turn in the larger his equity, his income from rental, or whatever may accrue from that land.

Now I pause again to remind you that the oil and mineral and the wealth under the surface is not intended to be covered by this bill. In order to make that entirely clear to every Indian, we are going to put in such a proviso. The bill is intended to safeguard the individual property rights in the completest way; to do this, we need new legislation. As I have already explained this morning, it became impossible to extend the trust period because the cost of administering there heirship lands is prohibitive. Under this plan the trust period can be carried on indefinitely because the title to the lands which pass after the death of those now living, that title goes into the community and what the heirs receive is—first, the right to use that particular land and they and their children and grandchildren, but—second, they receive a guarantee of the rental value of that amount of land. Having got this arrangement, which makes it possible to extend the trust period, then the Government can go forward and can buy up the white land within the area in question. The money spent on buying that land is not a loan, and the land is not encumbered with a mortgage—it is an outright gift by the Government to the community in behalf of the landless Indians. The landless Indians will have to get their share entirely through the buying of the new land—that is where they come in—and the buying of that new land is provided for through the granting of the two million dollars a year. This sum is just a beginning. More will have to be spent.

At this point I want to meet a thing that is constantly being said. They say this is Communism. But let me make it clear to you that that is no more Communism than the Empire State Building in New York. You have all seen pictures of that building. It is a building, which could not have been built unless a great many people pooled their investments. They all own a part and get a part of the dividends. The more they put in the more they take out. No one man ever built a big railroad. It was through the combined efforts of many investors. It is just a cooperative way of holding property and doing business. It is just a cooperative way of holding property and doing business, the way it is done in big business, the way that the railroads are owned and the steamship companies and the banking establishments, and all the other big properties of the country. There is nothing novel or new about this. In these organized Indian communities every Indian will have an equal vote. One will not cast a single vote because he is entitled to more income.

The effect of this changed arrangement, if it could be made universal, would be to save more than two million dollars a year on real estate costs to the Government. It would be enough to pay for new land in the first years at least. That much money turned over to the Government for Indian education would make an enormous difference in the welfare of the Indians.

The part you are interested in, I take it, is chiefly this—to be assured that the whole thing is optional—not mandatory. Be assured, as I can assure you, that the bill provides for the landless Indians out of new land to be bought and not out of land owned by Indians who own land. The bill provides for the permanent extension of the trust period with all that means—as permanent as it can, because you can never take away from Congress its powers to terminate the trust. But the bill takes the power away from the President and the Secretary of the Interior.

Now I think before going on to any other section of the bill it will be far better to stop right here and try to make sure that Title 3 is understood—the Land Title. There is a good deal more to say about self-government and about the loan system and the courts, but we want to be clear about the land part.

Mr. Siegel, Assistant Solicitor, reminds me that I ought to make very clear a point that I might not have made clear. I said awhile ago that the title to land, after the death of living Indians, passes to the community—that is in the law. The heirs receive all of these things I describe: exclusive use; right to the rental; ownership of the improvements; and the right to transfer title to heirs. But the underlying title passes automatically to the community. That will happen after the death of those now living. As for those now living—they keep same as theirs, or they pass their title as they choose. Most of them would pass their title because of the many advantages.

Now I will get on with the questions on this—or is there anyone who is prepared to make a clear cut statement against it? Now would be a good time to make it.

QUESTION: What happens to lands that Indians buy which are neither allotted nor restricted, and where an Indian has bought some additional land or land other than his allotment?

ANSWER: That land is not affected by this bill except, if an Indian wanted to, he could deed that land to the government and take in exchange these advantages. No part of this bill would apply to that land. He could pass his land title to the government and he would receive the corresponding advantages.

QUESTION: Does the bill which says enrolled or unenrolled include the newborn Indian?

ANSWER: Yes.

QUESTION: Is it not provided on Page 33, Section 11, of the bill that property within the community descend to the community, instead of reverting to the heirs of the deceased?

ANSWER: Yes, as I have explained already.

QUESTION: Where no community is formed, the lands of a restricted Indian at his death, according to the Bill revert to the tribe from whose lands the allotment was made. Is this not destroying the laws of descent and distribution so far as the Indians are concerned?

ANSWER: There the bill has been misunderstood. The language I admit is complicated legal language. That land that remains outside the consolidated area does not revert to the tribe. It is only within the consolidated area. Outside, the existing arrangement continues. I might as well at that point say this: That what we do here may prove to be very difficult, I mean about the outside lands. The heirs of this isolated allotment cannot live upon it and very often they cannot find a tenant. They want to liquidate the estate. Perhaps that would be best, so that to make the trust period permanent is going to be difficult. Probably within a year or two Congress would have to vest in somebody permission to liquidate the allotment. The bill does not provide that the title goes to the tribe where the land is outside the consolidated area. Most of your land would be outside.

QUESTION: When a community is formed, would a person living within the bounds of the community be permitted to vote for County, State or National offices, or be eligible to hold office?

ANSWER: Yes, he would be entitled to citizenship rights.

QUESTION: If an Indian lived in town and not within a chartered community within which his lands are located, would he be permitted to vote on the charter?

ANSWER: That is a new question: I never had thought of it. Certainly if he were to participate in the community, he would be allowed to vote. If the community were organized, it would decide whether or not that non-resident could vote, but in the matter of adopting a charter, I had never—I believe I shall ask Mr. Siegel to explain that.

MR. SIEGEL: I think that the bill provides in Section 2, Title 1, that the charter may be issued to two groups, first those within the existing reservation boundaries and second, those living on areas to be purchased for Indian colonies. The only voting will be done with respect to charters by groups living within existing reservation boundaries. There are no such in Oklahoma. However, the charters in which the Oklahoma Indians would be chiefly interested would be those to be issued to newly formed communities. Membership in such communities will be purely voluntary. That area might contain allotted land owned by Indians living somewhere else. I think it is clear that in the actual 3/5 vote necessary to adopt a charter, as the bill is now drawn, that vote would only be of those resident in the reservation area. But for eastern Oklahoma, it would almost always be the formation of a new colony or newly promulgate a new charter.

QUESTION: Those Indian allotments, which are restricted by the present roll, do not volunteer to join the charter community, what would become of them?

ANSWER: If they did not want to turn their land in, they would not have to. It would be up to them.

QUESTION: I am under the impression under this bill that it is the intention to segregate the Five Civilized Tribes, or is it true that the Five Tribes will be segregated to themselves?

ANSWER: As you know, each tribe has its special rights, claims and all that. When we talk of the Five Civilized Tribes we are talking about the Chickasaws, Choctaws, Cherokees, Seminoles and Creeks; each is separate. It is simply that they are covered by other legislation as a group. This bill does not segregate them. As you know, there is another bill separate from this which tries to correct some evils under which the Five Civilized Tribes are suffering by themselves. That is not in this bill.

QUESTION: Will Freedmen be eligible to membership in any form or character in the establishment of the communities and will they be given an equal right in such community?

ANSWER: I understand that Freedmen are not Indians. Is that correct? This bill is concerned only with enrolled Indians who would have rights under existing law. After the community is once formed, it is the judge of any new members that might come in.

QUESTION: Does not the bill provide that the proceeds from any suit now pending, wherein any of the Five Civilized Tribes are plaintiffs, be distributed as common property to members of the community, instead of same being paid to individual claimants?

ANSWER: The disposal of the proceeds from a suit now pending—this is now in the hands of Congress. What this bill does is to place that decision with the Indians. No longer with Congress. The proceeds are a tribal fund and would be spent according to the wishes of the tribe. If the whole tribe were organized into a community, it would control that fund. The Indians would decide on the disposal of the judgment.

QUESTION: In a checkerboard community as mentioned, who is considered undesirable that makes it necessary to be segregated, the Indian or White, and in your opinion is it necessary to segregate the Indian from the White because one race may contaminate the other?

ANSWER: I think the term segregation has been misunderstood. When we talk about the segregation of lands, we talk about getting them in the most effective condition for use. The people who live there will have just as much liberty to come and go. There are groups of people all over this country who own their land, who have peculiarities, but they come and go and deal and trade with the other people. I do not think segregation is the correct description of the plan. I believe that the Indian community built up under this measure would as a matter of fact break down the segregation which now surrounds a great many Indians. They would have that community as a base to go out into the world. The whole plan works against segregation.

QUESTION: What assurance do we have that Congress will appropriate moneys, not to exceed $2,000,000.00, for the purpose of carrying out the purpose of this bill? The Administration will change from one political party to another.

ANSWER: We cannot have any assurance of future action of Congress. What this bill does is authorize the appropriation of $2,000,000 per year. Its continuation would rely on the success of the undertaking. However, you have four years, that is $8,000,000 and that is some money, and possibly seven or eight years, unless you do not think Mr. Roosevelt will be reelected.

QUESTION: If this act should pass, as now drafted, will it not result in the segregation of Indians in Indian schools and they would have no right to go to schools maintained in Oklahoma without the payment of tuition, except, of course, those few outstanding students to be chosen by the Commissioner?

ANSWER: There are about 20,000 reservation Indians in other states now attending public schools. There is no reason why the Indians would not have the present advantages of the public schools. Furthermore, an Indian community once organized, could take the schools and turn them over to the state to run for the community and pay for it out of government funds.

QUESTION: Is not the title of this bill "Indian Self-Government" a misnomer? Should it not be changed to reflect exactly what it is—"Indian Self-Government Under the Rules and Regulations Provided by the Secretary of the Interior"?

ANSWER: I do not think so. I think that question is important enough to dwell upon it for a minute. Any Indian self-government at present is under rules and regulations of the Secretary subject to change by him or his successors. Under this new bill, once a charter is issued, the Secretary can neither revoke nor amend it. Only the Indians or Congress could do this. If a group of Indians petitions for a charter, the Secretary must grant it or issue a public finding stating under what conditions he will grant it. He must present this to Congress and Congress decides between him and the Indians.

QUESTION: If the Indians come together as a community, the question arises relative thereto, will the land be bought and Indians placed either here or elsewhere?

ANSWER: I expect there is lots of good land in Oklahoma. You can always buy land, of course, the land will be bought where Indians want to live. If an Indian tribe wanted to buy land in some other state, that could be done. It would be up to the Indians.

QUESTION: This is a question brought by Mr. Sam Anderson, Creek Secretary: "When the Creek area is settled, the government might put other Indians beside the Creeks."

ANSWER: I do not know the dimensions of the area and I would not say that the government would not put a colony for Cherokees on land which was once occupied by Creeks. Suppose Creeks and Cherokees wanted to get together, there is nothing to prevent that. That is up to the Indians themselves.

QUESTION: It is understood that if the Cherokees would agree to organize themselves and then should have a form of government of their own, could they have a Principal Chief and other officers of their own?

ANSWER: Of course, the Cherokees are now scattered over the country and could not organize a political government at present. They are just part of the life of the state. It can do nothing as it is now scattered so. Under this bill it could take out a charter which would give it control over any moneys that might rise. It could organize a community and thereby get the power to place its young people in government jobs and be given a voice in all expenditures of government money for Cherokees; and demand a removal of undesirable white influence. But it could not organize a territorial political government because it is scattered. If a colony were formed made of Cherokees and occupying 250,000 acres, that community could organize a municipal government under this bill.

Evening Session

MR. TEEHEE: The meeting will now come to order. We will resume questions. Let me just say I notice that numerous questions are being repeated. If you have sent up questions, and later more, that have not been answered in some other question, and a number of questions that have no relation to the bill under consideration. I think it is the desire of the Commissioner, for what time he has, to give attention to the bill under consideration. So if you have any questions outside of the issue which have relation to some other question, it is suggested that you address a letter to the Department of Washington, or the Superintendent here at Muskogee. But at this time direct your questions to the bill under consideration. We will resume here where we left off.

MR. COLLIER: Before I start on questions, I want to say that if we do not get finished to your entire satisfaction tonight, and if any of you are remaining over tomorrow, we will be glad to go forward tomorrow morning with you. We could even do this, we could break the meeting into three parts—one meeting with the Choctaws and Chickasaws—another with the Cherokees—and another with the Creeks and Seminoles. I would take one of the meetings—Mr. Siegel one—and Mr. Woehlke another, and then we would be able to explain some things in the bill more exactly than I may be able to do tonight. Let us know what you want to do about that later in the evening.

I call your attention to the second page of the explanation of the Wheeler-Howard Bill prepared by Mr. Harper, Secretary of the American Indian Defense Association. It is brief and clear and absolutely accurate. Now we will go on with the questions.

One signed by James Culberson of Durant.

QUESTION: Should a person accept an allotment in one of these cooperative communities and remain under its rules and regulations, would it not disfranchise him from participation in the State in which he might live?

ANSWER: No. An Indian in one of these communities does not lose his franchise any more than a white man living in Muskogee.

QUESTION: Would these Indians living in the organized community be subject to compulsory war service, either at home or abroad?

ANSWER: Indians are full citizens of the United States since 1924. As such they are, of course, liable for the performance of war services like all other citizens. The way to answer that question is—let us not get into any more wars.

QUESTION: Why is the Bill confined to Indians with one-fourth blood, or more? Should not the bill allow all enrolled Indians to participate regardless of their degree of blood?

ANSWER: It does. The limitation of one-quarter blood Indians deals only with new colonies created for the homeless Indians. All members of known and recognized tribes, the enrolled member and their children, will fully participate in the benefits of this Bill. No blood limitation is contained, except for the new colonies.

QUESTION BY A. E. RAIFORD: Where will land for Creeks be purchased, and how many acres for each member?

ANSWER: That depends where the good land is and where the Creeks want it. As for how much land—that depends how much money will be available and the number of Indians who will want to use the land. I want to stop a moment to say a few words about the way of obtaining new land. You already know the bill contains the authorization of two million dollars a year to purchase new land. There are other ways of getting your land besides that. The most important one you may not be familiar with at all.

The Government has undertaken to buy and to retire from commercial farming very large areas of land which is known as submarginal land. They are in States where Indians live—where there are homeless Indians—there are actually ten million acres of this submarginal land, so-called. Much of it is a great deal better than any but the best which you Indians now have and it is perfectly good for grazing and for subsistence farming. Now the announcement has already been made that this submarginal land, which the Government will buy and will take out of taxation, is to be made available to landless Indians. Landless Indians which might organize under this Bill and receive charters, could then enter into possession of submarginal lands in their part of the country. That manner of getting land may be more important than the buying of land, but, of course, that land would not be bestowed on Indians under the old allotment system—only under the new arrangement as proposed by the Wheeler-Howard Bill.

I am laying aside questions that are duplicates of those already answered.

QUESTION: When lands are condemned and purchased by the Department of the Interior for use in, and to become a part of, the various Indian colonies, how will the amount of the purchase price or value of the land so taken be arrived at?

ANSWER: There is a misunderstanding there. It is not proposed to condemn lands for these colonies. The land will be bought in the open market. When an Indian community becomes organized under a charter it is then endowed with the same powers of the condemnation, which are enjoyed by chartered municipalities, corporations and political subdivisions already. In other words, it can condemn land for right of way, roads and things of that kind for public use. When land is condemned for public use the Court fixes the value.

QUESTION: As I understand the so-called Wheeler-Howard Bill, the Indian Courts are to have broad jurisdiction. Will they also have jurisdiction of felony cases where Indians are accused?

ANSWER: The bill deals with two kinds of Indian Courts. First, when an Indian community organizes, if it be a community with a solid territorial area, like a county or town, then that community may institute its own local court just like a town does. There is a magistrate court, or police court, for handling matters between members of the community—a court of law and order arising in the community. That is a court created by the community to impose the ordinances of the community. That's entirely apart from the Court of Indian Affairs dealt with in Title 4 of the Bill.

The Court of Indian Affairs is a National Court. Its members will be appointed by the President, confirmed by the Senate, and its authority will be as great as that of the Federal District Court at present. It will take over the National jurisdiction of Indian matters from Federal District Courts. In addition, the Court of Indian Affairs appointed by the President will settle all controversies that arise as to the powers of the chartered Indian communities. If the Secretary of the Interior should try to violate the charter of the community, the community could then go to the Court of Indian Affairs to restrain him from interfering. If the community itself violates the charter and did not protect the rights of its members, the Secretary of the Interior can go to the Court of Indian Affairs and obtain an order directed to the community requiring it to live up to its charter. Also the Court would have jurisdiction over conflicts between Indian communities and the outside world, if they arose.

Also it will have jurisdiction over probate matters. These local courts would be similar to the local courts in towns. The Court of Indian Affairs will be a National Court which would go to the place where Indians are to hold tribal sessions, or have its settings. It could assign any one of its justices to deal with cases.

Also this is of importance that the bill creates a staff of public defendants for Indians. Lawyers who represent Indian communities and the individual Indians in cases arising before the Court and would be represented then without charge. Of course, you have already have Probate Attorneys here, but in most parts of the country the Indians have no representative when they appear in court. If they do not have money enough to hire a lawyer, they have to do without representation. The Bill provides for lawyers to be appointed by the Secretary for all Indians.

QUESTION: Suppose an Indian should still own his own allotment and has also bought say 300 or 400 acres more adjoining this allotment, all rented to white tenants. The owner is now living on a farm of 50 acres located 6 miles from this farm near his allotment, and said Indian does not wish to join this colony, but either or both farms are within this colony—then what?

ANSWER: That is a very complicated question—I shall restate it this way. The essence of the question is this. If an Indian owns land inside of what we call the consolidated area and does not want to live in the consolidated area and not have anything to do with the Indian community—what happens to his land then? In the first place he can keep it just like it is. Nothing will happen to it. In the second place, if he wants to be entirely away from that community, he can sell it to the community or exchange it for other land of equal value outside the community. Under the Bill, however, any Indian land within the consolidated areas of the community, after the owner dies—the present owner—the underlying title would pass to the community. Then the heirs would receive all the things I told you today—exclusive use, if they want it; the right to rental value, ownership of improvements; the right to transmit their equity to their heirs in turn. The comprehensive answer is that an Indian who wants to remain undisturbed will remain undisturbed in or out of the community.

QUESTION: Is there any minimum quantum of blood as to joining a community?

ANSWER: No—except as to where the community is created from the ground up for homeless Indians, but not affiliated with a recognized Indian Tribe. The Bill now says they must be of one-fourth Indian blood.

QUESTION: What degree of blood is required for the educational part of the program?

ANSWER: Nothing is said in the Bill about it. Any Indian who is recognized as a member of the Tribe is entitled to the educational benefits.

QUESTION: Can a full blood take his white wife into the community, and vice versa?

ANSWER: It depends on the status of the white wife now. If she is not a member of the Tribe he would have to get the consent of the community to bring her in, to have her share in the property.

QUESTION: If an Indian wants to join a community organization and his allotted land is mortgaged, will the community accept his equity in his allotment and permit him to become a member of the community, the community assuming the mortgage debt?

ANSWER: The mortgage has to be paid by someone. If he surrenders his allotment to the community, the community would have to pay off that mortgage. He would get a correspondingly lower share in the community assets. In other words, if his allotment is worth $2,000.00 and the mortgage is for $500.00, and he turns it into the community and the community pays the $500.00 to the bank, he would get an equity representing $1,500.00.

QUESTION: Why does the Bill prevent Indians of less than one-fourth Indian blood from becoming members of a community?

ANSWER: It does not. An Indian is eligible for membership if he wants to be. But where a new community is created by the Government for homeless Indians who have no tribal connections whatever, it seems necessary that there be put in some blood limitation. Otherwise you might have someone from Rhode Island of 1/80th degree Indian blood coming in.

QUESTION: Will an intermarried white citizen be eligible for membership in a community?

ANSWER: Yes, if the Tribe likes and the community wants to let him in.

QUESTION: Will all Indians, whether members of communities or not, be subject to the jurisdiction of the Court of Indian Affairs?

ANSWER: In crimes against the United States—yes. For example, an Indian who committed murder, either in the community or out, could be tried in the Court of Indian Affairs. There are ten crimes given in the Federal Statutes over which the United States Courts have original jurisdiction: larceny, rape, murder, arson—etc. The jurisdiction would be transferred from the Federal District Court to the Court of Indian Affairs.

QUESTION: If this Bill should become law, what will become of the tribal property of the Choctaws and Chickasaws, such as coal and asphalt deposits, surface of coal and asphalt lands, and claims against the Federal Government?

ANSWER: I think I answered that when I was on the subject of what the Choctaws might do if organized under a charter. The chartered community, if it included a whole tribe, would become owners of the tribal assets of their mines, surface lands, timber, minerals, and cash in bank. Communities would own tribal assets.

QUESTION: Where in the bill is the provision which would make Indians eligible for appointment to the Indian Service without taking Civil Service examination?

ANSWER: In Title 1, Section 8, Page 13 of the Bill. The Secretary of the Interior is directed in Section 8, which starts on page 12 of the Bill, to set up conditions which have to be met by an Indian in qualifying for a position in the Indian Service. It really means creating a special eligible list for Indians only. No white man may qualify on that list at all. It takes account of honesty, ability of the Indian, experience, etc. An Indian would go on that list and qualify to be a farmer, stockman, extension agent, teacher, or whatever he was qualified for, and then on page 14 it says:

> "Any Indian community may, through procedure set up in its charter, appoint a member to any vacant position under the Indian Service maintained for the administration of functions or services for Indians within the territorial limits of the community. The appointee shall not take office until he shall have previously received the certificate of approval of his fitness for the position in question from the Commissioner. The Commissioner shall issue such certificate of approval to any member of an Indian community recommended by the duly authorized representatives of the community and who is qualified for the position under the rules and regulations prescribed pursuant to this section."

This means that the Indian does not have to pass the civil service test. I told other Indians in the Congresses what the situation is. If you go back to the year 1900 you will find there were more Indians employed in the regular Indian Service in proportion to the total ratio than there are now. In other words, the ratio in the Indian Service was bigger in 1900 than it is today. We are not speaking of the E.C.W., the civil works or the road building, etc., but of the regular work. That is certainly not due to the desire of the administration to appoint whites rather than Indians.

We have the opposite desire. It is due entirely and exclusively to civil service. Hardly a day goes by in Washington that we are not confronted with this. An Indian with a fine record, good character, popular with his people, perfectly capable of filling a position—sometimes a small job and sometimes a bigger one—and he recommended for it by his Superintendent. We would recommend him for it but he cannot get on the civil service eligible list. He cannot pass the examination. He is out. It is beyond our power or control.

In the last year we have gotten a few concessions. For example, we can now appoint Indians as farm aids, home aids without civil service. We are doing it and are putting many Indians on instead of whites. We had to go to the President to get that concession for Indians. But in the main we cannot change the civil service, and the Civil Service Commission is entirely right in refusing to make any change. The general civil service is intended for the whole country and the Government is not the place where Indians ought to be required to go. They should have their own eligible lists and that is what this Bill gives them. In the Indian E.C.W. we are not controlled by the civil service and there one can see what the Indians can do if they are given a chance. As you know, we had about 14,000 Indians in camps over the country, only about 300 of whom were of the Five Civilized Tribes, because there is so little Indian land to work on here. These E.C.W. members in groups are doing a great variety of technical work—forestation, forest fire prevention, trail building, reforestation, the development of stock water and the erosion control to stop the wastage of soil, etc.

In that work we have today more than one-half of the supervisory jobs held by Indians. More than half of the top jobs are held by Indians and are held with great success and every month the proportion of Indians holding responsible jobs grows greater and they have been extraordinarily successful and efficient. We could not have done this under civil service at all—Indians would have been blocked. On the new building work about to start we are going to build to the tune of millions of dollars for school buildings. There will be numerous cases where there will not be anyone but Indians employed. All the skilled labor and executive work will be done by Indians. That is possible, because we do not have to obey civil service. Public works is not under civil service. We believe that this Bill would make all these real jobs in the regular Indian Service.

I am losing my voice and I am going to see if Mr. Siegel will answer the next question:

MR. SIEGEL: Question. After a charter is granted, A Indian becomes a member of the community—he has one child who has attained his majority and does not become a member of the community—while living as a member of the community another child is born to A and his wife. A dies while a member of the community. To whom does his proportionate share in the community property descend?

ANSWER: It is not required under the Act that the proportionate share which an individual receives in exchange for land transferred to the community, or tribe, should descend to a member of the community. It is possible that under Section

10, Title 3 of the Bill, wherein the Secretary of the Interior is permitted to prescribe rules and regulations governing the descent of Indian property, that non-members of an Indian community could be excluded, but that that section was not put in the bill for that purpose and I do not see any reason why it could not be made clear that there is no attempt to disinherit non-members of the community, or tribe. In other words, any property rights which an individual Indian now has will go to his heirs as before, except this—that there will be provided a ruling of descent and distribution which will prohibit the subdivision of that land into small units so small that nobody can use them. With regard to property which is now tribal and which may be transferred into a community, if a community is organized, the right to share in such property will go as heretofore, to the members of the tribe or community, so that, if the child spoken of here is not a member of the community or tribe, it would not share.

Let me repeat. With regard to property which has heretofore been allotted, or any property which is individual property now, that will descend to the heirs as under the present law with the provisions against subdividing it into small unworkable units. With regard to tribal or community property which has never been allotted, or individual property, that will go as heretofore to a member of the tribe or community.

QUESTION: If the Government buys land for the community that is now taxable in State, County and Municipality, will such land be non-taxable after becoming a part of the community?

ANSWER: Section 16 of Title 3 provides that all lands which are acquired for the new Indian reservations, or which are added to old ones, shall as long as title is held by the United States, or by an Indian Tribe or community, shall not be subject to taxation. The United States assumes all Governmental obligations of the State or County in which such lands are situated with respect to the maintenance of roads across such lands and furnishing of educational and other public facilities, execution of proper measures for the control of fires, floods, etc., and the Secretary of the Interior may enter into agreements with authorities of any State, or subdivision thereof, in which such lands are situated.

In other words, the Bill provides that all lands acquired for Indian Tribes or communities, shall not be subject to taxation, but the Federal Government shall perform all public services with regard to people residing on that land and may pay the State for such functions and the Secretary of the Interior may enter into contract with the State for the performance of any function which the Federal Government has undertaken to do. I wish to state frankly, we have never had a Supreme Court decision squarely holding that the Federal Government can take taxable land out of the tax status and place it into the tax-exempt status. The only case which deals with the question is the case which holds that the Secretary of the Interior has no authority now to take out of the tax roll, lands which were formerly tax exempt, but which were purchased with restricted and non-taxable funds. But the Supreme Court, in my opinion, made it plain that the case was solely one of the intention of Congress, and if the intention of Congress to remove such lands from taxation were made perfectly plain, then the Supreme Court, in my opinion, made it plain that those lands would be removed from taxation.

MR. COLLIER: You Cherokees know that in North Carolina you have brethren who would not take the Trail of Tears one hundred years ago. The Eastern Cherokees hid out in the mountains and were not moved to Kansas. They emerged from the wilderness with no land at all, but they went to work and saved money and acquired land—bought it. They formed a corporation under the laws of North Carolina to hold that land in common as a community. For a good many years they paid taxes on it, but about ten years ago they transferred title to the United States, and did not alter ownership at all in practical effect, but transferred title to the Government and then waged a successful battle against being allotted.

I think they are the one tribe that has a guarantee in law against being allotted and who are holding land in common. They do not pay taxes. The North Carolina Court has taken the position that the land now held belongs to the Government and is not taxable. In Arizona and New Mexico the Navajos have been buying land for several years. They are acquiring purchases off the tax rolls, which become tax exempt, so that while the matter may be a moot one, so far as the Supreme Court is concerned, actually Indian land is being taken off the tax rolls by this method right along, successfully.

QUESTION: Will babies born after 1907 be privileged to share in this land purchased for these colonies?

ANSWER: Surely, if they are members of the tribe.

QUESTION: Would Indians participating in a new colony have the right to designate the land to be acquired for them?

ANSWER: Of course, up to a certain point. The final decision on what lands to buy would have to be left with the Government. It would be agreed upon by the Indians and the Secretary of the Interior.

QUESTION: If a colony is established within the Creek Nation, with the money supplied by this Bill, and land is bought, will the Creek Nation be liable to the Government for the amount expended in the acquisition of such land? Will the Creek Nation have to reimburse the Government in the future, if there are funds available?

ANSWER: This land-purchase fund is a straight gratuity appropriation, not reimbursable and not a loan. But that does not quite answer your question: It compels me to talk a little about the suits in the Court of Claims and that will compel me to go outside the Bill. This Bill does not deal with Court of Claims suits. As you know, when an Indian Tribe goes to the Court of Claims, it sets up its claims and the Government sets up counterclaims. The Government pleads what they call off-sets and the effort of the Government is always to plead large off-sets—that is, of money spent allegedly for the benefit of the tribe in all the years gone by, to be deducted from the judgment. Last year some Indians of Montana got a $3,000,000 judgment and the Government got $4,000,000 set-off. So the Indians woke up one morning one million dollars in debt as the result of winning suit against the Government. That is the way it is worked now.

We are hoping to meet that situation through the present legislation. The way the Government deals with these claims against Indians is a perfect outrage. Delaying them a lifetime through all kinds of promises and lengthy off-sets. The way the thing is done now, we will still be settling their claims in the Court of Claims one hundred years from now. We propose to bring an end to this sort of thing with legislation, a bill which will create a special Indian Claim Court, we will call it, for handling Indian tribal claims against the Government. That same legislation will limit the amount of off-sets which the Government may impose against future judgments.

Under that legislation, the Government will not be able to set up any counterclaims, except in those cases that the Indians, at the time of the Government expenditure, agreed that these should be counterclaims and in addition, the Government will have to demonstrate actual benefits to Indians for such expenditures. That legislation is of very grave importance and of grave importance to you for the prompt prosecution of your particular claims. We have not attempted to cover that subject in this Bill because if we get the kind of thing I am describing the Indians can get their day in court promptly, decently and fairly and the Indians will get judgments against the Government that would stagger the imagination. They would run into the hundreds of millions of dollars. We did not want to burden that bill with this particular thing because we want to present this first then tackle the claims later.

Now to get back to the original case, whether the land bought for a tribe might be termed as a set-off against future judgment. Under existing laws, it might be, because any Government expenditure might be. We cannot promise it would not be. We cannot promise the Court of Claims would not admit it. We cannot give you a pledge. Under this new bill as we have proposed it, the General Claims Bill, it could not be unless the Indians stipulated that it should be at the time they received the land. By the way, if you want to know what is in that bill, you can read it in the hearings of the Senate Investigating Committee, dealing with Indian claims. The bill was drawn by the present Solicitor of the Interior Department, Nathan Margold.

I have rather wandered from the subject in answering this question but I know the question of claims is near to the heart of all of you.

MR. LANDMAN: At this time, I wish to announce that due to a pressing engagement, our presiding Chairman, Mr. Houston B. Teehee, is compelled to leave us and I want to extend our thanks and the thanks of this meeting to our presiding officer who is now compelled to leave. In his place we have requested Mr. W. F. Semple, Choctaw, to assume the responsibility of the Chair and to preside from here on.

MR. SEMPLE: Mr. Landman, ladies and gentlemen. I feel that I should take advantage of the opportunity afforded me to express my deep appreciation of the great honor extended to me to preside for a brief time over this meeting. An entirely unexpected honor and yet, I appreciate the fact we are gathered here to consider a matter of grave importance to those of the Five Tribes to whose interests we are devoted. I think we are fortunate and I am going to trespass upon your time long enough to say so—we are fortunate to have in charge of Indian Affairs and at the head of the Indian Administration, a man like Mr. Collier. He has expressed himself as being positively and definitely a friend and a far-seeing one insofar as the Court of Claims is concerned.

I know he has the best interest of the Five Tribes at heart and I believe he is the first commissioner in fifty years with a real determination to accomplish some lasting benefit for these Five Tribes and to correct some of the mistakes made in the past. I think we should cooperate with him and do our best to help with the work he has in mind in order that the Five Tribes' needs may be advantageously presented in this Bill. Mr. Collier is thoroughly devoted and is determined to do his utmost to benefit the Indians of the Five Tribes.

JOSEPH BRUNER: I'd like to ask a question: Does the bill provide for employment of Indians and where. Does the present bill provide that an Indian equally capable with a white man has preference over a white man?

MR. WOEHLKE: I believe that question was answered fully and exhaustively just a little while ago.

QUESTION: Would it be necessary for a tribe to have a National Council before they could vote on this bill?

ANSWER: There can be no formal vote on this bill by the Indian Tribes. There can only be an expressed opinion and naturally, if the tribe is not organized, it is impossible to completely organize in the short time which remains. Organization cannot be complete enough to make its voice really impressive and forceful. Therefore the thing the members of the Five Tribes should do is to express their individual opinions to the Members of Congress, to the Commissioner of Indian Affairs, the Committee on Indian Affairs of the House of Representatives and the Senate so that these committees may know what the opinion of the rank and file of the largest possible number of these tribes is, concerning this bill. It is very easy to have or to create an organization and give it a long name and in the name of that organization present resolutions and send them in. However, unless the organization can prove its actual membership, its voice will have little effect on the Indian Commissioner.

Therefore, the real influence on this legislation will have to be by letters written by the members of the tribe or by a petition signed personally and addressed to the Commissioner of Indian Affairs, or the Committees or to the Secretary of the Interior. Whether these letters or petitions be for or against the bill does not matter, so long as they are sent in as an expression of opinion. But there will be no formal vote—there can be no formal vote—on this bill at this time.

QUESTION: We have several questions here by Mr. C. W. Ward of the Organization of the Unrestricted Indians of the Muskogee Creek Nation. The first one is: If the Wheeler-Howard Bill is passed will it take precedence over the Supplemental Agreement of March 4, 1901?

ANSWER: That agreement of March 4, 1901 was a long involved document containing many things and it would take a careful analysis to find out points of conflict that might arise, but in a general way it can be said very authoritatively that if under the supplemental agreement, vested rights have been acquired, if claims against the United States are involved, the Wheeler-Howard Bill will not affect them, as the Commissioner has explained. On the other hand, concerning the provision for the taking over by the United States of the Tribal Council functions, etc., naturally the Wheeler-Howard Bill, by creating a new form of community organization, would take precedence over this supplemental agreement.

QUESTION: Would the bill affect any money now due the Creek tribe?

ANSWER: That has already been answered. It will have no effect whatever on any claims against the United States, now pending.

QUESTION: Article 2 of the bill as presented, will it conflict with Section 583, Article 17, concerning distribution of Tribal funds?

ANSWER: Our attorney informs me it will have no effect and will not be in conflict with this section.

MR. COLLIER: I want to supplement what Mr. Woehlke told you as to an expression of opinion by Indians. There are some tribes which are completely organized already and which are in position to act as tribes. For example, the Menominee Tribe has an organization which enables it to present its opinion authoritatively on this bill. The Pueblos of New Mexico are so organized as to act. So too, the Navajos, the Crows and many others. Down here, unfortunately, your tribal organizations which once were strong and representative have been crushed by the policy of the Government. It is quite strange to find the biggest group of Indians in the country without organization to speak for it officially or authoritatively.

Under this bill you can get such organization for the Five Tribes. As I understand it, this is the position you are in. Therefore, as Mr. Woehlke said, what the Congress will need to know is the wish of the greatest number of you. Any individual who can suggest a way to improve this bill may do so—any amendment will receive the hearty thanks of the Department and of the Committee, because both the Department and the Committees are seeking for ways to improve the bill and as I have remarked, this bill will be amended many times. We want items and we want them from anybody, Indians or white people, and we want to know what is the desire of the Indians.

Two days ago, at Anadarko, I got into a slight conflict with some of the Tribal Council. They had met in advance of our meeting and two of them had adopted resolutions which not merely objected to the bill but stated that the bill contained things which are really not in the bill at all. In other words, they gave reasons which had no connection with the bill, irrelevant considerations. These tribes contain very large numbers of landless Indians and I find they were against the bill because they had been told the bill took land from the one who retained his land and gave it to the one who had none. The resolution had been adopted. I gave them my own views about the procedure.

In the first place, I asked for a showing of hands to see how the Council was made and I found there were sixty members there who were owners of living allotments. But in that tribe there is only one landowner to each five landless Indians. I said, in my judgment, Congress would want to know the wishes of the whole tribe in cases like that. I could not rest on a verdict by a Tribal Council, when that verdict rested on erroneous facts in the first instance, on things which were not in the bill at all and where, admittedly, it did not speak for the great majority of the tribe, who were landless. That, in some way or other, we would have to arrange a referendum of the whole adult membership of these tribes. If there were a way to do that among the Five Tribes we would be glad to do it. Are there any further questions to be submitted on this particular subject?

MR. WALTER COLBERT: Mr. Chairman, I make a motion that we cooperate with Mr. Collier and endorse all his actions.

MR. SEMPLE: What's your pleasure?

MR. FRYE: Before presenting that motion I think there are some resolutions that should be presented to the Commissioner and I move now that any resolutions which they have prepared be now presented to the Commissioner.

MR. SEMPLE: Where are those resolutions?

MR. FRYE: They are in the hand of the members of the Kee-too-wahs.

MR. SEMPLE: Will you send them up?

(RESOLUTIONS presented and explained by full-blood Cherokee and interpreted by John Smith).

RESOLUTIONS OF KEETOOWAH SOCIETY, INC.,

> Whereas, the Honorable John Collier, Commissioner of Indian Affairs, is sponsoring a proposition, as an experiment to set aside a lot of land to be settled, improved and owned and occupied in common by as many Indians as so desired, they to live on, farm, raise livestock, poultry, fruits, berries etc., and to live in common on whatever is produced and raised on same. The Government proposing to purchase the land necessary to carry out the plan and to give the Indians employment in building houses, fencing, clearing and improving same, and
>
> Whereas, the Hon. Commissioner Collier is the first and only Commissioner of Indian Affairs ever to come out and announce himself in favor of the Government giving all Indians an early hearing before the Hon. U.S. Court of Claims on their claims against the Government, and whatever is found due them by said court to pay them and not be always about it, and
>
> Whereas, his proposition to colonize, if it might be called such, is largely experimental and not compulsory on anyone, but only optional, and since we live in an age of experimentation, the Government and every state having many experiment stations and many large companies and individuals are continually experimenting to find out new things, we see no harm in trying out such a plan or proposition.
>
> Therefore, considering everything in his plan and especially his advocacy of the government paying the Indians whatever is found due them by the Honorable Court of Claims.
>
> We, the Executive Committee of the Kee-Too-Wah Society, Inc., of the Cherokees in session assembled do hereby indorse Mr. Collier and his plan, and we take this opportunity to express our most sincere thanks for the interest and friendship he has shown for the American Indian.
>
> We also indorse the resolutions presented by the Nighthawk Kee-Too-Wah Society.
>
> Signed at Tahlequah, Oklahoma, this 21st day of March, 1934.
>
> James W. Duncan, Sec'y of the Society and member of the Executive Committee.
>
> Jim Rickey
> James Cochran
> Tom Greece
> Executive Committee, Keetoowah Society, Inc.

JOSEPH BRUNER raises question of order as to time spent on resolution of Kee-too-wah who are only a clan of a tribe and not representative of the body.

MR. SEMPLE: There will be no action taken—the resolutions are only to be read. What is your further pleasure?

MR. BRUNER: I move that we adjourn.

NED BLACKFOX (through interpreter Richard Glory) presented copies of various old treaties entered into by and between the United States and various Indian Tribes and asked consideration of their merit in connection with the bill.

MR. COLLIER: What the speakers have just said is not altogether aside from the mark. The United States, in these treaties, which he refers to, made undertakings and broke them. You have suits pending that are seeking damages on account of those broken treaties but money payment by itself cannot restore what was taken away from you when those treaties were broken, because the treaties pledged you freedom and self-determination. The right of organization of home rule. When those rights were taken away from you, there was not a way to restore them except by new legislation.

I think it is quite true to say that the Wheeler-Howard Bill does re-create the heart of the old treaties. It is the way in which lands can be restored to you which were wrongfully taken from you. It is the way in which your tribal life, insofar as it fits into the modern world, can be reborn and it will be given full recognition.

This legislation does not abrogate any treaty or diminish any treaty but it will not establish some of your most precious rights, pledged to you by treaties, then taken away in violation. Now before you adjourn, I want to leave a thought with you and I hope you will take it away. I spoke today of the fact that so far as I knew, there were only three Presidents who had cared a great deal about the Indian—Washington, Lincoln, in his last days, and Franklin Roosevelt. We have come to the time when the thought of the country is directed to your problems and your needs.

I carry you back to 1928 when the Indian Investigation by the Senate began. Some of you will remember how hard the Indian Bureau fought to prevent that investigation and you will remember how that investigation smashed into existing affairs and year by year that committee has gone on piling up its findings. I think there are twenty-eight printed volumes of those hearings. They are monumental pieces of work. First, under Senator Frazier, then under Senator Wheeler. Last year, the result of that investigation was summarized on the Senate Floor in an epoch-making speech by Senator King of Utah. I presume a good many of you have received copies of that great speech. It is the most valuable document on the Indian situation in existence in my judgment.

An administration had come into power in 1929 pledged to obtain various legislative reform but it did not fight for its program. It gave friendly service but it made no effort to put through its program in Congress, and finally President Roosevelt came in and appointed an extraordinarily strong man for Secretary of the Interior—Secretary Ickes, a man of great power to the Government, great force of character and mind—and I do not think there has ever been a Secretary of the Interior who cares about the Indian problem as he does. His interest goes back many years of time as a citizen. In addition, another man came into the cabinet under President Roosevelt—Secretary Wallace. Many of you may not know this, but Secretary Wallace has a burning interest in the Indian matter. It is one of the deepest things in his life. This interest in Indians is almost a religion with him and he has a great deal of wisdom about the Indian race and its needs.

So we have two powerful men in the cabinet, two dominant men of the cabinet who want to do the right thing. We have as Chairman of the House Committee, a man whom most of you know, Edgar Howard of Nebraska, who has been the pillar of strength of the Indians in the House for many, many years. In the Senate, we have Mr. Wheeler and you all know about Senator Wheeler. Both Committees are strong and they are made up of friends of the Indians.

Now it is a remarkable set-up that we have, with a President more popular than any president in our lifetime, with almost irresistible driving force, and with Congress itself all ready to go the limit in behalf of the Indians and with a Cabinet actively friendly to the Indians. I could mention other members of the Cabinet but I have said enough.

If you all are readers of the newspapers and magazines you will be aware of the fact that there is a vast amount of public attention focused on your problems right now. It is a time that the Indians have been waiting for a long, long number of years. The time when the Indian can get anything within reason. Nobody can tell how long that situation is going to last. There are many accidents that might occur and change public opinion. Crises may come that will take the Indian out of the national conscience. In the history of countries and peoples, there comes a time when everything is possible. There are moments of destiny and if they pass by—are not used—it may be too late. It is in the lines of Shakespeare that we all learned in school, that:

> "There is a tide in the affairs of man,
> Which, taken at the flood, leads on to fortune;
> Omitted, all the voyage of their life
> Is bound in shallows and in miseries."

The only reason why I think there is a need for reasonable haste in connection with this Indian legislation is that if you want it, now is the time to get it. If you wait too long then want it, the time may have passed and the opportunity gone. Our Indians in the United States are so far gone, his property so mismanaged, that the Indian cannot wait another twenty or thirty years until the clock again runs round to his hour. The present may be the last chance of the Indian. Especially is this true in Oklahoma. You are not going to get emancipation and a clearing up of your situation down here unless you have the attention of the country and the whole attention fixed upon your needs. The problem of Oklahoma Indians is going to be met by National Public opinion.

You have it now. You did not have it five years ago. You may not have it two years from now. Do not think I am asking you to rush into endorsement of this Wheeler-Howard Bill. Not at all. Personally, I am more interested in getting the opinion of hostile critics than I am in getting the endorsement of anybody for the Bill. I value very highly the interest of Mr. Bruner and Mr. Grady Lewis in picking out the flaws and I want them to keep on, but I am anxious to convey to you that this probably is your chance—this year or next year—and that if you slip up on it, pass it by, we may never be able to bring about a situation where you will again be in control of your own fate. You are now.

It is possible when the thing is looked back upon for years to come, you will see the whole length of history of the Indians pointing to the years 1934–35. Everything will lead to that point and away from that point. It is a moment to feel very serious and very much in earnest, to use your best brains and I can assure you that with all my heart, we are trying to find the right way, we are looking for a better way, if there is one. We want to improve these bills in their details, to make them better. If we can find a way to make them better fundamentally in some definite way, we will adopt it.

I have been very much inspired by these Congresses, which I have attended. Unfortunately this Congress was too brief. One day is not long enough. Wherever it has been possible to spend enough days, the way we did in the plains country where we spent four and one-half days and nights, the Indians have contributed the most fundamental and stimulating ideas. They have shown in every case that they have had the stamina necessary to solve their own problems. I know that it would be manifested here, could we remain two or three days. You have heard and we have discussed the bill briefly. We could hardly do more than touch upon it because we have not sufficient time.

I have had most of my staff out of Washington for about a month. Assistant Commissioner, the Director of Property, Director of Lands, the law force, everybody, until the wheels have nearly stopped in Washington. The time has come when we have got to get back there or something will go badly wrong administratively. I hope we at least have impressed you with the fact that we are seeking alongside of you for the answer. That we truly want to solve your problems. That we are not trying to have you act as yes-men to the administration.

I have felt here all day long a wonderfully generous tolerant happy spirit in you. The whole day has been for me a refreshing and encouraging one. I go away from here feeling strengthened and more responsible to the Indians. I am sure we all carry that feeling away and I have no doubt at all that when you arrive at your conclusion, after mature thought, consideration and discussion, it is going to be a wise conclusion which we will accept without hesitation and the Congress will accept.

MR. SEMPLE: What is the pleasure of the body?

Mr. Ward requests that the Organization of Unrestricted Indians of the Muskogee Creek Nation be allowed to read their Resolution.

MR. COLLIER: Any resolution which has a bearing on the Wheeler-Howard bill will be made a part of the record.

THE SUPREME ORGANIZATION OF THE UNRESTRICTED INDIANS
OF THE MUSKOGEE CREEK NATION
—1932—

Accepted by Petition to the Commissioner of the Five Civilized Tribes. Approved and Registered With Commissioner of [Indian] Affairs, Washington, D.C.

1110 East Randolph
OKMULGEE, OKLAHOMA

RESOLUTION
OF THE UNRESTRICTED INDIAN
ORGANIZATION

TO ALL TO WHOM THESE PRESENT SHALL COME GREETING:

WHEREAS, THE UNRESTRICTED INDIAN ORGANIZATION OF THE MUSKOGEE CREEK NATION Has assembled in The City of Beggs, County of Okmulgee, State of Oklahoma. This the 19, day of March, 1934, for the purpose of the discussion of the WHEELER-HOWARD INDIAN RIGHTS BILL (S. 2755; H.R. 7902) now pending in Congress. AND WHEREAS, The National Commissioner of Indian Affairs, Mr. John C. Collier, will be in the State of Oklahoma, between the dates of March, the 19, and 22, 1934, to Elect Delegates to confer with him on said bill.

WHEREAS, The said Commission to the Five Civilized Tribes, or its lawful successor, has presented to Congress, by Mr. Howard, on February 12, 1934, and referred to the committee on Indian Affairs, the above mention bill.

NOW THEREFORE, We the undersigned, Officers of The Unrestricted Indian Organization, of the Muskogee Creek Nation, with its duly Elected Delegates, to confer with The Honorable National Commissioner of Indian Affairs, Mr. John C. Collier, by Resolution. Be it inacted that this Resolution be adopted and approved, and become a part of the records [of the] local Convention of the Creek Tribe of Indians now assembled, of the Muskogee Creek Nation, on the 22, day of March, 1934, and the said resolution, be given to the Honorable John C. Collier, the National Commissioner of Indian Affairs.

BE IT FURTHER RESOLVED, that the Representatives of the Unrestricted Indian Organization, of the Muskogee Creek Nation, do now regret, of the inability of the Muskogee Creek Tribe of Indians, now assemble in a convention, of being able to approve or disapprove of the Wheeler-Howard Bill, and that said bill can only be discussed for further information.

FIRST, For the reason that on March the 4, 1906, The Creek National Council, of the Muskogee Creek Nation, was abolished. And the Creek Tribe of Indians are now divided into several local Organizations, further reasons that the Creek Tribe of Indians do not have a National Organization, and therefore this convention now assembled on this the 22, day of March, 1934, for the purpose of hearing the discussion of said bill, shall not be as of record as a National Convention, as far as the Creek Indians of Muskogee Creek Nation, is concerned.

BE IT FURTHER RESOLVED, That before the said bill now pending in Congress a National Issue, can be legally approved, or disapproved, The Creek Indians of the Muskogee Creek Nation, shall have to comply with the act of Congress March the 1, 1901, and were ratified by the Creek National Council in 1902, and the Act of April 26, 1906, as shown in Indian Land Laws, Page 487, Sec. 598, and that the said Act read as follows.

PROVIDES THAT NO ACT, ORDINANCE OR RESOLUTION (Except resolution of adjournment) of the Tribal Council or Legislative of any of said Tribes or Nation shall be of any validity until approved by the President of the United States. Further provides that no contract involving the payment or expenditure of any or affecting any property belonging to any of said tribes or nations made by them or any of them or by any officer thereof, shall be of any validity until approved by the President of the United States. And for such reason any resolution that may be passed on or vote taken in this convention, that is not in accord with the Act of Congress March the 1, 1901, could not expect the Indorsement or approval of the President, of the United States.

THEREFORE BE IT RESOLVED, That this convention now assembled, urge that in as much that the Restricted Indians have a Organization, and the Unrestricted Indians of the Muskogee Creek Nation, have a Organization. That the said Organizations should come together and perfect a National Organization, and that the said National Organization shall call a National Convention, that we may be able to intelligently pass on the WHEELER-HOWARD bill, or any other matters pertaining to the Muskogee Creek Nation, with a National committee from a National Convention, as by the act of Congress March the 1, 1901, Ratified by the Creeks May 25, 1901, as a Sect. 451, Art. 33, page 430, of Indian Land Laws.

BE IT INACTED, That the WHEELER-HOWARD bill be tabled until such time that a National Organization Council, can be perfected, as follows.

FIRST: President, Vice President, Secretary, Asst. Sect., Treasurer, Auditors, Interpreter, National Translator, and six (6) National Delegates, Whose Duties shall be to oppose all measures looking toward the territorialization or sectionization of our public domain. Or any change in our present relations, with the United States Government. They shall represent in all other matters the interest of the Muskogee Creek People members and citizens of the Tribe, in such a way as will be most for the welfare of the Indian race.

BE IT FURTHER RESOLVED, That the members of the National Organization Council, of the Muskogee Creek Nation, be elected from the Restricted Indian Organization, and the Unrestricted Indian

Organization, as near equal as possible, and the same be submitted to His Excellency, Franklin D. Ro[o]sevelt, President of the United States, for his approval.

Which is in accord with the supplemental agreement of March 1, 1901, and that no agreement pertaining to the Creek Tribal Affairs and the United States Government shall not be valid without the signature of Two-thirds majority of the said representatives of the Muskogee National Organization Creek Council, as the vote of the members and citizens of Creek Nation, National Organization Council, when such Organization have been perfected.

BE IT FURTHER RESOLVED, That this Organization, The Unrestricted Indian Organization, of The Muskogee Creek Nation, in compliance with the Act of Congress April 26, 1906, Sec. 598, send a copy of this resolution, to his Excellency, Franklin D. Roosevelt, President of the United States, as of our actions in this convention now assembled.

IN WITNESS WHEREOF, We the Members of the Unrestricted Indian Organization, of the Muskogee Creek Nation, and members and citizens of the Creek Nation, and as members of the Resolution Committee, have hereunto set our hands, the day and year above mention,

And present to you for your approval,

Respectfully submitted,

Lewis Adams
Chairman of the Committee,
Tvoma J. Adams
Sarah Grayson Naw Brown

(ATTESTED And APPROVED)
Date. March 19, 1934
C. W. Ward, Chairman of the Unrestricted Indian Organization.
Date. March 19, 1934
Washington Adams, Secretary of The Unrestricted Indian Organization.

DELEGATES AS REPRESENTATIVES OF THE UNRESTRICTED INDIAN ORGANIZATION
OF THE MUSKOGEE CREEK NATION
TO CONFER WITH MR. JOHN C. COLLIER, NATIONAL COMMISSIONER OF INDIAN AFFAIRS.

C. W. Ward
J. T. Ward — Creek Census Cort 3378, Rule #9333
Washington Adams — Creek Census Cort 3791

MR. WM. O. ADAMS of Bartlesville: I want to request permission to ask a few questions. I want to ask the Commissioner if the Wheeler-Howard Bill is coming up before the present session of Congress.

ANSWER: It is already before this session.

QUESTION: Do you think it will be voted on?

ANSWER: That, I cannot say. Nobody can say. Nobody can tell when Congress will adjourn.

QUESTION: Regarding the so-called Indian claims bill. Is that coming before them?

ANSWER: No, we may be able to get it introduced but there is no chance of counting on it at this session.

QUESTION: Of course you know how the Cherokees are scattered in Washington County. We have perhaps 1500 Cherokees including the Delawares and Shawnees and you said a few minutes ago that, should this bill pass that Indians scattered over the district would be branches of so-called colonies. According to your bill I believe we could form an organization. I hope we could if we could get a charter. We want to stay right there.

MR. COLLIER: I don't mean that every Cherokee would have to be organized under one organization but in many cases that is the way it would be done. Take a big tribe scattered over a large area—say 25,000 square miles in the Navajo country, organized into sub-divisions under their one charter. The same thing could be done in Oklahoma by any of the Five Civilized Tribes but there is no cut and dried way of doing this. The only thing to be sure about is that whatever organization be adopted, equity in tribal property must remain undisturbed. They could organize a group of the Cherokees at any time if they want to. They have no organization at present.

QUESTION: Could they join with another group if they wished.

ANSWER: That is entirely up to the Indians.

MR. BEN CARPENTER (Shawnee) asks to be recognized: I represent a little tribe of Indians—Shawnees, located in Craig County in the Cherokee Nation. We do not know that we need to organize. We get along and we are satisfied just like we are—we are satisfied now. Satisfied with the Government in every way. We fought for peace and we are tickled with just what we have got and we are thankful that the Commissioner got to come down here and talk to us Indians. That's all we ask. A little later on we might come in with them. Thank you very much.

MR. SEMPLE: The Chair will state that is the first tribe that I ever knew that is entirely satisfied. The Chair is authorized to state that the Commissioner's staff, particularly his legal staff, will be here in the Indian office tomorrow and can be seen by any people interested or any tribe who wants to come and see the Commissioner's legal staff and that they may be found on the third floor of the Federal Building in the Superintendent's office. They will be there for a while during the morning.

MR. COLBERT: Renewal of motion for adoption and approval of the Wheeler-Howard Bill.

[MR. SEMPLE:] Chair is inclined to believe the motion is not appropriate at this time inasmuch as there are many of the tribes who desire to deliberate further and the Commissioner would really like those who have constructive suggestions to be given time to make them so they will be heard and considered, so the Chair is inclined to think that we should not at this time either approve or disapprove the bill in question:

MR. BRUNER: Motion to adjourn.

CHAIR: The chair will state to those who desire to meet the Commissioner or the Commissioner's staff, you can find him by calling at the Indian office tomorrow. He will be gone by noon and those who want to see him will bring any suggestions and present them before noon tomorrow.

Motion for adjournment seconded. Meeting adjourned.

Moody Convention Hall,
Moody, Oklahoma.
March 9, 1934.

Mr. A. M. Landman,
The Five Civilized Tribes,
Muskogee, Oklahoma.
Dear Sir:

We the Cherokee Emigrant Indian Committee held a meeting during March 9, 1934, at Moody Convention Hall at Moody, Oklahoma.

We have decided that at the meeting that our wants is a Treaty. Which was made in December 29, day of 1835, 1836, 1846. Now this is our own Treaty so we cannot exchange with any other laws or make any other Treaty. In reference to our Treaty of 1835, -36,-46. Which the Treaty was made by our forefathers with the United States of America forever to our Homestead.

You promise to us that you will work faithfully with our problem that will come before you, and get whatever we call for. We are asking you to get our Treaty back just like it was before and let us run it ourselves.

Now, we are asking you to present us The Cherokee Emigrant [Indian Committee] to the Commissioner John Collier. And there will be a short speech made by The Principal Chief Of Cherokee Nation.

COMMITTEE

Names	Post-office
Noah Bunch	Stillwell Oklahoma
Sam Summerfield	Spavinaw Oklahoma
Famous Deul	Oaks Oklahoma
Charley Summerfield	Spavinaw Oklahoma
Leach Summerfield	Zena Oklahoma

CHAIRMAN OF COMMITTEE

White Youngbird	Oaks Oklahoma

Assign by Principal Chief of Cherokee Nation
Ned Blackfox, Oaks, Oklahoma
Ass. Chief of Cherokee Nation.
George Duck, Stillwell, Oklahoma

(Article 2.) Of the Treaty May 6, 1828 (7 Stat. 311) The United States in order to secure to the Cherokee nation a permanent agree[ment] to possess the Cherokee and to guarantee it to them forever seven millions (7,000,000) acres of land within described boundaries and in addition guarantee to the Cherokee Nation a perpetual outlet west in a free unmolested use of all the country line west of the Western boundaries of the above described limits, as far west as the sovereignty of the United States and the right soil extend.

(Article 1.) Of the Treaty of February 14, 1833 (7 Stat. 414) The United States by a correct description as to the seven millions acres of tract renewed the guarantee to such a tract, etc. contained in (article 2) of the treaty of 1828 with reservation respecting use by other Indians of the Salt Plains if within the limit of the outlet. The article concluded with the statement that "letters patent should be issued by United States as soon as practicable for the land hereby granted."

(Article 2) Of the Treaty of December 29, 1835 (7 Stat. 478). After reciting that by the treaties of 1828—1833. The United States guaranteed and secured to be conveyed by the patent to the Cherokee of Indians a described seven millions [acres] of land and had further guaranteed to the Cherokee Nation a perpetual outlet west etc. ceded an additional eight millions acres of land.

(Article 3) Of the same treaty of the United States. Also agreed—That the land above ceded by the treaty of February 14, 1833 including the outlet, and those ceded by this treaty, Shall all be included in one patent executed to the Cherokee Nation of the Indians of the President of the United States. According to the provision of the act of May 28, 1830. The Treaty Of May 6, 1828 and the supplementary treaty thereto of February 14, 1833 with the Mississippi the United States guaranteed and secured to be conveyed by patent, to the Cherokee Nation Of Indians that the agree to give Cherokee Nation of Indians Of Seven Millions of acres of land thus provided for and bounded, the United States further guaranty to the Cherokee Nation a perpetual outlet west and a free and unmolested use of all the country west of the western boundary of said seven millions acres, as far as west as a sovereignty of the United States and their right of soil extend.

(Article 7) Perpetual peace and friendship shall exist between the citizen of the United States and the Cherokee Indians. The United States agree to protect the Cherokee Nation from the domestic strife and foreign enemies and against intestine wars between the tribes. They shall endeavor to preserve and maintain the peace of the country, and not make war upon their neighbor and should hostilities commence by one or more tribes upon another, the Cherokee Council of the nation, when called upon by the authorities by the President of the United States shall aid the United States with as many warriors as may be deemed necessary to protect and restore peace in Indian country, and while in service they shall be entitled to pay and rations of the army of the United States. They shall also be protected against all intrusion and interruption from the citizens of the United States who may attempt to settle in the Country without their consent; and all such persons shall be removed from the same order to the President of the United States. But this is not Intended to Prevent the residence among them of useful farmers, mechanics, and teachers for the instruction of the Indians. According to the treaty stipulations, and the regulations of the government of the United States.

RESOLUTION

RESOLVED BY THE INDIAN WOMEN'S CLUB OF TULSA, OKLAHOMA

In view of the fact that many American Indians residing in the State of Oklahoma are highly educated, filling positions of responsibility, both in national, state, county and City offices, we feel that our people are fully competent to have charge of Indian affairs in all departments in the State of Oklahoma.

Therefore, we, the members of the Indian Women's Club of Tulsa, of nearly one-hundred members and representing ten different tribes, affiliated with the State and General Federation of Clubs, earnestly request the Secretary of the Interior, Honorable Harold Ickes, and the United States Commissioner of

Indian Affairs, Honorable John Collier, to give serious consideration to making such appointments in Oklahoma.

Respectfully submitted,
Mrs. Nan Lowery Hitchens, President
Mrs. Emily Wade Breshears, Secretary

LEGISLATIVE COMMITTEE.
Mrs. S. R. Lewis, Chair.
Lilah D. Lindsey
Lena F. Barnard

RESOLUTION

RESOLVED BY THE INDIAN WOMEN'S CLUB OF TULSA, OKLAHOMA.

Our attention has been called to the fact that many of our Indians in isolated districts are in dire need.

THEREFORE BE IT RESOLVED: That the United States Commissioner of Indian Affairs investigate and provide for our needy Indians in remote districts and urge the Field Agents to give special attention to that class of our people, since the Indians, as a rule are too timid to assert their rights or ask for assistance.

Respectfully submitted,
Mrs. Nan Lowery Hitchens, President
Mrs. Emily Wade Breshears, Secretary

LEGISLATIVE COMMITTEE.
Mrs. S. R. Lewis, Chair.
Lilah D. Lindsey
Lena F. Barnard

RESOLUTION

RESOLVED BY THE INDIAN WOMEN'S CLUB OF TULSA, OKLAHOMA

RESOLVED: That the Haskell Institution Indian School at Lawrence, Kansas, be made a University for Indian children with an advanced curriculum, second to none, thereby preparing our Indian students to compete with any students in fields of higher education.

Respectfully submitted,
Mrs. Nan Lowery Hitchens, President
Mrs. Emily Wade Breshears, Secretary

LEGISLATIVE COMMITTEE.
Mrs. S. R. Lewis, Chair.
Lilah D. Lindsey
Lena F. Barnard

RESOLUTION

RESOLVED BY THE INDIAN WOMEN'S CLUB OF TULSA, OKLAHOMA

RESOLVED: That some provision be made for a Home for Aged Indians who need a home and comforts in their declining years.

Respectfully submitted,
Mrs. Nan Lowery Hitchens, President
Mrs. Emily Wade Breshears, Secretary

LEGISLATIVE COMMITTEE.
Mrs. S. R. Lewis, Chair
Lilah D. Lindsey
Lena F. Barnard

State of Oklahoma,
Muskogee,
March 22, 1934

TO HONORABLE JOHN COLLIER, COMMISSIONER.

Honored Gentlemen:

We, the Cherokees by blood and the Citizens of the eastern part of Oklahoma and members of the Eastern Emmigrant and Western Cherokees legally organized under the laws of the State of Oklahoma, compromising Delaware, Adair, Cherokee, Sequoyah and the eastern part of Mayes County favor the immediate enactment of the Wheeler-Howard Indian Rights Bill (S. #2755, H.R. 7902).

We believe this is the only Bill that has ever been introduced in Congress to correct the allotment system, enabling the Indians to get their lands into usable [blocks] and providing the machinery and authority for restoring homes to the landless. Most essential parts, extends benefits to all the Indians, not exclusively to the allotted Indians. The Bill seeks to establish the legal conditions through which the Indians will be released from economic and social imprisonment, and will begin to work out a real happiness in America for all Indians.

James Foster, Vian, Oklahoma,
National Chairman.
C. F. Buzzard, Jay, Oklahoma,
Vice-National Chairman.
S. W. Peak, Jay, Oklahoma,
National Secretary and Interpreter.

Eli Teehee, Colcord, Oklahoma,
2nd Vice Nat'l Chairman.

CHIEF FIRE, Gore, Oklahoma

RESOLUTION

At a meeting of the Nighthawk Kee-too-wah Society, an organization of full-blood Indians with a membership of 6,000, held at their stomp grounds Northeast of Gore, in Sequoyah county, Oklahoma, on the 10th day of March, 1934, the following resolution was unanimously passed:

WHEREAS, Senate Bill #2755 introduced by Mr. Wheeler by request on the 6th day of February, 1934, in the Senate of the United States and entitled "A Bill," to grant to Indians living under Federal tutelage the freedom to organize for purposes of local self-government and economic enterprise; to provide for the necessary training of Indians in administrative and economic affairs; to conserve and develop Indian lands; and to promote the more effective administration of justice in matters affecting Indian tribes and communities by establishing a Federal Court of Indian Affairs.

WHEREAS, said Senate Bill #2755 was thoroughly discussed by the members of the Nighthawk Kee-too-wah Society, and said members, having a thorough understanding of the same, heartily approve the contents thereof, believing that it is to the best interests of this Society that this bill should become a law.

BE IT RESOLVED that it is the desire of our Society that Senate Bill #2755 be passed by Congress and become a <u>Law</u>.

BE IT FURTHER RESOLVED that a copy of this resolution be delivered to the Honorable John Collier, Commissioner of Indian Affairs when he visits Muskogee on the 22nd day of March, 1934, and that copies be sent to the Honorables T. P. Gore and Elmer Thomas, to each member of Congress from Oklahoma, to the Chairman of the Committee on Indian Affairs and to the Honorable Mr. Wheeler.

Sam Smith
John Redbird Smith
Wm. Rogers
Lincoln Towie

John Johnson
Tom Smith
Stake Smith

CHIEFS OF THE NIGHTHAWK KEE-TOO-WAH SOCIETY.

Meeting in United States Courtroom, March 23, 1934. Meeting had begun before stenographers arrived.

QUESTION: If a group organizes and incorporates itself, holding their land in different states, will that group be tax free?

ANSWER: Yes, the land that is tax free now would be kept tax free. The bill contemplates that when a community is formed it is for a definite reason, but not necessarily just to escape taxes.

QUESTION: My mother, who received an allotment, is on the roll and I am not. If she turned her property over to the community, would I ever inherit any of that?

ANSWER: You would inherit whatever she wanted you to have. Nothing can be done that will destroy inherited rights. Property must descend. The thing that descends might not be that particular property, but an equal value, regardless of whether or not you are in the community.

QUESTION: With reference to the Choctaw and Chickasaw communities, where there are two projects under the C.W.A., is it the purpose to continue those under this bill?

ANSWER: They could come under the bill. They are being done now because they are needed.

QUESTION: Is it the purpose of the Department to recommend payment to the tribes as a whole for the land taken for this community?

ANSWER: I had not thought of it. This particular thing grew out of an idle land proposition.

QUESTION: How are you to limit rights?

ANSWER: Where a colony like that was established on tribal land, the preference would be given to those not having any land, those born since allotment. The bill provides for unused land, new land, the preference would always be given to the Indian who has been out of luck until now. As to whether or not the Government would pay the tribe the money, I do not know. I do not see why the Government would do that.

QUESTION: How many acres in these projects?

ANSWER: About 3,000 in one; about 2,700 in the other.

QUESTION: Would it be admissible to offer for us as a preamble the old Cherokee Law as abrogated at Statehood, to be included in our operative Cherokee community.

ANSWER: I see no reason why those laws could not be considered; the charter would be formed as a matter of agreement between the Secretary and the community. I believe there is a similar case in New Mexico. The New Mexico Pueblos got their grants a long time ago in Spain, and subsequently they became laws under the territory of New Mexico, and the Supreme Court later declared that they were municipal corporations. These prior rights would be confirmed under charter. Your charter would do the same thing. I have no doubt that the Eastern Cherokees will want to incorporate in the charter their rights. The treaty would be fully concerned in drawing the charter. The Indians themselves will make the charter.

QUESTION: What steps would these communities have to take in going about organizing themselves?

ANSWER: As far as formal steps are concerned the way it is put down in the act; first, by petition saying that they want to organize. Then the Secretary must grant that petition by issuing the charter or issue a public finding as to why he cannot grant it. That finding goes to Congress as a report from the Secretary. The next step, supposing he did grant it—the tribe has either worked out its charter, or it will, and it would undoubtedly want to consult with the Superintendent and someone from Washington. When the charter was finally perfected, there would probably be a tribal committee appointed to frame it. When it was finished it would be submitted to a public vote of the adult members of that tribe or community.

QUESTION: Is the petition to be signed by those who want to organize?

ANSWER: Yes, the election is held and the charter cannot become a law, except by a vote of 3/5 of those who vote.

QUESTION: Is this situation not a bit peculiar in Oklahoma?

ANSWER: The voting will be done by those who reside within the territory for which the charter is to be issued; otherwise when a new colony is to be formed on entirely new land, the charter is set up and thrown open to groups of Indians of 1/4 or more degree blood; so that in most instances the colonies in Oklahoma will probably be composed of people not resident now of the territory to be established. There might not be any vote by them; the bill might be changed so that they would have a vote, but that would be extraordinary. It would be a very difficult task to find the voters. There will not be much voting done in Oklahoma, except where communities are to be established on lands now partly occupied by Indians, and then only by those resident in that territory. After a charter has been adopted, the power of amendment rests with the members of the community. Probably a charter if adopted for new communities will be made very elementary, then the members would proceed to perfect that charter. Probably every charter issued would be changed many times by the members of the community before they got what they wanted.

QUESTION: In your referendum vote on the charter, the question arises—would the women be entitled to vote?

ANSWER: The bill reads "adult members." If women are not in the habit of voting, they would not vote. There are some places where no women would vote, but that is another case of not wanting to raise the woman suffrage proposition in this bill.

QUESTION: Then if there were only 5 people who voted, and 3 voted for it and 2 against it, it would pass?

ANSWER: Yes.

QUESTION: If these 5 were the only ones out of a community of 10,000 to vote, would their vote control the entire community?

ANSWER: Yes, it would control the entire tribe. A community that had 10,000 people in it, and only 5 were interested enough to vote, they would never vote at all.

QUESTION: Supposing, which is the case here, a lot of the Indian population is located in the rocks and hills, and they want a charter. Supposing that while they made application, an examination reveals that the country in which they are located is an unfit place in which to try to fix a community.

ANSWER: Either they would tell the Department so, or the Department would tell them. Of course, if they still wanted to organize in that area, there is no reason why they should not be allowed to do it. It would be up to the Commissioner to find something more suitable. (*Here the Commissioner gave an illustration as to western tribes which have dealt with this problem.*)

QUESTION: In getting these communities, that does not confine it just to the State of Oklahoma, does it?

ANSWER: Oh no, not at all. Anywhere that they want to go, and can show the Government that the land is worth having.

QUESTION: Suppose that our people are capable of handling their own affairs and suppose that we obtained a charter. Now, is it possible through this bill for that organization as a whole to take over the work in the education, health, farm extension service, etc.? Could we become the Indian Bureau as far as the tribe is concerned?

ANSWER: Completely. When a tribe is capable of taking over, say, schools, health services, etc., then the Secretary transfers that authority along with the property to the tribe, and the tribe receives money from Congress. If the tribe does not make a success, it can be brought back. If it is a success, it can finally take over anything.

QUESTION: Then suppose that is as far as we want to go. Would we under the bill have to go into establishing these communities?

ANSWER: No. But suppose there was a group of Choctaws who wanted to go further into organizing. That also could be done, either by receiving a charter from the tribe, or if preferred they could get it straight from the Government.

QUESTION: Suppose we did not want to undertake the type of community outlined in the bill and wanted to establish one peculiarly fitting our own people.

ANSWER: That is exactly what you are expected to do. Conditions and customs are too different. I think the thing is going to be done very much the same way Spain worked it out under the laws of the Indies. (*Here the Commissioner gave in detail the condition of the tribes in Mexico.*)

QUESTION: Suppose that we had secured our charter, and wanted to go down here and establish a particular type of community along this line, concentrating the Indians in that community, but not taking their title away from them, and putting it into a community, so we can get those various services to them easier. We want to have cooperative marketing, but we still want to do everything to keep our children in the public schools. Can we do this under this bill?

ANSWER: You may establish such a community under this bill. The bill provides that such a community can enter into contractual relations with the State and by that method can actually use Federal money to procure State aid for themselves. Peculiar to the Indian situation, all of this can be done in a safe way; that is, the authority of Congress is ultimate. The guardianship by the Government is contemplated in the constitution. It is established very deep in our law, so that it is possible for all of this to be done, and if it does not succeed you can abandon it and fall back into the original guardianship.

QUESTION: If this bill fails, we go back under the Government?

ANSWER: Yes, same as the old system.

QUESTION: The original boundaries of the Creek Nation are—on the north and east by the Arkansas River; on the south by the Canadian River; and on the west by the Seminole Nation. In case the Creeks decide to keep their own original Creek Nation, would it be possible that they could do so under the bill as it is presented?

ANSWER: Part of it, yes, but possibly not all of it. It would cost too much to buy up all of that land. Moreover, would you have any use for all of that land?

QUESTION: Most of the land is occupied. Most of the Creeks would object to being moved out.

ANSWER: They would not be moved out. It is optional. If you multiply there is no reason to believe that you would not eventually get back all of that land. If the birth rate of the whites continues to diminish and the Indians continue to multiply, and the death rate among the Indian grows smaller in comparison to the whites, the Indians will soon take more land and the whites less.

CHICKASAW REPRESENTATIVE: We are glad to have had this chance to talk to you and hear the explanation of this bill, and at this time we want to publicly say that we are happy and glad to have had the opportunity to talk to you. They are beginning to get restless and want to go home. I want to repeat one little gem that was given this morning by Mr. Gibbs: "I am in favor of this bill, because every morning our children will be Indians."

ANSWER: I want to say one thing more. You may have seen in the morning paper a statement by Secretary Ickes about the bill warning Indians about being misled by real estate operators. There has been a great deal of that misleading in material in the Northwestern areas.

He did not mention one other thing which I think it is perfectly fair to mention. As far as I know the most systematic misleading that has been going on, has not been by those above named, but by another influence. A document in four pages has been broadcast and signed by Mr. Lindquist. Mr. Lindquist has been here in Muskogee, and most all over the Indian country attempting to fight this bill by organizing missionaries. I do know that in one place after another where I go, a missionary will come to me and ask if it is true that we are trying to put them out of business, and if it will be possible to do so. The statement of Mr. Lindquist is that the bill is an attempt to pull you all back into savagery; into the blanket, etc.; that it is an attempt to revive things as they were a long time ago.

I know perfectly well that the majority of the Indians are never going to sit down and read this bill word for word for themselves, and hence a lot of people are likely to believe Mr. Lindquist. I can only say that the description of the bill and the conclusions drawn from the descriptions are totally untrue, and do not have anything to do with the bill at all. The bill contains complete guarantee of the constitutional rights; it gives every Indian all constitutional rights. The bill is the most important step taken toward giving the Indian full opportunity of education in the white world. It is built for that purpose; to give Indians the opportunity to go out into the great world to get an education.

As to these communities, the bill is so drawn that the communities will be able to hitch up with every good thing going on in that part of the world, and the community itself will become possessed of financial organization, civic organization, so that the whole plan does nothing but set the Indian free; give him power. There seem to be some people who insist on working with the Indians and for them, but who are totally without faith in the Indians. They seem to be thinking that the Indian is no good and it is their duty to rescue the Indian from his no-good race. There are too many people like that who are working with Indians and who do not believe in them. Anyone who takes that view is going to be opposed to this bill.

I do not mean to imply that Mr. Lindquist and those associated with him want to kill off Indians or rob them, but they do seem filled with this idea—that the Indian is no good. You cannot love people very much if you do not believe in them. I say this because the propaganda is going on all the time, and the Indians want to be on their guard against it and insist upon knowing the facts.

[UNKNOWN SPEAKER:] On behalf of the little band of Indians whom I represent, the Red Men, and as to the great effort you have shown on behalf of these people and all the people called Red Men and Indians, on behalf of them we appreciate very much to see the good that you are trying to accomplish for the people. Most people I have found opposed to this bill are people who might be hard for them to prove their ancestral blood. Of course those that are known cannot be disputed, and we believe that the Commissioner of Indian Affairs is one white man with a red man's heart, and as far as my little band of Indians is concerned, we appreciate your efforts and think it is a great cause. The State of Oklahoma has demonstrated that they are trying to rid themselves of the Indians. The bill has been explained very thoroughly; the bill will be explained to the people whom I represent as best I know how. We thank you.

QUESTION: Some have indicated that because of this so-called segregation, there will be disfranchisement. Is that true?

ANSWER: The members of the Five Civilized Tribes are rather proud of the fact that they had the first opportunity to vote in the State and Nation. These two points we want made clear—the first, segregation; and another, disfranchisement. About disfranchisement—you understand clearly you have your franchise as citizens of the United States. In no way could you be deprived of it. Although the Oklahoma Indians have a franchise, yet because they have not been organized they have failed to secure protection. There are a lot of Oklahoma Indians. They would be an important element in the total vote, especially in primaries. The Indians of Oklahoma under this bill would become organized in such a way that they would be quite clear as to what they wanted done by the Government and Congress. They would be able to throw their vote in such a way that it would be just about controlling. I think that their use of the franchise would in the long run be made ten-fold in effectiveness by this bill. This is very important.

About segregation—Let me give you an example: It does not touch Indians. You have all been hearing about the Tennessee Valley Plan. The plan is for developing giant power and transporting it at lower prices. It has grown into what you may call the segregation plan, reaching about 200 miles in all directions from Knoxville, Tennessee. They are going to get various kinds of help; have their forests replanted, etc. That will become an organization within four different States. It has never occurred to the people there that they are going to be humiliated because of this segregation. They are going to have many advantages. They will build up their city and county life and their schools and become prosperous. That is the only kind of segregation that is really entailed in this bill, which means that the Indians are going to get a special, generous attention from the Government. The only meaning of segregation is not the one given by Mr. Lindquist, but is like that found in the Tennessee Valley now, where life is being planned in long-range understanding, to show that human life can be built up.

QUESTION: A citizen of Muskogee told me yesterday that under some plan of the Government they have asked about a million dollars for citizens in Muskogee to buy subsistence homesteads. Is this true?

ANSWER: As a matter of fact this plan of ours follows along after the subsistence homestead plan, and we have all over the country States, towns, counties clamoring for a chance to get in on the subsistence homestead scheme; that is, one for colonizing white people. Those who get in are very lucky people. The worst segregation is that caused by poverty.

REPRESENTATIVE of the Eastern Emigrant Cherokees: We hereby present to you in regard to the utmost favorable report to us, taking all consideration in due form, for our interest that we are deliberating pertaining to the situation by advising us the way, in stating the proposition, granting us for all procedure outlined by your suggestions, we now see fit, that, by you and by all the Department, not for your program, that our vast resources that we would be deprived by your assisting us as a party of our very earnest request from our own thinking, depending upon our Creator in trust, in gathering all special commendable relation to the Government, appealing to you now at the present time, to re-create, revive in our effort and your effort, so that according to various treaties is of true foundation of our civilization and progress—under these stipulations we are asking you to assist us in all features.

MR. COLLIER: Another example that bears on this segregation question: Beginning two or three years ago, everybody began to get wise to a condition in this country which is very serious; that is, wastage of soil by soil erosion, and it cost the country many billions of dollars every year. One of the first things President Roosevelt got busy on was this matter of soil erosion; and to begin with, $5,000,000 was set aside and large additional sums are to be set aside, and there was created a soil erosion service under the Government. It is not working everywhere; it is successfully working at present in twelve selected segregated areas. One is in Tennessee, one is in Wisconsin, one in Texas, one in the Navajo Reservation, and one in Southern Arizona, etc.

Before they go in to do their work, they require that all the land owners living inside the colonization area shall agree to certain things which require certain sacrifices. Everybody agrees that he won't overgraze his land; he must agree to come in and work with the Government in developing the engineering structures needed; and he must agree with respect to any timber that he owns, to cut it in such a way as to preserve the forest. After these agreements are signed up, only then does the soil erosion work begin and the people living in that area are segregated. Then the Government starts in with the work, not only of saving the soil but of helping in the development of industries and building up the whole economic life. This is exclusively within these twelve areas. The segregation is as complete as any Indian Reservation. I am in close touch with this service. They have been driven nearly crazy by petitions coming in from all over the United States. It never occurs to anybody that they are being segregated; they want this help. This is exactly the same thing that we are talking about. The Government is spending a million dollars at present at the Navajo Reservation, and is going to spend three million dollars more down there for that purpose. The segregation we are talking about in the soil erosion and in subsistence homesteads is nothing but a concentrated provision of needed help, which will lift that area to a higher plane of living. That is the purpose of this bill just as it is under soil erosion.

CHAPTER 11

MINUTES OF MEETING HELD AT MIAMI, OKLAHOMA, MARCH 24TH, 1934 BY COMMISSIONER OF INDIAN AFFAIRS COLLIER TO DISCUSS THE WHEELER-HOWARD INDIAN RIGHTS BILL WITH THE INDIANS OF THE QUAPAW AND OSAGE JURISDICTIONS

MR. ANDREWS, Supt. Quapaw Agency: The meeting will come to order now. We are gathered here to discuss things of vital importance to all Indians. It is one of those rare occasions when the Commissioner visits us, and so far as I know the first occasion of the Indians being consulted on matters concerning them. I think we will open this meeting by a little invocation by Mr. Victor Griffith, Quapaw.

Invocation by Mr. Griffith in the Quapaw Language.

We will have an address of welcome given by Mr. Ray McNaughton. Mr. McNaughton is an Indian belonging to this jurisdiction. Following Mr. McNaughton's address of welcome he will take charge of the meeting as chairman. Mr. McNaughton.

MR. MCNAUGHTON: Mr. Andrews, distinguished visitors and guests: It is indeed a privilege to appear before this audience here assembled to meet the representative of our Government who most directly has to deal with the Indian people, and were I to fail to at least say to our visitors and guests, and especially you people who are residents of reservations other than that in Ottawa County, something of the history of this jurisdiction, of this agency, something of the progress that has been made in the handling of Indian Affairs and welfare of the Indians, as well as the cause of this progress and of the changed and changing conditions, it seems to me I would be derelict in my duty.

Our Government in its wisdom from its very formation saw fit to deal with its Indian inhabitants in a manner separate and apart from the methods employed to deal with the other residents within its jurisdiction. In the Constitution of the United States it is provided that to the Federal Government is reserved the power to deal with the Indian Tribes. The Tribes now resident in Ottawa County, with the exception of the Modocs and a part of the Quapaws, have since the adoption of the Federal Constitution been within the jurisdiction of the United States. As to the Modoc, who is from the far West, and as to our Quapaw citizens, they came to the United States largely along with the Louisiana Purchase. These Quapaws resident in our country are probably the only natives of this particular jurisdiction.

The Cherokees, Senecas, Shawnees, Wyandottes, Ottawas, Peorias, Miamis, Weas, Kaskaskias, Piankishaws and Modocs all obtained their rights in this jurisdiction through lands that were purchased by the Government from the Quapaws or their brothers, the Osages, and later these lands were ceded or sold to these smaller tribes. These smaller tribes, that is the tribes named, excepting the Cherokees, were the remnants of small bands of Indians, those who were left from once powerful tribes that had been gradually driven back from the East and South.

These Indians, as they gradually moved westward met finally with the Indian policy on the part of the Federal Government about 1867, under which it was proposed that they would move the Indians then resident in the so-called western part of the then United States, and from the section in Illinois, Iowa, Indiana and Ohio into a country to be known as the Indian country. Soon after 1867 these lands were purchased and they were ideally located and situated for the purpose which the Government had in mind that was to cause our Indian people to properly be assimilated into the great mass of other

American citizens, in order that they might take their position and become a proper part of the governing body of this nation. This particular section, as I said, was ideally situated and located for this purpose. The Tribe of which I am a member, the Peorias, had come up from southern Illinois through a series of migrations, finally into Miami County, Kansas, and moved to here in the early seventies. Soon after removal of the small tribes of Indians to what is known as Ottawa County, shortly after 1867, the first agency was established here four miles west of Seneca. A little later the barracks that were used by the Government troops south of Baxter, Kansas, were transformed into an Indian school and an Indian school was established at Wyandotte. Later all those schools were consolidated and the agency was moved to Wyandotte and later to Miami.

The representatives of the Indian Office generally have been of the highest type of men. They have had the interest of our people at heart. They have strenuously endeavored to lift us up mentally as well as morally.

The lands of these various tribes were allotted beginning after the general allotment act in 1887. However, only a part of the lands in this agency were allotted under the act of 1887. The Confederated Tribes of Peorias, Miamis, Weas, was I believe the first tribe allotted. That allotment was 1890 and the restrictions on alienation expired in 1915 and were not extended. These were not trust patents but patents similar to those issued to the Quapaw Tribe in 1896. In other words fee patents were given them. Restrictions were extended as to part of our people in some tribes, particularly the Quapaw tribe, and it was extended to 1946.

My friends and distinguished guests, if while you have been in our community you have had occasion to visit our banks, our business houses, our lawyers' offices, our doctors' offices, and those of other professions, our mines, our farms, or other places of business, you have found that the Indians of Ottawa County, with the exception of a very small portion, have taken their place in the government and business of the county, State and Nation. We are proud of the accomplishments of our people. We feel we have been able to compete on equal terms with our white brethren. While many of our people have suffered reverses, that is also true of the white man, and I suggest to my people of Indian blood that if you go to the relief agencies in this county or any other county in which there are Indian residents in this section of the State, you will find a larger percentage of people of non-Indian blood asking for charity from the Government than you will our people. We are proud of our illustrious warriors who were our forefathers, even as our white friends are proud of Robin Hood and Daniel Boone, but we want our boys and girls to look up and look forward and take their places such as Vice-President Curtis, Senator Owen and Honorable W. W. Hastings, rather than to go back and to be of the hunting class.

Applause.

We welcome you, Mr. Commissioner, because we are appreciative of the things the Indian Office has done. We want to help; we want you as representative of the men who a great many of us, including myself, helped to put in power; we want you as a representative to help us with the new deal, because we realize that while we have gone forward, the limit is only the limit made by our own ability, and when you come to us as a representative of our Government and give us ways and means to still further raise ourselves up, you will have done us a great favor. It is a privilege to have you here with us and other representatives of your department. We are proud of the fact that we have a man in your high office who is so interested in our people as to go out and give us first hand information of what we may expect, and you may have first hand information of conditions that should be corrected. Doubtless there are many of our older people upon whom the protection should be continued, and we would be derelict in our duty as a nation if we fail to carry out that obligation, but I want to say to you, Mr. Commissioner, that so far as the average Indian citizen of Ottawa County, Oklahoma, is concerned he takes his place in every walk of life that every other man takes. He is of the governing class as well as the class of the governed. He is truly a representative citizen just as much as the descendants of the Scotch, Irish, French or German immigrant who came to our shores a short time ago. He needs no special privilege; he just needs a square deal. We believe, Mr. Commissioner, you are going to see that we get it.

Applause.

MR. COLLIER: Mr. Chairman and friends: Should it prove to be the case that a large number of Indian tribes whose representatives are gathered here—I think there are about ten tribes within this area and I presume some of their numbers are here—should it prove that this large group of Indian tribes represented have reached the point where they don't need any more Government aid and protection and don't require the expenditure of any more money by the Government, that will be good news to take back to Washington, because there are other Indians whose needs are so great that we will never have enough money to go around. I want to be very clear before I start on the general subject, that the legislation being put forward by the Administration, by President Roosevelt and his Secretary of the Interior, the legislation known as the

Wheeler-Howard Bill, is something that is being offered to each tribe if that tribe wants it, something that will be imposed on no tribe. Not only is it being offered only to those who want it, but the Administration has no desire to unduly influence any tribe or any member of any tribe into the direction of accepting the legislation. We are very much concerned with giving you the information so that you may act with your eyes open, with knowledge, so that you may either take something if you need it, or do without it if you don't need it, but not throw away an advantage if you do need it.

From one remark of the chair and the instant applause that met it, I am led to think that there is a certain misconception, which I have to deal with before anything else. The Chairman remarked that the Indians here did not want to be turned back into hunters; that they were citizens, responsible and powerful members of the general community and did not want to be turned back into hunters, that is, into old-fashioned reservation Indians, and there was an immediate applause. I think it must be in the minds of some of you at least that there is an idea that the Administration wants to turn you back into hunters, wants to put you back into some old condition and perhaps that this bill will have that effect. Such is not the case at all, as I hope to show you as we go ahead.

The Administration wants you to keep and enlarge all your citizenship, all of your participation in the world around you, all of your political and economic activities and power, and it is putting forward legislation designed to assist you to that end, and for those Indians who still need Government to aid and protection, whose properties still need to be kept off the tax rolls, who need educational help from the Government, who need financial help from the Government, for those Indians it is proposed to extend the aid, so that they may become whatever they want to be. But the Indians who don't need these things, don't want them, will be doing the Government and other Indians a kindness by saying so, because that will set free the limited money which we have, to be spent on those Indians who do have this need and do want it.

We have no desire to persuade you that you do need that thing that is being offered to the Indians at this time. As a matter of fact I believe you are going to conclude that you do need some of this help. I am not interested in persuading you that you do need it, but only in giving you the facts. I have been impressed by this, by the extraordinary haste of some Indian groups in registering their objections to the Wheeler-Howard Bill, or their desire not to be included in it. A half dozen of such protests were received so early that the bill had not had time to reach those Indians when the protests were filed. There wasn't a copy in existence in the neighborhoods where they were, and in another, a tribe got the bill one day and filed their protests the next, whereas it would take more than one day to thoroughly read and comprehend a 48-page bill. Such quick action, indicating panic or a feeling of fear, must mean that the tribes had certain ideas, preconceived ideas, or had been told things in advance about what the bill was going to contain and felt that something very dangerous was being threatened against them. I have met that in a number of parts of the country and tried to break down a fear and prejudice and to overcome ideas about the bill which are not correct.

The bill is different from those ideas, not the same thing at all. However, I think the best way to proceed is to ask you to let your minds travel along with me while I tell you, first, the reason why the Wheeler-Howard Bill was drawn up and introduced in Congress and then endorsed by the President, and then you will be able to see whether the matter has any bearing on your own situation or not.

You understand that the Government is responsible for the Indians all over the country, the Indians of Oklahoma and California, Washington, Oregon, Utah, Montana, South and North Dakota, Minnesota, Wisconsin, Michigan, Kansas, North Carolina, New Mexico, Arizona, all over; they are all of them, since the beginning of the Government, a peculiar responsibility of the Government. Nearly all of them have suffered great losses and wrongs at the hands of the Government in past years. Many of them expect and are entitled to a restitution for wrongs done them in the past, and in any event all of them are responsibilities of the Government, so declared in the Constitution of the United States and by repeated decisions by the Supreme Court and by innumerable acts of Congress, and this Wheeler-Howard Bill is drawn up for all of these Indians in so far as these Indians want to take part in it. It is intended to be applicable to all of them who want it. To understand the bill and even to see how it might apply to your life, you will have to think with me for a little while about all the Indians and their situation, because otherwise you won't get a true understanding of what the bill is intended to do, and what it is the new Administration is trying to accomplish.

I will pause here and find out whether everybody or nearly everybody understands English and whether there are a good many who do not understand English. Will those who do not understand English so indicate by raising their hand. (*No hands raised.*) Are there any here who need an interpreter? (*No hands raised.*) That is good. It will save us hours of time. Now to explain the reason for the Wheeler-Howard Bill—

LADY IN AUDIENCE: I don't think these Indians understood your question.

MR. COLLIER: Will somebody translate my question? I want to know how many Indians there are here who don't understand English. I think there are a good many Osages who don't understand English.

MR. GRIFFITH: I think all the Quapaws here understand English.

Henry Tallchief interprets to the Osages.

MR. COLLIER: There are six Osages who do not understand English. Is it possible for them to gather in one place so that the interpreter can interpret in a low voice while I talk.

Osages gather in one place.

Before I say anything more about the bill, just let me tell you and have it translated that the Wheeler-Howard Bill has nothing to do with oil or gas or zinc or lead or minerals. It has nothing to do with the ownership of those things, has nothing to do with the management of those properties. They are not affected by the Wheeler-Howard Bill.

Interpreted in Osage.

Now, to explain the bill I am going back a number of years to a time about fifty years ago. Up to that time, up to a time about when you middle-aged people were born, when I was born, the Indians held land under treaties with the Government. Many tribes had fairly large land holdings which they owned as a tribe, and the treaties guaranteed them the perpetual ownership of these lands. That was the condition fifty years ago.

Interpreted in Osage.

The tribes had a great variety of methods of individual tenure and ownership within their treaty-protected lands, but the fundamental title was in the tribe and was protected by the treaty.

Now, beginning one hundred years ago when the Government started to move the tribes from the East out here to Oklahoma—beginning one hundred years ago—the Government repeatedly broke its treaties with the tribes and took away all or part of the land which the tribes owned under treaties and gave them other land, frequently of poorer quality and smaller area. That happened again and again all over the country, and the result was a great many Indian uprisings and wars, which were very expensive to the Government, and likewise it was sort of a disgraceful thing for the Government to go on breaking treaties with the tribes, because that was breaking its sworn word of honor, but that was the way lands were taken away from the Indian in those days until about fifty years ago.

Interpreted in Osage.

As I say, the breaking of these treaties resulted in a great many Indian wars, and those wars were very expensive to the Government. About 1872 compilation was made in Congress about the cost of these wars, and it was found that for each Indian killed in an Indian war it cost the Government $1,000,000—$1,000,000 to kill one Indian in these wars, and they were altogether too expensive to keep up.

Laughter. Interpreted in Osage.

Our Chairman suggests that they could do it cheaper now by using the automobile.

Interpreted in Osage.

Well, to make a long story short, the land allotment law and scheme were adopted as a substitute for the breaking of treaties as a means of getting the Indian land away from the Indian without breaking treaties and without precipitating uprisings and wars.

Many of the officials who were responsible for the allotment system sincerely believed, first, that it was the only way left for the Government to proceed, and second, that it would have the effect of bringing the Indians into a new ambition and a new amount of industry and civilization. They sincerely believed that, but I nevertheless repeat my statement that the allotment system was adopted first and last as a means to get the Indians' lands away from the Indians peacefully and without breaking treaties, because the Government had experimented with the allotment of Indian lands for many years before the general allotment law was passed. The Government started experimenting away back in 1839 when they allotted the Brotherton Indians in New York, and the Brotherton Indians soon lost all their land, and again and again in the years after that the Government experimented in a small way, allotting this tribe and that tribe, and invariably the land passed from the Indian to the whites. The facts were known, they were of official record, they were known to everybody, and therefore I say that when the Government decided to make allotment wholesale and compulsory, the Government already knew what the effect was going to be. There is no escape from what I say, the Government knew what was going to be accomplished, and allotment did accomplish the thing which it was intended to accomplish.

Interpreted in Osage.

Now let us see what did happen following the allotment law and as a result of that law. I suppose that many of you cannot see clearly the details of this chart. I am anxious to know how far back it is visible. Half way back in the hall will somebody who can or cannot see that chart hold up their hands? Are you able to see it? No? Well, I hope during the lunch hour you will come up and look at it. I will give you the figures taken from the chart. It was in 1880 that the Government announced the policy of allotting all Indian lands. The policy was announced by the then Secretary of the Interior, Carl Schurz, one of our truly great statesmen. In that year, as the chart shows, the Indians were the owners of land totaling 155,000,000 acres. The preparations for adopting the allotment law were passed and allotment was commenced. The chart shows that in 1887 the lands had been reduced to 136,000,000 acres by throwing open about 20,000,000 acres to settlement by whites.

Now, allotment, as you know, worked in this way. The Government took the tribal land and gave to each man, woman and child then living and enrolled a parcel of that land. The amount varied all the way from ten acres up to hundreds of acres assigned to each enrolled member. Then there would be a large amount of tribal land left over, and that land was called surplus; that is, each living Indian had been given one piece of land and all the remaining land belonging to the tribe was called surplus land, on the theory, it would seem, that there were not going to be any more Indian children born after the date of allotment. They seemed to have that happy thought. The surplus land, so called, were then bought from the Indians, forcibly bought in most cases, and as a rule they paid $1.25 an acre, and it was thrown open to white entry, turned over to the whites.

Now we follow down the years—I won't take too long explaining, because you can come up and examine the chart—if you jump to 1887 up to the present year, to the last year, you find that the Indian lands—I am speaking of the whole country—have shrunk to a total of 47,000,000 acres. That represents a loss of 89,000,000 acres since 1887, 89,000,000 gone, 47,000,000 remaining.

Now I am giving you these facts only for one reason. If it were just a matter of history I wouldn't mention it. I am giving the facts to you because the allotment law is still at work and is still forcing the Indians to lose their land, and will still continue to do so until it is all gone.

The facts are worse than the chart shows, much worse, because, first, speaking generally, the lands that have been lost are the best lands, the best agricultural and grazing lands have passed to whites. There are exceptions as in the case of the Quapaws and Osages where minerals and oil were found on the allotted lands, and they have been held on to, but I am speaking of the grazing and agricultural lands, the surface, we are concerned at present only with the surface of the land. The bill does not touch the minerals.

In some Indian areas there are cases where the allotment law was not put in operation. It would take too long to give you the particular reason why it was not, in this or that case. I am afraid we will have to pause—I can't talk against the crying. I am sorry, because this bill is principally for the little ones like that, but I haven't got the voice and you haven't got the ears.

There were some areas where the allotment was not put into effect, as in the case of the Menominees of Wisconsin, the greater part of the Klamath in Oregon, all the Pueblo areas in New Mexico and Arizona, the great Navajo and Papago reservations where the land was not allotted. The unallotted land belonging to these Indians has not diminished but greatly increased since 1887 and is still increasing, and that increase in the unallotted area is contained within this total of Indian land as shown for 1933; so that if you limit your examination to the allotted area, and ignore the unallotted area, you find a loss very much greater than the chart shows. The loss of land in the allotted area has been more than 80%, more than 8/10 of all the lands, and the surface value that has been lost would be nearer 90%.

Now, if somebody says I have done an injustice in saying why the allotment law got started, which was to take the lands away from the Indians peacefully, then I will say that certainly by the year 1900, certainly by the year 1910, the whole world knew how allotment was working, yet the Government deliberately went forward and forced it on all the tribes, except these few. It knew then, if it didn't in 1860, but it went right on, and I assert that that was a great, faithless wrong perpetrated by the Government on the Indians.

And we know now that the loss of land is continuing and will go on to the end; and if the President, if Secretary Ickes and I were silent, we would in turn become partners in that great past wrong, and we are not going to be partners in that past wrong.

But if any single Indian tribe, or two, three or ten, wants to go on in the old way, it will be entirely for that tribe to so decide, and all the power we have got will be given in exempting that tribe and keeping things as they want. I don't think there will be many tribes, and I doubt if there will be any in the long run, who will want to be exempted.

I will have to get you to think with me a little longer about the allotment system, because when we see it clearly we see this bill clearly. As you know, the trust period was applied to each allotment for a certain number of years, and then it expired unless renewed by Congress. Frequently it was renewed. The Secre-tary of the Interior could terminate the trust period for each individual allottee by declaring him competent, giving him a fee patent. Many, of course, will remember how that was done in 1917 under Secretary Lane, when they forced the fee patent upon thousands of Indians, wholesale, and thereby the lands became taxable right away and could be mortgaged and sold and were very quickly lost. That happened all over the country, and the Secretary of the Interior at any time could do that under the existing law. As a rule, however, the trust period has been carried forward as it ran out.

It has been renewed, but this has always taken a fight, and it always gets harder and harder to procure an extension of the trust period. Your neighboring tribes, the Five Civilized Tribes, when they came to Congress four years ago had a terrible fight to get their trust period extended, and we all fought for them, yet they were half beaten, because about half of their land was brought under taxation and they only got about half of the land exempted.

It always gets harder, and there is a reason for that that may not be so familiar with you. Most of the Indians think the difficulty in extending the trust period grows out of the desire of the local community to tax the Indian lands. That is true in part; of course the county doesn't want any tax-exempt land and the State doesn't want it.

But there is a much more important reason than that. The reason lies in what happens after the original allottee dies. Then under the allotment law the heirs have to be determined, then the property must be partitioned among the heirs. If it is not capable of being partitioned and usually, of course, it is not—you can't take a 40 acre allotment, or 160 acres, and fence it out so each of 20 or 30 heirs has that portion, it is too small to use.

There then is one of two things the Secretary has to do. He has either got to sell the allotment and distribute the proceeds among the heirs, or he has got to rent it out and distribute the rental proceeds among the heirs. Now, in 98 cases in every hundred it has been found impossible to partition the allotment and in those 98 cases out of every hundred the department has had to decide either to sell the land at auction or to continue holding it to rent to whites, and millions of acres have been sold under these conditions of heirship land. At the present time there are seven million acres of dead allotments awaiting sale to whites.

When the Government does not sell this dead allotted land, but holds on to it and rents it, what is the situation? You have from two to 250 heirs, each of whom has an equity in a given dead allotment. If the thing is held across a generation, kept under trust to the second generation, you will have many hundreds of heirs to that allotment, and each heir as a rule has an equity in more than one allotment, in several allotments, sometimes twenty or thirty allotments, until we have arrived at this kind of a condition; that there are many of these dead allotments where the Government is collecting and paying out 1-1/2 cents a year to each of hundreds of heirs, 2 cents a year, 3 cents a year, and it will be paying tiny amounts like that from a dozen or fifty allotments to each heir.

The administrative job becomes more and more impossible the longer the trust period is continued, the longer the dead allotment is administered this way, and every year we see the cost of administering the allotment, especially the dead allotments, growing greater and greater, while the area owned by the Indian grows smaller and smaller. It is costing the Government millions of dollars a year in an expenditure that doesn't produce any good, doesn't save the lands. That money is taken out of the Indian health service and Indian school service and so on. At the Kiowa Agency the other day I had the figures presented as to how their expenditures were being used.

They are spending there seventy—no, eighty thousand dollars a year, at that agency. They are spending that on all the agency work, including health work, the agricultural extension and all relief activities, and of that $80,000, 65,000 is used up in the real estate work of handling these allotments, which are now mostly dead allotments. In other words, at that agency of each $80 spent, $65 goes to this real estate business, renting, collecting and disbursing these petty amounts for these tiny pieces of land that are scattered all over the county.

At the Five Tribes Agency, where they spend $300,000 a year, we were informed that 80% of the work done, $8 in every $10, goes to the administration of these allotments. Multiply that all over the country—I can't even tell you how many millions of dollars it represents. We haven't finished the budget analysis, but we know a great many millions of dollars is going to waste and does not result in getting an additional foot of land for any Indian. It doesn't result in saving any land, because in the long run the land goes anyway, and it forces the Government to bring the trust period to an end, because in hundreds and thousands of cases already the cost of administration of allotments is more than eating up the total income, sometimes amounting in one year almost to the total value of the allotment. The Government can't go on doing that, especially as the cost rises all the time. That is the fundamental reason why the trust period cannot be extended indefinitely under the allotment system. There is no hope of continuing to extend it. Again, I remind you I am not talking about oil and minerals, I am talking about the surface of the land.

Now where do we find ourselves? The Five Civilized Tribes received 101,000 allotments. At present 72,000 members of the Five Civilized Tribes are landless, totally landless, and the annual income in the Five Civilized Tribes if you leave out the oil payments that go to only a few of them, the annual per capita income is $47.00 a year. That is how much the average member of the Five Civilized Tribes has to live on in a year. That is the value of what he wears and eats and consumes. I read to the meeting day before yesterday down there at Muskogee a statement by a prominent Oklahoma citizen that there were no poor Indians in Oklahoma, that they were all fine, contented, that it was a slander against the State of Oklahoma to say otherwise. Well, it is a fact that in the recent studies, which took into account more than 15,000 members of the Five Civilized Tribes in whole great areas, that was the annual income, $47.00 a year, and 72,000 have no land.

In the country as a whole we don't know the number of totally landless Indians. We have been saying it is a hundred thousand, but our recent studies, which we have been able to make through a grant of Civil Works money, indicate that a hundred thousand is too small, very much too small, it is more than likely it is 150,000 of Indians who have been rendered completely landless by allotment.

Now, in the past, the Federal Government—not Congress but the executive—has followed the theory that when an Indian had been stripped of all his property, when he no longer owned anything which is under the trust of the Federal Government, he was no longer a ward and no longer had a claim under the Government, he had got to go somewhere else for protection, he had to go somewhere other than the Federal Government. We have served him for good and all, we have finished with him, we have plucked him clean. That was the theory of the previous Administrations. It was a convenient theory because it saved the Government a lot of money. It saved the Government millions of dollars a year to just kick these Indians out and say "You are civilized now, you are grand, we just admire you, we are proud of you. You are civilized, go to your county, go to your State, don't come to Uncle Sam for any more help." Nice. It flattered the homeless Indian. It flattered him and saved the Government a lot of money, but it was just as faithless and cynical as a lot of other policies toward the Indian.

Now I want to make this clear, and I don't care whether anybody likes it or does not like it, that the present Administration has reversed that policy, that we consider that the United States Government is responsible for the propertyless Indian, does owe him a service, and owes him more service than it owes the Indian who has still got property. This statement I make, not subject to the vote or referendum of any Indian tribe, because it deals with the fundamental, indissoluble responsibility of the United States toward the individual Indian, and no tribe or tribal council is entitled to set up a barrier between the United States and the landless, impoverished individual Indian, and we make that announcement to you knowing that it is going to mean a long fight to get the necessary money to do the decent thing, the human thing, by these 150,000 landless Indians.

Again I pause, to say that the landless Indian can and is going to be helped without depriving the landed Indian of anything he has got, but even after that has been explained by myself and our other emissaries from Washington, even after we have made it perfectly clear that there is no plan to take away any Indian's land and give it to another Indian and so on, that we are talking about getting new land, buying land for the landless Indian and getting a grant of money from the Federal Government to capitalize that landless Indian, so he can build up a home by his industry, even after we have made that perfectly clear still, again and again, somebody rises up and says "They were the Indians who squandered their heritage. You are proposing to give them equal treatment with us. We didn't squander our inheritance," and they have protested against this policy of helping the landless, propertyless Indians. I mean some Indians have done that.

The reason I have given you this history of the allotment system is to convey to you the fact that in the main, by and large, the loss of land by Indians under the allotment system has nothing to do with being thrifty or unthrifty. The allotment act intended for the Indians to lose their land, they have to lose their land under it. I don't mean there haven't been cases, let us say if you like, hundreds of cases, of thriftless Indians who got their fee patents and blew in the money. Of course a lot of white people would, too. Maybe Indians do it a little more, but that is so unimportant in relation to this chart, to this terrible, mandatory, inexorable loss of land, that we can afford to forget it.

Down at the Anadarko Agency the other evening one old chief took the stand and made an oration along the line I have stated. He said he thinks these Indians who squandered their land ought to be punished (as if they haven't been punished enough yet), and then alongside the table there came a young fellow—he was about twenty-one I guess. He said "I was born one hour after the rolls were closed," too late to be allotted, and it turned out that in this Cheyenne and Arapaho area, 2,100 had received allotments and 2,600 had not received any; 2,600 had been born too late to be allotted. Now, had they squandered their land? What they did, in being born too late, was, if you like, to disregard the theory of the men who made the allotment system, which was that there wouldn't be any more Indians born after allotment. But enough said.

It is the Government which created the landless Indian. The Government did it deliberately and knowingly, with its eyes open, and did it as a means of getting the Indian land in a respectable and peaceable way and no longer having to spend a million dollars to kill an Indian.

You are all conscious that the Government owes you, at least owes most Indians, restitution for past violations of treaties, and since 1920 the Government has recognized that it was delinquent in violating treaties and has allowed a great many tribes to come in to the Court of Claims and some of them have obtained large judgments and others are going to obtain larger judgments.

When a treaty was broken, it was usually by some act of an agent out in the field. Only a small part of the Government was consciously involved in these violations of treaty, but in this taking of your land by the allotment system the whole Government has been involved. It has gone on for forty-seven years in the full light of day, with the knowledge of the Administration and of Congress. I say that the moral responsibility of the Government for the evils wrought by the allotment system is greater than its moral responsibility for the evils wrought by violations of treaties. While under decision of the Supreme Court the Indians cannot go into the Court of Claims to obtain restitution for the injuries done under the allotment system—they can't do it—that does not relieve the Government of its moral and human obligation to make restitution, and the fundamental policy of this Administration is that restitution shall be made and that the allotted land which remains shall be saved from being lost like the rest of it has been lost.

In Oklahoma 23,000,000 acres were allotted; there remains 3,000,000 acres owned by Indians in Oklahoma. What about right here? The Osages—I am giving these figures in the rough—have a little over 400,000 acres in allotted land—I am talking about the surface now. That is all that is left out of 1,500,000 acres—just 400,000. What about the Quapaws? We have the exact figures here. The Quapaws who are said not to need any help from the Government. Of 190,922 acres of Quapaw land that were allotted, 155,700 acres are now owned by whites. The Quapaws still have 35,322 acres. If you take that 35,000, they have still only 10,000 belonging to living allottees; 24,390 acres of Quapaw land still owned by Indians are dead allotments, with all of these conditions I have told you concerning dead allotments. It either must be sold or the trust period must be ended. In other words, the Quapaws through allotment have lost 81% of their land, but some of them do not feel the loss so much because they have zinc and lead.

However, the zinc and lead mines, as I understand it, belong to individual allottees. They may out of their friendliness or out of their blood obligation contribute to the support of others. That is all. Sixty or seventy allottees, as I understand it, own the minerals. They will continue to own it. They are not touched by this bill. There are six hundred Quapaws, so it is quite evident that there must be a large number of Quapaws who haven't any land. Now if those Quapaws born after allotment or others who have lost their land through permitting lifting of restrictions, if they don't want to take part in the new land that is going to be bought, nobody will make them and nobody will even request it because there is going to be a terrific competition among landless Indians for the land-purchase-money that is contained in this bill. It ought to be very clear to you that it will not be to anybody's interest to come down here and persuade the Quapaws or other Indians to come in on these grants; on the contrary, there will be a lot of Indians in other parts of the country sitting around and praying that you will stay out because then they will have that much more that we can buy them.

I want to add one other thing before coming down to the terms of the bill. One of the reasons why the Indians generally are handicapped in the struggle of life is that they have no access to financial credit. This may not apply to you here. It would not apply, of course, to those whose lands are entirely unrestricted. Indians can't pledge their restricted property, are invalid unless the Secretary of the Interior underwrites them. As a result the Indians are denied financial credit.

That is true of all, generally speaking. The Government has been extending financial credit in the lordly amount of three or four hundred thousand dollars a year to the whole Indian population in the shape of implements, etc., under the reimbursable scheme, a sum totally inadequate to do much with. The Indians cried out against this condition, and the successive Indian Commissioners pointed out the handicap resting on the Indians, yet nothing has been done. A year ago the Senate Committee on Indian Affairs reported that something must be done to extend financial credit in a modern way in an adequate amount to the Indians. The Wheeler-Howard Bill, through an amendment you will find in the House hearings, does that. It sets up a system of financial credit. The amount authorized to be appropriated is only $5,000,000 in the Bill. The House Committee members indicated that they thought it ought to be $10,000,000 to start with. This money is not to be loaned by the Government, but is to be granted to the communities outright. It is to become a perpetual revolving fund and lend it out to the individual members of the community or partnership. If he wants to engage in a collective business enterprise, the provision for financial credit is almost as essential as the purchase of land. No element in our population can get along without financial credit, and the Indians must have that opportunity.

Now I shan't say anything at this point about that part of the bill that deals with Indian self-government, although later in the day we will. I can't say anything at this point about the educational part of the bill which provides a means for the ambitious Indian boy and girl to go forward in the professions, medicine, engineering, nursing, etc. I am going to hold myself to the land and allotment matter. That is basic. Once it is understood everything else becomes clear.

The bill provides $2,000,000 to be spent each year in buying new land for Indians, which means for the landless Indians and those who have not enough land to live on or to make a living with. That doesn't seem very much, but $2,000,000 a year in five years is $10,000,000, and the amount required will become apparent as the operation of getting the land goes forward. The Government is now starting in to buy up large areas of farm land and retire it from commercial farming. They call it marginal. Hundreds of millions of dollars are to be spent in buying up submarginal land and retiring it from commercial production, and it has already been announced that Indians may come in and buy this land, and if they like may enter into possession under say a year-to-year lease of such as they can use. That land to be bought is to be taken out of taxation and this land that is to be bought under this bill will be taken out of taxation. Where land is taken off the tax rolls over a county and state, the bill provides that the Federal Government shall assume complete responsibility of maintaining public service within the areas; roads, bridges, schools and so on. It does that in lieu of taxes. That means there will be states and counties competing to get the Government to take over this land, because they will be getting so much more back in services than taxes and be much better off.

This whole plan of land acquisition depends upon getting a land-holding system different from the present one. The Government isn't going to spend millions of dollars buying land and building houses on land in order to have it lost again as it was under the allotment scheme. Of course they are not going to do that. The Government is not going to spend millions of dollars buying land and improving it in order to have it get into the condition of the heirship lands at present, so that for every million of dollars it spends to buy the land it would have to spend a quarter of a million in administering it as it does now with the heirship lands.

The whole scheme of acquiring land hangs upon a reversal of the allotment system. Also, if the Government is to undertake to make the trust period permanent on the allotted lands, we have to get some change in the heirship allotment situation. Nobody can successfully ask the Government to take a permanent trusteeship of land where the administrative costs are greater than the income to the Indians. They won't do it. So that the Wheeler-Howard Bill sets up a new scheme of land holding which is optional, both as a means of saving the allotted land, making the trust period permanent and getting new lands. All of that is told in Title 3 of the Bill and is clearly explained in this memorandum which analyzes the bill paragraph by paragraph, and which uses language that is not legal, but that a layman can understand. But the bill itself has to be couched in legal phraseology.

I have expressed my opinion about the allotment system. It is bad business but, be that as it may, the Indian who got an allotment acquired a property right, what they call a vested right, an ownership of that piece of land. That ownership, that vested right, must of course be respected. It has to be respected. If the Government had any plan of destroying that property right, confiscating it, and got legislation of that sort, then the courts would at once throw it out as violative of the Constitution. That property right is as fully protected as any body in the country, not only protected by statute, but by the Constitution. That fact alone suffices to answer these wild rumors that the Government is going to take the land of those who have it and give it to those who haven't. The Government couldn't do that if they wanted to. If it was that crazy to want to try to do it, the court would declare the legislation null and void on the first test case.

Now I will describe what the bill does do. It says first that the Secretary of the Interior shall make studies, examinations and he shall determine and lay down on a map what area, if any, ought to be consolidated for Indian use. Usually allotment results in checkerboard ownership. An Indian owns some land, and next to him a white man, and after a while the Indian owns a dot of land and the white man owns an ocean of land all around it. The bill says the Secretary shall determine what area in the Indian country where there are allotments should be marked for consolidation. Consolidation will be brought about primarily by buying up white owned land in that area. Now there will be a good many allotments lying outside of that area. In Oklahoma most of the allotments would lie outside of any area that might be selected for consolidation. That is true of the Five Tribes and I expect it is true of the Quapaws. I do not know your land distribution very clearly, but from the map I would say that the most of the allotments would lie outside the area for consolidation. As to these lands that would lie outside of the area for consolidation, these allotted lands still held in trust, the only operation of the bill would be to make the trust period permanent, to take away from the Secretary of the Interior authority to lift the restrictions and to say that the trust would be continued until Congress might otherwise direct. Congress, of course, has to keep the final power. You can't take it away. So far as those lands are concerned, they would remain as they are with nothing but the continued trust period and certain other benefits which the owners would get in the shape of these loans and educational advantages and so on.

What about the allotments lying inside the area marked for consolidation? This may not interest you at all, because there may not be any such area either in the Osage or Quapaw or any of your country. But suppose there were? In those areas the owner of the allotment, if he so desired, could transfer his title to what is called the community, the Indian community, which would be an organized land-holding corporation. He could transfer the title to the community and would get in exchange a series of compensating advantages. What would those advantages be? First, life tenure of his own allotment; second, the right to designate that same piece of land, his allotment, to his heirs for their life tenure; third, the ownership of improvements would remain unaffected, they would be absolute and of course they would be transmitted by inheritance to the heirs; fourth, the individual who surrendered his allotment in this way would get what is called a certificate of membership entitling him to the use of other land in the community of equal area or value, in case he wanted to give up this particular land and not stay on it any more, but go somewhere else. He could take the land he wanted to use. Also, he would be entitled to the rental value of that land which he turned in to the community; that is, the rental from the land. Whatever was collected would be paid to him, and of course, as the rental value increased he would get more. In a nutshell, he would keep every tangible, practical element of ownership that he has got. Only the underlying title would pass to the community, let us say to the Government as a perpetual trustee. If the Indian has a strong sentiment that made him not want to do this, that wouldn't matter, that would be up to him. He would just hold on to it exactly like he is. I think the advantage would soon become so apparent that all the Indians would want to do this. The new land bought under the bill to fill in the consolidated area would be owned by the community, or by the Government as trustee for the community, and it would be assigned by preference to their heirs, the preferential right to keep the land which they had selected in a group, so that they would have individual ownership without the conflictions of the allotment system. It would be very much like what they have in Canada now and in a number of our western unallotted reservations where the ownership is just as secure as any white community, altho the fundamental title is in the tribe. Land passes from generation to generation back and forth between the Indians, all improvements are owned, all the proceeds of the land are owned, no land is ever lost because of this underlying community title over which the Government stands as a perpetual trustee.

Now what about the heirship lands, the dead allotments; they would also remain as they are, except that the Government would buy them up, proceed to purchase them and turn them in to the community, thereby getting rid of all this tangle of bookkeeping and multiplicity of equities, these uncertainties of heirship area of dead allotments, the Government either to pay cash outright for them or it could pay on the installment basis across a certain number of years, thereby at one stroke, as fast as this amalgamation took place, the Government would be able to step out from under this wasteful administrative costs, and money saved in that way could be reapplied for the real service needed by the Indians, health, education, and so on. One of the reasons why the bill appeals to the President and Congress is that it would solve the problem of getting money for Indian education and health which is so badly neglected. We would get it out of savings from the wasteful real estate operations.

What about those who would die after this enactment had been made law? I mean those in the consolidated area who died after this bill became law. The title would pass to the community in all cases under the act, and the heirs would receive these various things that I told you, the right to exclusive use, ownership of improvements, and to pass those rights on to the heirs, and the right of full rental value of the land that had passed in this way to the community. What do I mean when I say they would receive these rights, these guarantees? That question was brought up especially at Anadarko. Could the Government, having guaranteed these new rights, take them away? The answer is "No, no more than it can take away your trust patents." These certificates would be the same thing as trust patents. They will be evidences of property rights, a vested right which could not be cancelled by an act either of the executive or Congress any more than your patents could be. They would be protected by the same clause of the Constitution which guarantees that property cannot be taken without due process, the same one that protects your existing allotments. The status of a certificate referred to in this bill would not be one of a treaty or statute, but of a title. Those of you who are lawyers know the difference between a land title and a treaty or statute. It cannot be taken away without consent, compensation and all that. That in a nutshell describes the plan. For the lands lying outside the consolidated area nothing would happen except the trust period would go on. It is really very simple when you get beyond the legal jargon of the bill and look at it in a practical way.

Suppose the Secretary selected an area for consolidation and the Indians wouldn't want to be consolidated? Well, I think the answer, the practical answer, is even stronger than the answer could be in law. It is in these consolidated areas that new lands are going to be obtained for homeless Indians. There would be more than 100,000 of those Indians to take care of. For years and years to come there is going to be terrific competition from all over the country to have this or that area selected first and the purchase of land begun. Any area where the Indians are not actively seeking the benefits of the bill could be forgotten about. It would be just like the Public Works now. The Public Works doesn't thrust its money on anybody. For every grant the Public Works can make, there are ten they can't make. It is the same way here, but not quite that bad. The bill is an optional thing extended to the Indians, and even to the individual, not to speak of the tribe. The tribe can do without it better than the individual. Some features of the court section, almost all of that, are optional too.

You might say, why doesn't the administration go ahead and pass it, since it is only optional; why do you keep telling us that if a tribe wants to be excluded by an express statement, it will be? The answer is this, that we have adopted a policy of not recommending legislation without the knowledge and consent of the Indians. We intend for the Indians to be their own legislative committee. We may think we are right; so did the people who made the allotment act. Most of the terrible blunders in the past of Indian legislation would have been avoided if the administration had carried the thing back to the Indians before they put the bill thru. It would have taken a little more time, but the Indians would have seen to it that a lot of errors were not committed. Furthermore, they wouldn't have been permitted to carry this sense of eternal grievances they have about legislators in Washington who took up legislation and shot it through, and the Indians wake up and find next morning they had been legislated for. We are not going to do that any more. As this is the most important legislation affecting the Indians this administration will put forward, we are determined to lay it before all the Indians, hard work as it is to do that. It may seem like a terrible waste of time to some of the people, but it doesn't seem that way to us. Our purpose connects up with the thing that is going to be talked about later. The time has come for the Indians to be their own masters; they must accept this bill or reject it tribe by tribe. It is now 12 o'clock. I presume that is the time we are to adjourn.

MR. MCNAUGHTON: There is to be a luncheon at 12 o'clock at the Hotel Miami. You will get your tickets in the lobby of the hotel. The Ladies of the Methodist Church are having a chicken dinner on Central Avenue at the Consumer's Gas Company.

MR. COLLIER: I want you to know this—my statement will come to an end very shortly after lunch and then we will pass on to questions and discussions. I am not going to talk to you all day, and if we don't get done this afternoon and want to come back tonight, we will go on just as late tonight as they will let the lights burn.

Adjourned until 1:30 p.m.

MR. MCNAUGHTON: Kindly get your seats now. Will someone who knows the delegation who occupied these seats, tell me if they are still here?

ANSWER FROM THE AUDIENCE: They are Cherokees. They had to leave.

MR. MCNAUGHTON: Have any delegations from any of the tribes left the meeting or are all the delegations here that were here this morning? The Osages are present, are they not?

ANSWER: Yes.

MR. MCNAUGHTON: Wyandottes, Shawnees, Senecas, Peorias, and Miamis?

ANSWER: They are here, Mr. Chairman.

MR. MCNAUGHTON: I believe, Mr. Commissioner, they are all present. Are there any of the Modoc Tribe present? If there is I wish you would stand up. Now it is desired that if any of you folks have questions that you would like to ask with relation to any part of this bill, if you will kindly prepare them in writing and hand them up here so that after the close of the Commissioner's explanation, we will endeavor to answer your questions. After those questions have been answered, there will be an opportunity for such other discussion on the matter as seems proper. I am sure we are all interested in the Commissioner's explanation of this matter, and if you will keep these things in mind and ask the questions intelligently and not have duplications, all will reply. If you will kindly prepare those, they will be given attention.

MR. COLLIER: One more announcement. There may be delegations here which may not want to remain after the close of this session, because they live so far off; they may want to say things and talk before they go, and they will be given the opportunity this afternoon.

I will now conclude in the land matter, with two further items. I have explained that practically the whole plan was permissive, not compulsory. There is one place on page 31 of the bill, first line, which might allow compulsion. It says the Secretary of the Interior is authorized to transfer the title of an allottee to the community that is within the consolidated area. Several weeks ago we told the Indians at the Plains Indian Conference that this also should be made merely permissive—"that the Secretary of the Interior with the consent of the allottee may transfer the title."

One more item with respect to the allotments, which are agricultural. What I am saying does not relate to forest land or grazing land, but to agricultural land, farm land. There is no reason why agricultural allotments should not be left as they are, whether inside or outside the consolidated area, to be carried on just as under existing law. The one change that would have to be made would be to prohibit the subdivision of agricultural allotments into parcels too small to be used. I believe most of your allotments are agricultural.

I now pass on to a quick explanation of other parts of the bill, first about title 2, which deals with education. In brief, this is what that title does. It gives the Secretary of the Interior power and it orders him to help Indian young men or women with outstanding ambition, talent, and wants to have a career, as for example to be a nurse, teacher, engineer, doctor, lawyer, etc. The young person is to be financed in getting his or her education wherever the best education is to be had, either in a state college or a medical, law or a technical school. The money necessary to pay the tuition and living costs would be provided by the Government, one-half of it to be an outright gift to the student and one-half to be a loan to be repaid without interest, but not to be repaid unless the student has a job. Likewise, in that title there is given authority to the Secretary to put a young man or woman of real talent who ought to be a leader, thru college or technical school entirely on a gift basis. The object of this part of the bill is to furnish the Indians what they have not had before; that is, a chance at equal education with any white people in the country. We know the Indians are capable of excelling, of succeeding, of becoming distinctive along all lines of professional work. They can't, however, unless educational advantages are supplied them. Those advantages can only be supplied by going to the great colleges, medical schools and law schools and putting the Indian in there thru scholarships and paying his living expenses. That is Title 2 of the bill—education—and I may remark it is not a way to send the Indian back to the blanket. It is to enable the Indian to go out in the world.

Just a word about the court section—the last part of the bill. That has been very widely misunderstood by the newspapers, largely due to the fact I suppose that they did not read it. This last part of the bill establishes a Court of Indian Affairs, its members appointed by the President with the consent of the Senate. That Court of Indian Affairs will take over the cases that now go to the United States District Court. That court will travel and go where the Indians are. In addition it will have certain jurisdiction where an Indian group forms a chartered community. Controversies and suits between Indians in their chartered communities and white people would go to this Court of Indian affairs. That part of the jurisdiction of the court would apply where only the Indians organize under the bill and take out a charter. The court likewise is given the job of probate work, determining heirs. That job is transferred from the Bureau of Indian Affairs to the Court of Indian Affairs. It is properly a court function and it is put there. The Indians would be supplied with a staff of lawyers, practically public defendants, who would represent them without pay in litigation and trial before this court, lawyers appointed by the President. Even this part of the bill has been criticized as being a segregation. Well, claims against the United States are already handled in the United States Court and they would still be handled there under this bill. Litigation involving restricted property of a ward Indian can always be taken into Federal Court, and all this bill does is simply to provide a Federal Court especially formed so that it will suit the convenience of the Indians and go where they are.

Now we come to Title 1 of the bill, which is called "Indian Self-Government." Before I speak of it I must explain that ward Indians, Indians who are Federal wards, may organize to a certain extent under existing law. They may organize simply because the Secretary of the Interior allows them to. Their organization has no power except the power he gives it, and he can take it away whenever he wants to. That is not true of the Osages. They have their Tribal Council under statute, but the Tribal Council of the Osages hasn't very wide powers. Owing to the fact that the Indian restricted property cannot be hypothecated, mortgaged, and owing to this lack of authority to make contracts by ward Indians, the practical consequence is that Indians are denied the advantages of organization. I mean all kinds of organization now, organization for business, and organization for political purposes, for self-government, home rule. Under the existing law to a large extent we at Washington are compelled to govern both the tribal affairs and the personal affairs of the Indians. We are forced to do it in an arbitrary way, and in most matters there is no appeal from our decision. We are the court as well as the administration. Ours is the last word, so that without desiring to be absolute monarchs, we are pretty nearly all that. Commissioner Burke in a radio address several years ago spoke of this power in a way to indicate he liked to be an absolute monarch. Well, we don't believe in absolute monarchy applied to Indians or anyone else.

Now what does this entitle them to? It is absolutely and exclusively permissive. No Indian has to pay any attention to it at all, neither a tribe nor an individual, but to those Indians who do want to take on the power that goes with organization, Title 1 extends that opportunity and they can organize, whether for business or for pleasure or for politics. They can organize within the guardianship of the Government. They don't have to get out of the Government's guardianship in order to organize. They organize as wards, and when they organize, that organization becomes itself an agency of the United States Government, or as the bill says an instrumentality of the Federal Government, clothed with the protection and some of the authority of the United States Government.

The organization can be almost any kind of organization you can think of. It might be an organization to conduct business between any two or more Indians. It might be organized to take over the range and stock it with your own cattle and run the cattle through a cattle association, instead of renting the land to whites. It might be organized to obtain credit from the Government. The Indians could organize and form their own credit association to borrow money and form a bank. The credit association would lend the money to its members. In many parts of the country the organization would be more than that, because the Indians live in a solid territorial area. They would organize practically a town, a county government, and they would have the authority of the town and county government in their own local community; they would have their own county commissioners and clerks, promulgate their local ordinances just like a white town does. That wouldn't happen much here, but it would happen in Arizona and New Mexico where the Indians have great solid areas of land and there aren't many white people. Of course, this is permissive. The organization formed might as easily be territorial. It might be just what we would call functional, an organization to carry out a certain piece of work. It might be like any modern corporation. Our large public utilities are owned not by individuals but by corporations. A lot of different people pool their capital. That is the way the railroads are built, the big factories, granaries and so on.

For some reason this part of the bill which allows the Indians to organize along modern lines, has been called a scheme for segregating the Indians, just as if somebody would say the Standard Oil Company was a scheme for segregating John D. Rockefeller and his family. The Standard Oil Company was a scheme by which John D. Rockefeller and his family gathered up a great deal of money and power. That did not segregate them, and so I could go on illustrating innumerable organizations in white life. The person who is without organization is generally not very powerful; all the power and influence in American life is exercised through organization, by men who are members of organizations, and any race denied the right to organize is denied the right to protect itself, to increase its wealth or have any prestige or standing.

When a group of Indians under Title 1 decides it wants to become an organization or chartered group and obtain their charter from the Federal Government, certain other things go along with it. A lot of you Indian fathers and mothers and young people know how difficult it is for Indians to get employment in the Government Service. The Indians can be just as capable as white people, have just as much practical ability and moral integrity and so on, but they can't get the jobs. The reason is the Civil Service, the general Civil Service being applied to the Indian Bureau, and the Indians cannot qualify, haven't had the academic or college training or exceptional kinds of experience. If they qualify, they qualify at the bottom of the list, and the Secretary is compelled to appoint from the Civil Service register the employees at the top of the list to all the Indian jobs. Civil Service is becoming more rigid every year and therefore it is harder and harder for Indians to get employment in the Government Service, Indian Service or any other Government service. It is a serious condition. How are we going to meet it?

We meet it in this bill by saying, to put it briefly, that where an Indian who is a member of one of these organizations or chartered groups, where an Indian can show that he has the qualifications for holding any particular job carried out by the Indian Bureau, then he can have that job regardless of the Civil Service. The Civil Service is lifted, put aside so far as the Indians are concerned in these chartered communities. The bill goes into detail and directs the Secretary to prepare the standards and qualifications for Indians so that he may qualify on a list no white man is eligible to. When the community wants to nominate one of its members for a job, if he has the qualifications and if there is a vacancy, he must be put into the job, irrespective of whether the Secretary wants to or not. He has got to under the law.

Parallel to that is another arrangement where one of these communities is formed and the Indians have the power to compel the department to remove objectionable employees, if there are any, and the community is the judge. It still comes about here and there from time to time that there are employees whom Indians would like to have removed. They have no power to do it now. This gives them that power and makes the employees of the Indian Bureau responsible to the Indians.

Whenever the Indian Commissioner is preparing to spend money on Indian Service he has to come to the Indians first and present his plans, his budget, he has to do that before he goes to Congress. Whatever the group decides, whatever action they take about the matter is transmitted to Congress along with the recommendation of the Commissioner with the budget to Congress. That means every Indian community would know all that was being done in the way of expenditure and would be able to take part in changing an expenditure in any direction the community desired. That community will have money, tribal funds, community money. Under this bill not a dollar of tribal money can be spent except with the consent of the Indians. That is the point. We are still using Indian tribal funds in very large amounts to pay the expenses of the Indian Bureau. Secretary Ickes and I don't believe we ought to. We have protested against being compelled to do it; we have called it wrong and immoral. Nevertheless we are compelled to, and next year we are going to take $2,000,000 of Indian trust moneys and use them for Indian Bureau salaries and such things. In fifty years the Indian Bureau has eaten up about $100,000,000 of Indian trust money for its own keep. It is forced on us, because if we use Indian trust money, the Federal Treasury or the taxpayers are saving that much money. In case after case it has even gone beyond that and put the tribe in debt to the Government to pay for its salaries. It has used its last dime of trust money belonging to the Indian tribes. It is a great scandalous misappropriation of Indian moneys. The only way to stop it is the way we have in this bill, to give the Indians the power to stop it. That would stop it in a hurry. That is, the Indians who took the trouble to organize in a chartered community would control their own money, including money they would derive in the future from their own assets, which Congress controls under existing law.

If a charter were issued to an Indian group, the Secretary of the Interior could not take it away or modify it. It would be out of his hands. It would be the law by which he has to live. The tribe could give up its charter or amend its charter, but the department could not change it in any way.

The Indians who take advantage of the right to organize and who take out a charter, would keep all rights of citizenship now possessed. The Indian has those rights of citizenship by virtue of being a citizen of the United States. He would keep his voting rights, his right to hold public office and all other rights which he enjoys now. Let me make this clear. Suppose a white man is a voter and he is an office holder and so on. He joins, let us say, the Knights of Pythias, or the Elks or he becomes a stockholder in the General Motors Corporation. Yet he doesn't sacrifice his vote by doing that, his franchise or his citizenship rights. Those are inalienable, fundamental. In the same way an Indian who might want to organize under this plan would retain all his citizenship rights. I have to say that clearly because we are constantly being asked by Indians whether they would lose their status as citizens, their franchise, under this plan. Of course not.

It is to this section of the bill especially that the President refers in a part of a letter about the bill. He says that the section simply offers to the Indian the natural rights of man and offers to the Indian the advantage of the modern corporate system of managing property.

The Indian community which organized under Title 1 could go still further. It could take over the complete responsibility for one or more of the Indian Bureau services. It could, for example, take over the medical service and manage it. The Federal Government would pay the community the money out of the Treasury and the community would spend that money in maintaining its own medical service, its own farm extension service and so on. If the matter were not a success, then the thing would be turned back, the Indian Bureau would resume the service, the appropriation would go on uninterruptedly.

All of this from beginning to end would be optional, voluntary. A tribe might, or a group of Indians might say: "We don't care about it now, maybe ten years from now we would take advantage of it." All right, we will wait ten years. They may say: "We want just a little bit of power, just enough power to enable us to say how our tribal money shall be spent." All right, take that much. A group or tribe might not like it, then they can drop it; it would go back in the old way, it is entirely permissive, but it is of the greatest importance. To any Indian who wants to enter into his full human rights this would be the royal road toward power and citizenship.

I have now finished this brief explanation which undoubtedly has left a great many things unexplained to you. Let me make myself clear on one point. You will note that a record is being kept of all that I say and will be kept of everything everybody else says. That will be typed out and then it will be mimeographed and sent out to those of you who want it. A similar record has been kept of all the other congresses. This is the ninth of these meetings in different parts of the country. They all go back to Washington, to be delivered to the House and Senate Indian Committees and Judiciary Committees, the committees that have this bill under consideration. The things that are said here are exactly as binding upon us as the things we might say to the committees in Congress. The hearings of the House Committee on the bill have already been printed and contain an answer to almost any question that could arise in anybody's mind about the bill. In addition to that there will soon be the departmental report on the bill which will answer the questions, so that all of you will have access to documents of record, public and official, giving answer to all the questions I haven't answered and to any question that may not be answered when we are done tonight.

Before I stop for the questioning and discussion I want first of all to read you a part of a statement issued day before yesterday by Secretary of the Interior Ickes at Washington and carried in the newspapers. Secretary Ickes on March 22 at the office of the Interior Department, charges that there exists a nation-wide campaign of false propaganda by real estate, cattle and lumber interests to defeat the Wheeler-Howard Bill which proposes reformation of Indian affairs. This bill, he says, aptly termed the Indian bill of rights, seeks to correct as far as possible the generations of injuries the Indians have suffered at the hands of whites, at the hands of the federal Government as well. Real estate interests which have been buying up Indian lands for a song, cattlemen and lumber interests which for years have taken advantage of the inability of Indians to protect their own resources, are working through hired Indians to spread utterly false reports. They are spreading the report that the Wheeler-Howard Bill is a tyrannical scheme to take away the rest of the Indians' land, he states, and the Secretary adds that his interview is based upon the reports which have been coming in from the West, and he means principally the far northwest country. It is a fact that there has been an amazing amount of misconception of this bill, misconception so extreme and basic that is hard to think it is a matter merely of misunderstanding.

Day before yesterday we met all day and into the night with the Five Tribes down at Muskogee. The next morning we met all morning with them. The reporters were present throughout and the stenographers took down every word. I explained things to them very much as I have done to you, saying that in the long run they would have to decide whether they wanted to take advantage of this bill or not, but stating my own position which I stated to you, that the Indian tribe which in the long run decides not to accept the protection and aid of this bill, is going to lose its property and suffer worse things than it has suffered in the past. I stated it is my belief. I arrived here a few hours later, picked up the local paper, read a news dispatch sent out by the great news organization, the Associated Press, and at first I was bewildered. It was a news dispatch from Muskogee and the news dispatch said that John Collier at this meeting of the Indians only yesterday morning had told the Indians that the bill was going to be changed so as to cut out the Oklahoma Indians from the benefits of the bill, from everything except the educational section, that he promised them soon to mail back to them an amended bill cutting them out. That of course went all over the State and as far as I know it went all over the country. It was of necessity a fabrication from beginning to end because nothing of the sort happened. Nothing of the sort was said or could have been said by me. An Indian who went away from the Muskogee meeting must have read that dispatch and thrown up his hands with the idea that Washington had been down there tricking them once more.

The misrepresentation has been so persistent that I speak of it because I think you must be put on guard. The strangest misconceptions have been met almost everywhere. I have gone to these congresses and missionaries have come to me, good men and women, and asked me whether it could be true that this Wheeler-Howard Bill put the churches out of business and forbade the missionaries to work among the Indians. They have been told that by somebody all over the country. It is absolutely false and baseless, yet it has been believed.

Everywhere I have gone I have had Indians rise up and say that they didn't want this bill because it took away their land and gave it to the poor Indians; and we have sent out ourselves statement after statement denying this silly story, still these erroneous statements come back to us. Again and again we met the statement that this is the Administration's communizing plan, it is a scheme of sovietizing the Indians, to organize them into Soviets, Russian stuff and so on. They are not misunderstandings anybody could get from reading the bill. They are fabrications, but most Indians are not trained in reading the legal phraseology of bills. When they are told these things, they may not even possess a copy of the bill or they may have it and they can't quite understand this legal language and so they believe what they have been told.

Let us be perfectly frank about this. The Indians have lost a tremendous amount of property. That document shows what happened to the land, but they have also lost hundreds of millions of dollars of money the same way; especially down here in Oklahoma they have lost money in vast amounts. They have been everybody's victim here and in other parts of the country. There is a very large class of exploiters who make their living by exploiting Indians under the present unjust laws through litigation and through forced land sales and through paying low rentals on their land. These lessees pay low rentals and take advantage of the exemption from taxation of the Indian land, which advantage is thus transferred from the lessee to the Indian and the guardians. They don't want the existing situation changed. They know that under the existing arrangement and existing law the Indian is still at their mercy. Indian property is today worth at least a thousand million dollars in the country as a whole, and a thousand million dollars is a lot of value. Under existing law that thousand million dollars will pass to white people before many years, year-by-year, so there are many powerful organized interests in many States, which are fighting this bill. They will come to Congress and fight it out there.

Their method of attack is to throw the Indians into a panic wherever they can. Since we announced that this bill is to go through as the Indians' bill or not at all, that we are going to be guided by the Indians about the bill, why of course these influences have become all the more active because if they can confuse and misinform and stampede the Indians, they have got us caught as we have pledged ourselves not to put this bill through unless the Indians ask us to. We pledge ourselves to exclude from it any Indian tribe that wants to be excluded.

The time has come—and it is the first time I have thus spoken—for a frank statement that there is an embittered conflict between Indian interests and rights on one hand and powerful exploiting white corporations and individuals on the other hand. These exploiting white corporations are but a small minority in the communities where they are located, but they are there and they are active and they are unscrupulous. I have no more to say than that.

I should add that the Associated Press as soon as we called the attention of the New York office and the Oklahoma City office to this fact of the report of yesterday, they prepared to send out a correction of it, but I mention it only as an example of what is going on. They were not responsible; it was put over on the Associated Press by some interested party down in Muskogee, not in the Indian Bureau.

The time has come for questions and for remarks from those who have to go away, questions from members and resolutions or speeches from those who have to go away soon.

MR. THOMPSON: As attorney for the Quapaw Tribal Council and in good faith and just simply for the purpose of clarifying some questions in their minds, I desire to submit these questions.

MR. COLLIER: As questions come along I shall answer them, but some I shall turn over to members of our Washington staff, both in order to break the monotony of my talking and to save my voice. Before answering these questions Mr. Siegel of the Solicitor's office thinks I ought to hammer home a statement I made this morning concerning the heirship provision of the bill as applied to the areas marked out for consolidation. I had explained that the transfer of title to the community would be in all cases voluntary, by purchase or arrangement, but I also explained that as to the heirs to those who die after the enactment of the bill, their title, the title of their lands, would pass to the community and the heirs would receive perpetual use of the land, the right to transmit that perpetual use, the right of ownership of the improvements, the right to transmit that ownership, guarantee of the rental value and the right to transmit that and the right to use it or an equal area within the community and the right to transmit that.

Now there is a group of questions submitted from the Quapaw Council through its attorney, Mr. Thompson. I am going to get somebody to read these questions so I may rest my voice. Read them slowly so they will be clear.

MR. MCNAUGHTON: Is it not true that under the bill as now drafted, that if the act was passed by Congress, the line of inheritance from the holders of trust patents would be changed from the heirs as now determined under the laws of Oklahoma to the chartered community, or if no community has been chartered, to the tribe from whose lands the allotment was made, irrespective of whether the Quapaws voted to come under the terms and provisions of the act, except as to the certificates evidencing the Indian heirs' pro rata interest in the tribal or community property?

MR. COLLIER: It is involved, but I think we can break it down in answering it. Part of it is the very thing I have just been telling, that under the bill within a consolidated area the land, the title to the land after the death of the living Indians, would pass to the community and the heirs would get what I described, their share of the rental value of that land, their share of the improvements, their share of the life tenure of it or of another piece of equal value as that property and so on. That share which they would get would be evidenced by this certificate of membership.

MR. THOMPSON: That is in the event of community form; in the event a community is not formed it would then go back to the tribe, as I understand the bill.

MR. COLLIER: Now let us read that section. That is Section 8, isn't it, Mr. Siegel?

MR. SIEGEL: That is Section 11 of Title 3 I think he has reference to. May I say a word there? I think what the gentleman has asked is true, for the rights of the heirs are the same whether a community has been formed or a tribe, provided that the area has been marked for consolidation, that is to say if the lands are not so scattered that they couldn't form the basis of any community whatever and therefore would be left out of this section entirely, this provision would not go into effect. If they weren't so scattered they would go into the provision and into effect.

With reference to farm land, the rights acquired under Section 11 of Title 3 are exactly the same as those enjoyed under allotment now, that is the person is entitled to continue the exclusive use of the same piece of land and that land would go to his heirs without qualification. That will serve the purpose, or rather the Secretary of the Interior is endowed with the authority to approve any subdivision of that land in units, of course units which could be used.

Let me explain that is not true with reference to grazing and forestry land for the reason that grazing and forestry land must be used in larger units than are allotted to a single individual. Therefore the corporate idea prevails, of sharing in one larger unit rather than individual ownership and use, but with regard to farm land which can be used in individual allotment there is no reason why the original allotment system could not be continued providing there is no subdivision of that land in too small units. As Mr. Collier, I think, has already suggested this afternoon, the bill might be amended specifically to provide that with regard to agricultural land no change whatever might be made, even in name. I don't know, does that answer the question?

MR. THOMPSON: The right of use would descend only to a member, but would not descend to those having less than one-fourth Indian blood?

MR. SIEGEL: That is not true. I think Section 8 of Title 3 does provide that with regard to a certificate issued in exchange for land which is transferred to the community or tribe, such certificate will not descend to a non-member. That was inadvertent.

MR. COLLIER: And should be stricken out. In any event there is no such provision with regard to the interest of heirs in Section 4. I might add, however, that the Secretary of the Interior might have such authority under Section 10 of this title or such authority might be given the chartered community. A chartered community might exclude a non-member.

MR. THOMPSON: A non-member would be anyone not having one-fourth blood?

MR. COLLIER: The one-fourth limitation has to do with the creation of new communities from unaffiliated Indians. There they must have one-fourth or more Indian blood, but otherwise one becomes a member by virtue of being either an enrolled member of a tribe or a descendant of one. The provision with reference to one-fourth Indian blood relates only to new colonies or communities. There are lots of unaffiliated Indians in the country. Section 11 requires close reading in order not to be misunderstood. This is what it means now in plain language: That when an area is consolidated, then the land title passes to the community after the death of the living Indians. When an area is not consolidated, it doesn't, but goes on as at present. The language is involved, but that is the effect of the language.

MR. MCNAUGHTON: If the heirs as now fixed by law shall have a contingent interest in the land after the death of the present holder until such time as the Secretary shall determine that such lands be outside of any area classified for consolidation, is there any effective and certain date provided for in the bill when such determination shall be made, so as to determine when such contingent interest shall become vested?

MR. SIEGEL: I think the answer to that question is no. There is no definite time. The Secretary under Section 6 of Title 3 is directed to make that determination forthwith, but there is no guarantee it can be finished immediately. I am advised by the members of the Indian Bureau staff that this determination would not be very difficult to make and they ought to be through within a year or two. I am not sure; Mr. Collier probably could speak more accurately about it than I.

MR. COLLIER: I wouldn't guarantee when the final determination could be made, but it could be made with reasonable promptness and, if it were desired, a date could be set before which it must be finished. Making that determination of the consolidated area is not of itself a very complicated task, but the Secretary of the Interior would unquestionably want to know the desires of the tribe in question. It might take a while for that tribe to decide whether it wanted a certain area marked for consolidation, but you could set a five-year limit on it or any limit.

MR. MCNAUGHTON: Question 3. "If the Indians voted to accept the terms of the proposed act and should vote for and establish a charter under the act, is there then any question but what the line of inheritance would then be changed from the next of kin to the tribe or community?"

MR. COLLIER: I think that has been answered. Within the consolidated area which is also a chartered community, inheritance after the death of those now living would be the tribe and the heirs would receive these rights of tenure and ownership and all that. It is a consolidated area which is controlling, though, and not the community. There might be a community outside of any consolidated area.

MR. MCNAUGHTON: Question 4. "If the bill should pass as drafted, then would not the Court of Indian Affairs have exclusive jurisdiction in all actions in any way involving a restricted Indian allotment, where any person of any degree of Indian blood was involved, irrespective of whether or not a chartered community had been formed under the terms of the bill? See lines 4–6 on page 40."

MR. COLLIER: Answering that question, I read the language in this section: The Court of Indian Affairs shall have what is called in line 9, page 39, original jurisdiction over, among other things, "all actions, suits or proceedings involving the right of any person, in whole or in part of Indian blood or descent, to any allotment of land under any law or treaty." Mr. Siegel is of the opinion that that would give to the federal Court original jurisdiction over all restricted allotments.

MR. THOMPSON: You don't mean Federal Court, you mean the Court of Indian Affairs.

MR. COLLIER: With that Court of Indian Affairs rests original jurisdiction.

MR. THOMPSON: What I meant is the question: Would that be exclusive jurisdiction in that new court?

MR. COLLIER: Yes, as it now reads.

MR. SIEGEL: I should think that would be exclusive jurisdiction, not merely original, and no other court is endowed with jurisdiction over these matters. The special Indian court is established to take over jurisdiction, which Federal Courts have exercised, and also any jurisdiction which is not conferred upon the local community Indian courts.

MR. THOMPSON: Now if a controversy should come up in which we will say there was an Indian heir to a twenty-fifth of the allotment and the others were unrestricted or white, that sort would necessarily in this bill go in this Court of Indian Affairs?

MR. SIEGEL: I think so, yes.

MR. MCNAUGHTON: Question 5. "Commissioner Collier stated in substance at his Muskogee meeting on March 22, that the provisions of this bill would not affect oil or lead and zinc lands. Would it not have the same effect on such lands where the title was held by restricted Indians as to the rights of inheritance and the forum for the trial of actions as it would have on any other restricted Indian lands?"

MR. COLLIER: It is as far as I can see—I am merely taking words out of the Solicitor's mouth here. I will give my layman's answer first—that the bill as now drawn, if unamended, it seems to me would have brought these mineral things under all the provisions. It was not our intention so to do. It should not be done, at least not in areas where minerals are known to exist, and as we told the Blackfeet, there should be a special proviso put in to the effect that it does not affect minerals. It would affect the surface of the allotted land.

MR. THOMPSON: Mr. Commissioner, when I heard that remark, I thought you had in mind the Osage oil holdings in which, as I understand, the title to the oil was reserved in the tribe. You understand in the making of these lead and zinc leases the title to the lead and zinc is not reserved in the tribe as it was in the Osage tribe.

MR. COLLIER: Yes, I understand.

MR. THOMPSON: As it is under the Osage Act.

MR. COLLIER: Yes, I understand. Under the bill, where the title is individual as here, then that ownership would be reserved in the individual, that ownership of the lead and zinc.

MR. THOMPSON: Would the bill be amended so as to declare that?

MR. COLLIER: Yes, so as to put that outside of controversy. If we attempted to work out an absolution of all individual ownership of mineral values, it would be an awfully complicated thing and result in a great deal of resistance and no good would be accomplished by it. We never had any idea of it, but we should have made that clear in the original draft. We did make it clear in the hearings before the House Committee.

MR. MCNAUGHTON: Question 6. "Could a restricted Indian make a will, willing any part of his restricted allotment, except improvements, to his or her children, if the bill as now drawn was passed, irrespective as to whether or not the members of the tribe of which the allottee or holder was a member had voted to come under the provisions of the act?"

MR. SIEGEL: The same section which deals with the heirship provision which we discussed a moment ago also provides that no will will be approved which provides for any disposition inconsistent with that provided for in the section. However, all the rights, which are granted by that section, might be willed and, as I have already explained with regard to farm land, agricultural land, the rights enjoyed under this bill are no different from the rights enjoyed under the allotment system.

With regard to grazing and forestry land, the rights are in effect the same since the rights in it are merely to receive the income. The right to dispose of that land is also permitted, but it will not be the right to use and receive the income necessarily from the same piece of land because for economic reasons scattered small pieces of land must be used as one unit. With those qualifications I have just made, a will might be made disposing of any of the rights which are guaranteed under Section 11, but no other.

MR. THOMPSON: I have been asked by members of the tribe to advise them upon this question. Supposing the member has an allotment and they have two children. One child has an allotment which is valuable, the other child was born too late, as the Commissioner has suggested, and there are no improvements. Suppose the allottee desires to make a will, as he or she could now, subject to the approval of the Secretary of the Interior, willing that estate to the child who had no allotment, could he or she under this act make such a will?

MR. SIEGEL: Is that agricultural land you are speaking of?

MR. THOMPSON: Agricultural land, yes. As to the fee simple, not to the right of occupancy but as to the fee?

MR. SIEGEL: I think Mr. Collier suggested earlier this afternoon that there is no substantial difference between the rights guaranteed by this bill as to agricultural land and those guaranteed by the allotment system, but to make that perfectly plain, it is perfectly consistent with the purpose of this bill and we can amend the bill so that the allotment system with some modification would continue with regard to agricultural land. The answer to your question would be yes, with the only qualification that he could not will to so many devisees it would have to be divided up into small pieces nobody could use, but since that would not be true in your case, since there would only be two devisees, the answer would be yes.

MR. THOMPSON: Even under the terms of the bill, but you propose to amend it?

MR. SIEGEL: Even under the terms of the bill as it is. The only thing which passes to the community is the equitable title to the allotment now enjoyed, but all the rights which the Indian has by virtue of owning that equitable title, the right to use that particular piece of land, the right to receive the rental from it or an equal amount of land, the right to transmit it to his heirs and enjoy the improvements on it, the bulk of rights which you get by virtue of that title, all those rights are guaranteed by this bill so that the only difference with regard to agricultural land is difference in name only, as the Commissioner has suggested.

MR. THOMPSON: Suppose this child was 1/8 Indian blood?

MR. SIEGEL: That would make no difference absolutely, so even under the terms of the bill the answer would really be, he can.

MR. THOMPSON: So it couldn't be devised or willed or inherited by anyone not of Indian blood?

MR. SIEGEL: That isn't true either, unless the present laws were changed. There is not limit as to the right of will. I think under Section 10 of this bill, unless it is amended, the Secretary of the Interior would have the authority to eliminate such heirs, or possibility of heirship among such people, or if the authority were given the Commissioner, the Commissioner might be the authority to eliminate such people as possible heirs.

MR. MCNAUGHTON: Question 7. "If a chartered community was formed, would that community thereafter for any purpose be considered as a part of the State of which it was formerly a part, and would not an Indian living in that chartered community thereby be deprived of his rights and privileges as a citizen of the State?"

MR. SIEGEL: The Supreme Court has held that even on Indian reservations to which the Indian still holds the title, and which have been allotted and so on are part of the State, a State for example can issue its process against offenders against its own laws and against white men; for example, all offenses by a white man against a white man within such territory are offenses against white law, on the theory that these reservations are parts of the State, but the Federal Government reserves its right to extend its laws to the Indian in order to promote and protect the Indian under its guardianship. In other words the answer to your question is yes. And since citizenship of the Indian and the right to vote in the State would not be inconsistent with the guardianship of the United States or injure the effective guardianship of the United States in any way, the individual would not lose his citizenship in the State or his right to vote.

MR. THOMPSON: Of course you are familiar with the case of Worcester against the State of Georgia, Judge Marshall's decision arising out of the question as to whether a Cherokee Indian reservation within the confines of the State was subject to the laws of the State. As I understand that case Chief Justice Marshall held in his opinion that an Indian reservation within the confines of a State was not subject to the laws of the State. Neither was it entitled to the protection of the State. That decision does not seem to have been reversed.

MR. SIEGEL: About all that decision holds, I think, is that the State law will have no application to the Indian until Congress otherwise provides, because it would be inconsistent with the guardianship of the United States. But since the United States has granted citizenship to the Indian, it has never been thought that the exercise of the privileges of citizenship by an Indian in the State would be inconsistent with that guardianship. The Indians in those reservations since they have been granted citizenship in fact exercised the right of voting so that I don't think the principle of the Worcester case would apply.

MR. COLLIER: We have all over the country closed reservations where the Indians are living on tax-exempt land and are enjoying all the privileges of citizenship. They go to the common schools, they run for office and hold office and so on. Naturally where it is a matter of distributing relief, for example, the local county will discriminate against an Indian not taxed because it says "You are not contributing to the treasury of the county and we prefer the fellow who is." That is the condition now. He has all the privileges, but he may be discriminated against.

MR. THOMPSON: I had in mind that, since the bill, as I understand, provides that the community as organized takes over all governmental functions, including the control of the schools and highway system.

MR. COLLIER: It doesn't.

MR. THOMPSON: Well, assume that it did. Assuming that it took over all governmental functions and was a State in itself, then of course the right of citizenship in the State in which it was located would necessarily be inconsistent with the exercise of the rights in that community.

MR. COLLIER: Look at the way it is now. When it has taken over all these functions, then it would have the functions already exercised by the Bureau of Indian Affairs, wouldn't it? It is doing all that. The Bureau of Indian Affairs on closed reservations, any of those reservations in the Northwest, for example, is doing all these things. We maintain roads, schools, health service. The Indian Bureau is an instrument of the Federal Government and carries out these services in that area. The Indians living there are tax-exempt. They are today enjoying all the privileges of citizenship in their States. If the community took over these functions it would simply be substituted for the Indian Bureau as a Federal instrumentality. The status of the individual wouldn't be altered at all. I think I can illustrate that more clearly from the Eastern Cherokees.

The Eastern Cherokees formed themselves into a community, they were an incorporated body, their land is tax-exempt because they deeded it to the Government in order to have it exempted and they are taking on gradually more functions of self-government. They are not allotted. They are full citizens of the State and enjoy all its privileges and all the amenities of citizenship in the State. The only places where Indians are deprived of citizenship are in States whose constitutions do prohibit them, like New Mexico. Indians not taxed may not vote in the State of New Mexico. That is the condition now and it would be under this bill because the control is with the State, unless we can end it by getting some Supreme Court decision that would reverse that. In Arizona they have worked out a ruling in their Supreme Court that Indians who are wards may not vote. Those are the only two places where any discrimination does exist and no more would exist under this than does now, unless it were for this reason: There is now a definite resentment in many communities against the Indian as a non-taxpayer. The taxable values are kept out of the community and the Federal Government has not made itself responsible for maintaining its services, so that there is a deficiency of service for the white people in that community. This bill also obligates the Federal Government to maintain all the public services within these areas and that would take away this resentment growing out of the loss of tax money. In that way the Indian would get better treatment.

Furthermore, the chartered community may in turn contract with the State, the county, the school board and have them carry out any services within the community and pay them for doing it.

MR. THOMPSON: This bill seeks to subject the whites living within the community to the action of the community?

MR. COLLIER: Yes, insofar as it becomes a territorial community, a municipal government, of course anybody living in it would be subject to its ordinances.

QUESTION: "Could a tribe now rejecting the bill, now requesting to be excluded from it, ever get a chance to apply for a charter, that is, ever get a chance to be let into it again?"

Certainly, but there is this reason to think about it before you act: We are now riding the crest of a wave. We think we are going to be able to get this bill through Congress because it is a big thing and offers a far reaching and definite solution of problems. We are asking for a lot of money and we think we can get it because we say this money is going to get the results, going to save the land, going to re-establish the Indians. Also, we have the President actively in favor of it, and the President controls at present both Houses of Congress. What the situation would be at a later date I can't predict. If tribes were excluded from the bill, the appropriations would be correspondingly reduced and when they came back to be included in the bill it would be the same as coming back to be included in the appropriation, which would make larger appropriation necessary, hence there might be some difficulty later on in being admitted after the enthusiasm had passed and when perhaps the President wouldn't be there anymore or wouldn't have control of Congress. There is a certain risk.

It is conceivable even that this condition might arise: Let us just imagine that twenty big tribes said they didn't want to go in now, they are going to wait five years. The bill was passed in that form. Then we would have an appropriation of $500,000 for the expenses of chartering the communities and $2,000,000 appropriation for land purchase. The Indians who did come in would soon find that the amount of money appropriated was still not enough, not enough even for them. They would want it all. They would want more and it would be quite reasonable for them to set up a resistance against admitting more Indians that would result in causing or compelling the money to be spread thinner. So I would say that it is on the side of safety to come in if a tribe can convince itself that it is safe to come in; in other words, if a tribe can see clearly the optional nature of the whole bill and that even though it is brought into the bill, still it doesn't have to do anything unless it wants to, then the tribe would be in and whenever it got ready could take advantage of the facilities. That would be safer than coming back to the Congress later and asking to have the act amended to include that tribe.

MR. MCNAUGHTON: Any other questions or resolutions you desire, or statements?

MR. THOMPSON: May I ask just one more question on behalf of the tribe? They are anxious to know about when this matter will probably be reported out of the committee?

MR. COLLIER: That is difficult to say. We have delayed the proceedings by going out in the field for these congresses. There are still congresses to be held. There is one to be held in Utah and one in the Wisconsin-Minnesota country. That means that the Senate practically has not started its hearings yet. That goes before the judiciary jointly with the Indian committees, so I would expect that many weeks would have to elapse before it was reported in both Houses.

Furthermore, the committees are going to desire the reaction from the Indians after these congresses. They are going to want to hear from them just as we do. Now if it appears, if it should appear in two or three weeks or more that Congress is going to adjourn at a known day, say the first of June, I would expect that the committees would aim to report out a bill, this bill or something like it, early enough to pass it, early enough so that it wouldn't get lost in the eleventh hour rush. In that case if there were tribes which were still very much in doubt, there would be nothing to do except to put in a rider, broad language, saying that the following tribes are not to be affected by any provision in this bill, including those that know they want it. The bill could pass in that form. Then next year, if the tribes in the meantime had changed their mind or had made a decision, they could be included, if there is no opposition to such admission. So I can't say absolutely, and it is perfectly possible that the delay which we have invited by going out to these congresses may lose us the bill in this session. It might happen. We know we were running that risk, but we were interested in doing this thing with your knowledge, and even at the risk of a year's delay we will not be sorry we did it; so I can't promise the enactment of the bill. We would have put the bill through. With the active endorsement of the President a bill of this kind would go through like greased lightning, but now I don't know how it is going to be.

This is an important question. "You say it is your opinion that a tribe rejecting this bill, will, in time, lose property, etc. Why? And how?"

I am glad of this question because it enables me to explain why and how. Let us look at the tribes whose lands have been allotted. You can say the thing which has happened will continue to happen if conditions haven't changed. The trend shown on that chart, the steady shrinkage of the lands, will go on. Now why? First, the trust period runs out. It becomes more and more difficult to procure extension of trust periods. When the Five Civilized Tribes went back two years ago to secure extension, they got only half of what they asked for. Next time probably they can't get anything. The ending of the trust period sees the land go under taxation; it is mortgaged, sold and gone. Second, as the years go on, more and more land passes into the class of heirship land and is split up among these ever-growing numbers of heirs. As a result wasteful, unproductive, administrative costs rise to the sky. I explained how much the Indian real-estate business was costing the Government. At the Kiowa Agency it eats up all but $15,000 of the agency money each year. The agency has $80,000 and this administration eats up $65,000. And so in the aggregate it runs to $2,000,000 or $3,000,000 a year, which is regarded by the Government as a waste of money, and it is always increasing. Now we are up against it for money for the Indians. Let me illustrate. The condition of Indian health is not good in this country. The death rate continues to run twice as high as the white death rate. We are very badly undersupplied with doctors and nurses and hospitals in the Indian service. Our hospitals are so undersupplied with nurses that this condition is dangerous to the life of the nurses. The nurses are being worked to death and their mortality increased. We lose our best nurses.

We made an issue of that this year to get more money for health. We carried the case all the way to the President to get the President's endorsement, forwarded it to the House Committee, and what did we get? As a reward we got an increase of $75,000 for the whole United States, the point being that the total appropriation for the regular Indian service cannot be increased, it is being held absolutely down. As a matter of fact we are spending this year twelve and one-half million dollars less than two years ago. That amount has been taken away.

We have the same condition in education. We have today 15,000 Indian children, wards of the Government, with no school, denied schooling for the lack of money. Now Congress, seeing what it is that is taking the money, this administration of these heirship lands, and seeing the cost rise every year and that it isn't doing any good, is going to do one of two things: Either bring this thing to an end and get out, terminate the trust period, wash their hands and quit looking after thousands of Indians, or else they are going to say "The Government won't appropriate any more money." If these lands are to be administered they will have to be paid for by the Indians, which again is not feasible as the Indians are too poor. Therefore I would say it is quite certain that the shrinkage of allotted areas which has gone on, will continue to go on and that regardless of anything I might do or might promise or that Secretary Ickes might do or promise, the trust periods will not be extended. The heirship lands will be sold, the allotted lands will vanish away.

Furthermore, regarding the trust money belonging to tribes, which have totaled $750,000,000 and more since 1900 and which now total less than $20,000,000, I don't know any way to stop the misappropriation of those funds except to give the Indians the veto power of those appropriations. If Secretary Ickes and I can't stop it, I don't believe our successors can. We propose to give the Indians the power to say that we, the Government, can't use trust money unless the Indians consent to it.

I mentioned that our educational appropriation is too small just as our health appropriation is too small. The effect of both of those things is to pull the Indian down into a lower and lower social level. Those two things are almost as important as the loss of the land. I see no way to build up educational and health service except along the lines of this bill. That will save money and reapply it to those uses through the building-up of material prosperity of the Indians through the adding of new land and by capitalizing industry. The Indian is in a condition where he is sleeping—I don't mean the individual but the allotted Indian in general. We have to reverse that trend. I don't see how anybody else looking at the whole history can understand them and the law division and I who sit up there and have these pleas for alienation of land go over our desks every day, understand them. I don't think anybody at all can deny that allotted land is going to go, substantially all of it, and as I say, we cannot prevent the inevitable lifting of the trust and the forced sale of lands except by some method like this.

MR. MCNAUGHTON: How was the Indian trust money accumulated?

MR. COLLIER: Different ways, partly from this ceded land taken away from the Indians as part of the allotment, where they got $1.25 as a rule for it, partly it has been accumulated from royalties derived from tribal oil and minerals of all kinds, partly it has been derived from the sale of Indian timber from large Indian-owned forests, partly it has been derived from suits in the Court of Claims. You Osages know how your tribal money came and how much of it went away, $244,000,000 since 1915. I think you have about $25,000,000 of that left.

JOHN LOGAN: I am a member of the Six Nations, of the Western band of Seneca-Cayuga Indians. We have derived some funds from the State of New York, direct from the State of New York. Part is paid direct to the Indian Office. I mean one time it was paid direct to Indian Office and I had money; one time it was paid to Chief, but this you refer to was referred to Indian Office.

MR. COLLIER: Yes.

JOHN LOGAN: It is kind of complicated, I don't understand what you say once in awhile but you just go on and I will—

MR. COLLIER: Well about these tribal funds. There are many—

JOHN LOGAN: Yes, we got tribal money, tribal funds you refer to. I got a little building here and that would be whether it is validated or not.

MR. COLLIER: You are probably referring to some payment made under treaty.

JOHN LOGAN: Yes, sir. No, we have no treaty, I belong to the Western Band of Six Nations. We are Six Nations. I belong to Six Nations.

MR. COLLIER: The Six Nations haven't got any tribal fund I know about, none under the jurisdiction of the United States anyhow.

JOHN LOGAN: Well, Six Nations, Western Band from New York state, we got little fund from the United States. It is a Cayuga fund.

MR. COLLIER: Now I am talking about tribal funds. I want to rub this in: The amount of money paid in as tribal funds has been enormous. I gave you the figures, $750,000,000 since 1900, and I told you practically all of that was gone. All tribal money of most of the tribes is now gone, but there will be new tribal income hereafter from timber, from tribal minerals and above all from suits in the Court of Claims. I predict it will go the way of the old money unless the Indians get a voice in the manner of its disbursement. We want to give the Indians a voice in how it shall be spent. That is all this bill does.

QUESTION: Can a member of a tribe join the community plan, regardless of what tribe he belongs to, even though his tribe doesn't want him to?

JOHN LOGAN: I am a member of the Six Nations—

MR. COLLIER: If a community is formed, any member of the tribe can join it if he wants to, but if a tribe wants itself excluded from the bill, why that is that. Its members are of course shut out. That is the only way I can answer it. When a tribe comes into the bill, then its members, all of them, have the privilege, but of course if a tribe is excluded, it is excluded. They can't be both out and in.

This is Mr. Woehlke, the field representative of the Indian Office.

MR. WOEHLKE: Question: "Just what does this bill of rights propose to do with grazing and forestry on surplus lands as on the Klamath Indian Reservation?"

MR. COLLIER: That means on tribal lands.

MR. WOEHLKE: On forestry land which is tribal land it proposes to manage or to give a chance to manage those lands on a perpetual-yield basis, instead of as at present taking the capital assets of the tribe, which is the timber, and cutting it clean and distributing these capital assets among the members of the tribe where the money disappears as water goes into a thirsty soil. Instead of wasting the capital assets in this way, the bill proposes that the tribal land, the tribal forest, shall be so managed that it will produce an income for the tribe for all time to come, that the capital will remain there and only the interest from that capital will be spent for the benefit of the tribe, will be paid to the individuals as dividends.

So far as the grazing land is concerned, it is proposed under this bill to give the community the power to consolidate the grazing lands in grazing units, to take out the checkerboard, to arrange the tribal lands as grazing land, irrespective of individual ownership, into areas which can be advantageously used for grazing which, if they have to be rented because there isn't enough stock belonging to the tribe or the members thereof to use them, can be rented for far more money than they bring in this scattered condition.

If such a unified grazing area produced higher rentals, then the individuals who have a share in that grazing unit will of course receive larger dividends than they do at present from the use of their individual land.

QUESTION: "What does the bill provide in reference to employment of Indians in community government and handling the same?"

The bill provides that in any chartered community various services may be taken over from the Indian Bureau as the community is able and willing to assume and direct those services. It also is provided in the bill that the appropriation of these services will be transferred to the community, and the community shall have the right to fill the vacancies in the positions taken over with its own members or with persons of its own choice as those vacancies arise. Of course, as the Commissioner explained this morning, they will have to be qualified persons, but at the same time the bill also provides that the Secretary may describe and set the qualifications for persons of Indian blood for the service of these communities. This is done so as to remove in part the effect of the general civil service rules and regulations and standards on the selection of employees for the community service. As the Commissioner explained this morning, during the past thirty years the educational and other standards for the general civil service have been continuously lifted, while the education of the Indian population has not kept pace at the same speed, with the result that there have been fewer and fewer Indian applicants who were able to qualify under the general civil service, or if they did qualify they came in at the bottom of the eligible list, whereas the law provides that positions in the civil service must be filled from the top of the eligible list.

This bill provides that special qualifications for certain positions may be prescribed by the Secretary of the Interior with the idea in view that in many, many instances there are well qualified persons of Indian blood who understand the work, who understand their people, yet by reason of the technical educational qualifications of the general civil service are unable to find employment at the present time. With the rules or with the provisions of the bill giving the Secretary power to establish what you might call an Indian civil service, it will be very much easier to fill the ranks of the community service with persons of Indian blood.

QUESTION: "Who will pay for administration of community government?"

For the initial launching or the beginning, for the organization work of these communities as described in this bill, the bill carries an appropriation of half a million dollars. After organization, after the chartered community is working and has its various officials, the division of the cost would be about as follows: The services which were taken over, which were transferred to the community from the Indian Bureau, services such as the health work, the agricultural extension work, education and things of that character, services which the Indian Bureau now performs and which would be paid for through a federal appropriation just as they are now, except that the disbursement of the federal appropriation would be left to the community through a bonded disbursing officer. The expenses of the civil community organization, you might say of the town government, the pay the councilmen, if any—I mean if there were any pay—and the pay for whatever other community officials there might be, they would have to come out of the funds of the community itself, just as for instance today the Osages are paying their councilmen, if they do pay them, out of their own tribal funds. You will find that the bill provides that the community has the power to levy assessments and collect taxes for the conduct of its own business. But it also provides that instead of paying the assessment in cash, the individual may pay his assessment in work. That provision was put in there so that it would be possible to get community work done without having to place a tax lien on the property inside the community.

QUESTION: "Will you favor positions filled by Indians?"

I suppose the question means: Is it the policy of this administration to favor Indian employees for the Indian service? I believe you can find the answer in this bill. Certainly the bill would not provide an elaborate system for bringing Indians into the Indian service if the administration didn't favor that policy.

MR. COLLIER: I think you can say something more here. There is a certain kind of work now going on which is not under civil service; for example the work of the Indian emergency conservation camps is not under civil service. There we are free to give anybody whom we want the supervisory jobs, foremen, managers and executives. There are 14,000 Indians in these projects and more than half of all the technical supervisory employees are Indians. The proportion is increasing every month. That is not only because we want to do it that way, but we have found that the Indian men placed in the responsible positions were very efficient, responsible and capable, and the camps have been a great success largely, I think, as a result of the fact that we have employed Indians for the top jobs.

MR. SIEGEL: Question: "If this bill passes, could a mixed group of Indians of various tribes band together and form a colony and could they select territory in any state for their community?"

I see no reason why the members of various tribes could not be the nucleus of a new colony, their land to be purchased in any territory. They would not if their tribe were specifically exempted from the terms of this bill. They would not be successor to the rights, powers and privileges and assets of the tribes of which they are now a part.

MR. COLLIER: This is a long series of questions. "Are you," that is Collier, "an attorney?" No. "And if so"—I am not an attorney—"do you understand the import of the bill as drawn or are you merely assuming its good features which you stress?" I guess I understand it all right. If I hadn't, they would have found it out in the House Committee where they had me on the stand for five or six successive meetings.

QUESTION: "Who is really the author of this bill and did the Indians themselves suggest any part of it?"

The bill is the product of the joint labors of the Indian Office and the office of the Solicitor of the Interior Department. It represents the work of lawyers and non-lawyers. The essential ideas in the bill go back a number of years, in fact they were all put forward in 1929 by the then Secretary of the Interior, Dr. Wilbur, and the then Commissioner of Indian Affairs, Mr. Rhoads. They put them out in a very careful memorandum to Congress, but they never went forward and they never drew their ideas up in the form of a bill and did not support the idea actively.

I don't know that any one person can claim main credit, or discredit as you may think, for the bill. It represents the combined brains of a lot of people and before it is finished, I think before it is perfected finally, a great many more people would have to put their brains into it, Indians and friends of Indians.

I might add that there is a number of organizations who have been working in behalf of the Indians for years, like the American Indian Defense Association, the Indian Rights Association, and so on. They have all helped shape up the ideas that have gone into this bill and they are all supporting it.

QUESTION: "Did the Indians themselves suggest any part of it?"

The original suggestion for the incorporation of tribes, which is at the heart of this bill, was made in 1927 by the tribal council of the Klamath Indian tribe of Oregon. They put the idea out first. The Klamath Tribe then contributed a lot of detailed ideas and later the Menominee Tribe took it up and they have contributed more ideas. The Pueblo tribes and the Eastern Cherokees have been organized as bodies corporate for years and their experience underlies a good deal of this legislation. Senator Curtis, who was mentioned here today, has from time to time through a number of years contributed ideas that have gone into this bill. I could go on. Yes the Indians have contributed a whole lot to this bill.

QUESTION: "You say there is no attempt being made to coerce or influence any Indian tribe or individual to accept your community proposition, yet why do you say before the House Indian Committee that if opposition of the Indians is met by you in your present contacts with them, the matter will be only deferred until such time as 'we can swing them around?'"

Well that is obvious. I believe in this bill and I don't expect to stop preaching its virtues. I expect to give my views now and hereafter that it is a good bill. It is the kind of thing you want. You can't ask any more than that. That is very different from coercion.

QUESTION: "You say that under the bill the individual right cannot be taken away without his, the Indian's, consent. Then why, in your own statements to the House Committees, do you admit just the opposite?"

I don't. I said that the individual property right in allotment could not be taken away. That is obvious but I have added, and I thought I made it clear here, that there is a way, a legal and practical way, to deprive the Indian of his allotment, that is by forcing a fee patent on him, by declaring him competent, by throwing his land on the tax list and thus causing him to lose. In my statement to the House Committee I likewise developed this thought which I wish I had had time to develop today. You will find it at the beginning of part 1 of the House printed hearing. I gave a long list of arbitrary things which the Secretary of the Interior and the Commissioner of Indian Affairs can do under existing law, of course discretionary. We have the arbitrary power which we think we should not have, such power for example as to destroy an Indian's will, annul it. There is no appeal from what we do. We have such power as to force upon the Indian the ending of the trust period on his land. We have the power on Indian reservations to arrest and imprison Indians for long periods without trial and without any court of record. We have the power to forbid Indians from complaining in an organized way about their wrongs. We have the power to forbid investigators, attorneys and even Congressmen from going among the Indians on reservations. If they go in spite of our prohibition, we fine them $1,000 and put them in jail two years. I gave a long list of these arbitrary powers which can be used to annul the citizenship of Indians. I don't say we are using them that way, but we could use them and they have been used and we want them taken away from us.

QUESTION: "You say and stress the fact that this bill in no way affects oil, lead and zinc or other mineral rights. Does the bill really say that or is not that merely your own presumption? Did you not admit otherwise in your own statements to the House Committee?"

That is not a frank question because I have already answered it. I told you, I told the House Committee, that the bill was not clear, but the bill should be amended to exclude oil and minerals. That was way back before the House Committee. That has been answered already.

MR. THOMPSON: Mr. Collier, in that connection do I understand you to say that you are going to recommend that so far as the allotments are concerned where the Indians are individual owners of mines, that the bill will be so amended that it will not extend to that ownership?

MR. COLLIER: We have already done that and it will be so done. The bill in its present text does not even contain the credit provision. That has gone in as an amendment, but we are committed to it and there is no question about it.

QUESTION: "Are you really familiar with all the allotment laws?"

ANSWER: I won't answer that, I know enough of them. This is just a heckling question.

QUESTION: "Are we to understand that you advocate by this bill the perpetual restriction of the estates, properties etc. of Indians, regardless of their future progress?"

ANSWER: No, I don't advocate any perpetual bill; I advocate and the bill contemplates continuous restriction until otherwise directed by Congress; and I think that would be a good long time in many cases. Mr. Roe Cloud has got some questions now that have been handed up.

MR. ROE CLOUD: I have some hot questions. "If the Indian is not considered by you as inferior, why do you seek to place him in a community to himself?"

I think this question in the first place was based upon a misunderstanding and a misconception. It has been said here repeatedly that no Indians would be placed by themselves excepting those Indians who are at present unaffiliated and unadopted. You know there are a great many Indians who have been wandering as strays around the United States, particularly in the north. They are so-called landless, wandering Crees and Chippewas, quite a number of them. They can't be put into my reservation or your reservation because all the land is already claimed, therefore new lands have to be acquired. These lands that they are terming submarginal lands are to be provided in cooperation with the Secretary of Agriculture so that such lands will be taken out of general production which is causing overproduction and in turn causing the farmers of the nation to have a hard time today. If you can take those lands from being used to cause overproduction, it will cause the farm prices, I understand, to go up and everybody will be benefited.

Now these wandering landless Indians will get some of those lands for subsistence farming. Some of them are eating out of garbage cans in the cities and towns in the north of our country now. They will have opportunity to have a little piece of ground where they can farm, have a cow, a few chickens and have a decent home where they can help to support themselves. There are thousands of Indians such as that. To help them that way is not to consider them inferior in any respect. As a matter of fact it is placing honor upon them in supposing that they have the ability and capacity for self-government, for self-support. If we thought they were inferior and couldn't help themselves, why the last thing to do would be to try to help them because they are worthless and should not be helped; but on the contrary so capable are they and so deserving of respect are they that they deserve help. They are in a bad fix because of the misfortunes that have befallen them through the treatment beyond their control by powerful governments, both the Canadian and the United States government. The logical thing to do is to help them and take them away from these counties and states which have not money to look after them, and let the powerful federal government take care of them.

The misconception is also here, that the Indians who go into these chartered communities will be segregated all by themselves and have no dealings with the whites after that. The way I understand this bill where there is a checkerboard condition, an Indian here and white man next-door neighbor to him and so on all the way through, the chartered community can be interpreted as a reorganization. For instance in the Quapaw area here where you have white neighbors all around you, the Indians in this community could go into a chartered community and yet go about exactly as they are, merely forming a business organization so that they can participate in this five or ten-million-dollars capital loan system that will be set in operation. "In organization is strength" we are continually hearing, and I believe it is very true that if Indians can so organize in a business fashion, they can gain a great deal of common betterment, political betterment, and the white people of this community would be forced to listen to those Indians in their demands from an economic standpoint, from a political standpoint, from a business standpoint, because they too at last will be acting in a large way, they will be acting in a united way instead of in a single way. They can then command things instead of begging for things as they have been doing in all these years.

When Indians get organized, they can have the operation of their own education, health and other services. "If we are entrusted with the expenditure of large sums of money, that is one way of considering us with great respect and honor instead of considering us as inferior people." At present, the Indian Bureau, 2,000 miles away, does all this work for you; it does it because they still consider you inferior—"We can't handle our affairs, the white people got to handle them for us. They are smart and we are uneducated and we can't do it;" therefore we will put the expenditures, the budget estimates and the establishment of all these things in your hands and you try it. That is a great compliment. Never has such a compliment been paid to the Indian people.

Here is another question: "Indians and whites have been citizens of Oklahoma for twenty-seven years, as governed and of the governing class without racial controversy. For one hundred years the Indians and whites have intermarried in the Indian Territory. Why do you propose a change? Who is the bad apple in the barrel?"

That also is begging the question because it is based on, as I said, a misconception. Apparently the Indians have been getting along fine, marrying the white people, becoming like white people, making money and acting just like white people, so this question said. But look at that map over there, millions and millions of acres lost, hundreds of millions of dollars lost for the Indian people! As I said in my few remarks to the employees at the luncheon here, where among a thousand white men and one man dies among a thousand Indians at the same time two Indians die. The death rate among the Indians is twice that among the white people today under the present system. When you look at the loss of these lands and the loss of these moneys and the loss of human beings themselves at a fast rate such as we are going, where is our future? There is no equality, no betterment to be discovered there. A few of us, maybe a handful here and a handful there, may do well because we have made our adjustment, but we have to think of our hundred thousand brothers and sisters who are hungry, cold and homeless, of the future generations and build up these lands and capital resources in such a way that they shall not be doomed as we ourselves are doomed in the near future.

Now do we lose our so-called privileges in the future? If a chartered Indian community-member wants to marry a white person, what is to prevent them? A chartered Indian community member comes in contact with white people here at Miami, in Pitcher and Joplin; they get attached to one another, they get sentimental and they get married now. Why not in the future?

Now about that bad apple. Of all the Commissioners that ever came into office, John Collier is the only one who says we are all good apples. "You are worth our preserving. The perpetual use of your culture and your contributions to us who are white Americans is so great and so precious that I want to save it; I want to preserve it and I want to enrich it, make it more abundant and enlarge it so that the rest of the white people of the nation may enjoy what the Indians can contribute." That's what he says. If he had thought you are a bad apple and are going to spoil all the rest of the whites, would he come with his program among us today, offering lands, moneys, credit organizations and opportunity for self-government as we have never had before?

I know of no Commissioner of Indian Affairs that comes with such a love of the Indian people as to amount to a fervor of passion of service for them and bring to them opportunities and self-government and self-preservation as he has.

"If the Indian" (this is the third question) "If the Indian has been deprived of his land by the Government, why not the Government grant land to him, restriction taxation and against alienation?"

That is exactly what he is trying to do under this bill and in order to prevent a loss of any of these lands and moneys, he will fix it so that it will be perpetually inalienable. No power on earth except the Congress of the United States can cause us to lose our lands again under this bill. When he does that, he does it in the only way it can be done and that is by a system of self-governing communities under a perpetual trust period arrangement. If an Indian goes into that community and is so enterprising that he thinks he can do better by going out of that community and live among the whites, there is nothing to prevent him from doing that. He can dispose of his holdings, put his hands on his cash in his pockets, go out of the community, make an investment and compete with the white men out there. But we have found that at the present development of the Indian race he hasn't been able, speaking of this whole class of Indians, to compete with the organized white system as successfully as we wish him to do. Collier is trying to give us that time element, say a quarter of a century or more, when we can make a better adjustment with the white race, and in that time when we have developed ourselves and we have the capacity, we can vote ourselves into another kind of adjustment to our white neighbors such as may be more suitable than we are here proposing today.

If we really understood it, if we really understood this bill, we should discover that it takes nothing from us of that which we now have, but in addition to what we have, it gives us so much more that if such things were offered to an immigrant group of white people, Irish, Czechs or Italian or any of these people coming from across the ocean, how long do you suppose they would hesitate in grabbing them? If it were not for the whispering in the ear of interested people who want to continue to rob the Indians and work under the very system that causes that loss of lands, the Indians themselves would take it very gladly and say "Thank you very much indeed. I like your scheme. I will give it a trial and if it doesn't work, I can go back to my old system."

Applause.

MR. WOEHLKE: Question: "Is there any provision in the proposed act whereby two separate distinct tribes of Indians can take out a charter jointly together, where their reservations are located side by side?"

They can easily do that any time they are already, any time they want to.

QUESTION: "Would this act apply to any Indian tribes outside of the 48 States in the Union, for instance, such as the Kickapoo Indians of Old Mexico, who are now located there?" Delegates—Sac & Fox of the Missouri Tribe.

It all depends on the citizenship status of the Kickapoos of Old Mexico. If they have not lost their citizenship status and wanted to come back, then they would enjoy all the rights and privileges offered by this bill. If they have lost their citizenship status, then they could not possibly come under this bill.

MR. SIEGEL: Question: "The bill provides that the rights now owned by Indians if a community is chartered, will upon the death of the present owners pass to the community, with the right in the heirs to its use, or to its rental. Since it seems to be true that possible heirs have no vested rights, what assurance is there that the Secretary of the Interior, by exercising his power of establishing rules of descent, will not make rules which require the land to pass directly to the community to the exclusion of the usual heirs?"

I suppose the person has reference to the rights evidenced by a certificate. The answer is that the danger to which the person refers is a real one and possibly ought to be avoided by amending the section to which the person has reference.

MR. COLLIER: Question: "You contend there are about 100,000 Indians practically in the bread line in Oklahoma, landless and homeless. Is there not a greater proportion of whites in the same condition in Oklahoma? Why should not the Federal Government place the red man and his white brother together in the proposed Federal Municipal Corporation?"

ANSWER: Well, I reckon there are lots of whites in the bread line temporarily, although the proportion is not as high as among the Indians. It happens that Indians are wards of the Government, with a particular claim on it. Therefore they are able to get what we can get for the Indians. I might add under the subsistence homestead plan $25,000,000 is being loaned by the Federal Government in establishing white people in consolidated areas exactly like these proposed Indian colonies, and the demand for that $25,000,000 is so many times greater than that amount of money that they don't know what to do.

HOMER CHANDLER: As I understand it, this record is being made to be used in connection with the Congressional Record. It is my desire, speaking for and on behalf of the chiefs of these respective tribes, that this go into the record, Mr. Commissioner: "Miami, Oklahoma, March 24, 1934. To whom it may concern: We the undersigned officials and councilmen, the duly elected delegates of the Association of Indian Tribes, having been selected and elected as delegates by the members of said Association at a duly called meeting on March 12, 1934, to appear before and represent said Association before and with the Honorable John Collier, Commissioner of Indian Affairs, on March 24, 1934 when he appears in the city of Miami, Oklahoma for the purpose of conferring with the Indians of northeastern Oklahoma, do hereby select and designate Homer E. Chandler of Miami to act as spokesman for our said delegation at such meeting or meetings with Mr. Collier, and we hereby ratify each and every statement he may make in that respect to you."

MR. COLLIER: Could I see that a moment?

MR. CHANDLER: Now, Mr. Commissioner, we appreciate getting that into the record and as I said a while ago, here stands in these three rows, five chiefs of five tribes residing in Ottawa County, Oklahoma, the members of which are—a majority of the members of which tribes are under the superintendency of the local agency.

First permit me, Mr. Commissioner, for and on behalf of these chiefs to extend to you our appreciation of having this contact in this manner with you.

Perhaps, Mr. Commissioner, you will recall some time ago of receiving a lengthy resolution from the Association of Indian Tribes of Miami, Oklahoma, of which these men are members, and under date of November 30, 1933, Mr. Commissioner, we received from you a response which we appreciate.

The Association of Indian Tribes wants to say a few words in that regard. It is an organization here in Miami, Oklahoma in which every Indian can belong and in which there is now some 300 members and in which these five chiefs can—also with Mr. Griffin, Chief of the Quapaw Indians, is a member, thereby making six chiefs—and we have only one thing in view and only one thing and that is for and in the interest of the Indian, although we have been referred to, Mr. Commissioner, and I want to get this into the record, as an organization in which the officers are therein solely for personal gain for political purposes, which information, Mr. Commissioner, you can—is a matter of record in the Secretary's office, having been obtained here by a Mr. Bonneville some time ago, an inspector out of the Secretary of Interior's office.

Now, Mr. Commissioner, I wish to say that some three or four weeks ago these members of our association and chiefs as I have referred to procured copies of this bill. I believe some were mailed out by your office and they asked the respective Oklahoma delegations in Washington to forward them and they forwarded them and they have been studying them ever since. Last night they called a council. There were fifteen present, including the chiefs and the counsel of this Association. They were in session some three or four hours and they all more or less have some knowledge I might say of what the bill contains. They received that knowledge last night more than they have ever heretofore in view of the fact that they were in assembly together and had some discussion. They are asking me to speak for them and that is why I am here and that is why I made the record.

We have sat here and listened intensely and given our ear to what you have said, Mr. Commissioner, in connection with this bill, and I want to say for and in behalf of these chiefs that there are certain portions of that bill which is all right, in my opinion, and that is what they think, but there are others—taking the bill as in its entirety it is something that they disapprove. As I understand it, getting down to the fundamental principle of it, it means more or less incorporating or permitting Indians of 1/4 degree blood to incorporate, apply to the Secretary of the Interior and procure a charter and certificates of membership, all these. It gives me the thought of a corporation. I can't think of it any other way; and then the Secretary of the Interior places them upon this reservation, loans them this money that, Mr. Secretary, you spoke about this morning, gives them their own right to choose their own officers and places them under a court of their own, takes them away from the district court of Ottawa County, the county court of Ottawa and the Supreme Court of the State of Oklahoma and creates a court solely for that purpose. As I understand the bill, and I may be wrong, it provides for six or seven judges, as I understand, to act in a circuit at a salary probably of $7,500,000 per annum, I am not positive in that connection, and some ten attorneys to be appointed by the President of the United States to take care of their affairs. This proceeding these men disapprove. Now we have prepared a resolution here, Mr. Commissioner, by these men as chief of their tribes, which they desire to file and to be made a part of your record, and also the Shawnees have prepared a resolution and they desire to file that with you in order to be made a part of the Congressional Record.

MR. COLLIER: It may be filed, Mr. Chandler.

MR. CHANDLER: All right, thank you kindly. I want to file those now.

MR. COLLIER: Were they prepared recently?

ANSWER: Well, this morning after discussing the bill last night, Mr. Commissioner. Would you let the record show, Mr. Commissioner, that they would be made a part of the record?

MR. COLLIER: They will be made a part of the record, yes. For the record, Mr. Chandler, who was present at the meeting last night? How many were present?

MR. CHANDLER: Well, fifteen.

MR. COLLIER: And you say there are how many members of the Association?

MR. CHANDLER: Approximately 300, scattered here and there, from various tribes.

MR. COLLIER: The membership is individual of course?

ANSWER: Yes, yes sir, all memberships are eligible to become members and regardless of blood and regardless of the particular tribe to which they belong and where they might be located.

MR. COLLIER: Has the Association met on this bill?

MR. CHANDLER: They did March 12, 1934, and passed a resolution in opposition thereto and mailed your office at Washington a copy thereof.

MR. COLLIER: How large a meeting was that?

MR. CHANDLER: I would say there was 250 present.

MR. COLLIER: 250 individual members of the Association?

ANSWER: Yes.

MR. COLLIER: All of them of these tribes. How many people, how many members of these tribes are there? How big are these tribes in the aggregate?

ANSWER: You mean the chief officers?

MR. COLLIER: I am trying to get at the number of Indians in the several tribes who aren't members of the Association.

MR. CHANDLER: I don't know, Mr. Commissioner. That is a matter probably that can be furnished you by the Superintendent.

MR. COLLIER: Yes, no doubt.

MR. CHANDLER: Mr. Commissioner, those resolutions for and on behalf of the men for which, of which I have acted as spokesman are self-explanatory. That is their attitude. Now, Mr. Commissioner, would you permit me in closing to say a few words for and on behalf of these men and our Association?

MR. COLLIER: Proceed.

MR. CHANDLER: It is the sense—it is the belief of these Indians here in Ottawa County, Oklahoma that there is only three things to do for the solution of the Indian people, and I am speaking as an Indian myself and for—and I can safely say for and on behalf of every member of our association in addition to these chiefs, and that is to educate the young. The other is to put the able bodied to work and teach the Indian to instead of driving an automobile, to learn to drive a team to a plow.

Applause.

Another thing, Mr. Commissioner, in my closing remarks, and one we are vitally interested in. When you were appointed to that honorable office I assure you, it was my understanding that it was one of your theories to put as many Indian people in the service as possible—I may be wrong in that connection. Understand me of course, that I understand that there is a civil service commission and that at this day and time it is by competitive examination. Years ago perhaps some of you men that is in the service now, an Indian, regardless of what race he might be, could apply to Civil Service Commission and they would send him papers to his local postmaster and he could take a competitive examination, he could take an examination. If he made a satisfactory examination in a week's time approximately he would get an appointment to the service, but this day and time it is wrong, it is not that way, it must be by competitive—but Mr. Commissioner, it is our belief that more Indians should be employed in the Indian service and if there is anything you can do in that connection to perfect such a rule I can safely say for and on behalf of these Indians that they will greatly appreciate it, for we are really competent and qualified.

I want to say to you, Mr. Commissioner, that no doubt you have addressed some intelligent audiences while in this State, but I don't think you have ever addressed an audience that is superior to this audience in the way of intelligence. The Indian people today, some of them that is only 1/4 degree of blood, are in a position to take their place anywhere, any time, any place with any white man in the way of business. For example, take Mr. Roe Cloud there. There is an example. He has Haskell Institute up here. I don't know what degree of blood he is. There is one example. Take my friend, Ray McNaughton that sits beside him. He is one of the honored members of the bar, a Peoria Indian. His brother here, is a chief of the Peorias. The halls of Congress echo with their voices. They are both in the upper and lower houses. They fill the District Judges' chair throughout the State of Oklahoma. They are in the halls of our legislature. I say to you—I can say this, that I consider them one of the most intelligent set of people on the face of the earth.

Now and I say to you that I consider that supreme in the State of Oklahoma, exceeding any other State, in view of the fact that there are more Indian tribes in the State of Oklahoma than there are in any other State and, Mr. Commissioner, there are more Indian tribes in Ottawa County than any other county in the State of Oklahoma, as I understand it, or any other county of any other State in the United States. I may be wrong. In this country. Therefore why should we not be vitally interested? We are vitally interested, the men, the boys and girls, men and women belonging to the tribe, the Quapaw tribe and these respective tribes are able to pass almost any kind of civil service examination and I say to you with all respect to the white men, I want to say to you with all respect to the white men and to any other nationality that I say this, that every superintendency throughout the State of Oklahoma or the United States should be filled with a man of Indian blood.

Applause.

Let me tell you something else, Mr. Commissioner. You can go then to the superintendent among the Five Civilized Tribes, you can go then to Anadarko among the Arapahoes, the Kaws and all that kind of Indians. I don't know how it is in the western States. You can come here and any other place where there is a superintendency in this State or the United States and you will find men, Mr. Commissioner, who are able to fill the office of superintendent, who can speak the language of the people under their jurisdiction, speak their own language, that is what you can do. Don't you see what it would mean? As I said before, don't misconstrue my statement. Personally I have no prejudice against anybody in the Government service, that is their affair, but I say this, Mr. Commissioner, because we don't know when you are going to come back, we don't know how long you are going to stay, and for and on behalf of these people—this is the way they wanted me to tell it and in my humble way I am trying to tell it—I say to you, Mr. Commissioner, that if the United States Government would pay us through the Court of Claims upon those suits we have filed, and I am associated counsel in some of that litigation, that we wouldn't have to be put out here on a community but they could take that money and buy their own homes, their own cows and own chickens and do as they please.

Now, Mr. Commissioner, another thing I want to ask of you for and on behalf of these people, that we will appreciate anything you can do to push that litigation as fast as possible. Let me ask something, Mr. Commissioner, if it is proper without the written interrogation that has been used heretofore. Now suppose that they would pay those claims in the United States Court of Claims, if they would pay, if we would get a judgment on those lawsuits—of course Congress must lead and appropriate the money, sure they have got to do that before we could get it—now suppose some of those Indians who receive the pro rata part of that money were set up, would the Secretary of the Interior and would your office supervise those funds and restrict those funds, Mr. Commissioner?

MR. COLLIER: Congress under the present law, as you know, would determine the distribution. Congress would do that now. Under the new bill if the Indians were organized into a chartered community they would do it; in neither case would the Secretary. He doesn't do it now and neither then. Now it is Congress and then the Indians.

MR. CHANDLER: Paid through the local superintendents, would it not, to the Five Civilized Tribes for the restricted class of Cherokees?

MR. COLLIER: Of course what would be done—I don't imagine you will have a bill to provide for prorating the money. It is a privilege left to Congress.

MR. CHANDLER: Yes, sir. If a restricted Indian was in this community and they paid him his money derived from this lawsuit, would the Secretary of the Interior hold that money and say "I want to use it as community trust money and to take care of the Indians in this community?" That was the point.

MR. CHANDLER: No. I want to ask about one of these resolutions. It winds up: "The Eastern Shawnees"—the business committee of the Eastern Shawnee Tribe, here—"expresses its entire disfavor toward each and every provision of the said Wheeler-Howard Bill." Now I would like to ask whether—you were speaking about this employment of Indians; was it explained to them that this bill allows the employment of Indians outside of civil service? Are they opposed to that feature of the bill?

MR. CHANDLER: Mr. Commissioner, the chief and council are here and they can speak for themselves in that connection.

MR. COLLIER: It says they are opposed to each and every provision. Well, you were there, weren't you?

MR. CHANDLER: Yes, sir, I was there and we have had the bills and we went over the bills and they asked that the resolution be drawn accordingly and it was drawn.

MR. COLLIER: Can you tell us whether you had explained that provision?

MR. CHANDLER: Yes.

MR. COLLIER: And the provisions of the credit item?

ANSWER: Yes, sir.

MR. COLLIER: They don't want the financial credit either?

MR. CHANDLER: Yes, that is right, that is what they tell me.

MR. COLLIER: And they don't want the educational policies and so on?

MR. CHANDLER: They are against the passage of the bill, Mr.—

MR. COLLIER: It says "each and every provision." I am putting this into the record for the several committees.

MR. CHANDLER: That is what they said.

MR. COLLIER: I wish they would get up and tell me whether they mean that or whether they mean something else. Specifically do they object to this provision for scholarships for young Indians, to send them through college?

CHIEF BLUEJACKET of the Shawnee Tribe: We object to quite a few things that is in that bill.

MR. COLLIER: I am asking because these are the things in the bill. Do you object to that?

ANSWER: What?

MR. COLLIER: This provision of money to send Indian boys and girls to school, through nursing school and law school, medical school and engineering school and so on.

ANSWER: I don't know whether I quite understand that.

MR. COLLIER: You don't object to that?

ANSWER: No, sir.

MR. COLLIER: Do you object to this plan of setting up a $5,000,000 fund which will be a gift to the Indians and which will be used by the tribes to lend money to their communities? Are you opposed to that?

ANSWER: It is owing to how we get it.

MR. COLLIER: Are you opposed to the buying of land for the members of your tribe, other tribes, who have no land?

ANSWER: I am opposed to it in one way. I am opposed to buying land, setting up this Indian community whereby our children will get no special benefit from it.

MR. COLLIER: But you are not opposed to buying land for homeless Indians?

ANSWER: No.

MR. COLLIER: Are you opposed to extending the trust period on the allotted land, on the other Indian lands?

ANSWER: No.

MR. COLLIER: Then what does it mean when you say you look with entire disfavor on each and every provision of the said Howard-Wheeler Bill?

ANSWER: I don't quite understand that part of it.

MR. COLLIER: And I would like to know whether those things were explained to you, so that you knew you were voting against those things when you signed the resolution.

MR. CHANDLER: Mr. Commissioner, it was gone over carefully and they executed it and we desire that it should be made a part of the record.

MR. COLLIER: It will be made a part of the record.

MR. CHANDLER: Mr. Commissioner, in closing, I appreciate the attention you have given me as spokesman of these people and in conclusion let me reiterate that it is the desire of this Association that you comply with the last paragraph of your letter of November 3, 1933, wherein it is stated:

> "I am personally very much interested in the conditions on the Quapaw and adjacent reservations. As soon as the pressure of the present extraordinary amount of work on the decreased personnel will permit I shall send a personal representative to look over the conditions."

As spokesman of these respective chiefs we ask that you send that representative at your earliest convenience. Thank you for your attention. Let me reiterate that we want more Indians in the Indian Service.

MR. COLLIER: But you don't want the legislation that permits us to put them in the Indian Service.

Applause.

MR. CHANDLER: What do you mean in that regard? Explain your statement in that respect, Mr. Chairman.

MR. COLLIER: I mean just that. There is one and only one proposed bill which would allow the Indians to get the jobs other than through this civil service.

MR. CHANDLER: Do the Indians have to join these communities in order to get a job without civil service status?

MR. COLLIER: Yes, any Indian in the community will get the job.

MR. CHANDLER: As I understood you awhile ago, if any Indians prove themselves competent and able to hold those jobs upon the reservation community they could probably procure that employment with the civil service?

MR. COLLIER: Right.

MR. CHANDLER: Now those Indians have preference on the civil service rolls to positions in the service who have passed the examination.

MR. COLLIER: Indians who have eligibility possess—they would not possess a preference overriding the preference clause.

MR. CHANDLER: That is all. Mr. Commissioner, how many Indians are employed in your office over which you have supervisory capacity as Commissioner?

MR. COLLIER: I can't answer that offhand. The figures a year ago were around 2,000 in the whole Indian Service out of about 6,600.

MR. CHANDLER: I see. I mean in the office of the Commissioner.

MR. COLLIER: I imagine the proportion would be about the same.

MR. CHANDLER: How many, please?

MR. COLLIER: Oh, I don't know, I haven't counted them, but the number is very much too small.

MR. CHANDLER: Not very many, are there, Mr. Commissioner?

MR. COLLIER: Oh, no.

MR. CHANDLER: There aren't very many here at this agency?

MR. COLLIER: I am asking you to stick to the point. We are speaking of this legislation and your friends say they are opposed to it wholesale. They don't say "we would like to have that part of the bill amended so as to apply to all members."

MR. CHANDLER: I say, Mr. Commissioner, in conclusion that that bill will never pass as it is drawn and we will fight it from toenail to teeth.

Applause.

MR. MCNAUGHTON: Mr. Commissioner, the Chief of the Quapaw Tribe, Mr. Griffin, is here and I think the Chief of the Osages is here and probably these gentlemen may have a statement. Mr. Griffin, do you have a statement you would like to make?

MR. THOMPSON: Mr. Chairman, the chief requests me to state so that there will be no misconception, the Quapaw Tribe have been acting independently and not in connection with any association, that the tribe did file a formal protest with the House Indian Affairs Committee, but that the members of the tribe are—have listened with much interest to the explanation of the bill by the Commissioner. They have appreciated the courtesy with which he has attempted to answer their questions and they appreciate his sincerity and they aim to hold another meeting and take final action upon a resolution which they will submit to the Indian Affairs Committee and to the Commissioner in the near future, with not only their preconceived notions of the bill but after thoroughly discussing it from the angle that it has been discussed here, and they request that they be given a reasonable time in which they can make that resolution and submit it.

MR. COLLIER: It will be done.

MR. MCNAUGHTON: Chief Lookout of the Osages is here. Would he care—the Chief care to make any statement?

SIMON HENDERSON: The Chief asked me to say a few words. He says the Osage people, Mr. Collier, said they are represented by council, Chief, Assistant Chief, and this matter, this program, we are handicapped, we have no lawyer among our people.

MR. MCNAUGHTON: Will you give us your name please?

SIMON HENDERSON: Simon Henderson, speaking for the Osages. This is what I am interpreting for Chief Lookout. We listened here. Most of them here are uneducated, cannot write. We don't feel like we should commit ourselves one way or the other. I think on behalf of the people and the council that the instructions what we learned here—when we get back home we take this matter up and consider it and consider this program of Mr. Collier's far reaching, so at this time we are not prepared to say one way or the other. As soon as possible we will consider this and decide on the matter; and that is all the Chief wants to say at this time.

MR. MCNAUGHTON: We thank the Chief for his statement.

JAMES BUTLER: Mr. Commissioner, I am a good deal like the Osage Chief here.

MR. MCNAUGHTON: Mr. Butler, what tribe is yours?

MR. BUTLER: Cherokee Tribe. I think best just at this time not for the Cherokee Tribe—I refer specially to the full bloods, in the community which I represent—to express themselves until further meeting, but I want to say this to the people here. A short time ago, or in the summer, I saw the needs of the full bloods in my district. We couldn't get no help from no source because of a little land. I applied to the Commissioner, Mr. Collier, and in a very short time I received a letter from him that this would be taken up with the union agency at Muskogee. A short time after that we had another letter from him and he said this matter would be taken up and investigation made and I believe through his efforts that part of the needs among the full bloods were relieved. We got a contribution, they had work they could do and are passing through; and I think in matters of such importance, that far reaching, I do not think we are able just now to express ourselves until and unless we had further time to consider it.

MR. MCNAUGHTON: The Commissioner would be glad to hear from the representatives of any other tribe.

J. W. MCCRACKEN: Nowata, Oklahoma, Delaware Indian. I don't know whether I have any authority or not. Anyway I will speak as an individual. Senator Thomas sent me a copy of this bill some time ago and perhaps I didn't read it as carefully as I should have. I was for it, very favorably impressed, and my first impression of the bill was that fact that it was not compulsory for any tribe or any individual. It was simply a voluntary proposition if the Indian as an individual or tribe saw fit to join in these community organizations, and I was very much impressed with the thing, the opportunity that might be gained for the Indian by the help of the United States government. Since coming here this afternoon and since the explanation from our Honorable Commissioner of Indian Affairs it seems to me the thing is more complicated now than at any time since I read the bill originally. I may be wrong. I may be able to clarify those features from the remarks he has made and the answers to the different questions this afternoon and his sponsoring of the bill, but I don't just understand the different features of the bill as he explained.

Finally, the part as to the civil service impressed me as much if not more than any other feature of that bill. The Indian tribes throughout the United States, as I understand, I don't know if it is true of Oklahoma—I have been here all my life—notwithstanding the fact that the Indian perhaps could pass a creditable examination in many different departments of civil service, if they were just inclined in other words to butt in and go in and grab it if they got a chance, and I feel that like Mr. Chandler which he said awhile ago—he and I have always been on opposing sides of different things that came up in Indian matters in Oklahoma, different organizations—we usually are absolutely opposed to each other—but I think he is absolutely right on that question of civil service, that the Indian should be given some sort of examination as our soldiers and sailors are given, also that the Indian should be granted a position if it could be determined by the Secretary of the Interior or our Commissioner of Indian Affairs that the Indian is capable and qualified to fill the position to which he aspires.

Understand that I am not a stranger to civil service. I have had a little of that myself but not in the way, it was not the classified standard civil service examination. I passed the examination for postmaster. It is a first-class office, under President Wilson, you know how it was. I went ahead and passed those examinations. I wouldn't say they were down to the point if I was going into an engineering position, if I was going into the job of superintendent, teacher in a different department, teacher in an Indian reservation. That examination would be more complicated than the one we have in the lines of postal examination, and I think there is more or less politics played in that part of it, but I still think there should be some way, Mr. Commissioner, if the Indian could be given some advantage or some opportunity to give him a chance and to show his ability and everything being equal he should be given the opportunity to fill the position to which he aspires.

Going a little further, I have held responsible positions. I went out last July from serving two terms creditably as County Treasurer of my county. There are a lot of other Indians here who have filled responsible positions in this state. At the same time when it comes to getting something from the Department, out of your Department, through the Indian Department, through our Commissioner of Indian Affairs, through our Secretary of the Interior—

MR. MCNAUGHTON: Mr. McCracken, I don't want to unduly hurry you—

MR. MCCRACKEN: I just don't want to blow my own horn, I am just saying that these Indians should be given an opportunity on this civil service matter, and I think the bill is certainly entitled to be studied and every Indian here should go over all the provisions carefully before they determine what they are to do.

MR. MCNAUGHTON: Are there representatives of other tribes? Just a moment, this lady here, will you come forward? Will you give us your name please?

MRS. EUNICE W. STABLER.

MR. MCNAUGHTON: And what tribe?

MRS. STABLER: Omaha, Nebraska. In 1926 the Institute for Government Research was asked to make a detailed survey of Indian affairs. Two years later this committee reported to the Secretary of the Interior in a book entitled "Problems of Indian Administration." Behind this report were eight men and two scientific experts. This report revealed that the majority of the Indians on the various reservations were extremely poor. In other words this revealed in its pages another century of dishonor.

Other investigations followed, congressional and various welfare organizations. All faced the cold facts of truth contained in the authentic report submitted by this government research. I take it that this bill is the ultimate result of these investigations. This bill embodies a program of rebuilding of Indian life. Take the self-government phase of it. The bill states plainly it is optional with any tribe of Indians to become, to take this community phase into their reservation lives. It is not a thing of compulsory nature.

We hear much today about the government doing colonization work among various classes of people. The depression has brought on all classes of people asking aid from the government. I do not see why anyone should object to this phase of the bill because it does not, it will not, there is no danger to taking the Indian back to the blanket days. To colonize the Indian in such a way as does this bill does not necessarily deny him, deny her, taking his place in the outside world. To me it is a self-sustaining proposition for the landless and homeless Indian. We realize that land which we own is the basis of self-support. Depression has been for many years with the Indians. We have had no codes governing us, but we have had rules and regulations, some 3,000 pieces of legislation governing our life, and we are still wards, involuntary wards of the government, impoverished by the system inaugurated by our guardian, the government.

We take the educational phase of this bill. What is finer than the program proposed in this bill for our generation? Our hope is in our youth. It means schooling for all Indian children, when we are aware there are nearly 16,000 Indian children totally without any school facilities. It will provide schooling for all Indian children. It will provide college and university education for those who wish to go on.

We take the land feature of this bill, to restore lands to the Indians. We know that two-thirds of the Indians on two-thirds of the reservations are landless today. If that law of 1887 was a success they would not be landless, but it has failed to serve the Indian. Lands that were bought with restricted funds and with restrictive clause amounted to nothing. Deeds from one Indian to another with restrictive clause in the government amounted to nothing. They become taxable under state legislation. Taxes piled up. The Indian was unable to pay them. The lands were gone. Hence two-thirds of the Indians on two-thirds of the reservations are poor, extremely poor. This program may not fit in other reservations in Oklahoma, but surely it will fit in other reservations and we have 214 reservations throughout our nation.

I see no socialistic or communistic idea in this program. We have provided for in this bill a much-needed new agency, that of the judicial agency. For the first time in the history of the Indians we have a Secretary and a Commissioner of Indian Affairs who really have faith and confidence in the Indians that they wish to give him power and a voice in his own government.

Those of us who have experienced land litigations in the past have realized that there has been very little or no virtue at all in the courts for the Indian, so far as the Indian is concerned, regarding his property. I read in a paper, or perhaps it was a pamphlet called "Indians at Work" some time ago where one Senator had either an original letter or telegram to Commissioner Collier saying "We appreciate your effort in trying to solve the Indian problem, but it is like pouring water on a dirt floor, the more water you pour on it, the muddier it gets." I think such a statement as that is a challenge to the Indian race. If ever there was a time the Indians should think for themselves and not take the advice of people who have dominated and ruled over us, it is today. We have a commissioner who has a first hand knowledge, thorough understanding of this complex, complicated Indian problem.

Mr. Commissioner, I want to express my thanks for giving me this opportunity to say these few words and I am heartily in favor of every phase of this bill.

Applause.

JAMES WEBBER: A Delaware Indian of Dewey. Mr. Chairman and fellow citizens, I just want to cooperate with a few words. Mr. McCracken has said here a few minutes ago—I am truly glad of having this opportunity because I have been in this community for something like forty-two years. My interest is in the people, in the Indian people who are of the full-blood element and I have advocated for more than twenty years a corporate interest or some kind of law that could be carried through Congress and made in congressional act that the Indians could govern themselves. I believe that is one of the greatest things that have ever been placed before us.

In fact, it has been more than one year ago that I came to the office of Commissioner of Indian Affairs, a little over a year ago. At the time when Mr. Rhoads of Philadelphia was appointed to that position, the same position the Honorable Mr. John Collier now holds, and his letter to me at that time, I explained to my fellow members, said that we had the right but at the same time we were not given the power, the authority to act and govern our affairs like we ought to do.

I truly believe that if the average Indian will come right down and look into those things, take their affairs in hand and look into the educational system, handle the conditions or handle the financial part of their affairs, handle all other industries that might come under it even to the agricultural pursuits for their benefit, I believe it would be better for us to govern ourselves, although I feel that the interest that we have in this bill that is now proposed could be greatly modified perhaps because all conditions of every tribe is not exactly alike. There may be some difficulty. Anyway I want to voice that and I will say that we are going to offer you a letter giving this matter our further consideration. We will take it under advisement.

I thank you.

Applause.

MR. MCNAUGHTON: Will you give your name please.

LOUIS GOURD: A Cherokee. I have been greatly impressed with what has been said here this afternoon and what I may say at this time may not have any particular import except I desire to say this: The bill carries with it everything so far as I have been able to learn that is good. Now here is the thing I desire to say. If all the Indians of this country were of the standard class as our representative here at this time, I would say to the Commissioner "Let us go, we can go out into the world and we can compete with anybody; we will hold our part or we will starve to death trying it." But what I mean to tell you at this time is that I represent a community where there are full-blood Indians that have to be considered. I am of their blood, they are of mine, and those people down there you don't ordinarily see in a place like this. They won't make any particular effort to come from those hills down there where they are busy making ties and staves. People, you don't see those fellows here, but what I mean to say to you fellows is that, let us be mighty careful before we turn this thing down. We are being offered something we will never have a chance to hear again, I believe. We may not have an opportunity for such a thing again. I live in a part where I try to contract the things that are required of me in a limited way, but here are my ideas: I am living today as well as you are; now we are all right; today is taking of itself, but these homeless and landless Indians, young children are running around down there in the hills, I tell you they are barefooted, they can't attend the schools today because they live in rough, hilly country. Timber has been stolen on the reservation. They would share in the community. Now where are they going? Now I want to say that I will make it all right if my health holds up. I believe the next time you come around I will be here, but these Indian boys and girls that are coming up, they don't have these advantages, they don't live in this day.

I can go home now and I will be at home, I will not be disturbed by anybody, not like this young fellow come along, the uneducated boys and girls. They will not have a place to go, they will be kicked and cuffed and burned at the stake and killed and everything else will happen to them, so what I intend to say to you is let us be particularly careful about the decision we make concerning the passage of this bill. I for one want to say at this time that I am like the other fellow that is against it. I am teeth and toenail for it until I find out something really is wrong with it.

Applause.

MR. MCNAUGHTON: Do we have representatives of any other tribes?

MR. MCINTOSH: Creek. Friends, for the first time we have a man in the Commissioner of Indian Affairs office who has ever attempted to do anything for the Red man. You can go back during your entire life and here comes one who offers a chance to the Indian children to receive an education, those who cannot provide it, to receive food, clothing and shelter. Are we as individuals or groups—those Indians that are justly entitled— are we going individually here to oppose something that will deny someone who are entitled to this bill and who wants that particular thing? To my mind it is preposterous for any individual or group to undertake to oppose anything that some other group of individuals might want. In other words, at this time we have a man trying to do something for the Indian, one who has studied the Indian problem all of his life, and as I formerly said, the only one who has ever attempted to do anything for us, and he is entitled to the support of every person of Indian blood until he has proved himself that he has not the qualifications we know he has. To my mind to oppose something until we have had an opportunity to hear the facts is ridiculous. I am entreating you to not go on record in any way in opposing something anyone else wants. I think you should figure this thing out and write the Commissioner a letter and explain to him your views and not be persuaded by any person or group of individuals.

CHARLIE GOOD EAGLE: Quapaw. I want to explain my feeling as the Chief's statement was made by his attorney. The position to take is to approve it, and for myself look at the needs of someone else, more especially the young ones. I am looking forward to the future for our younger ones. I consider the things we possess today and wonder how long we are going to possess them. I am glad to hear this explanation of the bill. I had an opportunity the other day of hearing Mr. Collier at Anadarko. At that time the writer presented a resolution of approval and the chairman stepped upon the platform opposing it. On returning home different ones had asked me about the explanation of the bill and I gladly presented the copy I had and they said they never could see anything wrong with that bill, it couldn't hurt the Indian. The Indian was getting something he should have had years ago instead of the allotment system. As Mr. Collier told us at the Anadarko meeting, the government possibly thought the Indian population would never increase after that allotment act was enacted. Since that time we have increased in numbers and our land holdings have decreased. A great majority percentage of our people are landless today. A very small percent of all northern Quapaw Tribe possesses their allotments, a greater number of Indians does not possess land. That situation is to be remedied by the bill. Not only all phase of today but the future is taken care of.

Like the sentiment of the speaker who just preceded me, I want to make an appeal to all of you to consider it, to make your own decision, not listen to all rumors that is floating throughout this country. They may be your friends, they may not be your friends, but think for yourselves. The day and time come when we should do for ourselves. We have all made mistakes. The present generation have all made mistakes. Let us not make a mistake for our future generation, for our young that are to come in the future. I thank you.

Applause.

W. H. DOWNING: A Cherokee. I had the pleasure of attending yesterday a meeting with the Cherokees and we had the bill read to us and explained and we voted unanimously to accept it.

MR. WILLIAMS: Shawnee, Eastern Shawnee, Shawnee-Cherokee. We were told in the meeting this afternoon that the Eastern Shawnees last night voiced disapproval of this bill. Now I am an Eastern Shawnee living a few miles up here and I never even knew a meeting had been held. Now may I ask a representative of the Shawnees last night how many Shawnees were there?

MR. MCNAUGHTON: Is the gentleman who represented the Shawnees at the meeting present? Could you tell us how many members were present last night?

ANSWER: Three of them.

MR. WILLIAMS: Mr. Chairman, I do not believe that that action represents the majority of the Shawnees by any means.

MRS. ED HOLDEN: Shawnee. We have a council and they—we gave them the authority to tend to our business and whatever they do, why we stand back of them. Thank you.

LILLIAN MATHEWS: Now I happen to be an Osage Indian, but I am less than one-fourth and I would like to ask a question. Why is the Indian of one-fourth or less excepted in your educational phase of the bill?

MR. COLLIER: He is not.

MISS MATHEWS: Then I have misinterpreted.

MR. COLLIER: Only where new colonies are being formed.

MISS MATHEWS: So an Indian who is say 1/64 who shows ability to get a higher education can apply for a scholarship? I want to make perfectly sure about that answer. I am sure there is nothing like that in the bill. There is something concerning quarter or less.

MR. COLLIER: Oh, yes, they have got either to be members of communities, members of organized communities or one-fourth.

MISS MATHEWS: A member of an organized community if he is less than 1/4 can have a scholarship, but if he is not and less than 1/4 he cannot?

MR. COLLIER: That is the way it reads now.

MISS MATHEWS: I thank you.

MR. PALMER: I am a chief of the Western Miamis and I just got in here this afternoon and haven't had time to read the bill and don't know anything about it, but from what I understand from your talk I don't know how any of our tribe would object if the government gives them a thousand or two dollars. I believe people fighting this bill here, I don't imagine they would object if you would turn them around and give them a thousand dollars and not ask them for a note or anything else. I can't see anything wrong with it at the present time but I have called the council together, the Indians, and I think they will endorse the bill and I feel that way about it myself.

Applause.

MR. MCNAUGHTON: Now friends, I want us to remain just a few minutes longer and in conclusion Mr. Collier is going to have a few words further to say to you. I am sure he has appreciated your interest in this meeting and I am sure that as a chairman I have appreciated the manner in which you have conducted yourselves and the assistance you have given in the conduct of the meeting.

MR. COLLIER: Friends, this is the conclusion of a long series of congresses held in all parts of the country. This is the last one for the time being. We are going back to Washington from here.

I want to say first that just as it has been every other time, so this meeting has brought out important points concerning the bill. Every meeting has contributed new light and this meeting has contributed new light and has raised questions about ways to improve the bill, possibilities of amending it, needs of clarifying it and so on. Therefore from our point of view at least this meeting has been well worthwhile and we are appreciative of your thought and friendly attitude.

Now something else. This is an unusual time in Indian affairs and at Washington. You have a President who cares deeply about your problems. Very rarely has there been a President who cared much about Indian matters. Mr. Roosevelt does care. You have a Secretary of the Interior who for years before he became Secretary had been fighting for Indian rights. He is a man of extraordinary gifts, he is a man of extraordinary power, Mr. Ickes. For myself I can only say that you have someone who was picked in order to carry out a strong program for you and is entirely committed to the task of doing it as far as I have power. You have a situation in Congress such as has never existed before. The lady who spoke so well in this aisle, the Omaha lady, gave some indication of it. Over a long term of years things have been rolling up in Congress, based on a series of important investigations. She mentioned the investigation by the Institute for Government Research. That was followed by the long study carried out all over the country by the Senate Indian Investigation Committee, dealing with an immense amount of the Indian problem. That committee has brought out a series of reports, very carefully considered. Last year Senator King of Utah summarized the results of the work of that committee in a very great speech on the floor of the Senate, challenging Congress to do the right thing and pointing out what to do.

Things have been slowly mounting up. There has come into chairmanship of the House Indian Committee one of the life-long friends of the Indians and warriors for Indians, Congressman Howard, into the chairmanship of the Senate, Wheeler of Montana. The stage is set for you to get whatever is good, whatever is reasonable. You can have anything that is reasonable and well thought out now. It is a time when big changes are being made. The public mind has been all shaken up, first by the depression and then by the great uplift given by President Roosevelt. It is a time when Congress is ready to do big things.

The attention of the public is focused on your needs. That is a remarkable thing. There are only a few of you, 300,000 Indians in a population of 120,000,000 people, one Indian to every 400 people. What an awful lot of attention to give to one person in every 400, but if for example you go to the newsstand right now and buy a copy of Good Housekeeping just out, a magazine that goes into 2,500,000 homes, there you will find a great article telling about your situation and your needs, and it is only one of a great many big articles appearing in magazines and newspapers.

Now it is a time when it is possible to get results. The results have to be obtained in terms of legislation, no other way. It may not be possible a year from now or two years from now to get anything at all. It is possible now. The condition of the country and the country's mind may have changed. Things change very fast now. A year or two from now it may be impossible to gain the attention of Congress. We don't know how long the President himself will keep his control of both houses of Congress, much as we hope and pray that he will. There is an election coming next fall, we don't know what it is going to do. Now we have come forward with a bill that represents the best that we know how to do up to a month ago. It represents the careful thought of people who have worked with and for you for years, and it is sensible enough to have commanded the attention of the President and to have obtained his active, determined support.

It is a time when, as our friend over here said and as others have stated, for Indians to think seriously, earnestly, and not to be hasty, not to be what I will say frivolous, because it is the moment of destiny for you people, your children and your grandchildren. We aren't saying that this bill is perfect; on the contrary we have told you again and again today that it isn't, it is going to be amended. We are not even saying that there may not be some other way of getting at this that may be better than this way which has been proposed; if so and it can be presented, we will grab it and will put it in place of what we now offer. It is your thought that we want. It is also important that a dominant administration, in a position to get any reasonable legislation it wants very quickly and very easily, has decided to come out to the Indians, lay it before them and put the decision in their hands. That has never been done before.

Therefore I beg you, and I know I am going to be satisfied what you do, to go home, continue to study the bill, continue to discuss it, get all the light you can on it from everybody and don't lay off. Keep on studying it and discussing it and send your ideas in. It is the way you are going to prove yourselves truly to be American citizens.

Now I want to indicate the kind of thing that I consider very bad for the Indian cause. There comes a speaker here who states that he has explained this bill to a group of Indians. He is an intelligent man, capable of understanding the bill, capable of giving a clear explanation. He states that after he had explained the bill, the Indians have acted on it and presents the document which they signed. That document condemns absolutely every feature in the bill, all of them, just sweeping damning condemnation. Then those Indians are asked "Did you mean to condemn the Educational section?" "No." "Did you mean to condemn the credit section?" "No," and so on. They didn't mean it, and all that goes into the record and all that goes down to Washington.

It hurts the Indians for things like that to be done, and a good friend of the Indian, if an educated man, will not lead them to do things like that. It is an unfair and an unfaithful thing to do to trusting Indians. It is the kind of thing that Secretary Ickes referred to in that document I read you earlier today. It is not in the spirit of the present moment and not in the spirit of this bill or of the effort that is now being made, and it will not be viewed with favor by the committees of Congress, I assure you. I think it is right to say this just as I spoke of that Associated Press fabrication earlier in the day, because it is illustrative and typical of other cases, but there have been some.

We want ideas, we want the most drastic hostile criticism. We have welcomed things handed up by Mr. Thompson which were searching criticisms pointing in the direction of improvement. We want that, but it does no good to present a resolution signed by Indians who confessedly did not know what they were doing in order to knock out this serious effort by President Roosevelt to build up your life, to increase your property and educate your children and save you as a race.

I am going to place in the record without reading now because the hour is so late, President Roosevelt's own statement concerning the bill. You will get it in the newspapers or in the mimeographed copy of these proceedings.

I want to say something else. If every one of you tribes here gathered or represented should object to this bill and want to be thrust out, we not only would cooperate with you in bringing that result to pass, but we would be just as much interested in continuing to serve you in the old way as if you had endorsed the bill. Our responsibility in the Interior Department, the Indian Bureau, is a responsibility toward the Indians and for all of them, and if we were influenced, if we were made unfriendly toward an Indian group by the fact that the Indian group might disagree with us and reject something we are offering, if we allowed that to influence our attitude on things, we would be faithless to our trust. I can promise you that we are going to be just as much interested in the group that turns this bill down as we are in the group that endorses the bill. We wouldn't for the world want you to feel that you have got to endorse this bill or else you would incur the displeasure, lose the good will of the Administration. You will not. It is entirely up to you, up to you in your mature thinking, after you have brought into your mind the whole picture, including the picture of your landless fellow Indians, including the picture of your children and their unborn children, and then when you have thought deeply, the answer you give will be equally satisfactory, whether you agree with us or disagree with us. Thank you.

Applause.

MR. MCNAUGHTON: Mr. Commissioner, on behalf of the citizens of this community I want to assure you of our appreciation of your coming here. I want to assure you that these people here assembled realize your earnestness and your endeavor to do the thing that is best for the Indian and that he may take his proper place as a citizen and a part of the United States, and we hope that you will come again to see us and we hope that your efforts in the interest of the Indian, whether it be in this bill or something more satisfactory will be successful. (*Applause.*)

We stand adjourned.

EXHIBITS

(Copy) THE WHITE HOUSE (Copy)

WASHINGTON, D.C.

March 13, 1934.

My dear Mr. Howard:

My interest has been attracted to your bill, H. R. 7902, because of the virile American principles on which it is based. Opportunities for self determination for the Indians in handling their property by providing modern corporate management, participation in local government, a more liberal educational system through day schools and advanced health measures are provided in the bill.

Adequate provision is made for his training in the management and protection of his property, and the conservation of his health during the period that must intervene before the Indian may be intrusted with the complete management of his own affairs. In offering the Indian these natural rights of man we will more nearly discharge the Federal responsibility for his welfare than through compulsory guardianship that has destroyed initiative and the liberty to develop his own culture.

Sincerely yours,
(Signed) FRANKLIN D. ROOSEVELT
President.

(Copy)
Hon. Edgar Howard,
Chairman, House Committee on Indian Affairs.

RESOLUTION

WHEREAS: There is now pending before the Congress of the United States a certain bill commonly termed the Howard-Wheeler Bill, designed to inaugurate a new policy for the administration of the affairs of the several Indian tribes of the United States, and

WHEREAS: The Honorable John Collier, Commissioner of Indian Affairs, is now in the city of Miami, Oklahoma, where he has discussed and has further expressed his views and interpretations of said bill to the Indians of Northeast Oklahoma, with a view to obtaining their attitude toward the enactment of such legislation, and

WHEREAS: Having heard the lengthy presentation and interpretation of the several sections and general provisions of said bill and the extended discussions both pro and con in connection therewith and having otherwise given the entire matter very careful study and consideration it is the belief of this Association that this bill as drawn is not at all proper for adoption by any Indian tribe, faction or community thereof.

WHEREFOR: BE IT RESOLVED BY THE ASSOCIATION OF INDIAN TRIBES: That in view of the general uncertainty and the many discrepancies of said bill and the further evident fact that the bill, as a whole, so plainly suggests utter disrespect or disregard for our local, State and National Governments and tends to revive and urge race prejudice even tho' "the hatchet" of such prejudice and hatred has been buried for years and our Indian people generally are now looked upon as respectable, upright and progressive citizens, the Association of Indian Tribes hereby voices its emphatic DISFAVOR for the passage of or the enactment of the legislation intended by the provisions of the Howard-Wheeler Bill hereinabove referred to and further suggests that the extreme efforts now being extended toward the passage and enactment of such legislation be directed toward more sane, respectful and beneficial accomplishments in the interest of our American Indian citizenship.

Done at Miami, Oklahoma, the 24th day of March, 1934.

SGD. Walter Bluejacket
Chief of Shawnee Eastern

SGD. Willis McNaughton
Chief of Peorias

SGD. Guy Jamison
Chief of Ottawa Indians

SGD. William Smith
Chief of Cayuga Tribe

SGD. John H Logan
Chief of Seneca Indians

RESOLUTION

WHEREAS: There is now pending before the Congress of the United States a bill known as the Howard-Wheeler or "Collier New Deal" Bill, proposing the enactment of legislation intended to inaugurate a more liberal and beneficial administration of Indian Affairs, and

WHEREAS: The matter of this intended enactment of such legislation is and has been for some time the subject of considerable study and discussion by the various Indian tribes of these United States, and

WHEREAS: In order to gain a full understanding of the contents and import of said bill, in the interest of the several members of our tribe, a careful and extended study of same has been made, in open meetings of members and otherwise, after which the conclusion has been reached that the legislation intended as now outlined in the provisions of said bill would be prejudicial to the best interests of our Indian citizens rather than of any consequential benefit.

NOW THEREFORE, BE IT RESOLVED: That the Business Committee of the Eastern Shawnee tribe of Indians, residing in Ottawa County, Oklahoma, having been duly authorized so to do by regular and proper action of said Indian tribe, for and on behalf of the said Eastern Shawnee Indian tribe, hereby expresses its entire disfavor toward each and every provision of said Howard-Wheeler Bill and urges that such legislation be NOT enacted.

Done at Miami, Oklahoma, this 23rd day of March, 1934.

EASTERN SHAWNEE BUSINESS COMMITTEE
By
SGD. Walter Bluejacket
SGD. David Dunham
SGD. Edward H. Bluejacket
SGD. Ora Hampton
SGD. T. A. Captain

CHAPTER 12

TESTIMONY TAKEN AT HAYWARD, WISCONSIN, APRIL 23 & 24, 1934 WHERE INDIANS OF WISCONSIN, MINNESOTA AND MICHIGAN GATHERED FOR A TWO-DAY CONFERENCE TO DISCUSS THE WHEELER-HOWARD BILL OF INDIAN RIGHTS

Meeting opened by Mr. William Zimmerman Jr., Assistant to Commissioner John Collier.

MR. ZIMMERMAN: As you all know, this is one of the series of meetings that officials of the Indian agencies are holding in various parts of the country. We set the date rather late in the hope that Mr. Collier himself could be here, but it is unfortunate that hearings before the Senate and House committees have conflicted with this date. He sent many of us here to take his place, and we will do our very best to explain this bill to you. Before we discuss the bill, as long as Mr. Collier is not here, I would like to read a few extracts of a speech made by Mr. Collier at Rapid City:

MR. ZIMMERMAN: (*Reading*)

"I shall first talk about the fundamental conditions of our life as I understand it. And what are these fundamental conditions which I shall suggest are wrong conditions and ought to be put right? What are they? They are, first, that the Indians of the United States, including your tribes, have for two lifetimes been steadily losing their property, becoming poorer and poorer on the whole. That is on the side of your property. If you take the United States as a whole, the wealth of the people has been increasing year by year steadily until the depression of three years ago. And, during those same years the wealth of the Indians, instead of increasing, has been melting away. I shall give you the exact facts after a few minutes. They are terrifying facts.

"Now, the second big condition is this: That the Indians of the United States are living under a condition which puts them at the mercy of the Indian Bureau.

"The guardianship of the Federal Government over Indian life, which was intended to be a means of making the Indians both prosperous and free, has been having the opposite effect and has been making them poor while they were deprived of their freedom. Therefore, many people and some Indians have risen up and said that the only hope for the Indian is to put an end to the guardianship of the Government so that they may stand a chance in living. Some people have said the guardianship of the Government is injuring the Indian, is keeping them in a condition of slavery. Therefore, the responsibility must be brought to an end.

"You have all heard that line of talk, and I do not hesitate to say I am speaking honestly my own feelings, that if the guardianship of the United States has to continue doing the things it has been doing; if it has to go on the old way, I think it had better be stopped, thrown aside, and the Indian better do without it. But, that is not the answer. The cure for the evils done by the Government is not to abolish but to reform it and make it do good things instead of evil things, and that is true of the guardianship over Indians.

"The United States is not making a mess of its Indian guardianship because its employees are wicked or stupid. That is not the reason. They are not wicked and they are not stupid. But because the guardianship maintained by the United States is carried out under a body of laws which are wicked and stupid and which make slaves even of the Government employees hired to enforce the laws. There was a time when it was the policy of the United States Government to rob the

Indians. There was a time when it was the policy of the United States Government to crush Indian life and even to crush the family life of Indians, and during that time laws were passed and those laws are still the laws, though it is no longer the policy of the Government to rob you or to crush you, but they are the laws, and by them we must work and you must live."

MR. ZIMMERMAN: Let us go back to 1887. In round numbers the Indians at the time had 138,000,000 acres of land, among which was included some of the best land in the United States. It included some of the best farm lands, good grazing lands, and much land under irrigation, and much land rich in minerals. In 1887 Congress, over the protest of the Indians, enacted the general allotment act that since has been the "backbone" of Indian law. It is today the great basic law of Indian affairs. From 1887 until the present day the Indian has lost 91,000,000 acres, and the best land was included in the land that was lost. Much of the remaining acreage, in fact about 20 million acres, is desert or semi-desert. The allotment law was not applied equally, for as you know the Menominee and Red Lake reservations and some other reservations have never been under this law. In the Southwest the Navajos and other tribes where land was not allotted, the Indians have actually increased their holdings since 1887. Some of them have twice as much as they had then. Every one of the tribes which was spared from the allotment act has more land now than in 1887. In other words, the losses of land have fallen upon those tribes that were subjected to the allotment act, so that the allotted tribes have lost in land area more than two thirds of their total holdings since that year.

If you take the value of the land lost, the figures are even worse. The allotment operation was not brought to bear everywhere at the same time. It came sooner some places and later in other places, so that the effects of the allotment system are not equal in intensity everywhere. They are variable. If you take Oklahoma as an example, the amount of land owned by the Oklahoma tribes was twenty three million acres before allotment—and all of that except three million acres has passed away. You can take individual tribes like the Oneida of Wisconsin and find that practically one hundred per cent of the land has passed from the Indians to Whites, and the Oneidas are landless. More than one hundred thousand Indians in the allotment areas have lost all their land down to the last square foot and are entirely landless.

The question that faces the administration is how to change this allotment system so as to stop the futile loss of land by Indians, increase the amount of land owned by Indians and protect the rights and equities of those Indians who have not yet lost their lands. Let me repeat and emphasize that:

1. The future sale of Indian lands must be stopped.
2. New land or more land must be procured in large amounts in order to supply those Indians who have lost all their land and in order to supplement the inadequate land of those who still have some land.
3. You may say what you will about the allotment plan, but the fact remains that allotment has created individual valid property rights in individuals. It has created individual property rights and those rights must be respected.

Interpretation of the above by Mr. Frank Smart of Odanah, Wisconsin.

MR. ZIMMERMAN: *(continuing)* In Washington today there are many changes going on. Most of the Government agencies, bureaus and departments are acquiring more and more power and authority. I think that the Indian office is probably the only unit of the Federal Government that is trying to get rid of some power. This proposed bill will take away from the Secretary of the Interior and the Commissioner many of the powers that these men now have. Those powers can be turned over to the Indians. In order to do that the Indians must be organized. We take the position that it is very necessary for Indians to be permitted to organize, to organize for many different purposes. It is necessary for Indians to be allowed to organize to take care of their own local affairs, and again to organize to do business in a modern business world in competition with the modern white world. In the world at large, the white world, the unorganized people are powerless. They are victims. Only organized groups have power in the white world.

There are many kinds of organization in the modern world. For example, there are corporations, there are cattlemen's associations and stock associations. There are co-operative societies to run, for example creameries, to buy in quantities so as to cut out middlemen's profits; all kinds of co-operative economic organizations for mutual benefit. There are town governments which manage the local affairs of towns.

The ward Indian is shut out from all of these advantages of organization. He likewise, as you all know to your sorrow, is denied access to credit, financial credit. We propose that Indians shall be allowed and helped to organize for mutual benefit, for local self-government and for doing business in the modern, organized way. We are proposing that there shall be set up a new financial credit system through which the Government will extend financial credit to these organized groups of Indians. We are proposing that when the Indians do organize, and they will only organize if they want to when and if they do organize, that their organizations will be instrumentalities of the Federal Government. When the Indians do organize it will be under Federal laws enacted by Congress.

The time will come, probably very soon, when these changes going on in Washington will come to an end; when perhaps the country will settle down into some new pattern; perhaps in two or three years, nobody knows. But, the chance to change this Indian law is now. It is the chance of all time for the Indians to get whatever they are entitled to have. If you will use your best brains, frame an intelligent program and a clear and precise one you can get the most today. We are here today to discuss this bill with you. We are going to spend many hours trying to explain to you in detail every section of this proposed bill. Before we do that, I should like to read to you a letter which the President of the United States wrote about this bill. In about 150 words he summarizes the entire thing.

MR. ZIMMERMAN: (*reading President's letter*)

> "My Dear Mr. Howard:
>
> "My interest has been attracted to your bill, H. R. 7902, because of the virile American principles on which it is based. Opportunity for self-determination for the Indians in handling their property by providing modern corporate management, participation in local government, a more liberal educational system through day schools and advanced health measures are provided in the bill.
>
> "Adequate provision is made for his training in the management and protection of his property, and the conservation of his health during the period that must intervene before the Indian may be intrusted with the complete management of his own affairs. In offering the Indian these natural rights of man we will more nearly discharge the Federal responsibility for his welfare than through compulsory guardianship that has destroyed initiative and the liberty to develop his own culture.
>
> Sincerely yours,
>
> (Signed) FRANKLIN D. ROOSEVELT
> President
>
> Hon. Edgar Howard,
> Chairman, House Committee
> On Indian Affairs.

In those few words the President has covered the field of this bill. The Bill is divided into four main sections or titles. The first one sets up machinery by which Indians may organize for self-government; the second provides machinery by which Indians may be educated so that they may the better operate and manage business affairs; the third main title deals with the principal item of Indian property, namely land; the fourth deals with the proposed court of Indian affairs.

Before we take up each of these sections point by point, let me make clear our position in this matter. I hope you will keep your minds free of prejudice. For the moment, try to forget if you can any ideas you may have about the bill. Let us first explain it to you, and later we will give you all the chances you want to ask questions. We are not here to sell you anything, nor are we trying to ram anything down your throats. We realize this bill is not perfect by any means. Many changes have been made as a result of suggestions derived at previous Congresses like this one. We are here to explain this bill as we understand it, and you will be permitted to ask questions when the time comes.

I will now ask Mr. Woehlke to act as chairman for the rest of the morning.

Chair taken by Mr. Walter V. Woehlke, Field Representative to Commissioner John Collier.

MR. WOEHLKE: Mr. Commissioner, delegates and guests, you are up against a tough job. Here is a bill in technical legal language covering 52 pages. We want to discuss this bill in great detail and make it as clear to you as possible, and that is a big job. At Rapid City we had four days; we talked from 9 A.M. to 6 P.M., started again at 8 P.M. and continued until 11 to 12 P.M. almost every day. Here we have only two days to do the same job. At Rapid City they gave the Commissioner an Indian name of "Iron Man" because he had worn out four of the Sioux interpreters—literally talked them under the table. We won't do that here, but will ask you to do most of the talking. I believe we can safely do that because you people are more familiar with the bill. At Rapid City, one of the first congresses, the bill was new to all the Indians and most of the white people. They had learned of it only a short time previous to our visit. Since that time you have received a great deal of printed material concerning the bill and you must have discussed the various provisions of the act time and again, especially those parts which directly affect you. If you haven't, I am very sorry, because this thing is a most important development which may vitally affect all of you, and I do hope that prior to our arrival here you have gained a fair knowledge of what this bill proposes to do. I would like just briefly to run over some of the purposes which this bill aims to accomplish, and to discuss them from the standpoint of the objections that have been most frequently raised.

In the first place, this bill specifically forbids any further allotments of Indian lands in severalty; it prohibits the giving of another individual piece of land to any individual. Through this provision it turns the current which has been carrying the Indian and his property down hill for the last 50 years. It guides the current in a new direction. The bill has been criticized equally by Whites and Reds, but I believe that all have agreed that the allotment plan during its existence has served to cut down continually the land holdings of the Indian population of the United States.

There may be some dispute as to how much land has been lost and how much land belonging to Indians has been sold and the proceeds beneficially invested. But the fact remains that under the system of giving the individual Indian an individual piece of property which he could dispose of—under the system that included the sale of so-called "surplus" land which never was surplus—under that system the land holdings of the Indian people have constantly diminished and grown less and less wherever this system was applied. It is also admitted universally that where this system was not applied, the Indians have not lost any land. On the contrary, their land holdings have increased. That is point number one, and upon that conceded point this bill is based. It aims to stop the continuous loss of Indian lands. That is the primary purpose of the bill, and I believe that the objective is admitted by everybody to be of great benefit to the Indians. It is also a fact that a continuation of the present system of administering Indian lands must inevitably lead very rapidly to the complete separation of Indians from their lands through the manner in which the inheritance laws work out.

Many of you through sad experience know the inheritance laws and how they separate the Indian from his property. Whenever there is a death with the resulting split-up of the estate among the heirs then further among the heirs of the heirs, you reach a time when the land can no longer be divided into these very small parcels. Therefore, the only way in which the claims of the heirs can be satisfied is to sell the land and divide cash. You can always divide cash, but not so with land when the parcels become too small. So you can figure out for yourself how long it will be until the remaining portion of the 48 million acres still belonging to Indians will be all gone. They must be sold under the present system if there is to be satisfaction of the claims of the heirs. I think that also is universally admitted, that within comparatively few years the Indians on allotted reservations will be totally without land. The system is poor for another reason. What happens when a young man gets cash? White or Red, the results usually are the same. Up in the Sioux country in January I was addressing a meeting, and after two hours of talking, a young man got up and said: "I really have no right to speak here, but I speak to warn others. I got a fee patent, and I sold the land and bought an automobile. I wrecked the automobile, and now I have nothing but the pants I stand in."

That is the way it is going, and under this system that is the way it will continue to go, irrespective of what we would like to do about it.

Interpretation of the above by Frank Smart, Odanah.

MR. WOEHLKE: (*continuing*) I think the interpreter did a mighty good job of that, but I am going ahead with some more, and if he can translate it he is a better man than I think he is.

I think we have reached universal agreement on the fact that under the allotment system as it must be administered, the Indian land is going and will all be gone in a very few years. But in the meantime, it has another effect. Where you have all of these inheritance allotments split up into a lot of small pieces—millions of them—somebody must look after them. The Indian Bureau must act as a real estate agency. It must endeavor to rent or lease the small pieces and try to collect the fees, if possible. Three different accounting entries must also be made—on the books of the agency, on the books in Washington, and in the general accounting office—three complete sets of books. I have in mind an example where one superintendent had it figured that an heir was entitled to receive 52,382 parts of $114,386,982, and there were 60 other heirs, all to receive various amounts. Why, it took a group of clerks three days to figure these awful fractions, and as a net result one man got a two-cent stamp, and it cost the Government about $1.50 to pay him that two-cent stamp.

Now for the application of that to you. Congress makes certain appropriations for the benefit of the ward Indians. They are supposed to receive from these appropriations medical service, educational advantages, home demonstrations, etc., but a major part of that money is spent in these real estate transactions—in the effort to collect rent and lease money; in keeping track of these small parcels of land and in doing all the necessary bookkeeping.

It is an unprofitable real estate business for the Government and as the pieces of land become smaller, the receipts from that business are going down steadily so that you can figure out that by and by it will cost the Government more money to handle this business than the owners of the land get out of it; Congress is beginning to realize this fact.

On a certain reservation in Oklahoma where $80,000 annually is appropriated for the benefit of the Indians, it was found necessary to disburse $65,000 in these real estate transactions. You can readily see why it is absolutely necessary to take hold of this land proposition of the Indian—grab hold of it with both hands and wring its neck.

It is necessary to do something drastic to change the status of the Indian. It is necessary that Indians who now have land be protected from loss, and the landless Indian must be helped. That is what this bill proposes to do, but you can readily see that it would be foolish to have the Government pay out millions of dollars for the purchase of new lands and then throw them into the same sewer out of which they are at present draining. It would be altogether unjustified to buy new lands for the Indians unless the possessors of that land could be assured of its possession forever and a day—unless the repetition of the history of the past fifty years can be prevented—and that is what this legislation endeavors to do. It endeavors to provide ways and means of acquiring more land for the Indians who are now landless and to safeguard that land by placing the title to it in the community rather than in the individual. That is the purpose and main purpose of this bill, to which practically everything else is an accessory.

Before I go any further I would like to call your attention to Title 5, Page 51, of the Bill. In the words of Dr. Roe Cloud, Superintendent of Haskell Institute who should be right here running this meeting, through the operation of this bill not one Indian will lose anything by the Bill. Nothing is taken away from him, but both civil rights and property rights are added. He has nothing to lose and everything to gain.

However, to make certain that the adoption or acceptance of this legislation is entirely voluntary, we have at the suggestion of Congressman Howard, Chairman of the Indian Affairs Committee, added a new section under which any tribe or band which does not want to come under this legislation can within four months after its passage vote to exclude itself.

In my judgment that should remove the last bit of opposition to this bill since it is designed primarily to help the landless Indians, to protect those who still have land and to help them make use of their land by a large credit fund. Since that is the object of the bill, I don't see how there can be any opposition, especially in view of the fact that any tribes not wishing to assume the obligations can vote to exclude themselves.

A second section in this new title does another thing: It specifically states that no part of this bill shall be construed to impair, to diminish, or to do away with any right or claim that any Indian has against the United States Government on the basis of old treaties. Nothing in this bill would have affected these treaties anyway, but in order to make absolutely sure we added this new section which in plain language says that this bill is not in any way to interfere with the claims of any tribes against the Government of the United States, and it further provides that any appropriations made in this act for the benefit of the Indian people shall not be used as set-offs in any pending claims or future claims suits, so that if this bill appropriates $2,000,000 for land purchase and $150,000 is used for the purchase of land in a specific instance, that $150,000 can not be used as a set-off in the claim that the Indian tribe may have against the United States.

MR. WOEHLKE: *(continuing)* The Assistant Commissioner just told me that it would be a good idea to have the various delegates and delegations write out questions regarding parts of this bill which are not clear so that they can be answered from the platform. Just write out any questions which you would like to ask and hand them to the secretary, Mr. Daiker, the handsome gentleman over there, during the lunch hour.

This is a good idea, since very often the same point is not clear in the minds of 10 or 15 persons, and by having the questions written down we can avoid repetition. We hope you will have a number of questions in the possession of Mr. Daiker so that we can start answering them right after lunch.

And now to touch briefly on this question of Indian self-government:

You must remember for 250 years the white man and the red man have been fighting for possession of this country. It was war. Being greatly outnumbered, the red man naturally fought a losing battle. Not because his fighting ability was any less, but the numbers were too great to cope with. The Indians were put on reservations originally as prisoners of war, and guarded by soldiers. Every once in a while they got away and came out raiding, so Congress made many laws to control them. If a person was considered undesirable he could be thrown off the reservation. All kinds of laws were made restricting the freedom of the Indian. Now those old laws, obsolete as they are, are still on the statute books. The Indian as such has still not the power of organization which is the right of every American citizen.

What this bill proposes to do is to give the ward Indian the power to organize in any way he sees fit. It aims to allow him to form cooperative societies, livestock associations, corporations, etc., so that he may better his general living conditions.

If you will go back to the land problem for a moment—to the proposal to buy new lands without at the same time withdrawing from the restricted Indians the protection of the Government—if you go back to that point—you can see that it would be poor business on the part of the Government to buy a million pieces of land here and a million pieces there and in some other place, because if the ward Indians are to continue to have the services of the Government such as public health service, farming instructions, home demonstrations, education, etc.—if they are to continue to have all this, they should be so situated as to allow the services to be rendered at a reasonable cost. You can readily see that an Indian population entitled to these services, which is scattered over 10 or 15 counties with 10 or 15 miles between them and with a total distance of from 50 to 75 miles in every direction from the point where the services can be rendered—you can readily see that the cost would be so high that Congress would get tired and say "Let's quit."

So that the thing to do is to make the administering of these services as easy as possible by keeping these purchases in a close compact area. If that is done the next step is to bestow upon these compact areas the right of self-government—give these communities the power to run their own affairs in their own sweet way.

Self-government however is not a light thing. You all know that a lot of American communities have made a rather bad job of self-government. You can take a look, for instance, at the great city of Chicago where self-government has proved to be almost a flat failure. Now the objection is frequently raised that if a white community of the size of the city of Chicago cannot efficiently govern itself, how can an Indian community ever hope to do so? Well, we have got to make a try. The self respect of the Indian demands that we give him the chance, and I am dead certain that once an Indian community is given the right to run its own affairs it will do so efficiently and far better than a lot of whites are doing it now. But you must start sometime. You may get a few bumps, but what of it? I have never yet seen a child who started to walk without tumbling on his nose or on the other end a number of times. It may hurt, but the child soon learns, and by and by he is up and away under his own power. We never think of denying a child the right to learn to walk merely because we know it may fall down and get hurt in the process of learning. And you can't learn to walk by leaning against a wall. Just try it and see. The Indian has been forced to lean on the government and on the Indian Bureau far too long. It is about time for him to stand up and get under way on his own power.

We know from experience in E.C.W. camps in the past year that your young men are able and willing and anxious to work. In fact, they performed their work as efficiently if not more efficiently than their white brothers in the C.C.C. camps. It has been a revelation to see the marvelous accomplishments of the E.C.W. workers. It has given us a broader outlook and a more hopeful outlook when we have seen how rapidly these gangs of workers developed their own leaders, foremen, etc. We know then that the capacity for leadership is in the Indian race. It is there just as much and sometimes more than in other races. It is merely a question of how best to set free this capacity and put it to work, and that we propose to do through the system of organized communities to which it is proposed gradually to transfer various administrative and other services for the communities to do for themselves, whereas now they are being done for them by the government through the Indian Bureau.

In other words, the Commissioner proposes through this bill—the self-government section—gradually in the course of time to eliminate the Indian Bureau as a master and to transform it into a sort of advisory system, and to give the communities the chances to work out their own problems. I could go into the details of this particular section, but I won't do it now because Mr. Baumgarten informs me that dinner will be served at 12 o'clock sharp and we must get through here about 10 minutes to twelve, so we will omit any detailed discussion on this subject and bring it up again.

MIKE WOLFE: Mr. Chairman, if any announcements are made we would like to have them interpreted immediately. About ninety percent of us understand you, but there are some of us who don't understand English and we would like to have the announcements interpreted.

MR. WOEHLKE: The interpreter will announce them.

MR. WOLFE: I refer to those written questions which you mentioned some time ago.

MR. WOEHLKE: The interpreter will interpret them.

MR. WOEHLKE: Very briefly I want to wind up the discussion on the self-government part of the bill. The self-government as offered in this bill is purely voluntary. You have to come and take it if you want it. If you want a charter for a community, you have to ask for it, and you have to decide what you want in that charter and confirm it by a majority vote. Every aspect of this program is voluntary. You can go as far as you want to and as short a distance as you want to. It's just as though self-government were a river. You are on a bank. You have to walk to that river to get to it and you can test it out to see if you like it. You can begin by sticking your toe in the water, and if you like it you can go in still deeper and if you don't like it you can get out. It depends entirely on your willingness and ability to handle the proposition.

At Rapid City the Sioux interpreter from Pine Ridge at the end of four or five long days got up and said when he first heard of this new deal for the Indians he liked it. Then he began to worry about it. He said: "I began to see that what we need to put this program into effect is leaders and I looked around hard and long among my people, but I couldn't find any leaders and that is what we need if we are to make a success of it."

That might well apply to a great many other tribes I know of. The development of leadership among the Indians has been nullified for the past 50 years because there was no goal for the individual to strive for. Everything was being done for them. The development of leaders was suppressed by the system under which the Indians were governed. There was no chance for development because there was no object in developing—no incentive.

Realizing this, the committee and the Commissioner put into this bill Title 2 which deals with educational privileges. You will find in the amended bill that the amounts which are to be set aside for special Indian education—for the special training of your young men and women—that these appropriations have been very much increased. Now the figures stand at $200,000 and $50,000 where they were $50,000 and $15,000. We realize we must have leaders if this program is to be put through. Therefore these sums are to be authorized so that the most promising of your young men and women can be given professional training in administration, in medicine, in law, in agricultural and all kinds of technical subjects which are closed to them now because of the excessive cost of obtaining them. In part this money is to be a loan. Half is to be furnished by the men and women who receive the scholarships, but if they are unemployed payments can be suspended until such time as they are able to pay. We hope to develop a body of professionally trained Indian men and women that will take over the task of administration off the shoulder of the white people and put it where it belongs.

Now, let us look at the section which sets up a special system of Indian courts. As you know we already have the so-called Indian courts on the reservations where justice is administered in cases of minor law infractions. It is a purely informal system of courts with a loose organization and without the right of appeal. Under Title 4 the powers of the Indian community courts are limited and regulated. The manner of selecting judges is left to the community instead of to the Secretary of the Interior. The right of appeal is granted to those who feel the weight of a sentence and feel they have been injured. The right of appeal is given to a special Federal court of Indian affairs with seven judges equal to seven U.S. District Courts. The U.S. District Courts usually are too busy to give the Indian the time to which he is entitled.

It is in no sense an effort to create a special system of Indian judicial affairs, but rather it is an effort to provide the judicial facilities to which the Indian is entitled and which at the present time he is denied. Also, this particular title is subject to amendment and may be amended before the bill reaches the floor of the House and Senate. The Committee of Indian Affairs has sent letters to all U.S. district judges asking for their opinion of this title and a good deal depends upon what their attitude is as to what amendments shall be made.

I have given you a very rapid sketch of the proposed legislation and the time has now arrived to get ready for lunch. We reconvene in this hall at 1:30 P.M. At that time I hope you will have many of your questions ready. Mr. Marshall will start the session with a detailed analysis of the proposed land system and as soon as he is through we shall begin to answer the questions. I hope you will have many of them.

Session adjourned until 1:30 P.M.

1:30 P.M. April 23, 1934

MR. WOEHLKE: The meeting will come to order.

JOE MORRISON: Since the ideas and needs of the various bands are so far apart. I would like to ask that different meetings be held so that we will not interfere with one another. I think we could get along much better in this manner.

MR. WOEHLKE: We had already planned to hold different meetings tonight with the various groups and the announcements of those meetings will be made some time in the afternoon. It is not yet settled as to the locations, but we had planned to have meetings with delegations from Minnesota, and another one with delegations from Wisconsin, and another with the men from the Winnebago, Sioux and Potawotamie tribes and also those from Red Lake. These meetings will be held this evening and announcements as to where they will be held will be made from the platform this afternoon. Is that satisfactory?

JOE MORRISON: That is satisfactory.

MR. WOEHLKE: We will now proceed with the program as announced this morning. We will discuss in detail the provisions of the land title and that task falls to a man whom I know you will all like. He is a man who is descended from the illustrious John Marshall, Chief Justice who made the interpretation of the Constitution which prevails today. He is not only a technical forester, but writes books in his spare moments. Some years ago he proceeded up to Alaska and for almost two years lived in an Eskimo village. He wrote a book about it and that book later became a best seller. I know he doesn't know I know this and he probably hates to have me tell it, but when he got a lot of royalty, running into thousands of dollars, one-half of it went to the inhabitants up in that little village on the Polar Sea. He knows his business as a forester and he knows what he is talking about.

ROBERT MARSHALL (Director of Forestry): After everything nice the Chairman said about me, I hate to tell you that I am neither a lawyer nor a descendant of a chief justice, and I will say that if it was not for the lawyers and their technical phrases, I wouldn't have to speak on this since it is all contained in these 15 pages from page 27 to page 41. These pages would be perfectly clear if they weren't all tangled up with legal phrases as they are in any bill.

Interpretation of above by Frank Smart, Odanah.

MR. MARSHALL: Now, I think about everything that there is in this whole 15 pages I can summarize in 5 sentences—that is everything of importance from the standpoint of the average person. Now for the first sentence: 1. The Indians will keep the land they now own. 2. The Government will buy them more lands. 3. The lands will be owned in such a way that the Indians can really get the benefit of them. 4. They will be managed so as not to ruin them. 5. The tax free period will be continued indefinitely. A great deal must be explained in connection with those five sentences in order that you understand them, but those five sentences tell pretty much what those 15 pages mean.

Interpretation by Frank Smart.

MR. MARSHALL: That sums up pretty well what is contained in those fifteen pages, but it is early in the afternoon, and before you start your questions I will add a few more sentences. First, in regard to the matter of the Indians keeping the land they now own. The bill provides two phases of the same thing: 1. No more Indian lands can be sold to white men. 2. Those unsold ceded portions of the Indian reservations which by hook or crook have been thrown open by Congress and have become open for homesteading by White people—those lands which have not yet been sold or homesteaded will be returned to the Indian reservation and become a part of the Indian land.

When I say the Government will buy more land, that means two different sorts of land the Government will buy up in this part of the country—timber and farming lands.

Because of the allotment law in the past a great many solid timber blocks have been broken up by partial white ownership and Indian timber lands have been scattered throughout with white owned patches. You know that in order to be profitable, timber operations should be carried on in solid blocks and this has been impossible with white lands scattered throughout your holdings.

Under this bill it is proposed to buy up part of the white lands scattered throughout the reservations. Under the present system the white man controls your land, so to speak, and it is not a good thing for you. So it is proposed that the Government will buy up some of the white timber land and make it possible to block out solid blocks of Indian lands that you could operate yourselves. On most of the reservations it is not possible to make a living only on timber lands, valuable as they may be. However, probably most of you could make a living in timber lands if you also had farms to operate. The bill proposes to buy land for landless Indians and I know a great many of you people, particularly Chippewas who through no fault of your own have lost their land—will in time be provided with land through the bill. Another thing of importance—in cutting timber on your lands, enough seed trees will be left so that new trees may grow up, thus avoiding barren wastes so typical of many parts of this country.

I am now reading from the Bill of Indian Rights.

"On the death of the owner of restricted land, other than grazing or timber land, lying within an area classified for consolidation pursuant to the provisions of this section, the Secretary shall partition such land among the heirs, or devisees, if the lands are capable of partition without impairment of the beneficial use of the lands. If the land cannot be so partitioned, each heir or devisee shall receive a certificate entitling him to an undivided interest in land or other assets equal in value to the parcel he would otherwise inherit, and the title of the decedent shall pass to the chartered community within whose territorial limits the land is located, or, if no community has been chartered, to the tribe from whose lands the allotment was made.

"On the death of the owner of restricted grazing or timber land lying within an area classified for consolidation pursuant to the provisions of this section, each heir or devisee shall receive a certificate entitling him to an undivided interest in land or other assets equal in value to the parcel he would otherwise inherit, and the title of the decedent shall pass to the chartered community within whose territorial limits the land is located, or, if no community has been chartered, to the tribe from whose lands the allotment was made.

"It shall be the duty of the Secretary to determine what interests in lands or other assets shall be granted to such heirs or devisees in lieu of the parcels they would otherwise inherit. Any arbitrary and unreasonable determination may be set aside by any court of competent jurisdiction."

Each of you, I suppose, has different questions in your mind about this bill and I suppose it would be well to begin answering some of the questions.

MR. WOEHLKE: I think we will now begin to answer the large number of questions that have arrived at the desk.

QUESTION by the Bad River delegates: On the Bad River Reservation the allotted Indians all hold fee patents for their individual allotments. These fee patents have restrictions. Would it be compulsory for the allottee to surrender or relinquish his land to the community if the Department so ordered? We understand that the Constitution does not give the Secretary of the Interior the right to nullify or abrogate this fee patent without the owners' consent.

ANSWER BY MR. WOEHLKE: There must be a slight mixup in terms here. If it is a fee patent, I suppose it has no restrictions. It would be a trust patent, so let us assume the Bad River delegates are referring to trust patents. Would it be compulsory to relinquish the land to the community? I believe we have explained once or twice that the entire system of community organization is voluntary—that no one has the right to take private property from anybody else, and the Secretary of the Interior is just as much bound by the Constitution of the United States as any other citizen—therefore we can tell our friends from Bad River that it is perfectly impossible constitutionally to take land away from them and that the bill contemplates no such step. If there is to be any surrendering at all, it will be a purely voluntary process. The Indians would have to consent or it could not be done.

QUESTION by Bad River delegation: Will the Chair explain in detail how credit facilities will be made available for use by the chartered community?

ANSWER: The credit section of the bill authorizes the appropriation of $10,000,000 for a so-called "revolving fund." That is, a fund out of which loans are made which are then repaid to the fund and loaned out again to others, so that the fund itself never returns to the Treasury of the United States, but continues to be used for loan purposes.

Under the bill as drawn at the present time, loans from this fund would be made to chartered communities and to members of these communities for various purposes, a number of which are enumerated in the bill. For instance, for the building of homes, barns and fences, for the purchase of livestock, of implements, of fertilizer, and for any other purpose which would contribute to the economic success of the community and its members.

Under that provision you might set up in the chartered communities a credit union to which the government would loan a certain amount, and that union in turn would loan to its members or members of the community. You might have a livestock association which would borrow from this fund and repay in installments, so that for almost any activity of the community and members, these loans would be available.

The loans need not always be made on good security or on any security whatsoever. They may be made by the credit union on the character of the person who borrows it. The terms of repayment will be set by the organization; by, say, the credit union in the local community, and if these loans are repaid the money will become available again for loans to other members of the community, so the fund will be circulating right along. I think that just about describes the method of making loans.

QUESTION by Bad River delegates: Some of our members contend that they have the right to sell wholly or in part at any time, when the money derived from such a sale, to the individual's best judgment, any land held under a *restricted* fee patent when such a sale helps the business the individual chooses to follow. They also contend that they have the right under the constitution of the United States to will their lands to their heirs, the fee patent title remaining with the heirs.

ANSWER: If restricted, no; if unrestricted, yes.

MR. WOEHLKE: Now right here is where the chairman gets a rap on the jaw—listen to this question.

QUESTION by Bad River delegation: An exception is made to one of your remarks. When were the Chippewa Indians at war with the U.S. Government? Where they became prisoners of war? Was it not through deceit that we become wards of government?

ANSWER: I believe I made the general statement that the white race occupied the North American continent and that during this process of occupation it was at war with the Indian race. I believe in general that this is true, but at the same time during this 300-year-war a great many of the tribes cooperated with the United States Government, as for instance the Crows and other tribes who were never at war with the United States. Several tribes in the Southwest always remained peaceful and helped the U.S. Government. But after all it was a condition of war in which the whites fought against the Red race, even though there were various alliances back and forth. Now as to the question of deceit on the part of the Government, that is undoubtedly true.

On the reverse side of this paper appears this question: "If this so called self-government bill is accepted, how do we know that the Government will fulfill its promises? We have been deceived quite a few times!"

That is a very good question and it deserves an answer. Personally, none of us can guarantee that, but we can say that this administration has taken a new view, a new attitude toward the common man, whether White or Red. The first concern of our President is with the rights of man and not so much with the rights of property.

I am quite certain that I can guarantee that whatever promises are made to you by this administration will be kept by this administration. As to the future, you must realize that up until very recent years the Indian race had land and properties that the white man wanted—especially land. The huge reservations of the 70s and 80s were right in the path of the white wave that swept across them. No matter what kind of promises the Government would make, the citizens would proceed to override them and take what they wanted; and frequently the Government had to break its treaty promises and reduce your land holdings, because if it hadn't done so, the whites would have taken everything by force and the Government would be powerless to restrain them.

The point is this: Of late years the white race has discovered that it took away too much land from the Indian race. It bit off and swallowed so much of the Indian land that now it has a national stomachache—it can't digest all the land. Because it took so much land and put it into cultivation and production, it now is faced with a condition under which it produces so much from the soil—so many things like cotton and wheat and corn—so many of those commodities—that there is no market for most of it and the prices have gone to the devil and the land values have also gone to the devil. Everything has gone to hell largely because too much land was taken from the Indians and put under cultivation. All of us are suffering from these past mistakes as you have noticed from the action of Congress in limiting cotton production, in trying to limit wheat production, etc. The Government realizes this, and in fact is now willing to buy back at low prices some of the land that was taken away and give it back to the Indians. That is why I believe that the promises made now will be kept. The theory now is not to take away from you, but to give back to you.

QUESTION by Menominee delegation: Will this self-government bill revoke all laws governing the Indians prior to the enactment of this act?

ANSWER: No, it would not.

MR. BAUMGARTEN: We are now ready to announce the places in which the various meetings will be held tonight. The Minnesota Chippewas will meet in this auditorium at 8 P.M. The gentlemen in charge will be Mr. zimmerman , Mr. Reeves. The Wisconsin and Michigan Chippewas will meet 8 P.M. with Mr. Woehlke and Mr. Daiker in the dining hall, upstairs in what is known as the employees' sitting room. The Menominee and Red Lake groups will meet with Mr. Marshall in the room upstairs in the girls' building right across from the office at 8 P.M. The Winnebago, Sioux, Oneida and Stockbridge groups will meet with Dr. Roe Cloud at the same time in the girls' building in the other sitting room which will be pointed out to you. The Potawatomie group will meet with the Wisconsin and Michigan Chippewas.

MR. WOEHLKE: The next series of questions will be answered by an old friend of yours—a man born in a tepee and raised on buffalo milk, finally winding up with a Yale degree and becoming Superintendent of Haskell Institute—Dr. Roe Cloud.

DR. ROE CLOUD: Mr. Interpreter, tell them I don't go quite as far back as the buffalo milk—tell them that I began with duck soup. Now for the questions.

QUESTIONS by White Earth delegation: What does tutelage mean?

ANSWER BY DR. ROE CLOUD: It means instruction, guidance, education and nurture. It also has this added meaning—it means wardship and government control of Indians whenever we use that term.

QUESTION 2: What Minnesota Indians are included under Federal tutelage?

ANSWER BY DR. ROE CLOUD: Generally speaking I should say that all Indians in the United States—not only Minnesota—but all Indians are under Federal tutelage. In a more technical sense, the Supreme Court of the United States has said that wards and citizens are not incompatible terms—so that you and I as Indians can be wards and citizens at the same time and exercise under those terms the privileges that go with both names. The word citizen is often referred to. A fee-patent Indian and also one who has separated himself from tribal connections and gone out with the white people to live—he is supposed to be a citizen. Technically he still remains a ward of the Government even though he is separated from all tribal connections because in many, many instances he continues to participate in the tribal fund. A great many Minnesota Indians today are still wards and citizens in the sense that they still continue to share in the fund. In 1924 President Coolidge made us all citizens, but that didn't impose upon us those well known responsibilities that go with citizenship.

QUESTION 3: What distinction, if any, does the bill make between "tribal" and "community?"

ANSWER BY DR. ROE CLOUD: Of course the word tribal means the whole number of Indians in the tribe or in anything that has to do with land or property in which every member of that tribe participates. A person that has tribal relationship may have that relation with respect to both property and land.

The term community is well defined by this bill in two ways. A community is based upon a so-called economic unit. It may be defined in many different ways according to the locality and the kind of economic situation in which the Indians find themselves. In a grass area where I have been for the last month among the Sioux Indians, an economic unit is comprised of an area containing grass, meadow hay and water. An economic unit here in Wisconsin would likely be far different and its interpretation would vary from the Sioux country just to the extent you may have fishing opportunities, forestry opportunities, subsistence opportunities, etc.

A community is further distinguished by the word *charter*. Where you have a community there must be a charter.

QUESTION 4: After a community has been organized it develops that a considerable number of Indian members—say 75%—refuses to work. What can be done with them? Will the other 25% have to feed and care for them?

ANSWER BY DR. ROE CLOUD: I believe someone is letting his imagination run away with him, but I would like to say here that this new system—this new plan—provides in my judgment far more work opportunities to the Indian race than what you and I have experienced up to the present time.

Generally speaking Indians are considered lazy, largely because of two things: There is wide-spread unemployment on reservations everywhere. A reservation is the hardest place in the world to find work for the Indian. Therefore, having no employment, he stands around the streets or mopes along the road in his lumber wagon. The second factor is because of wide-spread sickness resulting from not having enough to eat—malnutrition as it is called. Maybe tuberculosis has set in and there is a dragging of the feet and a loss of ambition together with a generally weakened condition—he may not be strong enough to go to work.

Lately when these relief work opportunities have been given the Indian, he has demonstrated that he will work if he has the opportunity—as thousands proved this past winter.

In the second place, this new system sets up a new form of self-interest that we have never before experienced. Here is this $10,000,000 loan fund that you and I can utilize to get started in something. To make industry we must have land, labor and capital, and hitherto we have not had anything but labor. Now for the first time in our experience the Government favors giving you the other two.

In the third place, the bill says that beneficial use must be made of this land. The chartered communities must see to this. Drones are a problem in any community and I trust in the best judgment of the Indians to solve the problem themselves. It is a thing that cannot very well be legislated against, but I believe that it can be controlled with a lot of good horse sense.

Fourth, the chartered community brings to apply on the Indian the local public opinion. Up to the present when the Bureau asked us to go to work we said, "Well, those birds are way off in Washington and we don't care very much about the white man's opinion."

But let the Indian public opinion be focused upon some one member of the community and watch the reaction. We naturally respond to what our fellows think of us and it is a most powerful force to make us do something useful in life. So I say that 75% of any community is not going to be lazy by any means.

QUESTION 5: Would ceded reservations in Minnesota under this bill be classified and considered as reservation?

ANSWER: Yes.

QUESTION 6: In dealing with the Indians in this bill it defines the status of degree at 1/4 Indian blood. Then what provision is being made for those less then one-fourth Indian blood?

ANSWER BY DR. ROE CLOUD: Since the person of less than one-fourth Indian blood is excluded from the terms of the bill, I believe this is a good question to forward to the commission at Washington for final determination.

VOICE from the back part of the auditorium: Mr. Chairman, may we ask the speakers to be a little louder? It is difficult to hear in the back part of the hall.

QUESTION by the Leech Lake delegation: When a band of Indians accepts the plan of self-government, where will the community be established and who will be the selector of such location? Will it be the Indians or the Secretary of the Interior?

ANSWER: I should say that the selections of sites will be made by and with the advice of experts of the Government. The Government is helping the landless Indian with $2,000,000 for the purchase of lands. I do not question but what the Government will be very glad to listen to the desires of the Indians as to the place they would like to live, and in general this rehabilitation will begin where they already have any kind of land holding. Where there is a group of Indians that have no land whatsoever, they may wish to colonize and go to other places to live.

QUESTION: Can a person who belongs to another tribe on another reservation come over and join some other tribe on some other reservation?

ANSWER: If that is the case, any person having land in two different communities can consolidate their holdings wherever they want to live. In the case of a man and woman, the man may move to her holdings, or vice versa. This is merely a question of transfer that the communities can see to themselves.

QUESTION: What will be the money source for the development of these proposed communities?

ANSWER: The $10,000,000 appropriation will be the source for the development of these communities. If the community wants to use its own tribal money it may do so and whatever money profits are derived from the initiative of Indians in tribal ventures may also be used in furthering the development of the community.

QUESTION: The proposed bill provides funds for the use of those Indians who are eligible for higher education. Where will these youths obtain their elementary or preparatory training which will enable them to take advantage of this provision in the bill?

ANSWER: I wonder why that question was asked—because already the Government is providing most tribes with elementary education—for example at boarding schools, day schools, etc.—and wherever there is a tax supporting institution among whites, the Indians are permitted to attend. There will be available $250,000 and Indian boys and girls will be sent away after they have been discovered to have the capacity to become doctors and nurses, lawyers, engineers, accountants, business men and one thing and another.

MR. WOEHLKE: I wonder how the interpreter can possibly interpret all that.

Lengthy interpretation by Mr. Frank Smart, Odanah.

THOMAS ST. GERMAINE of Lac du Flambeau: Mr. Chairman, I believe that last question was perfectly legitimate. I happen to have the honor of being a graduate of the same school as Dr. Roe Cloud, and I would like to have this question elaborated on. The bill provides that the young people must reveal a capacity for higher education in order to be sent to large institutions, but how are they going to develop this capacity? Are they just going to jump right into it? If the Indian schools can prepare the youth up to the point of entering the University of Wisconsin, or Yale, or some other large school, all well and good, but it does not prepare the youth up to that point. Why do we have a Dr. Roe Cloud or a St. Germaine or perhaps one or two others who are graduates of big schools? Why do we have so few of them? Because the system of education has been so faulty, so low in grade that it does not prepare for entrance in to higher schools.

MR. WOEHLKE: It is the policy of the U.S. Government to provide elementary and high school education for Indians wherever possible.

MR. ST. GERMAINE: Where I come from there was only one boy who received a little help. Do you mean to say that in a community like that there is only one candidate who is eligible for higher education?

DR. ROE CLOUD: I think that Mr. St. Germaine's remarks are very well spoken and to the point. The Government has in the past few years conducted institutions in the elementary grades that were not accredited with the college requirements. The reason for that has been that the Government considered what it calls industrial education of more importance than simply getting Indians into college. Lately, however, the Government is seeing to it that Indian children receive instruction in public schools that are tax supported—the aim being to see that the Indian children get the standard training that is afforded the white children to enable them to enter universities and colleges. This bill, if passed, will provide a better chance for the Indian children to receive the necessary elementary training.

MR. WOEHLKE: I think we are getting far behind in our interpretation. Suppose we have the interpreter summarize what has been said during the last hour.

Interpretation by Mr. Frank Smart, Odanah.

MR. WOEHLKE: I think that was a marvelous piece of work and I think that we ought to reward the interpreter by taking a recess for 15 minutes.

Recess for fifteen minutes.

MR. WOEHLKE: The minutes of this conference will be mimeographed and a copy of them will be supplied to each delegate through his superintendent. If any of the other guests and visitors would like to have copies of these proceedings, will they please communicate with the superintendent of their district so that the proper number can be ordered. It will probably take three weeks before these copies will be ready. Upon request additional copies will be furnished for distribution among those Indians who did attend this conference.

I want to repeat the announcements of this evening's meetings. The Minnesota Chippewas are meeting in the building at 8 P.M.; the Wisconsin and Michigan Chippewas in the building in which the dining room is located; the Menominee and Red Lake groups in the girls' building upstairs; and the Winnebagos, Sioux, Stockbridge and Oneida groups in the same building upstairs. Visitors of course will be welcome up to the capacity of the rooms.

We will now proceed with the answering of questions, and our latest victim will be the distinguished Chief Counsel of the Office of Indian Affairs, a man who has been digging into the laws of the Indians for the past 30 years. What he doesn't know about Indian law isn't worth knowing, and you can take what he says as gospel truth.

QUESTION by White Earth delegation: Is there provision in H.R. 7902 for appeal from decisions rendered by the proposed Indian Court?

ANSWER BY MR. REEVES: Yes, page 47 and 48, Section 15 of the bill reads as follows: "The final judgment of the Court of Indian Affairs shall be subject to review on questions of law in the circuit of appeals of the circuit in which such judgment is rendered. The several circuit courts of appeals are authorized to adopt rules for the conduct of such appellate proceedings, and, until the adoption of such rules, the rules of such courts relating to appellate proceedings upon a writ of error, so far as applicable, shall govern. The said circuit courts of appeals shall have power to affirm, or, if the judgment of the Court of Indian Affairs is not in accordance with law, to modify or reverse the judgment of that court, with or without remanding the case for a rehearing, as justice may require; the judgment of the circuit court of appeals shall be final, except that it may be subject to review by the Supreme Court as provided in the United States Code, title 28, Sections 346 and 347."

QUESTION by White Earth delegation: Cite and interpret the so-called Curtis Act enacted in 1924, conferring citizenship upon the Indians of the United States, and state briefly how H.R. 7902 with its multitudes of provisions, can constitutionally be applied under grants provided for in the said act of 1924?

ANSWER BY MR. REEVES: That question has already been answered twice from this platform. It was referred to by both Dr. Roe Cloud and Mr. Woehlke. It was pointed out to you that citizenship and wardship are not incompatible. The Supreme Court has so held and the Act of June 2, 1924 in conferring citizenship upon the Indians in no way deprived you of any property rights, privileges and opportunities granted to you Indians. There is no inconsistency between the two in any manner whatever, and enactment of the bill would only extend to you additional facilities and privileges without dispossessing you of present property rights or rights as citizens.

QUESTION BY JOHN BROKER, White Earth: What effect will that have on the Indians if they want to run for office—for instance a county office?

ANSWER BY MR. REEVES: It should have none whatever.

QUESTION by White Earth delegation: Do you not think that you are taxing the endurance and good nature of your interpreter with too lengthy statements?

ANSWER BY MR. REEVES: That is an interesting question and I want to answer it by saying that I certainly do think so.

QUESTION by White Earth delegation: Will a future administration interfere with the provisions of this legislation in the event it is enacted into law?

ANSWER BY MR. REEVES: Mr. Woehlke has already assured you that no representative of the Government can guarantee what Congress will do in the future. If it enacts this measure, any future Congress has the power to supersede it with other laws. I am no prophet and can't look into the future any more than you can. Neither can we representatives of the Government guarantee absolutely what is ahead of you in the way of legislation.

QUESTION by White Earth delegation: Is the court provision workable? Would it not strip the Indians of their constitutional rights they now enjoy? Would findings of fact by this court be made unreviewable on appeal?

ANSWER BY MR. REEVES: The answer to the first part as to whether the provision is workable or not is undoubtedly yes. The answer to the remainder as to whether it would strip the Indians of constitutional rights is no.

QUESTION by Lac du Flambeau delegation: Referring to Title 3, page 28, line 21. Do we now own the water rights? It is our chief asset since about one-third of the area of our reservation is water.

ANSWER BY MR. REEVES: Turning to page 28, line 21 of the bill you will find that it provides that no lands, water rights or other assets owned by Indians shall be voluntarily or involuntarily alienated. Further, I might state that the water rights referred to deal primarily in connection with arid southwest lands where it is necessary to resort to artificial application of water to raise crops. That is primarily the water rights dealt with in this bill. With reference to the water rights among you Chippewa people, your rights depend upon whether the waters are navigable or non-navigable. As to areas within the reservation, if they are navigable waters they belong to the State—if non-navigable they belong to the tribe or individual Indians in the event the reservation has been allotted.

Interpretation by Frank Smart.

QUESTION BY ATTY. THOMAS ST. GERMAINE, Lac du Flambeau: This question is so vital to us that I would like to add a few more words. Navigable streams have been defined by our supreme court of Wisconsin as being any stream or lake that floats along—anything that floats a ship is a navigable stream. The reason our grandfathers preserved these waters in old treaties was to provide the Indians with hunting and fishing and to provide a storehouse for game. Now if you want to help these reservations your action should be this: Congress should enact a law whereby we could have exclusive jurisdiction of these waters. Otherwise self-government means nothing to us for we will have nothing to self govern with.

QUESTION BY JEROME ARBUCKLE, Bad River delegate: We want to know how this bill would affect our hunting and fishing on streams which the State contends are navigable.

ANSWER: It would have no immediate effect.

QUESTION BY CHARLES PICARD, Chairman, L'Anse Chippewa delegation: Does the passage of this H.R. 7092 bill nullify the citizenship act of 1924? Indians in Minnesota, Wisconsin and Michigan now are eligible to vote—run for, and do hold township, village, county and State offices as citizens of the State and the United States. Will this proposed law deprive them this suffrage?

ANSWER: That question has been asked elsewhere and I believe was answered fully.

QUESTION BY MR. PICARD: Sec. 2, Title 5 does not appear to protect rights acquired under treaty agreements. Will this bill annul these rights such as fishing and hunting, and holding our lands or allotments free from taxation indefinitely and forever?

ANSWER BY MR. REEVES: I do not propose to get into argument as to the decision of the courts in this matter. I do want to state however that my heart goes out in deep sympathy to the Chippewa Indians because of their losses—primarily of land. Unquestionably there have been treaty violations and to correct this matter Congress will have to change the laws—I cannot change that law—Congress will have to do it. But as to the hunting and fishing—if the streams are navigable the title is in the State and the State has the control, and if the waters are non-navigable the State has no jurisdiction.

QUESTION BY JEROME ARBUCKLE of Bad River Band: As concerns the Bad River band the title to the swamp lands etc. rest in the hands of the Indians, and as far as one parcel of that land is concerned, I have the patent to that land right here in my pocket. The State relinquished their claim to these lands of the Bad River and they were all allotted to individuals who today hold titles to them. The State claims no jurisdiction over our navigable rivers. If this bill takes away our hunting and fishing rights it takes everything away from us and will be of no benefit to us.

ANSWER BY MR. REEVES: This bill would take away no rights that you now have—none whatever. If the State has selected other swamp lands that is fine—in Minnesota the Indians did lose their swamp lands.

QUESTION BY JEROME ARBUCKLE: If the State contends it has jurisdiction over navigable waters, would we be liable to State law and arrest if we pass over these waters with game out of season?

ANSWER BY MR. REEVES: I think you would—I may be mistaken.

MR. ARBUCKLE: I would like to know what good our treaty is then.

QUESTION BY MR. ST. GERMAINE: Someone has said—in fact the Supreme Court has said that the treaty is the supreme law of the land. I don't know what they mean by that—perhaps they should have said all but an Indian treaty. An Indian treaty, it seems, can be twisted any old way to suit someone else. A mere interpretation by a certain group of men should not change the law. My thought is this: That interpretation of the law has never been argued by a member who really believes and knows that the Indians retain titles to these waters within reservation lands. Give us a chance—let an Indian go there and tell those gray haired men what they should know.

Chair taken by Mr. Woehlke.

MR. WOEHLKE: We are not only getting into navigable waters, Mr. Reeves, but we are getting into deep legal waters—but I don't believe that a discussion of the legal aspect of this thing will get us anywhere.

If you gentlemen from the Bad River or Lac du Flambeau reservations think that through the Wheeler-Howard Bill we are trying to take anything away from you, you are badly mistaken. It gives you greater security, adds to what you have, and takes nothing at all away from you. If you still believe we are trying to take something away from you then we have been very much at fault in explaining this bill to you. We have been trying to explain all day long that what we want to do is to add to what you have and to help you in your present difficulties.

If we haven't made that clear it is our fault, and we hope that tonight we can tackle some of these things and see if we cannot work out a remedy that will protect you in the vital rights to these waters. But don't let us mix it up with the discussion of this particular bill which is designed exclusively to help you and to add to what you have.

We have had orders from the cook to close at once or we won't get anything to eat. So therefore we recess until 9 o'clock tomorrow morning with the exception of the evening meetings.

Recess until (9 A.M. April 24, 1934).

Session Reopened at 9:00 A.M. April 24, 1934

Meeting opened by MR. WOEHLKE: I understand from various persons who met in this hall last night that several of them froze their feet, hands and noses, and I suggest they go to the hospital for treatment if they still hurt. Where we met it was nice and warm.

We will now endeavor to answer as rapidly, yet as completely as possible the remaining written questions. After we are through we would like to hear from the various delegations and I suggest in view of the limited time and the large number of reservations represented, that the delegations from these reservations select their spokesmen as soon as possible so that they will be ready when they are called upon. This will aid in losing as little time as possible. After that we want to throw the subject right on the table and have expressions of opinion from anybody who might feel moved to speak on it, so I want now to ask Chief Counsel Reeves to complete the answering of the questions which he has in his pocket.

QUESTION by Bad River delegation: After the charter is issued can the restricted fee patent allottee still dispose of his land as he sees fit after he has requested that the restrictions be removed?

ANSWER BY MR. REEVES: Depends entirely on whether the title you own is restricted fee or an absolute fee. If you have an outright fee title, one on which all restrictions are removed, or you have received a certificate of competency, then you have the right to sell it without the approval of any Government agency. If you still retain the restricted title you can sell with the order of the Secretary of the Interior. As to the right of making a will, you have that right under the law as it stands today.

QUESTION BY MITCHELL RED CLOUD, Chairman, Wisconsin Winnebago Claim Committee: This bill carries no provision whatsoever objectionable to the Winnebago tribes as a whole, but it does lack a provision by which an Indian can recover ownership, or grant right to reimbursement of taxes paid, where the loss of ownership is not through the fault of the Indian, but through the indifference and laxity of administration of the Federal agents in recent years.

Many Indians would benefit by such a provision. From 1915 on, lands were purchased with trust funds and patents in fee given, carrying a clause stating that these lands were the inalienable property of the buyer, and further stating that these lands would be exempt from taxation for twenty-five years. These rulings held good for a number of years. Then without warning, without consulting the Winnebagoes, a ruling was made that these lands were taxable, which compelled these Indians to pay back taxes amounting to hundreds of dollars which the Indians could not meet and thereby lost their lands.

ANSWER: The Winnebagoes in Wisconsin received fee titles with restrictions against alienation for a period of 20 years. That period automatically expired by lapse of time when the 20 year period ran out. The lands were nontaxable during that period but became subject to taxation upon expiration of such period. It also involves another troublesome angle—the purchase of land for an Indian with proceeds derived from the sale of other trust lands, which under earlier rulings of the courts were held to be nontaxable. After quite an interval, and after everyone had been convinced that the repurchased lands were nontaxable, a higher court overruled the lower court, holding it beyond the power of the Secretary of the Interior to sell land held in trust for an Indian and take the proceeds and buy another piece of land from a white man and render that repurchased land nontaxable. It was a bitter experience to Indians who had sold tax-exempt land, but fortunately Congress has remedied that situation a year ago by enactment of a statute which enables the Secretary of the Interior to do what he previously was unable to do.

QUESTION by Bad River delegation: In this bill and elsewhere the question of wards and non-wards has come up on several occasions. We would like to have the chair clearly define a ward and a non-ward and the status of each class. We have cases where an allottee has received a certificate of competency for 20 acres of his 80 acre allotment. Is he a ward or a non-ward or just a *restricted* citizen?

ANSWER: He is a ward—he is also a citizen.

QUESTION BY MITCHELL RED CLOUD, Winnebago: Other lands were lost through failure to make payments on drainage taxation where drainage ditches were forcibly made without the consent of the Indian land owners.

ANSWER: That has reference to a special situation in a so-called drainage area and assessments were levied against those lands but they were not sold for failure to pay.

QUESTION BY MITCHELL RED CLOUD, Winnebago: Will there be only one or several Federal Courts of Indian Affairs to facilitate early settlement of claims arising from unpaid treaty stipulation?

ANSWER: If you turn to pages 41 and 42 of the bill you will see that it provides for one Federal court of Indian affairs consisting of seven judges, any one of whom may sit individually in minor cases. It does not however give that court jurisdiction of claims of the Indians against the Government. That will remain where it now rests in the hands of the Court of Claims.

QUESTION by Fond du Lac delegation: My boy has an education. He saw service in the World War. He was during action. After getting back, shortly he got married, and he has five children and three of the children received payment while the other two youngest children were deprived of the annuity payment. Shortly after the Patterson decision came into effect they were all taken off the annuity roll for the reason that they were born off the reservation. Could they be put back on the annuity roll as adopted children of the Mississippi Chippewa Indians?

ANSWER: The answer to the last part of that question is yes. If they were or are re-enrolled by adoption of tribal authority they would be readmitted and recognized as members under the Patterson decision holding, in effect, that children born off the reservation were not born to membership in the tribe and unless the tribal authorities are willing to recognize them by adoption they are not automatically entitled to membership. That is a very troublesome question among you Chippewas—the right of children of nonresident members to enrollment for benefits. We have hoped to work out a solution to the problem, and under this new bill if it is enacted, I believe the problem will be left for the communities themselves to decide—they themselves will probably have to decide the right of membership in cases like this.

MR. WOEHLKE: From that very brief talk by Mr. Reeves you can see the immense complexity of the problems that constantly confront the office and the legal department, and I think it is a marvelous thing that we can get together in this way to consider and discuss all these matters face to face instead of sending letters to Washington and getting a brief reply perhaps 3 or 4 weeks later. We hope that in the future we will have a series of these Congresses so that we can have these heart-to-heart talks and get acquainted with one and another.

Chair taken by Mr. Daiker.

QUESTIONS by Red Cliff delegation: Has the Indian the right to vote for County and town elections?

ANSWER BY MR. DAIKER: Yes. That has already been answered.

QUESTION: How long will it last, if successful?

ANSWER: I take it this has reference to the right to vote. Of course it will last indefinitely.

QUESTION: In regard to old Indian claims—will the Indians lose rights or not, to prosecute claims?

ANSWER: They will not. That has been answered before, I believe.

QUESTION: What will be the ratio of assessments, in regard to holdings of members?

ANSWER: That will be determined by the communities under this bill.

QUESTION: Can a member hold a piece of land outside of the community and still be a member?

ANSWER: There is no reason why he should not be.

QUESTION: What would happen if a member refused assessment, or will he be forced?

ANSWER: That has been answered before, but I will say again that it will be left to the communities to determine how those assessments will be collected.

QUESTION: An Indian tribe or band that excludes itself or does not accept the proposed community—are they denied the benefits provided in the bill? Do they come under the jurisdiction of the State, as to citizenship?

ANSWER: The community that denies or refuses the bill of course excludes itself by its own action.

QUESTION: Under this bill can the Government take taxable unrestricted land located within the Indian reservation and owned by an Indian wishing to join a community and make it restricted or tribal land? Would the present owner gain anything, and what would he gain, by relinquishing his rights to said land?

ANSWER: If the land is taxable now the only way it can be taken off the list is to have it purchased by the Government and the title taken by the Government—the individual benefit to the Indian would be that the land would be taken off the tax list.

QUESTION: How will this bill affect an Indian taxpayer on a reservation should a charter be granted to said community?

ANSWER: That depends upon what status his land remains in—whether he retains the title to it as an individual—if so it is still taxable. If sold to the Government and the title taken by the Government it is no longer taxable.

QUESTION by Stockbridge delegation: Will the Stockbridge Indians come under this bill? We received patents in fee simple in 1910 but never received our trust fund. All or nearly all lands have been lost to the Indians either through sale or mortgage foreclosure. Of 11,440 acres patented to the Indians in 1910 only about 200 acres remain under Indian ownership today. These Indians still remain as a group on their old reservations paying rent or just staying by the good graces of some white man.

ANSWER: They will receive benefit to the extent that the limited funds will allow. So many Indians are to be provided for that it won't be enough to go around and take care of all needy cases. As to the land, that means setting up new communities with land to be purchased under the appropriations authorized in this bill.

QUESTION by Stockbridge delegation: Would a man who could not show one-fourth Indian blood but is now on the Indian roll come in under this new bill or would he be excluded?

ANSWER: That question is answered under Section 15, Title 1 of the Bill of Indian rights which reads as follows:

> "The term 'Indian' as used in this title to specify the persons to whom charters may be issued, shall include all persons of Indian descent who are members of any recognized Indian tribe, band, or nation, and all persons who are descendants of such members who were, on or about February 1, 1934, actually residing within the present boundaries of any Indian reservation, and shall further include all other persons of one-fourth or more Indian blood, but nothing in this definition or in this Act shall prevent the Secretary of the Interior or the constituted authorities of a chartered community from prescribing, by provision of charter or pursuant thereto, additional qualifications or conditions for membership in any chartered community, or from offering the privileges of membership therein to non-residents of a community who are members of any tribe, wholly or partly comprised within the chartered community."

QUESTION by Grand Portage delegation: There is objection to allowing members of an Indian community to buy their way out of the community. They fear it will defeat the object of the bill.

ANSWER: As a matter of fact I think that section on page 4 of the new bill—Section 3, Title 1—is one of the most controversial and disputed subjects, and there do seem to be people who believe that members should not be allowed to buy themselves out of the community. The bill says he has the right "to abandon the community and to receive some compensation for any interest in community assets thereby relinquished, the extent of which compensation and the manner of payment thereof to be fixed by charter provision."

QUESTION by Grand Portage delegation: Section 4, Paragraph J. Does this paragraph mean that the Indians will have to relinquish any rights previously given them under former treaties, such as their claims against the U.S. Government, or the money that is held in trust for them at Washington, in the office of the Indian Bureau?

ANSWER: No, this law does not affect treaty claims and that is provided for in the revised act, Title 5, Section 2 which reads as follows:

> "Nothing in this Act shall be construed to impair or prejudice in any way any claim or suit of any Indian tribe against the United States based upon any treaty obligation or other obligation heretofore incurred by the United States. It is hereby declared to be the intent of Congress that no expenditures for the benefit of Indians made out of appropriations specifically authorized by this Act shall be considered as offsets in any suit brought to recover upon any claim of such Indians against the United States."

ATTY. ST. GERMAINE of Lac du Flambeau: You could save the Flambeau delegation a lot of troublesome worry if you will allow the interpreter to interpret what you just read.

Interpretation by Frank Smart.

Further interpretation by Atty. St. Germaine.

HENRY WAKEMEUP, St. Croix Band: I am here in behalf of my people, the St. Croix Indians. Referring to the Wheeler-Howard Bill, I heard men talking over in the dining room, one stating that he was a good surveyor, also another stating that he was a surveyor. I will call myself a land locator—but I am a poor land locator—I always fail to locate any land for my people. I call them the landless Chippewas, and if this bill has any effect upon our treaty rights and claims, I will have nothing to do with it. I have been trying to explain to the Indians the contents of this bill, and when I explained my opinion of it, I had lots of opposition, and I used my own judgment and said if this bill has no effect upon going to Washington to present back claims I am with you.

MR. MARSHALL: I can assure you it will have no bad effects on presentation of old claims.

QUESTION by Grand Portage delegation: Will allotments which Indians turn in to the Indian community be purchased from the Indians, or will he be expected to turn in any allotments, or heirship allotments, which he may own, for the benefit of landless Indians without any compensation therefor?

ANSWER BY MR. MARSHALL: The bill does not provide that Indians with land shall give lands to Indians. A fund is set up with which the Government may purchase lands for them.

Questions by the Lac Courte Oreilles Indians—submitted by John Kingfisher:

QUESTION: What will be the source of income for the Indians after self-government is established?

ANSWER: The source of income may be from timber operations, from farming, hunting, fishing, mining, grazing, and in fact any activity that can be carried on. Also, you may be able to find work off the reservation. Under the new system you will find it more profitable to engage in lumbering activities, etc. since the land will be blocked off in more solid blocks, permitting you to conduct your activities with more profit.

QUESTION by Lac Courte Oreilles Indians: How will lands now owned by white people and held at prices too high be obtained?

ANSWER: There may be one acre in ten that you may not be able to buy, but you can usually pick up nine out of ten acres at fair prices. If the white people hold out for exorbitant prices the Government simply will not pay.

QUESTION: Can a person who holds or retains his individual allotment still enjoy the rights and privileges on tribal lands acquired under the bill?

ANSWER: Yes.

QUESTION: Will the Government in purchasing these lands pay the same price for lands such as lakeshore lands as it will for other lands of not equal value?

ANSWER: No, the Government will pay for the lands in proportion to what they are worth. If the Government was buying land and one eighty had no timber and another 80 had a good timber stand, more would be paid for the latter.

QUESTION: Does the Government intend to purchase enough land to restore to this reservation its original size?

ANSWER: I can't say officially the plans of the Government in this respect, but personally I think it is an exceptionally fine reservation to try to block out the old white holdings and block out a large timbering area. Of course if the whites demand three or four times what the land is worth, the Government will not do it.

QUESTION: Will the funds credited to section 16, commonly known as school sections, be paid to the tribes of the reservations in which these lands are located?

ANSWER BY MR. MARSHALL: I am not sure of the legal status of that, but as I understand it the lands credited to Section 16 have gone to the State—that the tribe cannot get those funds under this bill or under any other bill.

INTERVENTION BY MR. REEVES: The State acquired no right to Section 16 in the reservation. I didn't understand that Section 16 has passed to the State. That will be a question we will have to look up.

MR. MARSHALL: We could probably arrange to look this question up and let you know.

QUESTION: Will the Indians in the event that this bill passes be given a voice as to which lands shall be added to their reservation?

ANSWER: Yes.

QUESTION: What will become of that class of people who after this bill passes will vote themselves out of the self-government feature of the bill?

ANSWER: That question refers to the old tribes that do not want to come under that feature. The land section of the bill still applies as does the Indian court and the educational facilities. So far as the Government is concerned, they are still under the Indian Bureau.

INTERVENTION BY MR. WOEHLKE: You corrected a statement of mine yesterday—now I'll get back to you. I think Mr. Marshall is laboring under a slight misapprehension. I don't quite get the idea of voting a tribe or a band out of the self-government section. There is no such a thing as voting yourself out of this. You either accept the bill as a whole or you reject it as a whole including all the benefits. But if you decide to stay under the bill then it is strictly up to you to say whether you want any part of the self-governing features or none at all.

You can accept the entire bill and then after you have accepted it you can make your choice as to whether you want a chartered community, and if you do want a chartered community, how much power you want it to have. That thing is purely optional, and as I tried to explain to you yesterday, so far as the self-government goes, you can put your toes in the water or stay on the bank and watch the self-government river flow by—watch others wading in, and if you want to experiment you can make an easy start on it—perhaps to the extent of selecting your own judge for your community, and your own policeman, and see how it works. That might be the full extent of the amount of self-government that some of you can stand until you get better organized and until you understand the operation of this thing better. But it is either acceptance of the entire bill or rejection of the entire bill. You can't take out the part that bestows certain benefits and leave all the obligations that it bestows—that isn't good reasoning. Take the whole thing and experiment with self-government, or reject the whole thing.

If you want self-government you will have to ask for it even if you are under this bill. If you don't ask for it you will not get it.

QUESTION BY JAMES ANTELL of White Earth delegation: Under those conditions would we as delegates be allowed to ask for certain amendments before this bill comes up?

MR. WOEHLKE: Why, certainly. You know, I am wondering whether there is a physical culture teacher in the house. I think it might be well to get him up here to warm us up. It is awfully chilly when you sit down. Is there a teacher of that kind in the house?

VOICE FROM AUDIENCE: No, but we've got a fighting man here.

QUESTION BY GABRIEL SAICE, White Earth: Last night we were called to a meeting at 8 o'clock, but there were too many trappers, too many hunters there, so we didn't discuss the Wheeler-Howard Bill to amount to anything. That meeting had so much talk of hunting and trapping that I felt like going out to set my own traps but I didn't dare to because Mr. Emerson was too close. I think the questions so far have been answered to the letter, and when I was appointed a delegate to this session I made up my mine when I left my squaw in the wigwam, that if this thing looked good I would certainly try to get a home for her. Last night there was too much talk of muskrats and fish to get anywhere. I think when we get through here I can go home and report to my wife that she has a home.

QUESTION BY MARIE J. DENOMIE—Bad River Band: In the event that the Wheeler-Howard Bill becomes a law, and I join the community plan—I have a fee-patent allotment improved farm in which 60 acres was reserved for timber purpose over 75 years ago, which timber is now merchantable—what would be the status of my holding?

ANSWER: If she puts this in, she derives not only the great advantage of ceasing to pay taxes on it, but she will get back the equivalent of its value. The status of the land becomes the same as the trust status of our lands when they have not yet been fee patented. It will continue as long as this law exists and Congress does not change its Indian policy.

QUESTION from Reserve, Wis. (No name signed): How hard is it going to be for Indians not at present living on the reservations to establish their rights on the reservations later? Would it be proper for the department to notify the Indians to establish their rights now?

ANSWER: The bill excludes those who were not residing on reservations from 1932 to 1934. Otherwise there would be an ingress into the reservation of Indians who have made the proper adjustment to life among the Whites, and it is not the purpose of the Government to discontinue their successful careers among the Whites. It would be an unkindness to such Indians to encourage them to leave their careers among the Whites and come back to the reservations just to get some land. Also, if this were the case it would involve a great many more sums of money than are contemplated in the Bill. It would do no good to send out notices for them to come back and avail themselves of the rights of this bill because this thing goes back to 1932, and it is between the 1932–1934 period that they have to be residing on the Indian reservations.

Assistant Commissioner Zimmerman says there might be an exception as to the date period—this in regard to new reservations set up, and then I might add that the chartered communities are also given the right to make new rulings and regulations as to membership in the chartered communities—they might turn out to be other than that provided in this bill. In other words, the Indians themselves will have a chance to discuss the rights of membership.

QUESTION by Chippewas (Unsigned): Can the Pembina Indians belong to the White Earth Reservation? They originate from the Red Lake Band of Chippewa Indians. How are the Indians going to market their products derived from this Indian community to compete with the Whites? The Whites will not buy anything that the Indian wants to sell.

ANSWER: Mr. Reeves can be thinking about the first part of that question while I answer the second part. As to the question relating to the marketing of products, this question says that whites will not buy anything that the Indians want to sell. The way I picture this Indian community, it will be an organized affair where they will oftentimes handle merchandise, products from the soil, cattle, forest products, etc. It will be an organization handling a great quantity of commodities.

When you begin to do this under this organized plan it will certainly attract the buying public in the United States. In other words, the products of the Indians will be far more attractive to the public under this set-up than they are at present under the old market basket system. Under an organized system where you use real salesmanship such as these people will do when they get organized, the marketing problem assumes an entirely different aspect.

QUESTION by Michigan delegation of Saginaw, Swan Creek and Black River tribes: The preliminary paragraph of the bill would indicate that its provisions would apply only to "Indians living under Federal Tutelage." Does this mean that the provisions in regard to landless Indians for whom land is to be purchased, do not apply to those who having no restricted land, no trust funds, and who are not living on an Indian reservation, might be regarded as not living under Federal tutelage? This is true of most of the Chippewas, all of the Ottawas and Pottawatomies. If land is to be purchased for Michigan Indians, where can it be obtained? There is not public land remaining in the Lower Peninsula.

ANSWER: As to where the land is to be purchased—if no land can be gotten in the Lower Peninsula of Michigan, all I can see personally is that there are possibilities of colonization in this new bill. Where there is no land available, there is no reason why these Indians should not be allowed to colonize in some other sections of the country. There are lots of wide open spaces in these United States where they could go. Texas, for instance, where many Indian tribes would like to go, and where there is great opportunity. As to these Indians who have made adjustments among the whites—I spoke to one man last night who said that if he came back and started to borrow from this $10,000,000 fund, it would hurt his self-respect which has been developed to a high pitch. I congratulated him. I told him that he had made his adjustment and that it would be wise for him to stay where he is, that the bill was not intended for him. It is intended for landless Indians to get on their feet.

DR. ROE CLOUD: (*continuing*) I was asked by my group to bring out a certain point in regard to education. There has been passed in Congress recently a law which is important in the matter of Indian education. Up to the present time the Indian Bureau has been making contracts with counties where Indian kids go to school with White kids. The new legislation says that the Indian Bureau can make contracts with state boards of education instead of making contracts with various counties. The advantage is that it centralizes the administration affairs of the educational bureau. Where the bureau had to write hundreds of letters to county boards, etc., it can write to one state board and let the superintendent of education handle it through his office with all the different counties in the state. It simplified the administration and it does not deny one cent to the counties which they received in the past. I am told certain white people are disturbed lest they lose this tuition money, which is not true.

DR. ROE CLOUD: There is one question I would like to ask before I sit down and I will ask Mr. Reeves to answer it—and that is about the possibility of a member of a chartered community willing his land to whomsoever he will. I didn't get that very clear. What would be the rights of a person so far as willing his land is concerned inside the community?

MR. REEVES: As far as the right of the Chippewas to go back to Red Lake and participate in the rights there, it would depend upon being recognized by tribal authorities of the Red Lake Reservation. As far as Dr. Roe Cloud's query on wills are concerned, under law you have the right with approval of the Secretary of the Interior to will your restricted property. As to unrestricted property you can will it without the approval of the Secretary of the Interior. Under this new legislation, if one of these chartered communities is organized and you were a member, you would have the right to make a will transferring to your beneficiaries your personal property, your household effects, your house itself, but not the title to the land, which would of course pass to the community.

Now I would like to read and answer a letter containing questions by Mr. William Skenadore of Oneida.

MR. REEVES: (*reading letter*) "To the Honorable Committee From Washington, D.C. Gentlemen: Oneida delegation wants to know:

> "Is it necessary for Congress to enact new legislation, to reassert its obligation to the Indians—where the Supreme Court of the United States has held for over a century—that the Indians and their lands are under the protection of the Constitution, laws and treaties made in pursuance thereof—that the Indians are outside the province of state and territorial authority and they are, and their properties are withdrawn from the operations of the state laws—and that Congress cannot divert itself or to confer to another, its constitutional obligations to the Indians—and where the Supreme Court of the United States had denied the petition of a county to review the decisions of the lower United States Courts—where the lower courts had held that the United States is still the guardian and the protector of the Indians and their estates even though the Indians named in the complaint had exercised the privileges of citizenship and had received the fee simple patents to their lands after the expiration of the 25 years' trust period—and that it is not for any state or its municipal sub-divisions to decide when the emancipation of the Indian takes place? And please speak a little louder so that we can hear you in the back."

ANSWER BY REEVES: The answer to most of that is yes. Additional legislation by Congress is necessary and you will find it in this proposed bill. The Court of Indian Affairs on page 41 would give you a special Federal court to which you can take these questions and have them promptly decided.

MR. REEVES: Just before we left Washington we received a letter from Mr. Wm. A. Brunette of Mahnomen, Minnesota which contained these three questions:

1. The claim is made by many Indians that this bill will permit the Indian office to take money from the Chippewa Tribal funds to use in establishing Chartered Indian Communities in Minnesota.
2. The claim is made that the passage of this bill will interfere with the division of the Chippewa Tribal Funds at the expiration of the 50-year period from the passage of the Act of Jan. 14, 1889.
3. The claim is made that the passage of this bill will interfere with the prosecution of the Chippewa Claims now in process of presentation to the court of claims.

MR. REEVES: (*answering the three questions*) The answer to the first is no. The bill does not permit the Indian Office to do that. It will permit the community itself to use its own funds for that purpose and the Indian Office could not do it without your consent.

The answer to the second question is no, it will not. The 50-year period has not expired. Nothing in this bill interferes with the provisions of existing law as to the disposition of that fund.

The third question has been answered a number of times from this platform and the answer is no.

Interpretation by Frank Smart.

MR. WOEHLKE: We should hear from the various delegations and inasmuch as the remaining time is very short, and inasmuch as we have 25 delegations here, every one of which should have a chance to speak, I would suggest that we limit the time of each delegation to seven minutes and that the 6th minute will be indicated by one tap of the gavel so that the speaker will know he has one more minute left to speak. The end of the seven minutes will be indicated by two raps of the gavel. We will begin with the Leech Lake tribe. Is the spokesman ready? If not, we will call upon someone else.

SPOKESMAN from Leech Lake: We would like to have our remarks interpreted.

MR. WOEHLKE: In that case you may speak five minutes and five minutes will be allowed for interpretation. I would like to have Dr. Roe Cloud take charge of the meeting now.

Chair taken by Dr. Roe Cloud.

WILLIAM MORRELL, spokesman for Leech Lake delegation: Mr. Chairman, gentlemen of the commission, ladies and gentlemen: The delegation from Leech Lake appointed me speaker and the thought they want me to bring out for the information of the commission at this time deals with the subject of self-government for the Leech Lake Reservation.

The Leech Lake Reservation is so situated at this time that it is a hard problem for the delegates to decide which way to go—whether to accept or reject the proposal. Our allotments are located in the Chippewa National Forest of Minnesota. This obstacle, the National Forest of Minnesota, will not in our opinion relinquish their right to give us the opportunity to improve our allotments in this area. Therefore, the Leech Lake delegation wants the commission to give us an opportunity to take this back to the Indians at home and discuss this matter further and see what they will think about it, and see if we could get legislation through Congress to move this forest aside so that we can benefit by the bill.

MR. MARSHALL: The new chief of the U.S. Forestry Service is very sympathetic with your cause—you have a much better chance than in the past to make such consolidation. Certainly it would be better under this bill than it would be under the present set-up. Your best chance would come through working under the provisions of this bill to make deals with the United States Forestry Service.

MR. MORRELL: I want to thank the Commission if they will give us this opportunity to spend a little more time and give us time to look into this matter. I also want to enter on the records at this time a resolution.

The following resolution introduced:

> Hayward, Wisconsin, April 23, 1934
>
> Whereas, as there has been approved for immediate construction a Chippewa Indian Sanatorium at Gwah Ching and a general hospital at Cass Lake, to be constructed out of Federal Relief moneys, and,
>
> Whereas, the conditions at the Sanatorium and hospital at Onigum, Minnesota, are intolerable, and the Indians confined therein are suffering due to said conditions, and
>
> Whereas, it is imperative said conditions be immediately relieved, now therefore be it resolved by the Chippewa Indians of Minnesota through their duly elected delegates in council assembled at Hayward, Wisconsin, that construction of the Chippewa Indian Sanatorium at Gwah Ching, Minnesota as approved and the general hospital at Cass Lake, Minnesota be immediately begun without further delay and, be it further resolved that at least 50% of the laborers to be employed thereon be members of the Minnesota Chippewa tribe.
>
> (Signed) Wm. J. Morrell
> Wm. Butcher
> George W. Rogers
> Charles Ellis
> Joe Ah Pah Be Tung
> George Fairbanks

DR. ROE CLOUD: The next speaker will be from White Oak Point.

SIMON LEQUIER of White Oak Point, speaking Chippewa with interpretation by Frank Smart: When I was appointed a delegate, one of four delegates, we were not given instructions to accept or reject the bill. We are told to come here to listen and take back what we see here and we hear, and tell what has taken place. The reason why we cannot commit ourselves is that they are widening the national forest in that district. If we sell our lands we have to sell to the forestry at $1.50 per acre. Therefore we are stuck. We do not know what to do. On these grounds we cannot give any consent to accept or reject, but must take back to our people what we see and hear here.

GEORGE GARVIN, Winnebago Delegation: What I have to say is very brief. When I came to this meeting, previous to that time we held various meetings on the reservation and went to other communities to gather information about this bill. Now, although we have been authorized by our people to come here, we have not been invested with the authority to accept or reject the matter under discussion; but we were sent here to gather some information and to secure the opinion of other delegates from other places. The bill itself is very good, and the discussion brought out are quite favorable to us. It was the general opinion of the Indians that they were to be removed from their lands when that self-government plan was accepted, and it was with great determination that these people said that it was better for the White man to kill us off than to have taken our lands. I feel that we have been enlightened by this meeting and as I go back home I can inform my people what has taken place here.

DR. ROE CLOUD: The next speaker will be from Nett Lake.

PETER SMITH, representing Nett Lake Tribe: We have been sent here to this Council or Congress, but we have not been invested with the authority to accept or reject this bill, and there are other people that came from the same community or vicinity and they are here listening to the discussions. Our people have not given us the authority to reject or accept. We must go back home and be guided by whatever they decide. The majority rules, and it is their privilege to accept or reject—

it is their privilege and their problem. We are only their ears and their mouthpieces. The majority of our people do not understand this bill, and it will be our duty to go back and give them our understanding of it after listening to these discussions. I am not a very eloquent speaker, and if I continue to talk I might get myself twisted in circles, so I think I will quit. Thank you.

DR. ROE CLOUD: That last remark reveals him to be a very wise man. The next speaker will be from Grand Portage, Minnesota.

EDWARD M. WILSON, Grand Portage, Minnesota: I haven't much to say at this time. Last night I explained my views at the meeting, and I want very little to say this morning. This bill as I look at it is a Godsend to the Indian—blessing and salvation, and as we look over the many things Mr. Collier has done for the Indian. I think he is a perfect gentleman. In his fight for the Indian he has been very useful—very energetic—and always uppermost in his mind was the Indian.

Last Christmas he gave me a Christmas present. He hung it on the tree, and now I am going to reach up with both hands and accept that present that he has given to me, and I sincerely hope that Indians of Minnesota will participate in taking down that present from the tree.

DR. ROE CLOUD: We have next on the list a speaker from Mille Lac, and following that will be Fond du Lac and White Earth. I might say at this time that any speaker, although he may not want to quote his delegation for or against the bill, may state his own personal views on the bill. It will be interesting to hear some of these views.

JOE EAGLE, Mille Lac delegation: My statement is very short. I just want to tell why I am here. My people held a council last Saturday and delegated us to come here—but we were not invested with the authority to accept or reject the bill—but we were instructed to listen to what is being said here and get the opinions of other Indians in regard to this bill.

DR. ROE CLOUD: All right, we will hear now from Fond du Lac delegation.

HENRY LA PRAIRIE of Fond du Lac delegation: We have heard the bill discussed, and so far so good, but we were not sent here to reject or to take the measure. You know, Mr. Chairman, that a man in business will never sign or take any agreement or contract without first seeing the contents of that contract. The same applies to us, so we ask for time for further consideration upon this matter. I thank you.

DR. ROE CLOUD: We will postpone hearing from the White Earth delegations until after lunch. We will now adjourn until 1:30 P.M.

Session Re-Opened 1:30 P.M. April 24, 1934

DR. ROE CLOUD: Before we start the meeting, I would like to say that we have a distinguished visitor, a member of our tribe now located at Fort Peck, Mt., who has said he shall be pleased to occupy about a minute and a half of our time to express himself.

M. V. WOLFE from Fort Peck: As I stated last night at the meeting of the Michigan and Wisconsin Indians, I didn't know anything about the condition of my people. I created quite a stir when I gave some of my own observations. I had no instructions to come here. I just dropped down here to call upon my father and mother, and I never had instructions to talk about this bill. I don't even know what these committees sitting with my father are going to present, and Mr. Chairman and Commissioners, I am not taking anything back that I said last night. I feel that way, and if it is the will of the Chippewa people to accept this bill it is up to every one of you to make up your mind to accept it. But if you don't like it, then refuse it. I can't say any more to you. Thank you.

JOHN KINGFISHER of Lac Court de Oreilles delegation: Mr. Chairman and fellow Indians, I consider it very fortunate that our people of the Lac Court De Oreilles reservation have had the privilege of listening to the discussions and interpretations of this new bill. When this bill first came up I was appointed to a committee charged with the responsibility of explaining the bill to my people, and now I have the honor of representing my people at this Congress. Just recently I have been appointed a private in the rank of the Indian service, and since I have held that office I have been associated with a fine class of people on the reservation. We have Indians who are performing the duties of town officers with efficiency and with honor. They have been representing the people of that Indian community on the town board for nearly 10 years, and I am sure there isn't a man or woman on that town board that has ever pulled a crooked deal, and what finer example of Indian self-government can you find than that in the Town of Hunter?

There has been reason to complain of the fact that there was no say as to the disposition of property and funds, but now the government is giving them the right to voice their opinions as to what should be done with the property, both real estate and financial, and I think the biggest majority of the young people are prepared to accept this new self-government;

and to the opposing faction, I will say that I am sure that in the event this passes and is made a law that they will be broad-minded enough to submit to the will of the majority as all good citizens in the United States do.

DR. ROE CLOUD: We will now have the interpretation of that eloquent speech.

FRANK SMART: I was so swept off my feet by the eloquence of Mr. Kingfisher that I forgot to take notes, but I will try to interpret what he has said.

DR. ROE CLOUD: I want to present a question to the house. A certain visitor is here, and by special request he wants to have a few minutes to say a few words, and his name is George Selkirk, a Chippewa from the Twin Cities. Shall we hear him?

GENERAL ACCLAIM: Yes!

DR. ROE CLOUD: Come forward now and we will give you a few minutes.

MR. SELKIRK: Delegates and visitors, on account of the lack of time I will not attempt to go into this self-governing proposition, but I feel it is my duty to pay tribute to my race. If I had the vocabulary of a Shakespeare or Emerson and the oratory of Cicero or Daniel Webster, and the eloquence of some of our old Chieftains I would fill this hall and thrill your hearts with song. Oh! Master Light! Master Light! Give me the fluence of speech and the strength that these people may hear me with understanding. Great lines have been written about the American Indian, the child of Nature who believed in the Great Spirit, who worshipped the Great Spirit in the Sun, in the Moon, in the Stars in the heavens above, in the trees, in the flowers, in the grasses, in the hills, in the valleys, and all things on earth. This child of Nature lives a strenuous life. To him it is a matter of the survival of the fittest. Only the strong survive. The Indians are a fast vanishing race. No longer can he go on the plain and chase the buffalo or go into the forest and stalk the majestic moose as his forefathers did. This child of Nature has been assimilated by the great American melting pot and has come forth a new type of Indian—a type who is the real American—the American Indian of today is this being—a different being than the American Indian of yesterday. Today he accepts his part of the social ranks of the American people. Today he stands side by side with his competitors in the ranks of industry. You will find the American Indian in every walk of life on this continent.

You will find the Chippewa Indian from coast to coast, from Canada to the Gulf of Mexico; yet it has been said that the Indians today are in a starving condition. A picture has been painted about the White Earth Indians being in a starving condition—and a few moments afterward the Chippewa Indian was lauded as the greatest leader on the face of the earth. But, ladies and gentlemen, I come here not to argue—I come here to applaud you—I come here to advise you. I do not have the time to go into the details, into the faults I can find in this bill, but let me caution you. You are regarded as the smartest Indians on the face of the earth. I will go farther than that. The Chippewa Indians are not only the smartest Indians, but they have the reputation of being the best and kindest Indians on the face of the earth.

I feel that you are smart enough; that you have the understanding and insight to look into things, to investigate thoroughly; and before you accept or reject this proposition, dig into it carefully. Go slowly, and in conclusion, ladies and gentlemen, let me say that what the Chippewa Indian wants is not a new deal but a square deal. I thank you.

DR. ROE CLOUD: We are here to hear all sides of this question, and we are certainly glad to get that side of it indeed. I think it is true that the Chippewa is a very great and kind person. I married one—I ought to know. But I still contend that the Winnebago is the bravest Indian on this continent, and right at this time I want to call upon a distinguished member of that tribe, the Assistant Attorney General of the State of Wisconsin, Mr. Wm. J. Kershaw.

Brief acknowledgement and remarks by Mr. Kershaw.

DR. ROE CLOUD: I wish all of you could have traveled with me to every reservation in the United States and see the hardships that all tribes in the United States are experiencing, and the sort of hopelessness that fills their hearts when they look at the outlook. When this new bill is interpreted to them it makes them feel the thrill of a new hope and chance. There are a handful of Indians here and there, for example St. Paul and Minneapolis, who have made an adjustment among the whites and are happy. The bill is not intended for them but is meant for the luckless Indian who is still struggling for existence among his fellow Indians.

The Dawes Act was a wonderful thing in its inception, but it gave only 25 years to the Indian race to get ready. This is another Dawes Act but the time element is different. Instead of only 25 years it gives you generations to make the adjustment, and I say that given the time the Indian will make a success of it. This bill does exactly that.

MR. BAUMGARTEN: Before leaving it is requested that all delegates please bring their slips to the office in person. Also we would like to have some idea of the number that will be here for breakfast.

Resolution introduced by John Pemberton—Twin Lakes White Earth:

> "We the assembled delegation representing N 1/2 of White Earth Reservation comprising the following villages:
>
> Twin Lakes
> Rice Lakes
> Beaulieu
> Pine Bend
> Mahnomen
> Waubun
>
> "Came here for the sole purpose of hearing discussions on the Wheeler-Howard Bill in order that we may clarify certain objectionable phases of this bill—and after this hearing we may say that these phases have been made so clear that we are in a position to accept the bill as a whole.
>
> "We wish to reserve the right to go back to our respective communities and have our people pass on the finding of this conference."

JOHN PEMBERTON: I don't wish to take up any more time than is allotted me, but I just want to make a few remarks in regard to this bill. Since February 1 we have held our weekly councils in regard to this bill. There are a number of people in our community who have been misrepresenting this bill to a number of our older Indians—telling them not to accept it. So at our councils we held open house and challenged anyone to come and show us where it would be detrimental to accept this bill, and there has been no one who has been able to do so. As for the White Earth Indians, I do not see what we have to lose by accepting this bill.

DR. ROE CLOUD: We will next hear from the Ponsford delegation.

JOHN BROKER, Ponsford, White Earth delegation: I just wish to make a few remarks. We represent about 900 people in our community and we were instructed by that community to favor this legislation. Also we were instructed to use our best judgment in formulating our opinions, and in going on record in favoring the bill, I just want to make a few statements and give a few reasons why.

We have been under the Indian Bureau for a good many years—going back 60 years. The system used under the bureau is becoming obsolete, and we desire a change. There has been legislation passed through Congress by unscrupulous politicians for the purpose of exploiting the Indians on these reservations. During all that time of legislation the Bureau has never made a protest in behalf of the Indians. It seems in a great many instances that it has been a party to the deal. This system we want to get away from, and through the new deal and the features of this bill we hope to provide that change. It gives us a better school system. It gives us more voice in the management of our affairs and in the expenditures of our money, and we have considered that bill to be very much favorable to our community. We recognize that there will be changes and amendments in this bill before it reaches final passage. We just merely want to go on record as favoring passage of the bill, but of course we want to have access to all new information that comes up on the bill. I believe that is about the extent of my statements new.

ARTHUR C. BEAULIEU, White Earth: We were duly elected and sent here for the purpose of taking part in the discussion of this bill. We went pursuant to notice but were not instructed to accept or reject the bill, but to work in cooperation with other delegates coming from that section in taking the matter back to our people. In this decision there was only one dissenting vote—that of Edw. L. Rogers.

Summary interpretation by Frank Smart.

PETER GRAVES, Chairman, Old Council, Red Lake delegation: We represent what they call the Chiefs' Council of Red Lake. Our delegation comprises 7 persons. Our instructions are to guard against the subdivision of the Red Lake Indian Reservation. Our instructions are also to guard against any unfavorable decision that the bill might impose upon the Red Lake Band of Indians. This Chiefs' Council of the Red Lake Band is composed of the older Indians. We still maintain the belief that the greatest evil the United States Government ever perpetuated was to allot land in severalty to Indians in the United States. I don't like to have these different delegations think I am trying to advise them or anything like that. Our position is different from that of the allotted Indian, and it has not been any easy matter to have kept ourselves in the state to the present time.

There are many of us who still believe that if we once take our land in severalty on the Red Lake reservation, our doom is sealed. The bill that is in discussion at this time, known as the Wheeler-Howard Bill, is just the thing that the Red Lake Indians would want enacted so as to prevent them from dispossessing themselves of their homes.

I believe that one of the men who spoke here said it was a Christmas present. It certainly is more than a Christmas present, because at Christmas time we only give to each other little worthless trinkets, so to speak. Our delegation believes that we should accept this bill and urge Congress to have the bill enacted into law regardless of the opposition—opposition by those who in the future should never be called Indians. The old chiefs and old men that you profess to call ignorant in this day of civilization—those men had dreams of future men like Mr. Roe Cloud and Mr. Kershaw. They want to keep their reservations intact—keep their homes intact—make the future secure for their children. This dream of course is a bad dream. Very few will live up to be educated so that they can mix with the civilized races of this earth. I for one know that I am 99% behind what I should be now that I am grown up. I do not understand the action in instructing the delegates not to accept this bill at once after what the Indians have gone through, and in behalf of the Chiefs' Council we urge that this bill be enacted into law!

GEORGE WALTERS of White Earth delegation (*speaking in Chippewa with translation by Frank Smart*): I want to say a few words in regard to the subject under discussion here. At the time the councils were held in my locality I did not know that these papers were in existence (referring to papers explaining bill) until the time when I was elected a delegate. These papers were not presented to me. These other delegates here know all about this, but all the time as for myself, only five days before I started for this conference did I know something about this. I am located very near where they are, but they never notified me. And I kind of in a way understand that I as an Indian am being approached to ask these questions. On my account as an Indian the government is holding this conference, and I want to say at this time that I don't have a show at all at this conference. It is at this place that I hear of the contents of this bill for the first time, and there are Indians of my tribe at home that should hear this news. It is not right that individuals must be here personally to hear of this deal.

Why are we in such terrible and poor shape today? Am I responsible? The government is the cause of our privation. It is not the fault of the Commissioner of Indian Affairs we are in such privation. We are responsible for our own condition today. We did not follow the instructions of the Commissioner or the Government of the United States. I am the person that tried to hold back this person that wants to be a white man and there was not a single Indian that did not oppose me. The one that talked here previous he opposed me just the same. The White Indian is too susceptible to wrong doing. He always wants the money. That is the reason for such poverty. Our money in Washington is in very small amounts now and still we are writing the Government to ask them to give us some more. Isn't it a fact that future generations should be benefited by some of this money? What is being left for our children—for the future generation? And what then will they live on? All these allottees have sold their 160 acres and I don't believe any of them possess even a twig of a tree and I don't believe they have as much as one shot of gunpowder or a parcel of land!

DR. ROE CLOUD: Mr. Interpreter, will you tell him that the new bill will protect his land so that there need never be a loss, and also tell him it is safe for his children and grandchildren in future generations.

Interpretation by Frank Smart.

MR. GEORGE WALTERS: That is all I want.

PAUL H. BEAULIEU, speaking for Young Council of Red Lake Band: Mr. Chairman, I have but very few words to say, and I want to start out by congratulating the old Red Lake Indians upon the stand taken in regard to this bill. The Young Council made its stand quite some time ago. That stand was forwarded to the Commissioner on January 27. We still stand on that same thing, and from that you can read between the lines that we had accepted the Indian Rights Bill as a whole, although there might be features we do not approve of. However, as a whole we do approve of the bill. That is our stand and I don't think there is a Red Lake Indian that wants an allotment. I just wanted to correct any impression that might have been created here in this respect.

DR. ROE CLOUD: You mean that you stand for the bill as a whole, but that there might be some features you do not approve of or that you are not yet familiar with?

MR. BEAULIEU: Yes, but we can thrash that out later at home.

DR. ROE CLOUD: It is interesting to note that these Red Lake people who have never been allotted, and who have watched the experience of other tribes, now say they don't want to be allotted. I think that is exceedingly significant and important.

JEROME ARBUCKLE (*representing Bad River Band*): We have instructions from our band, and we have no authority to accept or adopt this bill, but we as individual members of the band accept that bill or approve it as a whole, but feel that there are certain questionable features. One is: When is the Indian going to be given the full rights of citizenship with the privilege of doing whatever a citizen does? No provision is made for this. We do not know how long we are going to be under Government supervision. We are classed as restricted citizens and it might be 100 years or longer before this is changed.

Another thing is that all possible legislation and help should be given us to insure us our swamp lands. That is all.

FRANK SMART: Before we go any farther let's all stand up and rest our weary bones—and take a deep breath.

Audience stands up.

VOICE FROM CROWD: These bones of yours look to be pretty well padded, Frank.

THOMAS L. ST. GERMAINE of Lac du Flambeau delegation: Before speaking I am instructed to ask two questions of the chair:

1. Are Federal funds being used in the administration of our affairs in Flambeau. Are funds of the Lake Superior tribe being used without letting us know?

ANSWER: No Lac du Flambeau tribal funds have been used for administration purposes for the past three years and no such funds are being used now.

2. We have a camp called an ECW camp and the enormous amount of money appropriated has been expended in a certain way. Now these boys would like to know if the thought of whoever is responsible for these projects, is to make a lot of truck trails as fast as you can as long as you can in a shorter space of time. That seems to be the thought that has been followed there. Also, in regard to workers, are the men to be graded, say for instance A, B, or C, and promoted if found qualified? There are a lot of men qualified there who are still on the same level.

ANSWER BY MR. WOEHLKE: I believe the first part of this question refers to the character of the truck trails built by the ECW. The regulations governing the expenditure of ECW funds limit the expenditure of these funds to a certain type of work, and in the case of truck trails the ECW administration insists that they must be what the name implies—namely truck trails, and not highways and roads. The money of the PWA is used for the construction of highways and through roads, whereas the ECW money is destined to be used solely for so-called conservation projects, and these truck trails are to be just what the name implies—trails over which a truck can reach a certain district in case of fire. In regard to the second part, I have no personal knowledge of this promotion matter in this district, but we shall be glad to take that up with the men in charge and find out what the situation is and let you know as soon as we can get the information.

ATTY. ST. GERMAINE: (*continuing*) I am not a member of the committee. When this bill was brought to us a council was held, and at that time I didn't want to be elected to that council, as I didn't have the time. But as soon as the boys were elected they asked me to aid and advise them, and I am still in that capacity. They have also asked me to speak for them, so briefly I shall speak. In order to relieve the interpreter who is an able interpreter and an overworked one, I shall speak in my own language. [*Not recorded.*]

MIKE LA FERNIER, Red Cliff delegation: A committee of five was appointed by our reservation to discuss the bill among the members and we were sent here to get information as to the conditions and terms of the bill. We have finally come to the conclusion that we approve of the bill—that is, the delegation here does, and later on we will have a local council and if the majority approve the bill I will endeavor to send a letter to our representative in Congress in order to hold approval of this bill. I wish to thank the Commissioner for explaining this bill to us.

CHARLES PICARD, L'Anse delegation: Ladies and Gentlemen, I am a delegate, one of the delegates of a committee consisting of four members, appointed by our people, the Lost Band of Chippewas of Lake Superior. We came to this notable gathering armed with pockets full of objections to the bill we were to consider. On the whole, however, our people were favorably impressed with the principles contained in that bill. Upon our arrival here we procured additional literature consisting of amendments to the original drafts of the bill as it was presented to us.

Studying those amendments we find that it has entirely eliminated all of the objections which our people instructed us to protest against. We have listened to all the deliberations and all of the speeches and we find that your troubles are identical with our troubles. We have had the benefit of a private conference with some of the experts of this commission representing the Commissioner. To these experts we have submitted our own local troubles, and we have offered plans to solve our local problems. We are satisfied that this commission will put forth its best effort to assist us in solving our own local difficulties, and it is not necessary for me to take up these local problems of ours, and I wish to say that I feel safe in saying that our people back home—numbering approximately 1,200 souls—will be pleased upon our report to them, to accept the bill and approve it in its entirety.

Not only do we feel that they will do so, but our delegation has pledged themselves to use their influence in persuading our members of our tribe in drawing up resolutions petitioning our Congressmen to stand back of the bill. I thank you.

HENRY RICHIE, Pottawatomie delegation: Mr. Chairman and representatives of the Government, I am very pleased to meet you all this afternoon. When I left home I didn't know much about this bill, but I was sent out to learn all I could about the bill, and I may say that I have learned a good deal.

I am not in a position to say what my people will do, but I am in hopes they will accept this bill. As far as I am concerned individually I think it is a good thing. This bill is being drafted by friends of the Indian, and not a thing in this bill is going to injure anybody that I can see. When I go back home I shall return with a message and explain the situation I have met here, and I think my people will accept it.

MITCHELL RED CLOUD, Winnebago delegation: Friends, fellow delegates, and members of the Commission—there has been so much said this afternoon about this bill that I am not going to say much, only to explain my personal opinion.

I have no authority as a delegate either to accept or reject the bill, but I shall speak on the self-government phase. There is a general impression among the public that the Indian will fail in the art of self-government. I believe the Indian can succeed because it is nothing new. They had experience in it long before the coming of the White race, and they governed themselves without the aid of jails, penitentiaries, insane asylums, etc. Most of us Indians, all tribes included, still retain the power and wisdom of the old chieftains. Most of us retain the wisdom of the old councils.

Therefore, I cannot see why the Indian should fail in self-government.

In some respects this bill is too good to be true, but we know that it is the outcome of long consideration and deep thought, and that the Indians will receive the benefit of justice. Justice may be blind, but Mr. Roosevelt and Mr. Collier are excellent eye doctors.

DR. ROE CLOUD: I am glad as chairman to say that this delegate looks with a broad, sympathetic view on this whole question, and it augurs well for the future especially when the delegate reminds us that the Indian is capable of self-government.

WILLARD ACKLEY, Mole Lake delegation: We are in favor of the bill in all phases.

HENRY WAKEMEUP, St. Croix delegation: Ladies and Gentlemen and friends of the commission. I am glad of the opportunity to talk to you and I want to ask the privilege of using my own Indian tongue. I can speak in English but I want to talk Chippewa for the benefit of my older Indian friends so that they can get the sentiment of our delegation. In the place that we come from the people are very scattered over a wide area and they have no land holdings that they might call their own granted by the Government, and this situation they complained of to Washington; but when they made these complaints to the authorities no one heard them.

Now when we held these small councils, I attended and heard the pleas of these old men—pleas to get something for their children, and their pleas won my sympathy. It is true enough that at one time I gave up fighting for my people, thinking it was a hopeless job, and now we have come here especially to find the best way to lead my people. I am not an Indian in the true sense of the word as we have heard in the discussions. Perhaps the chiefs who lead my people made a mistake somewhere because they never set aside a reservation for our people and for that reason we never owned any lands—we just missed out, and listening to the proposed bill I can see far enough ahead to know that the Indian can be benefited through this bill. When we heard they were going to present this bill, we said it was no good and we had many objections to it, but since hearing the deliberation of the different delegates and the explanations by the commission, I have changed my opinion of it. In it I can see the welfare of my people, and I hope the promises which it contains will be fulfilled.

MR. WOEHLKE: Unfortunately Dr. Roe Cloud has to leave in a short while. Also, he was afraid of pronouncing the name of the next delegation so he turned the gavel back to me and I don't like it so I am going to ask your old friend Mr. Balmer to take the floor.

Chair taken by J. W. Balmer.

WILLIS JACKSON, Mount Pleasant delegation: Mr. Chairman and fellow delegates, we have come here on a great mission. We have learned many points in this paper, this bill, although we had some instructions on it that were very brief; but just the same we had considered it and we sent in a resolution in regard to it and in that we accept the bill and we desired a change in our community. I have gained much information that I will be able to go back and perhaps give them in a detailed manner information regarding what is planned to help them in the future. And now in the manner of education, it is a vital proposition. It is required in our district very much and I am glad that it covers our request because the future generation has then a chance to compete with the elements he will meet on the way.

MR. BALMER: I am sure it is very gratifying to hear such common sense. I worked down in Michigan where this man is from and in the early days the Indians were designated as competent and non-competent. When the patents were first given out, many of them used to tell me how they were cheated out of their lands. A buyer would come in and say he just wanted to buy a few trees on the allotments, and the Indians would sign over their entire allotments. Many Indians told me this in Michigan. This new bill is going to give you a home for eternity if you want it. We have allotments similar to what you have here and the people are happy because that home will be continuous.

CHARLES FRECHETTE, Menominee delegation: Mr. Chairman, ladies and gentlemen and guests, it gives me great pleasure to tell this assemblage in a few words how the Menominee Indians are situated. They have a beautiful reservation. They are a happy tribe. They are wealthy and prosperous. They have various assets such as timber on their reservation. The reason for this is that the Menominee Indians were thoughtful enough to hold their land in one, and from that they are the happiest tribe in the State of Wisconsin. That explains the situation on the Menominee reservation.

Now then, for the last 6 years the Menominees have been advocating self-government and a voice of their own and during the last general council the tribe voted in favor of the Wheeler-Howard Bill of the Indian Rights. Now then, the delegates from the Menominee reservation will also accept the bill as a whole and also stand behind the Honorable Commissioner of Indian Affairs, John Collier, one hundred percent.

MR. BALMER: There is a similar situation in Red Lake. These people are also all big and fat and happy and smiling.

REV. C. AARON, Stockbridge delegation: Mr. Chairman, Honorable assistants of the great Commissioner, and my dear Indian friends, it happens that I bring up the tail end almost of this grand and glorious meeting. Some of you perhaps may think it would make our hearts sore, but it doesn't. I am glad to be behind such a wonderful gathering we have had here these past two days. Consider when a man goes to war. We know when the white man goes to war he doesn't start out by shooting with cannons. No, he takes the little guns first and then comes the cannon: I take great consolation in that gentleman.

I think it was Alexander the Great who once stood looking over the last of his people and said: "They have done wonderful—in fact, everything has been done, and what is there left for me to do?" I feel in a sense like that man. After being here at this conference for two days I see what my fellows can do. I see that they are able orators, and I am almost standing in the same place where they stood and gave such wonderful speeches. However, as a member of the Stockbridge tribe, formerly the Mohicans of the East, I accept this pleasure gratefully.

Many years ago our forefathers took up their bows and arrows in defense of what they called their rights. We their sons and daughters do in no ways condemn them, although historians and writers of fiction have done so these many years. Gentlemen, I believe however the time has arrived when you and I and every Indian in the United States should begin to act with an eye to future security. We should pick up and take off and begin to work where our forefathers left off. The tide of events may have turned against them, but their cause was always right, and it is up to you and to me to take action to bring our people to the level to which God has set for us.

But I do not believe we can or should resort to primitive means to accomplish this. Ill will, hatred, prejudice have all been laid aside and the silent road of glory leads through enlightenment through enactment of the provisions of the Wheeler-Howard Bill of Indian Rights.

My dear friends, I have studied that bill thoroughly. I also have followed our esteemed Commissioner as he has gone about through our land trying tirelessly to do everything to make the truth known to our people. My common sense tells me that John Collier is a member of the White Race, but my heart tells me John Collier is an Indian: Yes, indeed, John Collier is an Indian with a heart as big and broad as the day is long. The Indian is as capable as any class of people on earth—the only trouble is we haven't had the chance to prove it to the white man. We have been like a smudge. The blanket has been put over us and the smoke couldn't be seen, but through the provisions of the Wheeler-Howard Bill we see a new day dawning.

You like to fish, don't you? I do. What does it feel like when you prepare for fishing all through the weeks, worrying that when the day arrives it perhaps will be raining—how does it feel when you wake up and see the sun coming over the hills, dispelling all your fears? My friends, we have had plenty worry in the past, but now through the enactment of the bill, the sun is shining and I am sure that my people will merit every confidence and trust that the white man is placing in him. The Stockbridge delegation comes here with instructions to accept that bill to the man!

PAUL ABRAHAM, Pipestone Sioux: Here goes the biggest cannon—the last kick on the program. Before I start in I would like to finish a statement made by Dr. Roe Cloud and correct a statement made by Mr. St. Germaine. Dr. Roe Cloud says the Chippewas are the smartest Indians and the Winnebagoes are the bravest, but he forgot to add that the Sioux are the best looking.

With reference to the Sioux being driven west of the river, let me say the Sioux have heard the call of Horace Greeley, "Go West, boys, and be a man."

We bring you greetings from the Sioux country in the same sense that our forefathers have smoked the peace pipe with you. We are sent here by our people to participate in this great Congress and seek for the light in this new plan. Our understanding is that we should come here for information and not to argue, and if we didn't like the plan we should tell the Commissioner like a man that we will not accept the bill. We have been listening and keeping quiet, but we have been thinking a whole lot. Now I wish to advise that our delegation is in favor of the plan, but owing to ancient customs and the respect that we have for our people, we are going to go back home and interpret this plan to them and we are positive that they will accept the plan. But until then we will hold the matter in abeyance. But you may tell the Commissioner that the Sioux delegates of this great Congress have not yet stuck their toes in the water, but we hope that by the time the bill is passed we will be in up to our necks!

Further, we wish to say that we owe our obligations to Superintendent Baumgarten and this efficient corps of employees who gave their time unselfishly to make our stay here one long to be remembered. I thank you.

WILLIAM SKENADORE, Oneida delegation: I assure you it is a great pleasure to stand before this grand body of Indians, although I feel I wish to say this—that if the Winnebago Indians are the bravest and the Sioux are the best looking, we have overlooked the fact that the Oneidas have got the most money. In behalf of the Oneida Indians I will tell a little story which best tells how we felt toward the United States. A farmer went up to see the president of the last administration, and the president asked him to lunch. The farmer accepted the invitation and went to lunch with the president. While they were eating the president stepped out and a little while later came back and saw the farmer's plate empty.

Another course was ordered and the president stepped out again. When he came back the plate was empty again. "My, what an appetite you've got," the president said, "I wish I had it." When the farmer returned to his home he told about it. He said: "The president took everything we had. Took our stock, our land, our machinery, and now he wants my appetite!"

Resolution handed to chairman by William Skenandore:

> "The Oneida Indians of the Oneida Indian Reservation, in Wisconsin, assembled in Council at the Parish Hall, Oneida, Wisconsin, March 14, 1934, determined:
>
> Through their chiefs, to express our appreciation to the President, Franklin D. Roosevelt, through our new Commissioner of Indian Affairs, Honorable John Collier.
>
> That we, the Oneida Indians, have felt the spirit of the new deal in the administration of the affairs of the people of the entire country as being carried out as intended.
>
> That we will forever be thankful to you as the new Commissioner of Indian affairs, as the tried and true friend of the Indians, which they have sorely been in need of for a century. We have known for many years that you were studying and fighting hard to bring about a betterment of the conditions of the Indians throughout the country. And we are hoping and struggling with you so that you will realize our desires.
>
> We know it to be a fact that it was you who was instrumental in having the Indians to be included in the Emergency Relief and Civil Works Programs, which relief we have received this winter was surely appreciated by the Oneidas, which relief has never before been accorded to us.
>
> We believe the best time to encourage a fighter to win, is when he is in the midst of a battle. And we are with you, as Oneida Indians, in your struggle, by giving publicity to have Congress pass the Indian Rights Bill, which you were instrumental in getting introduced. And should it become a law and a reality, we are sure that, what Abraham Lincoln was to the colored people, you are going to be the Abraham Lincoln to the Indians.
>
> We understand the aims and substance of the Indian Rights Bill to be as follows:
>
> 1. Due to the destitution of Indians in general, brought about by the General Allotment Act of 1887.
> 2. That it is the intention of the new administration to have the Government re-assert its obligations and safeguard the Indians from extinction, and their properties.
> 3. To stop the divesting of the lands from the Indians.

4. To provide lands for those Indians that have become landless so that they again can have homes.
5. Extended trust periods not to expire as intended.
6. No more lands to be allotted to individual Indians.
7. No more taxation of Indian lands.
8. Indians nevermore to have the right to sell or mortgage their lands.
9. Education of Indians as lawyers, doctors, nurses, teachers, clerks, engineers, and other professions at the leading universities, colleges and schools.
10. Provide facilities for reforestation, grazing and farming of Indian lands.
11. Transfer authority over to the Indians from the Secretary of the Interior and Commissioner of Indian affairs, to the Indians for self-determination concerning their tribal affairs.
12. United States to provide funds and assistance to Indians in building up self-government again.
13. Secretary of Interior to issue charter providing the essentials of self-government, that of liberty of conscience, worship, speech, and free speech.
14. United States to build highways, bridges and local churches.
15. Courts to be established for civil and criminal cases.
16. Lawyers to be provided for Indians at all times.
17. Relieve Indians in distress.
18. Indians at liberty to abandon Indian community at any time.

The above proclamation approved unanimously by the five hundred Oneida Indians assembled in council. Signed March 17, 1934:

Wm. Skenandore, Presiding Chief Oneida Indians
Chief Richard Sannor
Chief Hipon John
Chief Nelson Skenandoah
Chief William Cornelius

MR. WOEHLKE: I have waited with this final word to you until I could find out just how your sentiment was drifting. Now we have spoken of the stream of self-government into which would run the creeks of various appropriations for the benefit of the Indians. We have spoken of wiggling your toes in it, or of going right into it, but as yet, my friends, there is no water—there is merely the possibility of having such a stream—it isn't there yet. The Wheeler-Howard Bill has not been passed, and while the Commissioner and his staff have been spreading this legislation before the Indian people all over the country so that he might inspect it—during that period powerful forces have been organized to defeat it in its entirety.

Those forces have been working day and night and they will jeopardize the passage of this bill at this session unless those who believe in the bill, who believe in the principles which it tries to accomplish, will not only approve the bill, but will go out and do battle for it just as the opposition is battling against it.

To many of the members of the House and Senate Committee there is arriving constantly a stream of letters from various individuals opposing this bill, and from those who will be benefited by it, those who favor it, there is hardly a word; until the committee has come to the conclusion that nobody wants this bill.

On top of that you have the natural resistance of the Government itself against any increased appropriations for the Indians, and you must remember that this bill carries not only authorization for heavy appropriations immediately, but it also carries authorization for large appropriations to be made year after year—appropriations, the total of which will be a very large sum, and naturally there is resistance toward the making of obligations the size of which are indeterminate and which may run up to very large sums in the future.

All these things combine to make it exceedingly difficult to push this legislation with its appropriations through Congress at the present session, unless your passive approval is followed by active work on behalf of this bill. As groups and as individuals, let your representatives in the House and Senate know just how you feel about it, and write them and tell whether you are for or against the bill, and do it early and often!

REV. C. AARON: In view of the remarks made by Mr. Woehlke, I suggest we all put some power behind this bill. We know this power is created through the pen and through the tongue. I believe that in this gathering here there are men who are really able with the pen and also men that are able with the tongue, and I would like to suggest that after you go home today or tomorrow from this gathering, please remember what he has said, and by pen or by tongue do what you can to make this bill go through. For myself, I am going to speak four times in Chicago and three times in Detroit in the next month that I might put this cause before those people that I might have the chance to speak for.

JOHN BROKER, Ponsford: In regard to education—I have noted at times in the schools that the Indian child is somewhat handicapped in learning the English language. If they had a class or some provision made for them whereby they could learn their own language I believe they would be better off. I have noted at times that they have been handicapped by learning an alien language. Could it be possible under this new program to have schools in the Indian language to preserve the language and the past history of our people.

I suggest that we take it up with the director of education to see if we can do it.

WM. BUCHER, Leech Lake: Our land is in the National Forest area and contains about 230 acres and in this area that has been marked off are graves of our forefathers.

We could hardly leave those graves; and for another thing there are two churches in this national forest area, and it is there we go to worship God in whom we believe, and it has become sacred ground to us. We want the commission to thoroughly understand that we want them to relieve the situation that our national forest that we want for our home, and which our forefathers had enough foresight to set aside for us. These Indian graves are very sacred to us, and another reason we hate to leave is because of our schools. We love them because our children are getting an education there.

MR. WOEHLKE: Mr. Baumgarten has arranged to have the Wheeler-Howard Bill translated into the Chippewa language and copies of this translation will be available at the office of the Superintendent probably within the next week, and if you desire copies, please get in touch with Mr. Baumgarten.

Now I would like to tell you how delighted and grateful Mr. Collier will be when we report to him about the character of this meeting, and when he is able to read the transcript of what was said here.

He will be exceedingly pleased, and I know that you in turn will not rest upon your oars, but that you will give him the support which in your judgment his efforts deserve, and now since Mr. Baumgarten has announced that dinner will be ready at 5:30 I think we will have to adjourn. I thank you.

TRIBAL DELEGATES

CASS LAKE	
White Earth	56
Grand Portage	3
Nett Lake	4
Leech Lake	6
Fond du Lac	9
Mille Lac	2
White Oak Point	3
KESHENA	
Oneida	8
Menominee	10
Stockbridge	3
MOUNT PLEASANT	
L'Anse	4
Saginaw, Swan River, and Black Creek	3
LAC DU FLAMBEAU	
Lac du Flambeau	11
St. Croix	2
Mole Lake	2
Red Cliff	6
Bad River	10
Lac Courte Oreilles	6
RED LAKE	11
TOMAH	
Pottawattomie	9
Winnebago	6

PIPESTONE

Md. Sioux

2

LAC DU FLAMBEAU

Jack Lynch
Charles Son
Fred LaCass
Chief Nigani
Ben Chosa
Alex Bobidosh
Louis St. Germaine
Frank Wildcat
Henry Catfish
Tom Devine
John Devine

WHITE EARTH

Geo. Selkirk
J. B. Fairbanks
Simon McKeig
Chas. E. Bonga
John Broker
Frank Broker
Frank Clark
Jes. Peake
Aundah be tung
Wm. A. Brunette
Louis Hamlin
James Antell
Felix Brisbois
Thos. Antell
Chas. Roy
John Pemberton
John Colman
Frank Peleran
Wm. Heisler
Martin Bellecourt
Clifford Warren
John Brown
Joe Morrison
Isaac Fairbanks
Thos. Shingobe
Robt. Beaulieu
E. L. Rogers
Harold H. Emerson
D. F. Porter
Chas. Morrison
Robt. Rice
A. C. Beaulieu
Geo. A. Barry
Wm. Leecye
Niles Beaupre
Albert J. Fairbanks
Wm. Weaver
Geo. Bigbeau
Paul H. Beaulieu
Chas. Murray
Lawrence Budreau
George Walters
Wm. Angwaush
James St. Clair
Peter J. Perrault
F. R. Fairbanks
Teddy Dunnell
Louis Vizenor
Chas. Angwaush
John Busch
Gabe Saice
Bishop Littlewolf
Joe Bellecourt
Geo. Aspinwall

NETT LAKE

Albert Smith
Peter Smith
Tom Fisher
Wm. Johnson

POTTAWATOMIE

Archie Megenuph
Frank Shepherd
Richard Mishigaud
Henry Richie
Reuben Young
Jim Pidgeon
Hilbert Shegonee
Joe Waubiness, Jr.
Frank Wandahsega

MENOMINEE

Albert Turtlelotte
Amos Striker
Mose Tucker
Simon Beauprey
C. J. Frechette
Peter White

	Edwin Warrington	Frank H. Gauthier
	Alex Crow	Roy Oskosh
Md. SIOUX		
	Sam Bluestone	Paul Abraham
	Walter Leith	Sophia Wilson
ST. CROIX		
	Jack Kasabin	Henry Wakefield
	John Matrios	
RED CLIFF		
	Geo. Gurnoe	Martin Buffalo
	Mike La Fernier	
FOND DU LAC		
	John Landry	Joe LePrairie
	John Labeirge	Lyzeme Savage
	Ben Bassett	Alex Neganub
	Ben Loon	Henry La Prairie
	Joe Smith	
WINNEBAGO		
	Jim Smoke	Geo. Garvin
	Mitchell R. Cloud	Fred White Eagle
	Scot Mokey	Henry Johnson
MILLE LAC		
	Joe Eagle	Chief Wodena
WHITE OAK POINT		
	Simon Lequier	Geo. Rogers
	James Smith	
MT. PLEASANT		
	John Jackson	Elijah Elk
	Willis Jackson	
GRAND PORTAGE		
	Ed Wilson	John Flat
	Sam Crawford	
L'ANSE		
	Chas. Picard	Wm. Curtis
	Chas. Cardinal, Sr.	John Hugo
ONEIDA		
	E. L. Hill	Andrew Beechtree
	Wm. Skenandore	Martin F. Wheelock
	Junas Schuyler	Wm. A. Cornelius
	Agnes Fox	Chas. S. Cornelius
RED CLIFF		
	Alex Roy	Alex Davidson
	Frank Basina	
LEECH LAKE		
	Wm. Morrell	Jos. Gorbow
	Wm. Losh	Chas. Ellis
	Wm. Butcher	Geo. Fairbanks
BAD RIVER		
	John Cloud	Wm. J. Denomie
	Kate Armstrong	E. C. Morrison

Marie Denomie	Wm. Bigboy
C. E. Morrison	Sam F. Denomie
Jerome Arbuckle	James Jacco
STOCKBRIDGE	
Rev. C. Aaron	Oderian Yoccum
Carl L. Miller	
RED LAKE	
Benj. Littlerock	Alfred Wind
Peter Sitting	Wm. Sayers
Wm. Dudley	Peter Graves
Paul H. Beaulieu	Pay she ge slig
Paym way way be nais	Joe Mason
Ben Ricebird	
MOLE LAKE	
Willard Ackley	Chas. Van Tile
LAC COURTE OREILLES	
John Kingfisher	John Mustache
John Mike	Mrs. J. Perkins
Peter Wolfe	John Quarderer
WINIBIGOSHISH	
Joseph Garbo	
LAC VIEW DESERT—Lac du Flambeau	
1 delegate	

CHAPTER 13

MEETING OF COMMISSIONER COLLIER WITH THE NAVAJO INDIANS AT FORT DEFIANCE, ARIZONA, JUNE 11, 1935

The meeting was called to order at 1:30 p.m.

Interpreter: Albert Sandoval.

TOM DODGE: The purpose of this meeting is to try to clarify our minds on the Wheeler-Howard Act before the voting takes place within the next few days. I think some of us are still more or less in the dark regarding this particular law and in order to try to clarify our minds we have called this meeting and for that purpose Mr. Collier, the Commissioner, is here and our new General Superintendent, Mr. Faris, and their aides. After discussing the Act then we will turn to other matters, but before doing that we want to concentrate all our minds on the Wheeler-Howard Act, so at this time I will call upon Mr. Collier, the Commissioner of Indian Affairs.

MR. COLLIER: Mr. Chairman and Friends of the Navajo Tribe:

I have come out from Washington on a very short trip lasting only three days. It is a time when it is very difficult to be away from Washington because there are many important Bills which are now at a critical stage in Congress and also because we are now appearing before the Allotment Board to ask for millions of dollars of new money for the Indians. In spite of those facts it seemed to me that it was my duty to come out and talk with the Navajo Tribe because next week you are going to vote upon an important matter which will influence your life for many years to come. And I felt that I should help as far as I could so that you would clearly understand and would vote with a knowledge of the real facts. It is wholly your own business to decide how you are going to vote; each one of you should freely decide and your decision will be sacred. I do want to help you to a clear understanding so that then you may decide wisely.

A good friend of mine, one of my very good friends, wrote me a letter which I received in Albuquerque yesterday. In this letter he said that he thought it was a mistake for me to come out and talk with you about the Indian Reorganization Act, the Wheeler-Howard Bill, because, he said, there has been a great deal of misunderstanding and a good deal of misrepresentation and the Indians think that the Bill is the "Collier Bill" and the Navajos may vote against it because of misunderstanding. And this good friend said that it would lower my dignity to come out and talk with you and perhaps argue with you and that then if the Navajo Tribe should vote against the Act my reputation would suffer. But my reply to that advice is as follows:

The Wheeler-Howard Act, for good or for ill, is very important to the Navajo Tribe. The Navajo Tribe is by far the largest and most important Indian group. And the question of the dignity of the Indian Commissioner, or of his reputation, is of no importance. He must do his duty by the Indians and therefore he must go and talk to the Navajos and tell them the truth as he sees it about this matter and so I am here and I shall not talk any longer than I have to and I shall try to help you understand the Act, this Wheeler-Howard Act.

Now I ask you to go with me in your thoughts backward a little bit, backward in the years, because that is the way we will understand the present. Forget for the moment all about the Wheeler-Howard Act and let us talk as though there was not any such thing as the Wheeler-Howard Act at all. Many years ago the Navajo Tribe was subdued by the government and taken away to Bosque Redondo and kept there for two years in prison. And then the Tribe came back to its homeland and it entered into a Treaty with the United States. The homeland which was given to the Navajo Tribe was the old Treaty Area of about five million acres, as I remember the figures. At that time the Navajo Tribe did not number more than about 10,000 members. In signing that Treaty with the government the Navajos surrendered all claim to any other land. They accepted that small area in final settlement. Those of you who know the Treaty will remember its language.

Then as the years went on the tribe grew more numerous, the government began to carry out services for the Indians, do things for the Indians, of one kind or another. It began to supply some schools and some doctors and some hospitals. It provided stockmen and farmers and Indian Agents. It began to serve you and help you. As your members increased it became clear that you must have more land and a great deal more land. And from time to time as a result of many struggles by you and by your white friends, from time to time additions were made to your lands, so that from having about five million acres you increased your holdings to more than twelve million acres. You still did not have enough land, and the struggle to get more land for you is still going on.

And then, you will remember, oil was found on your land. It happened that the oil was found on the Treaty Area, not on the new Executive Order area of the reservation. But it was thought at that time, twelve years ago, that there would be large discoveries of oil on your new lands, your Executive Order lands, and Secretary Fall prepared an order which denied that you owned this oil or other minerals on the Executive Order reservation. And that legislation proposed that even for the oil you would have to pay what practically was a tax to the States of Arizona and New Mexico amounting to 371/2% of your total royalty. And that same legislation had the effect of declaring that you did not have title to any of the Executive Order land but that you merely occupied it until the President got ready to take it away from you and turn you off of the land. Then there began a struggle that went on from 1922 to 1927 to prevent this order and subsequent proposed legislation which would have ruined you. And the legislation was finally defeated and your friends obtained different legislation which declared that the President could not take away any of your Executive Order land any more than he could take away Treaty land; in other words, which gave you substantially a title to the Executive Order area.

In the meantime the government went on increasing its services to you, more schools, more doctors, and so on. Then beginning about two years ago, it became possible to get larger government aid, a good deal more money and help for the Navajos. That was because of the money under Public Works, the money that was appropriated because of unemployment, because of the business depression. And so it became possible to go ahead fast in the development of wells, springs and reservoirs and irrigation works. And all of this service by the government, this work in the way of schools, hospitals, doctors, nurses, irrigation, water development, and so on, is going forward and is still increasing and will go forward, I hope, through many years to come. And in these same years the effort to get more land also has been pushed, so that last year, as you know, we obtained the Navajo-Arizona Boundary Bill and the consolidation and the additions of lands in Arizona, and at this very moment we are working to pass the New Mexico–Navajo Boundary Bill which you all know about, which will consolidate the lands and add more than a million new acres, and I believe that Bill will be passed. But, if it proves impossible to pass that Bill, if the white interests are strong enough to block it, nevertheless your friends will go forward and I believe that we are going to get you that new land, which really is your old land. If necessary and if there is no other way, we will seek authority to fall back on the allotment of Public Domain and to allot you all over that reserved area and get the land that way.

Now, all that I have been telling you and bringing to your minds, which is the regular established government work for you, all of that work will go right on no matter whether you adopt the Wheeler-Howard Act or whether you vote the Wheeler-Howard Act down. If you decide that you do not want the Indian Reorganization Act, then all of this work and all of this effort by the government will go on just the same, will be pushed just as hard as it would be if you did vote that you wanted the Wheeler-Howard Act. I am emphasizing this because I don't want one Navajo Indian to cast his vote for the Indian Reorganization Act under fear; under any idea that he will lose these services [unless] he votes for the Act.

Now I will tell you why I think you need the Wheeler-Howard Act. Between this day and the time when President Roosevelt and Secretary Ickes pass out of office, from now until then, I pledge you that the effort will go forward the way it is going forward and be made larger as far as we have the power. As long as this administration remains in office there will be no effort to take away any of your land but only an effort to give you more. As long as this administration remains in office there will be nothing done to bring any of your land under taxation but we will fight against every effort to bring your lands under taxation. As long as this administration remains in office we can pledge you that none of your land or timber or oil or anything else will be leased to white men or white companies without your consent. And as long as this administration remains in office your tribal rights will be respected, your tribal council will be consulted, its decisions will be respected, and your power over your own affairs will be increased, and as long as this administration remains in office your irrigated lands, your farm lands, will not be allotted in severalty, broken up in such a way that they will pass under taxation and be sold to white people. But this administration will not remain in office for many years. Possibly in two years we will be gone, and there will be a new administration from the President down. Nobody can foresee what the policies of that next administration will be with respect to your land, to the taxing of your land, to your tribal self-government or toward the allotment of your farmlands. Nobody can tell what the policy will be.

Now the fundamental purpose of the Wheeler-Howard Indian Reorganization Act, and the reason why the Navajo tribe needs that Act; the fundamental purpose, the great reason, is to establish as a matter of law, of right and law, all of these protections and advantages so that you can be sure to keep them no matter who is the next President; no matter who is the next Secretary or who is the next Commissioner. This applies, of course, what I am saying, to all of the Indian tribes—not only the Navajos—but we are talking about the Navajos now. But unless I can make this clear to you then I will fail to show you the real meaning of the Wheeler-Howard Act, and I must try to make it clear to you.

Under the existing laws, if you are without the Wheeler-Howard Act, you are largely at the mercy of the administration in power at the time. If it wants to go on helpfully to protect your lands and so on, it can do so. If it does not want to do that but wants to take away what you have and break down your protection, then it has the power to take away, to destroy and to ruin you. The purpose of the Wheeler-Howard Act is to change that situation and to guarantee through a solemn law of Congress the protections and the gains and the advantages that you have got and to make it impossible for a future administration to take away from you.

You have heard much, I expect, about things like the revolving loan fund and the fund for enabling Indian boys and girls to take college education and things of that kind, and they are important parts of the Act, but they are not the really important part.

Now, in the effort to make my point clear I am going to give you three examples, all of which will show you how the Wheeler-Howard Act will safeguard you. The first thing I want to do is to remind you that the Navajo tribe will soon be the owner of about 20,000 square miles of land. When the boundary bill is passed that will be about the amount of land you will own. And that land includes a very valuable forest, the Defiance Plateau forest. It includes great areas of valuable coal land and oil land and it includes 36,000 acres which have now been supplied with water, irrigable acres, 36,000. Fifteen thousand (15,000) of those irrigable acres have been added within the past two years through water development and irrigation. And the entire property is immune from taxation; does not pay taxes to the State of Arizona, Utah or New Mexico. Don't imagine that the white people in the years to come won't want to get that oil, that coal, that timber, that irrigated land. They will want to get it. They will want to impose taxes on it. Your situation today is exactly the same as the situation of the Oklahoma Indians twenty-five years ago. They had then a property as big as yours, as valuable as yours, which did not pay taxes and which the white people coveted. And the Sioux Indians of North and South Dakota thirty years ago had a property as big as yours, as valuable as yours, and the Sioux Indians were almost as numerous as you, about 30,000 of them. And white people of Oklahoma and of the Dakotas wanted to know how to put taxes on the land of the Sioux Indians and the Oklahoma tribes, and they found out how to do it. They passed what is known as the General Allotment Law. The law provided for allotting the land of these tribes in severalty, a little piece to each Indian. The acceptance of allotments was obligatory on the Indians; the tribe had to surrender its title and the individual Indians had to accept allotments. And the next step was to give a patent in fee to the individual Indian who had an allotment and then his land was taxed and he could sell it. And when the allottee died—the man, woman or child who got a parcel of land—then the land was sold by the government to the whites. This General Allotment Law was put into force against the protest of these tribes. They even went to the Supreme Court for protection and the Court could not protect them and they were allotted and I will tell you exactly what happened. In the year 1908, that is 25 years ago, the Five Civilized Tribes of Oklahoma had fifteen million acres of very fine land, fifteen million acres—more than the total area of the Navajo reservation. Today they own one million five hundred thousand acres. In other words they have lost nine-tenths of their land. They still own one-tenth of what they had in 1908, and nearly half of that land which remains theirs has been put on the tax rolls of Oklahoma.

Now I pause to beg you to pay very close attention to what I am saying. It is the truth and of absolute importance to you. This same Allotment Law, passed in order to take away the land from the Oklahoma Indians and the Sioux Indians, applies to all Indians, including the Navajo Tribe. The General Allotment Law today is a law for the Navajo Tribe as much as for the Sioux Tribe and for the Five Tribes of Oklahoma. It is simply that, as yet, to the present, no Secretary of the

Interior has taken the necessary steps to apply the law to the Navajo Tribe because in the past your land has not been sufficiently valuable, sufficiently coveted by white men, or sufficiently important from the taxation standpoint to be worth getting. But let me say this in addition, not only is the General Allotment Law universal, it applies to all Indians, it applies to the Navajos, but it can be construed to be mandatory upon the Secretary of the Interior. It is possible to state that it is his duty, his obligation, under the law, to allot the Navajo tribe.

Some years ago there was a reservation in the State of Washington, the Quinault Reservation, and it had not been allotted. It was a very valuable property because of its timber of a fine quality. Some members of that tribe, just a few of them, decided that they wanted to get a piece of that timber and sell it themselves and so they asked the Secretary of the Interior to allot the Quinault Reservation, and he refused and then these young Quinault Indians got a white lawyer and they went into the Federal Court with a mandamus petition for the Court to compel the Secretary to allot the Quinault Reservation. The Department of the Interior and the Department of Justice went before the Court and they said, "If we allot the Quinault Reservation it means ruin for the Quinault Indians." Nevertheless, the court ruled, and ruled correctly in law, that these individuals had a right to their allotments, and the Court ordered the Secretary to proceed and allot the whole Quinault Reservation. The Department appealed to the Supreme Court and lost. The higher courts ruled the same way, that the Department must go ahead and allot. And the Department obeyed the court and did allot and today much of the Quinault Reservation is a gray, smoking ruin and the Quinault Indians are going toward ultimate landlessness.

If any of you are not convinced of the truth of what I am telling you, go to any competent lawyer anywhere, let him look up the law and he will tell you the same thing.

Now there is the additional fact in your case which I think most of you have forgotten—something in your Treaty which I am going to remind you of. Your Treaty, and I am referring to the Treaty of 1868, contains a section which anticipates that the Navajo Indians shall be allotted in severalty. It is Article V of the Treaty. You all have access to the Treaty.

Any member of this tribe who wanted to go into court tomorrow with a mandamus to compel the Secretary to allot the Navajo Reservation, he would not only have all of the arguments used by the young Indians at Quinault, but he would have this undertaking in the Treaty, this unfulfilled Article V, which anticipates the allotment of this reservation. I don't mean to imply that any member of this tribe would be that kind of traitor to his people, but I am saying that in the years to come when the white people press harder and harder against your boundaries and the States get hungrier and hungrier to tax your lands, when that time comes, some Indian may be persuaded, may be bribed, to do this. Or some political Secretary of the Interior may be persuaded by the white politicians to do it.

Now, all of the rest of the Wheeler-Howard Act is unimportant compared to its first section. "That hereafter no land of any Indian reservation, created or set apart by treaty or agreement with the Indians, Act of Congress, Executive order, purchase, or otherwise, shall be allotted in severalty, to any Indian." That repeals the General Allotment Act, supersedes Section V of the Treaty, and that and that alone can protect you in the years to come.

Furthermore, I can tell you and prove to you that the opposition against the Wheeler-Howard Act, the hue and cry that has been raised against it by certain men in Washington, is chiefly an opposition to that Section I, to that and that alone.

There has just been handed to me a document passed around among you Navajo Indians this morning. I hold it here. It is a reprint from a page of the Congressional Record and a mimeographed letter signed by O. K. Chandler, an Oklahoma man. The reprint is a speech made by Mrs. Jenkins, a member of Congress from Indiana. The letter states the correct fact, that the speech in substance was written or supplied by a man named Bruner, Joseph Bruner, of Oklahoma. Joseph Bruner is the President of an organization which is now working at Washington and which carries on its letterhead the names of at least two Navajo Indians. And they are advocating the continuance of the allotment system and practically the abolishment of the guardianship by the government over the Indians. And they are attacking me and the administration because we stand for maintaining the tribal lands intact; for continuing the guardianship of the government; and they say because we are doing that we are not good Americans and we are pagans and atheists and communists and Turks and Chinamen, and all kind of funny things.

I merely refer to this, not because it is having any important influence but because I do want you to realize that source of the opposition against the Wheeler-Howard Act, which is from those people who apparently want to see all of the Indian lands allotted and who want to see the guardianship of the government over the Indians brought to an end and who want to see the government quit serving the Indians. And if they should persuade the Navajo Tribe to reject Section I of the Wheeler-Howard Act and remain subject to the allotment law, I prophesy that they will win their objective before many years have gone by. Your lands will be allotted by some future administration; they will be taxed; the white men will get them, and the guardianship of the government will be brought to an end. The last sentence of Article V of your Treaty provides that the United States, at some future date, shall pass a law governing how you will hold your land and the descent of your land from father to child. That law passed and it is the General Allotment Law of 1887, which has not yet been put into force but which is the law for you. Section I of the Wheeler-Howard Act repeals that General Allotment Law and lays it down that your land shall remain forever tribal, owned by the tribe and inalienable and free from taxation. I say "forever" so far as the President and the Department are concerned. Congress always in the future would have the power to bring the trust period to an end. That power cannot be taken away from Congress, but Section I, which repeals the Allotment Act, is a declaration by Congress itself that your land shall remain tribal, and therefore inalienable.

Now I have spent nearly all of my time on this one point because it is the thing I believe you have not clearly understood before. I would even say that the only reason I came out here was to tell you what I have told you about this one thing, Section I of the Wheeler-Howard Bill. The rest of the Bill is easy to understand and easy to explain, and I am just going to refer to the different parts of it very briefly.

The Bill says that once you become organized under the Bill your Tribal Council has power and the Secretary of the Interior cannot break down your Tribal Council, cannot over-ride it and cannot lease your land and your oil and the timber without the consent of the Tribal Council. Then it says that if you want to arrange it that way, you can call yourselves as a corporation and then you can borrow money from the government out of a revolving loan fund for any proper purpose that you want. Then there is another part that authorizes an appropriation of $250,000 a year for the cost of organizing these Tribal Councils and Tribal Corporations if you want to form them. You do not have to form them. Then there is this appropriation of money for enabling your boys and girls to go to College to train as doctors, nurses, engineers or anything they want to do. Then there is this authority of $2,000,000 a year for buying land. It is true that after the boundary bill is passed this particular money cannot be used to buy land outside of the boundary in New Mexico or Arizona, but there is a lot of land inside the proposed outside boundaries which we could buy for you that you do not own yet, and there is lots of land in Utah and Colorado which the Navajos might like to own, and we could buy that. Then there is a section that allows Indians to get jobs with the government regardless of Civil Service so that an Indian, if he is qualified and capable of doing the job, can get it even though he has not a college education and cannot get a Civil Service rating. That is a very important thing for you boys and girls.

I explained very fully last night to your Council about Section VI and I want to repeat it here but briefly because the interpreter is beginning to suffer. I explained that the Secretary of the Interior already has, under existing law, all of the power in the matter of stock reduction that he will have if you adopt this Act, and Section VI, in the matter of range control, has to do with allotted Indians over whose land he does not now have sufficient control and he needs to have it.

And finally there is Section XVIII, the one which requires a referendum to be held, the referendum which is going to be held next week, Section XVIII. There have been some misunderstandings about the Section which I want to correct even though it is hard on the interpreter. The way it reads now it says that the Act goes into force in a tribe unless 51 out of every 100 of the adult Indians vote against it. Somebody, and I believe this came from somebody in the Indian Office, has told the Indians that if a man or woman did not vote at all then his vote would be counted "yes." There is nothing like that in the Act and it is not so. When the Wheeler-Howard Bill was pending in Congress I urged that the vote or decision ought to be controlled by the majority of the votes cast, which is the proper way, so if 100 Indians vote and if 51 vote "no," then it is "no" because that is a majority, but Congress did it this way. We have prepared an amendment, introduced it, and the House has passed it, changing Section XVIII so that a majority of the votes cast, actually cast at the ballot box, will be decisive. The Bill has passed the House, will pass the Senate, will become law, and it will be retroactive, so it will control the vote in all the elections which have been held and all those that will be held. I repeat that this amendment is certain to be adopted. Therefore, you can take it for granted that at your election the majority of the votes cast will decide, and for that reason those of you who want the Wheeler-Howard Bill should certainly go to the polls and not stay at home.

Now, I am not going to talk any more, both because you are getting tired, and out of mercy to the interpreter. I want to end by saying what I started by saying. You can see that I believe in the Wheeler-Howard Act. It is not my Act; it is the act which the President promoted in Congress, which Congress passed, which is the Act of the whole government, but I believe in it. I am sure that you would be wise to adopt it. But it is entirely a matter for the individual judgment and conscience of each Navajo Indian. He or she must decide. No Indian will be punished or even frowned on for voting against the Bill or for working against it. If the Tribe votes against the Bill we will go on just as hard as we can, doing all we can just the same way we will do if the tribe votes for the Bill. The decision is for you to make and we are nothing but your advisers.

I am very grateful for your courteous, patient attention to my long talk.

TOM DODGE: We will have a 20 minute recess.

Recess

ALLEN NESHKI: Mr. Chairman, Mr. Collier, I want to ask you a question about this voting. Just how are we going to work it? When the first order came out the way we understood when it came to voting for the Bill, when they say "yes" they mark an "X" and when they say "no" they were to make a circle. That was the first order we heard. But there have been talks to the Navajos all over the reservation and it has been explained all over the reservation and just the other day Mr. McCray told us a different thing from what it was at first. Mr. McCray told them it was changed. Instead of putting an "O" for "no" they are going to have to make just the "X." On the paper are they going to have "yes" and "no" and when they vote for it under the "yes" are they going to put an "X" and when they vote against it are they going to put an "X" under the word "no?"

MR. COLLIER: It would seem to me it does not make any difference which form of ballot is used. You either vote "yes" or "no." Now about this change, I suppose Mr. Faris could tell you better about that than I.

ALLEN NESHKI: Of course, it is plain with the educated people but uneducated Navajos are going to find it difficult for them to make their vote when they use only one letter.

MR. COLLIER: I was told that some of the old people are worried because they had the "X" which is the kind of thing to be put on a grave-stone but a circle is a good thing. Money is round and the world is round, and they were being confused because they put a death mark in one place and a good mark in another so they changed it to put a death mark in both places. Mr. Faris will tell you about this.

MR. FARIS: We have at the office in Gallup two kinds of ballot. The original ballot came out with two squares. On one it said "yes" and on the other it said "no." It has been my pleasure and privilege to see and be with a number of tribes voting. The Pueblos and Apaches voted with that ballot and they had as few ballots to throw out as I have ever known in any election. In other words, of 5,000 or 6,000 ballots I don't think there were more than two or three spoiled or mutilated. I don't like to think that the Navajo Indians cannot do just as well as the Apaches, the Pueblos, or any other group of Indians that have voted on the Wheeler-Howard Bill. I am not afraid of it from that standpoint at all. I think many of you who go to the polls know which square you want to place the mark in or what mark you want to make. No matter what mark is used I believe you would know when you are voting "yes" or "no" and that is all there is to the voting. "Yes" or "no." Now if it be the wish of the Council here that the Navajo people cannot vote except on the single square, I have no feeling in the matter at all. We have those ballots and can send them out. If you think the people in general, the Navajos in general, are prepared to vote on the original ballot and mark it, as you want to mark it so we will understand if it means "yes" or "no" that is all right. The negative means "no" and the affirmative means "yes." If you want to use the single ballot, let's not say it is because the Navajos cannot understand the other ballot. We have the single ballot and we have more of them than we have of the other so if you want the single ballot then single ballot it will be.

ALLEN NESHKI: We would rather have the single ballot. It will be more convenient for the people who are uneducated and who cannot read. That is, if the members of the Council will vote on that.

MR. FARIS: Those who prefer the single ballot please hold up your hands. If you want the single ballot it will be a square like this in the center and in that square is the place for you to vote with an "O" for "no" and the "X" for "yes." There will be an interpreter at every voting place to interpret to the Indians and there will be two judges. Now, since there will be present here two judges, clerks and interpreters, that will be four to six Indians. The interpreters will know about the meaning of the marks and you can get your ballot and make it like you want to and fold it and put it in the box. No one will know how you vote. That is what we call voting secretly. Your own people will see that there is nothing in the box and when you come up to register they will take your name so we will know just who has voted and you cannot go somewhere else and vote again. There will be a padlock on the box that the judges may keep the ballots locked until they can count them after the voting is closed.

JOHN GORMAN: It would be a good idea if at every voting place they would have one judge for the Bill and one judge against the Bill because we feel that you white people kind of wiggle about and we feel suspicious.

HOWARD GORMAN: It would be a good idea if those votes were counted right there.

MR. FARIS: Every Superintendent knows those things and has had an opportunity to tell you. They know how the election will be handled. They have had that information for three months.

JOHN GORMAN: I have heard over this part of the reservation that some white men are taking the census and thumb prints now and they are telling the Indians they will give them money and food if they will put an "X" in that. We don't want anything like that going on.

MR. FARIS: We don't either. At every voting place they will keep a list of every person who comes in to vote and there will be that many votes in the box so there is no danger of that part of it. There is no desire on the part of the Commissioner, the Secretary, or anyone other than to have an honest expression of what you want. I cannot see how any Navajo in this crowd, after hearing the Commissioner talk an hour or an hour and a half as he has and coming out here at this time when it is so hard for him to get away, showing the interest that he has, can think that he would allow me or any other employee in the field to deal unfairly with you.

Now, I do not hesitate to tell you that I think the Wheeler-Howard Bill is good for the Navajo people and all other Southwest Indians. That does not keep you from using your judgment. But I do want to say this to you, that no one is paying one cent so far as I know for you to vote one way or the other, and I think that is another challenge to the judgment and honesty of the Navajo people. I don't think you should say that of each other nor allow others to say it of you.

I want to say this to you—that it is quite an honor to have the responsibility of administrator for this group of people. The position is not my position, it is your position. The success of that position is in your hands, not in mine so much as you may think. Whether I stay in it or whether I do not is a small matter, but whether you, as men and women of majority age, do the right thing toward the future is an important matter. That matter is in your hands.

NAL NISHI (Delegate from Leupp): As far as I am concerned my jurisdiction favors the Bill.

JOHN GORMAN: The understanding I have is that every government employee is compelled to vote for the Bill.

MR. FARIS: The government should expect every employee to do his duty. No employee has to vote any way except the way he wants to. I wouldn't know how they voted unless they wish to tell because they vote secretly and there would be no other way to know.

JOHN GORMAN: I was just asking the question.

MR. FARIS: Indian employees of the Navajo Reservation can vote "yes" or "no" as they wish and I won't know the difference.

JOHN GORMAN: There has been talk like that and I wanted to know.

MR. FARIS: I am very sorry that the employees felt it was not part of their duty to tell the Indians more about the election. I think you are taking it not quite so seriously as you should.

Let me say to you again that the election will be Friday and Saturday. We will do all in our power and I will expect the employees to do all in their power to see that you vote "yes" or "no" as you want to vote. I think I have made myself clear to all of you.

DESCHNA: Mr. Collier, I would like to ask a question. As you explained in the Reorganization Act there is a point I would like to ask a question about. If we accept the Bill will that give us our title, our rights, back in the way of the trust funds?

MR. COLLIER: Yes. If the tribe accepts the Wheeler-Howard Act and then organizes under the Act, from that time on the tribe will control its own trust funds. It will never be possible to spend it except with the consent of the Tribal Council. You don't control them now but you will have complete control of them if you adopt the Reorganization Act.

HOWARD GORMAN: Mr. Chairman, I would like to ask a question.

DESCHNA: There are two points to this. In accepting this Reorganization Act will we have title to our trust funds or is it after we incorporate?

MR. COLLIER: It is after you have organized as a tribe, not after you have incorporated. Not as soon as you vote but after you organize.

MAN IN CROWD: Why is it that those fellows who have been to Washington ask such a question as that? The people are under the impression that they know.

MR. COLLIER: The answer is very simple. They do know, I am sure, but they think some of you don't know and I have not had time to tell you everything so they ask the question to make sure that I do tell you.

JIMMY BECENTI: I attended at a meeting at Shiprock some time ago. At that time we understood that if the tribe rejected the Reorganization Act they would live the same as they have maybe the next twenty years and that this is the understanding we had. Now you tell them if they reject the Bill they are subject to allotment and taxation.

MR. COLLIER: If the tribe accepts the Bill then the tribe will live the way it wants to live. It can live the way it is living now or it can change its life, if it accepts the Bill. If the tribe rejects the Bill the same thing is true. The tribe can go on living as it is living now or can change its way of life according to its own decision, only, if the tribe rejects the Act, as I have already explained to you, then you remain subject to allotment. If you are allotted it will break up your life and it will break up your lands and it will change your life entirely if you are allotted. And I have already made it clear as I can, as I know how to make it, why you are in danger of being allotted unless you adopt the Act. You would not be allotted by Secretary Ickes but in my judgment some future Secretary would allot you or some member of your tribe would go into court and compel him to allot you.

JIMMY BECENTI: Another question about this allotment law. You mentioned a certain Secretary of the Interior who had the tribe do some crooked work in the past. Many administrations have passed out and if there were anybody in the Indian Affairs who had taken a notion and wanted to allot the Navajos, why didn't they do it then? Why is it after all this time is brought up?

MR. COLLIER: The allotment law has been on the books since the year 1887. Some tribes were allotted promptly. Other tribes were not allotted until after 1900. Other tribes were not allotted until after 1920. Until last year the Interior Department was going ahead and allotting other tribes, until Secretary Ickes put an end to it. The reason why the Navajos were not allotted in the years gone by was because their lands were not considered to be very valuable; there was no great pressure by white men to obtain possession of their lands. Also, their lands were not very valuable for the purpose of taxation so there was no great pressure by the States to tax them. The reason why the lands of the Five Tribes in Oklahoma were allotted 25 years ago was because they were valuable and white men wanted to get hold of them. The time has come now when your lands are valuable; when the States want to tax your land; when the cattlemen want to get on your land; when white companies want to get possession of your oil; and that is why you are in danger now. To state the thing in another way, there is just one way by which the white men can get your land and your timber and your oil away from you. There is just one way by which the white men can impose taxation upon you. One way and one way only, and that is to apply the allotment system to you, and any Secretary of the Interior any day could go into court and sue to compel him to allot you. Now, if your lands are valuable then you may expect them to be gotten away from you if it can be done. It can be done by allotting them. It is the power of the Secretary to allot them. Probably as a matter of law it is his duty to do so, and you had better get away from that danger as soon as you can.

HOWARD GORMAN: I would like to ask this question. The Commissioner said under Article V in the Treaty of 1868, that that Article advocates that the government will allot the land in severalty to the Indians. I think as far as I can see there are not any such words as those in Article V.

MR. COLLIER: I will read the article and see if the rest of you have as much difficulty in understanding the English language as Mr. Gorman.

"If any individual belonging to said tribe, or legally incorporated with it, being the head of a family, shall desire to commence farming, he shall have the privilege to select, in the presence and with the assistance of the agent then in charge, a tract of land within said reservation, not exceeding one hundred and sixty acres in extent, which tract, when so selected, certified, and recorded in the 'land-book' as herein described, shall cease to be held in common, but the same may be occupied and held in exclusive possession of the person selecting it, and of his family, so long as he or they may continue to cultivate it.

"Any person over eighteen years of age, not being the head of a family, may in like manner select, and cause to be certified to him or her for purposes of cultivation, a quantity of land, not exceeding eighty acres in extent, and thereupon be entitled to the exclusive possession of the same as above directed."

And then it goes on to tell about the certificate that is to be issued to him, not to be held in common anymore. Then it goes on and gives that other language I read about the passing of a future law for arranging all of this. That future law was passed and it was the Act of 1887.

What I said about this Treaty was that it clearly points toward the breaking up of the tribal land into individual tracts, an equal amount to each Indian, which thereafter shall no longer be held in common. It points toward allotment, and if an Indian should go into court to sue the Secretary to make him allot, he would have all of those arguments which were put forward by the Quinault Indians and in addition he would have the Treaty as an argument, making it even more probable that he would prevail and be able to force the Secretary to allot.

Let me ask the critics here. Do you want allotment? Do you believe it is a good thing? I would like to ask that question very insistently.

HOWARD GORMAN: I have the floor, Mr. Collier. I will answer that question after awhile. I am asking these questions because I am against the Bill. It seems that there are people that are in authority who if they really wanted to protect the rights of the Indians why don't they take that allotment bill that Secretary Fall put over and repeal it and throw it out instead of introducing a new bill called the Wheeler-Howard Bill.

MR. COLLIER: What is this Bill of Secretary Fall that was put over?

HOWARD GORMAN: That is what I would like to know.

MR. COLLIER: My answer is that there was never an allotment bill passed by Secretary Fall or advocated by Secretary Fall. You are a well-read man, Mr. Gorman, and know that Mr. Fall was not Secretary of the Interior in 1887 or in 1903. He was Secretary in 1920.

HOWARD GORMAN: Well, whoever it was, I want to know why you don't just throw that Bill out.

MR. COLLIER: Now, I will answer Mr. Gorman. The Allotment Act that I have been talking about was passed in the year 1887. It is called the General Allotment Act. Mr. Fall was Secretary of the Interior from 1920 into 1923, so that he did not have anything to do with passing the Allotment Act. Secretary Fall did some other bad things but don't let's blame him for what was done when he was only a young man.

Then Mr. Gorman said, if we think that Allotment Bill is a bad thing why don't Secretary Ickes and I get it repealed. And my answer is that is exactly what we have done and Section I of the Wheeler-Howard Act does repeal the Allotment Act, only you have to decide whether you want this Act to apply to you or not. You have got to either adopt Section I or reject it.

Now I think Mr. Gorman will agree that courtesy should be mutual and that if I am to answer questions he also should be prepared to answer a simple, direct question, and that is whether he believes that allotment should apply to the Navajos or whether it should not.

HOWARD GORMAN: I go back to 67 years ago when the Treaty was made by the United States Government and the Navajos, and those old people tell us that if we comply by the rules and regulations laid down by Washington and the Navajos that they would continue to give us land, which is true that the United States government has extended our reservation until it reaches beyond Tuba City and South and East and North. I do not think that this allotment act should be impressed upon the people so as to make them scared. I don't believe that at all. But my question is why should the Commissioner, a competent man, quote a Treaty, Article V, and say that that should apply to their land.

MR. COLLIER: I have answered that, and I come back to my question which should be answered. I think the delegates are entitled to learn your answer to that.

HOWARD GORMAN: We do not know the danger of it, Mr. Collier.

MR. COLLIER: Then I will answer it. I said to you people what lay back of the fight against the Wheeler-Howard Act, and you know it now.

DESCHNA: Mr. Chairman, I just want to make a few remarks at this time on the Indian Reorganization. Since 1868 we have been living under the provisions of the old Treaty and the laws that have been enacted by Congress. The Treaty has been and is now of great benefit to our people and for that reason we all respect it as one of the great documents of our history.

In my opinion the Treaty has been and is now the foundation stone of our tribal life since 1868. The Indian Reorganization Act instead of destroying that foundation piece is a new structure placed over it. It strengthens and enlarges the rights and privileges granted to our people by the Treaty. In other words, the building started in 1868 to protect and guard our tribal rights is now completed by this new Act.

As the Commissioner has just explained, the most important provision of the Act is contained in Section I. This strengthens the only weak spot there was in the Treaty. It eliminates the great danger of our reservation being allotted into small individual holdings under the existing laws and Article V of the Treaty. If the reservation should be allotted, then the tribe will be broken up and the individual members will be reduced to poverty and forced to become charges on the public, except the very few able individuals who may survive the destruction.

No reasonable and convincing argument has been presented against the Reorganization Act by those who are opposing it. Therefore, I do not understand all the individuals who are making such a great noise against the acceptance to the Act by the tribe.

The other sections are not so important to me as the first one, and I believe that one section alone is enough for intelligent people to accept the Act.

MR. COLLIER: And I am going to stay with this particular question if you will allow me. The Allotment Act applies to the Navajos. That nobody disputes. Section I of the Wheeler-Howard Act repeals the Allotment Act so that it will no longer apply to the Navajos, and on that question you are going to vote this week.

Earlier when I spoke I said that I knew where the opposition to the Wheeler-Howard Act came from at the Washington end. There is no secret about it there. And at Washington Tom Sloane and Mr. Bruner and Congressman McGroarty have been very outspoken. They want the Wheeler-Howard Act repealed by Congress because they want the allotment system extended all over the Indian country. They have been perfectly open about it and have made no secret about it. But I did not say that any Navajo Indian was opposing the Wheeler-Howard Act because he believes in the allotment system. I did not say that because I did not believe there was even one Navajo Indian who wanted the allotment system, but now I discover that even here among you are Indians who apparently do want the allotment system. And I can only say that if they should prevail with you—I am not talking about anything but this one thing now—Section I of the Wheeler-Howard Act, which repeals the General Allotment Act—if they should prevail with you, if allotment should come about, as sure as the sun rises it means that your lands go to the white people; that your tribal government is destroyed and that you perish. I leave the issue with you that way.

HOWARD GORMAN: Commissioner Collier said that this was not a Collier Bill. The way he is protecting this Bill, the way he is talking for it, I am beginning to think it is his Bill, and if Section I of this Act is the only thing that pertains to the Navajos why put nineteen sections in this Bill?

MR. COLLIER: Because it is not the only one that pertains to the Navajos.

HOWARD GORMAN: The thing that I am opposed to mostly, the thing that created this opposition in me is the thing that started to take place two years ago, since Collier went in. The thing has gone to extremes. He has taken our sheep, our goats, even our money, and it seems to me that the sooner Collier gets out the better it is. If we accept this Wheeler-Howard Act, after his time expires within two years, where would we be? Could we repeal this act? Those are the things that I am opposed to this Bill for.

Talking about this revolving fund. The first time they told us $10,000,000. It looks pretty good to us. Next time they cut it down to $5,000,000 and then $2,500,000. And pretty soon there won't be any money.

And about this money we are going to borrow. We have to have a charter before we can borrow this money. But you organize these Indians under a charter and you will have your hands full. I thought Mr. Collier knew these Indians and understand us but I am beginning to understand that he does not know them.

MR. COLLIER: Of course, it is not for me to discuss Collier as Commissioner. I don't think much better of him than Mr. Gorman does, although it does give me a slight sinking of stomach to hear that I have not only stolen your goats and your sheep but your money.

I wish that I could claim the credit for the Wheeler-Howard Bill because I would be remembered for a long time as the writer of that Bill. I would be very glad to claim the credit because the Wheeler-Howard Bill brings to an end the great robbery of the Indians through the allotment system and it will be remembered always by the Indians with gratitude. But the simple truth is that the Wheeler-Howard Bill was drawn by the two committees of Congress, the House Committee on Indian Affairs and the Senate Committee on Indian Affairs, and was not drawn by me, but by them was drawn and presented to the House and so it is not the Collier Bill.

All that Mr. Gorman says about the bad qualities of the present Indian Commissioner could be true and it would not have any bearing on the question of this Bill. Indian Commissioners come and they go and none of them lasts long and I won't last long, and this Act will be on the statute books after I have been forgotten, after I am dead and gone, and after it has become all the same as if I never had been born.

Now I think it is probably true, as Mr. Gorman says, that I do not know much about the Navajos. I never pretended to.

Here Mr. Gorman interrupts with the statement: "Oh, yes you did."

I could know more about the Navajos than Mr. Gorman, who sees them through the glass of religious prejudice, and I still would not claim to know much, but I do know you Navajos well enough to know that you are men with good heads and honest hearts and that you stand on your own feet. I do know you well enough not to address arguments to you as if you were little children. I talk to you as men. And so today I have seriously and truthfully discussed with you Section I of this Act and I believe most of you understood me. And I have briefly discussed the many other Sections of the Act which do pertain to the Navajos and which are of value to the Navajos. So I do not feel the need of going into any more detail in reply to Mr. Gorman. I think that you understand the situation just as well as I do.

HOWARD GORMAN: I want Mr. Collier to understand clearly that I am not looking through a religious glass. I am not looking at you Navajos through a communistic glass either.

MR. COLLIER: I think I might say one thing more, which is concerning the importance of not bearing false witness against one's neighbor. Surely the Navajos are entitled to have people tell them the truth. We should not bear false witness against one another. When I stand as I do for preserving the tribal lands of the Indians in the ownership of the tribes and for allowing the tribes to control what is done with their property and their money; when I stand for the right of the Indians to continue living on as Indians—and I do stand for those things—nobody has any right to get up and say "You are a communist." There is no connection in the world between trying to protect your lands from being grabbed by the white people and trying to protect your tribal organization from being trampled by the Indian Bureau; there is no connection between this effort and communism, and these men are educated men, and they know the truth as well as I do, and they know I am not a communist, and they ought not to go on saying a thing that they know is not true. We ought not bear false witness against our neighbors.

Robert Martin explains a chart which he holds up for the crowd to see.

TOM DODGE: The meeting is adjourned.

(6:15 p.m.)

INDEX